ESSENTIALS OF PHYSICAL ANTHROPOLOGY
Discovering Our Origins

ESSENTIALS OF PHYSICAL ANTHROPOLOGY
Discovering Our Origins

CLARK SPENCER LARSEN
The Ohio State University

W.W. NORTON & COMPANY
NEW YORK · LONDON

Copyright © 2010 by W. W. Norton & Company, Inc.

All rights reserved
Printed in the United States of America
First Edition

Composition by TexTech
Manufacturing by Quad/Graphics
Illustrations by Penumbra Design, Inc.

Editors: Jack Repcheck, Pete Lesser
Assistant Editor: Laura Musich
Senior Developmental Editor, Project Editor: Kurt Wildermuth
Senior Production Manager, College: Christopher Granville
Managing Editor, College: Marian Johnson
Design Director: Rubina Yeh

Library of Congress Cataloging-in-Publication Data

Larsen, Clark Spencer.
   Essentials of physical anthropology : discovering our origins / Clark Spencer Larsen.
      p. cm.
   Includes bibliographical references and index.

ISBN 978-0-393-93422-9 (pbk.)

1. Physical anthropology. I. Title.
   GN50.4.L367 2010
   599.9—dc22

                              2009023920

W. W. Norton & Company, Inc., 500 Fifth Avenue, New York, NY 10110
wwnorton.com
W. W. Norton & Company Ltd., Castle House, 75/76 Wells Street, London WIT 3QT

3 4 5 6 7 8 9 0

To Chris and Spencer,
with my deepest thanks for their help, encouragement,
and (unwavering) patience

About the Author

CLARK SPENCER LARSEN heads the Department of Anthropology at The Ohio State University, Columbus. A native of Nebraska, he received his B.A. from Kansas State University and M.A. and Ph.D. from the University of Michigan. Clark's research is in bioarchaeology, skeletal biology, and paleoanthropology. He has worked in North America, Europe, and Asia. He has taught at the University of Massachusetts, Northern Illinois University, Purdue University, and the University of North Carolina. Since 2001, he has been a member of the faculty at Ohio State, where he is Distinguished Professor of Social and Behavioral Sciences. He teaches introductory physical anthropology, osteology, bioarchaeology, and paleoanthropology. Clark has served as president of the American Association of Physical Anthropologists and as editor-in-chief of the *American Journal of Physical Anthropology*. In addition to *Our Origins* and *Essentials of Physical Anthropology: Discovering Our Origins*, he has authored or edited 25 books and monographs, including *Bioarchaeology: Interpreting Behavior from the Human Skeleton, Skeletons in Our Closet*, and *Advances in Dental Anthropology*.

Basic Contents

Detailed Contents

PART I — THE PRESENT: FOUNDATION FOR THE PAST 19

CHAPTER 2 EVOLUTION: CONSTRUCTING A FUNDAMENTAL SCIENTIFIC THEORY 21

CHAPTER 3 GENETICS: REPRODUCING LIFE AND PRODUCING VARIATION 41

CHAPTER 4 GENES AND THEIR EVOLUTION: POPULATION GENETICS 67

CHAPTER 6 BIOLOGY IN THE PRESENT: THE OTHER LIVING PRIMATES 123

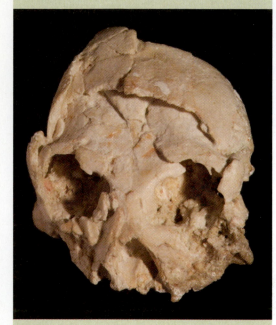

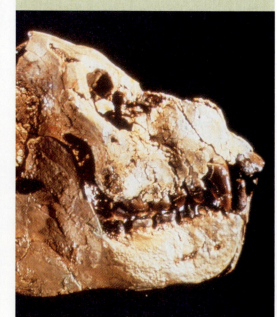

CHAPTER 9 EARLY HOMINID ORIGINS AND EVOLUTION: THE ROOTS OF HUMANITY 221

CHAPTER 10 THE ORIGINS AND EVOLUTION OF EARLY *HOMO* 251

CHAPTER 11 THE ORIGINS, EVOLUTION, AND DISPERSAL OF MODERN PEOPLE 273

CHAPTER 12 OUR LAST 10,000 YEARS: AGRICULTURE, POPULATION, BIOLOGY 317

To the Instructor

HOW THIS BOOK CAN HELP YOUR STUDENTS DISCOVER PHYSICAL ANTHROPOLOGY

It Is about Engagement

Teaching is about engagement—connecting the student with knowledge, making it real to the student, and having the student come away from the course with an understanding of core concepts. *Essentials of Physical Anthropology: Discovering Our Origins* seeks to engage the student in the learning process. Engaging the student is perhaps more of a challenge in the study of physical anthropology than in the study of other sciences, mainly because the student has likely never heard of the subject. The average student has probably taken a precollege course in chemistry, physics, biology, or geology. Physical anthropology, though, is rarely mentioned or taught in precollege settings. Commonly, the student first finds out about the subject when an academic advisor explains that physical anthropology is a popular course that fulfills the college's natural science requirement.

Once taking the course, however, that same student usually connects quickly with the subject, because so many of the topics are familiar—fossils, evolution, race, genetics, DNA, monkeys, forensic investigations, and origins of speech, to name a few. The student simply had not realized that these separately engaging topics come under the umbrella of one discipline, the subject of which is the study of human evolution and human variability.

In writing this book, I made no assumptions about what the reader knows, except to assume that the reader—the student attending your physical anthropology class—has very little or no background in physical anthropology. As I wrote the book, I constantly reflected on the central concepts of physical anthropology and how to make them understandable. I combined this quest for both accuracy and clarity with my core philosophy of teaching—namely, engage the student to help the student learn. While most students in an introductory physical anthropology class do not intend to become professional physical anthropologists, some of these students become interested enough to take more courses. So this book is written for students who will not continue their study of physical anthropology, those who get "hooked" by this fascinating subject (a common occurrence!), and those who now or eventually decide to become professionals in the field.

The book is unified by the subject of physical anthropology. But equally important is the central theme of science—what it is, how it is done, and how scientists (in our case, anthropologists) learn about the natural world. I wrote the book so as to create a picture of who humans are as organisms, how we got to where we are over the last millions of years of evolution, and where we are going in the future in light of current conditions. In regard to physical anthropology, the student should finish the book understanding human evolution and how it is studied, how the present helps us understand the past, the diversity of organisms living and past, and the nature of biological change over time and across geography. Such knowledge should help the student answer questions about the world. For example: How did primates emerge as a unique group of mammals? Why do people look different from place to place around the world? Why is it important to gain exposure to sunlight yet unsafe to prolong that exposure? Why is it unhealthy to be excessively heavy? Throughout their history, what have humans eaten, and why is it important to know?

I have presented such topics so that the student can come to understand the central concepts and build from them a fuller understanding of physical anthropology. Throughout the book, I emphasize hypothesis testing, the core of the scientific method, and I focus on that process and the excitement of discovery. The narrative style is personalized. Often I draw on my own experiences and those of scientists I know or am familiar with through their teaching and writing, to show the student how problems are addressed through fieldwork or through laboratory investigations.

Scientists do not just collect facts. Rather, they collect data and make observations that help them answer questions about the complex natural world we all inhabit. Reflecting this practice, *Essentials of Physical Anthropology: Discovering Our Origins* is a collection not of facts for the student to learn but of answers to questions that help all of us understand who we are as living organisms and our place in the world. Science is a way of knowing. It is a learning process. In this way, it is liberating.

HOW THE BOOK IS ORGANIZED

The book is divided into two parts. Following an introductory overview of anthropology and physical anthropology, Part I presents the key principles and concepts in biology, especially from an evolutionary perspective. This material draws largely on the study of living organisms, including humans and nonhuman primates. Because much of our understanding of the past is drawn from what we have learned from the present, this part lays the foundation for the presentation in Part II—the past record of primate and human evolution. In putting the record of the living up front, this book departs from the style of most other introductory physical anthropology textbooks, which start out with the earliest record and end with the living. This book takes the position that most of what we learn about the past is based on theory and principles learned from the living record. Just as all of Charles Darwin's ideas were first derived from seeing living plants and animals, much of our understanding of function and adaptation come from living organisms as models. Therefore, this book views the living as the window onto what came before. Individual chapters, however, can be taught in any order.

Part II presents evidence of the past, covering more than 50,000,000 years of evolution. Most textbooks of this kind end the record of human evolution at about 25,000 years ago, when modern *Homo sapiens* evolved worldwide. This textbook also provides the record since the appearance of modern humans, showing that important biological changes occurred in just the last 10,000 years, largely relating to the shift from hunting and gathering to the domestication of plants and animals. Food production was a revolutionary development in the human story, and Part II presents this remarkable record, including changes in health and well-being that continue today. A new subdiscipline of physical anthropology, bioarchaeology, is contributing new and profound insights into the last 10,000 years, one of the most dynamic periods of human evolution.

AIDS TO THE LEARNING PROCESS

Each chapter opens with a *vignette* telling the story of one person's discovery that relates directly to the central theme of the chapter. This vignette is intended to draw your students into the excitement of the topic and to set the stage for the Big Questions that the chapter addresses.

BIG QUESTIONS are introduced early in the chapter to help your students organize their reading and understand the topic.

CONCEPT CHECKS are scattered throughout each chapter and immediately follow a major section. These aids are intended to help your students briefly revisit the key points they have been reading.

LOCATOR MAPS are placed liberally throughout the book. College-level instructors tend to hope that students have a good sense of geography, but like a lot of people who do not look at places around the world on a daily basis, students often need reminders about geography. In recognition of this, locator maps in the book's margins show the names and locations of places that are likely not common knowledge.

DEFINITIONS are also presented in the text's margins, giving your students ready access to what a term means in addition to its use in the associated text.

At the end of each chapter, **ANSWERING THE BIG QUESTIONS** presents a summary of the chapter's central points organized along the lines of the Big Questions presented at the beginning of the chapter.

Physical anthropology is a visual field, in that anthropologists very commonly study objects, fossils, artifacts, and so on, by looking at them. This book helps your students visualize what they are reading about by including hundreds of images, many specially prepared for the book. These illustrations tell the story of physical anthropology, including key processes, central players, and important concepts. As much thought went into the pedagogy behind the illustration program as into the writing of the text. The highlight of these illustrations is six two-page spreads completed by the renowned biological science illustrator Kelly Paralis Keenan. These six stunning figures portray concepts, rather than just gathering facts about where or when fossils were found. One of my favorites involves the exciting discussion now playing out in physical anthropology regarding the origins of modern people. New discoveries in East Africa pinpoint the earliest modern humans as having lived in the modern country of Ethiopia, at a place called Herto. The two-page illustration of this important place in the human story tells what these people looked like and describes their behavior.

Join me now in engaging your students in the excitement of discovering physical anthropology.[1]

WHO HELPED

I owe much to the many people who made this book possible. First and foremost, I thank my wife, Christine, and son, Spencer, who helped in innumerable ways. They were my captive audience: without protest, they listened to my ideas at the dinner table, on family trips, and in other places where we probably should have been talking about other things. Chris read many drafts of chapters and gave great advice on when and where to cut, add, or rethink. I thank my parents, the late Leon and Patricia Larsen, who introduced me to things old and sparked my interest in the human past.

Jack Repcheck first approached me about writing a textbook on introductory physical anthropology. His powers of persuasion, combined with my interest in both the discipline and its presentation to college students, was instrumental in reeling me in and getting the project off the ground. Jack and others at W. W. Norton & Company made the process of writing the book a great experience. I first worked with the editors John Byram and then Leo Wiegman. I am indebted to Pete Lesser, who took on the project after Leo. Pete is a gifted editor and organizer. He gave direction on writing and production, provided very helpful feedback on presentation and pedagogy, and orchestrated the process of review, revision, and production—all without a hitch. Kurt Wildermuth edited the entire manuscript. His skill as an editor and staying on top of content from beginning to end added enormously to the book's presentation and readability. Mik Awake and Laura Musich's coordination of gathering permissions and acquiring images for the book are very much appreciated. Chris Granville skillfully guided the book through composition and manufacturing. Kelly Paralis Keenan at Penumbra Design developed the concepts for illustrations and did a great job of moving my primitive stick figures into elegant illustrations. Her two-page spreads bring to life some difficult concepts. Melissa Remis's and Nancy Tatarek's timely and efficient completion of the Test Bank and Instructor's Manual, respectively, is much appreciated.

Thanks go to graduate students and faculty colleagues at Ohio State University who helped in so many ways. I offer a very special thanks to Tracy Betsinger, who assisted in a number of aspects of the book. She read drafts of chapters at various stages, helped in figure selection, in glossary compilation, and as a general sounding board for ideas. Thanks to Jaime Ullinger, who provided the content and data for the box on PTC tasting. Tracy, Jaime, Jim Gosman, Dan Temple, and Haagen Klaus read parts or all of the manuscript and offered great advice. I had many helpful discussions with Scott McGraw about primate behavior, evolution, and taxonomy. Scott also provided advice on the production of the two-page spread on the diversity of primates inhabiting the Taï Forest, Ivory Coast. Doug Crews gave advice on the complexities of the biology and life history of primates, including humans.

Over the years, I have had helpful conversations with my teachers, colleagues, and students about areas of their expertise, and these discussions have influenced the development

---

[1] I am very interested in hearing your and your students' comments about the book, including problems, criticisms, and questions. Please feel free to contact me at Larsen.53@osu.edu.

of the book in so many ways. I am grateful to Patricia J. O'Brien and Milford H. Wolpoff, my respective undergraduate and graduate advisors. Both were instrumental in developing my interest in science and the great profession I work in. I especially thank Barry Bogin, Kristen Hawkes, Jim O'Connell, David Thomas, Bob Kelly, Jerry Milanich, Bruce Smith, Kris Gremillion, Bonnie McEwan, Matt Cartmill, Dale Hutchinson, Chris Ruff, Simon Hillson, Michael Schultz, Sam Stout, Doug Ubelaker, Dan Sellen, Clark Howell, Rick Steckel, Phil Walker, John Relethford, Mark Weiss, Margaret Schoeninger, Karen Rosenberg, Lynne Schepartz, Fred Smith, Brian Hemphill, Bruce Winterhalder, Meg Conkey, Desmond Clark, Erik Trinkaus, Katherine Russell, Vin Steponaitis, Mark Teaford, Richard Wrangham, Jerry Rose, Mark Cohen, William Bass, Loring Brace, Stanley Garn, Frank Livingstone, Phil Gingerich, T. Dale Stewart, Larry Angel, Mike Finnegan, Harriet Ottenheimer, Marty Ottenheimer, Roberto Frisancho, Randy Susman, Karen Strier, Joanna Lambert, Jim Hijiya, Cecil Brown, Bill Fash, Rich Blanton, Henry Wright, James Griffin, Bill Jungers, David Frayer, Bill Pollitzer, George Armelagos, Jane Buikstra, Elwyn Simons, Steve Churchill, Neil Tubbs, Bob Bettinger, Tim White, Dean Falk, Owen Lovejoy, Scott Simpson, David Carlson, Alan Goodman, Bill Dancey, Bill Bass, Debbie Guatelli-Steinberg, Clark Mallam, and Chris Peebles.

The book benefited from the expertise of many reviewers, and I have incorporated their comments wherever possible. I especially acknowledge the following authorities for their insight and suggestions for revision:

Sabrina Agarwal, University of California, Berkeley
Lon Alterman, North Carolina State University
Thad Bartlett, University of Texas, San Antonio
Owen Beattie, University of Alberta
Daniel Benyshek, University of Nevada, Las Vegas
Deborah Blom, University of Vermont
Emily Brunson, University of Washington
Victoria Buresch, Glendale Community College
Herbert Covert, University of Colorado
Douglas Crews, Ohio State University
Paul Erickson, St. Mary's University
Daniel Gebo, Northern Illinois University
Mark Griffin, San Francisco State University
Michael Grimes, Western Washington University
Gregg Gunnell, University of Michigan

Lauren Hasten, Las Positas College
Samantha Hens, California State University, Sacramento
Homes Hogue, Ball State University
Nina Jablonski, Pennsylvania State University
Karen Enstam Jaffe, Sonoma State University
Gail Kennedy, University of California, Los Angeles
Patricia Lambert, Utah State University
Michael Little, University of Binghamton
Chris Loeffler, Irvine Valley College
Sara Lynch, Queens College, City University of New York
Lorena Madrigal, University of South Florida
Debra Martin, University of Nevada, Las Vegas
William McFarlane, Johnson County Community College
Scott McGraw, Ohio State University
Ellen Miller, Wake Forest University
Ellen Mosley-Thompson, Ohio State University
Michael Muehlenbein, University of Wisconsin, Milwaukee
Dennis O'Rourke, University of Utah
Lesley M. Rankin-Hill, University of Oklahoma
Melissa Remis, Purdue University
Charles Roseman, University of Illinois
Lynette Leidy Sievert, University of Massachusetts
Fred Smith, Loyola University of Chicago
Richard Smith, Washington University
Sara Smith, Delta College
Christopher Stojanowski, Arizona State University
Margaret Streeter, Boise State University
Karen Strier, University of Wisconsin, Madison
Nancy Tatarek, Ohio University
Lonnie Thompson, Ohio State University
Christopher Tillquist, University of Louisville
Dennis Van Gerven, University of Colorado, Boulder
Ronald Wallace, University of Central Florida
David Webb, Kutztown University
Tim White, University of California, Berkeley
Janet Wiebold, Community Colleges of Spokane
Leslie Williams, Ohio State University
Sharon Williams, Purdue University
Milford Wolpoff, University of Michigan
Thomas Wynn, University of Colorado, Colorado Springs

Thanks, everyone, for your help!

Columbus, Ohio
January 2009

TOOLS FOR TEACHING AND LEARNING

The *Our Origins* teaching and learning package provides instructors and students with all the tools they need to visualize anthropological concepts, learn key vocabulary, and test knowledge.

For Instructors

CREATE DYNAMIC CLASSROOM PRESENTATIONS WITH THE *OUR ORIGINS* NORTON MEDIA LIBRARY CD-ROM

The ultimate tool for classroom presentation, this CD-ROM features all the drawn art, all the photos, and a complete set of PowerPoint lecture outlines for every chapter.

EASILY CONVERT YOUR BLACKBOARD COURSES TO *OUR ORIGINS*

Adopters of *Our Origins* have unlimited access to Norton's Blackboard course-packs. Provided at no additional cost to professors or students, these resources contain StudySpace assignments linked to the media elements inside them.

PREPARE FOR CLASS WITH THE *OUR ORIGINS* INSTRUCTOR'S MANUAL

Prepared by Nancy Tatarek (Ohio University), this innovative resource provides chapter summaries, chapter outlines, lecture ideas, discussion topics, suggested reading lists for instructors and students, and a video list.

QUICKLY AND EASILY CREATE TESTS WITH THE *OUR ORIGINS* TEST BANK

Prepared by Melissa Remis (Purdue University), this test bank contains multiple-choice, essay, and true/false questions for each chapter. It is downloadable from Norton's instructor website and available in *ExamView® Assessment Suite* format. Visit **wwnorton.com/instructors**.

For Students

EBOOK: SAME GREAT BOOK, HALF THE PRICE!

Our Origins is also available in an ebook format, which replicates actual book pages while providing links to helpful review tools. For details, visit **nortonebooks.com**.

ORGANIZE, LEARN, AND CONNECT WITH STUDYSPACE WWNORTON.COM/STUDYSPACE

This complete set of learning tools provides students with assignments that help them Organize their study, Learn course material, and Connect knowledge across chapters and to the world. Like the rest of the package, the *Our Origins* StudySpace focuses on physical anthropology's visual aspects. Features include:

- **ANTHROTOURS:** Using the power of *Google Earth*™, AnthroTours take students on flyovers of key locations discussed in the text. Students can explore Ethiopia's Great Rift Valley or trace the path of Darwin's voyage.

- **QUIZZES**, with photos and drawn art from the text.

- **FLASHCARDS**, many of which employ images, enabling students to study important fossils while memorizing key terms.

- **CHAPTER OUTLINES** help students organize their study and review.

- **EBOOK** links help students organize their reading and connect it to StudySpace assignments.

To the Student

PHYSICAL ANTHROPOLOGY IS ABOUT DISCOVERING WHO WE ARE

Thinking Like an Anthropologist

Who are we? Where do we come from? Why do we look and act the way we do? This book is a journey that addresses these and other big questions about us, *Homo sapiens*. This journey emphasizes humans' discovery of the fascinating record of our diversity and of our evolution, a record that serves as a collective memory of our shared biological presence on Earth. From here to the end of the book, I will share with you all kinds of ideas that add up our current understanding of human beings as living organisms. Along the way, you will experience scientific breakthroughs such as the human genome project and forensics (you might even watch *CSI* and *Bones* in a whole new way). You will gain new understandings of phenomena such as race and human diversity, global warming and its impact on our evolution and our well-being, the origins of human violence, global disease, and the growing worldwide obesity epidemic. Like an anthropologist tackling important questions, you will discover places on nearly every continent and come to see what life was like for millions of years before the present, before the emergence and evolution of humans.

Neither your instructor nor I can expect you as an introductory student to understand all the developments in physical anthropology. Both of us can, however, present you with a clear and concise framework of the field. By the time you are finished reading this book and completing this course, you will have a solid background in the basic tenets of the discipline. This knowledge will help you understand your place in nature and the world that we—more than six billion of us and growing—live in. The framework for developing your understanding of physical anthropology is the scientific method, a universal approach to understanding the very complex natural world. You should not assume that this book and this course are about only knowing the right answers, the "facts" of physical anthropology. Rather, they are also about seeing how physical anthropologists know what they know—understanding the scientific method. So as you read, keep in mind the key questions that scientists try to answer, their processes and methods for finding the answers, and the answers themselves.

In writing this book, I have focused on the big questions in physical anthropology, how scientists have tackled them, and what key discoveries have been made. I have not shied away from identifying the scientists who made these discoveries—real people, young and old, from all over the world. Whether you need to learn all these individuals' names and what they contributed to the growth of physical anthropology and to our knowledge of human evolution and variation is up to your instructor. But in the introductory physical anthropology class that I teach, I encourage my students to learn about the people behind the ideas. By seeing the field through these people's eyes, you can start thinking like an anthropologist.

Seeing Like an Anthropologist

Thinking like an anthropologist includes seeing what anthropologists see. We anthropologists are constantly looking at things—fossilized human teeth, ancient DNA, excavated stone tools, primate skeletons, and much more—and using what we see to understand biology in the past and in the present. The photos and drawn art throughout this book has been chosen to help you see what anthropologists see. I strongly encourage you to pay close attention to the visuals in the book and their captions, because much of our anthropological understanding is in the art program.

The Structure of the Book

The book is divided into three parts. Following an overview of anthropology and physical anthropology (chapter 1), Part I provides the basic context for how we understand human (and our nonhuman primate relatives') biology in the present (and how that helps us understand the past). From this section of the book you should come away with an understanding of evolution and the biology associated with it. Evolution as an idea has a long history (chapter 2). You will need to fully grasp the meaning and power of this theory, which explains humans' biological variation today and in the past. Part I also has the important job of providing you with an understanding of genetics (chapters 3 and 4). This information is a central part of the evidence for evolution, from the level of the molecule to the level of the population.

Part I also looks at the biology of living people, that of the other living primates, and the variation among primate species. I am keen on debunking the common notion that there are discrete categories—races—of human beings (chapter 5). In fact, nothing about the biology of people, present or past, indicates that we can be divided into distinct groups. After looking at how environment and culture help shape the way humans look and behave, I will look similarly at nonhuman primates (chapter 6). Because nonhuman primates' appearances are much more categorical than humans' are, nonhuman primate appearance lends itself to classification or taxonomy. In these chapters, we will look at what nonhuman primates do in the wild, what they are adapted to, and especially the environment's role in shaping their behavior and biology. By looking at living people and living nonhuman primates, we will be better equipped to understand the biological evidence drawn from the past.

Part II examines the processes and evidence physical anthropologists and other scientists use to understand the past (chapter 7), the evolution of prehuman primate ancestors that lived more than 50,000,000 years ago (chapter 8), and both the emergence of our humanlike ancestors and their evolution into modern humans (chapters 9, 10, and 11). Contrary to popular (and some scientific) opinion, human evolution did not stop when anatomically modern people first made their appearance in various corners of the globe. Rather, even into the last 10,000 years a considerable amount of biological change has occurred. Anthropologists have learned that agriculture, which began some 10,000 years ago, has been a fundamental force behind population increase. The downside of this shift to new kinds of food and the resulting population increase was a general decline in health. The later section of Part II (chapter 12) explores the nature and cause of biological change, including changes associated with health and well-being leading to today's world.

With this book plan in hand and our goals—thinking and seeing like anthropologists—in mind, let us set off on this exciting journey. Consider it a voyage of discovery, on which our shipmates include your instructor and your fellow students. If we work hard and work together, we will find perhaps the most interesting thing on Earth: ourselves.

One of the barrier islands along the Georgia coast, St. Catherines was the site of Spanish colonization in the sixteenth and seventeenth centuries.

CHAPTER 1

What Is Physical Anthropology?

I n the heat of the midday summer sun, our boat slowly made its way across the five miles of water that separate mainland Georgia from St. Catherines Island, one of a series of barrier islands dotting the Atlantic seaboard. Today, the island is covered by dense vegetation typical of the subtropical American South—palmettos and other palm trees, pines, hickories, and live oaks—and is infested with a wide array of stinging and biting insects. It is hard to imagine that this setting was once a focal point of the Spanish colonial "New World," representing the northernmost extension of Spain's claim on eastern North America. This was the location of the Roman Catholic church and mission Santa Catalina de Guale, where several hundred Indians and a dozen Spaniards lived and worked during the late 1500s and most of the 1600s.

What could possibly have motivated my field team and me to work for months under a blazing sun, fighting insects? Like any scientific investigation, our fieldwork was motivated by specific questions that we keenly wanted to answer. Buried in the sands of St. Catherines were the mortal remains—skeletons—of the native people who had lived at this long-abandoned place. These remains held answers to questions about the biology of modern people. Native Americans had lived in this area of the world for most of the last 10,000 years. We wanted to know about their biological evolution and variation: How had these people changed biologically over this time span? What caused these changes? What circumstances led to the changes that we hoped to identify and interpret?

When we first set foot on St. Catherines Island in the summer of 1982 to begin our work at Mission Santa Catalina, we were excited about our project, but little did we realize just what a spectacular scientific journey we were undertaking. The skeletons we sought turned out to provide wonderfully rich biological details about a little-understood region of the world, especially relating to the health consequences and behavioral consequences of European contact on native peoples. In setting up the research project, I had envisioned that our findings would provide a microcosm of what had unfolded globally—in the Americas, Asia, Africa, and Australia—during the previous 500 years of human history. During this period, significant biological changes had taken place in humans. Some of these changes were evolutionary—they resulted in genetic change. Other biological changes, nonevolutionary ones, reflected significant alterations in health and lifestyle, alterations that had left impressions on the skeletons we studied. Such study—of genetic and nongenetic changes—here and elsewhere in the world has proven fundamental to human beings' understanding of their biology in the early twenty-first century.

Like any scientific investigation, the research project at Mission Santa Catalina did not develop in a vacuum. Prior to our work there, my team and I had devoted nearly a decade to studying hundreds of skeletons we had excavated from the region, dating from before the arrival of Spaniards. We had learned from archaeological evidence that before AD 1000 or so, the people there ate exclusively wild animals, fish, and wild plants—they were hunters and gatherers. Never settling into one place for any period of time, they moved from place to place over the year, hunting animals, fishing on the coastline, and collecting plants. Then their descendants—the ancestors of the mission Indians—acquired corn agriculture, becoming the first farmers in the region. These people did lots of fishing, but farming produced the mainstay of their diet. This major shift in lifestyle led to the establishment of semipermanent villages. In comparison with the hunter-gatherers living before AD 1000, the later agricultural people were shorter, their skulls and limb bones were smaller, and they had more dental disease and more infections. All of this information—scientific discoveries about the prehistoric people, their biological changes, and their adaptations—set the stage for our return to the island to study the people who lived at Santa Catalina, the descendants of the prehistoric hunter-gatherers and later farmers. From our study of their remains, we learned that after the Spaniards' arrival the native people worked hard, they became more focused on producing and eating corn, and their health declined. The combination of declining quality of life and new diseases introduced by the Spaniards led to the native people's extinction in this area of North America.

The research just described is one small part of the broader discipline known as *physical anthropology*. My work concerns life on the southeastern United States Atlantic coast, but physical anthropologists explore and study *everywhere* humans and their ancestors lived. This enterprise covers a lot of ground and a lot of time, basically the entire world and the last 50,000,000 years or so! The territorial coverage of physical anthropology is so widespread and so diverse because the field addresses broad issues, seeking to understand human evolution—*what* we were in the past, *who* we are today, and *where* we will go in the future. Physical anthropologists seek answers to questions about *why* we are what we are as biological organisms. *How* we answer these questions is oftentimes difficult. The questions, though, motivate physical anthropologists to spend months in the subtropics of coastal Georgia learning about an extinct native people, or in the deserts of central Ethiopia finding and studying the remains of people who lived hundreds, thousands, or even millions of years ago, or at the high altitudes of the Andes Mountains studying living people and their responses and long-term adaptation to low oxygen and extreme cold, to name just a few of the settings you will learn about in this book. In this chapter, we will explore in more detail the nature of physical anthropology and its subject matter.

WHAT IS ANTHROPOLOGY?

When European explorers first undertook transcontinental travel (for example, Marco Polo into Asia in the late 1200s) or transoceanic voyages to faraway lands (for example, Christopher Columbus to the Americas in the late 1400s and early

1500s), they encountered people that looked, talked, dressed, and behaved very differently from themselves. When these travelers returned to their home countries, they described the peoples and cultures they saw. Building on these accounts, early scholars speculated on the relationships between humans living in Europe and those encountered in distant places. Eventually, later scholars developed new ideas about other cultures, resulting in the development of the discipline of anthropology.

Anthropology is the study of humankind, viewed from the perspective of all people and all times. As it is practiced in the United States, it includes four branches or subdisciplines: **cultural anthropology, archaeology, linguistic anthropology,** and **physical anthropology,** also called **biological anthropology (Figure 1.1)**.

Cultural anthropologists typically study present-day societies in non-Western settings, such as in Africa, South America, or Australia. **Culture**—defined as learned behavior that is transmitted from person to person—is the unifying theme of study in cultural anthropology.

Archaeologists study past human societies, focusing mostly on their material remains—such as animal and plant remains and places where people lived in the past. Archaeologists are best-known for their study of material objects—**artifacts**—from past cultures, such as weaponry and ceramics. Archaeologists study the processes behind past human behaviors—for example, why people lived where they did, why some societies were simple and others complex, and why people shifted from hunting and gathering to agriculture beginning more than 10,000 years ago. Archaeologists are the cultural anthropologists of the past—they seek to reassemble cultures of the past as though those cultures were alive today.

Linguistic anthropologists study the construction and use of language by human societies. **Language**—defined as a set of written or spoken symbols that refer to things (people, places, concepts, etc.) other than themselves—makes possible the transfer of knowledge from one person to the next and from one generation to the next. Popular among linguistic anthropologists is a subfield called **sociolinguistics**, the investigation of language's social contexts.

Physical (or biological) anthropologists study all aspects of present and past human biology. As we will explore in the next section, physical anthropology deals with the evolution of and variation among human beings and their living and past relatives.

No anthropologist is expected to be an expert in all four branches. Anthropologists in all four areas and with very different interests, however, acknowledge the diversity of humankind in all contexts. No other discipline embraces the breadth of the human condition in this manner. In fact, this remarkably diverse discipline differs from other disciplines in its commitment to the notion that humans are both biological and cultural beings. One central area of interest that many anthropologists share is the interrelationship between what humans have inherited genetically and culture. Anthropologists call this focus the **biocultural approach**. Anthropology also differs from other disciplines in emphasizing a broad comparative approach to the study of biology and culture, looking at all people (and their ancestors) and all cultures in all times and places—it is holistic.

culture Learned behavior that is transmitted from person to person.

artifacts Material objects from past cultures.

language A set of written or spoken symbols that refer to things (people, places, concepts, etc.) other than themselves.

sociolinguistics The science of investigating language's social contexts.

biocultural approach The scientific study of the interrelationship between what humans have inherited genetically and culture.

WHAT IS PHYSICAL ANTHROPOLOGY?

The short answer to this question is: *Physical anthropology is the study of human biological evolution and human biocultural variation.* Two key concepts underlie this definition.

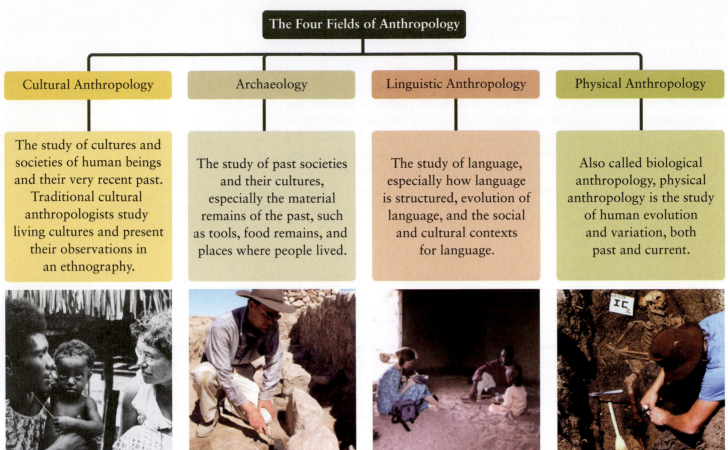

The Four Fields of Anthropology

Cultural Anthropology	Archaeology	Linguistic Anthropology	Physical Anthropology
The study of cultures and societies of human beings and their very recent past. Traditional cultural anthropologists study living cultures and present their observations in an ethnography.	The study of past societies and their cultures, especially the material remains of the past, such as tools, food remains, and places where people lived.	The study of language, especially how language is structured, evolution of language, and the social and cultural contexts for language.	Also called biological anthropology, physical anthropology is the study of human evolution and variation, both past and current.

(a)   (b)   (c)   (d)

FIGURE 1.1 ■ The Four Branches of Anthropology

(a) *Cultural anthropologists,* who study living populations, often spend time living with cultural groups to gain more intimate perspectives on those cultures. The American anthropologist Margaret Mead (1901–1978), one of the most recognizable names in cultural anthropology, studied the peoples of the Admiralty Islands, near Papua New Guinea. **(b)** *Archaeologists* study past human behaviors by investigating material remains that humans leave behind, such as buildings and other structures. In the Peruvian Andes, this archaeologist examines the remnants of a brewery used by the Wari Empire (ca. AD 750–1000). **(c)** *Linguistic anthropologists* study all aspects of language and language use. Here, Leslie Moore, a linguistic anthropologist working in a Fulbe community in northern Cameroon, records as a teacher guides a boy in memorizing Koran verses. **(d)** *Physical anthropologists* study human evolution and variation. Some physical anthropologists study skeletons from the past to investigate evolution and variation throughout human history. Those working in **forensic anthropology,** a specialty within physical anthropology, examine skeletons in hope of identifying the people whose bodies they came from. Such an identification may be of a single person or of thousands. For example, the forensic anthropologist pictured here was called on to help identify the estimated 30,000 victims of Argentina's "Dirty War," which followed the country's 1976 coup.

hominids A group of extinct and living bipedal primates in the family *Hominidae.*

Number one, every person is a product of evolutionary history, or all the biological changes that have brought humanity to its present form. The remains of humanlike beings, or **hominids,** indicate that the earliest human ancestors, in Africa, date to sometime around 6–8 million years ago (mya). Since that time, the physical appearance of hominids and their descendants, including us, has changed dramatically. Our physical appearance, our intelligence, and everything else that makes us distinctive biological organisms evolved in our predecessors, whose genes led to the species we are today. (Genes and species are among the subjects of chapters 3 and 4.)

Number two, each of us is the product of our own individual life history. From the moment you were conceived, your biological makeup has been determined mostly by your genes. (The human *genome*—that is, all the genetic material in a person—includes some 20,000–25,000 genes.) Your biological makeup is also strongly influenced by your environment. "Environment" here refers not just to the obvious factors such as climate but to everything that has affected you—the physical activities you have engaged in (which have placed stress on your muscles and bones), the food you have eaten, and many other factors that affect overall health and well-being. Environment also includes social and cultural factors. A disadvantaged social environment, such as one in which infants and children receive poor-quality nutrition, can result in negative consequences such as poor health, reduced height, and shortened life expectancy. The Indian child who lived after the shift from foraging to farming on the Georgia coast ate more corn than did the Indian child who lived in the same place before AD 1000. Because of the corn-rich diet, the later child's teeth had more cavities. Each child's condition reflects millions of years of evolution as well as more immediate circumstances, such as diet, exposure to disease, and the stresses of day-to-day living.

What Do Physical Anthropologists Do?

Physical anthropologists, scientists who study the evolution and variation of human beings, routinely travel to places throughout the United States and around the world to investigate populations. Some physical anthropologists study living people, while others study extinct and living species of our nearest biological relatives, **primates** such as lemurs, monkeys, and apes. I am among the physical anthropologists who travel to museum collections and archaeological localities to study past societies. When I tell people outside the field what I do for a living, they often think physical anthropology is quite odd, bizarre even. Frequently they ask, "Why would anyone want to study dead people and old bones and teeth?" Everyone has heard of physics, chemistry, and biology, but the average person has never heard of this field. Compared to other areas of science, physical anthropology is small. But smallness does not make it unimportant. It is practical and important, providing answers to fundamental questions that have been asked by scholars and scientists for centuries, such as *Who are we as a species? What does it mean to be human? Where did we come from?* Moreover, physical anthropology plays a vital role in addressing questions that are central to our society, sometimes involving circumstances that all of us wish had never come about. For example, the tragedy that Americans identify as 9/11 called immediately for the assistance of specialists from forensic anthropology.

Physical anthropologists study all aspects of human biology, specifically looking at the evolution and variation of human beings and their living and past relatives. This focus on biology means that physical anthropologists practice a *biological science*. But they also practice a *social science,* in that they study biology within the context of culture and behavior. Depending on their areas of interest, physical anthropologists might examine molecular structure, bones and teeth, blood types, breathing capacity and lung volume, genetics and genetic history, infectious and other types of disease, origins of language and speech, nutrition, reproduction, growth and development, aging, primate origins, primate social behavior, brain biology, and many other topics dealing with variation in both the living and the dead—sometimes the very long dead (**Figure 1.2**)!

primates A group of mammals in the order *Primates* that have complex behavior, varied forms of locomotion, and a unique suite of traits, including larger brains, forward-facing eyes, fingernails, and reduced snouts.

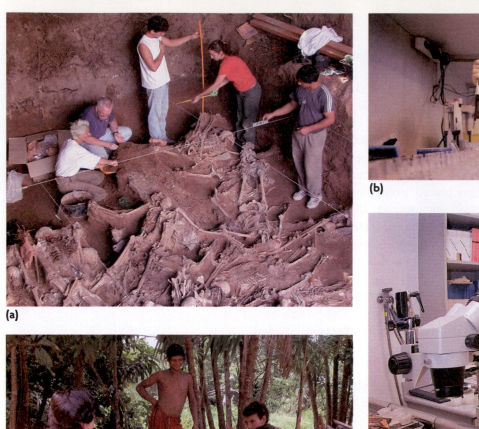

(a)

(b)

(c)

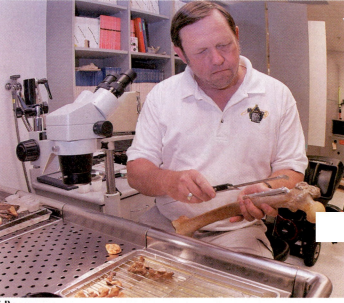

(d)

(e)

(f)

FIGURE 1.2 ■ **A Sample of What Physical Anthropologists Do**

(a) Forensic anthropologists investigate a mass grave in Argentina in hope of identifying some of the estimated 30,000 people who disappeared during the "Dirty War." **(b)** Geneticists analyze samples of human DNA for various anthropological purposes. DNA studies are used to determine how closely related humans are to other primate species, to examine human origins, and to determine individual identities. **(c)** A human biologist records the physical activities of a lactating woman (right, weaving basket) living in a rural community in the eastern Amazon, Brazil. These data will be used to calculate the woman's energy expenditure and understand how she copes with reproduction's great energy demands. **(d)** In a lab, a forensic anthropologist measures and assesses human bones. If the bones came from a contemporary grave, this forensic information might help identify the victim. If the bones belonged to a past population, physical anthropologists might use these data to gain insight into the population's health and lifestyle. **(e)** Laboratory investigations of human ancestors' bones help paleoanthropologists determine where these ancestors fit in the human family tree. **(f)** Primatologists, such as the British researcher Jane Goodall (b. 1934), study our closest living relatives, nonhuman primates. The behavior and lifestyle of chimpanzees, for example, help physical anthropologists understand our evolutionary past.

In dealing with such topics, physical anthropologists apply methods and theories developed in other disciplines as well as in their own as they answer questions that help us understand who we are, a point that I will raise over and over again throughout this book. The very nature of their discipline and their constant borrowing from other disciplines means that physical anthropologists practice an *interdisciplinary science*. For example, they might draw on the work of geologists who study the landforms and layering of deposits of soil and rock that tell us when earlier humans lived. Or they might obtain information from paleontologists, who study the evolution of life-forms in the distant past and thus provide the essential context for understanding the world in which earlier humans lived. Some physical anthropologists are trained in chemistry, so they can analyze the chemical properties of bones and teeth to determine what kinds of foods were eaten by those earlier humans. Or to learn how living humans adapt to reduced-oxygen settings, such as in the high altitudes of the Peruvian Andes Mountains, physical anthropologists might work with physiologists who study lungs' ability to absorb oxygen. The firm yet flexible identity of their science allows physical anthropologists to gather data from other disciplines in order to address key questions. Questions drive what they do.

WHAT IS SO DIFFERENT ABOUT HUMANS FROM OTHER ANIMALS?: THE SIX STEPS TO HUMANNESS

Human beings clearly differ from other animals. From humanity's earliest origin—about 6 mya, when an apelike primate began walking on two feet—to the period beginning about 10,000 years ago, when modern climates and environments emerged following what is commonly known as the Ice Age, six key attributes developed that make us unique. These attributes are bipedalism, nonhoning chewing, complex material culture and tool use, hunting, speech, and dependence on domesticated foods (**Figure 1.3**). The first development represents the most profound physical difference between humans and other animals, namely the manner in which we get around: we are committed to **bipedalism,** that is, walking on two feet. The next development was the loss of a large, honing canine tooth, like the one that apes typically use to shred their food (mostly plants) to the simple **nonhoning canine** with which we simply process food. Our ancestors' honing canine disappeared because they acquired the ability to make and use tools for processing food.

Today, our species *completely* depends on culture—and especially material culture—for its day-to-day living and its very survival. Culture, learned behavior transmitted from person to person, is a complex human characteristic that facilitates our survival by enabling us to adapt to different settings. **Material culture** is the part of culture that is expressed as objects that humans use to manipulate environments. For example, hammers and nails are forms of material culture that enable us to make cabinets, tables, and countless other forms of material culture. The material remains of past cultures go back hundreds of thousands of years, back to the first simple tools made from rocks more than 2.5 mya (**Figure 1.4**). Material culture today makes our lifestyles possible. Can you imagine your life without it? We could survive without modern additions to material culture, such as cars, computers, TVs, plumbing, and electricity, as our ancestors did before the last century.

bipedalism Walking on two feet.

nonhoning canine An upper canine that, as part of a nonhoning chewing mechanism, is not sharpened against the lower third premolar.

material culture The part of culture that is expressed as objects that humans use to manipulate environments.

FIGURE
1.3

The Six Big Events of Human Evolution:
Bipedalism, Nonhoning Chewing, Dependence on Material Culture, Speech, Hunting, an

Bipedalism   6 mya

The upright, bipedal (two-footed) gait was the first hallmark feature of our hominid ancestors.

Nonhoning Chewing   5.5 mya

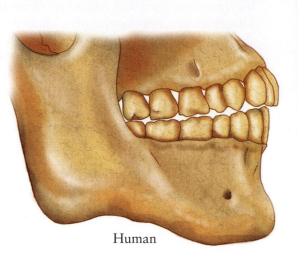

Human

Speech   2.5 mya

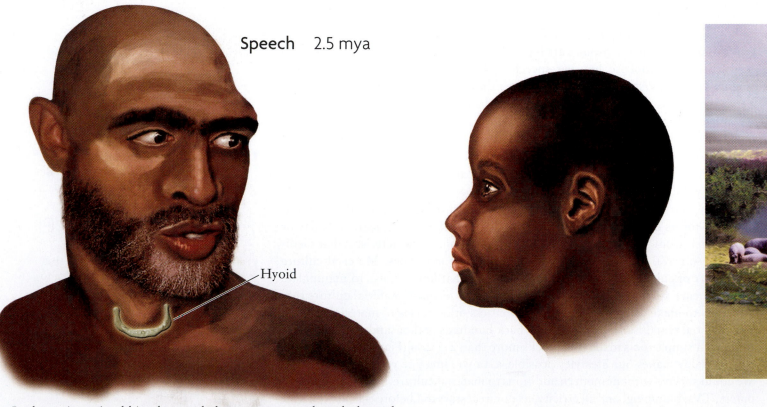

Hyoid

In the entire animal kingdom, only humans can speak and, through speech, express complex thoughts sid ideas. The shape of the hyoid bone is unique to hominids and reflects their ability to speak. Speech is part of the overall package in the human lineage of increased cognition, intelligence, and brain-size expansion.

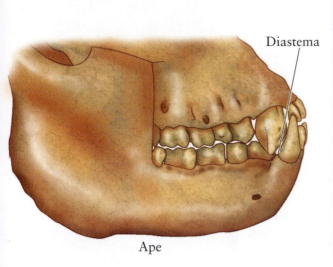

Diastema

Ape

Humans' nonhoning chewing complex (left) lacks large, projecting canines in the upper jaw and a diastema, or gap, between the lower canine and the third premolar. The chewing complex of apes such as gorillas (right) has large, projecting upper canines and a diastema in the lower jaw to accommodate them.

Material Culture and Tools   2.5 mya

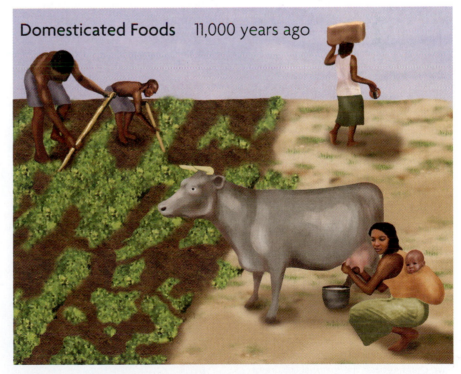

Humans' production and use of stone tools is one example of complex material culture. The tools of our closest living relatives, the chimpanzees, do not approach the complexity and diversity of modern and ancestral humans' tools.

Hunting   1 mya

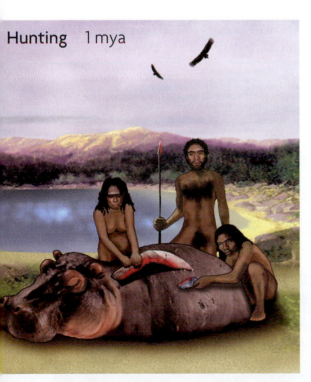

Humans' relatively large brains require lots of energy to develop and function. Animal protein is an ideal source of that energy, and humans obtain it by eating animals they hunt. To increase their chances of success in hunting, humans often employ tools and cooperative strategies.

Domesticated Foods   11,000 years ago

Humans domesticate a wide variety of plants and animals, controlling their life cycles, using them as food and other products.

FIGURE 1.4 ■ First Tools
The earliest stone tools date to 2.6 mya and are associated with early human ancestors in East Africa. The example shown here is from the Gona River area in the Afar region of Ethiopia.

What about living without basic material culture, such as shelter and clothing, especially in climates where it can be very, very cold in the winter? Without material culture, how would any of us get food? The answer to both questions is simple: we could not make it without some forms of technology—to regulate temperature, to acquire food, and so on. Some societies are much less technologically complex than others, but no society functions without any technology.

Anthropologists and animal behaviorists have shown that human beings are not, however, the only type of animal that has or can employ material culture. Primatologists have observed some chimpanzee societies in Africa, for example, making simple tools from twigs (**Figure 1.5**). In laboratories, chimpanzees have

FIGURE 1.5 ■ Tool-Making
Once thought to be a uniquely human phenomenon, tool-making has been observed in chimpanzees, the closest biological relatives of humans. As seen here, chimpanzees have modified twigs to scoop termites from nests. Other chimpanzees have used two rocks as a hammer and anvil to crack open nuts. More recently, gorillas were seen using a stick to test the depth of a pool of water they wanted to cross. Tool use such as this may have characterized the material culture of the earliest human ancestors.

been taught to use physical symbols that approximate human communication. Still, these and other forms of material culture used by nonhuman species are nowhere near as complex as those created by humans.

The other three key attributes of humanness—hunting, speech, and dependence on domesticated foods—appeared much later in human evolution than bipedalism, nonhoning chewing, and complex material culture and tool use. *Hunting* here refers to the social behavior whereby a group, adult men in general, organize themselves to pursue animals for food. This behavior likely dates back to a million or more years ago. Some nonhuman primates organize to pursue prey, but they do not use tools or travel long distances as humans distinctively do when they hunt.

An equally distinctive human behavior is speech. We are the only animal that communicates by talking. Unfortunately for research purposes, recording-and-listening technology was invented only about a century ago. For information about long-past speech, anthropologists rely on indirect evidence within the skeleton. For example, the hyoid bone, in the neck, is part of the vocal structure that helps produce words. The unique appearance of the human hyoid helps anthropologists conjecture about the origins of speech.

The most recently developed unique human behavior is the domesticated manner in which we acquire our food. Beginning about 10,000 years before present (yBP), humans began to raise animals and grow plants. This development led to our current reliance on domesticated species. This reliance has had a profound impact on human biology and behavior.

Human beings' unique behaviors and survival mechanisms, and the anatomical features related to them, arose through the complex interaction of biology and culture. Indeed, our ancestors' increasing dependence on culture for survival has made us entirely culture-dependent for survival. In the following chapters, we will therefore be looking at human origins and human behavior—the particulars of physical anthropology—from a biocultural perspective.

HOW WE KNOW WHAT WE KNOW: THE SCIENTIFIC METHOD

How do physical anthropologists make decisions about what their subject matter means? More specifically, how do we know what we know about human evolution and human variation? Like all other scientists, physical anthropologists carefully and systematically observe the natural world around them. These observations form the basis for identifying problems, developing questions, and gathering evidence—data—that will help answer the questions and solve the problems—that is, fill gaps in scientific knowledge about how the natural world operates. These data are used to test **hypotheses,** possible explanations for the processes under study. Scientists observe and then reject or accept these hypotheses. This process of determining whether ideas are right or wrong is called the **scientific method** (Table 1.1). It is the foundation of science.

Science (Latin *scientia*, meaning "knowledge"), then, is more than just knowledge of the facts about the natural world. Science is a way of acquiring knowledge—a way of knowing—through observation of natural phenomena. This repeated acquisition results in an ever-expanding knowledge base, one built from measurable, repeatable, and highly tangible observations. In this way, science is **empirical,** or based

data Evidence gathered to help answer questions, solve problems, and fill gaps in scientific knowledge.

hypotheses Testable statements that potentially explain specific phenomena observed in the natural world.

scientific method An empirical research method in which data is gathered from observations of phenomena, hypotheses are formulated and tested, and conclusions are drawn that validate or modify the original hypotheses.

empirical Verified through observation and experiment.

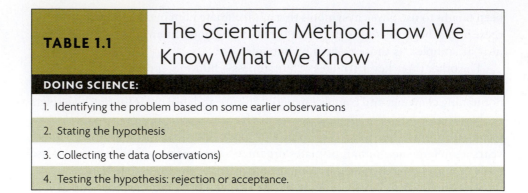

TABLE 1.1	The Scientific Method: How We Know What We Know
DOING SCIENCE:	
1. Identifying the problem based on some earlier observations	
2. Stating the hypothesis	
3. Collecting the data (observations)	
4. Testing the hypothesis: rejection or acceptance.	

theory A set of hypotheses that have been rigorously tested and validated, leading to their establishment as a generally accepted explanation of specific phenomena.

anatomical Pertaining to an organism's physical structure.

arboreal Tree-dwelling; adapted to living in the trees.

morphology Physical shape and appearance.

FIGURE 1.6 ■ Charles Darwin
George Richmond painted this portrait of Darwin in 1840.

on observation or experiment. After the systematic collection of observations, the scientist develops a **theory**—an explanation, not just a description, of phenomena. For many nonscientists, a theory is simply a guess or a hunch, but for a scientist, a theory is not just some stab at an explanation. Rather, a theory is an explanation grounded in a great deal of evidence, or what a lawyer calls the "evidentiary record." A scientist builds a case by identifying incontrovertible facts. To arrive at these facts, the scientist examines and reexamines the evidence, putting it through many tests.

The scientist thus employs observation, documentation, and testing to generate hypotheses and, eventually, to construct a theory based on those hypotheses. Hypotheses *explain* observations, *predict* the results of future investigation, and *can be refuted* by new evidence.

For example, the great English naturalist Charles Robert Darwin (1809–1882) developed the hypothesis that the origin of human bipedalism was linked to the shift from life in the trees to life on the ground (**Figure 1.6**). Darwin's hypothesis was based on his own observations of humans walking, other scientists' then-limited observations of nonhuman primate behavior, and other scientists' **anatomical** evidence, or information (about structural makeup) drawn from dissections, in this case of apes. Darwin's hypothesis led to an additional hypothesis, based on evidence that accumulated over the following century and a half, that the first hominids arose in the open grasslands of Africa from some apelike animal that was **arboreal**—that is, had once lived in trees.

Support for Darwin's hypothesis about human origins—and in particular the origin of bipedal locomotion—began to erode in 2001, when a group of scientists discovered the earliest hominids, from 5.2 to 5.8 mya, in the modern country of Ethiopia. Contrary to expectation and accepted wisdom, these hominids had lived not in grasslands but in woodlands. Moreover, unlike modern humans, whose fingers and toes are straight because we are fully terrestrial—we live on the ground (**Figure 1.7**)— the early hominids had slightly curved fingers and toes. The physical shape and appearance, what physical anthropologists call **morphology,** of the hominids' finger and toe bones indicate a lot of time spent in trees, holding onto branches, moving from limb to limb. These findings forced scientists to reject Darwin's hypothesis, to toss out what had been a fundamental tenet of physical anthropology.

This story does not end, however, with the understanding that the earliest hominids lived in forests. Instead, this new hypothesis generated new questions. For example, why did the earliest hominids arise in a wooded setting, and why did they "come out of the woods" as time went on? Later in this book, we will consider

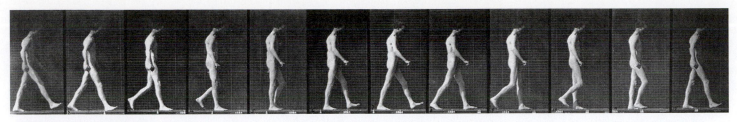

FIGURE 1.7 ▪ **Bipedalism**
These 1887 photographs by Eadweard Muybridge capture humans' habitual upright stance. Other animals, including primates such as chimpanzees, occasionally walk on two feet, but humans alone make bipedalism their main form of locomotion. As Darwin observed, this stance frees the hands to hold objects. What are some other advantages of bipedalism?

these questions. For now, the point is that science is a *self-correcting* approach to knowledge acquisition. Scientists develop new hypotheses as new findings are made. Scientists use these hypotheses to build theories. And like the hypotheses that underlie them, theories can be modified or even replaced by better theories, depending on findings made through meticulous observation. Over time, as observations and hypotheses and theories are tested and subjected to the test of time, science revises its own errors.

If a theory proves absolutely true, it becomes a **scientific law.** Among the few scientific laws, the well-known ones are the laws of gravity, thermodynamics, and motion. But scientific truth seldom gets finalized into law. Rather, truth is continuously developed—new facts are discovered and new understandings about natural phenomena are made.

As my crew and I traveled to St. Catherines Island, we were intent on discovering new facts and forming new understandings about the prehistoric farmers' descendants who were first encountered by Spaniards in the late 1500s. These facts and understandings would enable us to test hypotheses about human evolution and human variation. Once we completed the months of arduous fieldwork and the years of laboratory investigations on the remains that fieldwork uncovered, we would have some answers. The scientific method would guide us in providing insights into this part of the human lineage—human beings' most recent evolution—and how our species came to be what it is in the early twenty-first century.

scientific law A theory that becomes absolutely true.

ANSWERING THE BIG QUESTIONS

What is anthropology?

■ Anthropology is the study of humankind. In two major ways, it differs from other sciences that study humankind. First, anthropology views humans as both biological and cultural beings. Second, anthropology emphasizes a holistic, comparative approach, encompassing all people at all times and all places.

■ The four branches of anthropology are cultural anthropology (study of living cultures), archaeology (study of past cultures), linguistic anthropology (study of language), and physical anthropology.

What is physical anthropology?

■ Physical (or biological) anthropology is the study of human biology, specifically of the evolution and variation of humans (and their relatives, past and present).

■ Physical anthropology is an eclectic field, deriving theory and method both from within the discipline and from other sciences in addressing important questions about human evolution and human variation.

What makes us human and different from other animals?

■ Humans living today are the product of millions of years of evolutionary history and their own personal life histories.

■ Humans have six unique physical and behavioral characteristics: bipedalism, nonhoning chewing, complex material culture and tool use, hunting, speech, and dependence on domesticated foods.

How do physical anthropologists know what they know?

■ Physical anthropologists derive knowledge via the scientific method. This method involves observations, the development of questions, and the answering of those questions. Scientists formulate and test hypotheses that they hope will lead to theories about the natural world.

⊚ wwnorton.com/studyspace

KEY TERMS

anatomical
anthropology
arboreal
archaeology
artifacts
biocultural approach
biological anthropology
bipedalism
cultural anthropology
culture
data
empirical
forensic anthropology

hominids
hypotheses
language
linguistic anthropology
material culture
morphology
nonhoning canine
physical anthropology
primates
scientific law
scientific method
sociolinguistics
theory

ADDITIONAL READINGS

Molnar, S. 2005. *Human Variation: Races, Types, and Ethnic Groups.* Upper Saddle River, NJ: Prentice Hall.

Moore, J. A. 1999. *Science as a Way of Knowing: The Foundations of Modern Biology.* Cambridge, MA: Harvard University Press.

Spencer, F., ed. 1997. *History of Physical Anthropology: An Encyclopedia.* New York: Garland.

Stocking, G., ed. 1974. *The Shaping of American Anthropology, 1883–1911: A Franz Boas Reader.* New York: Basic Books.

Some Periodicals in Anthropology

General anthropology: *American Anthropologist, Annual Review of Anthropology, Current Anthropology.*

Archaeology: *American Antiquity, Antiquity, Archaeology, Journal of Archaeological Science, Latin American Antiquity, World Archaeology.*

Cultural anthropology: *American Anthropologist, Cultural Anthropology.*

Physical anthropology: *American Journal of Human Biology, American Journal of Physical Anthropology, Evolutionary Anthropology, Human Biology, Journal of Human Evolution, Yearbook of Physical Anthropology.*

The living primates—such as, here, orangutans and humans—have much in common, biological and behavioral. Their study provides essential context for understanding variation and evolution, now and in the past.

The Present: Foundation for the Past

Some physical anthropologists learn about human evolution by studying living plants and animals, including humans. Other physical anthropologists learn about human evolution by investigating the past, now represented mostly by fossilized bones and fossilized teeth. Together, living and past enable us to understand evolution in the largest context. The fossil record provides us with the history of humans and of humanlike ancestors, while the living record provides the essential picture through which to view that history. Charles Darwin, the pioneering force behind our knowledge about evolution and natural selection, developed his ideas by studying living plants and animals. He had the extraordinary insight to realize that his theories and hypotheses applied to past organisms. For Darwin, living organisms were key to interpreting the past because they displayed evidence of evolution's elements and mechanics. In the same way, living organisms provide insights—into fundamental forces such as reproduction, DNA synthesis, protein synthesis, and behavior—that are not available, at least in the same way, within the past record. Part I of this book lays out observations and principles based on the study of living populations, the essential background for understanding evolution. Part II then digs into the past, into the study of ancestors whose descendants are present in the world (all of us now living) and of those evolutionary lineages that did not survive.

(a)

(d)

(b)

(c)

During a round-the-world voyage from 1831 to 1836, Charles Darwin visited **(a)** Ecuador's Galápagos Islands. Among the unique life-forms he observed on the islands were **(b)** finches and, as in **(c)** Meredith Nugent's illustration from the 1830s, elephant tortoises. Darwin's observations provided the groundwork for his theory of natural selection, the basis of **(d)** his 1859 book, *On the Origin of Species*.

CHAPTER 2

Evolution: Constructing a Fundamental Scientific Theory

fossils Physical remains of part or all of once-living organisms, mostly bones and teeth, that have become mineralized by the replacement of organic with inorganic materials.

species A group of related organisms that can interbreed and produce fertile, viable offspring.

habitat The specific area of the natural environment in which an organism lives.

The nineteenth century was the century of scientific collecting. During the 1800s, the world discovered itself through collections. Expeditions large and small—involving scientists, explorers, and adventurers—crossed the continents and investigated land masses around the globe. These teams collected hundreds of thousands of samples: plants, animals, rocks, and preserved remains (or **fossils**—the subject of chapter 7). If it seemed worth picking off the ground or exposing in some other fashion, it was fair game. This kind of work, on one of these international expeditions, helped lay the foundation for the most important biological theory, arguably among the half dozen most important scientific theories—the theory of evolution.

In 1831, a 22-year-old Englishman and recent graduate of Cambridge University, Charles Darwin, was appointed the naturalist for a five-year voyage around the world on the ship HMS *Beagle* (**Figure 2.1**). Imagine that as your first job right out of college! Young Mr. Darwin, who was trained in medicine and theology, accepted a difficult task. He was to collect, document, and study the natural world—plants and animals, especially—everywhere the ship harbored. By the end of that voyage, Darwin had amassed a wonderfully comprehensive collection of plants, insects, birds, shells, fossils, and lots of other materials. The specimens he collected and the observations he made about the things he saw on that trip would form the basis of his lifetime of research. His discoveries would do no less than shape the future of the biological sciences, including physical anthropology. His ideas would provide the key to understanding the origin and evolution of life itself.

Soon after returning home from the voyage, Darwin began to formulate questions about the origins of plants and animals living in the many lands he and his shipmates had explored. His most prominent observations concerned the physical differences, or variation, between and among members of **species,** or like animals and like plants. He articulated the phenomenon best in his notes on finches, birds that live in the Galápagos, a small cluster of islands 965 km (600 mi) off the coast of Ecuador. Not only did these birds differ from island to island, but even within a single island they seemed to vary according to **habitat,** or surroundings. For example, finches living on an island's coast had a different beak shape than finches

BIG QUESTIONS

- How did the theory of evolution come to be?

- What was Darwin's contribution to the theory of evolution?

- What has happened since Darwin in the development of our understanding of evolution?

living in an island's interior (**Figure 2.2**). These observations raised two questions for Darwin: *Why* were the birds different from island to island and from habitat to habitat? *How* did different species of finches arise? After years of study, Darwin answered these questions with an idea called "descent with modification," or the theory of evolution.

Darwin also came to realize that the variations in physical characteristics of the different species of finches and other organisms were **adaptations**—physical characteristics that enhance an organism's ability to survive and reproduce. Darwin recognized many other adaptations in the natural world, and he concluded that adaptation was the crux of evolution. To connect these processes, he coined the term **natural selection.** According to this principle, biological characteristics that enhance survival increase in frequency from generation to generation. Members of a population endowed with these characteristics produce more offspring that survive to reproductive age than members of a population that are not endowed with these characteristics. Natural selection is thus the primary driver of evolution. Recognizing that the different species of finches all derived from a single common ancestor that had originated in South America, Darwin also postulated the process of **adaptive radiation:** out of one species branch closely related multiple species.

(a)

(b)

FIGURE 2.1 ■ **Darwin's Voyage**
(a) Charles Darwin ca. 1855, about 25 years after he set out on HMS *Beagle.* **(b)** In this 1890 illustration, the ship is passing through the Strait of Magellan, during the South American stretch of **(c)** its worldwide journey, whose ports of call are here mapped.

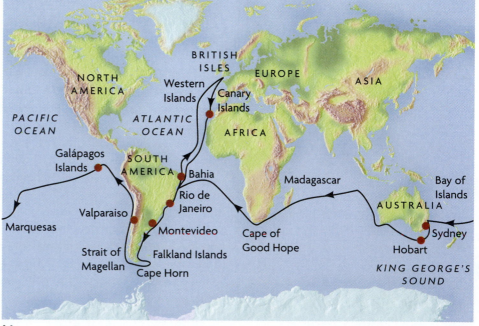

(c)

1. Geospiza magnirostris.
3. Geospiza parvula.
2. Geospiza fortis.
4. Certhidea olivasea.

FIGURE 2.2 ■ Darwin Finches
Darwin studied the physical variation in finches living on different islands of the Galápagos. Among other attributes, he studied beak shape, which varied from island to island. Eventually, Darwin related each beak shape to diet, especially to the texture of food and how the food was acquired. Finches with larger beaks typically consumed harder foods, such as seeds and nuts, while finches with smaller beaks ate softer foods, such as berries. Darwin concluded that each finch species had adapted to the particular environment and food resources of its island.

Darwin regarded evolution as simply biological change from generation to generation. Many evolutionary biologists today limit their definition of evolution to genetic change only. However, nongenetic developmental change—biological change occurring within an individual's lifetime—can give an adaptive advantage (or disadvantage) to an individual or individuals within a population. Moreover, genes control developmental processes, which likewise influence other genes.

In subsequent chapters, we will further explore these and other aspects of evolution. Although the core of this book is human evolution or how human biology came to be, understanding human evolution requires understanding the term *evolution* as it applies to all living organisms. In this chapter, we will take a historical approach to the term and the theory behind it. After reading about its intellectual history before Darwin, Darwin's contribution, and developments since Darwin, you should have a clear idea of what physical anthropologists and other evolutionary biologists mean by *evolution*.

adaptations Changes in physical structure, function, or behavior that allow an organism or species to survive and reproduce in a given environment.

natural selection The process by which some organisms, with features that enable them to adapt to the environment, preferentially survive and reproduce, thereby increasing the frequency of those features in the population.

adaptive radiation The diversification of an ancestral group of organisms into new forms that are adapted to specific environmental niches.

THE THEORY OF EVOLUTION: THE CONTEXT FOR DARWIN

Before Darwin's time, Western scientists' understanding of Earth and the organisms that inhabit it was strongly influenced by religious doctrine. In the Judeo-Christian view, the planet was relatively young, and both its surface and the life-forms on it had not changed since their miraculous creation. By the late 1700s, scientists had

FIGURE 2.3 ■ **James Hutton**
Hutton (here depicted ca. 1790) founded modern geology with his theory of the earth's formation. Hutton realized that the same natural processes he observed in Scotland had occurred in the past.

realized three key things about the world and its inhabitants: the Earth is quite ancient, its surface is very different than it was in the past, and plants and animals have changed over time. These realizations about the natural world provided the context for Darwin's theory of evolution.

To generate his theory, Darwin drew on information from five scientific disciplines: *geology, paleontology, taxonomy* and *systematics, demography,* and what is now called *evolutionary biology.* **Geology** is the study of Earth, especially with regard to its composition, activity, and history. This discipline has demonstrated the great age of our planet and the development of its landscape. **Paleontology** is the study of fossils. This discipline has detailed past life-forms, many now extinct. **Taxonomy** is the classification of past and living life-forms. This discipline laid the foundation for **systematics,** the study of biological relationships over time. **Demography** is the study of population, especially with regard to birth, survival, and death and the major factors that influence these three key parts of life. **Evolutionary biology** is the study of organisms and their changes. By investigating the fundamental principles by which evolution operates, Darwin founded this discipline. In the following sections, we will look at these fields in more detail.

Geology: Reconstructing Earth's Dynamic History

We now know that our planet is 4.6 billion years old and that over time its surface has changed dramatically. If you had espoused these ideas in, say, the late 1600s, you would not have been believed, and you would have been condemned by the Church because you had contradicted the Bible. According to a literal interpretation of the Bible, Earth is a few thousand years old and its surface is static. The Scottish scientist James Hutton (1726–1797) became dissatisfied with the biblical interpretation of the planet's history (**Figure 2.3**). He devoted his life to studying natural forces, such as wind and rain, and how they affected the landscape in Scotland. Hutton inferred from his observations that these forces changed Earth's surface in the past just as they do in the present. Wind and rain created erosion, which provided the raw materials—sand, rock, and soil—for the formation of new land surfaces. Over time, these surfaces became stacked one on top of the other, forming layers, or strata, of geologic deposits (**Figure 2.4**). From the (very long) time it took for these strata to build up, he calculated Earth's age in the millions of years. This was a revolutionary, indeed heretical, realization.

Hutton's idea—that natural processes operating today are the same as natural processes that happened in the past—is called **uniformitarianism.** Few paid much attention to Hutton's important contribution to our understanding of Earth's history until the rediscovery of the idea by the Scottish geologist Charles Lyell (1797–1875; **Figure 2.5**). Lyell devoted considerable energy to thinking and writing about uniformitarianism and its implications for explaining the history of our planet. His calculations of how long it would have taken for all known strata to build up created a mountain of evidence, an undeniable record, that Earth was millions of years old. Hutton and Lyell, relying on empirical evidence and personal observation to develop their ideas and to test clear hypotheses about the natural world, had revised the timescale for the study of past life.

FIGURE 2.4 ■ **Geologic Strata**
The succession of strata from oldest at the bottom to youngest at the top (as here, in Utah's Bryce Canyon) marks the formation of new land surfaces over time.

Paleontology: Reconstructing the History of Life on Earth

For hundreds of years, people have been finding the preserved—that is, fossilized—remains of organisms all over the world (see also the full discussion in chapter 7). To test his hypothesis that fossils are the remains of past life, the English scientist Robert Hooke (1635–1703) studied the microscopic structure of fossil wood. After observing that the tissue structure of the fossil wood was identical to the tissue structure of living trees, Hooke concluded that the fossil wood derived from once-living trees (**Figure 2.6**).

Fossils' potential to illuminate the past was demonstrated by the French naturalist and zoologist Georges Cuvier (1769–1832). Cuvier devoted considerable effort to learning the anatomy, or structural makeup, of many kinds of animals (**Figure 2.7**). Pioneering what we now call paleontology and comparative anatomy, he applied his extensive knowledge of comparative anatomy to fossils. By doing so, he reconstructed the physical characteristics of past animals—their appearance, physiology, and behavior. Although not very accurate by today's standards, these efforts provided early tools for understanding past life-forms as once-living organisms. Through detailed reconstructions, Cuvier demonstrated that fossils found in geologic strata in France were the remains of animals that had gone extinct at some point in the remote past. Cuvier's work provided the first basic understanding of the history of life, from the earliest forms to recent ones.

Cuvier observed that each stratum seemed to contain a unique set of fossils. What happened to the animals represented by each set, each layer? Cuvier concluded that they must have gone extinct due to some powerful catastrophe, such as an earthquake or a volcanic eruption. He surmised that following each catastrophe, the region was vacant of all life and was subsequently repopulated by a different group of animals moving into it from elsewhere. This perspective is called **catastrophism.**

FIGURE 2.5 ◼ **Charles Lyell**
Lyell (here depicted ca. 1845) rediscovered Hutton's work and the idea of uniformitarianism. Lyell's research, based on examinations of geologic strata, confirmed Hutton's estimate of Earth's very old age.

uniformitarianism The theory that processes that occurred in the geologic past are still at work today.

catastrophism The doctrine asserting that cataclysmic events (such as volcanoes, earthquakes, and floods), rather than evolutionary processes, are responsible for geologic changes throughout Earth's history.

(a)

(b)

FIGURE 2.6 ◼ **Robert Hooke**
(a) Hooke did pioneering biological research using a very simple microscope. He was the first to identify cells; in fact, he coined the term *cell*. **(b)** This illustration of cork wood cells appeared in Hooke's *Micrographia* (1667), the first major book on microscopy. His examinations of cells like this enabled Hooke to determine that fossils represented past life-forms.

FIGURE 2.7 ■ **Georges Cuvier**
(a) One of Cuvier's most important contributions to science was the concept of extinction. Here, Cuvier is depicted examining a fish fossil. **(b)** In his 1796 paper on fossil and living elephants, Cuvier suggested that mammoth remains represented a species different from any living elephant species and, therefore, mammoth remains were from a species that had gone extinct. This idea was revolutionary, because the common perception was that God had created all species, none of which had ever gone extinct.

(a)

(b)

We now know that Earth history does not consist of sequential catastrophes and resulting extinctions. Past catastrophes, such as the extinction of the dinosaurs 65 mya, have profoundly affected the direction of evolution.

However, such events are rare and do not explain even the sequence of fossils Cuvier observed, mostly in the region called the Paris Basin. In addition to confirming that fossils were the remains of life in the distant past, though, Cuvier revealed that the most recent geologic strata contain mostly mammals and earlier geologic strata contain mostly reptiles, including the dinosaurs.

Taxonomy and Systematics: Classifying Living Organisms and Identifying Their Biological Relationships

In the pre-Darwinian world, most scientists who studied life-forms realized the importance of developing a taxonomy—a classification of life-forms—for identifying biological relationships. Early efforts at taxonomy took a commonsense approach. Animals were placed within major groups such as dogs, cats, horses, cattle, and people. Plants were placed within major groups such as trees, shrubs, vines, and weeds.

As late as the seventeenth century, scientists generally believed that species were immutable. In their view, life had changed very little, or not at all, since the time of the single Creation. Thus, early taxonomists were not motivated by an interest in evolution. Rather, they were motivated by their desire to present the fullest and most accurate picture of the Creator's intentions for His newly created world. To construct the best possible taxonomy, the English naturalist John Ray (1627–1705) advocated personal observation, careful description, and consideration of plants' and animals' many attributes. Ray's attention to detail laid the

Pre-Darwinian Theory and Ideas: Groundwork for Evolution

Charles Darwin first presented his theory of evolution in his book *On the Origin of Species* (1859). Based on years of personal observation and of study, this unifying biological theory drew on geology, paleontology, taxonomy and systematics, and demography.

SCIENTIST	CONTRIBUTION (AND YEAR OF PUBLICATION)	SIGNIFICANCE
James Hutton	Calculated Earth's age as millions of years (1788)	Provided geologic evidence necessary for calculating time span of evolution
Charles Lyell	Rediscovered and reinforced Hutton's ideas (1830)	Provided more geologic evidence
Robert Hooke	Proved that fossils are organisms' remains (1665)	Revealed that fossils would provide the history of past life
Georges Cuvier	Extensively studied fossils (1796)	Revealed much variation in the fossil record
John Ray	Pioneered taxonomy based on physical appearance (1660)	Created the first scientific classification of plants and animals
Carolus Linnaeus	Wrote *Systems of Nature* (1735)	Presented the binomial nomenclature taxonomy of plants and animals
Thomas Malthus	Founded demography: only some will find enough food to survive (1798)	Provided the concept of characteristics advantageous for survival
Jean-Baptiste de Lamarck	Posited characteristics acquired via inheritance (Lamarckism) (1809)	Provided first serious model of physical traits' passing from parents to offspring
Erasmus Darwin	Also posited characteristics (determined by wants and needs) acquired via inheritance (1794)	Advanced the notion that physical changes occurred in the past

groundwork for later taxonomy, especially for the binomial nomenclature (two-name) system developed by the Swedish naturalist Carl von Linné (1707–1778). Von Linné, better known by his Latinized name, Carolus Linnaeus, gave each plant and animal a higher-level **genus** (plural, *genera*) name and a lower-level species (plural is also *species*) name (**Figure 2.8**). A single genus could include one or more species. For example, when Linnaeus named human beings *Homo*

genus A group of related species.

FIGURE 2.8 ■ Carolus Linnaeus
Linnaeus, a botanist, zoologist, and physician, is known for his contributions to the system of classification used today by all biological scientists, including physical anthropologists. He is also thought of as one founder of modern ecology.

CONCEPT CHECK

Darwin Borrows from Malthus

Five of Malthus's observations inspired Darwin's theory of natural selection.

Observation 1
For most organisms, every pair of parents produces multiple (sometimes many) offspring.

Observation 2
For most organisms, the population size remains the same. No increase occurs over time.

Observation 3
Population is limited by the food supply.

Observation 4
Members of populations compete for access to food.

Observation 5
No two members of a species are alike in their physical attributes—variation exists.

Theory: Evolution by Means of Natural Selection
Individuals having variation that is advantageous for survival to reproductive age produce more offspring (and more offspring that survive) than individuals lacking this variation.

sapiens—*Homo* being the genus, *sapiens* the species—he thought there were species and subspecies of living humans (an idea discussed further in chapter 5). The presence of more than one level in his taxonomy acknowledged different degrees of physical similarity. Today, we recognize that *sapiens* is the one living species in the genus *Homo* (**Figure 2.9**).

Like Ray, Linnaeus was committed to the notion that life-forms were static, fixed at the time of the Creation. In later editions of his book, he hinted at the possibility that some species may be related to each other because of common descent, but he never developed these ideas. His taxonomy is still used today, although viewed with a much stronger sense of present and past variation. The system's flexibility aided evolutionary biologists in their study of biological diversity, and the focus on taxonomic relationships over time is now called systematics.

Demography: Influences on Population Size and Competition for Limited Resources

After returning to England and while developing his ideas on natural selection, Darwin read the works of all the great scientists of the time. Probably the most important influence on his ideas was *An Essay on the Principle of Population*, by the English political economist Thomas Malthus (1766–1834) (**Figure 2.10**). First published in 1798, Malthus's book made the case that an abundance of food—enough to feed anyone born—would allow human population to increase geometrically and indefinitely.

TAXONOMIC CATEGORY	TAXONOMIC LEVEL	COMMON CHARACTERISTICS
Kingdom	Animalia	Mobile multicellular organisms that consume other organisms for food and develop during an embryo stage.
Subkingdom	Eumetazoa	All major animals (except sponges) that contain true tissue layers, organized as germ layers, which develop into organs in humans.
Phylum	Chordata	Group of vertebrate and invertebrate animals that have a notochord, which becomes the vertebral column in humans and other primates.
Subphylum	Vertebrata	Animals with vertebral columns or backbones (including fish, amphibians, reptiles, birds, and mammals).
Superclass	Tetrapoda	Vertebrate animals with four feet or legs, including amphibians, birds, dinosaurs, and mammals.
Class	Mammalia	Group of warm-blooded vertebrate animals that produce milk for their young in mammary glands. They have hair or fur and specialized teeth.
Subclass	Theria	Group of mammals that produce live young without a shelled egg (including placental and marsupial mammals).
Order	Primates	Group of mammals specialized for life in the trees, with large brains, stereoscopic vision, opposable thumbs, and grasping hands and feet.
Suborder	Anthropoidea	Group of primates, including monkeys, apes, and humans, but not prosimians. They have long life cycles and are relatively large-bodied.
Family	Hominidae	Group of anthropoids, including the humans, great apes, and human ancestors. They have the largest bodies and brain sizes of all primates.
Genus	*Homo*	Group of hominids including modern humans, their direct ancestors, and extinct relatives (e.g., Neandertals). They are bipedal and have large brains.
Species	*sapiens*	Modern and ancestral modern humans. They have culture, use language, and inhabit every continent except Antarctica.
Subspecies	*sapiens*	Modern humans alone.

FIGURE 2.9 ■ **The Place of Humans in Linnaeus's Taxonomy**
Linnaeus's system organized living things into various levels of hierarchical classification. Kingdom, at the top of the taxonomy, is the largest classification. The five kingdoms of the natural world—animals, plants, fungi, protists, monera—include all living organisms. Through descending taxonomic levels, each group's size gets progressively smaller. For example, there are fewer organisms in a genus than there are in a phylum. Additionally, these classifications reflect organisms' relationships to one another. For example, organisms within a genus are more closely related than are those from different genera.

In reality, the *Essay* argued, there simply is not enough food for everyone born, so population is limited by food supply. Who survives to reproductive age? Those who can successfully compete for food. Whose children thrive? Those of survivors who manage to feed their offspring. Applying Malthus's demographic ideas to human and nonhuman animals, Darwin concluded that some members of any species successfully compete for food because they have some special attribute or attributes. That an individual characteristic could facilitate survival was a revelation!

Evolutionary Biology: Explaining the Transformation of Earlier Life-Forms into Later Life-Forms

By the late 1700s, a handful of scientists had begun to argue that contrary to religious doctrine, organisms are not fixed—they change over time, sometimes in dramatic ways. Simply, life evolved in the past and evolution is an ongoing, undirected process. Building on this concept, the French naturalist Jean-Baptiste de Monet (1744–1829), better known by his title, Chevalier de Lamarck, speculated that plants and animals not only change in form over time but do so for purposes of self-improvement. Lamarck believed that in response to new demands or needs, life-forms develop new anatomical modifications, such as new organs. His central idea—that when life-forms reproduce, they pass on to their offspring the modifications they have acquired to that point—is called *Lamarckian inheritance of acquired characteristics*, or **Lamarckism** (**Figure 2.11**). We now know Lamarck's mechanism for evolution to be wrong—offspring do not inherit traits acquired by their parents—but his work was the first major attempt to develop a theory built on the premise that living organisms arose from precursor species. Lamarck was also convinced that humans evolved from some apelike animal.

Among the other scholars who believed that life had changed over time was the English physician, naturalist, and poet Erasmus Darwin (1731–1802), grandfather of Charles Darwin. Like Lamarck, he hypothesized about the inheritance of characteristics acquired thanks to wants and needs, but he, too, was wrong about the mechanism for change.

FIGURE 2.10 ■ Thomas Malthus
Malthus, the founder of demography, theorized that population size was limited by food supply. Can you think of other factors that might limit population size?

Lamarckism First proposed by Lamarck, the theory of evolution through the inheritance of acquired characteristics in which an organism can pass on features acquired during its lifetime.

THE THEORY OF EVOLUTION: DARWIN'S CONTRIBUTION

Darwin's remarkable attention to detail enabled him to connect his voluminous reading with his personal observations from the *Beagle* voyage. For example, while in Chile, Darwin had observed firsthand the power of earthquakes in shaping the landscape. Hutton's and Lyell's uniformitarianism led him to recognize that the accumulation of such catastrophes over a long period of time explains, at least in part, the appearance of the present-day landscape. This understanding of Earth's remarkably dynamic geologic history laid the groundwork for Darwin's view of evolution as a long, gradual process.

That process, he saw, could be reconstructed through the fossil record. He had read carefully Cuvier's studies of fossils, and in South America he saw fossils firsthand. Some of these fossils resembled living animals native to South America, such as the armadillo, ground sloth, and llama. This evidence strongly suggested that an earlier species had transformed into the modern species, most likely through a succession of species over time. Drawing on Malthus's ideas about reproduction, population, and variation, Darwin wrote: "it at once struck me that under these circumstances [i.e., specific environmental conditions] favorable variations would tend to be preserved and unfavorable ones to be destroyed. The result of this would be the formation of new species." Another revelation.

(a)

FIGURE 2.11 ■ **Jean-Baptiste Lamarck**
(a) Lamarck developed an early theory of evolution involving the inheritance of acquired characteristics. Although his mechanism of evolution was wrong, Lamarck's recognition of the dynamic nature of life in the past made an important contribution to the development of evolutionary theory.
(b) According to the classic (though incorrect) example of Lamarckism, giraffes stretched to reach food at the tops of trees, their necks grew as a result, and they passed on these long necks to their offspring.

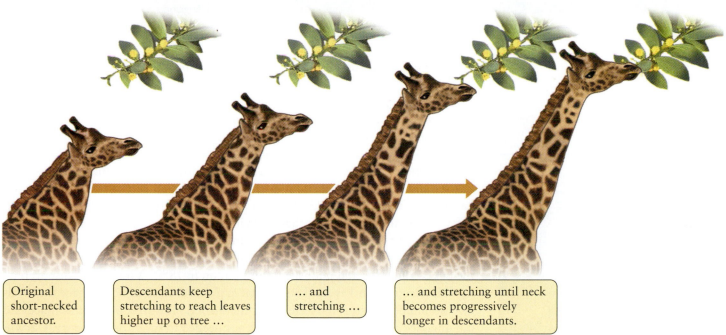

| Original short-necked ancestor. | Descendants keep stretching to reach leaves higher up on tree … | … and stretching … | … and stretching until neck becomes progressively longer in descendants. |

(b)

Darwin hypothesized that surviving offspring had attributes advantageous for acquiring food. Because these offspring survived, the frequency of their advantageous characteristics increased over time. Meanwhile, as environmental conditions changed—such as when rainfall decreased—offspring lacking adaptive attributes suited to their survival in the new environment died off. Building on these observations and their implications, Darwin deduced that natural selection was the primary mechanism of evolution. Over a long period of time, through generations' adaptation to different environments and different foods, a common ancestor gave rise to related species.

FIGURE 2.12 ■ Writing a Masterpiece Darwin wrote most of *On the Origin of Species* at his beloved home, Down House, in Kent, England.

Darwin's background research had begun in the 1830s. It was not until 1856, however—fully two decades after his voyage around the world—that Darwin had gathered enough evidence and developed his ideas enough to begin writing his great work about evolution by means of natural selection, *On the Origin of Species* (**Figure 2.12**). His colleagues had warned him that if he did not write his book soon, someone else might receive credit for the idea. Indeed, in 1858, Darwin received from the English naturalist and explorer Alfred Russel Wallace (1823–1913) a letter and a 20-page report outlining Wallace's theory of evolution by means of natural selection (**Figure 2.13**). Independently from Darwin, Wallace had arrived at most of the same conclusions that Darwin had. Both men had been aware of their shared interest in the subject, and both men formulated their theories simultaneously. Concerned that Wallace would publish first, Darwin completed *Origin* over the next 15 months and published it in London in 1859. Who, then, "discovered" natural selection, the key mechanism that explains evolution? Some argue that Wallace should be given primary credit for the theory. However, because Wallace had not amassed the extensive body of evidence needed to support the theory, Darwin is generally recognized as the discoverer.

FIGURE 2.13 ■ Alfred Russel Wallace Although Darwin often gets sole credit for the development of the theory of evolution through natural selection, Wallace (here depicted ca. 1860) contributed substantially to evolutionary theory. Wallace was the leading authority on the geographic distribution of animals, for example, and was the first to recognize the concept of warning coloration in animals. In addition, he raised the issue of human impact on the environment a full century before it became a concern for the general public.

SINCE DARWIN: MECHANISMS OF INHERITANCE, THE EVOLUTIONARY SYNTHESIS, AND THE DISCOVERY OF DNA

Mechanisms of Inheritance

Having articulated and supported his theory of evolution by means of natural selection, Darwin turned to the next fundamental question about natural selection:

how do the traits that are being selected for (or against) pass from parent to off-spring? Like other scientists of his day, Darwin believed that each body part contained invisible particles called **gemmules.** Darwin hypothesized that representative gemmules for all body parts resided in the reproductive organs. During fertilization, each parent contributed his or her gemmules to the potential offspring. The father's and the mother's gemmules then intermingled to form the characteristics observed in their progeny. Called **blending inheritance,** this process was a popular notion at the time.

Unknown to Darwin, research elsewhere in Europe was calling into question the idea of blending inheritance. In 1865, just six years after the publication of *On the Origin of Species,* Gregor Mendel (1822–1884), an Augustinian monk living in a monastery in what is now Brno, Czech Republic, published in an obscure local scientific journal the results of his work on inheritance (**Figure 2.14**). Mendel had spent the previous eight years crossbreeding different varieties of garden pea plants. Over the course of his experiments, he grew some 28,000 plants. These plants enabled him to identify and carefully observe seven characteristics, or traits, that were especially informative about breeding and its outcome over generations (**Figure 2.15**). From his results, Mendel inferred that a *discrete* physical unit was responsible for each characteristic. This unit passed from parent to offspring, and in this way the characteristic was inherited. In fact, the discrete unit could be traced through generations, and its passage (the inheritance) was determined by mathematical laws.

Mendel also discovered that the garden peas' traits did not blend. For example, plants and their offspring were either tall or short. Over time, the short plants diminished in frequency and eventually disappeared. Later scientists determined that the physical unit of inheritance—now known as a **gene**—has two subunits, one from the father and one from the mother, each called an **allele.** Each allele is either

FIGURE 2.14 ▪ Gregor Mendel
Mendel, the father of modern genetics, was a Christian monk by profession but a scientist by nature. His observations provided the foundation for our understanding of genetics (the subject of chapters 3 and 4).

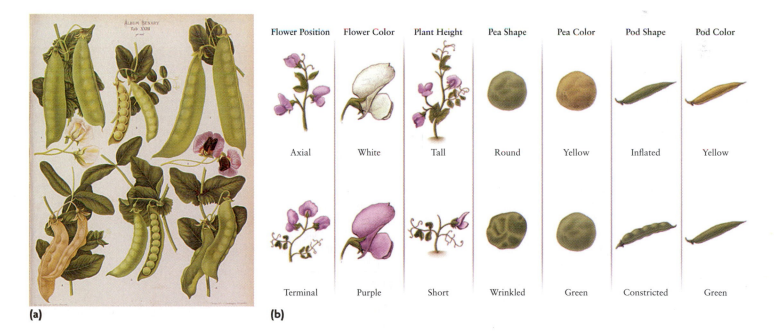

(a) (b)

FIGURE 2.15 ▪ Mendel's Peas
(a) This illustration—from the 1876 catalog of one of Mendel's seed suppliers—shows some of **(b)** the seven characteristics Mendel studied, each of which had two variants. Flower position, for example, could be axial or terminal, while flower color could be white or purple.

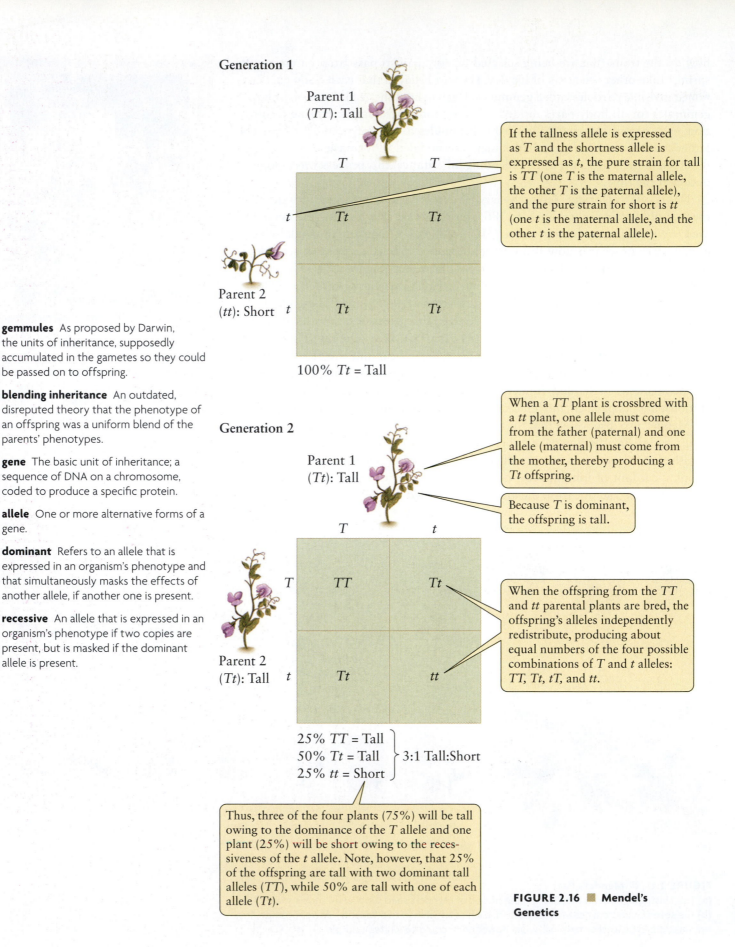

Generation 1

Parent 1
(*TT*): Tall

If the tallness allele is expressed as *T* and the shortness allele is expressed as *t*, the pure strain for tall is *TT* (one *T* is the maternal allele, the other *T* is the paternal allele), and the pure strain for short is *tt* (one *t* is the maternal allele, and the other *t* is the paternal allele).

	T	*T*
t	*Tt*	*Tt*
t	*Tt*	*Tt*

Parent 2
(*tt*): Short

100% *Tt* = Tall

Generation 2

When a *TT* plant is crossbred with a *tt* plant, one allele must come from the father (paternal) and one allele (maternal) must come from the mother, thereby producing a *Tt* offspring.

Parent 1
(*Tt*): Tall

Because *T* is dominant, the offspring is tall.

	T	*t*
T	*TT*	*Tt*
t	*Tt*	*tt*

Parent 2
(*Tt*): Tall

When the offspring from the *TT* and *tt* parental plants are bred, the offspring's alleles independently redistribute, producing about equal numbers of the four possible combinations of *T* and *t* alleles: *TT*, *Tt*, *tT*, and *tt*.

25% *TT* = Tall
50% *Tt* = Tall } 3:1 Tall:Short
25% *tt* = Short

Thus, three of the four plants (75%) will be tall owing to the dominance of the *T* allele and one plant (25%) will be short owing to the recessiveness of the *t* allele. Note, however, that 25% of the offspring are tall with two dominant tall alleles (*TT*), while 50% are tall with one of each allele (*Tt*).

FIGURE 2.16 ■ **Mendel's Genetics**

gemmules As proposed by Darwin, the units of inheritance, supposedly accumulated in the gametes so they could be passed on to offspring.

blending inheritance An outdated, disreputed theory that the phenotype of an offspring was a uniform blend of the parents' phenotypes.

gene The basic unit of inheritance; a sequence of DNA on a chromosome, coded to produce a specific protein.

allele One or more alternative forms of a gene.

dominant Refers to an allele that is expressed in an organism's phenotype and that simultaneously masks the effects of another allele, if another one is present.

recessive An allele that is expressed in an organism's phenotype if two copies are present, but is masked if the dominant allele is present.

dominant or recessive. In garden peas, the allele for tallness is dominant and the allele for shortness is recessive. If one parent provides a "tall" allele (*T*) and the other parent provides a "short" allele (*t*), then the offspring having one of each allele (*Tt*) would be tall because of the presence of the "tall" allele—the dominant allele is physically expressed, whereas the recessive allele is hidden. The pure strain for tall (*TT*) includes one tall maternal allele (*T*), and one tall paternal allele (*T*). The pure strain for short (*tt*) includes one short maternal allele (*t*) and one short paternal allele (*t*) (**Figure 2.16**).

While Darwin's theory had generated immediate excitement in the scientific community and among the public and was supported by leading scientists of the time such as Thomas Henry Huxley (**Figure 2.17**), Mendel's crucial discovery (now known as **Mendelian inheritance**) went unnoticed. His writing was not widely distributed, and his work was simply ahead of his time. But in 1900, three scientists working independently—the German botanist Carl Erich Correns (1864–1933), the Austrian botanist Erich Tschermak von Seysenegg (1871–1962), and the Dutch botanist Hugo de Vries (1848–1935)—discovered Mendel's research and replicated his findings. The Danish botanist Wilhelm Ludvig Johannsen (1857–1927) called the pair of alleles (e.g., *TT, Tt, tt*) the **genotype** and the actual physical appearance (tall, short) the **phenotype.**

Mendel's theory of inheritance forms the basis of the modern discipline of genetics (the subject of chapters 3 and 4). It makes clear that the physical units—the genes, and the two component alleles of each gene—responsible for physical attributes are located in the reproductive cells, eggs and sperm. When microscope technology improved in the late nineteenth century, the cell structure and the units of inheritance were defined (see chapter 3).

Beginning in 1908, the American geneticist Thomas Hunt Morgan (1866–1945) and his associates bred the common fruit fly in experiments that built on Mendel's pea breeding. All genes, they discovered, are transmitted from parents to offspring in the ratios identified by Mendel. The genes are on **chromosomes,** and both the hereditary material and its carriers are duplicated during reproductive cell division.

The Evolutionary Synthesis, the Study of Populations, and the Causes of Evolution

The combination of Darwin's theory of evolution and Mendel's theory of heredity resulted in an **evolutionary synthesis.** Darwin's theory provided the mechanism for evolution (natural selection), and Mendel's theory showed how traits are passed on systematically and predictably (Mendelian inheritance). The melding of natural selection and Mendelian inheritance led biologists to ask further questions about evolution, specifically about the origins of particular genes, genetic variation in general, and change in physical characteristics over time. *Why* do some genes increase in frequency, some decrease in frequency, and some show no change? *How* do completely new genes appear? These questions and a focus on population—viewed as the *gene pool*—provided the basis for a newly emerging field in evolutionary biology called **population genetics** (among the subjects of chapter 4).

Natural selection, the guiding force of evolution, could operate only on variation that already existed in a population. How did new variation—new characteristics—arise in a population? Through his experiments with fruit flies, Morgan showed that a new gene could appear as a result of spontaneous change in an existing gene.

Mendelian inheritance The basic principles associated with the transmission of genetic material, forming the basis of genetics, including the law of segregation and the law of independent assortment.

genotype The genetic makeup of an organism; the combination of alleles for a given gene.

phenotype The physical expression of the genotype; it may be influenced by the environment.

chromosomes The strand of DNA found in the nucleus of eukaryotes that contains hundreds or thousands of genes

evolutionary synthesis A unified theory of evolution that combines genetics with natural selection.

population genetics A specialty within the field of genetics; it focuses on the changes in gene frequencies and the effects of those changes on adaptation and evolution.

FIGURE 2.17 ■ Thomas Huxley Huxley (1825–1895), an English biologist, was known as Darwin's Bulldog because he so forcefully promoted Darwin's theory of evolution by natural selection. Among Huxley's contributions to evolutionary theory was the concept that humans evolved from an apelike animal.

(a)   **(b)**

FIGURE 2.18 ■ **Fruit Fly Mutations**
Thomas Hunt Morgan's research on fruit flies focused on a variety of mutations. **(a)** The normal fruit fly has two wings, while **(b)** the four-wing mutation has two wings on each side.

mutation A random change in a gene or chromosome, creating a new trait that may be advantageous, deleterious, or neutral in its effects on the organism.

gene flow Admixture, or the exchange of alleles between two populations.

genetic drift The random change in allele frequency from one generation to the next, with greater effect in small populations.

deoxyribonucleic acid (DNA) A double-stranded molecule that provides the genetic code for an organism, consisting of phosphate, deoxyribose sugar, and four types of nitrogen bases.

This kind of genetic change is called **mutation** (**Figure 2.18**). The only source of new genetic material, mutation is another cause of evolution.

Gene flow, a third cause of evolution, is the diffusion, or spread, of new genetic material from one population to another of the same species. In other words, genes from one gene pool are transferred to another gene pool. Take, for example, the gene that causes sickle-cell anemia (this disorder is discussed extensively in chapter 4). Among West African blacks, it has a frequency of about 10%. Among American whites, it has a frequency of 0%. Because West African blacks and their descendants have long reproduced with American whites, the frequency among people descended from both West African blacks and American whites of the gene that causes sickle-cell anemia is approximately 5%, halfway between that of the two original populations. Over time, as the two populations have mixed, gene flow has decreased genetic difference.

Genetic drift, the fourth cause of evolution, is random change in the frequency of alleles—that is, of the different forms of a gene. Such change affects a small population more powerfully than it affects a large population (**Figure 2.19**). Over time, it increases the genetic difference between two genetically related but not interbreeding populations.

By the mid-twentieth century, the four causes of evolution—natural selection, mutation, gene flow, and genetic drift—were well defined, thanks to a synthesis of ideas drawn from the full range of sciences that deal with biological variation. In effect, evolutionary synthesis unified the branches of biology and its affiliated sciences, including genetics, taxonomy, morphology, comparative anatomy, paleontology, and the subject of this book, physical anthropology. Similarly, evolution unites living and past worlds. All organisms are related through common descent, and organisms more closely related than others share a more recent common ancestor.

DNA: Discovery of the Molecular Basis of Evolution

Once chromosomes were recognized as the carriers of genes, scientists sought to understand the structure of **deoxyribonucleic acid (DNA),** the chemical that makes

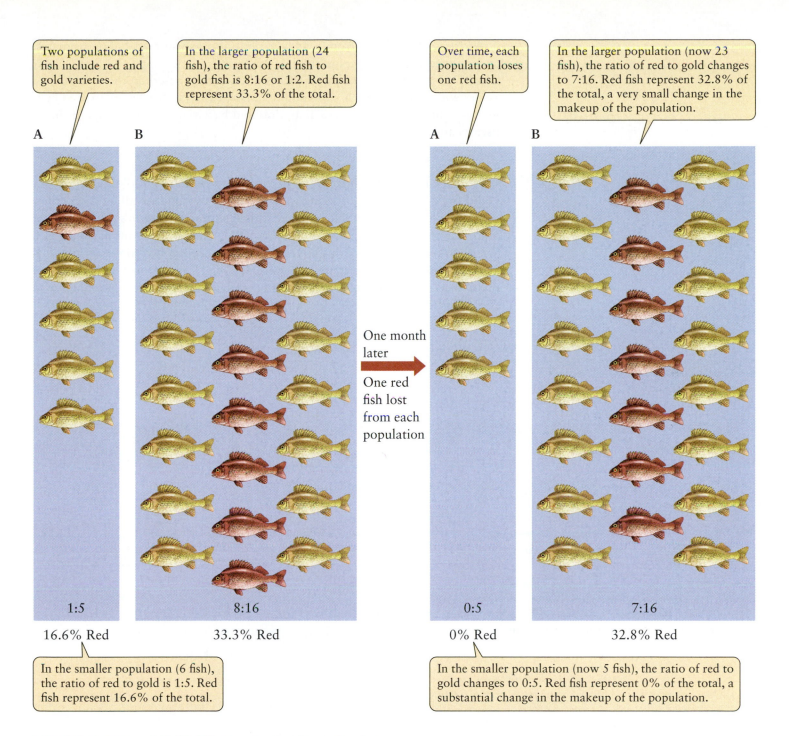

FIGURE 2.19 ■ **Genetic Drift's Effects on Small and Large Populations**

up chromosomes. In 1953, the American geneticist James Watson (b. 1928) and the British biophysicist Francis Crick (1916–2004) published their discovery that DNA molecules have a ladderlike, double-helix structure. Crucial to their discovery was the work of the British X-ray crystallographer Rosalind Franklin (1920–1958), who used a special technique, X-ray diffraction, to produce high-quality images of DNA. The combined efforts of Franklin, Watson, and Crick opened up a whole new vista for biology by helping explain how chromosomes are replicated.

Analysis of the DNA from a wide variety of organisms, including primates, has provided both new perspectives on biological relationships and a molecular "clock" with which to time the branches of evolution (based on the similarity of species within those branches). In addition, DNA analysis has begun to shed light on a growing list of illnesses such as viral and bacterial infections, cancer, heart disease, and stroke.

Little did Darwin realize just what a powerful foundation his evolutionary theory would build for science, ushering in modern biology and its allied disciplines, including physical anthropology. Long after his death, Darwin's search for the biological mechanisms involved in evolution would continue to inspire scientists. The questions Darwin and his colleagues asked, especially about how physical attributes pass from parents to offspring, laid the foundation for the study of inheritance—the science of genetics—and eventually the DNA revolution. Darwin would have been impressed.

ANSWERING THE BIG QUESTIONS

How did the theory of evolution come to be?

- In developing his theory of evolution by means of natural selection, Darwin drew on geology, paleontology, taxonomy and systematics, demography, and what is now called evolutionary biology.
- Scientists working in these disciplines had shown that
  —Earth is quite old and has changed considerably over its history,
  —fossils represent the remains of once-living, often extinct organisms and thus provide a record of the history of life on the planet,
  —life evolves over time,
  —groups of related species provide insight into evolutionary history,
  —the number of adults in a population tends to remain the same over time.

What was Darwin's contribution to the theory of evolution?

- Darwin's key contribution was the principle of natural selection. Three observations and inferences allowed him to deduce that natural selection is the primary driver of evolution:

—the number of adults in a population tends to remain the same over time even though, for most organisms, parents tend to produce multiple and sometimes many offspring,
—variation exists among members of populations,
—individuals having variation that is advantageous for survival and reproduction increase in relative frequency over time.

What has happened since Darwin in the development of our understanding of evolution?

- Gregor Mendel discovered the principles of inheritance, the basis for our understanding of how physical attributes are passed from parents to offspring.
- Mendel's revelation that attributes are passed as discrete units, which we now know as genes, laid the groundwork for our understanding of cell biology, our understanding of chromosomes, and eventually the field of population genetics.
- We now know that evolution—genetic change in a population or species—is caused by one or a combination of four forces: natural selection, mutation, gene flow, and genetic drift.
- We now know that each chromosome in an organism's cells consists of DNA molecules. DNA is the blueprint for all biological characteristics and functions.

KEY TERMS

adaptations
adaptive radiation
allele
blending inheritance
catastrophism
chromosomes
demography
deoxyribonucleic acid (DNA)
dominant
evolutionary biology
evolutionary synthesis
fossils
gemmules
gene
gene flow
genetic drift

genotype
genus
geology
habitat
Lamarckism
Mendelian inheritance
mutation
natural selection
paleontology
phenotype
population genetics
recessive
species
systematics
taxonomy
uniformitarianism

ADDITIONAL READINGS

Alvarez, W. 1997. T. rex *and the Crater of Doom*. Princeton: Princeton University Press.

Bowler, P. J. 2003. *Evolution: The History of an Idea*. Berkeley: University of California Press.

Gould, S. J. 1992. *Ever since Darwin: Reflections on Natural History*. New York: Norton.

Huxley, R. 2007. *The Great Naturalists*. New York: Thames & Hudson.

Moorehead, A. 1969. *Darwin and the Beagle*. New York: Penguin Books.

Repcheck, J. 2003. *The Man Who Found Time: James Hutton and the Discovery of the Earth's Antiquity*. Cambridge, MA: Perseus Publishing.

Ridley, M. 2004. *Evolution*. Malden, MA: Blackwell Science.

Wilson, E. O. 2006. *From So Simple a Beginning: Darwin's Four Great Books* [*Voyage of the H.M.S. Beagle, The Origin of Species, The Descent of Man, The Expression of Emotions in Man and Animals*]. New York: Norton.

On the surface, a human being and a chimpanzee might not seem to have much in common. However, they share 98% of their DNA. Chimpanzees are humans' closest living relatives, and both primates often employ similar facial expressions and body movements.

CHAPTER 3

Genetics: Reproducing Life and Producing Variation

There is a revolution going on in science: the discovery of DNA and the identification of its molecular structure have brought about a "DNA Revolution." At no time in history have humans learned so much so quickly about the biology of plants and animals. In addition to bringing about developments in agriculture and food production, medicine, and other areas that affect billions of people every day, the information derived from DNA has transformed a number of scientific disciplines. Consider forensic science, where fingerprints and blood types were once the primary evidence. Thanks to DNA, far smaller samples—of tissue, bone, hair, and blood—can be used to identify victims' remains and to identify criminals with far greater accuracy. DNA in samples saved from old crime scenes has helped free scores of individuals convicted of crimes they had not committed. Beyond forensics, DNA analysis has helped determine family relationships. It has helped genealogists reach into the past to chart ancestry. It has even been used to detect the presence of diseases, such as leprosy and syphilis, in ancient skeletons. Given the long and growing list of ways in which DNA can be used, no wonder former U.S. president Bill Clinton referred to the human DNA sequence, right after it was presented to the public in 2003, as "the most important, most wondrous map ever produced by mankind."

When I studied introductory biology in college, in the early 1970s, knowledge of DNA was just a tiny fraction of what it is today. Evolution was understood in terms of entire organisms and their biological history. Now, DNA provides us with the information—a whole new window—whereby we can *see* how organisms are put together and *what* is actually evolving. Powerful stuff! In anthropology, it has meant new insights into primate evolution. Before we can tie together the growing strands of DNA and evolution, though, we need to back up and examine the foundational work in genetics—the study of heredity.

Although the great nineteenth-century biologists discussed in chapter 2 knew a lot about variation in species, they did not fully understand how this variation is produced or how it is transmitted from parents to offspring. For example, how do an organism's attributes grow from a fertilized egg? The answers to questions about variation—its origin and continuation—lie in the cell, its structures, and the myriad functions it performs from conception through full maturity. And governing each cell is the genetic code.

BIG QUESTIONS

- What is the genetic code?
- What does the genetic code (DNA) do?
- What is the genetic structure of human variation?

THE CELL: ITS ROLE IN REPRODUCING LIFE AND PRODUCING VARIATION

Cell Types

The cell is the basic unit of life for all organisms (**Figure 3.1**). Every organism has at least one cell (that is the baseline definition of an organism). Organisms with just one cell are called **prokaryotes.** Those with more than one cell—all past and living plants and animals—are called **eukaryotes.** Prokaryotes—the earliest form of life on Earth—first appeared around 3.7 billion years ago (bya). Eukaryotes evolved much later, first appearing some 1.2 bya, and their quite complex structures require enormous amounts of energy to survive and to reproduce. Membranes enclose eukaryotic cells' two main parts, the **nucleus** and the **cytoplasm,** between which various communications and activities happen (**Figure 3.2**).

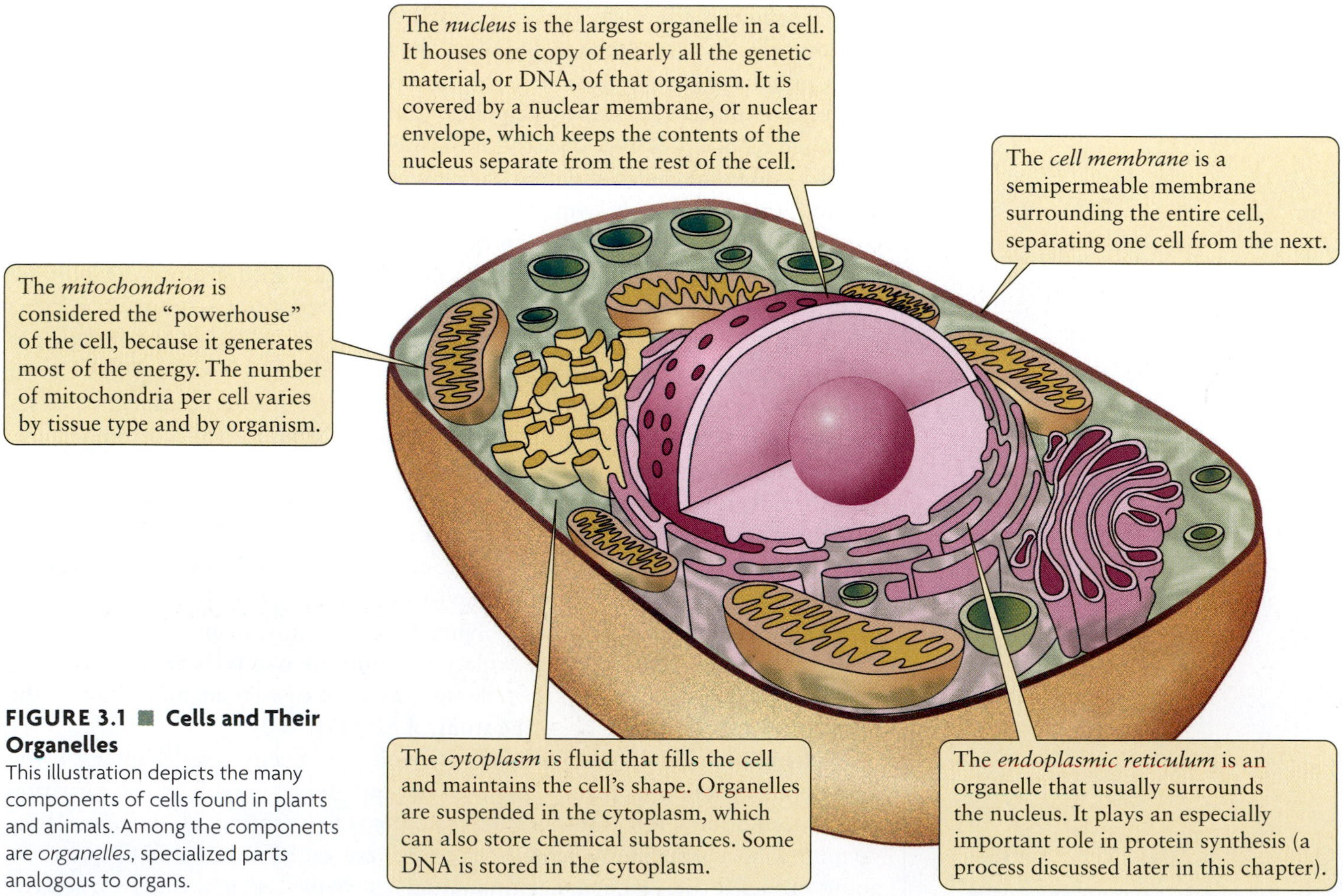

The *nucleus* is the largest organelle in a cell. It houses one copy of nearly all the genetic material, or DNA, of that organism. It is covered by a nuclear membrane, or nuclear envelope, which keeps the contents of the nucleus separate from the rest of the cell.

The *cell membrane* is a semipermeable membrane surrounding the entire cell, separating one cell from the next.

The *mitochondrion* is considered the "powerhouse" of the cell, because it generates most of the energy. The number of mitochondria per cell varies by tissue type and by organism.

The *cytoplasm* is fluid that fills the cell and maintains the cell's shape. Organelles are suspended in the cytoplasm, which can also store chemical substances. Some DNA is stored in the cytoplasm.

The *endoplasmic reticulum* is an organelle that usually surrounds the nucleus. It plays an especially important role in protein synthesis (a process discussed later in this chapter).

FIGURE 3.1 ■ Cells and Their Organelles
This illustration depicts the many components of cells found in plants and animals. Among the components are *organelles,* specialized parts analogous to organs.

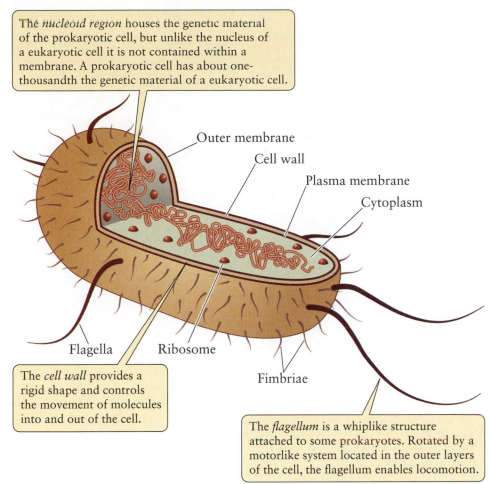

The *nucleoid region* houses the genetic material of the prokaryotic cell, but unlike the nucleus of a eukaryotic cell it is not contained within a membrane. A prokaryotic cell has about one-thousandth the genetic material of a eukaryotic cell.

Outer membrane

Cell wall

Plasma membrane

Cytoplasm

Flagella

Ribosome

Fimbriae

The *cell wall* provides a rigid shape and controls the movement of molecules into and out of the cell.

The *flagellum* is a whiplike structure attached to some prokaryotes. Rotated by a motorlike system located in the outer layers of the cell, the flagellum enables locomotion.

(a)

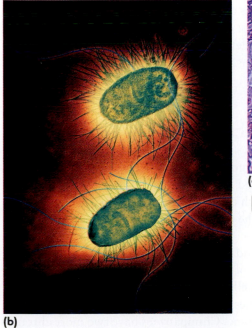

(b)

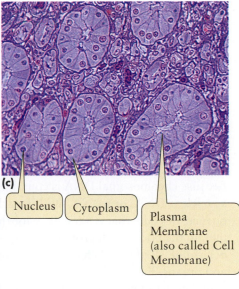

(c)

Nucleus

Cytoplasm

Plasma Membrane (also called Cell Membrane)

FIGURE 3.2 ■ Prokaryotes and Eukaryotes
(a) The many types of bacteria that we encounter in our daily lives are prokaryotic cells like this one. **(b)** For example, *Escherichia coli* (*E. coli*), two single cells of which are shown here, is a bacteria that aids digestion in the intestines of mammals, including humans. **(c)** This image shows the eukaryotic cells of a primate's kidney.

somatic cells Diploid cells that form the organs, tissues, and other parts of an organism's body.

gametes Sexual reproductive cells, ova and sperm, that have a haploid number of chromosomes and that can unite with a gamete of the opposite sex to form a new organism.

genome The complete set of chromosomes for an organism or species that represents all the inheritable traits.

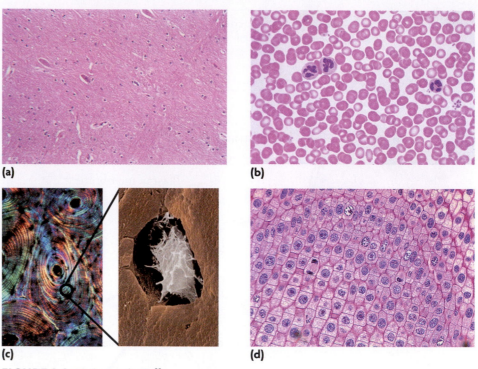

(a) (b)

(c) (d)

FIGURE 3.3 ■ Somatic Cells
Somatic cells in different tissues have different characteristics, but most somatic cells share a number of features. Every somatic cell has a nucleus, which contains a complete copy of the organism's DNA. As a result, throughout the organism's body there are millions of copies of that DNA. Note the nuclei in these images of human anatomy: **(a)** brain tissue, **(b)** red blood cells (the larger cells are white blood cells, and the small dots are platelets), **(c)** osteocyte (bone cell), **(d)** skin cells.

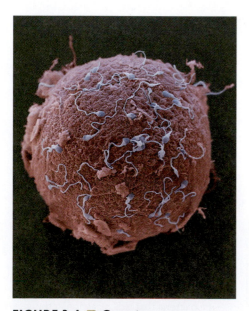

FIGURE 3.4 ■ Gametes
Sperm (male gametes) surround this ovum (female gamete). Only one of the sperm will penetrate the external membrane and fertilize the ovum.

In all animals and plants, there are two types of eukaryotic cells. **Somatic cells,** also called body cells, comprise most tissues, such as bone, muscle, skin, brain, lung, fat, and hair (**Figure 3.3**). **Gametes** are the sex cells, sperm in males and ova (or eggs) in females (**Figure 3.4**). The root of somatic cell and gamete production is in the chromosomes, located in the nucleus of each cell. In humans, somatic cells have 46 chromosomes and gametes have 23 (**Figure 3.5**).

THE DNA MOLECULE: THE GENETIC CODE

The chemical that makes up each chromosome, DNA, is the body's genetic code. Because chromosomal DNA is contained in the nucleus of the cell, it is referred to as nuclear DNA, or nDNA. Within each chromosome, DNA molecules form a sequence, or code, that is a template for the production of a protein, or part of a protein, in the body. Each protein has a specific function, and collectively the proteins determine all physical characteristics and govern the functions of all cells, tissues, and organs. Each DNA sequence, each protein-generating code, is a gene, and the complete set of genes in an individual cell is called the **genome.**

Although the number of chromosomes varies according to species (see Fig. 3.5), all organisms share much the same genome. Chimpanzees have two more chromosomes than humans, but the DNA in chimpanzees and in humans is about 98%

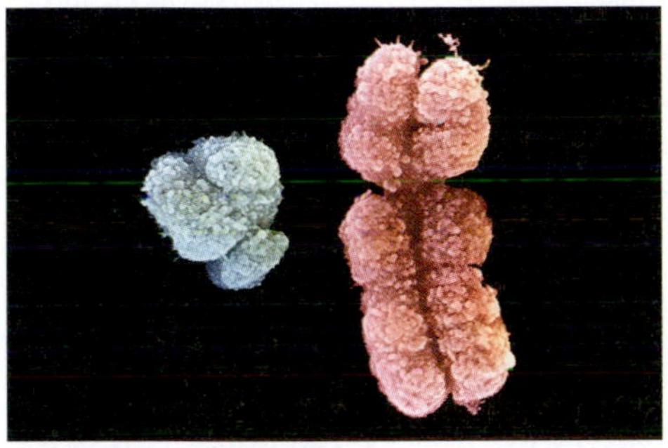

Organism	Chromosome Number	Organism	Chromosome Number
	Camel: 70		Potato: 48
	Guinea pig: 64		Petunia: 14
	Salamander: 24		Algae: 148
	House fly: 12		Ring-tailed lemur: 56
	Apple: 34		Black-and-white colobus monkey: 44
			Orangutan: 48

(b)

FIGURE 3.5 ■ Chromosomes
(a) To get an idea of the incredibly minute size of chromosomes, consider that this pair has been magnified 35,000 times. If a penny (approximately 2 cm, or .8 in, in diameter) were magnified 35,000 times, it would be approximately 700 km, or 435 mi, in diameter, wider than the state of Arizona. **(b)** An organism's complexity is not related to its number of chromosomes, as this comparison illustrates. While humans have 46 chromosomes, other primates have more (e.g., ring-tailed lemurs) or fewer (e.g., black-and-white colobus monkeys).

identical. Even baker's yeast is 45% similar to human DNA. Within any organism, nuclear DNA is **homoplasmic,** meaning it is the same in each and every cell—the DNA in a skin cell matches the DNA in a bone cell. (An exception to the rule is mature red blood cells, which have no nuclei and, hence, no DNA.)

homoplasmic Refers to nuclear DNA, which is identical in the nucleus of each cell type (except red blood cells).

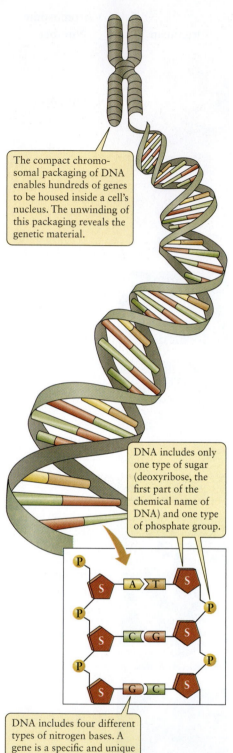

The compact chromosomal packaging of DNA enables hundreds of genes to be housed inside a cell's nucleus. The unwinding of this packaging reveals the genetic material.

DNA includes only one type of sugar (deoxyribose, the first part of the chemical name of DNA) and one type of phosphate group.

DNA includes four different types of nitrogen bases. A gene is a specific and unique sequence of these bases.

FIGURE 3.6 ■ **The Structure of DNA**

A small but significant amount of DNA is contained in tiny organelles, called **mitochondria,** within each cell's cytoplasm. These structures use oxygen to turn food molecules, especially sugar and fat, into **adenosine triphosphate (ATP),** a high-energy molecule that powers cells and, in turn, powers every tissue in the body. The number of mitochondria in a cell varies according to the cell's activity level. For example, the cells in highly active body tissues, such as muscles, contain far more mitochondria than do cells in relatively low-functioning tissues, such as hair.

The mitochondrial DNA (mtDNA), a kind of miniature chromosome containing 37 genes, is inherited just from the mother. That is, the mtDNA comes from the ovum. Each of us, then, carries our mother's mtDNA, she carries or carried her mother's mtDNA, and so on for generation after generation. In theory, a maternal lineage, or **matriline,** can be traced back hundreds of thousands of years. (Ancient matrilines in fossil hominids are one subject of chapter 10.) Unlike nuclear DNA, mtDNA is **heteroplasmic,** meaning it can differ among different parts of a person's body or even within the same kinds of cells.

DNA: The Blueprint of Life

The DNA molecule is the blueprint of life. It serves as the chemical template for *every* aspect of biological organisms. As Watson and Crick discovered, the molecule has a right-twisted, double-helix, ladderlike structure (see "DNA: Discovery of the Molecular Basis of Evolution" in chapter 2). Understanding this structure is key to understanding the growth of any organism and the transmission of genes from parents to offspring. The starting point for looking at the DNA molecule in any detail is to unravel a chromosome and look at a tiny segment of it under super-magnification. Its ladderlike structure consists of two uprights and many rungs. The uprights of the ladder are made up of alternating sugar and phosphate molecules, while the rungs are composed of paired nitrogen bases linked by a weak hydrogen bond (**Figure 3.6**).

On each side of the ladder, every unit of sugar, phosphate, and nitrogen base forms a single **nucleotide** (**Figure 3.7**). While the sugar and phosphate are the same throughout DNA, the base can be **adenine** (A), **thymine** (T), **guanine** (G), or **cytosine** (C). Owing to the bases' unvarying chemical configurations, adenine and thymine always pair with each other, and guanine and cytosine always pair up. In other words, apart from the rare errors in matching, adenine and thymine are **complementary bases** and guanine and cytosine are complementary bases. This means that if on one side of the ladder the sequence is ATGCAG, on the other side the sequence will be complementary, TACGTC. This predictability of base pairings assures the high reliability of one key function of the DNA molecule, that of self-reproduction.

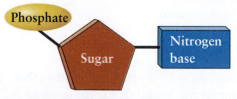

FIGURE 3.7 ■ **Nucleotide**
A nucleotide is the building block of DNA, made up of a phosphate group, a sugar, and a single nitrogen base.

THE DNA MOLECULE: REPLICATING THE CODE

One function of the DNA molecule is to replicate itself. **Replication** takes place in the nucleus and is part of cell division, leading to the production of new somatic cells (**mitosis**) or the production of new gametes (**meiosis**). Replication thus results in continued cell production, from the single-celled **zygote** (the fertilized egg) to two cells, then four cells, and so on, into the fully mature body with all of its many different tissues and organs—within which cells are continuously dying and being replaced.

In replication, DNA makes *identical* copies of itself, going from one double-stranded parent molecule of DNA to two double strands of daughter DNA. This means that where there was one chromosome, now there are two (**Figure 3.8**).

complementary bases The predictable pairing of nitrogen bases in the structure of DNA and RNA, such that adenine and thymine always pair together (adenine and uracil in RNA) and cytosine and guanine pair together.

mitochondria Energy-producing (ATP) organelles in eukaryotic cells; they possess their own independent DNA.

adenosine triphosphate (ATP) An important cellular molecule, created by the mitochondria and carrying the energy necessary for cellular functions.

matriline DNA, such as mitochondrial DNA, whose inheritance can be traced from mother to daughter or to son.

heteroplasmic Refers to a mixture of more than one type of organellar DNA, such as mitochondrial DNA, within a cell or a single organism's body, usually due to the mutation of the DNA in some organelles but not in others.

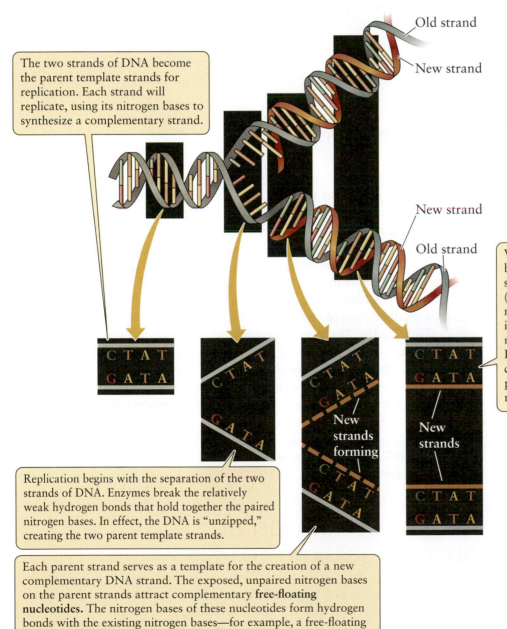

Old strand

New strand

The two strands of DNA become the parent template strands for replication. Each strand will replicate, using its nitrogen bases to synthesize a complementary strand.

New strand

Old strand

When all the nitrogen bases of the parent strands are paired with (formerly free-floating) nucleotides, replication is complete. There are now two complete DNA molecules, each consisting of one parent strand and one new strand.

New strands forming

New strands

Replication begins with the separation of the two strands of DNA. Enzymes break the relatively weak hydrogen bonds that hold together the paired nitrogen bases. In effect, the DNA is "unzipped," creating the two parent template strands.

Each parent strand serves as a template for the creation of a new complementary DNA strand. The exposed, unpaired nitrogen bases on the parent strands attract complementary **free-floating nucleotides.** The nitrogen bases of these nucleotides form hydrogen bonds with the existing nitrogen bases—for example, a free-floating nucleotide with a cytosine base will attach itself to a guanine base.

FIGURE 3.8 ■ The Steps of DNA Replication

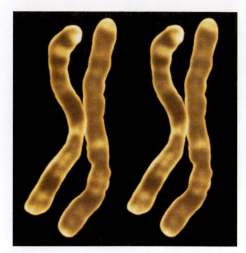

FIGURE 3.9 ■ **Chromosome Pairs** Homologous chromosomes are virtually identical in their physical and chemical structure. Each pair of chromosomes has the same genes, but the pair may have different alleles for specific genes.

The first function of DNA is to replicate itself. Templates from the original (parental) strand of DNA yield two exact (daughter) copies.

STEP	ACTIVITY
1. Strand of DNA unzips to form templates.	Weak nucleotide bonds between bases break, exposing two parental strands of DNA.
2. Templates plus nucleotides yield daughters.	Free-floating nucleotides in the nucleus match with the newly exposed template strands of DNA.

Chromosome Types

Within somatic cells, chromosomes occur in **homologous,** or matching, pairs (**Figure 3.9**). Each pair includes the father's contribution (the paternal chromosome) and the mother's contribution (the maternal chromosome). These nonsex chromosomes are called **autosomes.**

The **karyotype,** or complete set of chromosomes, includes all of the autosomes and one pair of **sex chromosomes,** so called because they determine an offspring's biological sex. The X chromosome, the larger of the two, contains genetic material that determines both male and female characteristics. The Y chromosome contains a small amount of genetic material, which determines only male characteristics (**Figure 3.10**). The interaction of gametes during fertilization determines the combination of chromosomes in the offspring. If an X-carrying sperm fertilizes an X-carrying egg, the offspring will be female. If a Y-carrying sperm fertilizes an X-carrying egg, the offspring will be male. Therefore, the male parent's gametes determine the sex of his offspring because the Y chromosome is present in males only; it is passed from father to son.

The Y chromosome can be highly informative about paternity over many generations. This **patriline** is analogous to the matriline-based mtDNA, which is passed on only by females.

autosomes All chromosomes, except the sex chromosomes, that occur in pairs in all somatic cells (not the gametes).

karyotype The characteristics of the chromosomes for an individual organism or a species, such as number, size, and type.

sex chromosomes The pair of chromosomes that determine an organism's biological sex.

patriline DNA whose inheritance can be traced from father to daughter or son, such as the Y chromosome, which passes from father to son.

MITOSIS: PRODUCTION OF IDENTICAL SOMATIC CELLS

An organism starts life as a single cell, the zygote, which then produces identical copies of itself many, many times. A single human zygote, for example, eventually results in more than 10 trillion cells, each having the *exact* same DNA (**Figure 3.11**).

1
2
3
4
5
6
7
8
9
10
11
12
13
14
15
16
17
18
19
20
21
22
X

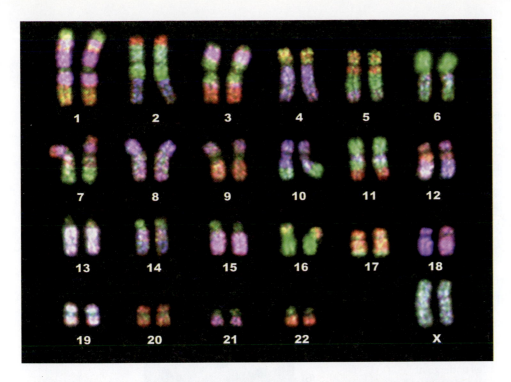

FIGURE 3.10 ■ **Karyotype**
Contained within each somatic cell, the human karyotype consists of 46 chromosomes of various sizes in 23 pairs. Of those 23, one pair determines the person's sex. Here, the label "X" means that these sex chromosomes are both X's and thus belong to a human female.

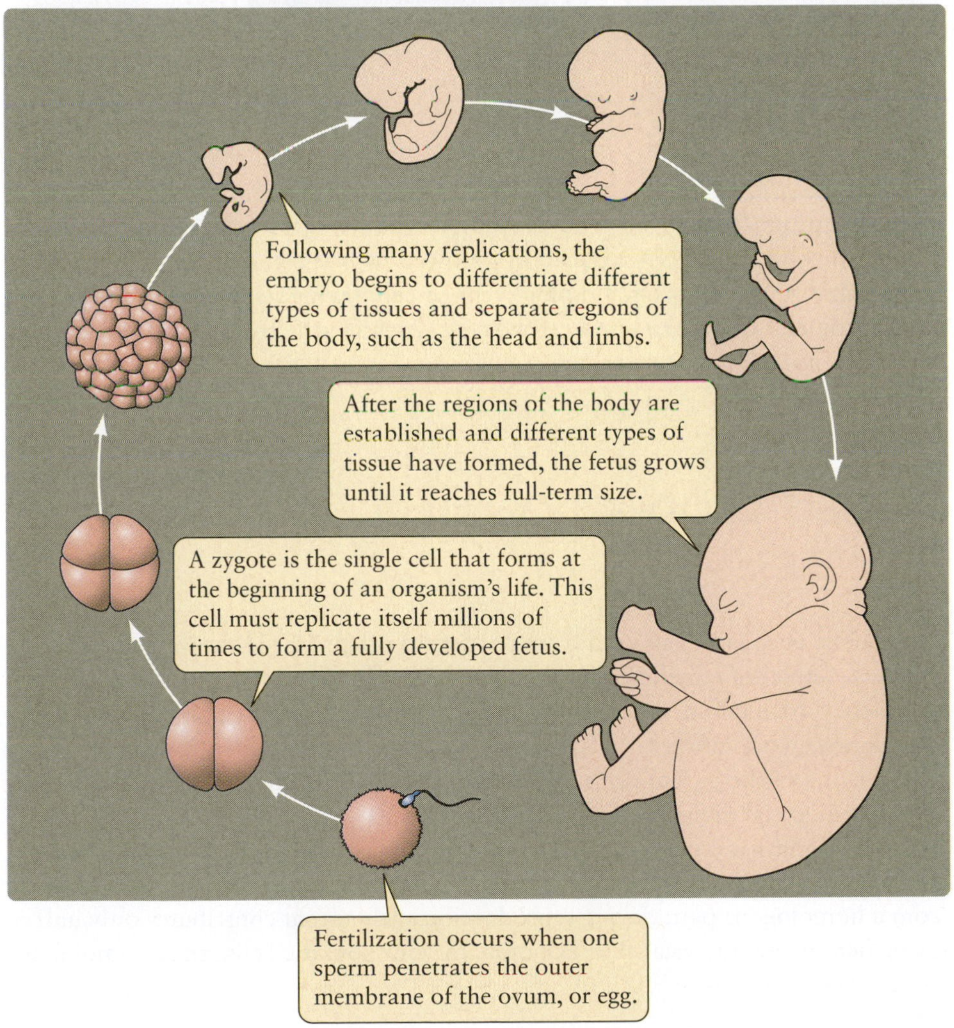

Following many replications, the embryo begins to differentiate different types of tissues and separate regions of the body, such as the head and limbs.
After the regions of the body are established and different types of tissue have formed, the fetus grows until it reaches full-term size.
A zygote is the single cell that forms at the beginning of an organism's life. This cell must replicate itself millions of times to form a fully developed fetus.
Fertilization occurs when one sperm penetrates the outer membrane of the ovum, or egg.

FIGURE 3.11 ■ **Embryonic Development**
The stages of human development from fertilization to a full-term infant.

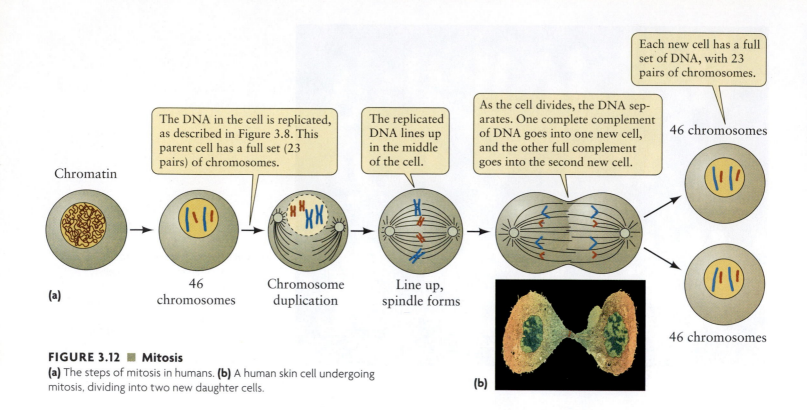

The DNA in the cell is replicated, as described in Figure 3.8. This parent cell has a full set (23 pairs) of chromosomes.

The replicated DNA lines up in the middle of the cell.

As the cell divides, the DNA separates. One complete complement of DNA goes into one new cell, and the other full complement goes into the second new cell.

Each new cell has a full set of DNA, with 23 pairs of chromosomes.

Chromatin

(a)

46 chromosomes

Chromosome duplication

Line up, spindle forms

46 chromosomes

46 chromosomes

(b)

FIGURE 3.12 ■ Mitosis
(a) The steps of mitosis in humans. **(b)** A human skin cell undergoing mitosis, dividing into two new daughter cells.

diploid A cell that has a full complement of paired chromosomes.

Here, the production of identical daughter cells from an original parental cell, mitosis, involves one DNA replication followed by *one* cell division (**Figure 3.12**). In this kind of cell division, a **diploid** cell—a cell having its organism's full set of chromosomes—divides to produce two cells, each of which also has the full set of chromosomes.

MEIOSIS: PRODUCTION OF GAMETES (SEX CELLS)

haploid A cell that has a single set of unpaired chromosomes, half of the genetic material.

The genetic code is transmitted from parents to offspring via the female and male gametes. Gametes, remember, have only half the chromosomes that are in somatic cells—they are **haploid,** containing one chromosome from each pair. Unlike mitosis, the production of these cells, meiosis, does not result in identical copies of the parent cell and the parent cell's DNA. Meiosis involves one DNA replication followed by *two* cell divisions (**Figure 3.13**).

Meiosis plays a critical role in the inheritance of biological characteristics and the variation seen in offspring. Because each gamete contains just one chromosome from a homologous pair, during reproduction each parent contributes only half of his or her genetic material. For example, in your somatic cells, each homologous

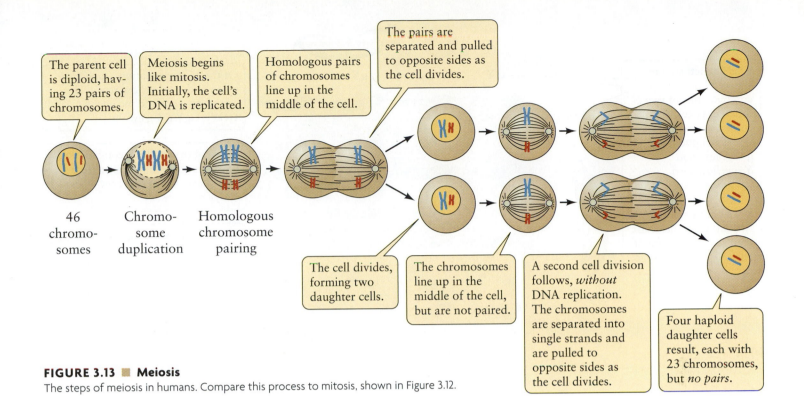

The parent cell is diploid, having 23 pairs of chromosomes.

Meiosis begins like mitosis. Initially, the cell's DNA is replicated.

Homologous pairs of chromosomes line up in the middle of the cell.

The pairs are separated and pulled to opposite sides as the cell divides.

46 chromo-somes

Chromo-some duplication

Homologous chromosome pairing

The cell divides, forming two daughter cells.

The chromosomes line up in the middle of the cell, but are not paired.

A second cell division follows, *without* DNA replication. The chromosomes are separated into single strands and are pulled to opposite sides as the cell divides.

Four haploid daughter cells result, each with 23 chromosomes, but *no pairs*.

FIGURE 3.13 ■ Meiosis
The steps of meiosis in humans. Compare this process to mitosis, shown in Figure 3.12.

pair includes one chromosome from your mother and one chromosome from your father. Each of your gametes, however, contains only one chromosome, which is either your mother's or your father's. Whether a particular gamete contains your mother's chromosome or your father's chromosome is completely random. In addition, homologous chromosomes often exchange parts when they pair up and intertwine. This exchange of parts is called **cross-over.** The outcome of such reshuffling is that gene variants on the maternal chromosome are now on the paternal chromosome (or vice versa), a common development called **recombination.** Genes that are close together on a chromosome are much less likely to recombine. These units or blocks of genetic material are called **haplotypes.** Geneticists prefer to study haplotypes because they do not recombine and are passed on for many generations, potentially hundreds, over time. Groups of related haplotypes, called **haplogroups,** are an important tool for studying both long-term evolution and populations' histories.

In rare instances, during meiosis nonhomologous chromosomes exchange segments. These rare exchanges are called **translocations.** The most common form in humans, involving both chromosome 13 and chromosome 14, affects about 1 in 1,300 people. Translocations cause infertility, Down syndrome (when one third of chromosome 21 joins onto chromosome 14), and a number of diseases, including several forms of cancer (some leukemias). On occasion, chromosome pairs fail to separate during meiosis or mitosis. These **nondisjunctions** result in an incorrect number of chromosomes in the person's genome. A loss in number of chromosomes

cross-over The process by which homologous chromosomes partially wrap around each other and exchange genetic information during meiosis.

recombination The exchange of genetic material between homologous chromosomes, resulting from a cross-over event.

haplotypes A group of alleles that tend to be inherited as a unit due to their closely spaced loci on a single chromosome.

haplogroups A large set of haplotypes, such as the Y-chromosome or mitochondrial DNA, that may be used to define a population.

translocations Rearrangements of chromosomes due to the insertion of genetic material from one chromosome to another.

nondisjunctions Refers to the failure of the chromosomes to properly segregate during meiosis, creating some gametes with abnormal numbers of chromosomes.

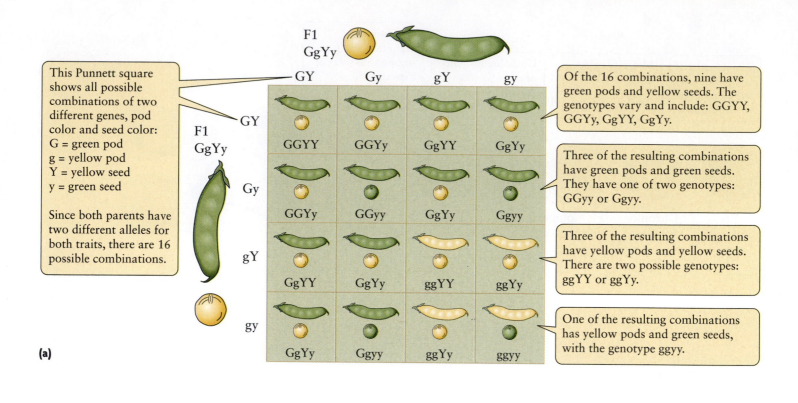

This Punnett square shows all possible combinations of two different genes, pod color and seed color:
G = green pod
g = yellow pod
Y = yellow seed
y = green seed

Since both parents have two different alleles for both traits, there are 16 possible combinations.

Of the 16 combinations, nine have green pods and yellow seeds. The genotypes vary and include: GGYY, GGYy, GgYY, GgYy.

Three of the resulting combinations have green pods and green seeds. They have one of two genotypes: GGyy or Ggyy.

Three of the resulting combinations have yellow pods and yellow seeds. There are two possible genotypes: ggYY or ggYy.

One of the resulting combinations has yellow pods and green seeds, with the genotype ggyy.

(a)

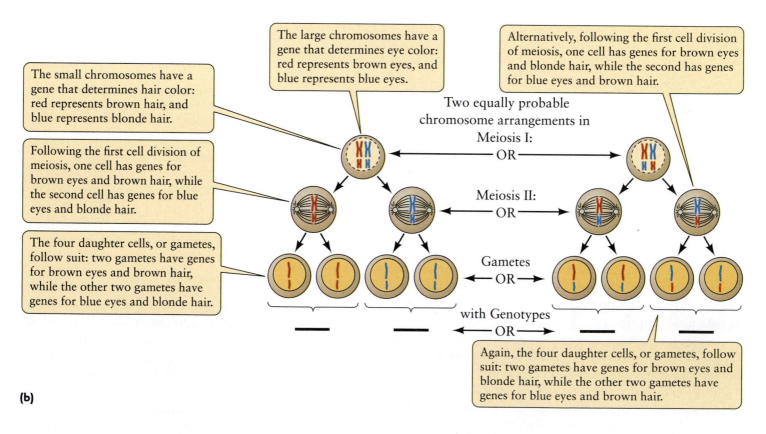

The small chromosomes have a gene that determines hair color: red represents brown hair, and blue represents blonde hair.

The large chromosomes have a gene that determines eye color: red represents brown eyes, and blue represents blue eyes.

Alternatively, following the first cell division of meiosis, one cell has genes for brown eyes and blonde hair, while the second has genes for blue eyes and brown hair.

Following the first cell division of meiosis, one cell has genes for brown eyes and brown hair, while the second cell has genes for blue eyes and blonde hair.

The four daughter cells, or gametes, follow suit: two gametes have genes for brown eyes and brown hair, while the other two gametes have genes for blue eyes and blonde hair.

Two equally probable chromosome arrangements in Meiosis I:
— OR —

Meiosis II:
— OR —

Gametes
← OR →

with Genotypes
← OR →

Again, the four daughter cells, or gametes, follow suit: two gametes have genes for brown eyes and blonde hair, while the other two gametes have genes for blue eyes and brown hair.

(b)

FIGURE 3.14 ■ Law of Independent Assortment

Through his research with pea plants, Mendel created several laws pertaining to inheritance. (a) His second law, the Law of Independent Assortment, asserts that traits linked to different chromosomes are inherited independently from one another. (b) Hair color, for example, is inherited independently from eye color.

is a **monosomy**. A gain in number of chromosomes is a **trisomy**, the most common being trisomy-21, or Down syndrome (in this form, caused by an extra or part of an extra chromosome 21). As with many chromosomal abnormalities, the age of the mother determines the risk of the offspring's having Down syndrome. For 20- to 24-year-old mothers, the risk is 1/1,490. It rises to 1/106 by age 40 and 1/11 beyond age 49.

As Mendel had recognized (see "Since Darwin: Mechanisms of Inheritance, the Evolutionary Synthesis, and the Discovery of DNA" in chapter 2), each physical unit (that is, gene) passes from parent to offspring independent of other physical units. This independent inheritance—often called Mendel's **Law of Independent Assortment** (**Figure 3.14**)—applies to genes from *different* chromosomes. However, what happens when genes are on the *same* chromosome? Simple—because meiosis involves the separation of chromosome pairs (homologous chromosomes), genes on the same chromosome, especially ones near each other on that chromosome, have a greater chance of being inherited as a package. They are less subject to recombination. This gene **linkage**—the inheritance of a package of genes (such as haplotypes) from the same chromosome (**Figure 3.15**)—is an exception to Mendel's Law of Independent Assortment.

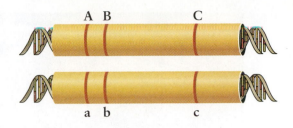

FIGURE 3.15 ■ **Linkage**
Since genes A, B, and C are on the same chromosome, they have a better chance of being inherited as a unit than of being combined and inherited with genes a, b, and c, which are together on a separate chromosome and thus also have a good chance of being inherited as a unit. Meanwhile, because they are close together, genes A and B (like genes a and b) stand a better chance of being inherited together than do genes B and C (like genes b and c). If, for example, eye color and hair color were on the same chromosome, especially if they were close together on that chromosome, they would most likely *not* be inherited separately with all the combinations examined in Figure 3.14.

PRODUCING PROTEINS: THE OTHER FUNCTION OF DNA

In addition to replicating itself, DNA serves as the template for protein synthesis. Proteins are the complex chemicals that make up tissues and bring about the functions, repair, and growth of tissues (**Table 3.1**). While some work within cells—for example, the enzymes that unzip DNA during replication—others, such as hormones, work within the whole body. Proteins consist of **amino acids,** of which there are 20. Each kind of protein is defined by its particular combination and number of linked amino acids. Most of the human body is comprised of proteins, and the body produces 12 of the amino acids. The other eight, also called **essential amino acids,** come from particular foods.

monosomy Refers to the condition in which only one of a specific pair of chromosomes is present in a cell's nucleus.

trisomy Refers to the condition in which an additional chromosome exists with the homologous pair.

amino acids Organic molecules combined in a specific sequence by the ribosomes to form a protein.

essential amino acids Those amino acids that cannot be synthesized in the body; they must be supplied by the diet.

TABLE 3.1	The Seven Types of Proteins	
NAME	**FUNCTION**	**EXAMPLE(S)**
Enzymes	Catalyze chemical reactions	Lactase—breaks down lactose in milk products
Structural Proteins	Give structure or support to tissues	Keratin—hair; collagen—bone
Gas Transport Proteins	Carry vital gases to tissues	Hemoglobin—oxygen
Antibodies	Part of immune system	Anti-A and Anti-B in ABO blood system
Hormones	Regulate metabolism	Insulin regulates metabolism of carbohydrates and fat
Mechanical Proteins	Carry out specific functions or work	Actin and myosin—help muscles contract
Nutrients	Provide vital nutrients to tissues	Ovalbumin—main protein of egg whites

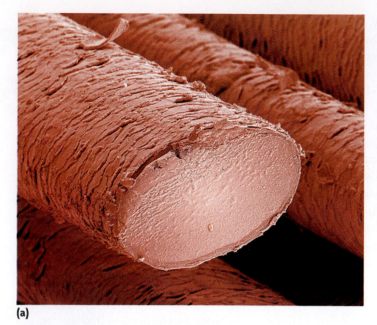

(a)

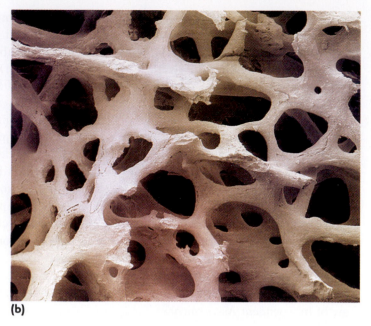

(b)

FIGURE 3.16 ■ **Structural Proteins**
While culture and environment strongly influence the development of biological structures, those structures are initially determined by structural proteins. Two important structural proteins are keratin and collagen. **(a)** In humans, keratin is the primary component of hair (pictured here), skin, and fingernails. In other mammals and in amphibians, birds, and reptiles, it also contributes to structures such as hooves, claws, beaks, scales, and shells. **(b)** Collagen is the most abundant protein in humans and other mammals and is essential for connective tissues, such as bone (pictured here), cartilage, ligaments, and tendons. In addition, collagen strengthens the walls of blood vessels and, along with keratin, gives strength and elasticity to skin. In its crystalline form, collagen is found in the cornea and lens of the eye.

structural proteins Proteins that form an organism's physical attributes.

regulatory proteins Proteins involved in the expression of control genes.

transcription The first step of protein synthesis, involving the creation of mRNA based on the DNA template.

translation The second step of protein synthesis, involving the transfer of amino acids by tRNA to the ribosomes, which are then added to the protein chain.

ribonucleic acid (RNA) A single-stranded molecule involved in protein synthesis, consisting of a phosphate, ribose sugar, and one of four nitrogen bases.

uracil One of four nitrogen bases that make up RNA; it pairs with adenine.

messenger RNA (mRNA) The molecules that are responsible for making a chemical copy of a gene needed for a specific protein, that is, for the transcription phase of protein synthesis.

ribosomal RNA (rRNA) A fundamental structural component of a ribosome.

Two main categories of proteins are constantly being synthesized. **Structural proteins** are responsible for physical characteristics, such as hair form, eye color, tooth size, and basic bone shape (**Figure 3.16**). The other category, **regulatory** (also called *functional*) **proteins**, includes enzymes, hormones, and antibodies. Enzymes regulate activities within cells, hormones regulate activities between cells, and antibodies are key to fighting infections.

Protein synthesis is a two-step process (**Figure 3.17**). The first step, **transcription,** takes place mostly in the cell's nucleus. The second, **translation,** takes place in the cytoplasm. Transcription starts out just like the first step of DNA replication: a double strand of parental DNA unzips. Rather than producing daughter strands of DNA, the now-exposed bases in the DNA molecule serve as a single template for another kind of nucleic acid, **ribonucleic acid (RNA)**. RNA has the same nitrogen bases as DNA, except that **uracil** (U) replaces thymine (T). Uracil always matches with adenine (A), while guanine (G) continues to pair with cytosine (C).

Only one of the two DNA strands serves as the template for the production of RNA. This strand attracts free-floating RNA nucleotides. The strand of RNA—now called **messenger RNA (mRNA)**—then splits off from the DNA template, leaves the nucleus, and moves into the cytoplasm.

In the translation step, the mRNA attaches itself to structures called **ribosomes.** The mRNA is a "messenger" because (in the form of its own open bases) it carries the code for the protein being synthesized from the nucleus to the ribosomes. Ribosomes are made up of another kind of ribonucleic acid, **ribosomal RNA (rRNA)**. Once the mRNA is attached to the ribosome, the transcription step of protein synthesis is complete.

Floating in the cytoplasm is yet another kind of ribonucleic acid, **transfer RNA (tRNA)**. tRNA occurs as triplets, or **anticodons,** that seek complementary triplet strands of mRNA, known as **triplets** or **codons.** For example, a triplet of AUC mRNA would pair with the complementary UAG tRNA. The three bases of the tRNA triplet represent a specific amino acid.

As the tRNA strand builds off the mRNA template, the amino acids are chemically linked together by a **peptide bond,** resulting in a chain of amino acids. A chain of these peptide bonds is called a **polypeptide.** Although a single polypeptide may function as a protein, in many cases multiple polypeptides must bind together and fold into a three-dimensional structure to form a functional protein. For example, hemoglobin, a molecule found on the surface of red blood cells, is comprised of two pairs of polypeptide chains. Once the protein has formed, it breaks away from the tRNA and commences with its task, either structural or functional.

All of the DNA involved in protein synthesis is **coding DNA,** the molecule segments encoded for particular proteins. The total length of DNA in humans is about three billion nucleotides. Each of the 20,000 to 25,000 genes has about 5,000 nucleotides, so (according to the math) only about 5% of the DNA contains coding material. Thus, most human DNA is **noncoding.** Often interspersed with coding DNA from one end of the chromosome to the other, this noncoding DNA seems to have no function. In protein synthesis, the noncoding DNA is cut out before translation. Recent studies by anthropological geneticists have suggested that noncoding DNA located close to genes that control brain function may have a role in the overall wiring of the brain cells to each other. Most research, however, focuses on the DNA that is coded for particular body structures or particular regulatory functions. This DNA makes up the two main types of genes, structural and regulatory.

transfer RNA (tRNA) The molecules that are responsible for transporting amino acids to the ribosomes during protein synthesis.

anticodons Sequences of three nitrogen bases carried by tRNA, they match up with the complementary mRNA codons and each designate a specific amino acid during protein synthesis.

triplets Sequences of three nitrogen bases each in DNA, known as codons in mRNA.

codons The sequences of three nitrogen bases carried by mRNA that are coded to produce specific amino acids in protein synthesis.

peptide bond Chemical bond that joins amino acids into a protein chain.

polypeptide Also known as a protein, a chain of amino acids held together by multiple peptide bonds.

coding DNA Sequences of a gene's DNA (also known as exons) that are coded to produce a specific protein and are transcribed and translated during protein synthesis.

noncoding DNA Sequences of a gene's DNA (also known as introns) that are not coded to produce specific proteins and are excised before protein synthesis.

CONCEPT CHECK	The Two Steps of Protein Synthesis

The second function of DNA is to synthesize proteins, which are responsible for all the structures and functions of the body.

STEP	ACTIVITY
1. Transcription (nucleus)	Parental strand of DNA unzips, exposing two daughter strands of DNA. Free-floating RNA nucleotides match one exposed daughter strand of DNA. The strand of messenger RNA (mRNA) moves out of the nucleus and into the cytoplasm.
2. Translation (cytoplasm)	The mRNA attaches to a ribosome in the cytoplasm. Triplets of transfer RNA (tRNA), with exposed bases and each carrying an amino acid specific to its set of three bases, recognize and bind with complementary base pairs of mRNA. The amino acids, linked by peptide bonds, form a chain called a polypeptide. The protein forms, either as a single polypeptide or as multiple polypeptides bound together.

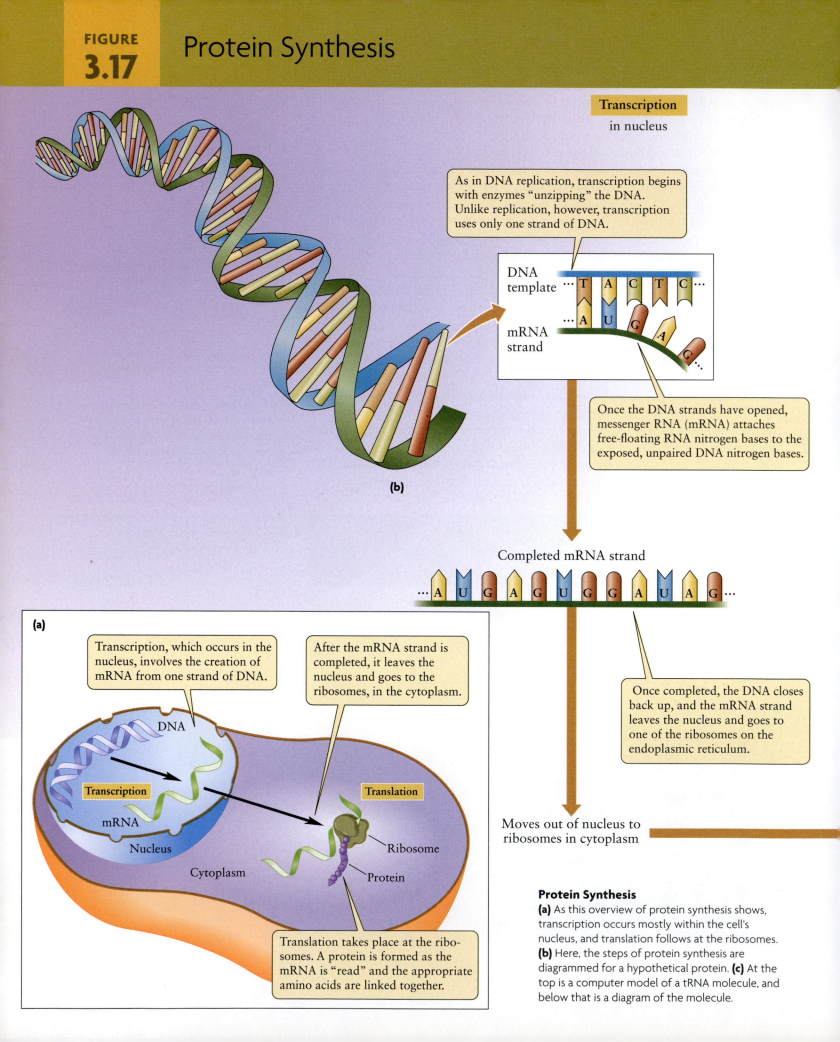

FIGURE 3.17 Protein Synthesis

Transcription in nucleus

As in DNA replication, transcription begins with enzymes "unzipping" the DNA. Unlike replication, however, transcription uses only one strand of DNA.

DNA template ...T A C T C...

mRNA strand ...A U G A G...

Once the DNA strands have opened, messenger RNA (mRNA) attaches free-floating RNA nitrogen bases to the exposed, unpaired DNA nitrogen bases.

(b)

Completed mRNA strand

...A U G A G U G G A U A G...

Once completed, the DNA closes back up, and the mRNA strand leaves the nucleus and goes to one of the ribosomes on the endoplasmic reticulum.

Moves out of nucleus to ribosomes in cytoplasm

(a)

Transcription, which occurs in the nucleus, involves the creation of mRNA from one strand of DNA.

After the mRNA strand is completed, it leaves the nucleus and goes to the ribosomes, in the cytoplasm.

DNA

Transcription

mRNA

Nucleus

Cytoplasm

Translation

Ribosome

Protein

Translation takes place at the ribosomes. A protein is formed as the mRNA is "read" and the appropriate amino acids are linked together.

Protein Synthesis
(a) As this overview of protein synthesis shows, transcription occurs mostly within the cell's nucleus, and translation follows at the ribosomes. **(b)** Here, the steps of protein synthesis are diagrammed for a hypothetical protein. **(c)** At the top is a computer model of a tRNA molecule, and below that is a diagram of the molecule.

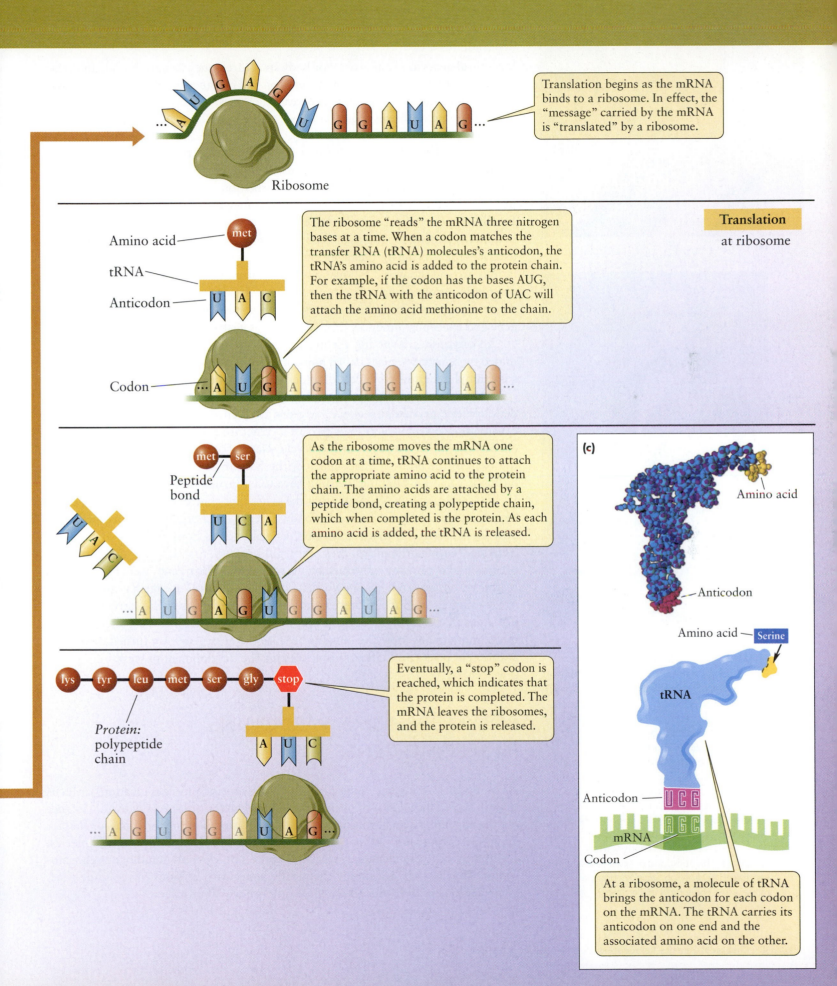

Translation begins as the mRNA binds to a ribosome. In effect, the "message" carried by the mRNA is "translated" by a ribosome.

Ribosome

Translation
at ribosome

Amino acid — met

tRNA

Anticodon — U A C

Codon — ...A U G A G U G G A U A G...

The ribosome "reads" the mRNA three nitrogen bases at a time. When a codon matches the transfer RNA (tRNA) molecules's anticodon, the tRNA's amino acid is added to the protein chain. For example, if the codon has the bases AUG, then the tRNA with the anticodon of UAC will attach the amino acid methionine to the chain.

Peptide bond — met — ser

U C A

U A C

...A U G A G U G G A U A G...

As the ribosome moves the mRNA one codon at a time, tRNA continues to attach the appropriate amino acid to the protein chain. The amino acids are attached by a peptide bond, creating a polypeptide chain, which when completed is the protein. As each amino acid is added, the tRNA is released.

(c)

Amino acid

Anticodon

Amino acid — Serine

tRNA

Anticodon — UCG

mRNA — AGC

Codon

lys — tyr — leu — met — ser — gly — stop

Protein: polypeptide chain

A U C

Eventually, a "stop" codon is reached, which indicates that the protein is completed. The mRNA leaves the ribosomes, and the protein is released.

...A G U G G A U A G...

At a ribosome, a molecule of tRNA brings the anticodon for each codon on the mRNA. The tRNA carries its anticodon on one end and the associated amino acid on the other.

GENES: STRUCTURAL AND REGULATORY

Structural genes are responsible for body structures, such as hair, blood, and other tissues. **Regulatory genes** turn other genes on and off, an essential activity in growth and development. If the genes that determine bones, for example, did not turn off at a certain point, bones would continue to grow well beyond what would be acceptable for a normal life (**Figure 3.18**).

Chickens have the genes for tooth development, but they do not develop teeth because those genes are permanently turned off. Humans have a gene for complete body hair coverage, but that gene is not turned on completely. The human genes for sexual maturity turn on during puberty, somewhat earlier in girls than in boys. Finally, regulatory genes can lead to either lactose intolerance or lactose persistence in humans (among the topics of chapter 4). In this instance, the gene that produces lactase—the enzyme for the digestion of milk—is turned off for most human populations around the world following weaning, usually by about age four. However, most humans of northern European and East African descent have inherited a different regulatory gene, which creates lactose persistence. A person who lacks this gene and eats dairy products experiences great gastrointestinal discomfort.

An organism's form and the arrangement of its tissues and organs are determined by regulatory genes called **homeotic (*Hox*) genes**. These master genes guide, for example, the embryological development of all the regions of an animal's body, such as the head, trunk, and limbs (**Figure 3.19**). This means that in the process of development, particular sets of *Hox* genes are turned on in a particular sequence, causing the correct structure or part of a structure to develop in each region. For example, genes responsible for the development of legs have to be switched on for the back of the body in quadrupeds or the bottom of the body in humans. Similarly, the genes for building the skull have to be turned on for the top of the body. Until recently, scientists thought that the genes that control the development of the key structures and functions of the body differed from organism to organism. We now know, however, that the development of various body parts in complex organisms—such as the limbs, eyes, and vital organs—that are very different from organism to organism is governed by the *same* genes. *Hox* genes were first found in fruit flies, but research has shown that common ancestral lineage has given organisms—ranging from flies to mice to humans—the same basic DNA structure in the key areas that control the development of form. Flies look like flies, mice look like mice, and humans look like humans because the *Hox* genes are turned on and off at different places and different times during the development process.

POLYMORPHISMS: VARIATIONS IN SPECIFIC GENES

Along each chromosome, a specific gene has a specific physical location, or **locus** (plural, *loci*). This locus is of intense interest to geneticists, especially in understanding the appearance and evolution of genetic variation (among the topics of chapter 4). Alleles, the genetic subunits (see "Mechanisms of Inheritance" in chapter 2), are slightly different chemical structures at the same loci on homologous chromosomes. That is, they are simply chemically alternative versions of the same gene. Some genes have only one allele, while others have 20 or more.

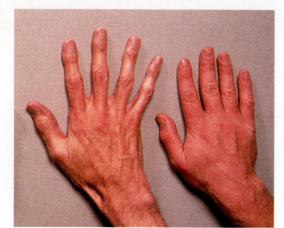

(a)

(b)

FIGURE 3.18 ■ Marfan Syndrome
(a) The hand on the right shows normal finger growth. The hand on the left has much longer and thinner fingers due to Marfan syndrome, a pathological, hereditary disorder of the regulatory genes that control connective tissue. As a result of Marfan syndrome, uncontrolled bone growth leads to long and thin fingers and toes, long and thin arms and legs, and increased stature. Organs such as the lungs and heart can also be negatively affected. **(b)** In the 1960s, a scientific paper asserted that U.S. president Abraham Lincoln (1809–1865) was afflicted with Marfan syndrome. This still-controversial assessment was based entirely on Lincoln's unusual tallness and the length of his limbs.

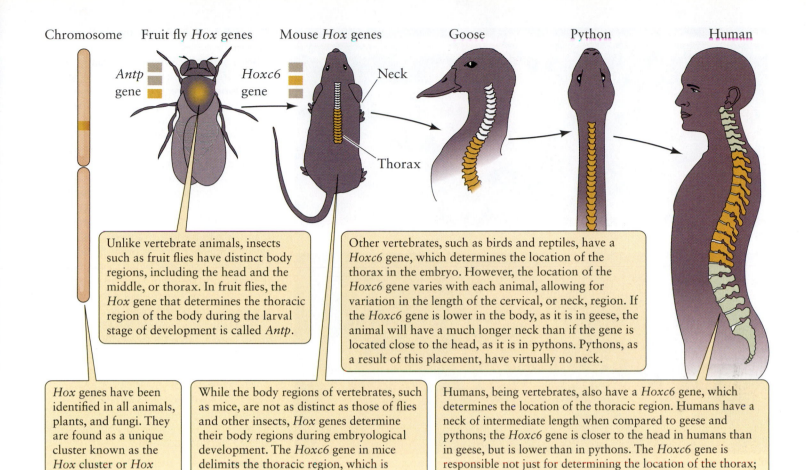

Chromosome **Fruit fly *Hox* genes** **Mouse *Hox* genes** **Goose** **Python** **Human**

Antp gene

Hoxc6 gene

Neck

Thorax

Unlike vertebrate animals, insects such as fruit flies have distinct body regions, including the head and the middle, or thorax. In fruit flies, the *Hox* gene that determines the thoracic region of the body during the larval stage of development is called *Antp*.

Other vertebrates, such as birds and reptiles, have a *Hoxc6* gene, which determines the location of the thorax in the embryo. However, the location of the *Hoxc6* gene varies with each animal, allowing for variation in the length of the cervical, or neck, region. If the *Hoxc6* gene is lower in the body, as it is in geese, the animal will have a much longer neck than if the gene is located close to the head, as it is in pythons. Pythons, as a result of this placement, have virtually no neck.

Hox genes have been identified in all animals, plants, and fungi. They are found as a unique cluster known as the *Hox* cluster or *Hox* complex.

While the body regions of vertebrates, such as mice, are not as distinct as those of flies and other insects, *Hox* genes determine their body regions during embryological development. The *Hoxc6* gene in mice delimits the thoracic region, which is indicated by the thoracic vertebrae.

Humans, being vertebrates, also have a *Hoxc6* gene, which determines the location of the thoracic region. Humans have a neck of intermediate length when compared to geese and pythons; the *Hoxc6* gene is closer to the head in humans than in geese, but is lower than in pythons. The *Hoxc6* gene is responsible not just for determining the location of the thorax; in humans, this gene determines the development of the entire thoracic region, including mammary glands.

FIGURE 3.19 ■ Homeotic (*Hox*) Genes
Discovered in 1983 by Swiss and American researchers, these regulatory genes are coded to produce proteins that turn on many other genes, in particular those that determine the regions of the body during embryological development. Without these genes, or if there are mutations in these genes, body development may be altered. For example, a mutation in the *Hox* genes of a fruit fly can cause a leg instead of an antenna to grow from the head.

Human blood type is one genetic trait with different alleles. Each person has one of four blood types—A, B, AB, or O—and these four types comprise the ABO blood group system, first discovered in 1900 (**Figure 3.20**). Because it has more than two variants, a genetic trait such as this one is called a **polymorphism** (Greek *poly,* meaning "many"; Greek *morph,* meaning "form"). Each person has one A, B, or O allele on one chromosome of the homologous pair and another A, B, or O allele on the other chromosome of that pair. The combination determines the person's blood type.

Although Mendel did not know about chromosomes, he recognized that physical units of inheritance—which we now know to be the alleles—segregate in a very patterned fashion. That is, his experiments with garden peas showed that the father contributes one physical unit and the mother contributes the other. This is Mendel's **Law of Segregation** (**Figure 3.21**). For example, a person with blood type AB will pass on either an A or a B to a child, but not both. The other allele will come from the other parent. This discovery was revolutionary because it explained how new variation arises in reproduction.

locus The location of an allele, or gene, on a chromosome.

polymorphism Refers to the presence of two or more separate phenotypes for a certain gene in the population.

Law of Segregation Mendel's First Law, which asserts that the two alleles for any given gene (or trait) are inherited, one from each parent; during gamete production, only one of the two alleles will be present in each ovum or sperm.

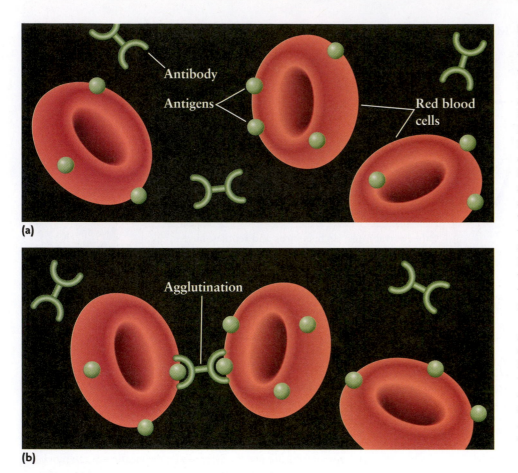

(a)

(b)

FIGURE 3.20 ■ **Antibody–Antigen System**

When a person receives a blood transfusion, the transfused blood must have the same blood type as the recipient's own to avoid an antibody–antigen reaction. **(a)** Each red blood cell has structures on its surface, known as **antigens**, that identify the cell as being type A, B, AB, or O. If the wrong type of blood is given to a person, the body's immune system recognizes the new antigens as foreign. Special proteins called **antibodies** are then produced in the blood in response to the "invaders." **(b)** The antibodies attach themselves to the foreign antigens, causing agglutination, or clumping, of the blood cells. Because the coagulated blood cannot pass through blood vessels properly, the recipient's tissues do not receive the blood they need. If not treated, the person might die.

For all the blood types in the ABO blood group system, **Table 3.2** shows the antigens, antibodies, and acceptable and unacceptable blood types. For example, type A blood, which can result from AO alleles or AA alleles, has A antigens on its surface and anti-B antibodies, which will react with B or AB blood. (Genotypes and phenotypes are defined and discussed below.)

TABLE 3.2	The ABO Blood Group System				
PHENOTYPES	**GENOTYPES**	**ANTIGENS**	**ANTIBODIES**	**UNACCEPTABLE BLOOD TYPES**	**ACCEPTABLE BLOOD TYPES**
A	AO, AA	A	anti-B	B, AB	A, O
B	BO, BB	B	anti-A	A, AB	B, O
AB	AB	A, B	none	none (universal recipient)	A, B, AB, O
O	OO	none (universal donor)	anti-A, anti-B	A, B, AB	O

single nucleotide polymorphisms (SNPs) Variations in the DNA sequence due to the change of a single nitrogen base; also known as point mutations.

microsatellites Specific loci in nuclear or organellar DNA that have repeated units of 1–4 base pairs in length; they can be used in various genetic studies.

Some of the most exciting contemporary DNA research has revealed a whole new array of genetic markers. Showing a tremendous amount of variation within and between human populations, these **single nucleotide polymorphisms (SNPs)** are known from well over 1,000,000 sites on the human genome. Closer examination of the human genome has also revealed that DNA segments are often repeated, sometimes many times, and for no apparent reason. These **microsatellites** are highly individualistic, forming a unique DNA signature for each person. Microsatellites have quickly become the most important tool for individual identification, and they have proven especially valuable in forensic science. For example, they have been used to identify victims of the 9/11 attacks as well as genocide and mass-murder fatalities in the Balkans, Iraq, and Argentina.

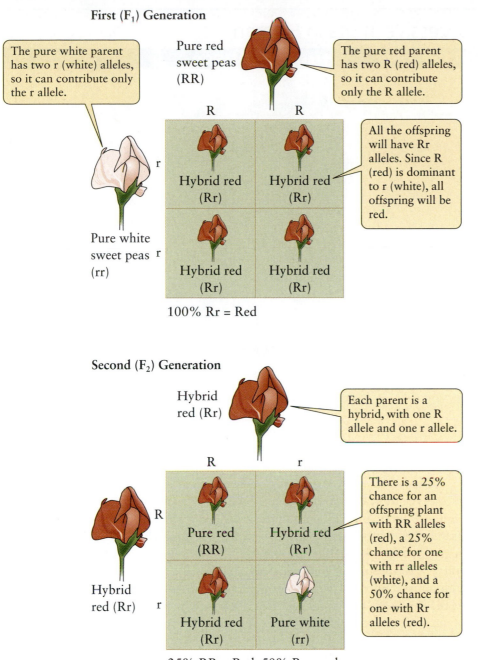

First (F₁) Generation

The pure white parent has two r (white) alleles, so it can contribute only the r allele.

Pure red sweet peas (RR)

The pure red parent has two R (red) alleles, so it can contribute only the R allele.

R   R

Pure white sweet peas (rr)

r

Hybrid red (Rr)   Hybrid red (Rr)

Hybrid red (Rr)   Hybrid red (Rr)

All the offspring will have Rr alleles. Since R (red) is dominant to r (white), all offspring will be red.

100% Rr = Red

Second (F₂) Generation

Hybrid red (Rr)

Each parent is a hybrid, with one R allele and one r allele.

R   r

Hybrid red (Rr)   r

Pure red (RR)   Hybrid red (Rr)

Hybrid red (Rr)   Pure white (rr)

There is a 25% chance for an offspring plant with RR alleles (red), a 25% chance for one with rr alleles (white), and a 50% chance for one with Rr alleles (red).

25% RR = Red, 50% Rr = red, 25% rr = White

FIGURE 3.21 ■ Law of Segregation
Mendel's first law, the Law of Segregation, declares that the mother and father contribute equally to an offspring's genetic makeup. For each gene, a person has two alleles (which can be the same or different). One allele is from the person's mother, and one is from the person's father.

Remember that meiosis (see Figure 3.13) creates four gametes, each of which has only one set of chromosomes, no pairs. Each gamete, having this one set, can pass on only one allele for each gene. If the gamete that the father contributes to fertilization has the allele for brown hair, for example, that is the only allele the father will contribute to the offspring. The other allele, for brown or a different color, will come from the mother.

Genotypes and Phenotypes: Genes and Their Physical Expression

The two alleles, whether they are chemically identical (e.g., AA) or chemically different (e.g., AO), identify the genotype—the actual genetic material in the pair of homologous chromosomes. Chemically identical alleles are called **homozygous.** Chemically different alleles are called **heterozygous.** When alleles are heterozygous, the dominant one will be expressed in the phenotype—the visible manifestation of

antigens Substances, such as bacteria, foreign blood cells, and enzymes, that stimulate the immune system's antibody production.

antibodies Molecules that form as part of the primary immune response to the presence of foreign substances; they attach to the foreign antigens.

homozygous Refers to the condition in which a pair of alleles at a single locus on homologous chromosomes are the same.

heterozygous Refers to the condition in which a pair of alleles at a single locus on homologous chromosomes are different.

TABLE 3.3	Dominant and Recessive Traits in Humans	
TRAIT	**DOMINANT EXPRESSION**	**RECESSIVE EXPRESSION**
Cleft in chin	No cleft	Cleft
Dimples	Dimples	No dimples
Earlobes	Free lobe	Attached lobe
Eye shape	Almond	Round
Eyebrow size	Broad	Slender
Eyebrow shape	Separated	Joined
Eyelash length	Long	Short
Finger mid-digital hair	Hair	No hair
Freckles	Freckles	No freckles
Hair on back of hand	Hair	No hair
Hairline	Widow's peak	Straight hairline
Hitchhiker's thumb	Straight thumb	Hitchhiker's thumb
Interlaced fingers	Left thumb over right	Right thumb over left
Tongue rolling	Roller	Nonroller

the gene. (**Table 3.3** lists a number of simple dominant/recessive traits visible on the human body. If you have a dominant trait, at least one of your parents must have the trait. If you have a recessive trait, there is a chance that neither of your parents possesses the trait. For more on dominance and recessiveness, see "Mechanisms of Inheritance" in chapter 2.) For example, individuals who are AA or who are AO have the same phenotype—A expresses dominance over O, and both individuals are blood type A. The recessive allele is not expressed. When you know simply that a person's blood type is A, you cannot tell whether that person's genotype is AA or AO. Rather, the blood type refers to the phenotype and not the genotype. If the person is AO, then the O allele is hidden because that allele is recessive. For the recessive allele to be expressed, each of the homologous chromosomes must have the recessive allele. For example, the alleles for type O blood are OO. For a person to have type O blood, both alleles in the pair of homologous chromosomes have to be O.

Sometimes alleles exhibit **codominance,** where neither chemically different version dominates the other. In the ABO blood group system, the A and B alleles are codominant and both are expressed. If someone has type AB blood you know that person's phenotype and genotype.

codominance Refers to two different alleles that are equally dominant; both are fully expressed in a heterozygote's phenotype.

THE COMPLEXITY OF GENETICS: POLYGENIC VARIATION AND PLEIOTROPY

For a long time, the general impression about genes has been that they represent specific locations of DNA coded to produce specific proteins. Much of research genetics,

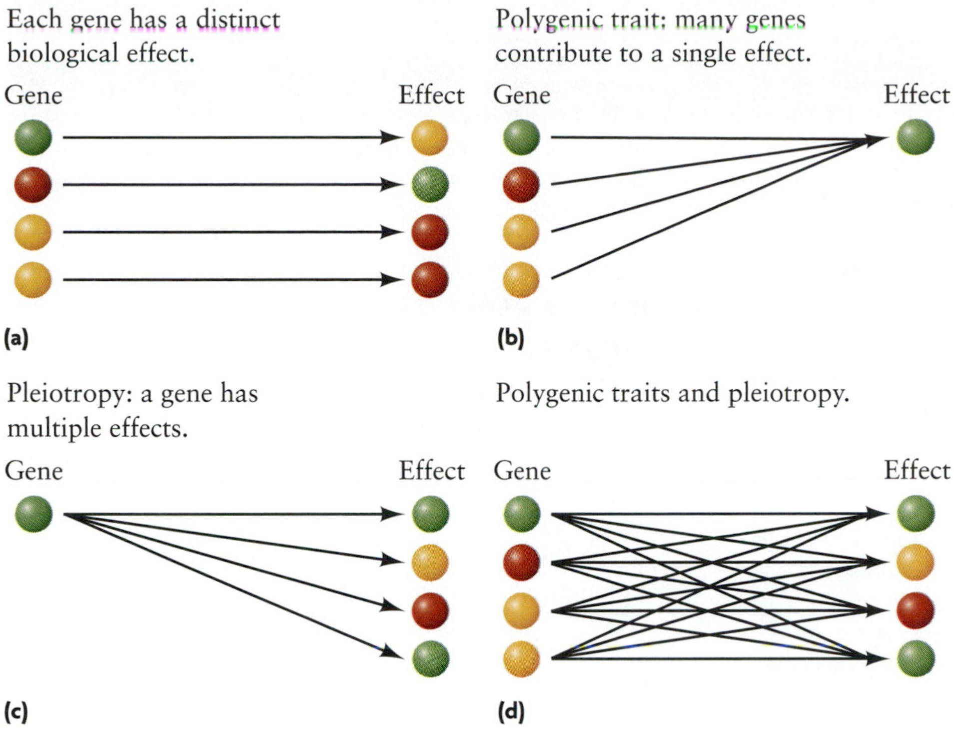

Each gene has a distinct biological effect.

Gene   Effect

(a)

Polygenic trait: many genes contribute to a single effect.

Gene   Effect

(b)

Pleiotropy: a gene has multiple effects.

Gene   Effect

(c)

Polygenic traits and pleiotropy.

Gene   Effect

(d)

FIGURE 3.22 ■ Polygenic Traits and Pleiotropic Genes
(a) Mendel's simple rules of inheritance **(b)** do not apply when traits are affected by many genes. Eye color, for example, is determined by at least three genes. Because this trait is polygenic, some children's eye colors are very different from their parents'. **(c)** Pleiotropic genes affect more than one physical trait. The PKU allele, for example, affects mental abilities and the coloration of hair and skin. A person who inherits this allele will be afflicted with the disease phenylketonuria, in which a missing enzyme leads to mental retardation as well as reduced hair and skin pigmentation. **(d)** One trait can be affected by several genes, and each of those genes can affect several other traits as well.

including in anthropological genetics, is based on this "one gene—one protein" model. However, the relationship between genes and their physical expression—especially their phenotypes—turns out to be more complex than previously thought. Many traits are **polygenic**, determined by genes at two or more loci; however, the genes cannot be identified individually, and the physical manifestations are influenced by environmental factors. In humans, thousands of traits such as height, skin color, head form, tooth size, and eye shape have multiple genetic components and are strongly influenced by environmental factors. For some of these traits, scientists can determine only the relative proportions of genetic and environmental contributions. A trait's **heritability**, the proportion of its variation that is genetic, can be calculated this way:

polygenic Refers to one phenotypic trait that is affected by two or more genes.

heritability The proportion of phenotypic variation that is due to inheritance rather than to environmental influence.

$$\text{heritability (}h^2\text{)} = \frac{\text{genetic variation}}{\text{(genetic variation + environmental variation)}}$$

Heritability estimates are presented as values ranging from 0, where none of the variation is genetic in origin, to 1, where all of the variation is genetic. In traits with heritability estimates greater than .5, most of the variation is genetic. For example, in the United States the heritabilities for height and weight are estimated to be .6 and .3, respectively. Tooth size has among the highest levels of heritability, about .7, and brain size and fingerprints are even higher, at .9. Physical anthropologists and other evolutionary biologists are very interested in heritability for one simple reason: *because only heritable traits respond to natural selection, they are the primary driving force of evolution.*

Measurement of heritability, however, is complicated by **pleiotropy**—a single allele can have multiple effects. In fact, most complex traits are polygenic and pleiotropic (**Figure 3.22**).

pleiotropy Refers to one gene that affects more than one phenotypic trait.

ANSWERING THE BIG QUESTIONS

What is the genetic code?

■ The genetic code is DNA, packaged in individual chromosomes.

■ One type of DNA exists in the cell's nucleus (nuclear DNA), and the other type exists in the cytoplasm (mitochondrial DNA). Nuclear DNA provides most of the genetic code.

What does the genetic code (DNA) do?

■ DNA serves as the chemical template for its own replication. DNA replication is the first step toward the production of new cells: somatic cells and gametes.

—Mitosis results in the production of two identical somatic cells. In humans, each parental or daughter cell has 46 chromosomes in 23 homologous pairs.

—Meiosis results in the production of four gametes. In humans, each parental cell has 46 chromosomes, and each gamete has 23 chromosomes.

■ DNA serves as the chemical template for the creation of proteins.

—Proteins are combinations of amino acids. They are responsible for all physical characteristics (structural proteins), the regulation (regulatory or functional proteins) of activities within cells (enzymes), the regulation of activities between cells (hormones), and the fighting of foreign antigens (antibodies). Thus, proteins comprise the entire body and determine all of its functions, from conception through maturity.

—The two types of proteins are governed by the two corresponding types of genes, structural and regulatory.

—*Hox* genes are regulatory genes that control the development of body parts, such as limbs and internal organs, and their locations relative to each other.

What is the genetic structure of human variation?

■ Each chromosome has a linear sequence of nucleotides that are coded to produce specific bodily structures and functions. These linear sequences are genes, and each gene has a particular locus on each chromosome—and the same locus on the like (homologous) chromosome.

■ Each pair of homologous chromosomes consists of a paternal chromosome and a maternal chromosome.

■ An individual's genotype, or actual genetic composition, is identified on the basis of two alleles, one from the father and one from the mother. Alleles can be chemically identical or chemically different. The genotype is expressed physically as a phenotype.

■ For most traits, no direct map yet exists for the translation of genotype to phenotype. That is, one gene may result in the construction of one functional protein, or multiple polypeptides each produced by a different gene may form the functional protein. The genetic basis for such a protein, therefore, is difficult to determine.

■ Most physical characteristics are determined by more than one gene (polygenic), and some genes can have multiple effects (pleiotropy).

The DNA Revolution has made it possible to understand in much greater detail the underlying principles of inheritance laid out so eloquently by Gregor Mendel a century and a half ago. In presenting the great breadth of knowledge about how genetic variation is transmitted from parents to offspring and maintained developmentally within individuals, this chapter has laid the groundwork for the topic of the next chapter, the study of genetic change in populations.

Ⓢ wwnorton.com/studyspace

KEY TERMS

adenine

adenosine triphosphate (ATP)

amino acids

antibodies

anticodons

antigens

autosomes
coding DNA
codominance
codons
complementary bases
cross-over
cytoplasm
cytosine
diploid
essential amino acids
eukaryotes
free-floating nucleotides
gametes
genome
guanine
haplogroups
haploid
haplotypes
heritability
heteroplasmic
heterozygous
homeotic (*Hox*) genes
homologous
homoplasmic
homozygous
karyotype
Law of Independent Assortment
Law of Segregation
linkage
locus
matriline
meiosis
messenger RNA (mRNA)
microsatellites
mitochondria
mitosis

monosomy
noncoding DNA
nondisjunctions
nucleotide
nucleus
paleogenetics
patriline
peptide bond
pleiotropy
polygenic
polymerase chain reaction (PCR)
polymorphism
polypeptide
prokaryotes
recombination
regulatory genes
regulatory proteins
replication
ribonucleic acid (RNA)
ribosomal RNA (rRNA)
ribosomes
sex chromosomes
single nucleotide polymorphisms (SNPs)
somatic cells
structural genes
structural proteins
thymine
transcription
transfer RNA (tRNA)
translation
translocations
triplets
trisomy
uracil
zygote

ADDITIONAL READINGS

Mielke, J. H., L. W. Konigsberg, and J. H. Relethford. 2006. *Human Biological Variation.* New York: Oxford University Press.

O'Rourke, D. H., M. G. Hayes, and S. W. Carlyle. 2000. Ancient DNA studies in physical anthropology. *Annual Review of Anthropology* 29: 217–242.

Portugal, F. H. and J. S. Cohen. 1977. *A Century of DNA: A History of the Discovery of the Structure and Function of the Genetic Substance.* Cambridge, MA: MIT Press.

Relethford, J. H. 2003. *Reflections of Our Past: How Human History Is Revealed in Our Genes.* Boulder: Westview Press.

Sapolsky, R. M. 2004. Of mice, men, and genes. *Natural History* May: 21–24, 31.

Sykes, B. 2001. *The Seven Daughters of Eve: The Science That Reveals Our Genetic Ancestry.* New York: Norton.

Weiss, M. L. 2000. An introduction to genetics. Pp. 47–85 in S. Stinson, B. Bogin, R. Huss-Ashmore, and D. O'Rourke, eds. *Human Biology: An Evolutionary and Biocultural Perspective.* New York: Wiley-Liss.

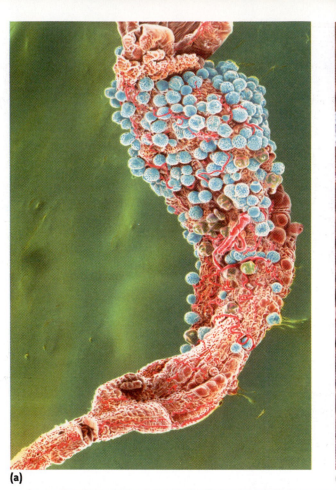
(a)

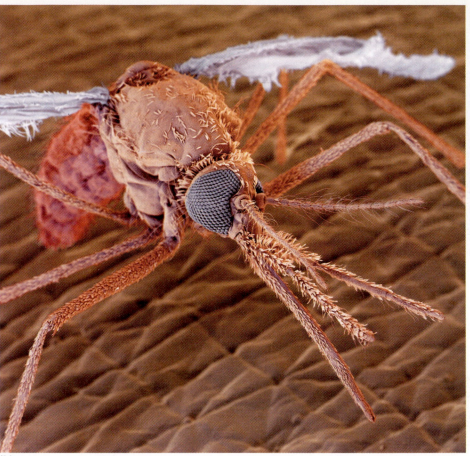
(b)

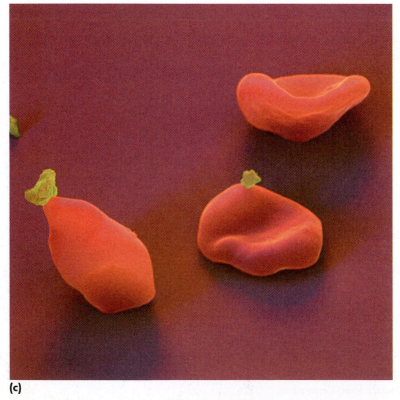
(c)

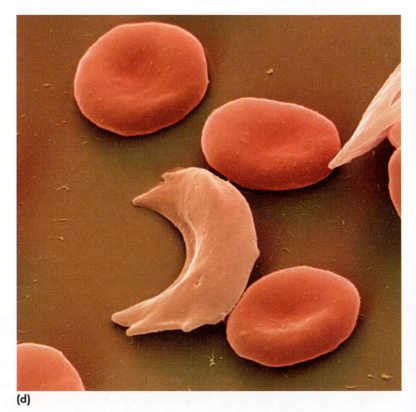
(d)

The connection between malaria and sickle-cell anemia helps illustrate the relationship between genes and evolution: **(a)** Malarial parasites, here infecting a mosquito's stomach, **(b)** may be transmitted when a mosquito bites a human to draw blood. **(c)** The parasite-borne disease that results, malaria, causes human red blood cells to become pear shaped. **(d)** The genetic disorder sickle-cell anemia causes human red blood cells to become sickle shaped. A person who inherits two alleles for sickle-cell anemia will have this disorder. A person who inherits one allele for it will not have sickle-cell anemia but will, thanks to natural selection, be immune to malaria.

CHAPTER 4

Genes and Their Evolution: Population Genetics

One of the great stories about genetics comes not from a research program of a famous scientist in charge of a large laboratory filled with technicians, graduate students, and postdoctoral fellows, and funded by a multimillion-dollar grant, but rather from a student with a simple hypothesis and a passionate interest in testing the hypothesis. At Oxford University in the late 1940s, a 20-something Anthony Allison was finishing his coursework in basic sciences and was about to start his clinical medical training. Allison had grown up in Kenya; his interest in anthropology reflected his intellectual curiosity, but his desire to become a doctor was motivated by an ambition to help improve native Kenyans' quality of life. While at Oxford, he was exposed to the ideas of the English scientists R. A. Fisher and J. B. S. Haldane and the American scientist Sewall Wright, pioneers of the new field of population genetics and advocates of the novel idea that gene frequencies were tied to natural selection.

Following a bout of malaria, Allison decided to help Kenyans (and other peoples) by seeking a cure for this disease. In 1949, he joined an expedition to document blood groups and genetic traits in native Kenyans. On this expedition, Allison discovered that in areas affected by malaria, especially along Kenya's coast (southeast) and near Lake Victoria (southwest), a remarkably high 20% to 30% of the population carried the gene for sickle-cell anemia. But in the highlands (west), where there was no malaria, less than 1% of the people carried the gene. In what he described as a "flash of inspiration," he hypothesized that individuals with the sickle-cell gene were resistant to malaria and that natural selection was operating on the gene. But how? he wondered.

Before pursuing these ideas, Allison completed his medical education. In 1953, with just enough money to buy passage back to Kenya and for food and simple lodging, he spent a year researching the relationship between malaria and sickle-cell anemia. He generated lab and field data, looking at malaria infection rates in people with and without the sickle-cell gene. His results showed that carriers of the gene are much more likely to survive malaria than are noncarriers. Natural selection was favoring the carriers.

The next year, Allison published three landmark scientific articles in rapid succession, laying out the proof for his hypothesis. Gene frequencies *are* tied to

BIG QUESTION

■ What causes evolutionary (genetic) change?

natural selection: carriers of the sickle-cell gene survive longer and produce more offspring than do noncarriers. In Allison's words, "disease is an agent of natural selection." Although his ideas met with strong skepticism, eventually Allison's hypothesis was accepted by most scientists. His research enabled generations of geneticists and anthropologists to further investigate genes and their evolution, all of these researchers asking why some gene frequencies remain the same while others change over time.

Human populations exhibit some remarkable biological differences, and the science of genetics helps biologists answer questions about those differences. The questions and the answers are founded on Darwin's discovery that phenotypes—the physical manifestations of genes—change over time. In addition, Mendel's research on garden peas revealed how the inheritance of genes produces variation in phenotypes. These two revolutionary scientific discoveries inform our understanding of biological variation and its evolution.

Before considering this chapter's big question, we need to look at populations and species, the units that evolutionary biologists work with.

DEMES, REPRODUCTIVE ISOLATION, AND SPECIES

To show how genetic variation is produced, the previous chapter focused on the individual and the transmission of genes from parents to offspring. When physical anthropologists and geneticists study the genetics of individuals, they focus on the reproductive population, or **deme:** members of a species that produce offspring. That is, evolution is about groups of organisms that have the potential to reproduce. When physical anthropologists talk about populations, they often refer to the **gene pool,** which is all the genetic material within a population. When geneticists talk about the gene pool, they are even more specific, referring to all the variation within a specific genetic locus. For example, some people carry the sickle-cell gene and some do not.

The concept of the breeding population is also central to the definition of *species*. A species is comprised of all the populations (and their individual members) that are capable of breeding with each other and producing viable (fertile) offspring. Species, therefore, are defined on the basis of **reproductive isolation** (**Figure 4.1**). In biological terms, if two populations are reproductively isolated, members of one population cannot interbreed with members of the other. Reproductive isolation is largely related to geographic isolation. If two populations of the same species become isolated, such as by a mountain range or a large body of water, enough genetic differences could accumulate for two entirely different species to emerge.

In the living world, we can observe members of a species to verify that they can produce offspring. Obviously, we cannot do this with fossils. Rather, we have to infer reproductive isolation in fossil populations on the basis of physical resemblance between fossils. Fossil remains that share the same characteristics in morphology of teeth and bones likely represent members of the same species (**Figure 4.2**). (This important concept will inform the discussion of primate evolution in chapters 8 through 12. Fossils are the subject of chapter 7.)

deme A local population of organisms that have similar genes, interbreed, and produce offspring.

gene pool All the genetic information in the breeding population.

reproductive isolation Any mechanism that prevents two populations from interbreeding and exchanging genetic material.

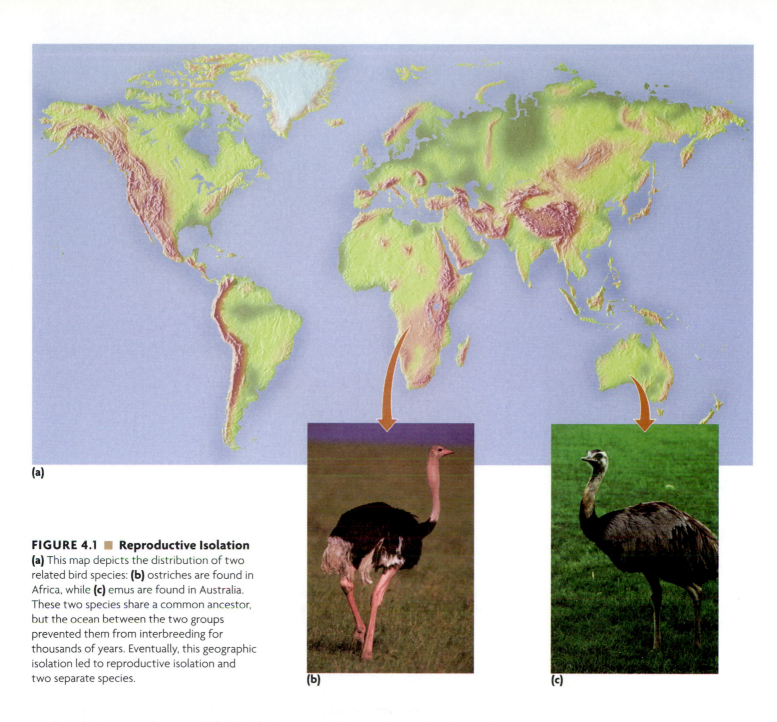

FIGURE 4.1 ■ Reproductive Isolation
(a) This map depicts the distribution of two related bird species: **(b)** ostriches are found in Africa, while **(c)** emus are found in Australia. These two species share a common ancestor, but the ocean between the two groups prevented them from interbreeding for thousands of years. Eventually, this geographic isolation led to reproductive isolation and two separate species.

Population genetics (see "The Evolutionary Synthesis, the Study of Populations, and the Causes of Evolution" in chapter 2) is the study of changes in genetic material—specifically, the change in frequency of alleles (genes). Genes are the records from which evolution is reconstructed, both over the course of a few generations (**microevolution**) and over many generations (**macroevolution; Figure 4.3**). Geneticists strive to *document* genetic change and to explain *why* it occurred. Such documentation and explanation are the central issues of evolutionary biology. Population geneticists, physical anthropologists, and other evolutionary biologists tend to focus on genetic change over time. For example, if a trait in a population has two alleles, *A* and *a*, and the parent generation is 60% *A* and 40% *a* and the next generation is 65% *A* and 35% *a*, scientists would want to know why the evolution occurred—why the frequency of the *A* allele increased in the population.

microevolution Small-scale evolution, such as changes in allele frequency, that occurs from one generation to the next.

macroevolution Large-scale evolution, such as a speciation event, that occurs after hundreds or thousands of generations.

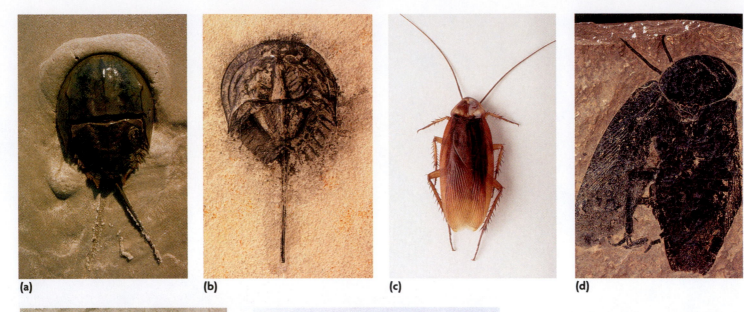

(a) (b) (c) (d)

(e) (f)

FIGURE 4.2 ▪ **Living Fossils**
Fossilized remains might represent animals and plants that lived thousands or millions of years ago, but a number of such organisms have counterparts that live today. Compare the forms of the following organisms: **(a)** living horseshoe crab and **(b)** fossil of *Mesolimulus walchii*, the ancestor to the modern horseshoe crab; **(c)** living cockroach and **(d)** a 49,000,000-year-old fossil cockroach; **(e)** living American opossum ("playing possum," i.e., feigning death); and **(f)** fossil skull of *Didelphis albirentris*, an ancestor to modern opossums. Which features have been maintained and which have been lost?

| **equilibrium** A condition in which the system is stable, balanced, and unchanging.

Just as interesting, however, are instances in which frequency does not change over time—that is, when the frequencies of a population's alleles for a particular trait are in a state of **equilibrium.** For example, in areas of West Africa where malaria is common, the frequency of the sickle-cell gene remains relatively constant. What factors—forces of evolution—account for deviations from equilibrium?

HARDY-WEINBERG LAW: TESTING THE CONDITIONS OF GENETIC EQUILIBRIUM

In 1908, Godfrey Hardy (1877–1947), an English mathematician, and Wilhelm Weinberg (1862–1937), a German obstetrician, independently recognized that some

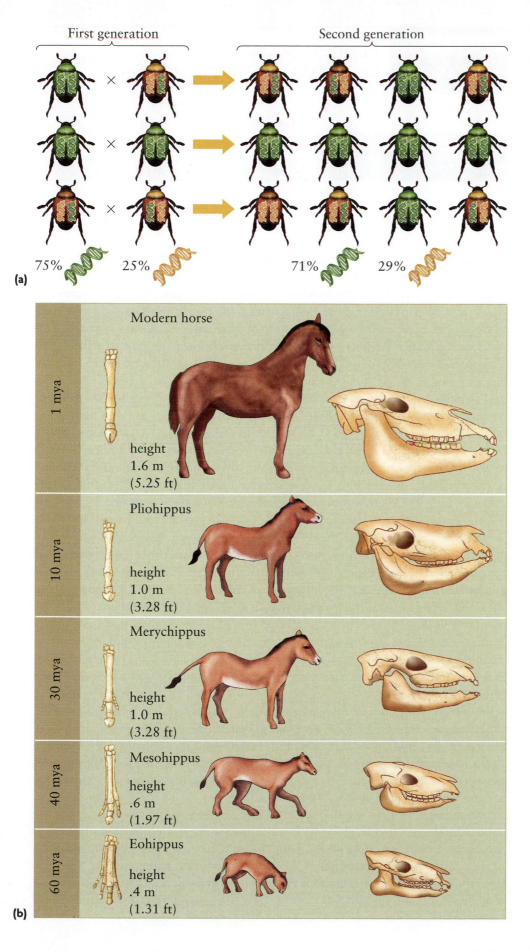

First generation

Second generation

75%   25%   71%   29%

(a)

(b)

Modern horse

1 mya

height
1.6 m
(5.25 ft)

Pliohippus

10 mya

height
1.0 m
(3.28 ft)

Merychippus

30 mya

height
1.0 m
(3.28 ft)

Mesohippus

40 mya

height
.6 m
(1.97 ft)

Eohippus

60 mya

height
.4 m
(1.31 ft)

FIGURE 4.3 ■ Microevolution and Macroevolution
(a) Microevolution is change in gene frequency over a few generations. For example, the beetles in this diagram have either of two colors, represented by two alleles. In the first generation, 75% of the color alleles are green and 25% are brown. In the second generation, 71% of the color alleles are green and 29% are brown. Thus, the frequencies of the green and brown alleles have undergone a microevolutionary change. **(b)** Macroevolution is substantial change over many generations, the creation of new species. For example, over 60,000,000 years, the eohippus—a small, dog-sized animal, with multitoed feet, that inhabited rainforests—evolved into the modern horse. Among the species' large-scale changes were increases in overall body size and height as well as the loss of toes. Horses' single-toed hooves enable them to run more efficiently in the open grasslands they naturally inhabit.

TABLE 4.1	Punnett Square for Hardy-Weinberg Equilibrium		
		FEMALES	
		A (p)	**a (q)**
MALES	**A (p)**	AA (p^2)	Aa (pq)
	a (q)	Aa (pq)	aa (q^2)

Hardy-Weinberg law of equilibrium A mathematical model in population genetics that reflects the relationship between frequencies of alleles and of genotypes; it can be used to determine whether a population is undergoing evolutionary changes.

alleles are in a state of equilibrium. If no mutation or natural selection or gene flow occurs, if the population is large, if mating is random, and if all members of the population produce the same number of offspring, then genotype frequencies at a single gene locus will remain the same after one generation. Moreover, the equilibrium frequencies will be a function of the allele frequencies at the locus. This is called the **Hardy-Weinberg law of equilibrium.** In the simplest case (**Table 4.1**), a single locus has A (dominant) and a (recessive) alleles, with respective frequencies of p and q. In assessing the population as a whole, it is assumed that males and females have both alleles. The Hardy-Weinberg law predicts the genotype frequencies for the next generation after one mating, where p^2 is the genotype frequency for the AA homozygous alleles, $2pq$ is the genotype frequency for the Aa (heterozygous) alleles, and q^2 is the genotype frequency for the aa homozygous alleles. In other words, the total population (100%) should be the sum of the frequencies of three genotypes, expressed by the simple mathematical equation $p^2 + 2pq + q^2 = 1$. If a hypothetical population were 60% A ($p = .6$) and 40% a ($q = .4$), the genotype frequencies in the next generation would work out to AA = .36, Aa = .48, and aa = .16. The frequencies can be expressed as decimals or percentages, but they are expressed most often as decimals. Since the three genotypes are the only genotypes for the gene in question in the population, the frequencies must add up to 1 or 100%. So, if the frequency of AA is .36 (or 36%), the frequency of Aa is .48 (or 48%), and the frequency of aa is .16 (or 16%), together they add up to 1 (or 100%).

In the absence of evolution, the frequencies of the genotypes will in theory remain the same forever. In this way, the Hardy-Weinberg equilibrium hypothesizes that gene frequencies remain the same because no evolutionary change takes place (**Figure 4.4**).

By determining the genotype frequencies for a population at different points in time, however, the Hardy-Weinberg equation establishes whether evolution is operating on a particular gene. If the genotype frequencies change from one generation to the next, the population is not in equilibrium—it is evolving. If the frequencies remain the same, the population is in equilibrium—the population is not evolving, at least with respect to the locus being studied.

What might cause a population to change its allele frequencies and go out of equilibrium? As noted in chapters 2 and 3, genes are passed from generation to generation by interbreeding within populations in particular and among members of the same species in general, and genetic changes result from one or a combination of the four forces of evolution: mutation, natural selection, genetic drift, and gene flow.

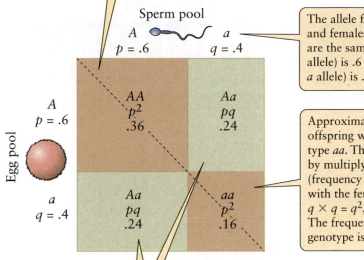

Approximately 36% of the offspring will have the genotype *AA*. The estimate is made by multiplying the male *p* (frequency of *A* allele = .6) with the female *p* (.6). Thus, $p \times p = p^2$, and $.6 \times .6 = .36$. The frequency of the *AA* genotype is represented by p^2.

Sperm pool

A $p = .6$ a $q = .4$

The allele frequencies for males and females in this population are the same: *p* (frequency of *A* allele) is .6 and *q* (frequency of *a* allele) is .4.

Egg pool

A $p = .6$

| AA p^2 .36 | Aa pq .24 |

a $q = .4$

| Aa pq .24 | aa p^2 .16 |

Approximately 16% of the offspring will have the genotype *aa*. This estimate is made by multiplying the male *q* (frequency of *a* allele = .4) with the female *q* (.4). Thus, $q \times q = q^2$, and $.4 \times .4 = .16$. The frequency of the *aa* genotype is represented by q^2.

Approximately 48% of the offspring population will have the genotype *Aa*. This estimate is made by multiplying the male *p* (.6) with the female *q* (.4) *and* the male *q* (.4) with the female *p* (.6). Thus, $p \times q = pq$ and $q \times p = pq$; $.6 \times .4 = .24$ and $.4 \times .6 = .24$. Since both $p \times q$ and $q \times p$ must be included, the two results are added together. $2pq = 2 \times .24$ (or $.24 + .24$) $= .48$. The frequency of the *Aa* genotype is represented by $2pq$.

FIGURE 4.4 ■ **Gene Frequencies in Equilibrium**

As this Punnett square illustrates, the Hardy-Weinberg equilibrium captures gene frequencies in a static moment, when no evolutionary change is taking place. Crossing the males (sperm pool) and females (egg pool) of the population produces theoretical genotype frequencies of the next generation.

Once evolutionary change takes place, the actual genotype frequencies will differ significantly from the theoretical genotype frequencies expressed in this Punnett square. For example, if the population later turns out to be 5% *AA*, 65% *aa*, and 30% *Aa*, an evolutionary force has most likely altered its genotype frequencies.

MUTATION: THE ONLY SOURCE OF NEW ALLELES

During cell reproduction, DNA almost always replicates itself exactly. Sometimes, however, the replication process produces an error or a collection of errors in the DNA code. If the problem is not at once detected and corrected by a set of enzymes that monitor DNA, a mutation results. The mutation can be any heritable change in the structure or amount of genetic material.

Because so much of any person's DNA is noncoding (see "Producing Proteins: The Other Function of DNA" in chapter 3), many mutations do not affect the individual's health, well-being, or survival. A new sequence of *coding* DNA that results from mutation may have profound consequences, positive or negative. For example, the mutation might code the DNA for a protein with an altered or different function than that performed by the protein coded for in the original parent strand of DNA, or the mutation might create a sequence that results in either no protein or an abnormal protein (**Figure 4.5**). Mutations occur at random, and they can occur in any cell, but the ones with consequences for future generations take place in gametes. Gametes may transfer mutations to offspring,

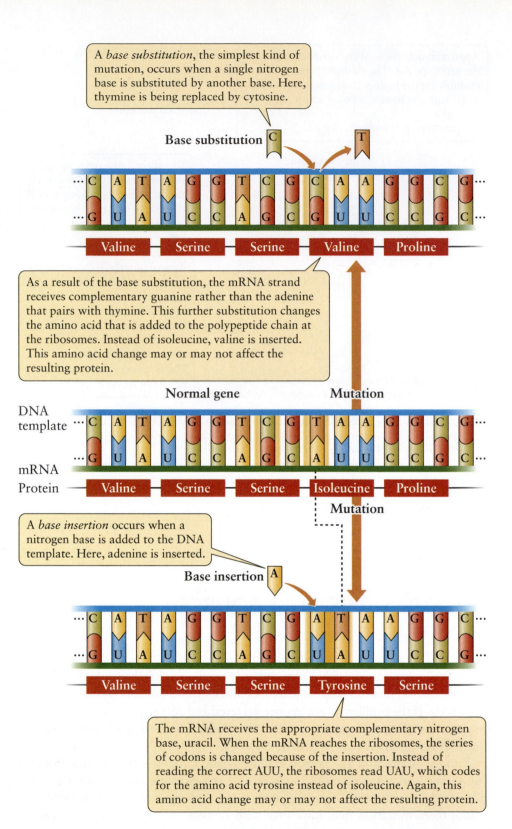

A *base substitution*, the simplest kind of mutation, occurs when a single nitrogen base is substituted by another base. Here, thymine is being replaced by cytosine.

Base substitution

Valine — Serine — Serine — Valine — Proline

As a result of the base substitution, the mRNA strand receives complementary guanine rather than the adenine that pairs with thymine. This further substitution changes the amino acid that is added to the polypeptide chain at the ribosomes. Instead of isoleucine, valine is inserted. This amino acid change may or may not affect the resulting protein.

Normal gene　　　　　**Mutation**

DNA template

mRNA

Protein — Valine — Serine — Serine — Isoleucine — Proline

Mutation

A *base insertion* occurs when a nitrogen base is added to the DNA template. Here, adenine is inserted.

Base insertion

Valine — Serine — Serine — Tyrosine — Serine

The mRNA receives the appropriate complementary nitrogen base, uracil. When the mRNA reaches the ribosomes, the series of codons is changed because of the insertion. Instead of reading the correct AUU, the ribosomes read UAU, which codes for the amino acid tyrosine instead of isoleucine. Again, this amino acid change may or may not affect the resulting protein.

FIGURE 4.5 ■ DNA Mutations

During the transcription phase of protein synthesis, errors in the DNA template can affect the resulting protein. Two types of DNA mutation are illustrated in these diagrams.

depending on what happens during meiosis in the parents. Regardless of their causes or outcomes, *mutations are the only source of new genetic variation in a population.*

Mutations involving incorrect base pairing are called **point mutations**. A **synonymous point mutation** creates an altered triplet in the DNA, but the alteration carries with it the original amino acid. Because the amino acid is the same, the protein formed is the same. A **nonsynonymous point mutation** results in a matchup that brings along a different amino acid. Such a mutation can have dramatic results for the individual carrying it. For example, a mutation on human chromosome 11 converts a GAG codon into a GTG codon. The GAG codon is encoded to produce the amino acid valine, whereas the GTG codon is encoded to produce glutamic acid. This substitution leads to the abnormal hemoglobin that results in sickle-cell anemia (discussed later in this chapter).

As a result of the shifting base pairs caused by base insertion, the reading frame of a gene is altered or stopped entirely. This **frameshift mutation** produces a protein having no function. Such a mutation usually involves a small part of the DNA sequence, often just a base pair or a relatively limited number of base pairs.

Other kinds of mutations can affect far more of the genome. **Transposable elements** are genes that can copy themselves to entirely different places along the DNA sequence. If such a gene inserts itself into another gene, it can fundamentally alter the other gene, doing real damage. If, as is strongly likely, the gene transposes itself to a noncoding area of the DNA sequence, little or no significant alteration will occur.

Large parts of DNA sequences or entire chromosomes can be affected by mutations. An entire piece of chromosome can be moved to another chromosome, can be placed differently on the same chromosome, or can be positioned in a chromosome backward. The impacts of these mutations are highly variable and depend on the mutations' loci.

In the most extreme mutations, entire chromosomes can be duplicated (a trisomy) or lost altogether (a monosomy). Examples of trisomies are Down syndrome, with its extra twenty-first chromosome (see "Meiosis: Production of Gametes [sex cells]" in chapter 3) and **Klinefelter's syndrome,** a common sex chromosome variant that appears in about 1 of 500–1,000 births.

All mutations fall into either of two types: **spontaneous mutations** have no known cause (**Figure 4.6**); **induced mutations** are caused by specific environmental agents, usually associated with human activity. These agents, or **mutagens,** are increasingly becoming known. For example, ionizing radiation (X-rays) and various toxic chemicals have been linked to mutations in animals and humans. Most mutations are spontaneous, however, and are simply DNA copying errors. The human mutation rate is higher in male sex cells (sperm) than in female sex cells (eggs), but is generally on the order of one per million per nucleotide per generation. The human genome includes about three billion base pairs, about 1.5% of which are protein coding, so the average mutation rate in humans is .45 mutations in protein-coding genes per generation, or about one new, potentially significant mutation in every other person born.

For individuals, most mutations are relatively harmless, while a few may have profound consequences. For populations, mutations are inconsequential unless they offer selective adaptive advantages.

point mutations Replacements of a single nitrogen base with another base, which may or may not affect the amino acid for which the triplet codes.

synonymous point mutation A neutral point mutation in which the substituted nitrogen base creates a triplet coded to produce the same amino acid as that of the original triplet.

nonsynonymous point mutation A point mutation that creates a triplet coded to produce a different amino acid than that of the original triplet.

frameshift mutation The change in a gene due to the insertion or deletion of one or more nitrogen bases, which causes the subsequent triplets to be rearranged and the codons to be read incorrectly during translation.

transposable elements Mobile pieces of DNA that can copy themselves into entirely new areas of the chromosomes.

Klinefelter's syndrome A chromosomal trisomy in which males have an extra X chromosome, resulting in an XXY condition; affected individuals typically have reduced fertility.

spontaneous mutation Random changes in DNA that occur during cell division.

induced mutations Refers to those mutations in the DNA resulting from exposure to toxic chemicals or to radiation.

mutagens Substances, such as toxins, chemicals, or radiation, that may induce genetic mutations.

(a)

(b)

(c)

(d)

FIGURE 4.6 ■ **Spontaneous Mutations**

Spontaneous mutations can affect only physical appearance or can have health consequences, sometimes extreme ones. **(a)** A mutation called leucism has made this American alligator white. On its head are some spots of alligators' normal, dark color. **(b)** The mutation that gives some cats white fur and blue eyes can also produce deafness and timidity. **(c)** Cheetahs normally have spotted coats, but a genetic mutation has produced stripes on this cheetah's back. **(d)** Mutations can affect the wing count, eye color, and eye placement of fruit flies. A mutation has given this fruit fly abnormally placed, or ectopic, eyes, one of which is visible here as the red area on the wing.

fitness Average number of offspring produced by parents with a particular genotype compared to the number of offspring produced by parents with another genotype.

NATURAL SELECTION: ADVANTAGEOUS CHARACTERISTICS, SURVIVAL, AND REPRODUCTION

Darwin's theory of evolution by means of natural selection provided the conceptual framework for understanding adaptation. That framework has become even more powerful over the last 150 years because it has allowed for many refinements. The principle of natural selection is based on Darwin's conclusion that individuals with advantageous characteristics will survive in higher numbers and produce more off-spring than members of a population lacking advantageous characteristics. Natural selection, therefore, focuses on reproductive success, or **fitness.** In particular, fit-ness is defined as some measure of the propensity to contribute offspring to future generations, usually by the next generation. Fitness can be defined in reference to individuals in a population or to specific genotypes. For our purposes, fitness is defined on the basis of genotypes. This means that some genotypes have more (or less) fitness than other genotypes. The implication is that fitness differences can result in changes to allele frequencies. For example, if the genotype for darker coloring confers an adaptive advantage over the genotype for lighter coloring, the dark-color genotype will likely increase in frequency over time.

Patterns of Natural Selection

Evolutionary biologists have identified three alternative patterns by which natural selection can act on a specific trait. **Directional selection** favors one extreme form of a trait—more children are produced by individuals who have that extreme trait, so selection moves in that direction. Human evolution, for example, has clearly favored larger brains (for more on these topics, see chapters 9 and 10). **Stabilizing selection** favors the average version of a trait. For example, living humans whose birth weights are in the middle of the range have a better chance of surviving and reproducing than do those born with the lowest and highest weights. In **disruptive selection**, the pattern of variation is discontinuous. Individuals at both extreme ends of the range produce more offspring than do the remainder of the population. Given enough time, this pattern can result in a speciation event, as those in the middle fail to survive and reproduce and two new species arise at the extremes (**Figure 4.7**).

directional selection Selection for one allele over the other alleles, causing the allele frequencies to shift in one direction.

stabilizing selection Selection against the extremes of the phenotypic distribution, decreasing the genetic diversity for this trait in the population.

disruptive selection Selection for both extremes of the phenotypic distribution; may eventually lead to a speciation event.

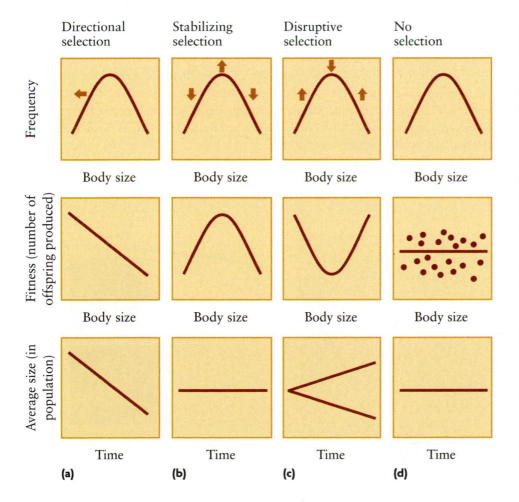

FIGURE 4.7 ■ Types of Selection
(a) Top: In the population represented here, smaller body size is more favorable than larger body size, so the frequency of smaller body size will increase thanks to directional selection. **Middle:** The fitness of individuals with smaller body sizes will be greater than that of individuals with larger body sizes. **Bottom:** Over time, the population's average body size will decrease.
(b) Top: In this population, medium body size is favored, so the frequency of medium body size will increase thanks to stabilizing selection. **Middle:** The fitness of individuals with medium body sizes will be much greater. **Bottom:** However, the population's average body size will remain relatively stable over time.
(c) Top: Here, owing to disruptive selection, the frequencies of small and large body sizes will increase, while the frequency of medium body size will decrease. **Middle:** The fitness levels are highest at the extremes and lowest in the middle. **Bottom:** Over time, the population will split between those with large bodies and those with small bodies.
(d) Top: In the absence of selection, the population will have a range of sizes. **Middle:** Fitness levels will vary independently of size. **Bottom:** The population's average body size will not change over time.

FIGURE 4.8 ■ Peppered Moths
This genus includes two species: *Biston betularia* (light) and *Biston carbonaria* (dark).

melanic Refers to an individual with high concentrations of melanin.

nonmelanic Refers to an individual with low concentrations of melanin.

Natural Selection in Animals: The Case of the Peppered Moth and Industrial Melanism

Perhaps the best evidence ever documented of natural selection operating on a heritable trait concerns the peppered moth, *Biston betularia,* a species common throughout Great Britain (**Figure 4.8**). This moth is nocturnal, eating and breeding by night and attaching itself to trees, especially in the upper branches, during the day. Prior to the mid-1800s, all members of the species had a peppered appearance, their white coloring sprinkled with black. Trees throughout Great Britain were covered with lichen, and the moths' coloration provided excellent camouflage against the trees' variable-colored surface and thus protected the moths from their major predator, birds. In 1848, a naturalist exploring the countryside near Manchester, England, spotted a completely black variety of the moth. A new species name, *Biston carbonaria,* distinguished this **melanic** (dark) form from the **nonmelanic** (light) form. The frequency of the melanic form remained relatively low for a couple of decades, but climbed rapidly in the late nineteenth century. By the 1950s, 90% or more of peppered moths were melanic (**Figure 4.9**).

This rapid increase in melanic frequency was a case of evolution profoundly changing phenotype. Directional selection had favored the melanic form over the nonmelanic form, and the melanic form exhibited a greater fitness. But what was this form's adaptive advantage?

The selecting factor was the Industrial Revolution. With the rise of industry throughout England and elsewhere in the middle to late nineteenth century, mills, fueled entirely by coal, spewed coal particles from smokestacks—50 tons per square mile per month, in some places—blackening the sky and covering the landscape. The trees survived this pollution onslaught, but the lichen covering the trees did not. The trees' surfaces went from light-colored to black, greatly altering the peppered moth's habitat. This pollution crisis provided a huge selective advantage for the melanic moths, which were now perfectly camouflaged against blackened trees. Nonmelanic moths became easy prey.

How did the genetics of this evolutionary change work? Breeding experiments revealed that, in a classic case of Mendelian genetics, the color difference between

FIGURE 4.9 ■ Changes in the Peppered Moth Gene Frequency
The frequency of the melanic gene in peppered moths increased from 1848 through 1948. The frequency of the nonmelanic gene decreased during that same period.

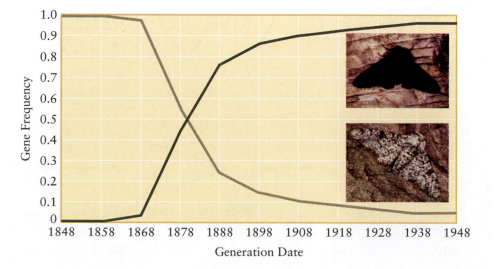

the two *Biston* species was determined by one locus. The nonmelanic variety had a genotype of *cc* (homozygous recessive), while the melanic variety was either heterozygous, *Cc,* or homozygous, *CC.* The dominant allele, *C,* likely first appeared as a mutation, perhaps in the first half of the nineteenth century or earlier, long before the first melanic moth was observed, in 1848. The C allele may have been in the population, maintained by the mutation's reoccurrence. Recent estimates suggest that the frequency of the nonmelanic variety was only 1–10% in polluted regions of England, and no more than 5% around Manchester. Plugged into the Hardy-Weinberg equilibrium, this information in turn suggests that 46% of the population had the *CC* genotype, 44% had the *Cc* genotype, and 10% had the *cc* genotype (**Table 4.2**).

Beginning in the late 1960s and early 1970s, the stricter pollution laws, changes in coal burning, and decline of mill-based industry in Great Britain profoundly affected the moth population, once again illustrating natural selection. That is, in areas that were no longer polluted, the frequency of *Biston carbonaria* dropped. In Manchester, for example, the frequency of the melanic moth decreased from 90% in 1983 to well under 10% in the late 1990s. Plugged into the Hardy-Weinberg equilibrium, these numbers reveal that the *CC* genotype decreased to 0.25%, the *Cc* genotype decreased to 9.5%, and the *cc* genotype increased to 90% (**Table 4.3**). This rapid evolutionary change reflected the return of the trees' original coloration, which conferred a selective disadvantage—predation visibility—on the melanic variety. This postscript adds even more power to the story of how natural selection brought about biological changes in the genus *Biston.*

TABLE 4.2	Moth Genotype Frequencies—Industrialization Period	
PHENOTYPE	**MELANIC**	**NONMELANIC**
Phenotype Frequencies	.90	.10
Genotype	$CC + Cc$	cc
Genotype Frequencies	$p^2 + 2pq$	q^2
Allele Frequency Calculations:		
Step 1		$q^2 = .10 \; (q^2 = f*(cc))$
Step 2		$q = \sqrt{q^2} = \sqrt{.10} = .32$
Step 3	$p = 1 - q = 1 - .32 = .68$	
Genotype Frequency Calculations:	$p^2 = f(CC) = .68^2 = .46$	
	$2pq = f(Cc) = 2 \times .68 \times .32 = .44$	
	$q^2 = f(cc) = .32^2 = .10$	
Check:	$p^2 + 2pq + q^2 = 1$	
	$.46 + .44 + .10 = 1$	
*f = frequency		

TABLE 4.3 — Moth Genotype Frequencies—Postindustrialization Period

PHENOTYPE	MELANIC	NONMELANIC
Phenotype Frequencies	.10	.90
Genotype	$CC + Cc$	cc
Genotype Frequencies	$p^2 + 2pq$	q^2
Allele Frequency Calculations:		
Step 1		$q^2 = .90 \; (q^2 = f*(cc))$
Step 2		$q = \sqrt{q^2} = \sqrt{.90} = .95$
Step 3	$p = 1 - q = 1 - .95 = .05$	
Genotype Frequency Calculations:	$p^2 = f(CC) = .05^2 = .0025$	
	$2pq = f(Cc) = 2 \times .05 \times .95 = .095$	
	$q^2 = f(cc) = .95^2 = .90$	
Check:	$p^2 + 2pq + q^2 = 1$	
	$.0025 + .095 + .90 = .99 \approx 1$	

*f = frequency

Natural Selection in Humans: Abnormal Hemoglobins and Resistance to Malaria

positive selection Process in which advantageous genetic variants quickly increase in frequency in a population.

sickle-cell anemia A genetic blood disease in which the red blood cells become deformed and sickle shaped, decreasing their ability to carry oxygen to tissues.

hemolytic anemias Conditions of insufficient iron in the blood due to the destruction of red blood cells resulting from genetic blood diseases, toxins, or infectious pathogens.

abnormal hemoglobin Hemoglobin altered so that it is less efficient in binding to and carrying oxygen.

The above case of industrial melanism is an example of **positive selection,** whereby an organism's biology is shaped by selection for beneficial traits. Natural selection for beneficial traits in humans is best understood by studying genes that control specific traits. Of the 90 or so different loci that are targets of natural selection (**Figure 4.10**), among the most compelling examples is the sickle-cell gene—the *Hemoglobin S* (or simply *S*) gene—which causes **sickle-cell anemia** (**Figure 4.11**). Millions of people suffer from such **hemolytic anemias,** which involve the destruction of red blood cells. A low number of red blood cells can produce health problems because of the resultant lack of hemoglobin, the chemical in red blood cells that carries oxygen to all the body tissues. The *S* gene yields a specific kind of **abnormal hemoglobin.**

Sickle-cell anemia has been known since the early 1900s, and the genetics behind it were documented in the 1950s. The *S* gene is a simple base-pair mutation (**Figure 4.12**). Genetically, people with normal hemoglobin have the alleles *AA,* the homozygous condition. People who carry the sickle-cell gene on one allele only are *AS,* and people who have the homozygous form of the disease are *SS. AS* individuals are for all practical purposes normal in their survival and reproduction rates. There is no cure for sickle-cell anemia, and in the absence of modern medical treatment, some 80% of people who are *SS* die before the reproductive years, usually considerably earlier. The *SS* genotype results in many red blood cells' having a sickle shape caused by the abnormal hemoglobin, in sharp contrast to the round appearance of

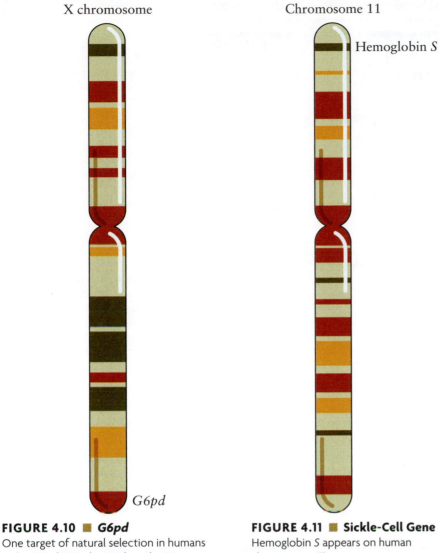

X chromosome

Chromosome 11

Hemoglobin *S*

G6pd

FIGURE 4.10 ■ *G6pd*
One target of natural selection in humans is the *G6pd* gene, located on the X chromosome.

FIGURE 4.11 ■ **Sickle-Cell Gene**
Hemoglobin *S* appears on human chromosome 11.

red blood cells in people with normal hemoglobin (**Figure 4.13**). The cells' abnormal shape prevents them from passing through the **capillaries,** the narrow blood vessels that form networks throughout tissues. When the clogging of capillaries cuts off the oxygen supply in vital tissues, severe anemia and death can result.

capillaries Small blood vessels between the terminal ends of arteries and the veins.

THE GEOGRAPHY OF SICKLE-CELL ANEMIA AND A POSSIBLE ASSOCIATION WITH MALARIA Beginning in the mid-twentieth century, the medical community observed that many people living in equatorial Africa—as many as 20% to 30%—had the *S* gene. This finding represented a huge puzzle: since the gene was so bad for survival, why was its frequency so high? In other words, one would expect strong selection against this nonbeneficial gene. The solution to the puzzle began to emerge with the discovery that high heterozygous (*AS*) frequencies appear in regions of Africa where malaria is endemic. In other words, where malaria—a potentially lethal parasitic infection in which the parasite is introduced to a human host by a mosquito—is always present, there is a high frequency of carriers of the

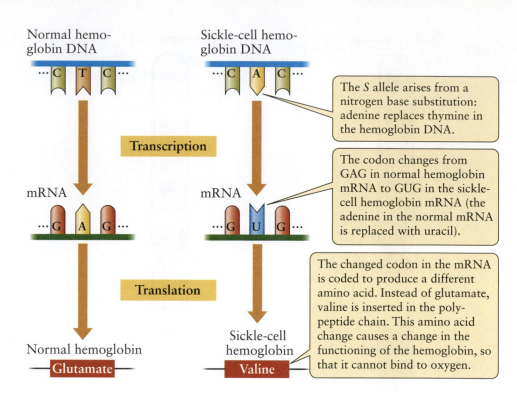

Normal hemo-globin DNA

···C T C···

Sickle-cell hemo-globin DNA

···C A C···

The S allele arises from a nitrogen base substitution: adenine replaces thymine in the hemoglobin DNA.

Transcription

mRNA

···G A G···

mRNA

···G U G···

The codon changes from GAG in normal hemoglobin mRNA to GUG in the sickle-cell hemoglobin mRNA (the adenine in the normal mRNA is replaced with uracil).

Translation

Normal hemoglobin

Glutamate

Sickle-cell hemoglobin

Valine

The changed codon in the mRNA is coded to produce a different amino acid. Instead of glutamate, valine is inserted in the poly-peptide chain. This amino acid change causes a change in the functioning of the hemoglobin, so that it cannot bind to oxygen.

FIGURE 4.12 ■ Sickle-Cell Mutation
Sickle-cell anemia begins with a single nitrogen base mutation—a base substitution. The abnormal hemoglobin that results is less efficient at binding oxygen and causes red blood cells to become sickle shaped.

balanced polymorphism Situation in which selection maintains two or more phenotypes for a specific gene in a population.

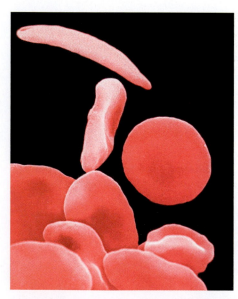

FIGURE 4.13 ■ Sickle-Shaped Red Blood Cells
This image shows normal red blood cells, which are round; a long, slender sickle-shaped cell (at top); and other irregularly shaped cells. The abnormal cells are very fragile and easily damaged or destroyed.

gene (**Figure 4.14**). Moreover, *AS* people (sickle-gene carriers) die of malaria in far fewer numbers than do *AA* people.

As described at the beginning of this chapter, Anthony Allison discovered that in low-lying, wet areas of Kenya (where the number of mosquitoes was great and the rate of malaria was high), the frequency of the sickle-cell gene was considerably higher than in highland or arid areas. He developed the simple but elegant hypothesis that the infection and the genetic mutation were related. Individuals homozygous for normal hemoglobin (*AA*) were highly susceptible to dying from malaria; individuals homozygous for sickle-cell anemia (*SS*) did not survive to reproduce; however, individuals heterozygous for normal hemoglobin and the sickle-cell mutation (*AS*) either did not contract malaria or suffered a less severe malarial infection. That these frequencies were being maintained indicated that the *AS* heterozygote was a **balanced polymorphism**. It was also a fitness trade-off: carriers could pass on the sickle-cell gene, but they received immunity from malaria.

THE BIOLOGY OF SICKLE-CELL ANEMIA AND MALARIAL INFECTION Why do people who are heterozygous for the sickle-cell gene survive malaria or not contract it at all? Unlike *SS* red blood cells, *AS* red blood cells do not sickle under most conditions (that is, except when severely deprived of oxygen). They are, however, somewhat smaller than normal cells, and their oxygen levels are somewhat lower. For reasons not yet understood, the *AS* red blood cells are simply a poor host—a nonconducive living and reproduction environment—for the parasite that causes malaria.

THE HISTORY OF SICKLE-CELL ANEMIA AND MALARIA In the late 1950s, the American physical anthropologist Frank B. Livingstone (1928–2005) sought to

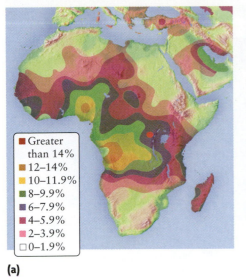

(a)

- Greater than 14%
- 12–14%
- 10–11.9%
- 8–9.9%
- 6–7.9%
- 4–5.9%
- 2–3.9%
- 0–1.9%

(b)

- Areas where malaria is present

FIGURE 4.14 ■ **Distributions of the Sickle-Cell Allele and Malaria**
In equatorial Africa, **(a)** the distribution of the sickle-cell allele coincides with **(b)** areas of high malarial parasite concentration.

strengthen the case for natural selection by historically linking sickle-cell anemia and malaria. Livingstone asked two important questions: *Where and when did the sickle-cell gene first appear in equatorial Africa?* and *What conditions led to the gene's being naturally selected?* He hypothesized that the Bantu, a group of peoples who speak Bantu languages, carried the mutation with them when they migrated south (**Figure 4.15**). Prior to the Bantu's arrival, the region was an unbroken forest. Bantu populations introduced agriculture there, clearing large swaths of the forest for cultivation. The peoples' iron-working technology made possible the creation of tools for cutting down large trees, plowing fields, and planting crops—mostly yams and cassava.

Even under the best conditions, tropical forests are fragile ecosystems. Once their trees have been cleared and their fields have been planted, their relatively poor soil, which normally soaks up rainwater, becomes thin or disappears. As a result, pools of water collect and become stagnant, providing ideal conditions for the breeding of parasite-carrying mosquitoes (**Figure 4.16**). This picture became clear to Livingstone as he developed his research: the newly created ecological circumstances fostered mosquito reproduction and the spread of malaria, and the growing host of humans made possible by agriculture-fueled population growth provided the food resources needed by the mosquitoes. The infectious disease gave those individuals with a very rare mutation—the sickle-cell allele—an adaptive advantage and the ability to survive and reproduce in these new environmental circumstances. Due to the advantage the heterozygous condition provides, the *S* allele was maintained and passed from generation to generation. For this reason, sickle-cell anemia predominantly affects those whose descendants came from the malarial environments in large parts of equatorial Africa. Outside of such malarial environments, the *S* allele never became advantageous.

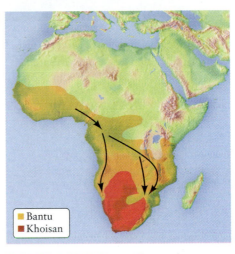

- Bantu
- Khoisan

FIGURE 4.15 ■ **Bantu Expansion**
As this map shows, in about 2000 BC the Bantu people moved from more northern aspects of Africa into the equatorial regions of the continent.

OTHER HEMOGLOBIN AND ENZYME ABNORMALITIES Sickle-cell anemia turns out to be just one of a number of **hemoglobinopathies** and other genetic abnormalities in Africa, Asia, and Europe that provide a strong selective advantage in regions of endemic malaria (**Figure 4.17**). Heterozygous carriers of abnormal hemoglobins apparently make poor hosts for malarial parasites.

hemoglobinopathies A group of related genetic blood diseases characterized by abnormal hemoglobin.

(a)

(b)

FIGURE 4.16 ■ The Spread of Malaria
As the Bantu cleared forests for agricultural fields, **(a)** pools of stagnant water **(b)** became an ideal breeding ground for mosquito larvae, which carried the malarial parasites.

- ■ Hb *C*
- ■ Hb *E*
- ■ Hb *S*

FIGURE 4.17 ■ Distribution of Hemoglobinopathies
This map shows the distribution of hemoglobin *E* in Southeast Asia. People with hemoglobin *E*, an uncommon but severe blood abnormality, may have mild hemolytic anemia or other mild effects. Like hemoglobin *S*, hemoglobin *C* appears primarily in equatorial Africa. Like hemoglobin *E*, hemoglobin *C* has generally minor effects, most often mild hemolytic anemia.

thalassemia A genetic blood disease in which the hemoglobin is improperly synthesized, causing the red blood cells to have a much shorter lifespan.

glucose-6-phosphate dehydrogenase (G6PD) An enzyme that aids in the proper functioning of red blood cells; its deficiency, a genetic condition, leads to hemolytic anemia.

Thalassemia, a genetic anemia found in Europe (especially in Italy and Greece), Asia, and the Pacific, reduces or eliminates hemoglobin synthesis. In some homozygous forms of the mutation, hemoglobin becomes clumped inside the red blood cells. The spleen then destroys the red blood cells, resulting in severe anemia. In the areas around the Mediterranean where the genetic frequency is highest—as high as 80%—the presence of malaria makes a strong case for a selective advantage for heterozygous individuals, for whom the condition and malaria are not lethal.

An association has long been recognized between deficiency of the enzyme **glucose-6-phosphate dehydrogenase (G6PD)** and malaria. A recessive hereditary mutation leads more males than females to lack the gene that is coded to produce this enzyme (see Figure 4.10). Without the G6PD enzyme, a person who takes sulfa-based antibiotics or eats fava beans risks the destruction of red blood cells, severe anemia, and occasionally death. Because of the connection with fava beans, this severe hemolytic disease is called favism. Its 130 genetic variants occur in high frequencies in some populations, the highest being 70% among Kurdish Jews. Heterozygote carriers have a strong selective advantage because they produce some of the enzyme but are protected from malaria (here again, the parasite cannot live in the abnormal red blood cells).

Analysis of genetic data by the anthropologist Sara Tishkoff indicates that the mutation for the disease arose between about 4,000 and 12,000 yBP, at the same time as the abnormal hemoglobins. Populations whose descendants did not encounter malaria do not have the *G6pd* mutation or abnormal hemoglobins. Today, for example, malaria appears throughout the tropical regions of the Americas, but Native Americans are 100% homozygous for normal alleles at the *G6pd* and hemoglobin loci. That these particular genes do not appear to have mutated in the New World strongly suggests that malaria was introduced to North and South America only after the Europeans' arrival. Indeed, the introduction of malaria and other Old World diseases—by either Spaniards or their African slaves—likely played an instrumental role in the precipitous decline in the native populations.

If malaria had been introduced in the Americas much earlier than the last few centuries—say thousands of years ago—and the mutations occurred, there might have been time for a natural selection to develop for the mutations. If the mutations did appear before the Europeans' arrival, however, they would have exhibited a clear selective disadvantage in the absence of malaria and been weeded out of the gene pool. Thus, red blood cell polymorphisms in the abnormal hemoglobin and *G6pd* loci reflect the fundamental interactions, among environment, genes, and culture, that have resulted in the modern human genome. The genes provide an important record about human evolution and the role of natural selection in shaping genetic variation.

GENETIC DRIFT: GENETIC CHANGE DUE TO CHANCE

One of the four forces of evolution (see "The Evolutionary Synthesis, the Study of Populations, and the Causes of Evolution" in chapter 2), genetic drift, is random change in allele frequency over time. Provided that no allele confers a selective advantage over another, a random change can lead to a change in gene frequency, such as one allele being lost and the other becoming fixated—or fixed, the only allele of its kind, in the population. This force, this kind of change, makes possible the measuring of evolution as a statistical probability.

Coin tosses can demonstrate the effects of genetic drift (**Table 4.4**). Imagine that heads and tails are two alleles in a population. If there are only two members of the population (two coin tosses), there is a great chance that both will be heads. In effect, the "heads" allele will become fixed in the small population, while the "tails" allele will be lost. As the population size (number of coin tosses) increases, it becomes less likely that one allele will become fixed and the other lost. In very large populations (1,000,000 coin tosses), both alleles may be present in equal proportions.

How does such statistical probability translate to populations? Now imagine that before the election of your student government you have been asked to predict the winners. The best way for you to predict would be to ask each voting-eligible student how he or she planned to vote. It is *highly* likely that the outcome of such a comprehensive poll would be close to the actual election results. The shortcomings of this approach might include the very large size of the target population. No one would interview, for example, 50,000 students! The second-best approach would be to select a sample, preferably a random sample that represented the entire student body. If you selected five students out of the 50,000, chances are very slim that those five would represent all the ethnic, national, regional, and economic backgrounds of the student body. In fact, chances are very high that this sample (.01% of the total population) would provide a voting outcome very different from the actual one. If you interviewed 500 students (1% of the population), the chances of representation would be much greater, and if you chose 5,000 students (10% of

TABLE 4.4 — Heads versus Tails: Genetic Drift and Probability

COIN TOSSES	HEADS	TAILS	HEADS:TAILS RATIO
2	2	0	2:0
10	4	6	4:6
50	22	28	11:14
100	55	45	11:9
200	199	201	199:201
500	253	247	253:247
1,000	501	499	501:499
5,000	2,500	2,500	1:1
10,000	5,000	5,000	1:1
100,000	50,000	50,000	1:1
500,000	250,000	250,000	1:1
1,000,000	500,000	500,000	1:1

the population), they would be greater still. The larger the sample size, the greater the probability of an accurate prediction.

Variations in human populations work the exact same way, except that genetic drift operates over a period of time rather than at a single point. The probability of an allele's frequency changing in a relatively short period of time increases with decreasing population size. The larger the population, the less divergence from the original gene frequency over time (**Figure 4.18**).

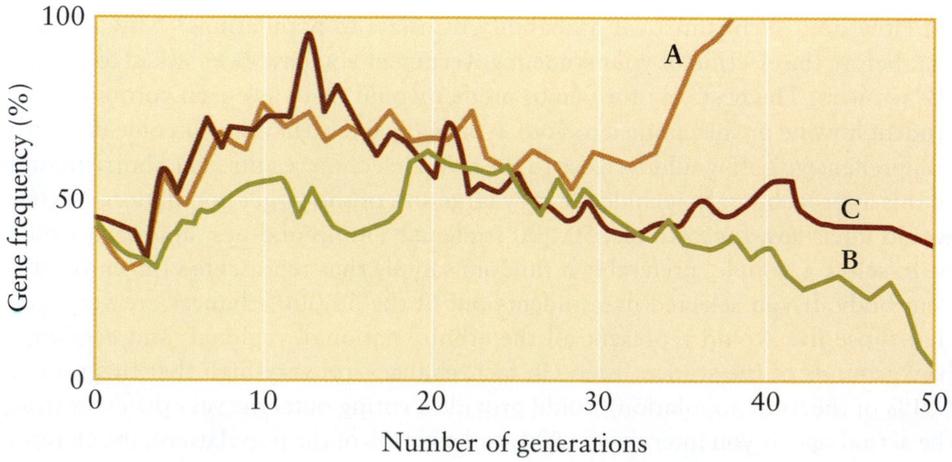

FIGURE 4.18 ■ Genetic Drift over Time
The effects of genetic drift appear in this graph, which plots the frequencies over time (by generations) of one gene in three differently sized populations. Assume that population A is the smallest of the three and population C is the largest. At the start, each population has the gene at 50% frequency. Around 38 generations, population A has drifted significantly; the gene is fixed at 100% frequency, a 50% increase. At 50 generations, population B has also drifted. Its gene frequency has declined by 40%. Although the frequency in population C has changed over time, it is still approximately 50% after 50 generations, owing to the largeness of the population.

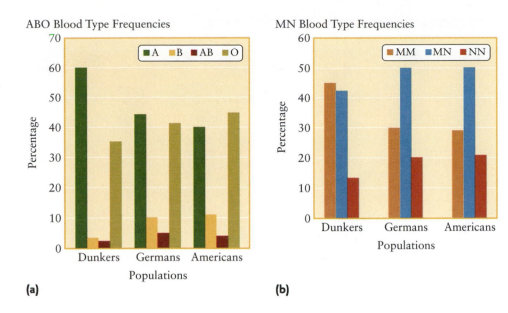

ABO Blood Type Frequencies

MN Blood Type Frequencies

(a)

(b)

FIGURE 4.19 ■ **Genetic Drift in the Dunker Population**
Comparisons of ABO and MN blood type frequencies among Dunkers, Germans, and Americans reveal genetic drift: **(a)** Dunkers have a higher percentage of blood type A and lower percentages of blood types O, B, and AB than do Germans and Americans. **(b)** Dunkers have a higher percentage of blood type M and lower percentages of MN and N.

How does this effect play out in real life? Among humans, for example, genetic drift might occur in a small group that is **endogamous,** discouraging reproduction outside the group. (An **exogamous** society extends reproduction outside its community.) Within such a group, the chances are great that the frequencies of genetic markers will differ from those of a larger population. When the Dunkers, a small religious sect that discourages outside marriage (and thus reproduction), first emigrated from Germany to Pennsylvania, in 1719, the group included just 28 members. Over the next few decades, several hundred more arrived in Pennsylvania; the breeding population remained quite small. Comparisons of contemporary blood type percentages among Dunkers, Germans, and Americans reflect significant changes in the Dunkers and a likely lack of change in the larger populations (**Figure 4.19**). That is, blood type frequencies among Germans and Americans remain basically the same as they were in the 1700s. The Dunkers' original frequencies were probably much like those of the Germans, but the small Dunker population meant a much greater chance for genetic drift. The frequencies diverged dramatically over time simply due to chance.

Founder Effect: A Special Kind of Genetic Drift

Founder effect, one form of genetic drift, occurs when a small group (fewer than several hundred members) of a large parent population migrates to a new region and is reproductively isolated. The new region is either unoccupied or occupied by species with which the small group cannot breed. Because the founding population is so small, there is a very good chance that its genetic composition is not representative of the parent population's. Thanks to the founder effect, as the founding population grows its gene pool diverges even further from the source (**Figure 4.20**). For example, around 12,000 yBP a very small number of individuals—perhaps just a few hundred—migrated from East Asia to North America (this movement is among the topics of chapter 10). Today, Native Americans have very high frequencies of type O blood—in many places the frequency is 100%—while

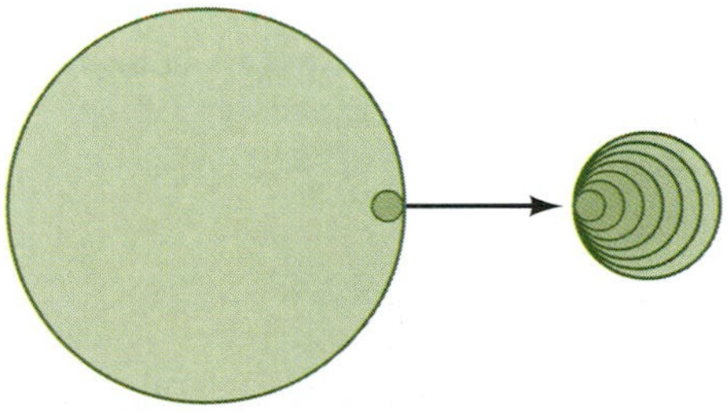

endogamous Refers to a population in which individuals breed only with other members of the population.

exogamous Refers to a population in which individuals breed only with nonmembers of their population.

founder effect The accumulation of random genetic changes in a small population that has become isolated from the parent population due to the genetic input of only a few colonizers.

FIGURE 4.20 ■ **Founder Effect**
The large circle on the left represents a parent population, from which a very small proportion is removed to begin a new population. Over time, the founding population grows, and its gene pool looks less and less like that of the parent population.

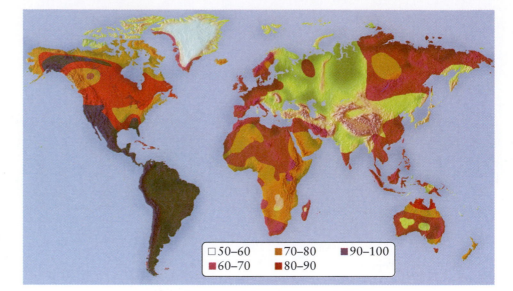

FIGURE 4.21 ■ O Blood Type Distribution
Native Americans in North and South America have much higher percentages of type O blood than do East Asians, with whom they share ancestors.

50–60   70–80   90–100
60–70   80–90

FIGURE 4.22 ■ Huntington's Chorea
The woman in the wheelchair suffers from Huntington's chorea, a degenerative genetic disorder.

Huntington's chorea A rare genetic disease in which the central nervous system degenerates and the individual loses control over voluntary movements, with the symptoms often appearing between ages 30 and 50.

admixture The exchange of genetic material between two or more populations.

East Asian populations have among the world's lowest frequencies of it (**Figure 4.21**). This discrepancy strongly suggests that the original East Asian immigrants, the founding "Native Americans," had a higher frequency of type O blood than their parent population had.

Founder effect has also been documented in several genetic diseases that affect humans. Among the best known is **Huntington's chorea,** a genetic abnormality caused by an autosomal dominant gene (**Figure 4.22**). The gene is located on chromosome 4 at the locus that codes for the Huntington protein, and a person needs only one allele from a parent to have the disease. At the end of the normal gene is a sequence of three DNA bases, CAG (the code for glutamine). If the sequence is repeated numerous times, usually more than 35 times, the individual has the mutation. Huntington's chorea causes degeneration of parts of the brain that control body movement and abilities such as speech production, triggering involuntary jerky movements of the arms and legs as well as dementia. These multiple and debilitating symptoms normally do not manifest until late in life or after the reproductive years, usually after about age 40. Fortunately, the disease is quite rare, affecting only five to eight people per 100,000.

Why had such a debilitating disease not been removed from the gene pool via natural selection? Since the effects of the gene are not expressed until later in life, people might not have known they had the disease until after they had passed on the detrimental allele to their offspring.

Today, most human populations are not small and isolated, and they interbreed relatively freely with surrounding groups. Whenever interbreeding occurs across population boundaries, gene flow occurs.

GENE FLOW: SPREAD OF GENES ACROSS POPULATION BOUNDARIES

Another force of evolution, gene flow (or **admixture;** see "The Evolutionary Synthesis, the Study of Populations, and the Causes of Evolution" in chapter 2) is the transfer of genes across population boundaries. Simply, members of two

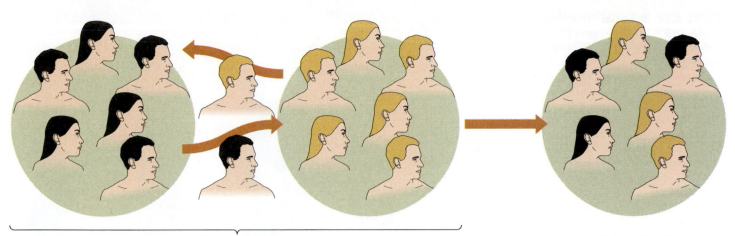

Generation 1   Generation 2

FIGURE 4.23 ■ Gene Flow
New genetic material can be introduced into a population through gene flow from another population. Say, for example, that a population in one place has genes for only brown hair. Members of that population interbreed with an adjacent population, which has genes for only blonde hair. After interbreeding for a generation, both populations have genes for blonde and brown hair. As a result, when people from either population interbreed with yet another population, they may contribute alleles for brown, blonde, or both.

populations produce offspring (**Figure 4.23**). The key determinant for the amount of gene flow is accessibility to mates—the less the physical distance between populations, the greater the chance of gene flow. While mutation increases genetic variation between two populations over time, gene flow decreases such variation. Anthropologists and geneticists have found that for many kinds of biological traits, ranging from cranial shapes to blood types to microsatellite DNA markers (see "Polymorphisms: Variations in Specific Genes" in chapter 3), similarity increases the closer one population is to another population.

Migration does not necessarily bring about gene flow. For example, when East Asians first migrated to North America (see "Founder Effect: A Special Kind of Genetic Drift," above), they reached a continental land mass where no humans had ever lived. Written records suggest that Vikings first traveled from Greenland to Newfoundland around AD 1000, but there is no evidence that they interbred with the native people. The first significant gene flow involving Native Americans and Europeans seems to have occurred when or soon after Christopher Columbus and his crew arrived in the New World, in 1492. From that point on, gene flow has been extensive.

Gene flow and genetic variation are also highly influenced by social structure (**Figure 4.24**). Endogamous societies—for example, Australian aborigines—have relatively little genetic diversity because few individuals migrate into the community and thus little new genetic material is introduced. Exogamous societies have relatively high genetic diversity because proportionately more genetic material is brought into the gene pool.

Gene flow has always affected human evolution, but its effects have increased greatly over time. Originally, human populations tended to be small and isolated (among the topics of chapter 12). Only during the last 10,000 years, with the development of agriculture and with major population increases, have humans had widespread interaction.

Specific genetic markers in living populations, such as the ABO blood group system, provide evidence of gene flow across large regions. For example, the frequencies

FIGURE 4.24 ■ **Social Structure in MtDNA and Y Chromosome Diversity**
In *patrilocal* societies, generally speaking, males stay in the birthplace, females migrate out, and female mates come from elsewhere. In *matrilocal* societies, females stay in the birthplace, males migrate out, and male mates come from elsewhere. To test the hypothesis that the out-migration of females and the out-migration of males produce different patterns of genetic diversity, the geneticist Hiroki Oota and colleagues studied six groups in Thailand, three of them patrilocal and three matrilocal. They found predictable patterns in the diversity of mtDNA and of Y chromosomes. Since mtDNA is passed from mother to daughter, the patrilocal groups showed high mtDNA variation (brought about by females' movement into new villages), and the matrilocal groups showed low mtDNA variation (brought about by females' remaining in place). Since the Y chromosome is passed from father to son, the patrilocal societies showed low Y chromosome variation (from males' not migrating), and the matrilocal societies showed high Y chromosome variation (from males' moving to new villages and introducing new Y chromosomes).

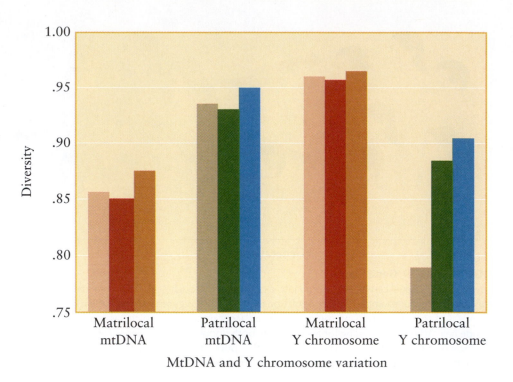

MtDNA and Y chromosome variation

CONCEPT CHECK What Causes Evolution?

Evolution is caused by one or a combination of four forces: mutation, natural selection, genetic drift, and gene flow. Although all four forces are important, natural selection accounts for most evolution.

CAUSE	DEFINITION	EXAMPLES
Mutation	Heritable change in structure or amount of DNA	Sickle-cell anemia Huntington's chorea Klinefelter's syndrome Down syndrome
Natural selection	Favoring of individuals with characteristics that enhance survival and reproduction	Sickle-cell anemia Industrial melanism Thalassemia G6PD deficiency Lactase deficiency
Genetic drift	Genetic change due to chance	Klinefelter's syndrome Blood types Hemophilia Achromatopsia Porphyria
Gene flow	Transfer of genes across population boundaries	Blood types

of type B blood change gradually from East Asia to far western Europe. This clinal—that is, sloping—trend was first noted, in the early 1940s, by the American geneticist Pompeo Candela (1906–1956), who made the case that the gradient from east to west reflects significant gene flow that occurred as Mongol populations migrated westward from AD 500 to 1500. That is, if Mongols had higher frequencies of the B allele, they might have passed on that allele as they interbred with local populations.

Subsequent data on blood groups, however, have revealed sharp distinctions in frequencies between adjacent populations. These distinctions suggest that, in addition to gene flow, genetic drift within small, isolated groups contributed to the frequency variations.

This chapter and the previous one have discussed inheritance, the genetic code, and genetic change in terms of evolution. Prior to the emergence of evolutionary approaches to the study of human variation, many scientists believed that human variation could be understood through discrete categories called races. The next chapter will address the study of biological diversity, the uses and misuses of biological classification, and the ways that variation in living people reflects adaptations to diverse and sometimes extreme environments across the earth.

ANSWERING THE BIG QUESTION

What causes evolutionary (genetic) change?

- Deviation from the proportions of gene frequencies and genotype frequencies as defined by the Hardy-Weinberg law of equilibrium is explained by one or more of the four forces of evolution: mutation, natural selection, genetic drift, and gene flow. These forces result in genetic change over time.

- Mutations are DNA coding errors that are biochemically manifested as permanent changes in the structure or amount of genetic material within cells. Mutations are the only source of new genetic material.

- Although a mutation can occur in any cell, only mutations in gametes have implications for offspring, and therefore they have greater importance for evolution than do mutations in somatic cells.

- Natural selection begins with variation among the individual members of a population. Members with advantageous characteristics survive and reproduce in greater numbers than do members lacking the same characteristics. Allele frequencies can increase, decrease, or remain the same owing to natural selection. Advantageous characteristics can be visible physical attributes (e.g., the peppered moth's color); invisible, biochemical attributes (e.g., in regions of endemic malaria, the heterozygote advantage of hemolytic anemias or enzyme deficiency); or some combination of the physical and the biochemical.

- Genetic drift is change in gene frequency due to chance. Within smaller populations, chances are greater that gene frequencies will change randomly. Drift was likely an important force in most human evolution, since prior to 10,000 yBP most human populations included fewer than several hundred individuals.

- Gene flow is the transfer of genes across population boundaries. In humans, gene flow became a major force of evolution mostly within the last 10,000 years, when population sizes increased and created greater opportunities for contact and reproduction.

wwnorton.com/studyspace

KEY TERMS

abnormal hemoglobin
admixture
balanced polymorphism
capillaries
deme
directional selection
disruptive selection
endogamous
equilibrium
exogamous
fitness
founder effect
frameshift mutation
gene pool
glucose-6-phosphate dehydrogenase (G6PD)
Hardy-Weinberg law of equilibrium
hemoglobinopathies
hemolytic anemias

Huntington's chorea
induced mutations
Klinefelter's syndrome
macroevolution
melanic
microevolution
mutagens
nonmelanic
nonsynonymous point mutation
point mutations
positive selection
reproductive isolation
sickle-cell anemia
spontaneous mutations
stabilizing selection
synonymous point mutation
thalassemia
transposable elements

ADDITIONAL READINGS

Gillespie, J. H. 2004. *Population Genetics: A Concise Guide*. 2nd ed. Baltimore: Johns Hopkins University Press.

Kettlewell, H. B. D. 1973. *The Evolution of Melanism*. Oxford, UK: Oxford University Press.

Livingstone, F. B. 1958. Anthropological implications of sickle cell gene distribution in West Africa. *American Anthropologist* 60: 533–562.

Mielke, J. H., L. W. Konigsberg, and J. H. Relethford. 2006. *Human Biological Variation*. New York: Oxford University Press.

Ridley, M. 2004. *Evolution*. Malden, MA: Blackwell Science.

Modern humans' skin colors range from very light to very dark. If all the variants were lined up from lightest to darkest, it would be hard to determine the dividing lines between so-called racial categories. In fact, the number of racial categories differs by whom you ask, from three to ten or more. Although skin color is an easily observable form of variation among humans, it is not the main form. Most of our variation as a species is invisible to the naked eye and does not divide up into discrete categories.

CHAPTER 5

Biology in the Present: Living People

I was first introduced to the biology of living people in high school, when my biology teacher assigned the section on race in our textbook. From that reading and class discussion about it, I learned that in America race is complex and important, especially with regard to poverty and inequality. I also learned that, from a biological perspective, race is a useful way to classify human beings. The teacher informed the class that each human belongs to one of three races: "Caucasoid," "Negroid," and "Mongoloid," referring respectively to Europeans and western Asians, Africans south of the Sahara Desert, and all other Asians and Native Americans. Simple.

Is racial categorization all that simple? Can human variation be classified? Is race a means of understanding why humans differ in appearance and biology around the world? If the answer to these questions is no, is there a better way to comprehend the enormous variation among humans today? In addressing these questions in this chapter, I will show that race, as it was presented in my high school biology class, has historical roots. These historical roots have led to a largely incorrect understanding of human biological variation.

In fact, race symbolizes the misperceptions that many Americans and others around the world have about human variation. Traits that are often seen as racial in origin are actually adaptations that have been strongly influenced by natural selection. As interpreted by anthropologists, human biological variation consists not of categories but of an evolutionary continuum. A key, underlying concept here is humans' flexibility toward their environmental circumstances, a process that begins before birth and continues through adulthood. The study of living human biology, then, emphasizes the enormous developmental flexibility that characterizes *Homo sapiens*.

IS RACE A VALID, BIOLOGICALLY MEANINGFUL CONCEPT?

Brief History of the Race Concept

The idea of race—that human variation can be classified—is a recent invention. Early written records do not employ the concept. For example, even though ancient Egyptians represented sub-Saharan Africans in their art, they never referred to the Africans' race. The Greek historian Herodotus (484?–420? BC) traveled widely, but never wrote about race. Similarly, the great Venetian historian and traveler Marco Polo (1254–1324), who saw more of the known world than anyone else of his day, recorded huge amounts of information about his sojourns in Asia without mentioning race.

The American physical anthropologist C. Loring Brace has argued that the race concept got its start in the fourteenth century, during the Renaissance. Before that time, people traveled gradually, either by walking or on horseback. A day's journey averaged 25 miles (40 km), over which travelers could observe subtle changes in human variation, such as in skin color, from place to place. When Renaissance-era travelers began covering long distances via oceangoing vessels, they also began categorizing people into discrete groups. In simply taking off from seaports, covering vast bodies of water, and landing at their destinations, these travelers noted obvious and sometimes profound physical differences in people—say between western Europeans and equatorial Africans—without all the gradations that came between.

The early scientific articulation of the race concept—namely that living humans could be lumped into different taxonomic groups—first emerged in the eighteenth century. By the 1700s, Europeans had encountered most of the biological diversity of the world's populations. Building on Linnaeus's taxonomy of organisms (see "Taxonomy and Systematics: Classifying Living Organisms and Identifying Their Biological Relationships" in chapter 2), the eminent German anatomist Johann Friedrich Blumenbach (1752–1840) developed a biological taxonomy of human races, published as his MD thesis at the University of Göttingen in 1775. Blumenbach based his taxonomy on human skin color and other physical traits but mainly on features of the skull, such as the facial projection (**Figure 5.1**). After studying several hundred skulls he had collected from around the world, he concluded that there were five races of people: Mongoloids, Malays, Ethiopians (Africans), American Indians, and Caucasoids. These types were static—they did not change over time. And while Blumenbach had focused on skulls, his racial taxonomy was subsequently applied to the living populations represented by those skulls. More than any other work, Blumenbach's study set the tone for the popular perception of human variation: that human beings come in categorical types called races.

Debunking the Race Concept: Franz Boas Shows That Human Biology Is Not Static

Franz Boas, the founder of American anthropology (see chapter 1), was among the first scientists to challenge the taxonomic approach to human biological variation. Specifically, he wanted to test the widely held notion that head shape and other so-called racial markers were static entities, essentially unchanging through time.

In the early 1900s, he and his researchers studied some 18,000 immigrant families, calculating the cephalic index—the ratio of head length to head breadth—of parents born in Europe and their children born in the United States. Their results revealed that the adults' and children's head shapes differed, not by a lot but by a degree that could be expressed mathematically. This finding undermined the idea, prevalent at the time, that racial types were innately stable. Because the differences that had been cited among various races were not immutable, Boas concluded, the race concept was invalid.

So-Called Racial Traits Are Not Concordant

Single biological traits, such as cranial shape, had seemed like such a firm basis for racial categories in part because it is so easy to classify when focusing on just one characteristic. What happens when human populations are grouped according to multiple characteristics? In the early 1970s, the American geneticist R. C. Lewontin (b. 1929) tested the race concept by studying global genetic variation. If human races existed, most genetic diversity would be accounted for by them. Focusing on blood groups, serum proteins, and red blood cell enzyme variants, Lewontin found that the so-called races accounted for only about 5% to 10% of the genetic diversity. In other words, most variation occurred *across* human populations regardless of "racial" makeup.

Subsequent studies by other scientists—of wide-ranging characteristics such as genetic traits and cranial morphology—have all shown the same thing: so-called races account for a very small amount of biological variation. Multiple biological traits do not lead to clear-cut racial classifications because traits simply do not agree in their frequency or distribution. One trait might cut across human populations in one way, but another trait cuts across them in another way.

Human Variation: Geographic Clines, Not Racial Categories

If race is not a valid way to account for human diversity, how do we speak meaningfully about the enormous range of variation in all kinds of human characteristics around the globe? One important finding from physical anthropologists' study of human variation is that specific biological traits generally follow a geographic gradient called a **cline**. Think, for example, of two patterns discussed in chapter 4: First, the frequencies of type B blood change gradually from East Asia to far western Europe. Second, the human gene that causes the disorder sickle-cell anemia, hemoglobin *S*, increases in frequency in areas where the parasitic disease malaria is endemic, and it decreases in frequency (to nearly zero) in areas where malaria is not endemic. Because living humans are a single, geographically diverse species, their variation is continuously distributed in ways like these and not grouped into discrete categories.

Among the best examples of clinal variation are the skin pigmentations of living people. From equatorial to higher latitudes, skin color changes in a gradient from dark to light. Exceptions exist, such as the relatively dark skin of Native Americans in the Canadian Arctic, but the single strongest factor in determining skin pigmentation is exposure to ultraviolet radiation (discussed below).

Human variation, then, cannot be subdivided into racial categories. As said best by the physical anthropologist Frank B. Livingstone, "There are no races, there are

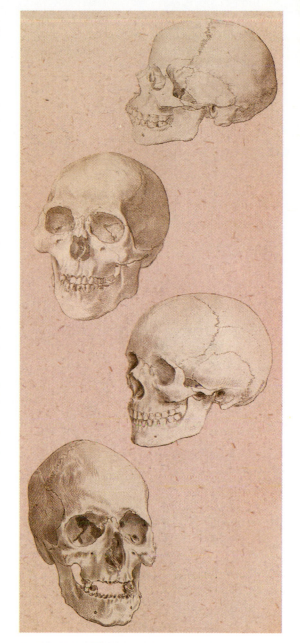

FIGURE 5.1 ■ Blumenbach's Skulls
Johann Blumenbach created a classification system for humans based on the shapes of crania he collected. Here, he has sketched the four skulls representing four of his five main groups: (from top to bottom) African (*Aethiopis*), Asian or Mongoloid (*Tungusae*), Caucasoid (*Georgianae*), and American Indian (*Americani Illinoici*). This scheme as applied to living humans is still prevalent in the popular perception of human variation. What differences do you see in these skulls?

cline A gradual change in some phenotypic characteristic from one population to the next.

only clines." Human variation can be understood far more meaningfully in terms of **life history,** the biology of growth and development.

LIFE HISTORY: GROWTH AND DEVELOPMENT

Various factors, genetic and external, influence the human body's growth (increase in size) and development (progression from immaturity to maturity). DNA provides a blueprint that schedules growth, but environment and events very much influence the actual development from conception through death.

The Growth Cycle: Conception through Adulthood

The bodies of large mammals such as adult humans are made of more than ten trillion cells, which are produced over the course of about 2^{38} mitoses (or cell divisions; see "Mitosis: Production of Identical Somatic Cells" in chapter 3). Mitoses result in all the various types of tissues (bone, blood, and muscle, for example) and organs (brain, stomach, heart, and so on), and they begin from the moment of fertilization. The human growth cycle, from embryo to fetus to child to adult, consists of three stages:

1. The **prenatal stage,** which includes the three periods, or trimesters, of pregnancy and ends with birth;
2. The **postnatal stage,** which includes the *neonatal* period (about the first month), *infancy* (the second month to the end of **lactation,** usually by the end of the third year), *childhood* (ages 3–7), the *juvenile* period (ages 7–10 for girls and 7–12 for boys), *puberty* (days or weeks), and *adolescence* (5–10 years after puberty);
3. The **adult stage,** which includes the reproductive period (from about age 20 to the end of the childbearing years, usually by age 50 for women and later for men) and *senescence* (the period of time after the childbearing years).

Prenatal Stage: Sensitive to Environmental Stress, Predictive of Adult Health

In humans, the prenatal stage, or pregnancy, lasts nine months. In the first trimester, or three-month period, the fertilized ovum multiples into millions of cells. Distinctive cell groupings first represent different kinds of tissues, then give rise to the tissues, the organs, the brain, and the various physiological systems. By the end of the second month, the embryo is about one inch (2.5 cm) long but is recognizably human. Because growth and development are at their most dynamic during this trimester, the embryo is highly susceptible to disruption and disease caused by mutation or environmental factors. Specific **stressors,** or potentially harmful agents, include the mother's smoking, consuming alcohol, taking drugs, and providing inadequate nutrition.

In the second trimester, the fetus mainly grows longer, from about eight inches (20.3 cm) at the end of the first month of this trimester to about 14 inches (35.6 cm), or three-quarters the length of an average newborn.

The third trimester involves rapid weight growth and organ development. During the final month, the lungs develop and most reflexes become fully coordinated. The fetus's wide range of movement includes the ability to grasp and to respond to light, sound, and touch.

This trimester culminates in birth, the profoundly stressful transition from the **intrauterine** environment to the external environment. Half of all neonatal deaths occur during the first 24 hours. Most of these deaths are caused by low birth weight (less than 5.5 lbs, or 2.5 kg), which is generally linked to one or a combination of multiple stressors, such as maternal malnutrition, smoking, and excessive alcohol consumption. Because individuals of low socioeconomic status tend to be exposed to environmental stresses, their children are prone to low birth weights and early deaths. And a poor intrauterine environment predisposes the person to developing specific diseases later in life.

Postnatal Stage: The Maturing Brain, Preparing for Adulthood

Each of the five postnatal periods has a different **growth velocity,** or rate of growth per year (**Figure 5.2**). During infancy, the period of most rapid growth, the **deciduous** (or primary) **dentition** erupts through the gums (**Figure 5.3**). By the time an infant has completed **weaning**—when the infant shifts from consuming only milk (theoretically provided by the mother) to consuming external foods—all 20 deciduous teeth have erupted. The time of weaning varies, but the process is usually finished by the end of the second or third year in preindustrial, traditional societies and earlier in industrial, contemporary societies. **Motor skills** such as walking and running develop during the first two years. **Cognitive abilities** also progress rapidly during this time, reflecting the very rapid growth and development of the brain during infancy (**Figure 5.4**).

During childhood, general growth levels off, but the still rapidly growing brain requires the child to have a diet rich in fats, protein, and energy. The child learns behaviors important to later survival, but still depends on adults for food and other resources. Because the child's dentition and digestive systems are immature, adults must specially prepare food that is soft and easy to chew.

By about age six, permanent teeth begin to replace primary teeth, and brain growth is completed (**Figure 5.5**). These hallmark developmental events occur nearly simultaneously, as they do in many other primate species. The eruption of the first permanent molar signals the ability to eat adult food, very high nutritional requirements ceasing once the brain reaches its final weight.

During the juvenile years, growth slows. The full-size brain makes possible formalized education and social learning. In industrialized societies, learning in grade school accelerates.

Adolescence presents a number of profound biological developments. Sexual maturation commences with puberty, and its visible characteristics are the beginning of breast development and menstruation (**menarche**) in girls, the deepening of the voice and emergence of facial hair in boys, development of secondary sexual characteristics (changes to genitals), and **sexual dimorphism** of girls' and boys' body sizes. Unlike other primates, humans experience increased growth velocity

intrauterine Refers to the area within the uterus.

growth velocity The speed with which an organism grows in size, often measured as the amount of growth per year.

deciduous dentition Also known as baby teeth or milk teeth, this is the first set of teeth, which form in utero and erupt shortly after birth.

weaning The process of substituting other foods for the milk produced by the mother.

motor skills Refers to the performance of complex movements and actions that require the control of nerves and muscles.

cognitive abilities Refers to the capacity of the brain to perceive, process, and judge information from the surrounding environment.

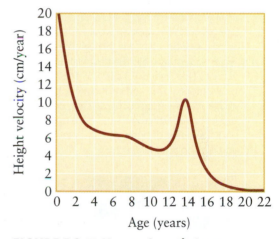

FIGURE 5.2 ■ Human Growth Curve
During postnatal life, a human grows at different rates. The highest rate of growth (on this graph, 20 cm/year) occurs during the first few months following birth. Growth velocity decreases through the rest of life, apart from a mid-growth spurt (here, approaching 7 cm/year) around age eight and an adolescent growth spurt (10 cm/year) following the onset of puberty.

menarche Refers to the onset of menstruation in an adolescent female.

sexual dimorphism A difference in a physical attribute between the males and females of a species.

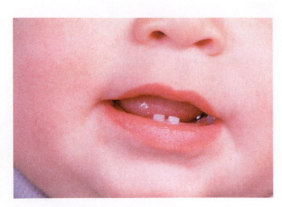

FIGURE 5.3 ■ Deciduous Teeth
Deciduous, or baby, teeth form in the fetus and erupt shortly after birth.

during this time. When nutrition is adequate and stressors are minimal, the adolescent growth spurt can add as much as three and a half inches (8.9 cm) to boys and somewhat less than three inches (7.6 cm) to girls. Boys complete their growth later than girls, whose growth spurts peak earlier than boys'. Growth spurts either do not happen or are minimized in very highly stressed populations, such as the Quechua Indians, who live in high altitudes of Peru and suffer from cold, overwork, malnutrition, and hypoxia (a condition discussed below).

Prior to the completion of growth, the ends of the long bones—the humerus, radius, and ulna in the arm, and the femur, tibia, and fibula in the leg—are separate growth centers called **epiphyses.** The epiphyses are separated from the main shaft, or **diaphysis,** by a growth plate containing cells that produce **nonmineralized** bone substance. As long as bone cells are producing bone substance and the epiphyses

FIGURE 5.4 ■ Growth Curves of Body Tissues
This chart shows the varying growth curves of the brain, body, dentition, and reproductive system in humans. The brain grows the fastest, reaching full cognitive development around age six. In fact, humans have such a large brain that much of it needs to be attained after birth; if the brain reached full size before birth, women would not be able to pass newborns' heads through their pelvic regions. Dentition has the next highest growth velocity (see Figures 5.3 and 5.5). The body grows more slowly and continues until as late as age 20. The reproductive system does not begin substantial growth and development until the onset of puberty, but it reaches completion around age 20.

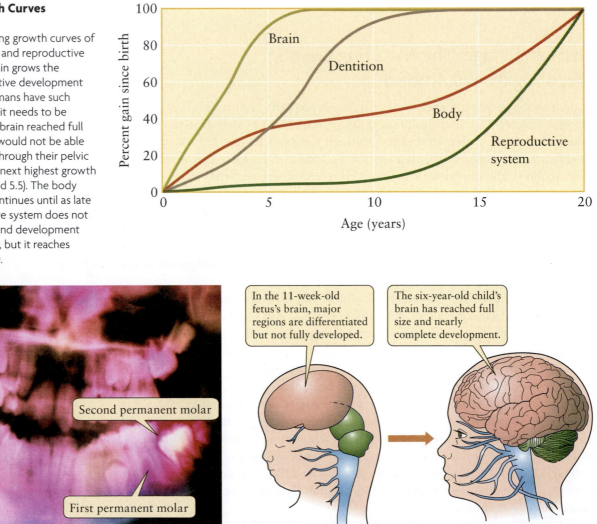

FIGURE 5.5 ■ Molar Eruption and Brain Development
(a) Permanent teeth form during the early years of life and begin to erupt around age six. In this X-ray image, the first permanent molars, called the six-year molars, have erupted. The second permanent molars, the twelve-year molars, are still forming and will not erupt for another six years. The crowded anterior dentition, or front teeth, includes the deciduous teeth and new permanent teeth waiting to erupt and take their places. **(b)** Brain growth and development finish at around the same time.

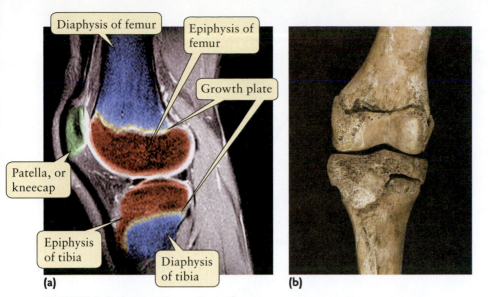

(a) Diaphysis of femur

(a) Epiphysis of femur

(a) Growth plate

(a) Patella, or kneecap

(a) Epiphysis of tibia

(a) Diaphysis of tibia

(a)

(b)

FIGURE 5.6 ■ **Long Bone Growth**
(a) This MRI of a child's knee shows the joining of the femur, or upper leg bone, with the tibia, or lower leg bone. Long bones like these begin as three separate bones—the diaphysis, or shaft, and two epiphyses, or ends—separated by a growth plate. **(b)** In this photo of a child's knee joint, the epiphyses have not yet fused to the diaphysis. The line of union may be visible for several years after the attachment occurs; when it eventually disappears, the bone appears as a single element.

epiphyses The end portions of long bones; once they fuse to the diaphyses, the bones stop growing longer.

diaphyses The main midsection, or shaft, portions of long bones; each contains a medullary cavity.

nonmineralized Refers to bone reduced to its organic component.

remain unfused, the long bone will continue to grow. The bone continuously grows in width throughout life, but once the epiphyses have fused to the diaphyses the growth in length stops and the individual's height is set (**Figure 5.6**).

Biologically, adulthood is signaled by the completion of sexual maturity, the reaching of full height, and the fusion of the epiphyses. The social and behavioral maturity associated with adulthood, however, are difficult to define. In fact, sociologists and social psychologists argue that social maturity is a lifelong process, developing earlier in some biologically mature individuals than others.

While bone growth and epiphyseal fusion are influenced by genes and sex hormones (androgens and estrogens), the amount of growth and the terminal length of bones are strongly affected by environment, especially by nutrition and general health. Negative environmental effects in the present and in the historical past, such as downturns in nutrition, have been documented worldwide. The American economic historians Dora Costa and Richard Steckel have shown, for example, that between 1710 and 1970 substantial changes occurred in the heights of American males of European descent (**Figure 5.7**). Initially, a gradual increase in heights likely reflected improved living conditions and food availability. The sharp decline in heights around 1830 coincided with the urbanization trend. As people moved from rural, agricultural settings to overly crowded cities, they were exposed to more diseases that were easily passed from person to person. In addition, high population densities caused great accumulations of garbage and waste, which may have polluted water supplies and thus exposed people to more bacteria, viruses, and parasites that caused infection and disease. As living conditions improved at the beginning of the twentieth century, as trash removal became mandatory and sewers were constructed, height increased. Today, Americans' heights are among the greatest in the country's history, thanks to reliable food supplies, unpolluted water, and access to medical care.

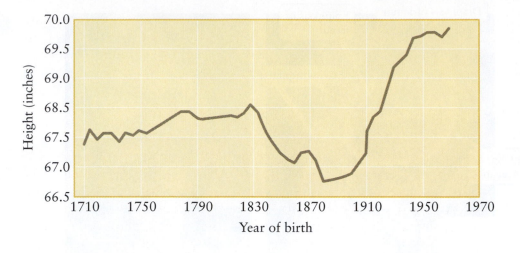

FIGURE 5.7 ■ Changes in Height

Beginning in the 1700s, the heights of soldiers, students, and slaves were routinely collected for identification or registration purposes. By combining these data with subsequent figures, Costa and Steckel discovered patterns of increase and decline in the heights of American-born males of European descent. From about 67.5 inches in the early 1700s, heights rose to about 68.5 inches around 1830, then sharply declined by two inches per year over the next 70 years. After the late 1800s, heights increased by a couple of inches per year throughout the twentieth century. Simply, the extraordinarily poor sanitation and health conditions in nineteenth-century cities resulted in increased disease, stress, and attenuated growth. The subsequent increase in Americans' heights reflected improvements in sanitation, nutrition, and health.

secular trend A phenotypic change, such as an increase in height, due to multiple factors.

This twentieth-century growth in tallness, sometimes called the **secular trend,** has been noted in many other countries as well. Multiple factors have contributed to particular causes from place to place, but the collective increase in stature has resulted from improvements in disease control and nutrition. In wealthy nations, the increase in height has come to a stop or slowed considerably, most likely because growth has reached its genetic limit. In many less wealthy (and thus less healthy) nations, growth potential has not been reached, and growth periods are comparatively slow. For example, as the American anthropologist Barbara Piperata has documented, in Brazil's Amazon River basin the suboptimal nutrition and exposure to infectious disease have resulted in less-than-optimal growth (**Figure 5.8**).

The growth and development of males, prenatally and postnatally, are more sensitive to environmental insult than are the growth and development of females.

FIGURE 5.8 ■ Height and Economically Disadvantaged Populations

As these graphs show, some populations of **(a)** Brazilian boys and **(b)** Brazilian girls grow less than the 5th percentile of American children. In countries such as Brazil, as in late nineteenth-century America, poor environmental conditions have led to slowed growth and shorter adult height.

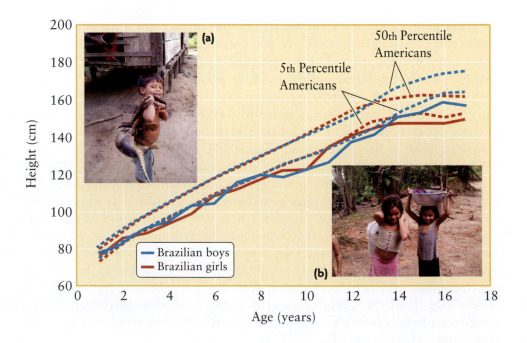

Human biologists have found much evidence of these differences in developing countries, but they have not been able to explain the mechanisms at work. In terms of evolution, it would make sense for females to have developed buffers from stress because females' roles in reproduction, including pregnancy and lactation, are much more demanding than males'.

Adult Stage: Aging and Senescence

Throughout life, the body continuously grows and develops. By adulthood, its basic structure has been formed, so during this period most growth and development involve the replacement of cells and of tissues. In fact, over a person's lifetime nearly every cell and tissue in the body is replaced at least once every seven years.

Aging basically means "becoming older," but it refers collectively to various social, cultural, biological, and behavioral events that occur over a lifetime but do not by themselves increase the probability of death. **Senescence**, which accompanies aging, is a biological process characterized by a reduction in **homeostasis**, the body's ability to keep its organs and its physiological systems stable in the face of environmental stress. Senescing persons are increasingly susceptible to stress and death and have a decreased capacity to reproduce. For example, older adults produce less body heat than younger adults and hence are more uncomfortable in cold temperatures.

Whereas the previous life stages are generally predictable in their timing (mostly due to genetic programming), the chronology of senescence is highly variable. **Menopause,** the loss of ovarian function, is a key element of female senescence, marking the end of the reproductive phase and the end of childbearing. As a human biological universal, menopause usually occurs by age 50, but it varies by several years in different populations. Male senescence is different in that men normally produce sperm well into their 70s and 80s. However, the number of well-formed sperm and their motility decline by half after age 70. Male and female individuals older than 70 years, having lived through senescence, are considered elderly.

As discussed in chapter 3, bone loss is a senescence universal. That is, after age 40 humans suffer increased bone porosity and reduction in bone mass. The increased susceptibility to bone fracture that comes with this loss is called **osteoporosis** (Figure 5.9). In extreme cases, osteoporosis can weaken bone to the point that it easily fractures under small amounts of stress. This fragile nature commonly leads to fractures such as broken hips or to "compression" fractures of vertebrae, in which the bone simply cannot support the normal body weight and collapses. The collapse of several vertebrae can give the person a hunchback. Far more common in women than in men—because a loss of the hormone estrogen is linked to bone loss—osteoporosis shows less age variation than menopause does. Other factors that can predispose people to this condition are smoking, chronic diseases, and some medications.

For every stage from conception through senescence, humans (and other primates) have evolved strategies for enhancing their survival and reproductive potential, the prime movers of natural selection. In the next section, we will examine behaviors that are central to this adaptive success.

aging The process of maturation.

senescence Refers to an organism's biological changes in later adulthood.

homeostasis The maintenance of the internal environment of an organism within an acceptable range.

menopause The cessation of the menstrual cycle, signifying the end of a female's ability to bear children.

osteoporosis The loss of bone mass often due to age, causing the bones to become porous, brittle, and easily fractured.

FIGURE 5.9 ■ **Osteoporosis**
(a) As this graph shows, men and women reach their maximum bone mass around age 30. **(b)** The loss of bone mass becomes evident in the grayish areas of X-rays such as this one. Notice the porous pelvic bones, which with normal bone mass would be solid white.

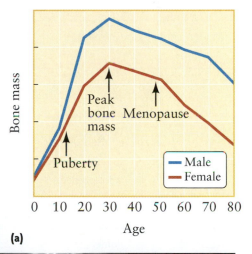

(a)

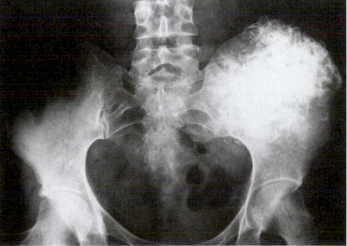

(b)

Life History Stages in Humans: Prenatal, Postnatal, and Adult*

A life history is the biological story, from conception to death, of an individual, a population, or a species. A life history provides insight into how energy is allocated to key events, such as reproduction, brain growth, and the care of offspring. It also sheds light on the interactions between genes and environment at crucial stages.

STAGE	PERIOD	TIMING AND CHARACTERISTICS
Prenatal	First trimester	Fertilization to twelfth week; embryo development; organ development
	Second trimester	Fourth through sixth lunar month; rapid growth in length
	Third trimester	Seventh month to birth; rapid growth in weight and organ development
Postnatal	Neonatal	Birth to 28 days; first exposure to extrauterine environment; most rapid postnatal growth and development
	Infancy	Second month to 36 months; rapid growth; breast-feeding; deciduous tooth development; other milestones (e.g., walking); weaning at end of period
	Childhood	Three to seven years; moderate growth; eruption of first permanent molar; completion of brain growth
	Juvenile	Seven to 10 years (girls), seven to 12 years (boys); slower growth; self-feeding; cognitive transition in learning and increased ability to learn
	Puberty	Days to few weeks at end of juvenile years; activation of sexual development; marked increase in secretion of sex hormones
	Adolescence	Five- to 10-year period after puberty; growth spurt (earlier in girls than boys); completion of permanent dental development and eruption; development of secondary sex characteristics; interest in adult social, sexual, and economic behaviors
Adult	Prime	Twenty years to end of reproductive years; stability in physiology, behavior, and cognition; menopause in women, commencing at about age 50
	Senescence	End of reproductive years to death; decline in function of many tissues and organs; homeostasis more easily disrupted than in earlier years; grandmother social behaviors

*Adapted from Table 11.1 in Bogin, B. and B. H. Smith. 2000. Evolution of the human life cycle. Pp. 377–424 in S. Stinson, B. Bogin, R. Huss-Ashmore, and D. O'Rourke, eds. *Human Biology: An Evolutionary and Biocultural Perspective*. New York: Wiley-Liss.

Evolution of Human Life History: Food, Sex, and Strategies for Survival and Reproduction

Two behaviors make possible the survival and adaptive success of humans and other primates: acquisition of food and reproduction. Unlike the other primates, humans acquire food and reproduce within the contexts of culture and society. For example, humans have created social institutions—especially kinship and marriage—and beliefs and rules supporting these institutions. Anthropologists are keenly interested in the relations between humans' sociocultural behaviors and the evolution of our unique life history, especially in comparison with other primates' life histories.

PROLONGED CHILDHOOD: FAT-BODIED MOMS AND THEIR BIG-BRAINED BABIES Humans have a relatively prolonged childhood. However, within this life period the spans of infancy and lactation are quite short. The mother's brief intensive child care allows her, theoretically, to have more births and to invest her resources among all her children.

The cost of this fertility advantage is the large amount of food the mother must provide for her children. The energy demands of the children's maturing brains require that this food be highly nutritious: rich in fats, protein, and energy. For only the first several years of each child's postnatal life, before the eruption of that child's first permanent molar, can the mother provide these resources, via lactation, from her own stored body fats and other nutrients.

GRANDMOTHERING: PART OF HUMAN ADAPTIVE SUCCESS Humans are also the only primates that experience, at the other end of the life history, prolonged postmenopausal survival. Some apes have a postmenopausal period, but it is briefer than humans'. Ethnographic evidence from cultures around the world shows that postmenopausal women, most often grandmothers, play important roles in caring for children, provisioning food to children, and providing essential information about the world to various members of their social groups. Because older people can become key repositories of knowledge about culture and society, longevity may have a selective advantage in humans but not in other primates.

ADAPTATION: MEETING THE CHALLENGES OF LIVING

Humans adjust remarkably well to new conditions and to challenges. As in other organisms, such adaptations—functional responses within particular environmental contexts—occur at four different levels. *Genetic* adaptation, as discussed in previous chapters, occurs at the population level via natural selection. Here, the biological change is inherited and is not reversible in a person (e.g., someone with sickle-cell anemia). *Developmental* (or *ontogenetic*) adaptation occurs at the level of the individual during a critical period of growth and development, childhood especially. The capacity to make the change is inherited, but the change is not inherited and is not reversible. For example, children living at high altitudes develop greater chest size prior to reaching adulthood than do children living at low altitudes. The expanded chest reflects the need for increased lung capacity in settings where less oxygen is available (discussed further below). *Acclimatization* (or *physiological* adaptation) occurs at the individual level, but unlike developmental adaptation it can occur anytime during a person's life. In this kind of adaptation, the change is not inherited and can be reversed. For example, exposure to sunlight for extended periods of time results in tanning (also discussed further below). Lastly, *cultural* (or *behavioral*) adaptation involves the use of material culture to make living possible in certain settings. For example, wearing insulated clothing keeps people from freezing in extreme cold.

functional adaptations Biological changes that occur during an individual's lifetime, increasing the individual's fitness in the given environment.

The American physical anthropologist Roberto Frisancho applies the term **functional adaptations** to the biological adjustments that occur within the individual's lifetime (that is, developmental adaptations and acclimatizations). Most functional adaptations are associated with extreme environmental conditions, such as heat, cold, high altitude, and heavy workload. Some of these conditions appear to have brought about genetic changes in humans. That is, over hundreds of generations humans have adapted to settings in which specific attributes enhance the potential for survival and reproduction. Skin pigmentation, for example, is related genetically to solar radiation exposure.

All adaptations have one purpose: *maintenance of internal homeostasis,* or maintenance of the normal functioning of all organs and physiological systems. Not to maintain homeostasis in body temperature, for example, or in oxygen accessibility, or in strength of the bones of the skeleton has severe consequences for the individual, including work impairment and loss of productivity, decline in quality of life, and even death. The maintenance of homeostasis involves all levels of any organism's biology, from biochemical pathways to cells, tissues, organs, and ultimately the entire organism.

To determine how humans maintain internal homeostasis, anthropologists employ indirect approaches and direct ones. *Indirect* approaches involve the study of populations in their natural environments, such as the Quechua Indians living in highland Peru or Eskimos living in Greenland. The observation of living populations as they engage in various activities in various settings provides great insight into functional adaptations, helping establish associations between specific biological attributes and environmental settings or circumstances. *Direct* approaches, by contrast, involve the replication of environmental conditions and of human responses to these conditions. In the course of such experiments, anthropologists determine cause-and-effect relationships, such as body response to temperature extremes.

Climate Adaptation: Living on the Margins

HEAT STRESS AND THERMOREGULATION Like all other mammals, humans are **homeothermic,** meaning they maintain a constant body temperature. A constant core temperature is essential for normal physiology, including brain function, limb function, and general body mobility. Humans can tolerate a body temperature higher than their normal 98.6 °F, but a body temperature above 104–107 °F for an extended period leads to organ failure and eventually death. Extremely hot weather can thus result in many deaths, such as in the summer of 2003, when at least 35,000 and perhaps as many as 50,000 people died in Europe during one of the hottest seasons ever recorded. Severe heat stress is experienced mostly in tropical settings, where it is hot much of the year, and during hot spells in temperate regions.

A body experiencing heat stress attempts to rid itself of internally and externally derived heat sources. Internal heat is produced by the body's metabolism, especially during activities involving movement, such as physical labor, walking, and running. External heat is derived from the air temperature. The initial physiological response to an elevated temperature is **vasodilation,** the dilation (expansion) of the blood vessels near the body's surface. By increasing blood vessels' diameter, the body is able to move more blood (and associated heat) away from the body's core to the body's surface. The red face of a person who is in a hot environment is the visible expression of vasodilation.

Sweating is another response to heat. Sweat is mostly water produced by the eccrine glands, which are located over the entire body's surface. Evaporation of

homeothermic Refers to an organism's ability to maintain a constant body temperature despite great variations in environmental temperature.

vasodilation The increase in blood vessels' diameter due to the action of a nerve or of a drug; it can also occur in response to hot temperatures.

the thin layer of water on the skin results in cooling of the surface. Humans can sweat a remarkably high volume of water, and this physiological process is central to humans' long-term functional adaptation to heat.

Sweating is less effective in areas of the body having a dense hair cover than in areas of the body having little or no hair. This relationship suggests that sweating evolved as a thermoregulatory adaptation in association with the general loss of body hair. Humans' loss of body hair is unique among the primates, indicating that the thermoregulatory adaptation of hair loss and sweating occurred in human evolution only.

Humans have a strong capacity to adapt to excessive heat. Individuals who have not often experienced such heat are less able to conduct heat away from their cores and less able to sweat than are individuals living in hot climates. Individuals exposed for the first time to a hot climate, however, rapidly adjust over a period of 10 to 14 days. This adjustment involves a lowering of the body's core temperature, a lowering of the threshold for when vasodilation and sweating begin, and a reduction of the heart rate and metabolic rate. Overall, women are less able to tolerate heat than are men, in part due to a relatively reduced ability to move blood to the skin through vasodilation and the presence of greater body fat.

Human populations who have lived in hot climates for most of their history—such as native equatorial Africans and South Americans—have the same number of sweat glands as other populations. However, heat-adapted populations sweat less and perform their jobs and other physical functions better in conditions involving excessive heat than do non-heat-adapted populations.

BODY SHAPE AND ADAPTATION TO HEAT STRESS The relationship between body shape and temperature adaptation was first described in the 1800s by a combination of two biogeographic rules, one developed by the German biologist Carl Bergmann (1814–1865) and the other developed by the American zoologist Joel Allen (1838–1921). **Bergmann's Rule** states that heat-adapted mammal populations will have smaller bodies than will cold-adapted mammal populations. Relative to body volume, small bodies have more surface area, facilitating more-rapid heat dissipation. Conversely, large bodies have less surface area, thus conserving heat in cold climates (**Figure 5.10**). Consequently, human populations adapted to hot climates tend to have small and narrow bodies (discussed further in chapter 9). **Allen's Rule** states that heat-adapted mammal populations will have long limbs, which maximize the body's surface area and thus promote heat dissipation, whereas cold-adapted mammal populations will have short limbs, which minimize the body's surface area and thus promote heat conservation.

Exceptions exist to Bergmann's and Allen's rules, but by and large these rules explain variation in human shapes that goes back at least 1,500,000 years. Populations living in hot climates tend to have small, narrow bodies and long limbs. Populations living in cold climates tend to have large, wide bodies and short limbs. This long-term association between body shape and climate means that body shape is mostly a genetic adaptation. However, body shape also involves childhood developmental processes that respond to climatic and other stressors, such as poor nutrition. For example, poor nutrition during early childhood can retard limb growth, especially of the forearm and lower leg, resulting in shorter arms and legs. Ultimately, then, body shape and morphology reflect both evolutionary and developmental processes.

COLD STRESS AND THERMOREGULATION Severe cold stress is experienced mostly in places close to Earth's magnetic poles, such as the Arctic; at altitudes higher than

Bergmann's Rule The principle that an animal's size is heat-related; smaller bodies are adapted to hot environments, and larger bodies are adapted to cold environments.

Allen's Rule The principle that an animal's limb lengths are heat-related; limbs are longer in hot environments and shorter in cold environments.

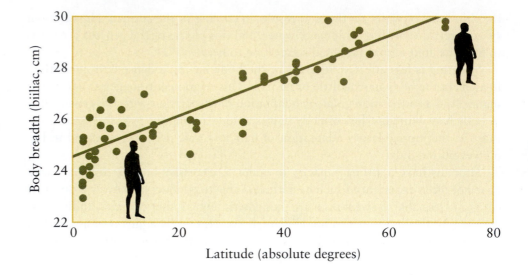

FIGURE 5.10 ■ Bergmann's Rule
This graph illustrates Carl Bergmann's biogeographic rule: as latitude increases (and temperature decreases), body breadth (as measured by the maximum breadth between the pelvic bones) also increases. Bergmann's Rule applies to all warm-blooded animals (including humans), which need to maintain a constant body temperature. Physically and physiologically, humans can adapt to a wide range of climates, but since humans are able to move about the earth, human body size may not strictly adhere to the latitude in which a person is living.

hypothermia A condition in which an organism's body temperature falls below the normal range, which may lead to the loss of proper body functions and, eventually, death.

vasoconstriction The decrease in blood vessels' diameter due to the action of a nerve or of a drug; it can also occur in response to cold temperatures.

basal metabolic rate (BMR) The rate at which an organism's body, while at rest, expends energy to maintain basic bodily functions; measured by the amount of heat given off per kilogram of body weight.

10,000 feet (3 km); and during cold spells in temperate settings. **Hypothermia,** or low body temperature, occurs in excessively cold air or immersion in cold water. During the great *Titanic* disaster, in 1912, many hundreds of passengers and ship's crew members escaped the sinking vessel, but died from hypothermia after floating in the northern Atlantic Ocean (28 °F) for two hours before rescue ships arrived.

Maintaining homeostasis against cold stress involves heat conservation and heat production. The human body's first response to cold stress is **vasoconstriction,** the constriction of the blood vessels beneath the skin. Decreasing the diameter of the blood vessels reduces blood flow and heat loss, from the body's core to the skin. The chief mechanism for producing heat is shivering.

Humans adapt to cold, but the adaptation includes cultural and behavioral factors, practices that societies living in extremely cold settings pass from one generation to the next. That is, people teach their children how to avoid situations involving heat loss. They teach them what clothing to wear, what kinds of shelters to build, and how to keep the interiors of shelters warm. Cold-adapted cultures also know that alcohol consumption contributes to the loss of body heat, increasing the chances of hypothermia and death.

After being exposed to survivable cold for more than a few days, humans shiver less, produce more heat, and have higher skin temperatures. Overall, adjusting to cold means becoming able to tolerate lower temperatures—simply, feeling better in the cold.

To measure heat production, anthropologists take a specific kind of measurement called the **basal metabolic rate (BMR).** Indigenous people living in cold settings, such as the Indians at high altitudes in the Peruvian Andes, have significantly higher BMR than do other human populations. Inuit are among the most studied populations on Earth, owing to their adaptation to the very cold, dry conditions in the Arctic Circle, where average winter temperatures range from –50 °F to –35 °F and even summer temperatures usually do not climb above 46 °F. In part, the Eskimos' high BMR is produced by their diet, which is high in animal protein and fat (about 9 calories per gram) and low in carbohydrates (about 3 cal/gm). Like most cold-adapted populations, however, the Inuit have adapted physiologically by developing a capacity for tolerating excessive cold. For example, their peripheral body temperatures, in the hands and feet, are higher than other peoples' because of a higher rate of blood flow from the body's core to the skin.

Eskimos conform to Bergmann's and Allen's rules, having large, wide bodies and short limbs. Moreover, they have developed a technology that conserves heat: their traditional housing focuses on insulation, so that even the walls of ice-constructed "igloos" include whale rib rafters that are covered with alternating layers of seal skin and moss. Heat conductivity from a fire built beneath the main floor of the house serves to warm cold air as it rises, which is a simple but highly efficient way to heat a small interior environment.

SOLAR RADIATION AND SKIN COLOR One of the most profound environmental factors that humans deal with daily is solar radiation, or the sun's energy output, which plays a central role in the evolution and development of skin color (**Figure 5.11**). In daylight, skin—the largest organ and the most conspicuous feature of the human body, accounting for 15% of total body weight—is exposed to ultraviolet (UV) radiation, a component of solar radiation. The American anthropologists Nina Jablonski and George Chaplin have shown that the best predictor of skin color, as measured by **skin reflectance,** is UV radiation exposure. That is, the darkest skin (low skin reflectance) is associated with the highest UV radiation, and the lightest skin (high skin reflectance) is associated with the lowest UV radiation. UV radiation is highest at noon, during the summer, at the Equator, and in higher altitudes, and skin becomes darker (more pigmented) at these times and in these settings. As a result, individuals living in low latitudes or equatorial regions of the globe have some of the darkest skin pigmentation due to the more direct and prolonged UV light throughout the year. As latitude increases, the amount of UV radiation decreases and so, too, does the amount of melanin in the skin; therefore, the lightest-skinned individuals are usually in the highest latitudes. In general, populations between 20°N latitude and 20°S latitude have the darkest skin.

When first exposed to UV radiation, light skin reddens—the process commonly called sunburn. With ongoing exposure, the **melanocytes** increase the number and size of **melanin** granules. In addition, the outer layer of epidermis thickens. This darkening—that is, tanning—and thickening serves to retard penetration of the epidermis and dermis by UV radiation, protecting the individual from sunburn and possibly cancer. Because melanin is a natural sunscreen, individuals with high melanin content receive the most protection. Thus, people with dark skin, such as in equatorial Africa, are able to tolerate more exposure to sun than are those with light skin. Dark-skinned people have a **sun protection factor (SPF)** of 10 to 15; light-skinned people have an SPF of between 2 and 3. Around the world, populations with the most melanin have the fewest skin cancers and malignant melanomas. However, these effects occur largely during or after the late reproductive years, suggesting that skin cancer is not an element of natural selection.

SOLAR RADIATION AND VITAMIN D SYNTHESIS The body needs UV radiation for the synthesis of vitamin D, a steroid hormone that regulates calcium absorption and mineralization of the skeleton. Today, we obtain some vitamin D through fortified foods and by eating fatty fish such as salmon, but most vitamin D is produced in the skin. UV radiation in the form of UV photons penetrates the skin and is absorbed by a cholesterol-like substance, *7-dehydrocholesterol,* in the epidermis (keratinocytes) and dermis (fibroblasts) layers (see Figure 5.11). This process produces a previtamin D that eventually converts to vitamin D, which is released from the skin and transported via the circulatory system to the liver and kidneys. There, more chemical reactions produce the active form of vitamin D. Without this

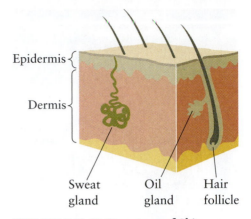

Epidermis

Dermis

Sweat gland   Oil gland   Hair follicle

FIGURE 5.11 ■ **Structure of Skin**
Skin's two main layers are the *epidermis,* which is external, and the *dermis,* which is internal. The epidermis makes the skin waterproof and contains *keratinocytes,* building blocks that manufacture the protein keratin, and *melanocytes,* specialized cells that produce the skin pigment, *melanin.* The dermis, a thicker layer of tissue, contains hair follicles, sweat glands, blood vessels, and oil glands.

skin reflectance Refers to the amount of light reflected from the skin that can be measured and used to assess skin color.

melanocytes Melanin-producing cells located in the skin's epidermis.

melanin A brown pigment that determines the darkness or lightness of a human's skin color due to its concentration in the skin.

sun protection factor (SPF) The rating calculated by comparing the length of time needed for protected skin to burn to the length of time needed for unprotected skin to burn.

FIGURE 5.12 ■ Rickets
Photographed in Hungary in 1895, these children are suffering from rickets, a disorder in which poorly mineralized bones, especially the weight-bearing leg bones, become soft, are prone to fracture, and can warp or bow. Rickets was especially prevalent in the 1800s in Europe and America. In urban settings, in particular, indoor work and air pollution decreased access to sunlight and exposure to UV radiation.

hypoxia A condition in which an organism is not able to breathe in adequate amounts of oxygen, leading to low levels of oxygen in the blood, shortness of breath, and, in extreme situations, death.

form, the bones do not mineralize properly, resulting in a condition called rickets in children and osteomalacia in adults (**Figure 5.12**).

Pregnant women and new mothers are at especially high risk of osteomalacia because a fetus or a nursing infant depletes the body's vitamin D and calcium. One telltale sign of osteomalacia in women is malformed pelvic bones, which result when poorly developed bone is unable to withstand the forces of body weight. Women with abnormal pelvic bones have trouble giving birth because the space for the fetus's passage during birth is restricted. Since a key element of natural selection is a greater number of births, this decreased reproductive capacity means that the trait—malformed pelvic bones caused by osteomalacia—is not advantageous.

Melanin, the primary influence on vitamin D synthesis, can be advantageous or nonadvantageous. That is, because melanin provides protection from solar radiation, substantial amounts of this pigment can inhibit vitamin D production. As a result, at high latitudes where there is less UV radiation, lighter skin, with less melanin, is favorable, because it allows more solar radiation to be absorbed, enabling vitamin D production. Skin needs to be dark enough to protect from UV radiation but light enough to allow solar radiation sufficient for vitamin D production.

Prior to 1 mya, all of our ancestors lived in what is now Africa, and their skin was likely pigmented highly so that it would block dangerous UV radiation. The American physiologist William Loomis has hypothesized that as human ancestors moved out of Africa into the more northerly latitudes of Europe and elsewhere, their dark skin would not have produced enough vitamin D to bring about calcium absorption and skeletal development. Therefore, in those latitudes natural selection strongly favored alleles for light skin.

HIGH ALTITUDE AND ACCESS TO OXYGEN At high altitudes, generally defined as greater than 10,000 ft (3 km) above sea level, a fall in barometric pressure reduces oxygen molecules. The primary environmental stress in such places is **hypoxia,** the condition in which body tissues receive insufficient amounts of oxygen (**Figure 5.13**).

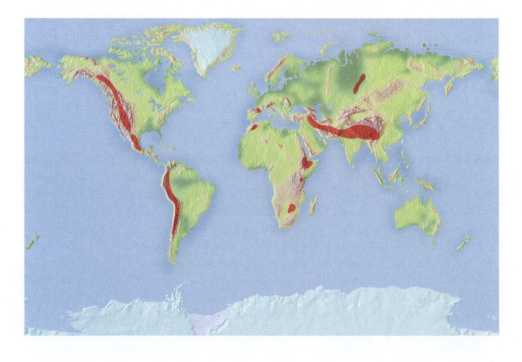

FIGURE 5.13 ■ High Altitudes
As this map shows, each continent except for Australia and Antarctica has at least one high-altitude area (shaded in red). A lack of oxygen is among the conditions to which humans must adapt at high altitudes.

Adaptation: Heat, Cold, Solar Radiation, High Altitude

Humans display both short-term adjustments and long-term adaptations to environmental extremes. These responses are crucial for maintaining homeostasis.

SETTING	EXPOSURE AND ADAPTATION	CHARACTERISTICS
Heat	First exposure	Vasodilation, profuse sweating, but effects reduce with continuous exposure.
	Functional adaptation	Less sweating, normal work performance.
	Genetic adaptation	Narrow body, long limbs.
Cold	First exposure	Vasoconstriction, shivering, but effects reduce after continuous exposure brings warmer skin temperature.
	Functional adaptation	Tolerance to cold and to lowering of skin temperature, metabolic heat lower than that of nonadapted populations, peripheral body temperature higher than that of nonadapted populations.
	Genetic adaptation	Large, wide body; short limbs.
Solar/UV radiation	First exposure	Reddening of skin (sunburn), followed by increased melanin production by melanocytes.
	Functional adaptation	Tanning, thickening of skin.
	Genetic adaptation	High melanin production (dark skin).
High altitude	First exposure	Hypoxia results in headache, nausea, loss of appetite, fatigue, and breathlessness, but symptoms disappear after a few days.
	Functional adaptation	Greater diameter of arteries and veins and greater relative blood flow to body tissues, greater lung volume, more efficient use of oxygen, larger chest size in some populations (reflecting greater lung volume).
	Genetic adaptation	High oxygen saturation in hemoglobin.

Secondary stresses include high UV radiation, cold, wind, nutritional deprivation, and the rigors of living in highly variable, generally rugged terrain.

The severity of hypoxia increases as a person moves higher, and the associated risk increases because all body tissues and physiological processes require an uninterrupted oxygen supply. Hypoxia results in mountain sickness, with headache, nausea, loss of appetite, fatigue, and breathlessness occurring at about 8,000 ft (2.4 km) during rest and about 6,500 ft (1.9 km) during physical activity. For some individuals living at sea level or in prehypoxic conditions who travel to high altitudes or otherwise experience hypoxia, mountain sickness becomes a life-threatening condition. For most people, the symptoms disappear within the first few days of exposure as the body begins to more efficiently use reduced amounts of oxygen in the air and homeostasis is restored. Extra red blood cells and oxygen-saturated

FIGURE 5.14 ■ **Tibetan Nomads**
Tibetan nomads, such as this woman being pulled by yaks as she ploughs a field, live in high-altitude areas and are shorter than Tibetans living in lowlands. Among the nomads' physical and physiological adaptations to their environment are large lungs, better lung function, and higher oxygen saturation in arteries.

hemoglobin are produced. The hemoglobin transports oxygen to body tissues, while an expansion in the diameter of arteries and of veins allows increased blood flow and increased access to oxygen.

Additional physiological changes represent a long-term response to hypoxia. A person who moved to the high-altitude settings of the Himalayas, for example, would function better there over time. A young child who moved there would, through growth and development, develop greater lung volume and the ability to use oxygen more efficiently. Human populations who have lived at high altitudes for many generations—such as those in the Peruvian Andes—have larger chest cavities than do populations at low altitudes, reflecting the high-altitude populations' inherited increases in lung volume. However, these populations are generally shorter than their low-altitude counterparts. Widespread growth retardation results from the increased energy required to live in cold environments with little oxygen and poor nutrition. But some biological attributes associated with living at high altitudes may offer selective advantages. For example, the American physical anthropologist Cynthia Beall and colleagues have found that Tibetan women with alleles for high oxygen saturation in their hemoglobin, a factor that enhances the body's access to oxygen, have more surviving children. Thus, hypoxia at high altitudes can be an agent of natural selection (**Figure 5.14**).

Nutritional Adaptation: Energy, Nutrients, and Function

MACRONUTRIENTS AND MICRONUTRIENTS Climate is only one key area in which humans adapt. We also adapt to *diet,* or the kinds of foods we eat, and *nutrition,* the deriving of nutrients from those foods. Such adaptation is crucial to acquiring the necessary energy and nutrients for reproduction, growth, and development.

Each body function requires a certain amount of energy and particular nutrients, and a lack of energy or of nutrients can hamper body functions. Like many other primates (the other primates are discussed in chapter 6), humans are omnivorous, eating a wide range of both plants and animals. This dietary plasticity enhances our access to the nutrients we need for function and survival, and in terms of adaptability and evolution it reflects humans' unique combination of biology and culture.

Nutritionists have developed two sets of dietary recommendations: those based on energy requirements and those based on nutrient requirements. Measured in calories, the minimum energy needed to keep a person alive is called the **basal metabolic requirement.** A person needs additional energy for other functions, such as work and exercise, thermoregulation, growth, and reproduction (pregnancy and lactation). The **total daily energy expenditure (TDEE)** consists of the basal metabolic requirement plus all the other energy requirements, and we fulfill all these energy requirements by consuming specific **macronutrients** (carbohydrates, fats, and proteins) in food and **micronutrients** (vitamins and minerals) in food as well as in multivitamins. **Table 5.1** shows the daily minimum amounts of micronutrients required by adult men in different countries. The lack of these essential vitamins and minerals, even those required in small amounts, can have devastating effects. For example, lack of folate in a pregnant woman can lead to

basal metabolic requirement The minimum amount of energy needed to keep an organism alive.

total daily energy expenditure (TDEE) The number of calories used by an organism's body during a 24-hour period.

macronutrients Essential chemical nutrients, including fat, carbohydrates, and protein, that a body needs to live and to function normally.

micronutrients Essential substances, such as minerals or vitamins, needed in very small amounts to maintain normal body functioning.

TABLE 5.1	Recommended Daily Intakes for Selected Nutrients for Adult Men			
NUTRIENT	**UNITED STATES**	**CANADA**	**UNITED KINGDOM**	**FAO/WHO[1]**
Protein (g)	56	61	72	52.5
Calcium (mg)	800	800	500	400–500
Phosphorus (mg)	800	800	—	—
Iron (mg)	10	8	10	8–23
Vitamin A (µg)	1000	1000	750	600
Vitamin D (µg)	5	2.5	2.5	2.5
Vitamin C (mg)	60	60	30	30
Folate (µg)	400	220	—	200
Vitamin E (mg)	10	9	—	—
Vitamin B-12 (µg)	3.0	2.0	—	1.0
Magnesium (mg)	350	250	—	—
Zinc (mg)	15	9	—	11
Iodine (µg)	150	160	—	—

SOURCE: Derived from Table 9.1 in Leonard, W. R. 2000. Human nutritional evolution. Pp. 295–343 in S. Stinson, B. Bogin, R. Huss-Ashmore, and D. O'Rourke, eds. *Human Biology: An Evolutionary and Biocultural Perspective.* New York: Wiley-Liss, Inc. Leonard's data is derived from Gibson, R. 1990. *Principles of Nutritional Assessment.* Oxford, UK: Oxford University Press.
1. Food and Agriculture Organization/World Health Organization.

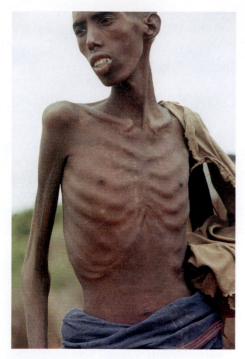

FIGURE 5.15 ■ Malnutrition
Malnutrition is a substantial problem in many parts of the world. Both of its forms—undernutrition, or insufficient consumption of calories and/or micronutrients, and overnutrition, or excessive consumption of calories and/or micronutrients—can have detrimental health consequences. Chronic undernutrition is a persistent problem for populations of many developing nations. This emaciated Somalian man, for example, has not been able to consume enough food to sustain normal body weight.

neural tube defects, such as spina bifida, in the fetus. Many foods we commonly eat in the United States, such as cereal, bread, and milk, are fortified with some of these essential nutrients.

HUMAN NUTRITION TODAY The majority of human populations across the world are undernourished (consuming fewer than 2,000 calories per day), especially in developing nations of Africa, of South and Central America, and across large regions of Asia (**Figure 5.15**). In the later twentieth century, governments across the world collaborated on increasing agricultural production to relieve famine and starvation. Currently, resources are directed at enhancing the nutritional attributes of key grains, particularly rice and corn. As a result of these international efforts, grains are more readily available and of better quality. This focus on grains has contributed, however, to a growing decline in the diversity of foods consumed by human populations, especially in nutritionally stressed settings. Increased agricultural production might help meet populations' caloric needs, but attention is shifting to increasing the availability of additional micronutrients—such as vitamin A, vitamins B_6 and B_{12}, vitamin D, iodine, iron, and zinc—through meat and other animal products.

Among the consequences of poor nutrition is the suppression of the immune system. Owing to poor living circumstances and poor sanitation conditions, meanwhile, undernourished populations are especially susceptible to the spread and maintenance of infectious disease. Thus, undernutrition and infection work hand-in-hand—each exacerbates the other, and the combination is much worse for the health and well-being of the individual than is either one alone.

Universally, undernourished populations experience stunted growth, resulting in shortness for all age periods. The American economist David Seckler has hypothesized that shortness in height is an adaptation to reduced food supplies, one with no costs to individual health. The record shows quite the opposite, however: individuals who are undernourished typically have poor general functioning, reduced work capacity, ill health, and shortened life expectancy. Short individuals might require fewer calories and nutrients, but the associated health cost is huge.

Moreover, it is highly unlikely that undernourished populations' shortness is a genetic adaptation. Where energy and nutrition became adequate or abundant following periods of disruption and deprivation, body size rebounded. For example, in many countries, especially in Europe and Asia, World War II had a profoundly negative impact on growth. In the Netherlands, 1944 and 1945 were known as the "starving years." Following the war, children and adults began growing again thanks to the return of adequate nutrition (**Figure 5.16**).

OVERNUTRITION AND THE CONSEQUENCES OF DIETARY EXCESS Much of the above discussion about nutrition focused on shortfalls and the consequences of not getting enough of some nutrient or food or energy. Increasingly around the world, the problem is becoming just the opposite: too much food and too many of the wrong kinds of food. These dietary choices have negative consequences for health and well-being (**Figure 5.17**). In the U.S., adults have increased their body weight by an average of 24 pounds (11 kg) over the last four decades, and over 50% of adults are overweight. The average weight of six- to 11-year-old children increased from 65 pounds (29 kg) in 1963–65 to 74 pounds (33 kg) in 1999–2002. Today, 20% of American children are overweight or obese. Obesity was mostly unknown in the 1950s, but since the early 1990s it has become a "growing" problem, not only in the U.S. but in some areas of the Pacific, most of Europe and the Middle East, Latin America, and South Africa.

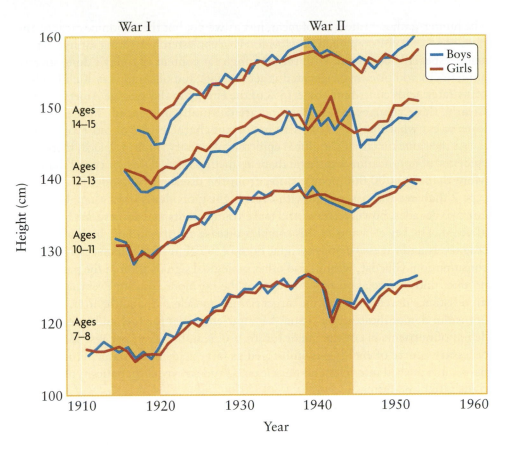

FIGURE 5.16 ■ **Malnutrition and Height**
Height is a sensitive indicator of diet and health. During periods of insufficient nutrition, growth can be slowed or arrested, leading to reduced adult stature. If, however, proper nutrition is restored before adulthood, a recovery period can follow, during which growth "catches up" to where it should be. This graph shows the heights of boys and girls of various ages in Germany during and after World Wars I and II. During the wars, food shortages negatively affected growth in height. Following the wars, food was more abundant and growth was not inhibited. What might account for the general increase in growth from 1910 through 1950?

The reasons for the increase are complex, but they basically boil down to the increased ability to produce inexpensive food, most of which is high in fat, and advances in transportation technology, which provides greater access to cheap food sources. More and more people, in other words, are expending less and less energy to consume a poor diet, rich in calories and low in micronutrients.

As the obesity rates have climbed, so has **hypercholesterolemia,** or high cholesterol, a predisposing factor for coronary heart disease. The cholesterol levels of traditional hunter-gatherers (and of our ancestors) averaged 125 mg/dl (milligram per deciliter of blood), but the average level of Americans today exceeds 200 mg/dl.

hypercholesterolemia The presence of high levels of cholesterol in an organism's blood; this condition may result from the dietary consumption of foods that promote high cholesterol or through the inheritance of a genetic disorder.

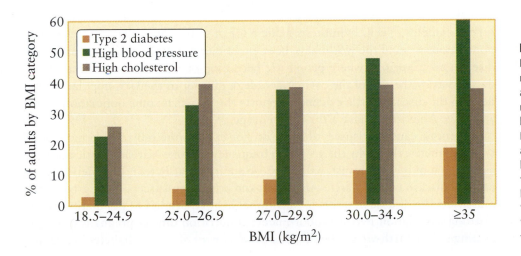

FIGURE 5.17 ■ **Overnutrition**
Like undernutrition, overnutrition has many negative consequences for health and well-being. As this graph shows, the risks of diabetes, high blood pressure, and high cholesterol increase substantially as BMI increases. BMI, or body mass index, is a statistical measure of weight according to height. A BMI between 18.5 and 24.9 indicates that a person has normal weight for his or her height. A BMI between 25 and 29.9 means "overweight," while 30 or above means "obese," where excess weight is so extreme that health and function are compromised.

The hunter-gatherers ate a lot of meat, just as we do, but the nondomesticated animals of 15,000 yBP contained very low levels of cholesterol-elevating saturated fatty acids, especially compared with the very high fat content of today's domesticated animals. In addition, hydrogenated vegetable fats and oils and very high levels of trans-fatty acids contribute some 15% of the energy in the average American diet. Clearly, these changes in consumption are culturally influenced. That is, people learn to eat what they eat. This is an important characteristic of our evolution.

At the same time that the global epidemic of obesity is taking place, there is an epidemic of non-insulin-dependent diabetes mellitus (NIDDM), or **type 2 diabetes**. More than 100,000,000 people suffer from the disease worldwide. Historically, type 2 diabetes was associated with overweight individuals older than 40. In the last two decades, however, more and more young adults and adolescents have been affected. The key elements of this complex disease are abnormally high blood glucose levels and excessive body weight, both of which result from excessive caloric consumption. Glucose, weight, and other biological signals prompt the pancreas to produce and secrete abnormal amounts of the hormone insulin. Eventually, insulin resistance develops at specific target tissues: muscle, fat, and the liver. The lack of insulin denies these target tissues key nutrients used for fuel and storage. This denial of nutrients is not the major health problem, however, because glucose—a necessary source of energy—is still stored as fatty acids in fat tissue. From the fat tissue, it is pushed into liver and muscle cells, and so type 2 diabetics typically become fatter and fatter.

The major health problem is that the extra glucose increases the blood's viscosity, and the thickened blood damages blood vessels in the kidneys, eyes, and extremities. In advanced stages of the disease, the kidneys function poorly, vision is reduced, and blood does not flow adequately to the hands, arms, feet, and legs. There is also a great chance of cardiac disease and stroke.

Is there an adaptive component to the disease? In the early 1960s, the American geneticist James V. Neel noted the high percentages of type 2 diabetes among Native Americans. In the early twentieth century, the disease had been virtually nonexistent in Native Americans, but after World War II it increased to the point of affecting more than half of some Native American tribes. Neel hypothesized a "thrifty genotype," one that during times of plenty stored energy efficiently in the form of glucose in fat tissue. For Native Americans, who lived a feast-or-famine lifeway, such a thrifty genotype for a rapid insulin trigger would have been a benefit. For populations that lived an abundant lifeway, the consequences of type 2 diabetes would have triggered a selection against the thrifty genotype.

Given the data in the 1960s, when only some populations around the world had type 2 diabetes, Neel's hypothesis made a lot of sense. Since that time, however, populations around the world have been experiencing an alarming increase in the disease, all in regions where people are becoming obese. Current projections indicate that by the end of the current decade, a quarter of the U.S. population will develop the disease. Little evidence supports the idea that some populations, such as Native Americans, have a thrifty genotype.

If genetic causes or susceptibilities do not explain the remarkable increase in type 2 diabetes, then why the very high frequency in some Native Americans, such as the Pima of the Southwest, half of whose adults are afflicted? To understand the cause of disease among Native Americans and other high-susceptibility groups, one must view the disease in terms of nutritional history. Studies of populations show a strong association between poor maternal nutrition during pregnancy (usually leading to low-birth-weight babies) and development of type 2 diabetes in later life

type 2 diabetes A disease in which the body does not produce sufficient amounts of insulin or the cells do not use available insulin, causing a buildup of glucose in the cells.

rigidity (bone) Refers to the strength of bone to resist bending and torsion.

osteoblasts Cells responsible for bone formation.

Nutritional Adaptation

Food and the nutrition it provides are critical aspects of human life. Both under- and over-nourishment have negative consequences for all human populations.

CONDITION	CHARACTERISTICS
Undernutrition	Too few calories and/or specific nutrients; reduced growth, slower growth, susceptibility to infection, predisposition to adult disease (e.g., cardiovascular disease) and early adult death.
Overnutrition	Too many calories, resulting in excess stored fat (obesity); associated health risks include type 2 diabetes, osteoarthritis, hypertension, cardiovascular disease, stroke, early adult death.

among the offspring. The American anthropologist Daniel Benyshek and his colleagues make the strong case that Native Americans and other populations with high incidence of type 2 diabetes share a common history of severe nutritional deprivation. Moreover, the effects of malnutrition are perpetuated for generations, even in subsequent generations no longer experiencing malnutrition. That is, the metabolism of children gestated under such conditions becomes permanently "programmed," leading to comparable developmental programming effects in their children, and thereby continuing the cycle for generations.

The incidence of type 2 diabetes is relatively low in other Native American populations, such as those inhabiting the Aleutian Islands, Alaska. Unlike native populations in the American Southwest, Aleutian Islanders lack a history of severe malnutrition. Clearly, the disease is related to activity and diet. During adulthood, too little activity and too many calories are risk factors for any population. But the impact of poor diet on the growing fetus is crucial for understanding the high prevalence of type 2 diabetes in humans today.

Workload Adaptation: Skeletal Homeostasis and Function

Homeostasis depends on the health of all the body's tissues, including the bone tissues. The skeleton must be maintained so that it can support the body and enable the body to move. Without this essential framework, where would tendons, ligaments, and muscles be attached and how would they get the leverage needed for their use?

Bones' growth and development are subject to a range of factors. Strongly controlled by genes, they are also affected by various physiological processes, disease, and nutrition. As discussed above, poor nutrition in childhood may result in short stature, both in children and in the adults they become. Various mechanical forces also affect bones' growth and development. The bones of the arms and legs, for example, are subject to bending and torsion, or twisting, whenever they are used. Bones' **rigidity,** or strength, is a functional adaptation to these forces, preventing fracture in the course of normal use (**Figure 5.18**). During growth and development, physical activity stimulates bone-forming cells, called **osteoblasts,** which produce

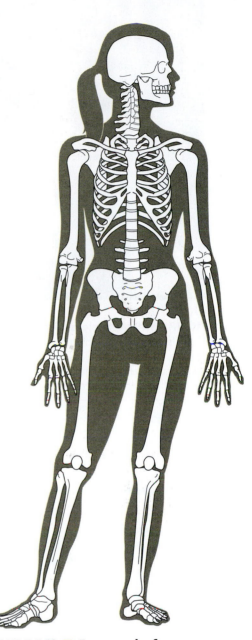

FIGURE 5.18 ■ **Framework of the Human Body**
Just as a building needs its framework, the human body needs the skeleton for support and rigidity. In addition to maintaining the body's shape and enabling its movement, the skeleton protects the many vital organs (such as by encasing the brain in the cranium). It makes possible the production of red blood cells (within the marrow cavities of bones). And it serves as a storage facility for minerals, which can be retrieved at any time (but which minerals would you expect to be stored in bone?).

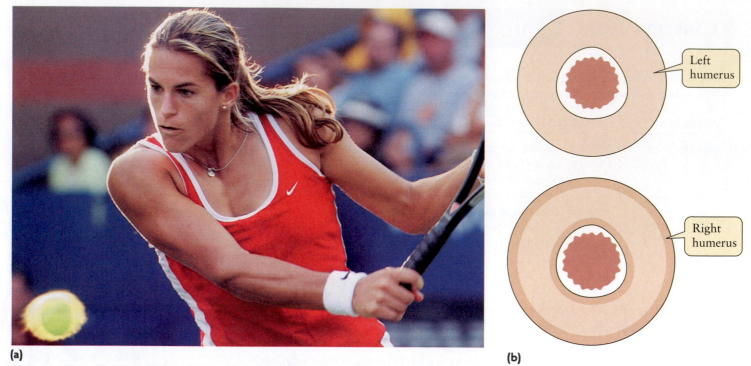

(a)

(b)

FIGURE 5.19 ■ Skeletal Remodeling and Athletics
The "playing" arms of athletes in certain sports undergo remodeling as a result of stress. **(a)** A baseball pitcher or a tennis player (such as, here, the professional player Amelie Mauresmo) typically has a dominant arm, which is used to a much greater degree than the nondominant arm. **(b)** The upper arm bone, or humerus, of the dominant arm may be much stronger than that of the nondominant arm. In these cross-sections, note the greater diameter of the right humerus.

bone mass The density of bone per unit of measure.

osteoclasts Cells responsible for bone resorption.

Wolff's Law The principle that bone is placed in the direction of functional demand; that is, bone develops where needed and recedes where it is not needed.

bone mass where it is needed to maintain the rigidity of specific bones and bone regions. In the absence of physical activity, other cells, called **osteoclasts,** remove bone mass. A principle called **Wolff's Law** lays out the homeostatic balance of osteoblastic and osteoclastic activity, in which bone mass is produced where it is needed and taken away where it is not needed.

Wolff's Law also accounts for the remodeling of bone that occurs during life, the changing of certain bones' shapes as the result of particular activities. Because the movements of tendons, ligaments, and muscles put stress on individual bones, repetitive actions eventually can cause those bones to reinforce themselves by adding more material. Just as you need to reinforce a shelf if it starts to buckle under the weight it holds, so the body is likely to try preventing a bone from breaking under added weight or stress (**Figure 5.19**).

At the other end of the spectrum, people who are physically inactive—such as from partial or full immobilization—have less dense bones because osteoblasts are not stimulated to produce bone mass (**Figure 5.20**). The resulting decline in bone density may weaken the skeleton. For example, the skeletons of astronauts who have been in outer space for extended periods of time have remarkable loss in bone density. Around the world, children who are less physically active tend to have smaller and less developed bones than children who are more physically active. Children with less bone mass due to habitual physical *in*activity become predisposed, as adults, to osteoporosis and fracture. Similarly, according to a biomechanical engineers' study of military recruits' leg bones, young men and women who have better-developed muscles and greater bone mass are less susceptible to fractures than are young men and women who have less-developed muscles and less bone mass.

Studying the larger picture of human variation, anthropologists have learned that highly physically active human populations—those that do lots of walking, lifting, carrying, or anything else that "stresses" the skeleton—have bones with optimum density. In addition, the diameters of long bones in populations with active lifestyles are greater than those in populations that are physically inactive. These greater diameters provide the bones with higher rigidity, increasing their ability to resist bending and torsion (this phenomenon is discussed further in chapter 11).

Excessive Activity and Reproductive Ecology

The biological benefits of physical activity are clear. Exercise improves physical fitness by contributing to bone strength, helping lower blood pressure and cholesterol, increasing heart function and lung function, and so on. Exercise that becomes an excessive workload, however, can hinder female reproductive function, a crucial factor in evolution. Many studies have shown that an excessive workload, such as regular intense aerobic exercise, can interrupt menstrual function, resulting in lower fertility. Even milder levels of physical activity have reduced the reproductive potential of some women. For example, a study of a large number of women from Washington State revealed that those who engage in more than an hour of exercise per day and whose body weights are 85% that of the average American woman are five to six times more likely to not be able to conceive within one year than are women who do not exercise and have normal weight. Two important implications stand out from this and other studies on workload and ovarian function. First, human populations requiring heavy work by reproductive-age women will have reduced birthrates. Second, and in the larger picture of human adaptation and evolution, amount of work is an important selective factor—a population with relatively high fitness will likely not require excessive energy expenditure, at least for reproductive-age women.

Anthropologists have shown that the classification of humans into different types, or races, simply does not provide meaningful information about variation. While race may be an enduring social concept, it is not valid biologically. Understanding human variation in an evolutionary context—that is, understanding people's remarkable adaptability to a wide range of environmental circumstances throughout the stages of growth, from conception through old age and senescence—is far more productive than attempting to classify different types of the human organism. Just as humans represent a continuum, so they are part of a larger continuum that includes their fellow primates, with whom they share a range of characteristics, many common adaptations, and much evolutionary history. As we will explore in the next chapter, the nonhuman primates provide an important record of adaptability and flexibility, one of the great success stories of mammalian evolution.

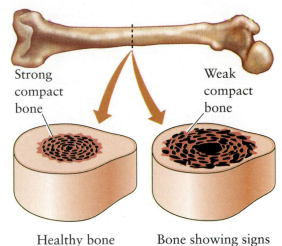

Strong compact bone

Weak compact bone

Healthy bone

Bone showing signs of osteoporosis

FIGURE 5.20 ■ Bone Disuse
When bones are not used routinely or for extended periods of time, bone density can decrease. Typically, the loss occurs on the inner surface of the bone, making the bone more fragile. The outer, compact bone becomes thinner as the bone marrow, or medullary cavity, in the middle increases in diameter. In this drawing, the osteoporotic bone, on the right, has a much thinner outer compact bone and a larger bone marrow cavity than does the healthy bone.

ANSWERING THE BIG QUESTIONS

Is race a valid, biologically meaningful concept?

- Race is a typological leftover from pre-evolutionary, taxonomic interpretations of biological variation. Race is neither a useful nor an appropriate biological concept.
- Human variation is clinal. In general, traits (skin color, cranial form, and genetic polymorphisms) do not correlate in their distribution. There would have to be a concordance of traits for races to exist.

What do growth and development tell us about human variation?

- Differentiation and development of all the body organs occur during the prenatal stage of life. Environmental stress during this stage predisposes the individual to disease later in adulthood.
- The postnatal stage—from infancy to childhood to the juvenile period to adolescence to adulthood—involves growth acceleration and deceleration. Childhood and adolescence are long events, in which adult behaviors are learned, individuals become completely mature, and the reproductive capacity develops.
- Old age and senescence have long been ignored as an important life stage. The length of the period is unique to humans. Individuals older than 50 play important roles in the care of young, in food provisioning for the young, and as sources of information for other members of their kin groups and societies.

How do people adapt to environmental extremes and other circumstances?

- Humans are remarkably responsive to their surrounding environments. Some adaptations to the environment are genetic (e.g., skin color), whereas others occur within the individual's lifetime and either have a genetic basis and are irreversible

(e.g., lung volume in high altitude) or have a genetic basis and are reversible (e.g., skin tanning). Biological change associated with all forms of adaptation occurs to maintain homeostasis.
- Most functional adaptations—adaptations that occur during the individual's lifetime—have important implications for evolution, such as selection for darker skin near the equator and for lighter skin in northern latitudes.
- Skin color (pigmentation) is subject to forces of evolution. Evolution of skin color is strongly influenced by environmental circumstances, especially by the amount of UV radiation. UV radiation is the catalyst for the skin's synthesis of vitamin D. Light skin evolved in areas with reduced UV radiation.
- Adaptation in high altitudes where less oxygen is available includes increased lung volume and a circulatory system that more efficiently transports oxygen throughout the body. Some differences between high-altitude populations and other populations may be evolutionary (genetic), such as high oxygen saturation in the high-altitude populations.
- Undernutrition is not the result of adaptation—the body either receives adequate nutrition and access to energy (calories) and nutrients or it is deficient in these resources. Nutritional deficiencies promote growth disruption, disease, and reduced fertility. Much of the human population globally is deficient in energy, nutrients, or both. In developed and underdeveloped nations around the world, obesity is a growing health threat, and associated health problems include high blood pressure, type 2 diabetes, osteoarthritis, various cancers, and heart disease.
- The key element of workload adaptation is skeletal function and maintenance of bone strength. Strength of bone and its ability to support the body are determined by density and distribution of bone tissue in cross-section.
- High levels of physical activity have a negative effect on women's reproductive potential.

ⓢ **wwnorton.com/studyspace**

KEY TERMS

adult stage	basal metabolic rate (BMR)
aging	basal metabolic requirement
Allen's Rule	Bergmann's Rule
anthropometry	bone mass

cline
cognitive abilities
deciduous dentition
diaphyses
epiphyses
functional adaptations
growth velocity
homeostasis
homeothermic
hypercholesterolemia
hypothermia
hypoxia
intrauterine
lactation
life history
macronutrients
melanin
melanocytes
menarche
menopause
micronutrients

motor skills
nonmineralized
osteoblasts
osteoclasts
osteoporosis
postnatal stage
prenatal stage
rigidity (bone)
secular trend
senescence
sexual dimorphism
skin reflectance
stressors
sun protection factor (SPF)
total daily energy expenditure (TDEE)
type 2 diabetes
vasoconstriction
vasodilation
weaning
Wolff's Law

ADDITIONAL READINGS

Barker, D. J. P. 1996. The origins of coronary heart disease in early life. Pp. 155–162 in C. J. K. Henry and S. J. Ulijaszek, eds. *Long-Term Consequences of Early Environment: Growth, Development and the Lifespan Developmental Perspective.* Cambridge, UK: Cambridge University Press.

Bogin, B. 1999. *Patterns of Human Growth.* 2nd ed. Cambridge, UK: Cambridge University Press.

Brace, C. L. 2005. *"Race" Is a Four-Letter Word: The Genesis of a Concept.* New York: Oxford University Press.

Crews, D. E. 2003. *Human Senescence: Evolutionary and Biocultural Perspectives.* Cambridge, UK: Cambridge University Press.

Frisancho, A. R. 1993. *Human Adaptation and Accommodation.* Ann Arbor: University of Michigan Press.

Gould, S. J. 1996. *The Mismeasure of Man.* New York: Norton.

Jablonski, N. G. 2006. *Skin: A Natural History.* Berkeley: University of California Press.

Marks, J. 1995. *Human Biodiversity: Genes, Race, and History.* New York: Aldine de Gruyter.

Stinson, S., B. Bogin, R. Huss-Ashmore, and D. O'Rourke, eds. 2000. *Human Biology: An Evolutionary and Biocultural Perspective.* New York: Wiley-Liss.

Wolpoff, M. H. and R. Caspari. 1997. *Race and Human Evolution: A Fatal Attraction.* New York: Simon & Schuster.

At Gombe National Park, Tanzania, in 1972, one of her research subjects examines Jane Goodall, who sometimes hid bananas for the chimpanzees beneath her shirt. A world-renowned primatologist, Goodall established the Jane Goodall Institute, dedicated to preserving wildlife worldwide. Projects spearheaded by the Institute, such as sanctuaries in Africa for orphaned chimpanzees, provide opportunities for continued research and educational outreach, as well as jobs for local communities.

CHAPTER 6

Biology in the Present: The Other Living Primates

Of all the scientists mentioned in this book so far, Jane Goodall (see "What Do Physical Anthropologists Do?" in chapter 1) may be the most famous. But when Goodall began doing what she most loves— observing primates and talking about them[1]—about the only people who had heard of her were family and friends in her native England. Since childhood, Goodall had dreamed of living in Africa, and in 1957, after graduating from secretarial school and holding a series of odd jobs, she traveled with a friend to Kenya. Within two months, she had met the famous fossil hunter Louis Leakey (fossils are the subject of chapter 7; you will hear more about Leakey in chapter 9), who eventually employed her at the museum in Nairobi.

Leakey was interested in human origins and had long thought that studying chimpanzees in the wild would be a window onto the behavior and social organization of early humans. After getting to know the energetic and highly competent Goodall, he decided she was the right person to pursue this line of inquiry. She enthusiastically agreed to live among and study chimpanzees in Gombe, a remote area along the shores of Lake Tanganyika, in western Tanzania. This venture would have been discouraging to most. No one had ever observed chimpanzees in the wild for an extended period or in the kind of detail needed to record behavior and draw conclusions. Moreover, living in the jungle was no easy undertaking—it was full of uncertainty and danger.

The outcome proved even more amazing than Leakey might have imagined. A few months after reaching her field site in 1960, Goodall was able to **habituate** the chimpanzees to her presence, observe them for hours on end, and record their behaviors in unprecedented detail. Her findings bowled over the anthropological world. Chimpanzees proved highly intelligent, for example, and close social bonds existed between chimpanzee mothers and their offspring and between chimpanzee siblings. Goodall also discovered behaviors that other scientists found quite hard to believe, mainly because the behaviors did not fit expectations about the species. First, Goodall documented in words and on film how chimps made stick probes to harvest termites from termite nests, and how they crumpled up leaves to make a

habituate Refers to the process of animals becoming accustomed to human observers.

Gombe National Park, Tanzania

---

[1] Throughout this chapter, *primates* refers to nonhuman primates except where otherwise specified.

BIG QUESTIONS

- What is a primate?

- What are the kinds of primates?

- What is special about primate societies and social behavior?

- How do primates acquire food?

primatologists Researchers that study nonhuman primates.

kind of sponge, with which they soaked up rainwater from the crooks of trees and then squeezed the water into their mouths. That chimps used tools was an exciting discovery because it narrowed the perceived behavioral chasm between humans and apes, our closest living relatives. Second, Goodall discovered that chimpanzees regularly hunted other primates and animals. Chimps were not vegetarians!

A skilled scientist, formulating hypotheses, testing them with careful field observations, and drawing conclusions based on her observations, Goodall single-handedly began an entirely new direction in primate studies. Many of the scores of **primatologists**—those who study primates—working around the world today owe their intellectual origins to her or to people who have emulated her style of careful scientific inquiry. Among the diverse disciplines that incorporate primate studies are anthropology, biology, ecology, psychology, paleontology, anatomy, genetics, and medicine. Animal and plant conservationists also study primates, in large part because the tropics—where many primate species live—are disappearing by the hundreds of thousands of acres around the world annually, mostly due to forest clearing and human encroachment. Primates serve as a barometer of species losses and extinctions; if primates are disappearing, then so are many other animals.

Still, research by Goodall and other primatologists shows that as an order primates have adapted to a wide range of environments. Living primates inhabit many kinds of landscapes and widely diverse climates, as past primates did. Some primates live in the bitter cold of northern Japan, others in the humid tropics of Brazil (**Figure 6.1**). Individual types of primates vary in their adaptive ranges. Humans and macaques can live in a range of terrestrial environments, whereas others are limited to tropical settings. Apes today, for example, are narrowly adapted in that they cannot live outside tropical environments. Other important characteristics of the primate order are intelligence, variable diets, complex social behavior, and longevity.

Many types of primates have some of the same diseases as humans or ones closely related to human diseases, and so the study of primate diseases can save human lives, such as by leading to vaccine production. Chimpanzees are susceptible to polio, for example, and the vaccine for this once-dreaded disease, which killed and debilitated millions around the world, was developed in the 1950s via research on chimps.

In addition, the anatomical similarity between apes and humans provides important clues about human origins (discussed further in chapter 8). Comparisons of apes' and humans' muscles and bones, for example, suggest what the common ancestor and the earliest hominid may have looked like.

In this chapter, we will consider how primates are defined, how they are classified (taxonomy), where they live (geography), their physical characteristics (anatomy), and key aspects of their social behavior, especially in the important linkage between social organization, ecology, and diet (socioecology). All of this information will provide the context for Part II of this book, which is about the origins and evolution of primates and of humans.

WHAT IS A PRIMATE?

When Linnaeus first defined the order *Primates,* in the eighteenth century (see "Taxonomy and Systematics: Classifying Living Organisms and Identifying Their Biological Relationships" in chapter 2), he did so purely for classification purposes

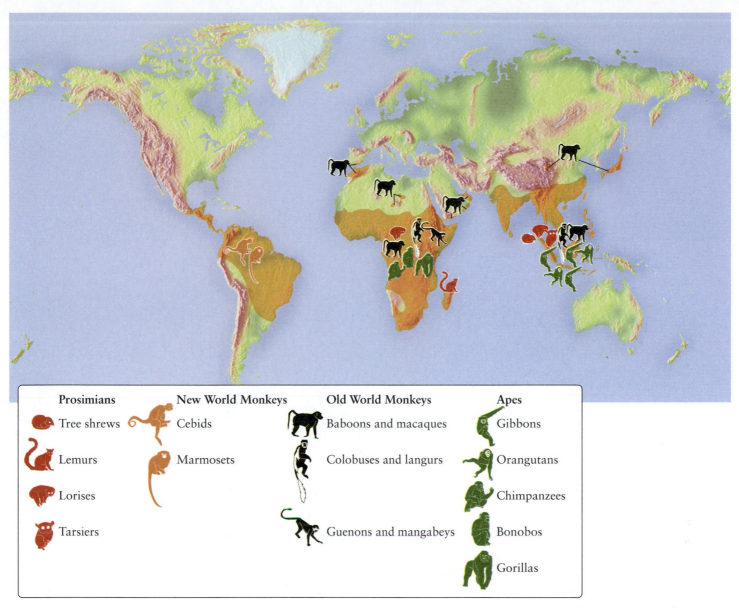

Prosimians

🔴 Tree shrews

🔴 Lemurs

🔴 Lorises

🔴 Tarsiers

New World Monkeys

🟤 Cebids

🟤 Marmosets

Old World Monkeys

⚫ Baboons and macaques

⚫ Colobuses and langurs

⚫ Guenons and mangabeys

Apes

🟢 Gibbons

🟢 Orangutans

🟢 Chimpanzees

🟢 Bonobos

🟢 Gorillas

and focused on descriptive traits. Physical anthropologists, however, define primates on the basis of behavioral, adaptive, or evolutionary tendencies. The eminent British anatomist Sir Wilfrid E. Le Gros Clark (1895–1971) identified three prominent tendencies:

1. Primates are adapted to life in the trees—they express **arboreal adaptation** in a set of behaviors and anatomical characteristics that is unique among mammals;
2. Primates eat a wide variety of foods—they express **dietary plasticity**;
3. Primates invest a lot of time and care in few offspring—they express **parental investment**.

In addition to these tendencies, the physical and behavioral characteristics discussed below identify primates as a separate order of mammals.

Meanwhile, the panoramic view on the next two pages (**Figure 6.2**) provides a sense of primates' remarkable diversity. Depicted in the Taï Forest, in Ivory Coast,

FIGURE 6.1 ■ Primate Distribution
As shown on this map, primates inhabit every continent except Antarctica and Australia. New World primates live in North and South America, while Old World primates live in Europe, Africa, and Asia. Although they are often considered tropical animals that live in forested settings, primate species exist in a wide range of environments.

arboreal adaptation A suite of physical traits that enable an organism to live in trees.

dietary plasticity A diet's flexibility in adapting to a given environment.

parental investment The time and energy parents expend for their offspring's benefit.

Generalized Skeletal Structure

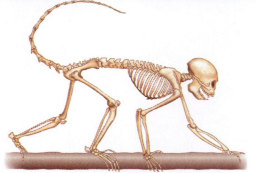

Primates have a generalized skeletal structure. The bones that make up the shoulders, upper limbs, lower limbs, and other major joints such as the hands and feet are separate, giving primates a great deal of flexibility when moving in trees. In this monkey skeleton, note the grasping hands and feet, the long tail, and the equal length of the front and hind limbs relative to each other.

Enhanced Touch

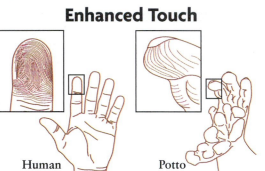

Human   Potto

Primates have an enhanced sense of touch. This sensitivity is due in part to the presence of dermal ridges (fingerprints and toe prints) on the inside surfaces of the hands and feet. The potto, a prosimian, has primitive dermal ridges, whereas the human, a higher primate, has more derived ridges, which provide better gripping ability.

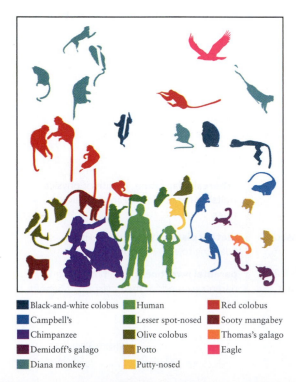

■ Black-and-white colobus	■ Human	■ Red colobus
■ Campbell's	■ Lesser spot-nosed	■ Sooty mangabey
■ Chimpanzee	■ Olive colobus	■ Thomas's galago
■ Demidoff's galago	■ Potto	■ Eagle
■ Diana monkey	■ Putty-nosed	

Emerging canopy

Main canopy

Understory

Enhanced Vision

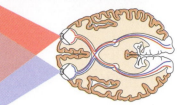

Overlapping visual fields

Primates have an enhanced sense of vision. Evolution has given primates better vision, including increased depth perception and seeing in color. The eyes' convergence provides significant overlap in the visual fields and thus greater sense of depth.

Reduced Smell

Primates have a reduced sense of smell. The smaller and less projecting snouts of most primates indicate their decreased reliance on smell.

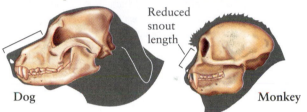

Reduced snout length

Dog

Monkey

Dietary Versatility

I1
I2
C
P3
P4
M1
M2
M3

Primates have dietary plasticity. Part of the record of primate dietary adaption is found in the teeth. The red colobus monkey dentition shown here is typical of a catarrhine dentition with a 2/1/2/3 dental formula. Note the differences in morphology of the four different tooth types: incisors (I1, I2), canines (C), premolars (P3, P4), and molars (M1, M2, M3).

Taï Forest

West Africa, are one kind of ape (chimpanzee), eight kinds of monkeys (black-and-white colobus, Campbell's, Diana, lesser spot-nosed, putty-nosed, red colobus, olive colobus, sooty mangabey), and three kinds of prosimians (potto, Demidoff's galago, Thomas's galago). All but the prosimians are active during the day. (The humans are, of course, primates as well. The eagle is an important predator of monkeys, especially the red colobus.)

Arboreal Adaptation—Primates Live in Trees and Are Good at It

Many animals—such as squirrels, nondomesticated cats, some snakes, and birds—have successfully adapted to living in trees. Primates, however, display a unique combination of specific arboreal adaptations. Even the few primates that spend all or most of their time on the ground have retained, over the course of their evolution, a number of features shared with an arboreal common ancestor.

PRIMATES HAVE A VERSATILE SKELETAL STRUCTURE Primates get around in trees using an unusually wide range of motions involving the limbs and body trunk. One has only to watch many of the primates perform their acrobatics in the forest canopy to appreciate this versatility, a function of the primate body's anatomy. That is, the bones making up the shoulders, limbs, hands, and feet tend to be separate. These separate bones are articulated at highly mobile joints.

Atop the list of separate bones is the collarbone (the clavicle), which acts as strut, keeping the upper limbs to the sides of the body. The lower forelimb (the ulna and radius) and the fingers and toes (the phalanges) also have separate bones. The forearm rotates from side to side with relative ease, and the hands' and feet's dexterity is unparalleled among mammals.

One of the most important attributes of the primate hand is the **opposable** thumb—on either hand, the tip of the thumb can touch the tips of the other four fingers. Thus, the primate can grasp an object or manipulate a small one. Humans have the longest thumb, or pollex, among primates and therefore the greatest opposability (**Figure 6.3**). This elongated thumb is part of the unique adaptation of the human hand for what the English anatomist and evolutionary biologist John Napier calls the **power grip** and the **precision grip.** In the power grip, the palm grips an object, such as a hammer's handle, while the thumb and fingers wrap around it in opposite directions. In the precision grip, the thumb and one or more of the other fingers' ends provide fine dexterity, as when holding a screwdriver, picking

opposable Refers to primates' thumb, in that it can touch each of the four fingertips, enabling a grasping ability.

power grip A fistlike grip in which the fingers and thumbs wrap around an object in opposite directions.

precision grip A precise grip in which the tips of the fingers and thumbs come together, enabling fine manipulation.

FIGURE 6.3 ■ Grips and Opposable Thumbs
Apes and humans have two kinds of grips: power and precision. **(a)** The power grip shown here, as a human holds a hammer, preceded the evolution of the precision grip. **(b)** The apes' precision grip is not nearly as developed as humans'. **(c)** The finer precision grip of humans—in part due to the greater opposability of their thumbs—lets them finely manipulate objects.

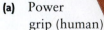

(a) Power grip (human)

(b) Precision grip (ape)

(c) Precision grip (human)

up a small object (such as a coin), or writing with a pen or pencil. The American paleoanthropologist Randall Susman has identified in early hominids the anatomy that would have supported a power grip and a precision grip (discussed further in chapter 9).

Many primates also have opposable big toes (the halluxes). Humans are not among these primates, mainly because of changes in the foot that took place when our prehuman ancestors shifted from a quadrupedal locomotion to bipedalism (**Figure 6.4;** see also "What Is So Different about Humans from Other Animals?: The Six Steps to Humanness" in chapter 1). To walk or run, humans need all five

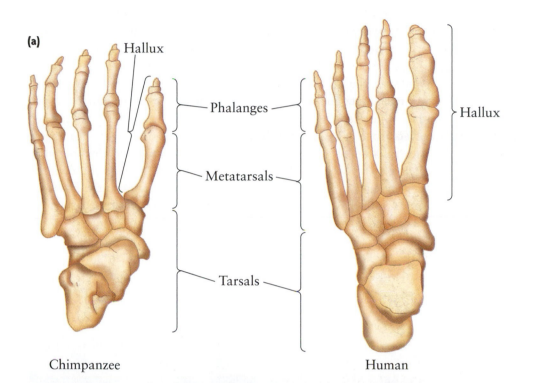

(a)
Hallux
Phalanges
Metatarsals
Tarsals
Hallux
Chimpanzee
Human

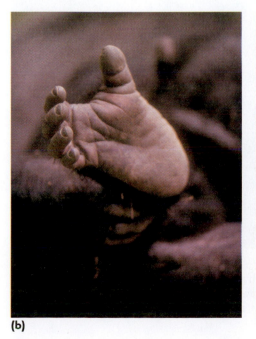

(b)

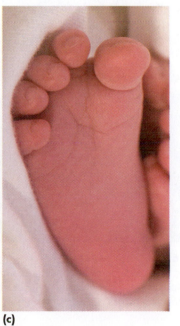

(c)

FIGURE 6.4 ■ Opposable Big Toes
Nonhuman primates' opposable big toes, like their opposable thumbs, enable their feet to grasp things such as tree branches. Humans lack this feature due to their adaptation to life on the ground. **(a)** Its curved hallux makes **(b)** the chimpanzee foot look more like a human hand (not shown) than like **(c)** a human foot.

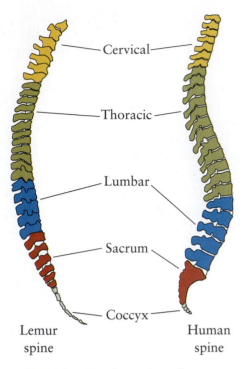

Cervical

Thoracic

Lumbar

Sacrum

Coccyx

Lemur
spine

Human
spine

FIGURE 6.5 ■ **Primate Vertebrae**
The five types of vertebrae in primates,
including lemurs and humans, create a
flexible column allowing a wide range of
movement. The cervical, thoracic, and
lumbar vertebrae are the true, or movable,
vertebrae, responsible for bending, twisting,
and stretching. The sacral vertebrae are much
less movable, as they form part of the pelvis.
In most nonhuman primates, the vertebrae
of the coccyx form the tail; in humans, these
vertebrae are reduced to three to five very
short, fused segments. Notice, too, the
s-shaped spine in humans versus the c-shaped
spine in other primates, such as the lemur.

preadaptation An organism's use of an
anatomical feature in a way unrelated to
the feature's original function.

diurnal Refers to those organisms that
normally are awake and active during
daylight hours.

rhinarium The naked surface around the
nostrils, typically wet in mammals.

toes firmly planted on the ground. The mobility of recent humans' toes has been
even further reduced by the wearing of shoes.

The body trunk of primates is also distinctive. The backbone has five functionally distinct types of vertebra—from top to bottom, the cervical, thoracic, lumbar,
sacral (forming the sacrum of the pelvis), and coccyx vertebrae—which give it a
greater range of movements than other animals have (**Figure 6.5**). The body trunk
also tends to be vertically oriented, such as when the primate climbs, swings from
tree limb to tree limb, or sits. The vertical tendency in a prehuman ancestor was
an essential **preadaptation** to humans' bipedality.

PRIMATES HAVE AN ENHANCED SENSE OF TOUCH The ends of the fingers and
toes are highly sensitive in primates. This enhancment helps inform primates about
texture and other physical properties of objects, such as potential food items. On
the inside surfaces of the fingers and toes and on the palms and soles, respectively,
of the hands and feet, the skin surface is covered with series of fine ridges called
dermal ridges (fingerprints and toe prints). These ridges further enhance the tac-
tile sense, and they increase the amount of friction, or resistance to slipping, when
grasping an object, such as a tree branch. On the backs of the ends of the fingers
and toes, most primates have nails instead of claws (**Figure 6.6**). Made of keratin,
the strong protein also found in hair, these nails may protect the ends of the fingers
and toes. They may aid in picking up small objects. Most importantly, however,
they provide broad support to the ends of the fingers and toes by spreading out the
forces generated in the digits by gripping.

PRIMATES HAVE AN ENHANCED SENSE OF VISION Primates' enhanced vision
stems from two developments in the order's evolutionary history. First, very early in

FIGURE 6.6 ■ **Fingernails**
Finger pads with nail support help primates, such as this orangutan, securely hold tree branches
that are smaller than their hands. By contrast, claws enable nonprimate mammals to dig into tree
bark, an especially helpful ability when limbs or tree trunks are larger than the animals' paws.

(a)

FIGURE 6.7 ■ **Primate Vision**

(a) Primates' forward-facing eyes enable depth perception, a vital adaptation to life in the trees that has a selective advantage beyond arboreal life. Consider what would happen if a primate attempted to leap from one branch to another without being able to determine the distance between the two branches. Now imagine a human leaping over a (relatively) narrow chasm without knowing how far to leap. **(b)** In most primates, such as the gibbon, the eye orbit is fully enclosed. In animals such as the lemur, a postorbital bar lines the back of the eye orbit but does not fully enclose it. In other animals, such as the raccoon, the eye orbit is open, with no bone enclosing it at the rear.

Gibbon

Lemur

Raccoon

(b)

primate evolution, the eyes rotated forward from the sides of the head to the front of the head (**Figure 6.7**). As a result, the two fields of vision overlap, providing the primate with depth perception. (Along with the eyes' convergence, fully enclosed or partially enclosed eye orbits evolved.) Second, color vision evolved. Crucial for spotting insects and other prey within the surrounding vegetation, color vision likely evolved as early primates shifted from a nocturnal adaptation to a **diurnal** adaptation.

PRIMATES HAVE A REDUCED RELIANCE ON SENSES OF SMELL AND HEAR-ING For most primates, enhanced vision led to greatly reduced senses of smell and hearing. Most higher primates have lost the **rhinarium** (the external wet nose, which most mammals have) and the long snout. Some of the prosimians—the more primitive primates, such as lemurs and lorises—have retained the rhinarium, and they continue to rely on a well-developed sense of smell. The reduction in snout length resulted from a loss of internal surface area of the nasal passage, the location of the chemistry involved in smell. But some primates, such as baboons, have retained a large snout to accommodate massive canine roots, especially in adult males (**Figure 6.8**).

FIGURE 6.8 ■ **Baboon Snout**
Baboons do not rely on olfaction. Their snout remains large because of oversized canines. (See also Figure 6.13.)

Dietary Plasticity—Primates Eat a Highly Varied Diet, and Their Teeth Reflect This Adaptive Versatility

PRIMATES HAVE RETAINED PRIMITIVE CHARACTERISTICS IN THEIR TEETH One fundamental anatomical feature in primates that reflects their high degree of dietary diversity is the retention of primitive dental characteristics, especially of four functionally distinctive tooth types: incisors, canines, premolars, and molars (**Figure 6.9**). Primates' mammalian ancestors had these same tooth types and so must have eaten a range of foods.

PRIMATES HAVE A REDUCED NUMBER OF TEETH Because the numbers of the different types of teeth are the same in the upper and lower jaws and the left and right sides of the jaws, anthropologists record each species' **dental formula** with respect to one quadrant of the dentition. Primates' early mammalian ancestor, for example, had a dental formula of 3/1/4/3: three incisors, one canine, four premolars, and three molars, in one quadrant of its dentition. As indicated in **Table 6.1,** the Old World higher primates (anthropoids) have a dental formula of 2/1/2/3. Most New World primates have retained one more premolar and have a dental formula of 2/1/3/3. Some primates, such as tarsiers, have different numbers of teeth in the upper and lower jaws. Over the course of the order's evolution, primates' teeth have tended to reduce in number, and the dental formula can be very useful in studies of ancestral primate species. For example, if fossilized remains of a primate ancestor have a dental formula of 2/1/3/3, the ancestor was likely related to New World monkeys and/or prosimians (tarsiers, lemurs, lorises), since these primates have retained the extra premolar.

> **dental formula** The numerical description of a species' teeth, listing the number, in one quadrant of the jaws, of incisors, canines, premolars, and molars.

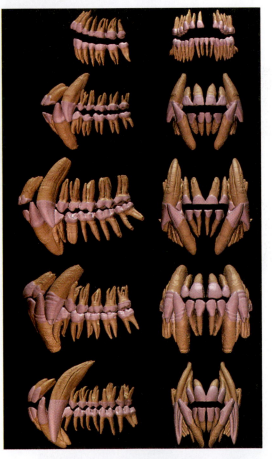

FIGURE 6.9 ■ Primate Dentitions
These five sets of dentitions represent, from top to bottom, human, chimpanzee, gorilla, orangutan, and baboon. Notice that humans do not have the large projecting canines evident in the other four dentitions. In the side view, the large upper canines fit into a diastema, or space, between the lower canines and the third premolars. Each time the jaws are closed, the upper canines are sharpened against the lower third premolars.

CONCEPT CHECK	What Makes Primates Good at Living in Trees?

Primates show a series of behavioral and anatomical tendencies that make them especially good at living in trees.

CHARACTERISTIC	FEATURES
Versatile skeletal structure emphasizing mobility and flexibility	Separation of bones in articular joints associated with mobility: clavicle; radius and ulna; wrist; opposable thumb; opposable big toe in many primates
	Five functionally distinct vertebrae types: cervical, thoracic, lumbar, sacral, coccygeal
Enhanced sense of touch	Dermal ridges at ends of fingers and toes; nails instead of claws
Enhanced sense of vision	Convergence of eyes; color vision

TABLE 6.1	Primate Dental Formulae	
The major primate groups are distinguished dentally by the number of incisors, canines, premolars, and molars.		
	UPPER	**LOWER**
Tarsiers	2.1.3.3	1.1.3.3
Lemurs	2.1.3.3	2.1.3.3 (although there is much variation with lemurs)
Lorises	2.1.3.3	2.1.3.3
New World Monkeys	2.1.3.2 *or* 2.1.3.3	2.1.3.2 *or* 2.1.3.3
Old World Monkeys	2.1.2.3	2.1.2.3
Great Apes and Humans	2.1.2.3	2.1.2.3

PRIMATES HAVE EVOLVED DIFFERENT DENTAL SPECIALIZATIONS AND FUNCTIONAL EMPHASES The premolars and molars of primates have undergone little evolutionary change compared with those of other mammals. This evolutionary conservatism reflects the continued purpose of these teeth, especially of the molars: grinding and crushing food. Specialized attributes of some primates' teeth reflect particular food preferences. For example, some primates have high, pointed cusps on the occlusal, or chewing, surfaces of their molars, for puncturing and crushing insects. Others have crests on their molars, for shearing leaves. The many primates that eat fruit and seeds tend to have low, round cusps on their molars, for crushing and pulping.

The molars of monkeys, apes, and humans have distinctive occlusal surfaces (**Figure 6.10**). Old World monkeys have four cusps on upper and lower molars, with two of the cusps on the front and two of the cusps on the back of the tooth's

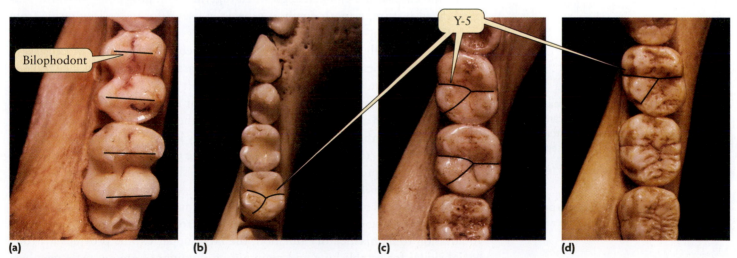

(a)   (b)   (c)   (d)

FIGURE 6.10 ■ Primate Molars
The morphology of lower molars in primates has two main variants: Old World monkeys' bilophodont pattern, such as in **(a)** the colobus monkey, and apes' Y-5 pattern, such as in **(b)** the gibbon, **(c)** the chimpanzee, and **(d)** the orangutan. Like the dental formula, molar morphology can be used to determine whether fossilized remains of a primate represent an ancestor of Old World monkeys or of apes and humans.

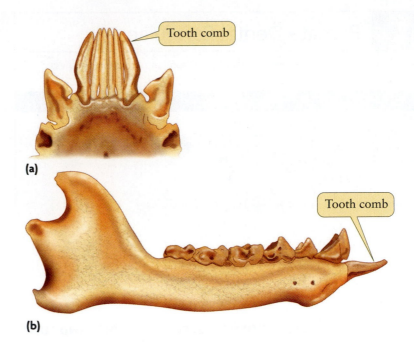

FIGURE 6.11 ■ **Tooth Comb**
Lemurs and lorises possess this unique morphology of lower incisors and canines—here seen from **(a)** below and **(b)** the side—useful for scraping and for grooming fur.

loph An enamel ridge connecting cusps on a tooth's surface.

bilophodont Refers to lower molars, in Old World monkeys, that have two ridges.

Y-5 Hominoids' pattern of lower molar cusps.

tooth comb Anterior teeth that have been tilted forward, creating a scraper.

canine-premolar honing complex The dental form in which the upper canines are sharpened against the lower third premolars when the jaws are closed.

diastema A space between two teeth.

sectorial (premolar) Refers to a premolar adapted for cutting.

occlusal surface. Each pair of cusps, front and back, is connected by an enamel ridge, or **loph.** This is called a **bilophodont** (meaning "two-ridge-tooth") molar. Apes and humans have a lower molar with five separate cusps that are separated by grooves. A Y-shaped groove is dominant, with the fork of the "Y" directed toward the outside of the tooth. This is called a **Y-5** molar. Apes' and humans' upper molars generally have four cusps, separated by grooves.

While most primates' incisors are flat, vertically oriented, and used to prepare food before it is chewed by the premolars and molars, many prosimians' lower incisors and canines are elongated, crowded together, and projecting forward. This specialized feature, a **tooth comb,** is especially useful for extracting resins from trees (**Figure 6.11**).

The horizontally oriented canine is one of three different kinds of canines in primates. The vertical, incisor-shaped canine appears only in humans. The projecting, pointed canine appears in all monkeys and all apes. In Old World monkeys and apes, the canines are part of a **canine-premolar honing complex,** in which the upper canine fits in a space, or **diastema,** between the lower canine and lower third premolar. This configuration slices food, especially leaves and other plants. When the primate chews, the movement of the back of the upper canine against the front of the lower first premolar creates a continuously sharpened edge on each of the two teeth (**Figure 6.12**).

The lower third premolar is **sectorial,** meaning that it has a single dominant cusp and a sharp cutting edge. The upper canine tends to be large, especially in males. In addition to its masticatory function, the large upper canine provides a strong social signal for establishing and maintaining dominance among male members of the primate society, such as in baboons, and as a warning signal to potential predators (**Figure 6.13**).

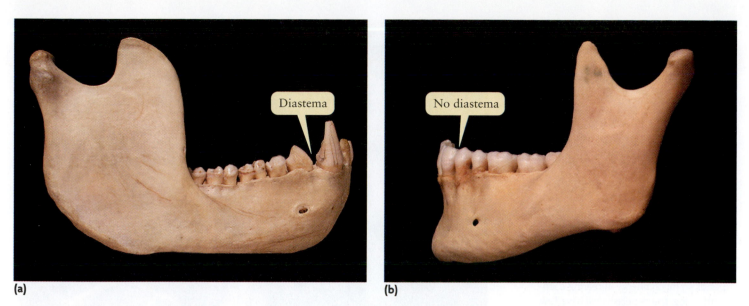

(a)   Diastema

(b)   No diastema

FIGURE 6.12 ■ **Honing Complex**

(a) In Old World monkeys and apes, the lower jaw has a diastema to accommodate the very large upper canines. **(b)** Humans lack such a space, because they do not have large, projecting upper canines.

CONCEPT CHECK

What Gives Primates Their Dietary Flexibility?

Primates display a broad range of dietary adaptations. Although prosimians' and anthropoids' teeth have evolved specializations, such as the tooth comb in lemurs, the overall retention of a nonspecialized, primitive dentition reflects the order's diverse diet.

CHARACTERISTIC	FEATURE
Multiple tooth types	Incisors, canine, premolars, molars
Reduced number of teeth	Fewer premolars and molars

Thickness of tooth enamel varies across primate species. Orangutans and humans have thick enamel, whereas chimpanzees and gorillas have thin enamel. Thick enamel reflects an adaptation to eating tough, hard foods. Although humans today rarely eat hard foods, they have retained this primitive characteristic.

Parental Investment—Primate Parents Provide Prolonged Care for Fewer but Smarter, More Socially Complex, and Longer-Lived Offspring

Female primates give birth to fewer offspring than do other female mammals. A single female primate's births are spaced out over time—sometimes by several years, in the cases of some apes. Primate mothers invest a lot of time and energy in caring

FIGURE 6.13 ■ **Canine Size**

In some primate species, such as baboons, the canines differ in size between males and females. Because the canines can be used as weapons, the fierce appearance of these large teeth serves to warn competitors and predators.

FIGURE 6.14 ■ Parental Investment
Because a female primate generally expends so much energy in rearing each of her offspring, she generally will have few offspring. Here, a chimpanzee mother holds her baby.

olfactory bulb The portion of the anterior brain that detects odors.

for each of their offspring (**Figure 6.14**). By caring for their offspring, providing them with food, and teaching them about social roles and social behavior generally, primates increase the chances of their species' survival.

Primates require longer development periods than do other mammals in part because they are more intelligent. That primates' brains are so large and complex reflects the crucial importance of intelligence—brain power—in primate evolution (**Figure 6.15**). The back portion of the brain where visual signals are processed is expanded in primates, whereas areas of the brain associated with smell (**olfactory bulb**) and hearing are considerably smaller than in other mammals. Among all primates, humans have the largest brain relative to body size and the

CONCEPT CHECK	Primate Parenting

Compared with other mammals, primates display unique parenting characteristics. These relate to the fact that primate offspring are more intelligent and behaviorally complex than are other mammals' offspring.

CHARACTERISTIC	FEATURES
Fertility	Birth to relatively few offspring at a time, commonly just one
Birth interval	Relatively long period between births
Preadult care	Elongated and intensive

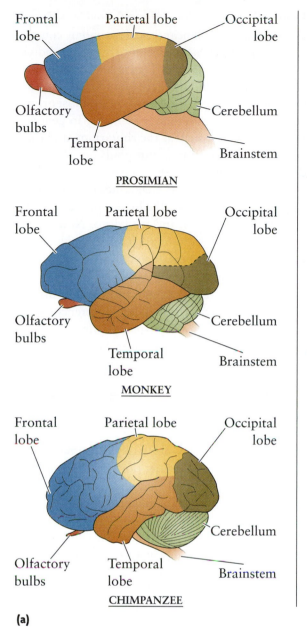

PROSIMIAN

Frontal lobe · Parietal lobe · Occipital lobe
Olfactory bulbs · Temporal lobe · Cerebellum · Brainstem

MONKEY

Frontal lobe · Parietal lobe · Occipital lobe
Olfactory bulbs · Temporal lobe · Cerebellum · Brainstem

CHIMPANZEE

Frontal lobe · Parietal lobe · Occipital lobe
Olfactory bulbs · Temporal lobe · Cerebellum · Brainstem

(a)

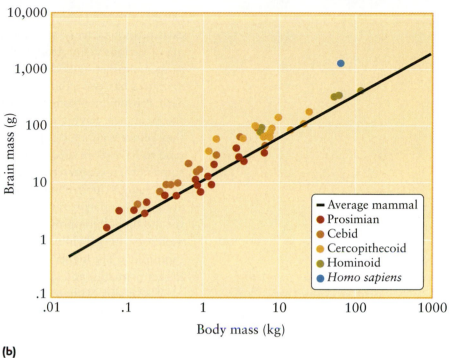

(b)

FIGURE 6.15 ■ Primate Brain Morphology
(a) The main regions of the brain are delineated in these drawings of primates' brains. The drawings are out of scale to show differences in anatomy. **(b)** As this graph shows, primates with the greatest body mass also have the greatest brain mass and thus the greatest intelligence. Most primates also have a larger brain relative to body size than the average mammal, a reflection of primates' higher intelligence. The *Homo sapiens* dot is way off the line because humans have a much bigger brain relative to body mass.

most elaborate neural connections between different regions of the brain. This combination of greater mass and complexity provides humans with greater intelligence compared with other primates and has led humans to develop language and advanced culture.

WHAT ARE THE KINDS OF PRIMATES?

Today, more than 200 taxa—number of species—of primates live in various parts of the world. If we count subspecies, there are more than 600 kinds of primates, from the mouse lemur, which weighs less than a pound (.5 kg), to the gorilla, which weighs several hundred pounds. Primates' physical diversity is reflected in different classification systems, prominent among them the Linnean-based taxonomy consisting of various major groups. Each group includes hierarchically arranged subdivisions, culminating at the bottom with genus and species (**Figure 6.16**). The order *Primates* has two suborders, prosimians (*Prosimii*) and anthropoids (*Anthropoidea*). Prosimians—sometimes called lower, or lesser, primates—are the most primitive primates, having undergone relatively little evolutionary change. In general, they retain a number of primitive characteristics, such as the rhinarium, and they tend to have more specialized diets and behaviors than anthropoids do. However, some of their characteristics are derived—that is, relatively more evolved—such as living lemurs' tooth comb, which evolved recently. The different kinds of prosimians are lorises, galagos, tarsiers, and lemurs. Anthropoids—the higher primates—are the monkeys (cercopithecoids, or Old World monkeys, and ceboids, or New World monkeys), apes (hylobatids, or lesser apes, and pongids, or great apes), and humans (hominids). The higher primates fall into two infraorders, platyrrhines (New World higher primates) and catarrhines (Old World higher primates).

The major primate groups and the various taxa included in them are distinguished by their anatomical and adaptive characteristics. These differences—for example, the differences between an ape and a monkey—matter, first, because they are a means of understanding the variation among primates. Second, the key characteristics of the different primate taxa appear at specific points in the evolutionary record. Paleontologists look for these characteristics in their study of the origins and evolution of the different primate groups. For example, when did the Y-5 molar, a defining characteristic of apes, first appear? When did bipedalism first occur? When did monkeys living in the New World first differ noticeably from those living in the Old World? Such questions are central to the study of primates and of their evolution. They can be answered only by knowing the attributes unique to different primate taxa.

In addition, it is important to know about the physical differences between primate taxa because the variation in the living primates provides models for understanding the morphology, the behavior, and the adaptation in the evolutionary past. For example, the Y-5 lower molar pattern seen today in apes and humans first appeared in anthropoids 20–30 mya. This morphology indicates that apes originated at that time. (Humans have the pattern, but evolved after apes.) Similarly, characteristics that define bipedality in humans—long lower limbs and short upper limbs—first appeared 5 mya or so. When they find these anatomical characteristics in fossilized remains (fossils are the subject of chapter 7), anthropologists are able to identify the origins of humanlike ancestors. And knowing how those ancestors walked helps complete a timeline of adaptation.

Add Hominin?: Genetic vs. Anatomical Classification

Clearly, then, taxonomy is an important tool for interpreting primate variation. How a primate is classified is important and not just a simple exercise. In the last several decades, taxonomists have focused increasingly on genetic relationships as a means of classifying primates. From this perspective, among the hominoids, humans and African great apes (gorillas, chimpanzees, and bonobos) are more closely related to each other than they are to the Asian great apes (orangutans). In addition, DNA comparisons reveal that chimpanzees and humans are more closely related than either is to gorillas. Therefore, anatomical and genetic classifications produce somewhat different results (**Table 6.2**). The anatomical classification includes three families: hylobatids (gibbons), pongids (great apes), and hominids (humans). By contrast, the genetic classification includes two families: hylobatids (gibbons) and hominids (great apes, including humans). It includes three subfamilies: pongines (orangutans), gorillines (gorillas), and hominines (chimpanzees, bonobos, and humans). And it divides the hominines into tribes: panins (chimpanzees, bonobos) and hominins (humans). In fact, the basic difference between the two classifications is that in the genetic system humans (and their ancestors) are called **hominin** instead of hominid.

Which classification scheme is better? Many anthropologists are shifting to genetic classification, whose advantages include a more accurate reflection of the genetic similarities and differences among apes and humans. For identifying genetic (i.e., evolutionary) relationships, genetic classification is better. For understanding the adaptation of anatomical variations, however, anatomical classification is better. As is emphasized throughout this book, humans have taken a very different adaptive trajectory than apes, and so humans are unique in some key ways, such as in how they walk, think, and communicate. Therefore, because this book focuses on adaptation, it uses anatomical classification.

With these terms in mind, we can look at the major features of the different primate taxa, starting with the prosimians.

hominin Humans and human ancestors in a more recent evolutionary taxonomy; based on genetics.

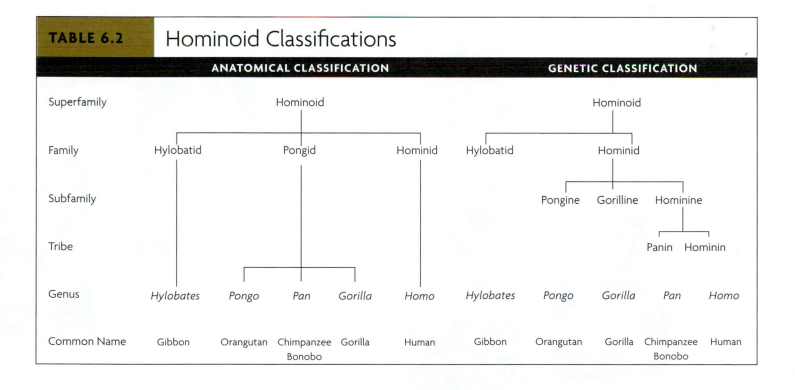

TABLE 6.2	Hominoid Classifications

	ANATOMICAL CLASSIFICATION					**GENETIC CLASSIFICATION**				
Superfamily			Hominoid					Hominoid		
Family	Hylobatid		Pongid		Hominid	Hylobatid		Hominid		
Subfamily							Pongine	Gorilline	Hominine	
Tribe									Panin	Hominin
Genus	*Hylobates*	*Pongo*	*Pan*	*Gorilla*	*Homo*	*Hylobates*	*Pongo*	*Gorilla*	*Pan*	*Homo*
Common Name	Gibbon	Orangutan	Chimpanzee Bonobo	Gorilla	Human	Gibbon	Orangutan	Gorilla	Chimpanzee Bonobo	Human

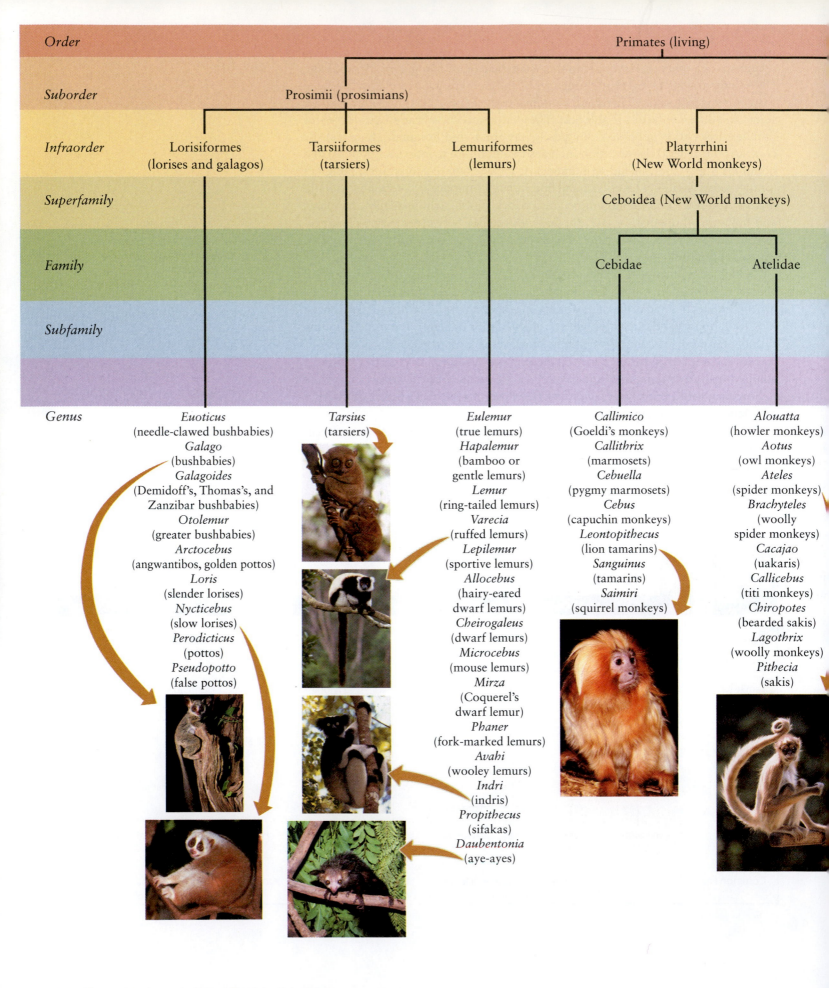

Order				Primates (living)	
Suborder		Prosimii (prosimians)			
Infraorder	Lorisiformes (lorises and galagos)	Tarsiiformes (tarsiers)	Lemuriformes (lemurs)	Platyrrhini (New World monkeys)	
Superfamily				Ceboidea (New World monkeys)	
Family				Cebidae	Atelidae
Subfamily					
Genus	*Euoticus* (needle-clawed bushbabies) *Galago* (bushbabies) *Galagoides* (Demidoff's, Thomas's, and Zanzibar bushbabies) *Otolemur* (greater bushbabies) *Arctocebus* (angwantibos, golden pottos) *Loris* (slender lorises) *Nycticebus* (slow lorises) *Perodicticus* (pottos) *Pseudopotto* (false pottos)	*Tarsius* (tarsiers)	*Eulemur* (true lemurs) *Hapalemur* (bamboo or gentle lemurs) *Lemur* (ring-tailed lemurs) *Varecia* (ruffed lemurs) *Lepilemur* (sportive lemurs) *Allocebus* (hairy-eared dwarf lemurs) *Cheirogaleus* (dwarf lemurs) *Microcebus* (mouse lemurs) *Mirza* (Coquerel's dwarf lemur) *Phaner* (fork-marked lemurs) *Avahi* (wooley lemurs) *Indri* (indris) *Propithecus* (sifakas) *Daubentonia* (aye-ayes)	*Callimico* (Goeldi's monkeys) *Callithrix* (marmosets) *Cebuella* (pygmy marmosets) *Cebus* (capuchin monkeys) *Leontopithecus* (lion tamarins) *Sanguinus* (tamarins) *Saimiri* (squirrel monkeys)	*Alouatta* (howler monkeys) *Aotus* (owl monkeys) *Ateles* (spider monkeys) *Brachyteles* (woolly spider monkeys) *Cacajao* (uakaris) *Callicebus* (titi monkeys) *Chiropotes* (bearded sakis) *Lagothrix* (woolly monkeys) *Pithecia* (sakis)

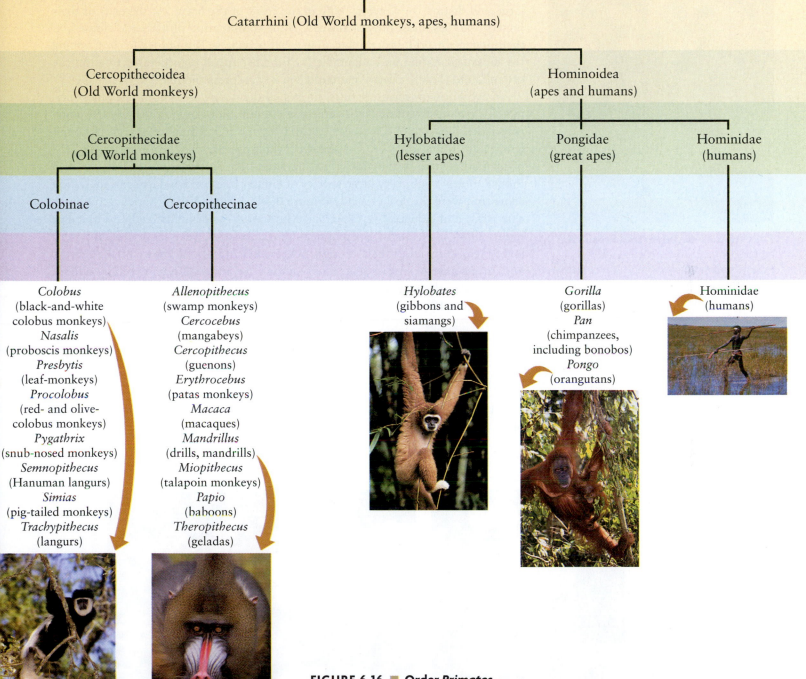

Anthropoidea (monkeys, apes, humans)

Catarrhini (Old World monkeys, apes, humans)

Cercopithecoidea
(Old World monkeys)

Hominoidea
(apes and humans)

Cercopithecidae
(Old World monkeys)

Hylobatidae
(lesser apes)

Pongidae
(great apes)

Hominidae
(humans)

Colobinae

Cercopithecinae

Colobus
(black-and-white
colobus monkeys)
Nasalis
(proboscis monkeys)
Presbytis
(leaf-monkeys)
Procolobus
(red- and olive-
colobus monkeys)
Pygathrix
(snub-nosed monkeys)
Semnopithecus
(Hanuman langurs)
Simias
(pig-tailed monkeys)
Trachypithecus
(langurs)

Allenopithecus
(swamp monkeys)
Cercocebus
(mangabeys)
Cercopithecus
(guenons)
Erythrocebus
(patas monkeys)
Macaca
(macaques)
Mandrillus
(drills, mandrills)
Miopithecus
(talapoin monkeys)
Papio
(baboons)
Theropithecus
(geladas)

Hylobates
(gibbons and
siamangs)

Gorilla
(gorillas)
Pan
(chimpanzees,
including bonobos)
Pongo
(orangutans)

Hominidae
(humans)

FIGURE 6.16 ■ **Order *Primates***

This classification of primate species uses the Linnaean taxonomy and places primates into two major groups: prosimians and anthropoids. Shared adaptive physical features help determine the degree of relatedness among primate species.

Prosimians: The Lesser Primates

FIGURE 6.17 ■ **Terrestrial Prosimians**
Not all primates are completely arboreal. Ring-tailed lemurs, for example, are terrestrial during the considerable periods of time in which they forage for food. Although native to Madagascar, the lemurs shown here live on St. Catherines Island, Georgia, as part of a project aimed at preserving the species through the establishment of an independent breeding population.

In acquiring food, prosimians rely heavily on their highly developed sense of smell. As a result, they have enlarged nasal passages, a rhinarium, scent glands, and a large and distinctive olfactory bulb in the front of the brain. At the ends of their fingers and toes, most prosimians have some combination of nails and claws, and their fingers are far less dexterous than other primates'. Ring-tailed lemurs, among the most fascinating and adaptable prosimians, spend considerable time on the ground, and their hands are humanlike in key respects (**Figure 6.17**).

In evolutionary terms, lemurs, lorises, and galagos are among the oldest primates (primate evolution is the subject of chapter 8). Many of the primitive characteristics they retain have been around for many millions of years. Although lemurs are found only on the island of Madagascar, they represent some 21% of primate genera worldwide. Until humans first occupied the island, about a thousand years ago, very large species of lemurs lived on Madagascar, including some that were the size of a cow (**Figure 6.18**). Lorises live in Africa and Southeast Asia, and galagos live in Africa. Many of these animals feed and breed at night. Their most distinctive physical characteristics, very large eyes and very large eye orbits, reflect their strongly nocturnal adaptation (**Figure 6.19**). Lemurs and lorises have primitive dentitions—some have 36 teeth, having retained three premolars in their dental formula. They also have the specialized tooth comb (see Figure 6.19).

Tarsiers, which live in Southeast Asia, are primitive overall. However, some of their characteristics are more derived than other prosimians', making tarsiers look more like higher primates, the anthropoids. For example, tarsiers' teeth are like anthropoids'—the canines are large and projecting, the lower incisors are relatively small, and the upper central incisors are large. Rather than having four lower incisors, two on the left and two on the right, tarsiers have only two. Like some of the other prosimians, they have retained three premolars on each side of the upper and lower jaws, giving them 34 teeth. Their name refers to the presence of two highly

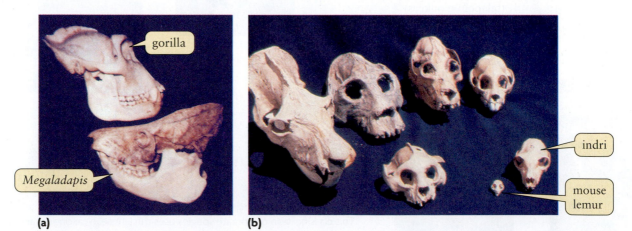

(a)   (b)

FIGURE 6.18 ■ *Megaladapis*
(a) These skulls belonged to a species of very large lemurs, the now extinct *Megaladapis,* on Madagascar. Skulls of *Megaladapis* were larger than a modern gorilla's, though *Megaladapis*'s body was smaller than a gorilla's. **(b)** In the right foreground, the skulls of a modern mouse lemur (middle) and an indri (right) represent the range of sizes in living lemurs. The crania in the back row and the skull to the left of the mouse lemur's show the range of sizes in extinct lemurs. The sizes of living and extinct lemurs overlap somewhat, but *Megaladapis,* the largest extinct lemur, was substantially larger than any living lemur.

elongated tarsal bones in their feet. These long bones give extra leverage for leaping in search of prey, such as small birds. Tarsiers' eyes and eye sockets are enormous, reflecting their nocturnal adaptation (**Figure 6.20**). Their brain's smallness and relatively simple structure make it more similar to lemurs' and lorises' brains than to the higher primates'.

Anthropoids: The Higher Primates

Anthropoids differ from prosimians in a number of ways. In general, anthropoids have larger brains, they are more dimorphic sexually in body size and other anatomical characteristics, they have fewer teeth (premolars, in particular), their eyes are convergent and enclosed by a continuous ring of bone, and they see in color.

The two infraorders of anthropoids—platyrrhines, or New World monkeys, and catarrhines—are named for the morphologies of their noses (**Figure 6.21**). Platyrrhine (from the Greek, meaning "broad-nosed") nostrils are round and separated by a wide nasal septum, the area of soft tissue that separates the nostrils. Catarrhine ("hook-nosed") nostrils are close together and point downward. (To understand nostril orientation, look at your own nostrils in a mirror. They should be directed downward since you are a catarrhine.)

The one superfamily of platyrrhines is the ceboids. The two ceboid families, cebids and atelids, are widespread in Latin America, from southern Argentina to

FIGURE 6.19 ■ Nocturnal Prosimians
Unlike the anthropoids, many species of prosimians (such as the red-bellied lemur, pictured here) are nocturnal. The largeness of their eyes improves nocturnal vision by enabling more light to enter the eyes. Darkness protects nocturnal prosimians from predators, but makes it difficult for them to socialize with other members of the same species. As a result, many nocturnal prosimians vocalize during the night. Sound travels easily in humid night air, so members of a species can communicate even if they cannot see each other.

(a)

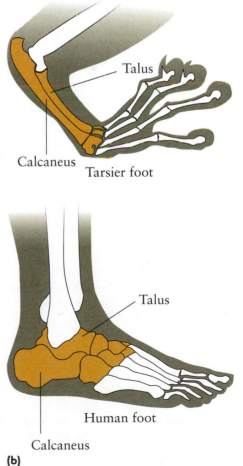

(b)

FIGURE 6.20 ■ Tarsier's Eyes and Feet
(a) Tarsiers are unique among prosimians in that their eyes have a fovea, a region of the retina that enables the sharp central vision needed for seeing details. This trait is unusual in nocturnal animals, because dim light typically prevents them from seeing things that clearly. **(b)** Thanks to their elongated tarsals (shown in color), especially the talus and calcaneus bones, tarsiers are superb leapers.

Platyrrhines
New World

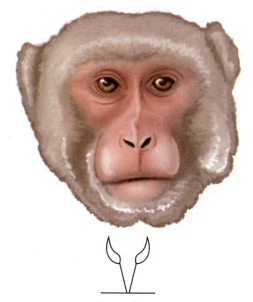

Catarrhines
Old World

FIGURE 6.21 ■ **Platyrrhines vs. Catarrhines**
In addition to their differently shaped noses, these two groups differ in their numbers of premolars; platyrrhines have six upper and six lower premolars, while catarrhines have four upper and four lower premolars.

prehensile tail A tail that acts as a kind of a hand for support in trees, common in New World monkeys.

FIGURE 6.22 ■ **Prehensile Tails**
Atelines, such as muriquis or woolly spider monkeys (shown here), are the only primates with a fully prehensile tail. (Opossums and kinkajous are among the other mammals with a fully prehensile tail.) The prehensile tail is very muscular, and its undersurface has dermal ridges, like fingerprints and toe prints, that improve the tail's grip.

Mexico. Ceboids are arboreal, spending nearly all their time in trees. They use suspensory locomotion, in which all four limbs grasp onto branches and help move the body from one tree or branch to another. Within the atelids are two subfamilies, one of which, the atelines, is distinctive in that each of its four types (howler monkeys, spider monkeys, woolly monkeys, and woolly spider monkeys) have a **prehensile tail** (**Figure 6.22**). In addition to locomotion functions in the trees, the prehensile tail can be used to suspend the body from a branch so the hands and feet can be used to feed. Ceboids have a diverse diet, ranging from insects (i.e., they practice insectivory) to fruits (frugivory) and leaves (folivery). Smaller ceboids obtain protein from insects, whereas larger ones obtain it from leaves.

The Old World monkeys, cercopithecoids, are the most diverse and most successful nonhuman primates. They inhabit a wide range of habitats throughout Africa and Asia, but mostly live in the tropics or subtropics. Some are arboreal and some are terrestrial. Cercopithecoids have bilophodont upper and lower molars, a narrow face, a sitting pad on the rear, and a long body trunk that terminates with a nonprehensile tail. Their canines are highly dimorphic sexually—male's canines are larger than female's canines, sometimes considerably so.

Cercopithecoids are divided into two subfamilies, colobines and cercopithecines (**Figure 6.23**). Colobines are closely related, medium-sized primates with a long tail and a wide array of coloration. They are mostly arboreal and live in a variety of climates, though not in dry areas. Colobines are folivores, and their anatomical features have adapted to accommodate a diet rich in leaves. The high, pointed cusps of their molars shear leaves and thus maximize the amount of nutrition obtained from them. Conversely, cercopithecines have rounded, lower cusps on their molars, as their diet is rich in fruit, which does not need as much processing to extract its

(a)

(b)

(c)

(d)

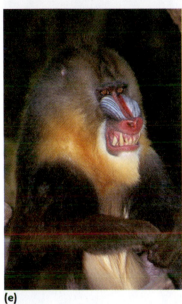
(e)

(f)

(g)

(h)

FIGURE 6.23 ■ Old World Monkeys
Colobines include **(a)** black-and-white colobus monkeys, **(b)** gray langurs, **(c)** proboscis monkeys, and **(d)** douc langurs. Cercopithecines include **(e)** mandrills, **(f)** De Brazza's monkeys, **(g)** olive baboons, and **(h)** vervet monkeys.

nutrients. Colobines' large, three- or four-chambered stomach, resembling a cow's stomach, contains microorganisms that break down cellulose, again to maximize the amount of nutrition extracted from the leaves. By contrast, cercopithecines are often called "cheek-pouch monkeys," because inside each cheek they have a pouch that extends into the neck and serves as a kind of stomach. While foraging, they store food in their cheek pouches, which are especially useful when they need to

(a)

(b)

(c)

(d)

(e)

FIGURE 6.24 ■ **Great Apes and Lesser Apes**
The great apes—**(a)** chimpanzees, **(b)** bonobos, **(c)** orangutans, and **(d)** gorillas—tend to be larger than other primates. All but gorillas are smaller than humans, with whom they are highly similar genetically. While great apes have a variety of social groupings (discussed below), lesser apes—**(e)** gibbons and (not pictured) siamangs—are unique in that they form pair bonds, in which one male, one female, and their offspring are the basic social unit.

gather food quickly in a dangerous area. Arboreal cercopithecines tend to have a longer tail, while terrestrial species have a short or no tail.

The most studied cercopithecoids are the cercopithecines, which include baboons and baboonlike monkeys (geladas, mandrills, macaques). Many cercopithecines live in savannas of East Africa. Some of them have highly dexterous fingers, adapted

| **brachiators** Organisms that move by brachiation, or arm-swinging.

for picking up small seeds from the ground. Because these primates live in habitats similar to those of early hominids (see chapter 9), they provide anthropologists with the means of understanding both the origins and evolution of early human social behavior and some physical attributes characteristic of primates living in open grasslands.

The hominoids are, in addition to humans, great apes and lesser apes (**Figure 6.24**). Humans live on every continent. Today, the only great ape that lives in Asia is the orangutan. The lesser apes live in Southeast Asia. The great apes of Africa—the chimpanzee, the closely related bonobo (or pygmy chimpanzee), and the gorilla—are restricted to small equatorial areas. All of these hominoids have large brains, broad faces, and premolars and molars with little occlusal surface relief. They all have a Y-5 lower molar pattern. All apes have the canine-premolar honing complex. None of the hominoids have an external tail.

All apes, hylobatids and pongids alike, have very long forelimbs (arms) compared with the hindlimbs. The fingers and toes are also quite long, for grasping trees and branches of various shapes and sizes. These characteristics are important adaptations used in the forest in a range of suspensory postures and movements (**Figure 6.25**). Gibbons and siamangs are skilled **brachiators,** using their upper limbs to move from tree limb to tree limb. Chimpanzees, bonobos, and gorillas are efficient at various suspensory postures, but their large sizes—especially in adult males—lead them to spend significant amounts of time on the ground in feeding and in locomotion. They employ a specialized form of quadrupedalism called knuckle-walking, in which the very strong arms are used to support the upper body weight while positioned on the backs of the fingers' middle phalanges. The knuckles bear the weight, while the fingers are flexed toward the palms (**Figure 6.26**).

In orangutans and gorillas, males have enormous masticatory muscles, which are accommodated by a large, well-developed sagittal crest, the ridge of bone running along the midline (mid-sagittal) plane of the skull. The sagittal crest is the terminal attachment site for the temporalis muscle (**Figure 6.27**). Gorillas devote

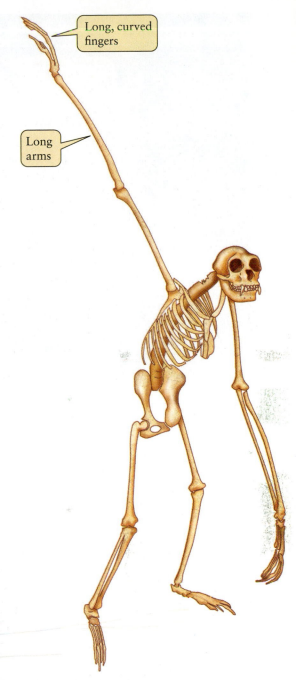

Long, curved fingers

Long arms

FIGURE 6.25 ■ **Suspensory Apes**
That the great apes and lesser apes regularly use suspensory locomotion can be seen in various features of their skeletal anatomy. For example, this gibbon's arms are long compared with its legs, its fingers and toes are long, and its fingers are curved and thus have enhanced grasping ability. If an ancestral primate's forelimbs were considerably longer than its hindlimbs, the animal was likely suspensory.

FIGURE 6.26 ■ **Knuckle-Walking**
This unique type of quadrupedalism enables chimpanzees and gorillas, like the gorilla pictured here, to move very quickly. In contrast, orangutans typically use fist-walking, supporting their upper body weight on the palms, which are closed in fists.

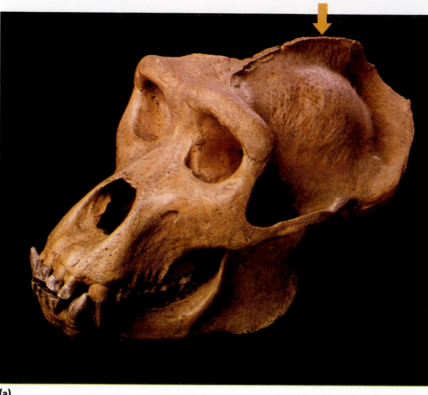

(a)

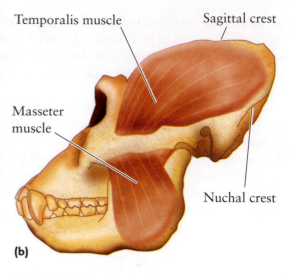

Temporalis muscle

Sagittal crest

Masseter muscle

Nuchal crest

(b)

FIGURE 6.27 ■ **Sagittal Crest**
(a) This ridge of bone is located at the sagittal suture along the midline of the cranium. **(b)** The more highly developed the sagittal crest is, the more highly developed the masticatory muscles are. This feature appears in gorillas and orangutans, as well as a variety of other animals, especially carnivores. It has been found in some human and primate ancestors.

CONCEPT CHECK	Prosimians and Anthropoids Differ in Their Anatomy and Senses

Prosimians tend to be more primitive than anthropoids are.

CHARACTERISTIC/ ADAPTATION	PROSIMIAN TENDENCIES	ANTHROPOID TENDENCIES
Smell	More developed	Less developed
Vision	Nocturnal for many	Diurnal
Touch	Claws in some	Nails
	Less developed	More developed
Diet	More specialized	More generalized
	More teeth in some	Reduced number of teeth
Intelligence	Less developed	More developed
	Small brain	Large brain

considerable time to eating leaves and plant stems. In contrast, chimpanzees are omnivorous—they eat fruit, leaves, bark, insects, and meat, depending on the season, their habitat (ranging from dense rainforests to savanna-woodlands), and local tradition. When meat is not available, chimpanzees' body weight goes down, suggesting that they rely on animal sources for protein.

Humans' general body plan resembles that of the large-bodied apes of Africa, a fact that has been recognized since at least the middle of the nineteenth century, when Thomas Huxley wrote his famous treatise on primate anatomy and human evolution, *Man's Place in Nature* (Huxley's research is discussed further in chapter 9). Humans have several unique anatomical attributes, however, many of which are related to the fact that humans are the only obligate, or restrictedly, bipedal primate (see "What Is So Different about Humans from Other Animals?: The Six Steps to Humanness" in chapter 1).

The skeletal indicators of bipedalism are found in the skull and the postcranial skeleton. In bipeds, the foramen magnum—the large opening for the passage of the spinal cord to the brain—is located at the bottom of the skull. The skull sits atop the body, whereas in quadrupeds it is on the front of the body. The major postcranial characteristics associated with bipedality are in the pelvis. The pelvis of the human (the biped) is short and directed to the side of the body, whereas the pelvis of the ape (the quadruped) is long and directed to the back of the body. These differently shaped pelvises reflect the different positions and functions of two gluteal muscles—gluteus medius and gluteus minimus—which attach across the hip joints of both human and ape. Ape gluteal muscles act as thigh straighteners, or extensors, but human gluteal muscles abduct the thigh on the side of the hip that supports the body weight when a person walks. The muscles' contraction on the abducted side keeps the hip stable while the other leg swings forward (**Figure 6.28**). (Next time you walk, notice how only one foot is on the ground at any one time, and feel how on that side of your hip the gluteal muscles have contracted.)

Among the other anatomical differences between humans and apes (discussed more fully in chapter 9) are the relative lengths of the limbs (**Figure 6.29**). In addition, unlike apes, humans do not hone their canines and premolars.

So far, we have concentrated on the anatomical differences among the different taxa of living primates. Of course, primates are not just about bones and teeth and other physical components. Like their anatomical variation, primates' behavioral variation reflects millions of years of evolution, during which adaptive strategies have enhanced the survival and reproduction of individuals and societies.

PRIMATE SOCIETIES: DIVERSE, COMPLEX, LONG-LASTING

Diversity of Primate Societies

Primate societies are diverse in several ways. First, *primates express themselves socially through a range of behaviors*. Some of the more obvious behaviors include touching, hugging, mouthing, mounting, lip smacking, vocalizing, greeting, and grooming. Far more so than any other animal, primates use these social signals to express different kinds of relationships, many of them complex and reciprocal. These signals can serve as a kind of "currency" for items or activities they are in-

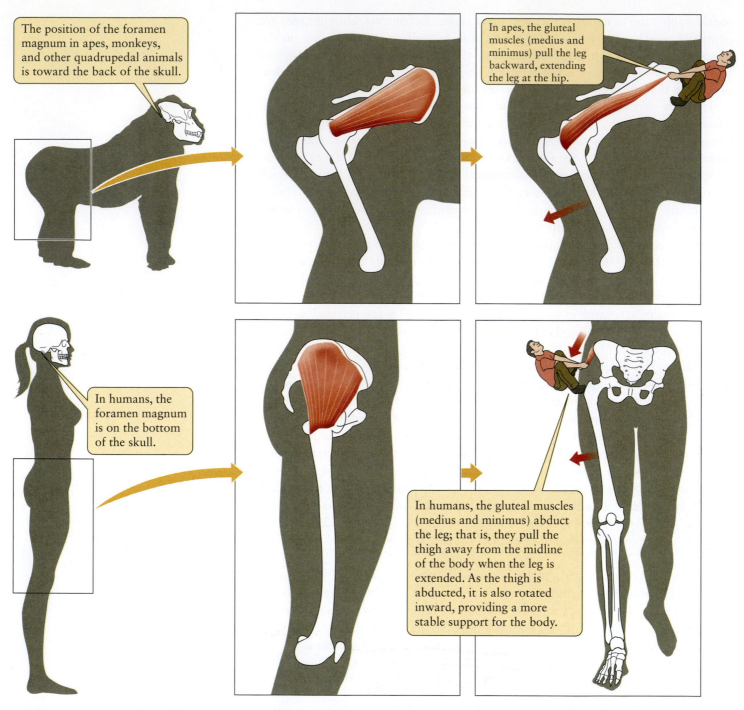

FIGURE 6.28 ■ **Quadrupedalism vs. Bipedalism**
Various morphological features indicate these two forms of locomotion.

terested in, such as grooming another individual to establish an alliance at the moment or in some future event.

Second, *many primate societies are complexly organized.* Within any primate group, individuals representing different kinships, ranks, ages, and sexes often form alliances.

Third, *primates form various social relationships for the long term.* Primates form relationships for immediate payoff (e.g., access to food or to mates), but

FIGURE 6.29 ■ Limb Proportions
In suspensory apes (left), the arms are long
compared with the legs. In humans (right), the
arms are relatively short because they are
no longer used in locomotion. In addition,
humans' fingers and toes are relatively shorter
and straighter than apes', again as a result of
bipedalism.

they also establish and maintain long-term alliances that at first glance do not appear to be beneficial, especially with regard to reproductive success. For example, chimpanzee males who groom each other frequently, travel together, or engage in other cooperative activities might later compete, for food or mates, against other groups.

Primate Social Behavior: Enhancing Survival and Reproduction

The theory underlying the study of primate social behavior is simple. Basically, natural selection favors primate behaviors that enhance survival and reproduction. In this way, the genes of individuals who engage in those behaviors pass from generation to generation. Primatologists explore the relationships between specific social behaviors and reproductive fitness. Such behaviors may be purely natural or they

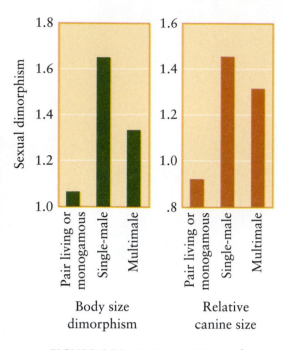

FIGURE 6.30 ■ **Competition and Dimorphism**

Among primates, as shown in these charts, sexual dimorphism in body size and in canine size is directly related to group composition. Here, a value of 1.0 indicates no sexual dimorphism. In primate species with monogamous pairs (such as gibbons), there is less competition for females and thus little sexual dimorphism. In primate species with multiple females but only a single male (such as gorillas), there is substantial competition among males to hold the dominant position and thus great sexual dimorphism. In primate species with multiple males competing for multiple females (such as chimpanzees), the sexual dimorphism is not as extreme as in single-male groups.

polygynous Refers to a social group that includes one adult male, several adult females, and their offspring.

polyandrous Refers to a social group that includes one reproductively active female, several adult males, and their offspring.

may be learned. In other words, sometimes primates are not conscious of their actions, and other times they strategize, learning by observation and imitation. These extremely important processes are highly elaborated in primates.

Males and females have very different reproductive roles and very different life histories in adulthood. Males provide the sperm to produce offspring. Females provide the ova to conceive the young, grow the young within them, give birth, and nurse the young. Overall, females expend far more energy in the creation of and caring for offspring than males do. As a general rule for many animals, including primates, those members of the sex that expends less energy in this way (the males) compete more aggressively among themselves for sexual access to members of the sex that expends more energy (the females).

When male primates compete for females, whether they are competing singly or in groups, the males' bodies adapt. Sexual dimorphism in body size and in canine size is considerably higher in such societies than in societies where males do not compete. This difference reflects the fact that to compete for females successfully, males must be big and aggressive (**Figure 6.30**). In these societies, males are generally unrelated. In societies where males are related, live in the group in which they were born (the natal group), and compete with related males, sexual dimorphism tends to be lower than in groups where males disperse and compete with nonrelated males.

The availability of reproductive-age females powerfully influences the organization of a primate society. Generally, a group's ratio of reproductive-age females to reproductive-age males will be four to one.

Finally, although all the life periods of primates are longer than those of other animals, humans have the longest life span. The average human life lasts nearly 70 years, longer than that of the chimpanzee (44 years), the gibbon (30 years), the baboon (29 years), and the lemur (27 years). And the American anthropologist Timothy Gage suggests that humans are the only primate to have "baby booms"—that is, variation in numbers of offspring in a population, fluctuating from large numbers to small numbers over time.

Primate Residence Patterns

Animals such as birds and nonprimate mammals tend to be regimented in their social structures and residence patterns. By contrast, individual primate species combine different patterns, and their social groups are strongly influenced by factors such as food availability, environment, and competition. Although it is thus exceedingly difficult to fully understand primate social behavior, primatologists have identified six main types of primate residence patterns (**Figure 6.31**):

1. *One-male, multifemale.* This haremlike organization consists of one reproductive-age male, several mature females, and the immature offspring. The society is **polygynous,** meaning that the one male has more than one partner. Some howler monkeys, some langurs, and some Old World monkeys, such as gelada baboons, practice this social system.
2. *One-female, multimale.* This group consists of one reproductive-age female, several mature males, and the immature offspring. The society is **polyandrous,** meaning that the one female mates with nonpolygynous males. The males often cooperate with the females in parenting activities. Only some New World monkeys practice this social system, and only rarely.
3. *Multimale, multifemale.* This group consists of many adults, male and female, and the offspring. Both sexes mate promiscuously.

Competition for mates tends to be relatively low, especially among males. Many Old World monkeys, a few New World monkeys, and chimpanzees fit in this category.

4. *All-male.* In some species, such as baboons, males form at least temporary groups, typically before joining or forming groups that include males and females. All-male groups commonly exist together with multimale, multifemale groups.

5. *One-male, one-female.* This group consists of an adult male, an adult female, and their immature offspring. Mating is typically **monogamous,** so each partners' reproductive success is tied to that of the other, and the male invests a relatively large amount of time and energy in the young (e.g., through protection and food acquisition). Gibbons, siamangs, a couple of ceboids (owl monkeys and marmosets), and several species of prosimians practice this form of society.

6. *Solitary.* Solitary primates go it alone—rarely are individuals seen with others. Interaction between adult males and adult females occurs only for sexual activity. Only orangutans and a few prosimians are solitary. An orangutan male has greater reproductive success if he maintains a territory with areas traversed by two or more females. Orangutan sexual dimorphism is predictably quite high—adult males are twice the size of adult females and have large canines, large cheek pads, and very loud calls over long distances. Males that have been relatively unsuccessful at competing for access to females tend to be more solitary than more successful males.

monogamous Refers to a social group that includes an adult male, an adult female, and their offspring.

FIGURE 6.31 ■ **Primate Residence Patterns**
Primates exhibit these six social groupings, which in many cases can change. In some species, for example, groups break apart if food is scarce and reunite when food becomes more ample.

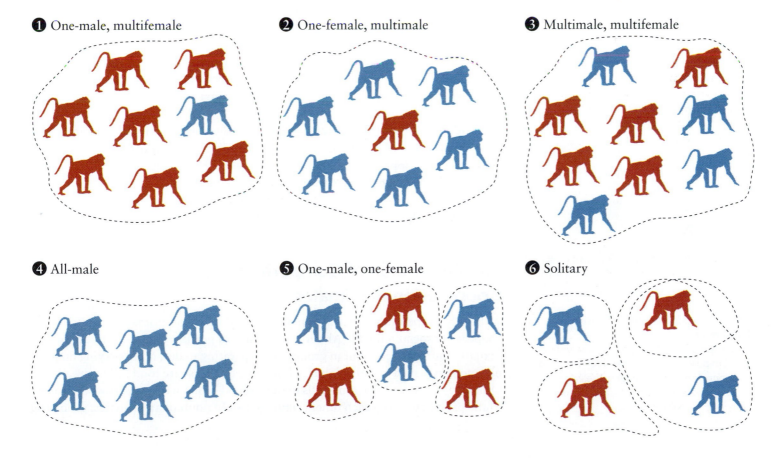

❶ One-male, multifemale   ❷ One-female, multimale   ❸ Multimale, multifemale

❹ All-male   ❺ One-male, one-female   ❻ Solitary

sexual selection The frequency of traits that change due to those traits' attractiveness to members of the opposite sex.

infanticide The killing of a juvenile.

FIGURE 6.32 ■ Primate Vocalizations
Male howler monkeys, such as the one in action here, are among the male primates that vocalize to protect their territories, their resources, and/or their females. Despite the name, howler monkeys roar more than howl, and their notorious calls can be heard over great distances. Howler monkeys are the loudest land animal and the second loudest of all animals, outdone only by the blue whale.

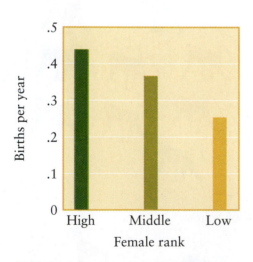

FIGURE 6.33 ■ Female Dominance Hierarchy
This graph compares the birth rates among high-, middle-, and low-ranked female gelada baboons. The higher the rank, the greater a female's access to resources, and the more offspring she will bear.

Primate Reproductive Strategies: Males' Differ from Females'

Because reproduction makes very different demands on males and females in terms of energy expenditure and time investment, each sex has a different set of reproductive strategies and interests. As discussed above, males' primary strategy is to physically compete for access to reproductively mature females, resulting in a strong degree of natural selection in males for both large bodies and large canines. This form of natural selection is called **sexual selection.** Another male strategy is **infanticide,** the killing of a nursing infant, primarily by a foreign male who has driven the single male out of a one-male, multifemale group. The American primatologist Sarah Blaffer Hrdy has hypothesized that the new male kills the nursing infant so that its mother stops lactating, resumes ovulation, and becomes sexually receptive to him. As a result, the new male enhances his reproductive fitness, largely at the expense of the previous male.

In some primate societies, males compete through distinctively loud vocalizations, which indicate territory and warn away predators and potential competitors. For example, according to the American primatologist Dawn Kitchen, male black howler monkeys in Guatemala howl in extremely loud choruses that inform other groups of the howlers' relative strength (**Figure 6.32**).

Whereas males compete with each other for mates, females compete with each other for resources that enable them to care for young. In various New World and Old World monkeys, including macaques and some baboons, the competition for resources happens within the context of stable dominance hierarchies. Hierarchical ranks usually pass from mother to daughter, and younger sisters usually rank higher than older sisters. The higher the rank, the greater the ability to acquire important resources, such as food. Higher-ranked females also tend to have more offspring, such as in gelada baboons in East Africa (**Figure 6.33**). In some primates, higher-ranked females have a greater number of offspring because they begin reproducing months before lower-ranked females. For example, dominant yellow baboons in Kenya start reproducing some 200 days before lower-ranked ones.

In addition, some female primates are relatively more selective in choosing mates than are others, making the selection on the basis of characteristics such as disposition, physical appearance, and position in social hierarchy. Some adult females' social behaviors encourage support for and investment in their offspring by other members of the group. And some adult females protect their infants from aggression, as when they attempt to prevent infanticide.

The Other Side of Competition: Cooperation in Primates

Although competition is central to primate social behavior, primates are also highly cooperative social animals. About half the size of gorillas and not very dimorphic sexually, chimpanzees hunt in groups of cooperating males, often preying on juvenile monkeys, such as red colobus. Chimpanzees also share food following a hunt. Other primates issue warning calls to their social group when predators approach. Many primates groom each other (**Figure 6.34**). In nonhuman primates, grooming

Male and Female Reproductive Strategies

Reproductive strategies differ in male and female primates. Males compete for mates, but females both compete for resources and invest time and energy in care of offspring.

SEX	REPRODUCTIVE STRATEGY AND OUTCOME
Males	*Behavior:* Physical competition for access to females *Outcome:* Selection for large body size and for large canines; selection for loud vocalization ability in some territorial primates
	Behavior: Sometime killing of nursing young (infanticide) *Outcome:* Suppressed lactation, resumption of ovulation, and receptiveness to new male partner
Females	*Behavior:* Acquisition of resources for raising young, usually in competition with other females *Outcome:* Higher-ranked females provide more resources than low-ranked females do.

involves one individual picking through the skin and hair of another individual, removing insects or other foreign objects, sometimes eating these materials. Among this practice's functions are bonding two members of a social group, calming the primate being groomed, or appeasing that primate if he or she has a higher position in a dominance heirarchy.

Some cooperative behaviors are **altruistic,** in that they appear to reduce the reproductive fitness of the individuals performing them but enhance the recipients'

altruistic Refers to a behavior that benefits others while being a disadvantage to the individual.

(a) **(b)**

FIGURE 6.34 ■ Grooming
Among many primates, including **(a)** chimpanzees and **(b)** humans, grooming is one of the most important social bonding behaviors. While helping ensure proper hygiene and good health, it can also cement social bonds between individuals, resolve conflicts, and reinforce social structures or family links.

(a)

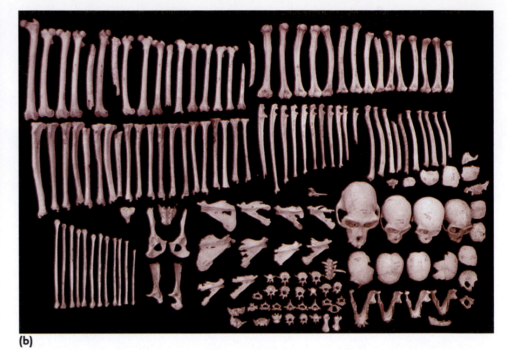

(b)

FIGURE 6.35 ■ Predation on Primates
(a) Large eagles are the chief predators of arboreal primates around the world. Analysis of the contents of eagles' nests has revealed precise information about predation rates.
(b) Within the eagles' nests, fewer bones are found from primates that live in large groups and thus are protected from predators. Prosimian bones are relatively abundant, because primates that live in small groups or are solitary lack the protection afforded by large groups. This photo shows the bones primatologists found in just one eagle nest.

 kin selection Altruistic behaviors that increase the donor's inclusive fitness, that is, the fitness of the donor's relatives.

reproductive fitness. For example, adult baboons might give warning calls to their social group, or even attack predators, and in doing so place themselves at jeopardy. Grooming, food sharing, and caregiving are also altruistic, because one primate invests time and effort in another.

If primates are focused on perpetuating their individual genes, why should a primate engage in altruistic behavior? Altruism seems not to be directed haphazardly, but rather is directed primarily at relatives. According to the British evolutionary theorist William Hamilton's hypothesis of **kin selection,** the evolutionary benefits of an altruistic behavior to the kin group outweigh costs to the individual acting altruistically. A primate will most strongly and consistently act altruistically when living with relatives. This is particularly true among cercopithecoids, such as baboons and macaques, where females live mostly in the natal group, or in chimpanzees, where males live in the natal group. The primatologist Richard Wrangham has observed groups of cooperating (related) male chimpanzees attacking groups of male chimps unrelated to them. He has also observed groups of cooperating male chimps patrolling territorial boundaries. Such behaviors in living chimpanzees may be the best model for early hominid behavior and for the origins of human aggression.

Cooperation has many advantages, but it ultimately provides most primate taxa with their distinctive behavioral characteristic: primates live in social groups. And the primary reason for these social groups is probably that while many primates are proficient predators, primates are preyed upon by a range of predators. Defense from predators would seem to be an important form of cooperative behavior. While primatologists have observed the kinds of warning calls and direct physical defenses described above, however, the evidence of primates' protecting each other from predators is slim. It is difficult to directly observe predation, for example, because predators tend to be afraid of humans and they avoid primate groups being studied.

Many primates are preyed upon by large birds, such as eagles. The American primatologists Susanne Shultz and Scott McGraw have studied eagles' nests, since the remains left in them—representative samples of "meals"—provide proxy information about what the eagles hunt and how often (**Figure 6.35**). The results show that predation rates are lower among larger primate groups than among smaller primate groups. Predation is a very strong selective pressure, and mutual cooperation—sociality—has been favored among primates because of the protection it provides.

GETTING FOOD: EVERYBODY NEEDS IT, BUT THE BURDEN IS ON MOM

Primates acquire their food through a wide variety of foraging practices, which entail looking for food, then handling and processing the food for consumption. The American physical anthropologist Karen Strier estimates that on average foraging can take up over 50% of a primate's waking time. This burden is especially great on mothers. Not only do mothers need to eat food that will provide the energy for gestation and lactation, but they also need to look for food and then handle and process it for their young to consume. In a few primate species, the father is involved in caring for and providing food for the young, but generally the mother is the sole provider of her offspring's food. The American primatologist P. C. Lee estimates that in adult female primates, a mother's energy requirements are between two to five times higher than a nonmother's. For the female primate, success in caring for young, both before and after their birth, is very much tied to adequate nutrition. Females with good nutrition have young at an earlier age, have healthier young, experience shorter intervals between births, and live longer than those with suboptimal nutrition.

Three key factors contribute to a female primate's success at feeding: quality, distribution, and availability of food. *Quality* refers to food's providing energy and protein that are readily digestible. Mature leaves and mature grasses, for example, are of relatively little value to many primates because the cellulose and dietary fiber are much harder to digest for nutrients than are the cellulose and dietary fiber of young leaves and young grasses. As discussed above, sharp-crested teeth and compartmentalized stomachs have evolved in some primates, especially in leaf-eating monkeys. For example, folivorous Old World monkeys have sharper crests connecting the cusps on the fronts and backs of the occlusal surfaces of their bilophodont molars.

Distribution refers to the locations of food across the landscape. Ideally, the primate would have to expend relatively little energy to acquire food. In terms of evolution, behaviors that minimize the costs of acquiring food are selected for. Many primates focus on patches of food, such as a fruit-bearing tree or a group of such trees, whose fruit provides a ready and concentrated source of nutrients. However, a small patch will support only a relatively small group. All primates are able to adjust the size of the feeding group in relation to the amount of food available in a patch. Some primates, such as chimpanzees, can be enormously flexible in making such adjustments.

Food *availability* can be highly fluid, depending on season and rainfall. The farther a region is from the equator, the more defined are its seasons and the less available are fruit and leaves, primates' main food sources. Thus, primates are generally restricted to equatorial regions.

ACQUIRING RESOURCES AND TRANSMITTING KNOWLEDGE: GOT CULTURE?

Primates and humans acquire food in vastly different ways. While primates can acquire food using only their bodies, humans depend on technology—material culture—to acquire food. But this distinction does not mean that primates have no material culture.

In the 1960s, Jane Goodall became the first to question that assumption when she observed adult chimps poking twigs into a termite hill, withdrawing them, and eating the termites that clung to the twigs (**Figure 6.36**). Goodall realized that one fundamental assumption about what it means to be human—namely, that material culture (and culture in general) is exclusive to human beings—seemed incorrect. Other scientists then realized that living chimpanzees' tool use may be the best model for understanding our prehuman ancestors' earliest cultures (among the topics of chapter 9).

Based on Goodall's pioneering research and a great deal of work since, anthropologists have identified two central features about chimpanzees' tool use. First, most of the tools chimpanzees produce are for acquiring and consuming food. Among the rare examples of primate tool use unrelated to food is that of chimpanzees in Gombe throwing stones as part of a dominance conflict between adult males. One of chimps' most fascinating food-based innovations, observed by the American primatologist Jill Pruetz, is the creation and use of a spearlike object—a trimmed, pointed twig—to skewer prosimians for food (**Figure 6.37**). Second, tool production and tool use are sometimes highly localized. For example, although some adjacent chimpanzee groups in West Africa use stones to crack open hard-shelled nuts, this tool use has not been seen anywhere else in Africa.

Chimpanzees clearly have material culture, and its general, widespread nature suggests that it dates back to antiquity. Sites in the Ivory Coast of West Africa contain chimpanzee tools from 4,000–5,000 yBP, but tool use likely started earlier than that.

What about other primates? Field observations by the Swiss anthropologist Carel van Schaik and his associates show that, like chimpanzees, orangutans in Borneo and Sumatra habitually use probes to obtain insects for food. Across the Atlantic in South America, some capuchin (Cebus) monkeys use stones to dig for food and to crack open nuts. The complexity here is far less than that of human technology,

FIGURE 6.36 ■ Chimpanzee Tool Use
When "fishing" for termites (which are highly nutritious), a chimpanzee selects a branch or twig thin enough to pass through holes of a termite nest, then removes all extra branches and leaves and inserts the twig into the nest. Simple and disposable, even primitive, tools like this might have been used by our ancestors long before the appearance of stone tools some 2.5 mya.

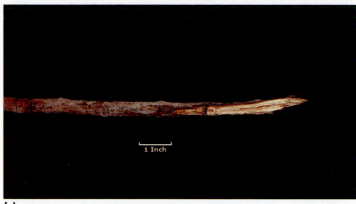

(a)

FIGURE 6.37 ■ **Chimpanzee Spears**
(a) A chimpanzee made this spear from a tree branch, sharpening one end with its teeth. (b) Chimpanzees who make such spears use them to thrust into the hollows of trees and kill bushbabies. Here, an adolescent female holds a dead bushbaby. This method is primates' first use of tools to hunt other mammals.

(b)

but these simple behaviors show that chimpanzees are not the only primates that interact with the environment through tools they make.

Material culture in any society, human or primate, is but one part of culture. Broadly defined, culture is learned, transmitted knowledge. Teaching an individual how to make a simple stick tool is one example of material-based culture, while teaching someone how to whistle is an example of nonmaterial-based culture. Some of the best evidence for culturally transmitted knowledge consists of characteristic behaviors that are not material-based. For example, chimpanzees in Mahale, Tanzania, use an unusual grooming technique called a hand clasp. The two participants face one another. Each one holds a hand up over their heads and clasps the other's hand, forming an A-frame, and each one uses his or her free hand to pick parasites and other detritus off the other participant (**Figure 6.38**). In addition to grooming, chimpanzee populations display different kinds of vocalizations unique to specific groups and regions. These group-specific patterns of grooming and of vocalization are just a sample of the many behaviors identified by primatologists that represent nonmaterial aspects of primate culture.

This chapter has discussed the nature of primates, their anatomical characteristics, their social behaviors, their methods of acquiring food, and the growing realization that they have material culture and nonmaterial culture. All of this information lays the foundation for understanding the next part of this book, on the roughly 50,000,000 years of primate and human evolution.

FIGURE 6.38 ■ **Hand Clasp Grooming**
The distinctive type of grooming depicted here has been observed only in groups of chimpanzees in Tanzania. Here, the paired chimpanzees grasp each other's wrist, while in other groups they grasp each other's hand. Such specific social customs are unique to individual groups of chimpanzees and thus must be learned within each group, a fundamental aspect of culture.

What is a primate?

- Primates, an order of mammals, are best defined on the basis of their evolutionary trends: they are arboreal, have highly flexible diets, and invest a great deal of time in their young. Overall, they are generalized—primates have specialized in not specializing.
- Their physical characteristics reflect primates' adaptation to life in the trees. A highly versatile body structure facilitates great mobility and manual dexterity. Vision is highly developed, but the senses of hearing and smell are greatly de-emphasized in most primate taxa.
- Primates' highly varied diet is reflected in a generally nonspecialized dentition including functionally distinctive tooth types.
- Primates' prolonged care for young reflects the fact that primates have a lot to teach, especially in the area of complex social behaviors.

What are the kinds of primates?

- The more than 200 primate species living today are subdivided into two suborders, prosimians and anthropoids. Prosimians are the lesser, or lower, primates. Anthropoids are the higher primates.

What is special about primate societies and social behavior?

- Primate societies are highly diverse, ranging from solitary animals to complex multimale, multifemale groups. Most primates live in some kind of social group and do so on a long-term basis.
- Male reproductive strategies emphasize competition between males for access to reproductive-age females. Female reproductive strategies emphasize care of young and access to food for young and for the support of mothers' and their offspring's nutritional needs.
- Primates living in larger groups are better able to protect themselves from predators than are primates living in smaller groups.

How do primates acquire food?

- Primates' wide variety of habitats require them to use a wide variety of food-foraging strategies. Chimpanzees are the only primate known to systematically hunt other animals, including other kinds of primates.
- Primates rely entirely on their bodies for acquiring and processing food for consumption. Humans rely on extrasomatic means—material culture—to acquire and process food. Chimpanzees, orangutans, and some New World monkeys employ rudimentary technology, reflecting socially transmitted knowledge.
- Some primates (chimpanzees, for example) have material culture. They and other primates have displayed some learned behavior and cultural tradition, such as forms of social grooming and vocalization that are unique to specific groups and regions.

KEY TERMS

altruistic	olfactory bulb
arboreal adaptation	opposable
bilophodont	parental investment
brachiators	polyandrous
canine-premolar honing complex	polygynous
dental formula	power grip
diastema	preadaptation
dietary plasticity	precision grip
diurnal	prehensile tail
habituate	primatologists
hominin	rhinarium
infanticide	sectorial (premolar)
kin selection	sexual selection
loph	tooth comb
monogamous	Y-5

ADDITIONAL READINGS

Campbell, C. J., A. Fuentes, K. C. MacKinnon, M. Panger, and S. K. Bearder, eds. 2006. *Primates in Perspective*. New York: Oxford University Press.

Falk, D. 2000. *Primate Diversity*. New York: Norton.

Goodall, J. 1986. *The Chimpanzees of Gombe: Patterns of Behavior*. Cambridge, MA: Harvard University Press.

Hart, D. and R. W. Sussman. 2005. *Man the Hunted: Primates, Predators, and Human Evolution*. Jackson, TN: Westview Press.

McGrew, W. C. 1998. Culture in nonhuman primates. *Annual Review of Anthropology* 27: 301–328.

Peterson, D. 2006. *Jane Goodall: The Woman Who Redefined Man*. New York: Houghton Mifflin.

Stanford, C. B. 2001. *The Hunting Apes*. Princeton: Princeton University Press.

Strier, K. B. 2007. *Primate Behavioral Ecology*. 3rd ed. Boston: Allyn & Bacon.

Wrangham, R. and D. Peterson. 1996. *Demonic Males: Apes and the Origins of Human Violence*. Boston: Mariner Books.

PART II

The Past: Evidence for the Present

Living organisms have resulted from millions of years of both natural selection and other evolutionary forces. This living record has provided natural historians and biologists, Charles Darwin first and foremost, with important information about how evolution works and what forces are behind it. Fundamental as it is, however, the living record provides a limited picture of evolution, a record of just the *surviving* lineages. The other fundamental part of the evolutionary picture is found in the past, thanks to the fossil record, which portrays the lineages and extinct species that gave rise to living species. The focus of the remainder of this book, the fossil record, is the basis for documenting and interpreting biological history. Because fossils are the only source of evidence for what past organisms were like, where they lived, and how they behaved, living *and* past records are essential for understanding evolution—one is incomplete without the other.

Part II begins with a look at what fossils are and how they can be interpreted. Once this window onto the past has been opened, we will explore the diversity and abundance of primate species, starting with the first true primates (prosimians), followed by the origins and evolution of the first higher primates (anthropoids); then the appearance, evolution, and diversity of the first apes (hominoids); and, beginning around 6–7 mya, the origins and evolution of primitive, humanlike ancestors (hominids).

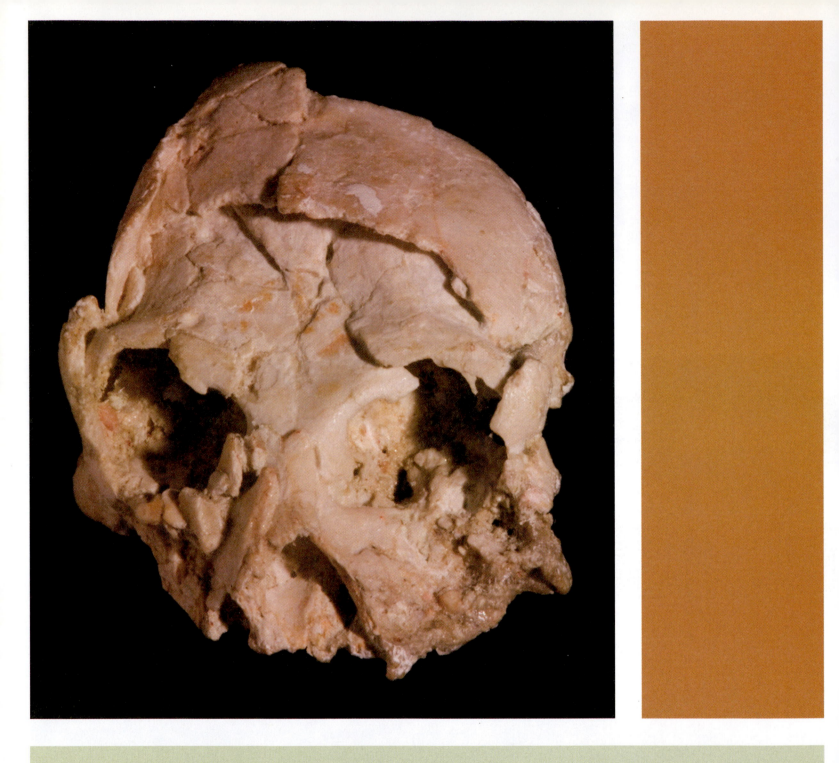

This skull, *Catopithecus,* dates from about 36 mya. It is from northeastern Africa's Fayum Depression, a region in which many fossils have been found. Fossils like this one help scientists understand what past animals were like and are essential evidence of the evolution of life.

CHAPTER 7

Fossils and Their Place in Time and Nature

Although Charles Darwin's theory of evolution was based mostly on his observations of living species, Darwin certainly knew about fossils. His extensive reading must have included the ancient Greek historian Herodotus, who had recognized the shells preserved in rock as the remains of organisms. Darwin was no doubt familiar with discoveries of fossils in the Americas. He even had a hand in prospecting for fossils in Argentina, noting in his journal that "the great size of the bones . . . is truly wonderful." He likely heard about discoveries in the United States, such as by the American president Thomas Jefferson (1743–1826), who reported on an extinct ground sloth found in Virginia (**Figure 7.1**). Darwin definitely knew the work of the French paleontologist Georges Cuvier (discussed in chapter 2), who had meticulously studied and published on the fossils of many different plants and animals around Paris.

Though Darwin and these other figures made important contributions to scientific and anthropological thought, none of these people fully appreciated the importance of fossils as a record of the past. Cuvier recognized the fact that fossils are the remains of once-living organisms. Darwin saw the significance of the similarity in features between living ground sloths and the extinct forms in Argentina. But fossils' larger role in reconstructing the history of life and a time frame in which to place that history was not at the forefront of either Cuvier's or Darwin's thinking. In science, it sometimes takes one person with just the right combination of background, experience, and intellect to put together various lines of evidence and draw conclusions from this evidence that result in a breakthrough. The breakthrough setting the stage for fossils as a fundamental source of information about the past came not from a respected scientist but from an engineering surveyor with a remarkable attentiveness to detail and pattern. Unlike many of the great scientists of the eighteenth and nineteenth centuries, the Englishman William Smith (1769–1839) was born into a family of very modest means. At 18, he apprenticed as a surveyor, and he eventually worked for a coal-mining and canal-construction company. In the mines, he observed that layers of rock—**strata**—were always positioned the same way relative to each other. He deduced this pattern from the colors and other physical properties of each stratum. He also realized that each stratum

strata Layers of rock, representing various periods of deposition.

BIG QUESTIONS

- What are fossils?

- What do fossils tell us about the past?

- What methods do anthropologists and other scientists use to study fossils?

contained a unique collection of fossils representing long-extinct life forms. From these observations, he hypothesized that the relative positions of strata and the kinds of fossils found in the layers were the same throughout England. He called his hypothesis the *Principle of Faunal Succession,* and he tested it with a research program that correlated strata and fossils throughout Britain.

Smith was fired from his job in 1799, likely because of his distractions from his surveying work. Despite going into abject poverty and spending time in debtors' prison, he continued recording data across the country, ultimately, in 1815, producing the first geologic map of the British Isles. What motivated him? Like the other scientists we have studied, Smith was motivated by questions about the natural world around him. And he believed that fossils provided an important record of past life and of time's passage. Although his passion was to produce a geologic map, he recognized fossils' importance in the creation of a time frame for once-living organisms. The scientific world grew to realize what an important thing he had accomplished, and in the last years of his life Smith was recognized by the leading scientists of the time. Owing to his pursuit of answers to questions, fossils became a means of documenting the evolution of life on Earth and a means of reconstructing geologic time.

Fossils are the very heart of the study of evolution. They provide us with the only direct physical evidence of past life and its evolution, from the simple bacterial organisms that lived over three billion years ago to the complex organisms that

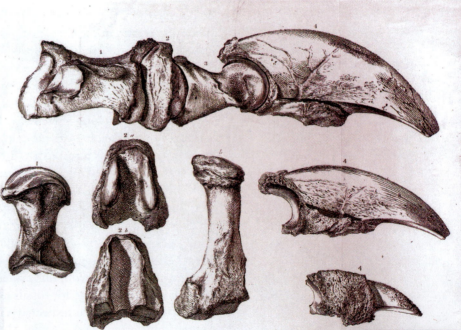

FIGURE 7.1 ■ *Megalonyx jeffersoni* **Fossil Claws**
In 1796, Thomas Jefferson (right) discovered the bones of an extinct ground sloth. The paper he presented on his finding to the American Philosophical Society helped launch the field of vertebrate paleontology in America.

evolved later (**Figure 7.2**). The scientific study of fossils centers around two components: time and environment. Placement of fossils in time allows us to document **phylogeny,** or biological change and evolutionary relationships. Placement of fossils in their environmental contexts helps us understand the factors that shaped the evolution of the organisms the fossils represent.

In this chapter, you will learn about the study of fossils, or paleontology, and the vast chronology within which scientists place the fossil record. You will also learn how paleontologists—the scientists who study fossils—determine how long ago organisms lived and what their environments were like.

phylogeny The evolutionary relationships of a group of organisms.

FIGURE 7.2 ▪ Kinds of Fossils
Information about past organisms comes from various sources, such as **(a)** 250,000,000-year-old bacteria (*Bacillus permians*) recently revived by scientists; **(b)** stromatolites, which resemble bacterial colonies that dominated life on Earth for more than two billion years; and fossils: **(c)** ammonite, **(d)** trilobite, **(e)** fern, **(f)** crab, **(g)** soft-shelled turtle, **(h)** fish, and **(i)** tyrannosaurus skeleton. Fossils like these have been found all over the world.

FOSSILS: MEMORIES OF THE BIOLOGICAL PAST

What Are Fossils?

Fossils (Latin *fossilis*, meaning "dug up") are the remains of organisms. More specifically, they are the remains of organisms that have been wholly or partially transformed into rock through a long process of chemical replacement. In the replacement process, the minerals in remains, such as calcium and phosphorus, are very gradually replaced with rock-forming minerals like iron and silica.

Taphonomy and Fossilization

taphonomy The study of the deposition of plant or animal remains and the environmental conditions affecting their preservation.

Fossils can derive from any body parts, but bones and teeth are by far the most common sources, providing more than 99% of the fossil record. **Taphonomy**—the study of what happens to an organism's remains—describes the multiple circumstances that must (and must not) occur for a dead organism to become a fossil (**Figure 7.3**). An organism will *not* become a fossil, for example, if its remains are left exposed for any length of time. If the remains are exposed for more than a day or so after death, scavengers such as dogs, wolves, or birds may eat the soft tissues. Maggots will quickly consume flesh. Once the flesh is gone, the bones of the skeleton will weather, break, or disappear. Because of the unlikelihood of a quick burial not brought about by humans, very few once-living organisms end up as fossils.

If an organism is buried soon after its death, such as under soil sediments deposited by water, the remains will be at least partly protected from scavengers. To become fossilized, however, the remains must stay in an oxygen-free (anoxic) environment, where scavengers cannot access the body and where bacterial activity and decomposition are limited.

Even in this ideal burial environment, other factors can lead to the decay or alteration of the remains. For example, groundwater or acidic soils can dissolve bones and teeth, and ground pressure or geologic activity can distort the appearance of any potential fossils.

Types of Fossils

sedimentary Rock formed when the deposition of sediments creates distinct layers, or strata.

Fossils are found in various types of rock, but most commonly in **sedimentary** rock, which is produced by water carrying and then dropping tiny bits of rock, sand, and soil over time. In South Africa, for example, sediments were washed, blown, or dropped into caves. Coincidentally, as the sediments built up, carnivores dropped the remains of animals, including early hominids, in the caves. Sediments subsequently buried the remains and filled the caves, preserving fossils for millions of years.

Fossilization has also occurred when volcanic activity has buried animal remains in volcanic ash. Occasionally, volcanic ash preserves footprints, such as the spectacular tracks left by three hominids around 3.5 mya at Laetoli, Tanzania (**Figure 7.4**).

Though fossils do not contain the original biological materials that were present in life, even fossils that are millions of years old preserve vestiges of the original

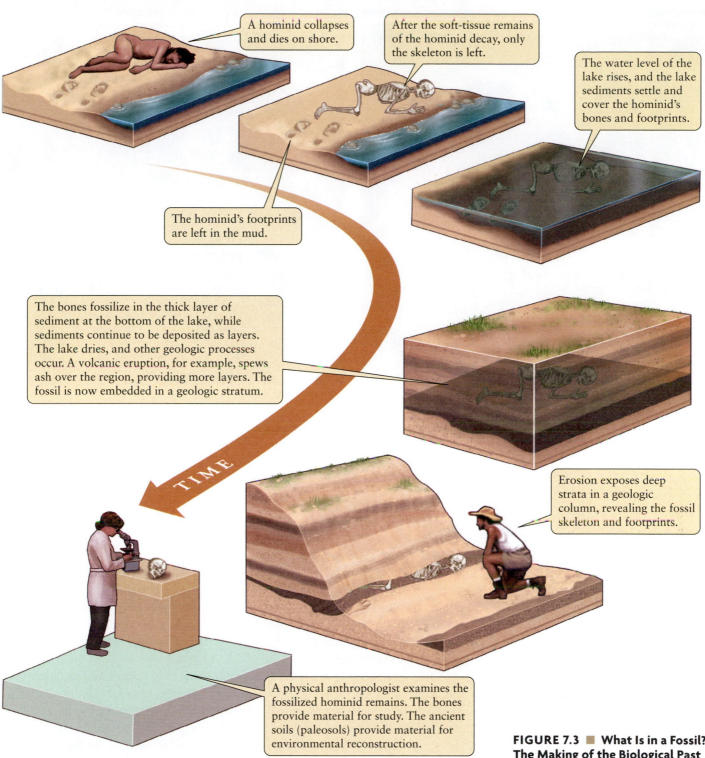

A hominid collapses and dies on shore.

After the soft-tissue remains of the hominid decay, only the skeleton is left.

The water level of the lake rises, and the lake sediments settle and cover the hominid's bones and footprints.

The hominid's footprints are left in the mud.

The bones fossilize in the thick layer of sediment at the bottom of the lake, while sediments continue to be deposited as layers. The lake dries, and other geologic processes occur. A volcanic eruption, for example, spews ash over the region, providing more layers. The fossil is now embedded in a geologic stratum.

TIME

Erosion exposes deep strata in a geologic column, revealing the fossil skeleton and footprints.

A physical anthropologist examines the fossilized hominid remains. The bones provide material for study. The ancient soils (paleosols) provide material for environmental reconstruction.

FIGURE 7.3 ■ What Is in a Fossil?: The Making of the Biological Past

tissue. DNA within this tissue can be used to identify genetic information. Also, chemicals within original bone tissue or tooth tissue may be used for dietary reconstruction. Chemical constituents of bone, for example, have been extracted from early hominids from South Africa and Europe. The chemical analysis shows that early hominids ate a range of foods including meat and plants.

(a) **(b)**

FIGURE 7.4 ■ Ancient Footprints at Laetoli
(a) Fossilized footprints of our human ancestors in Laetoli, Tanzania, provide information about **(b)** bipedal locomotion in early hominids. What information about locomotion can anthropologists learn from footprints? (Figure 7.4b: "The Fossil Footprint Makers of Laetoli," © 1982 by Jay H. Matternes.)

Limitations of the Fossil Record: Representation Is Important

To form a complete picture of life in the past, we need fossils that represent the full range of living things from the past to the present. Representation, then, is the crucial factor in creating a fossil record. The fuller and more representative the collection of fossils from specific animals and plants in any site or region, the richer will be our understanding of the various populations of these animals and plants within that site or region.

Some fossil species are remarkably representative. Paleontologists have found hundreds of fossils from some 55 mya, for example, representing many different kinds of early primates and animals of the period (see chapter 8). By contrast, many taxa are known from very limited fossil records, such as for the earliest apes of Africa (from around 20 mya). Key stages in the record of past life are missing because (1) paleontologists have searched for fossils in only some places—they simply have not discovered all the fossil-bearing rocks around the world; (2) fossils have been preserved in some places and not in others; and (3) rock sequences containing fossils are not complete in all places.

The Fayum Depression, in Egypt, helps illustrate these limitations. There, paleontologists have examined an unusually rich record of early primate evolution from about 37 mya to 31 mya (primate evolution is the subject of chapter 8). Hundreds of early primate fossils have been found in the Fayum geologic strata. The record ends at about 31 mya, however, when the rock stops bearing fossils. Did primates stop living there at 31 mya? Probably not. Rather, the geologic activity necessary for fossilization—the depositing of sediments—probably stopped after 31 mya. Without deposition and the burial of organisms, no new fossils were created.

Elsewhere in Africa, geologic strata dating to the same time period as the Fayum are exceedingly rare, or they do not contain fossils. Primates might have lived in those areas, but sedimentation or fossilization or both simply did not occur.

Similarly, the record of early hominid evolution in Africa is mostly restricted to the eastern and southern portions of the continent. In all likelihood, early hominids inhabited all of Africa, certainly by 4 mya, but they were not preserved as fossils throughout the continent. (Early hominid evolution is the subject of chapter 9.)

When fossil records are especially well represented over time, they help us discuss aspects of evolutionary theory, such as the timing and tempo of change. These records can indicate whether evolution is the gradual process that Charles Darwin wrote about in his *Origin of Species* (see chapter 2), or if its pace can speed up or slow down.

Fully interpreting the information in fossils means knowing both where the fossils were found and their ages. Without being able to place fossils in time, anthropologists cannot trace the evolution of past life.

JUST HOW OLD IS THE PAST?

Time in Perspective

Most of us have limited perspectives on time. We tend to think about yesterday, today, and tomorrow or perhaps next week. Long expanses of time might extend to our earliest memories. Because most of us were born after World War II, that conflict seems like part of the distant past. "Ancient" history might mean the beginning of the American Revolution, in 1775, or Columbus's arrival at the Americas, in 1492.

For scientists that deal with the distant past—such as geologists, paleontologists, physical anthropologists, and archaeologists—recent centuries constitute a tiny portion of time. Indeed, when put in the context of Earth's age—4.6 billion years—several centuries aren't even an eye blink in time. An appreciation of the history of life and (more immediately for this book) of primate and human evolution must be grounded in an understanding of the deep time involved. That is, to reconstruct and interpret evolutionary changes, it is crucial to place each fossil in time, answering the question *How old is it?* Without an answer to that question for each and every fossil, it is not possible to order the fossils in chronological sequence. Simply, without a chronological sequence, there is no fossil record.

Throughout Part II of this book, our normally narrow perspective on time broadens to include the vast record of natural history. The following discussion is a first step toward that broader sense of time.

Geologic Time: Earth History

The evolutionary history of life on Earth involves deep time, as represented by the geologic timescale (**Figure 7.5**). By placing all past life forms—as represented by fossils—on that scale, paleontologists record the major changes and events in the evolution of plants and of animals (**Figure 7.6**). Paleontologists order the evolution of major life forms, as geologists order Earth history, in a series of three **eras**—the **Paleozoic**, the **Mesozoic**, and the **Cenozoic**—each subdivided by a series of **epochs**. Collectively, these eras and their epochs cover the last 545,000,000 years. During

eras Major divisions of geologic time that are divided into periods and further subdivided into epochs.

epochs Divisions of periods (which are the major divisions of eras) in geologic time.

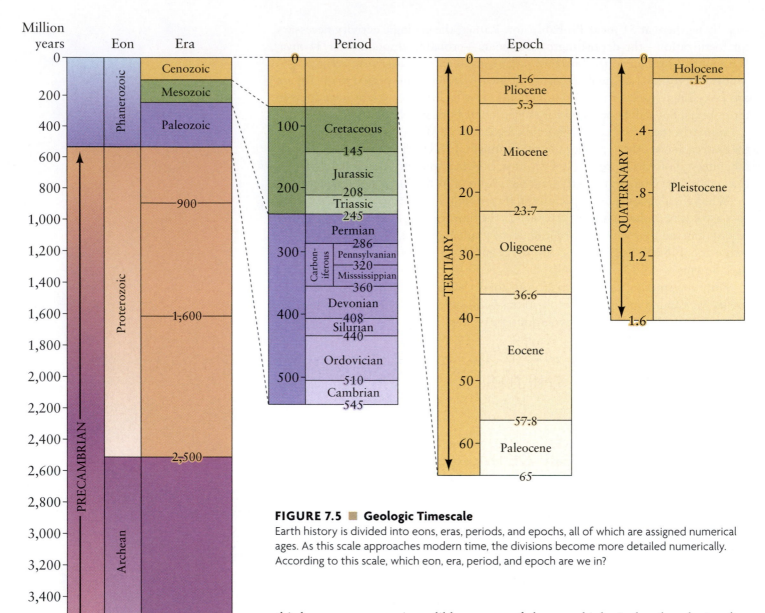

FIGURE 7.5 ■ Geologic Timescale
Earth history is divided into eons, eras, periods, and epochs, all of which are assigned numerical ages. As this scale approaches modern time, the divisions become more detailed numerically. According to this scale, which eon, era, period, and epoch are we in?

this long expanse, an incredible amount of change—biological and geologic—has occurred.

In the upcoming chapters, we will look at some of the biological evolution during this eon, especially in the Cenozoic era. Some of the most profound geologic changes have taken place within the Mesozoic and Cenozoic eras, or within the last 200,000,000 years. At the beginning of this time frame, the supercontinent we call **Pangaea**—the original continent from which our continents derive—began a process of separation, still ongoing (**Figure 7.7**). By the time true primates appeared, 145,000,000 years later, the Atlantic Ocean had formed, separating North America from Europe and South America from Africa. The gaps between North America and Europe and between South America and Africa continue to widen as the continental (**tectonic**) plates drift apart.

Pangaea A hypothetical landmass in which all the continents were joined, approximately 300–200 mya.

tectonic Refers to various structures on Earth's surface, such as the continental plates.

Relative and Numerical Age

The events described above and the idea that Earth could be hundreds of millions of years old seemed preposterous to most scholars living even a few hundred years ago. Before the eighteenth century, not many people could fathom that time

FIGURE 7.6 ◼ **Evolution of Life**
Earth's geologic timescale demonstrates the evolution of major organisms. As shown in this chart, modern humans are one of the most recent organisms to have developed; our roots go much deeper, however, as our ancestors appeared millions of years ago.

stretched more than several thousand years before the present, past what geologists call "historical" time, the time since written records began. In 1654, the archbishop of Armagh, James Ussher, added up all the generations of religious patriarchs listed in the Old Testament of the Bible and reported that Earth was created at midday on Sunday, October 23, 4004 BC. Ussher's pronouncement became the definitive answer to the question raised by many—*How old is planet Earth?*

Other scholars turned to nonhistorical sources of information, determining that a geologic past began long before the historical past. Niels Stensen (also known by his latinized name, Nicolaus Steno), a Dane serving as the court physician to the grand duke of Tuscany, studied the geologic formations around Florence, Italy, and the fossils they contained. Hypothesizing that the fossilized shark teeth that he found

(a) 200 mya

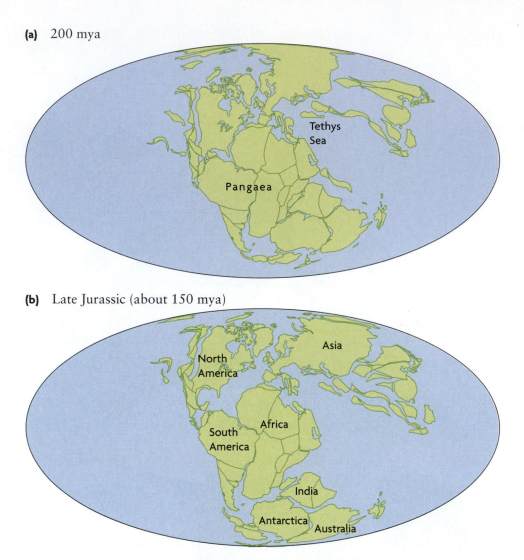

(b) Late Jurassic (about 150 mya)

(c) Late Cretaceous (about 70 mya)

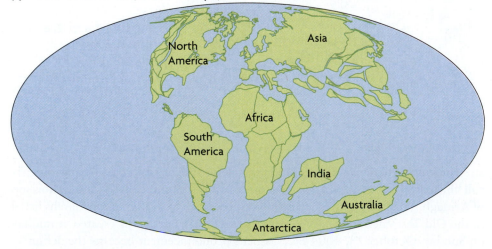

FIGURE 7.7 ■ Movement of Continents

Earth's continents have been moving for hundreds of millions of years and continue to drift. At the end of the Paleozoic (545–245 mya), all the land on Earth formed **(a)** a single mass, which we call Pangaea. Beginning in the Late Triassic (245–208 mya), this supercontinent began to break up into **(b)** separate continents. The initial split seems to have occurred in the northern part of Pangaea, creating the North Atlantic; the southern part, including South America, Africa, the Antarctic, and Australia, remained closed. At the end of the Cretaceous (145–65 mya), **(c)** most of the continents were separate and the Atlantic Ocean was complete; however, the continents had yet to reach their present-day positions.

Steno's law of superposition The principle that the lower the stratum or layer, the older its age; the oldest layers are at the bottom, and the youngest are at the top.

far under the ground were prehistoric, Stensen concluded that in a series of geologic layers—the stratigraphic sequence—higher rocks are younger than lower rocks.

Steno's law of superposition laid the foundation for relative dating, which states the relative age of one event (such as the formation of a geologic stratum) or object (such as a fossil or an artifact) with respect to another (**Figure 7.8**). That is, the

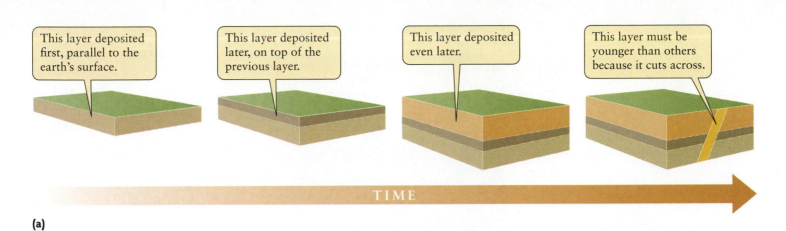

This layer deposited first, parallel to the earth's surface.

This layer deposited later, on top of the previous layer.

This layer deposited even later.

This layer must be younger than others because it cuts across.

TIME

(a)

event recorded or object found on the bottom is the oldest, that above next oldest, and so forth. By contrast, the numerical age of an event or object is expressed in absolute years, such as 2,000 years ago, 1.3 billion years, 4004 BC, or 2008. Developed long before numerical aging, relative aging can be accomplished through several methods.

Relative Methods of Dating: Which Is Older, Younger, the Same Age?

STRATIGRAPHIC CORRELATION Geologic correlation of strata from multiple locations—matching up strata based on physical features, chemical compositions, fossils, or other properties—in a region helps place the passage of time in a large context. This highly sophisticated method, first developed by William Smith, involves matching up physical and chemical characteristics of strata with the fossils found in those strata. Chemical characteristics make **stratigraphic correlation** possible across vast regions. For example: any volcanic eruption produces ash with an individual and highly specific chemical signature. The eruption's force, together with powerful winds, can spread the ash over hundreds or even thousands of kilometers, as when Krakatoa, an island volcano in Indonesia that erupted in 1883, sent ash as far as 3,700 miles (6,000 km) away. When an ash layer exists above or below a fossil, that fossil can be judged younger or older than the ash, depending on their relative positions. Such correlations, from various lines of evidence, involving millions of places around the world, have resulted in the geologic timescale.

CHEMICAL DATING Soils around the world have specific chemical compositions, reflecting their local geologic histories. For example, some soils contain **fluorine**. Once a bone is buried in fluorine-bearing soil, the bone begins to absorb the element. A bone that has been buried for a long time will have more fluorine in it than will a bone that has been buried for a short time.

Fluorine dating, one of the first **chemical dating** methods, was proposed by the English chemist James Middleton in 1844 (**Figure 7.9**). The Croatian paleontologist Dragutin Gorjanović-Kramberger applied fluorine dating to human and animal remains found in Krapina, Croatia, in the late 1890s and early 1900s (**Figure 7.10**). Hypothesizing that the bones buried in strata at the site had absorbed fluorine, he wanted to determine if the human bones, all representing humans called Neandertals (see chapter 10), were the same age as the animal bones. The animal bones

(b)

FIGURE 7.8 ■ Steno's Law of Superposition

(a) This law, formulated by **(b)** Niels Stensen, states that the youngest strata are at the top and the oldest strata are on the bottom. In which situations would this law not apply?

stratigraphic correlation The process of matching up strata from several sites through the analysis of chemical, physical, and other properties.

fluorine dating A relative (chemical) dating method that compares the accumulation of fluorine in animal and human bones from the same site.

chemical dating Dating methods that use predictable chemical changes that occur over time.

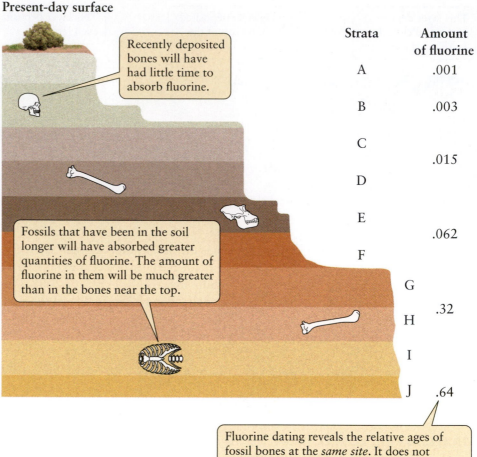

Present-day surface

Recently deposited bones will have had little time to absorb fluorine.

Fossils that have been in the soil longer will have absorbed greater quantities of fluorine. The amount of fluorine in them will be much greater than in the bones near the top.

Strata	Amount of fluorine
A	.001
B	.003
C	
D	.015
E	
F	.062
G	
H	.32
I	
J	.64

FIGURE 7.9 ■ **Fluorine Dating**
Bones absorb fluorine from surrounding soil.

Fluorine dating reveals the relative ages of fossil bones at the *same site*. It does not provide absolute dates, and it cannot be used to compare fossils from different sites because fluorine levels in soil vary from place to place.

FIGURE 7.10 ■ **Dragutin Gorjanović-Kramberger**
The Croatian paleontologist used fluorine dating at a site in Krapina, Croatia. The significance of this dating method was demonstrated by his results, which suggested that extinct animals and Neandertals had coexisted.

were from long-extinct, Pleistocene forms of rhinoceroses, cave bears, and cattle. Some scientists believed that the Krapina Neandertals were not ancient, however, but had been living at the site in recent times only. They considered the Neandertals simply different from people living in Croatia in the late nineteenth and early twentieth centuries. If Gorjanović-Kramberger could show that the two sets of bones—human and animal—contained the same amount of fluorine, he could prove that the Neandertals were ancient and in fact had lived at the same time as the extinct animals. When the simple chemical analysis revealed that the Neandertal bones and the animal bones had very similar amounts of fluorine, this pioneering study had shown human beings' deep roots.

BIOSTRATIGRAPHIC (FAUNAL) DATING Gorjanović-Kramberger recognized that different strata include different kinds of fossils. He regarded these findings as chronologically significant. That is, the forms of specific animals and plants change over time, so the forms discovered within individual layers can help determine relative ages. **Biostratigraphic dating** draws on the first appearance of an organism in the fossil record, that organism's evolutionary development over time, and the organism's extinction. Pliocene and Pleistocene African rodents, pigs, and elephants and Eurasian mammals of all kinds have been especially useful for biostratigraphic dating because they show significant evolutionary change. By determining when certain animals lived, scientists have developed biostratigraphic markers, or **index fossils,** for assessing age. For example, giant deer—sometimes called Irish elk—provide useful information based on their extinction. That is, because the species appears to have died out in northern Europe around 10,600 yBP, the presence of Irish elk fossils in a northern European site indicates that the site predates 10,600 yBP.

Mammoths—relatives of modern elephants—first lived and evolved in Africa, then spread to Europe, Asia, and North America around 2.5 mya. Mammoths went extinct in Africa, but continued to evolve elsewhere. After 2.5 mya, their molars became increasingly complex. Paleontologists have determined how these teeth changed from the species' emergence to its complete extinction. Therefore, when paleontologists discover fossilized mammoth teeth, they can determine the relative age of the site simply by looking at the molars. Likewise, changes in molar shape and size have helped paleontologists develop relative ages for Pliocene-Pleistocene pigs in East Africa and South Africa (**Figure 7.11**).

biostratigraphic dating A relative dating method that uses the associations of fossils in strata to determine each layer's approximate age.

index fossils Fossils that are from specified time ranges, are found in multiple locations, and can be used to determine the age of associated strata.

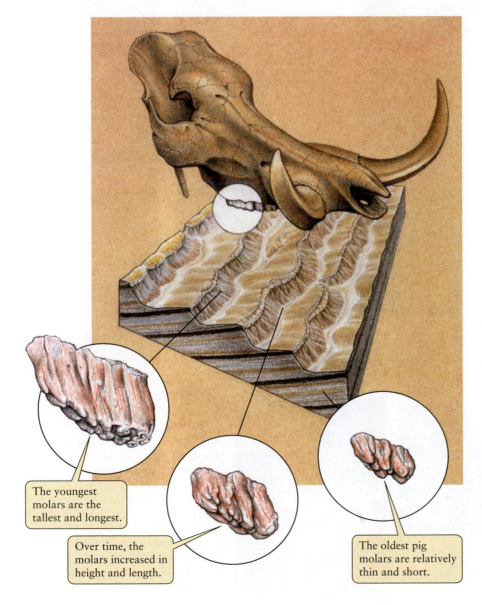

The youngest molars are the tallest and longest.

Over time, the molars increased in height and length.

The oldest pig molars are relatively thin and short.

FIGURE 7.11 ■ **Fossil Pig Molars**
Changes in the size and shape of these teeth can be used for biostratigraphic dating, in a method developed by the American paleontologists Jack Harris and Tim White. Over time, the molars became taller and longer.

In addition, fossil pig molars found in conjunction with layers of volcanic ash may be used for absolute dating, if paleontologists can determine the age of the ash. (On techniques for doing this, see "The Revolution Continues: Radiopotassium Dating," below.) Because the teeth and the volcanic layer are associated chronologically, the teeth can then be used as time markers when found at other sites. ("Pig Dating: Stratigraphic Correlations," © 1985 by Jay H. Matternes.)

(a)

(b)

(c)

(d)

(e)

(f)

(g)

(h)

(i)

(j)

(k)

(l)

(m)

(n)

(o)

(p)

(q)

(r)

(s)

FIGURE 7.12 ■ Cultural Artifacts
Among the remains of material culture that can be used to determine the time periods of archaeological sites are **(a)** an Oldowan chopper, **(b)** an Oldowan flake tool, **(c)** an Acheulean hand axe, **(d)** an Olorgesailie tool, **(e)** a Galeria tool, **(f)** a Mousterian Levallois flake tool, **(g)** Mousterian tools, **(h)** a Solutrean tool, **(i)** an Upper Paleolithic point, **(j)** a Neolithic flake tool, **(k)** a Neolithic axe head, **(l)** Neolithic scrapers, **(m)** a Mayan pot, **(n)** post-Neolithic Clovis points, **(o)** a post-Neolithic spade, **(p)** an American Indian stone maul, **(q)** an Inuit fishing spear, **(r)** a Ford Model T, and **(s)** an Apple iPod.

CULTURAL DATING Material culture can provide information for **cultural dating.** The first evidence of material culture—primitive stone tools called **pebble tools**—dates to 2.6 mya. Although individually distinctive in appearance, pebble tools are not especially useful for bracketing small amounts of time, mainly because their forms changed so slowly. For example, a pebble tool from 2.5 mya is very much like one produced at 1.8 mya. However, the presence of a certain kind of tool enables paleontologists to say that the site (and its hominid occupants) dates to a certain age (**Figure 7.12**).

Beginning in the later Pleistocene, stone tools and other components of material culture changed more rapidly. The various regional cultures in Europe collectively known as the Upper Paleolithic provide a number of "time-specific" artifacts, such as the small sculptures known as Lion Men. The first of these artifacts was found in a cave in Germany in 1939, neglected for 30 years in part because of World War II, and only recently restored (**Figure 7.13**).

In the Holocene, artifacts such as ceramics became even more "time-specific." In fact, ceramics were invented during this period.

Absolute Methods of Dating: What Is the Numerical Age?

THE RADIOMETRIC REVOLUTION AND THE DATING CLOCK When we say that the American Civil War took place after the American Revolution, we have provided relative ages for the two wars. That is, we have related the ages without specifying them. When we say that the American Civil War began in 1861 and the American Revolution began in 1775, we have provided numerical ages. That is, we have pinpointed the wars' beginnings in terms of years, a measure of scaled time. We know these dates thanks to written records, individuals having recorded all sorts of events associated with both wars (**Figure 7.14**). Since the time that Niels Stensen and his

FIGURE 7.13 ■ **Lion Man**
The discovery of another sculpture like this one, made of mammoth ivory and about 30 cm high, would provide a relative date for the archaeological site. The site would have to be at least 30,000 years old because the sculptures are that old.

> **cultural dating** Relative dating methods that are based on material remains' time spans.

> **pebble tools** The earliest stone tools, in which simple flakes were knocked off to produce an edge used for cutting and scraping.

RELATIVE AGE	NUMERICAL AGE	
Iraq War	Iraq War	
Gulf War (Persian Gulf)		2000
Falkland War (Argentina-England)	Gulf War (Persian Gulf)	
	Falkland War (Argentina-England)	1980
Six-day War (Arab-Israeli)		
Vietnam War	Vietnam War	
	Six-day War (Arab-Israeli)	
Bay of Pigs Invasion (Cuba-U.S.)	Bay of Pigs Invasion (Cuba-U.S.)	1960
	Korean War	
Korean War		
	World War II	1940
World War II	Spanish Civil War	
Spanish Civil War		
		1920
World War I	World War I	
	Russian Revolution	
Russian Revolution	Russo-Japanese War	
Russo-Japanese War	Boer War	1900
Boer War (South Africa)		

FIGURE 7.14 ■ **Relative vs. Numerical**
Wars of the twentieth and twenty-first centuries can be ordered relatively or numerically. The relative chart simply shows the order of events and does not specify when these events occurred or how long they lasted. The numerical chart provides dates and gives at least a rough sense of the wars' starting points and durations.

dendrochronology A chronometric dating method that uses a tree-ring count to determine numerical age.

radiocarbon dating The radiometric dating method in which the ratio of ^{14}C to ^{12}C is measured to provide an absolute date for a material younger than 50,000 years.

isotopes Two or more forms of a chemical element that vary in the number of neutrons in the nucleus and by the atomic mass.

half-life The time it takes for half of the radioisotopes in a substance to decay; used in various radiometric dating methods.

contemporaries began studying geologic features and fossils, scientists have been recording relative ages. By doing so, they have established the sequence of events in the geologic timescale—proving that the Eocene came before the Miocene, for example, and that ceramics were invented long after Neandertals lived in Europe. However, unlike historians, who often work with records containing dates, premodern geologists, paleontologists, and anthropologists had no means of providing numerical dates. Geologists could only group geologic events, paleontologists could only group species' lives, and anthropologists could only group peoples' lives and cultural events.

In the 1920s, the American astronomer A. E. Douglass (1867–1962) developed the first method for numerically dating objects and events, specifically ones including or involving wood. In studying sunspots and their impact on climate, Douglass noted that in temperate and very cold regions tree growth stopped in the winter and reactived in the spring. This intermittence resulted in layers of growth, visible as a concentric ring pattern in the cross-section of a tree. Douglass's **dendrochronology,** or tree-ring method of dating, involved counting the number of rings, each of which represented one year of growth (**Figure 7.15**). Tree-ring dating was first used on tree sections found in archaeological sites in the American Southwest. It works only when wood is as excellently preserved as it is in the Southwest, however, and thus can be applied in only a limited number of areas in the world.

Widely applicable numerical dating became possible in the nuclear age, following World War II (1939–45). In 1949, the American chemist Willard Libby (1908–1980) discovered **radiocarbon dating,** an accomplishment for which he won a Nobel Prize. Scientists now had a means of determining the numerical age of past life forms via the decay of radioactive elements.

The radiocarbon method, sometimes called the carbon-14 method, involves dating of carbon **isotopes.** Isotopes are variants of an elements based on the number of neutrons in the atom's nucleus. Some isotopes of an element are stable—in theory, they will last for an infinite amount of time, at least with respect to maintaining the same number of neutrons. Some isotopes are unstable—over time, they decay radioactively, transforming themselves to stable isotopes of either the same element or another element. Carbon has one radioisotope (unstable or radioactive isotope), identified as ^{14}C because it has an atomic mass of 14 (six protons and eight neutrons) in its nucleus. Carbon has two non-radioisotopes (stable isotopes), ^{12}C (carbon-12) and ^{13}C (carbon-13), which have an atomic mass of 12 (six protons and six neutrons) and 13 (six protons and seven neutrons), respectively. The radiocarbon method focuses on what happens to the radioisotope, ^{14}C. Over 5,730 years, half of the ^{14}C decays into ^{14}N. Over the next 5,730 years, another half of the ^{14}C decays again into ^{14}N, and so on, until eventually most of the radioisotope will have decayed. The number representing the time it takes for half of the radioisotope to decay is called the **half-life** (**Table 7.1**).

All living plants and animals (including you) absorb about the same amount of ^{14}C in their tissues, through the ingestion of very small amounts of atmospheric carbon dioxide (CO_2). Once a plant or animal dies, it stops absorbing ^{14}C, and the ^{14}C begins to decay—the clock starts ticking. This means that over time, the ratio of ^{14}C to ^{12}C changes, because the ^{14}C is decaying over time but the ^{12}C is not in the material being dated (**Figure 7.16**).

The advantage of the radiocarbon method is that it has a precise baseline for the start of the clock—the death of the organism. The disadvantage for dating major events in primate and human evolution is that ^{14}C has a fairly short half-life, rendering its dates most accurate for only the last 50,000–70,000 yBP. Dates

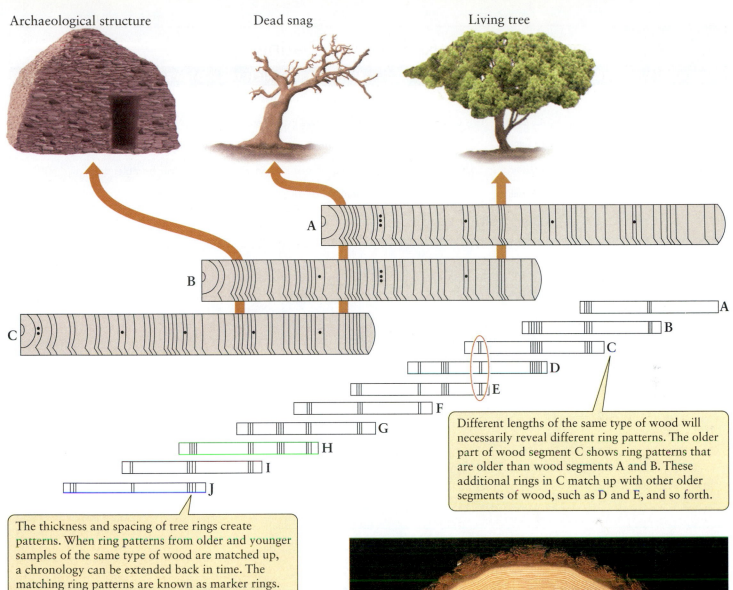

Archaeological structure   Dead snag   Living tree

Different lengths of the same type of wood will necessarily reveal different ring patterns. The older part of wood segment C shows ring patterns that are older than wood segments A and B. These additional rings in C match up with other older segments of wood, such as D and E, and so forth.

The thickness and spacing of tree rings create patterns. When ring patterns from older and younger samples of the same type of wood are matched up, a chronology can be extended back in time. The matching ring patterns are known as marker rings.

(b)

(a)

FIGURE 7.15 ■ Dendrochronology
(a) Tree-ring patterns **(b)** can be used to date relatively recent archaeological sites.

TABLE 7.1	Isotopes Used in Radiometric Dating		
PARENT → DAUGHTER	**HALF-LIFE (YEARS)**	**MATERIAL IN WHICH THE ISOTOPES OCCUR**	
$^{14}C \rightarrow {}^{14}N$	5,730	Anything organic (has carbon), such as wood, shell, bone	
$^{238}U \rightarrow {}^{206}Pb$	4.5 billion	Uranium-bearing minerals (zircon, uraninite)	
$^{40}K \rightarrow {}^{40}Ar$	1.3 billion	Potassium-bearing minerals (mica, feldspar, hornblende)	
$^{40}Ar \rightarrow {}^{39}Ar$	1.3 billion	Potassium-bearing minerals (mica, feldspar, hornblende)	
$^{235}U \rightarrow {}^{207}Pb$	713 million	Uranium-bearing minerals (zircon, uraninite)	

^{14}C is produced in the atmosphere.

^{14}C is oxidized and forms carbon dioxide.

$^{14}CO_2$ is used by plants in photosynthesis. ^{14}C is incorporated in plant tissues.

Most ^{14}C is absorbed by the oceans.

Animals consume plants, and the plant ^{14}C is incorporated in animal bone and other tissues through metabolic processes.

When animals die, their metabolism ceases, and their tissues stop incorporating ^{14}C. ^{14}C begins decaying to ^{14}N. The proportion of ^{14}C begins to decrease.

FIGURE 7.16 ■ **Radiocarbon Dating**
This dating method was the first generation of radioisotope methods. Such dating methods remain among the most important for the determination of numerical dates.

can be determined for another 25,000 years beyond that, but they are less precise owing to the small amount of ^{14}C left.

THE REVOLUTION CONTINUES: RADIOPOTASSIUM DATING All organic materials contain carbon and thus can be dated through the radiocarbon method. By contrast, nonorganic materials such as rocks contain other elements that can be dated radiometrically. Because the radioisotopes of these elements have very long half-lives, the radiometric clock is considerably longer for these nonorganic materials than for carbon-based materials. **Igneous** (volcanic) rock, for example, contains the radioisotope ^{40}K (potassium-40). ^{40}K decays very slowly from its unstable form to a stable gas, ^{40}Ar (argon-40)—its half-life is 1.3 *billion* years. It is usually not possible to date rocks much younger than 200,000 yBP, but ^{40}K's long half-life presents no limitation on the other end of the range. **Radiopotassium dating** certainly accommodates all of primate evolution.

The great strength of this method is the presence of volcanic rock in many places throughout the world. During a volcanic eruption, the heat is so extreme that it drives off all argon gas in the rock. The ^{40}K solid that is in the rock sealed by lava then begins to decay to ^{40}Ar gas, and the gas accumulates, trapped within the rock's crystalline structure. To date that rock—which could then be millions of years old—a scientist measures, with sophisticated instruments, the amount of gas (^{40}Ar) relative to the amount of nongas (^{40}K) in the rock. The more gas there is, the older the rock.

The radiopotassium method was first used to date the volcanic rock associated with an early hominid skull found by the British archaeologist Mary Leakey (1913–1996) in the lowest strata of Olduvai Gorge, in Tanzania, in 1959. At that time, scientists assumed that hominids had been around for perhaps a half-million years but not longer. When the associated volcanic rock at Olduvai proved to be 1,800,000 years old, that dating nearly quadrupled the known time frame for human evolution. Since then, radiometric methods have helped paleontologists fine-tune the chronologies of primate evolution and human evolution.

In the last 10 years, scientists have developed an alternative method of radiopotassium dating, whereby they measure the ratio of ^{40}Ar gas to ^{39}Ar gas. In the argon-argon method, volcanic rock is bombarded with "fast" neutrons in a nuclear reactor. Like ^{40}K, ^{39}K is present in the volcanic rock, and the two isotopes, ^{40}K and ^{39}K, occur in the same amounts relative to one another, no matter how old the rock may be. The neutron bombardment converts the ^{39}K to ^{39}Ar. Because the ^{39}Ar serves as a proxy for ^{40}K, the ratio of the ^{40}Ar to ^{39}Ar reveals the rock's absolute age. This method's advantages over the potassium-argon method are that it requires less rock and the potassium does not have to be measured. Now routinely being used by paleontologists and geologists to date early hominids (see chapter 9), the method has made it possible to date hundreds of hominid (and other) fossils from between 5,000,000 yBP to *Homo sapiens'* origin, more than 100,000 yBP.

Note, though, that radiopotassium can be used to date only igneous rock, not sedimentary rock.

NON-RADIOMETRIC ABSOLUTE DATING METHODS Several other, non-radiometric methods provide absolute dates (**Figure 7.17**). Among these methods, **amino acid dating** is the most useful in more-recent settings. This method is based on the decay of protein molecules following an organism's death. Amino acids, the compounds that make up proteins (among the subjects of chapter 3), come in two forms, L-isomers and D-isomers, respectively known as left-handed amino acids and right-handed amino acids. Basically, this distinction means that when a protein is viewed under high-power magnification with a specialized light called **polarized light,** the molecules bend light to the left (and are called L-isomers) or to the right (D-isomers). Most living organisms' tissues are comprised of L-isomers. Once an organism dies, these L-isomers begin to transform to D-isomers. The longer the

igneous Rock formed from the crystallization of molten magma, which contains the radioisotope ^{40}K; used in potassium-argon dating.

radiopotassium dating The radiometric dating method in which the ratio of ^{40}K to ^{40}Ar is measured to provide an absolute date for a material older than 200,000 years.

amino acid dating An absolute dating method for organic remains such as bone or shell, in which the amount of change in the amino acid structure is measured.

polarized light A kind of light used in amino acid dating because it allows amino acid changes to be observed and measured.

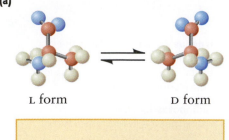

(a)

L form   D form

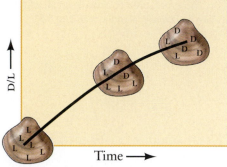

D/L

Time →

(d)

(b)

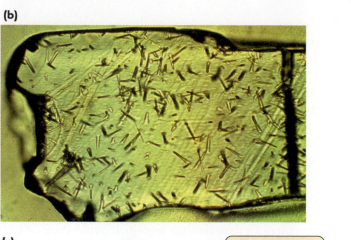

(c)

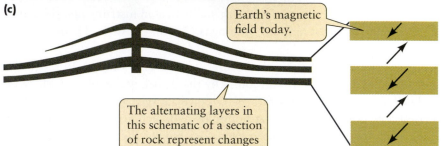

Earth's magnetic field today.

The alternating layers in this schematic of a section of rock represent changes in polarity over time.

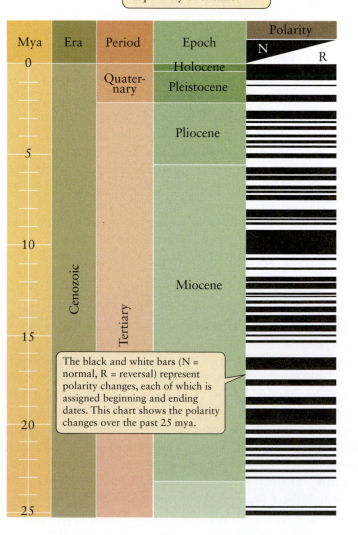

The black and white bars (N = normal, R = reversal) represent polarity changes, each of which is assigned beginning and ending dates. This chart shows the polarity changes over the past 25 mya.

FIGURE 7.17 ■ **Non-Radiometric Absolute Dating Methods**

These methods produce chronological dates, but do not involve the measurement of radioactive decay. **(a)** Amino acid dating is based on changes in the form of amino acid molecules (from L to D) over time. **(b)** Fission track dating employs the number of tracks left behind by isotope decay. **(c)** Paleomagnetic dating derives from changes in Earth's polarity. **(d)** Luminescence dating is related to the amount of light released when an object with stored energy is heated.

organism has been dead, the greater the number of Ds, and so the fossil's date is based on the ratio of L to D.

The limitation of amino acid dating is that the rate of the chemical decomposition resulting in the shift from L to D—a process called **racemization**—is largely determined by the temperature of the region. That is, a region with a higher average temperature will have a faster rate of chemical decomposition than will a region with a cooler average temperature. The age range for amino acid dating is generally 40,000–100,000 yBP, but has been extended to 200,000 yBP in tropical settings and to 1 mya in cooler settings. The method has provided useful dates for

racemization The chemical reaction resulting in the conversion of L amino acids to D amino acids for amino acid dating.

| CONCEPT CHECK | How Old Is It? |

Fossils are the primary source of information for documenting the evolution of past life. Paleontologists have developed various means for determining a fossil's age.

METHOD	BASIS	MATERIAL	DATE RANGE
Relative Age			
Law of Superposition	Older is lower	Just about anything	Just about any time
Stratigraphic Correlation	Like strata from different regions are related to the same event	Rocks and fossils	Just about any time
Biostratigraphic (Faunal) Dating	Evolution of animals	Bones and teeth	Just about any time
Chemical Dating	Fossils absorb chemicals, such as fluorine, in soil	Bones	Less than 100,000 yBP
Cultural Dating	Artifacts are time-specific	Technology generally	Up to about 2.5 mya
Numerical Age			
Dendrochronology	Tree growth	Specific tree types	12,000–8,000 yBP
Radiocarbon Dating	Carbon-14	Anything organic	75,000–50,000 yBP
Radiopotassium Dating	Potassium-40	Volcanic rocks	More than 200,000 yBP
Amino Acid Dating	Racemization	Bones, shells	1 mya–40,000 yBP
Fission Track Dating	Fission tracks on rock crystal	Volcanic rock	Up to 3 mya
Paleomagnetic Dating	Shifts in Earth's magnetic field	Sedimentary rocks	Up to 5 mya
Electron Spin Resonance Dating	Concentrations of radioisotopes	Bones, teeth	Several thousand to more than 1 mya
Luminescence Dating	Trapped energy	Sediment, stone, ceramics	Up to 800,000 yBP

a variety of sites, but it is best known in human evolutionary studies for dating Border Cave, in South Africa (70,000–145,000 yBP).

Fission track dating is based on the radioactive decay of naturally occurring ^{238}U (uranium-238). When the isotope decays, fragments produced in the decay, or fission, process leave a line, or track, measuring just a few atoms wide on the rock crystal. Thus, the greater the number of tracks, the older the material being dated. This method can date materials from the last several million years and has been used for dating volcanic ash and obsidian (volcanic glass).

Paleomagnetic dating is based on changes in Earth's magnetic field, which change the planet's polarity. In essence, movement of the planet's liquid (iron alloy) outer core creates an electric current that results in the magnetic field. When the magnetic field shifts, the magnetic north and south poles shift. The poles' shifts have been well documented. In the last 6,000,000 years, for example, there have been four "epochs" of polar changes, or four different well-dated periods. Because certain metal grains align themselves with Earth's magnetic field as they settle and help form sedimentary rock, geologists can examine the orientation of these fragments to determine the planet's polarity at the time of the rock's formation. In addition, when molten igneous rock is produced, each new layer records the polarity, which can later be determined from the hard igneous rock. The South African caves where so many early hominid fossils have been found (see chapter 9) contain mostly sedimentary rock and therefore are ideally suited for paleomagnetic dating.

Electron spin resonance dating relies on the measurement of radioisotope concentrations (e.g., of uranium) that have accumulated in fossils over periods of time. Once buried, remains such as bones and teeth absorb radioisotopes and so record the radioactivity in the surrounding burial environment. The older the fossil, the greater the concentration, and this method can date material from a few thousand to more than a million years old.

Luminescence dating is based on the amount of the sun's energy trapped in material such as sediment, stone, or ceramic. When such an object is heated—as in, for example, an early hominid's campfire—the energy it contains is released as light. The next time that same material is heated—as in the laboratory to derive a date—the amount of light released (measured as electrons that are from natural radiation, such as from uranium) reveals the amount of time since the material was first heated. This method can date materials back to about 800,000 yBP.

Scientists must consider various factors when choosing an absolute dating method, among them the material involved and the time range in which the fossilized organism likely lived. Some methods date the fossil, some date the *context* of the fossil, and others date either the fossil or the context. Radiocarbon, for example, can be used to date either the remains of the once-living organism or an associated organic substance, such as wood. To determine the age of a human skeleton, the bones can be dated directly. If, however, it can be proved that the deceased was buried at the same time a fire was lit nearby, the fire pit can be dated.

Genetic Dating: The Molecular Clock

The DNA in living organisms is an important source of information for retrospectively dating key events in their species' evolution, including divergence from closely related species and phylogenetic relationships with other organisms. In light of the well-founded assumption that a species accumulates genetic differences over time at a more or less constant rate, it should be possible to develop a chronology

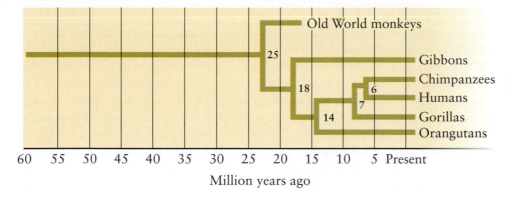

showing the amount of time since two species diverged in their evolution. Simply, more closely related species should have more similar DNA than less closely related species have. The American geneticist Morris Goodman and others developed the molecular clock for dating the divergences of the major primate taxa. This record indicates that Old World monkeys first diverged from all other primates at about 25 mya; gibbons diverged at about 18 mya, orangutans at about 14 mya, gorillas at about 7 mya; and the split occurred between chimpanzees and early hominids about 6 or 8 mya (**Figure 7.18**). Molecular anthropologists and paleoanthropologists studying the respective genetic and fossil records (among the subjects of chapter 8) find a general consistency in the dates for the origins of the major primate groups. As geneticists and anthropologists learn more about the primate genome, this method of retrospective dating is becoming increasingly refined.

In summary: anthropologists and other scientists that deal with deep time have various methods and research tools for answering questions about when past organisms were alive. Some of these methods and tools directly date fossils, and others date the fossils' geological contexts. Relative and absolute dating have brought about a far greater understanding of the evolutionary record than was imagined when fossils were first being discovered centuries ago. Placing fossils in order creates a detailed picture of the past, of the evolutionary sequence of events for specific organisms and for groups of organisms.

In addition to determining the ages of fossils, anthropologists seek to understand what the habitats were like in which past plants and past animals lived. This is a new area in the study of the past, and it is becoming increasingly clear that understanding environmental contexts—reconstructing past environments to shed light on the circumstances driving evolutionary change, such as major climate change—is crucial to understanding evolution in general and local adaptations in particular. In the next section, we will explore ways in which anthropologists reconstruct environments and landscapes.

RECONSTRUCTION OF ANCIENT ENVIRONMENTS AND LANDSCAPES

For much of the history of paleontology, the focus has been on evolutionary relationships (phylogeny). In studying the origins and morphological evolution of the various life forms, paleontologists have asked questions such as *Which (now fossilized) species gave rise to primates? To the first apes? To the first hominids? To the first modern humans?* Phylogenetic questions remain central to the study of evolution, but

FIGURE 7.19 ■ **Life in the Trees**
(a) The skeleton and body reconstruction of *Oreopithecus* show that the ape's long arms were adapted to a suspensory form of locomotion. **(b)** Gibbons have a similar body style, adapted to life in the trees. What differences in skeletal anatomy would you expect in a primate that lived primarily on open grassland?

foraminifera Marine protozoans that have variably shaped shells with small holes.

the evolution of past organisms is not truly meaningful unless it is correlated with the circumstances under which the organisms lived and the processes that underlay their evolutionary changes. Scientists need to ask additional questions—for example, *Which conditions drove natural selection and other processes that account for the appearance, evolution, radiation, and extinction of past primates and humans?* This question pertains especially to the ecology of the setting the primates lived in—their habitat. Using models derived from the study of living animals, paleontologists can look at the bones of extinct animals and determine how they functioned during life and in what kinds of habitats they functioned. For example, as discussed in chapter 6, the long arms and short legs of apes are now well understood to be part of the species' adaptation to life in the trees—the apes are skilled at suspensory forms of locomotion. Therefore, when paleontologists find fossil apes with long arms, such as the Miocene ape *Oreopithecus*, they can infer that these primates lived in a habitat where trees were the dominant form of vegetation (**Figure 7.19**).

The Driving Force in Shaping Environment: Temperature

Temperature is perhaps the single most important feature of climate. Therefore, if scientists can reconstruct the temperature for a particular geologic stratum, they come very close to characterizing a past climate. Scientists cannot measure temperature in the past, but they can identify and study the impacts of different temperatures on biology and geologic chemistry. Hot climates leave very different biological and chemical signals than do cold climates.

Because of this close linkage of temperature with biology and chemistry, paleoclimatologists have reconstructed temperature changes for much of the Cenozoic (and before). Some of the best information on climate history—and especially temperature—is based on the study of **foraminifera** and other ocean-dwelling microorganisms (**Figure 7.20**). These microorganisms' tiny shells are preserved in sediments on the ocean floor worldwide, and their chemical compositions tell important stories about temperature change over time. While the microorganisms are alive, they ingest two of the three stable isotopes of oxygen, ^{18}O and ^{16}O, from the ocean water. Atmospheric temperature directly affects the water's temperature, which in turn affects the amount of ^{18}O in the water. When temperature declines, the amount of ^{18}O in the water, and therefore in the microorganism, increases. When temperature increases, the amount of ^{18}O decreases. Geologists have taken core samples of sediments from the ocean floor and have tracked the ^{18}O content in the microorganisms within those sediments, producing a record of global temperature change (**Figure 7.21**).

Based on the isotope signatures of ancient sediments, we know that temperatures were high in the Paleocene, preceding the appearance of true primates, and that they peaked at the beginning of the Eocene, about 55 mya. This warm period was followed by a gradual decline in temperature throughout the Eocene. At the boundary between the Eocene and Oligocene, about 34 mya, temperature sharply declined, then rose, then sharply declined again. Moderate ups and downs followed in the Oligocene and into the Middle Miocene. After a sharp decline about 17–15 mya, temperature leveled off for the remainder of the Miocene. Climate was drier and more seasonal about 10–5 mya, coinciding with the appearance of early hominids.

One of the most profound temperature changes, and thus dramatic alterations of climate and habitat, began at the end of the Miocene, around 6 mya. Sea levels are at their highest during warm periods; during cold periods, more water is tied up in ice and glaciers than during warm periods. This cold period likely added a permanent ice sheet on the continent of Antarctica; so much water was tied up in glacial ice that the Mediterranean Sea was nearly dry. During the Pleistocene (1.6 mya–15,000 yBP), periods of massive glaciation, or glacials, were followed by periods of relative warmth, or interglacials. Studies of such cold-and-warm patterns indicate that the time we live in, the Holocene, is not a separate epoch but simply another interglacial. More severely cold weather might be just around the corner!

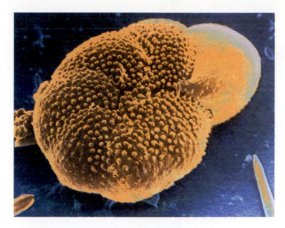

FIGURE 7.20 ■ **Foraminifera**
The chemical composition of these microorganisms found in sediments on the ocean floor provides information on past climates.

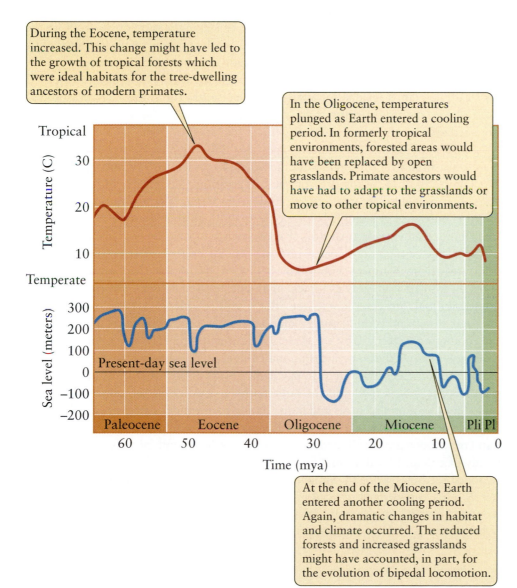

During the Eocene, temperature increased. This change might have led to the growth of tropical forests which were ideal habitats for the tree-dwelling ancestors of modern primates.

In the Oligocene, temperatures plunged as Earth entered a cooling period. In formerly tropical environments, forested areas would have been replaced by open grasslands. Primate ancestors would have had to adapt to the grasslands or move to other topical environments.

At the end of the Miocene, Earth entered another cooling period. Again, dramatic changes in habitat and climate occurred. The reduced forests and increased grasslands might have accounted, in part, for the evolution of bipedal locomotion.

FIGURE 7.21 ■ **Global Temperature and Climate Changes**
Changes in temperature during the Cenozoic have been documented by measuring ^{18}O in foraminifera shells.

Chemistry of Animal Remains and Ancient Soils: Windows onto Diets and Habitats

C₃ plants Plants that take in carbon through C₃ photosynthesis, which changes carbon dioxide into a compound having three carbon atoms. Tending to be from more temperate regions, these plants include wheat, sugar beets, peas, and a range of hardwood trees.

C₄ plants Plants that take in carbon through C₄ photosynthesis, which changes carbon dioxide into a compound with four carbon atoms. These plants tend to be from warmer regions with low humidity and include corn, sugarcane, millet, and prickly pear.

Chemical analysis of the bones and teeth in fossils provides important information about past animals' diets and habitats. The reconstruction of diets and habitats is based on the plants those animals ate. Edible plants employ either C_3 photosynthesis or C_4 photosynthesis. The type of photosynthesis determines how the plant extracts and uses carbon from atmospheric carbon dioxide (CO_2). In East Africa, to take one example, C_3 **plants** include trees, bushes, and shrubs associated with a relatively wet, wooded environment; C_4 **plants** are associated with open grasslands typical of tropical savannas. Because C_3 and C_4 plants extract and use carbon differently, the two stable isotopes of carbon in the plants (^{12}C and ^{13}C) have different ratios. C_3 plants have lower ratios of ^{12}C to ^{13}C than do C_4 plants. That is, the values for the stable isotope ratios are lower for C_3 plants than for C_4 plants.

When animals eat the plants, those ratios are transmitted to the body tissues (including bones and teeth) through digestion and metabolism. Thus, scientists can determine which kind of plant the animal ate based on the ratio of ^{12}C to ^{13}C in the animal's remains. The amounts of ^{12}C and ^{13}C are determined by placing a very tiny piece of bone or of tooth in an instrument called a mass spectrometer.

Similarly, the soils in which edible plants grow express different ratios of ^{12}C to ^{13}C. The plant's residue following decay preserves the stable carbon isotopes. Worldwide, the ratios in the soils, like those in the animals, tend to be lower in forested settings than in grasslands.

Numerous remains of Miocene apes and Pliocene and Pleistocene hominids and other animals have been found in Kenya (discussed further in chapters 8 and 9). The study of these fossils' isotopic compositions has greatly informed scientists' environmental reconstructions. Today, the Serengeti grasslands of Kenya are dominated by C_4 grasses. It has long been assumed that the first hominids and their immediate apelike ancestors lived in such a setting. New evidence from the study of the ancient soils (paleosols) and animal bones in Kenya and elsewhere indicates an environment with relatively low $^{12}C/^{13}C$ ratios (C_3 plant dominance). This means that if C_4 grasses typical of an open grassland were present, they were quite minimal. However, sometime after 6 mya, C_4 plants became dominant for a range of mammals, indicating a marked shift in ecology. Recent work at a site in Lemudong'o, Kenya, by the American anthropologist Stanley Ambrose and colleagues shows that 6 mya the animals there, unlike the ones there today, lived amongst large trees and water. In particular, birds of prey that roost in large trees (such as the strigid owl) and the large number of colobine monkeys argue for a woodland habitat. Paleosols and fauna dating to around 5.6 mya at early hominid sites in the Middle Awash Valley of Ethiopia show a similar record of open woodland or wooded grasslands around lake margins. The combined evidence from the study of paleosols and animal fossils indicates that the earliest hominids lived in wooded settings, probably for some time after 5 mya (discussed further in chapter 9). This knowledge is crucial because it helps us understand the environmental context in which our humanlike ancestors rose, and that rise is fundamental to who we are as biological organisms.

This chapter presented several key concepts for understanding the past, primarily the importance of fossils as windows onto the past. Once placed in time, fossils document and enable us to interpret change over time—they become the central record of evolution. In the upcoming chapters, we will apply this knowledge about fossils and how to evaluate them, as we examine nonhuman and human primate evolution. We will look at the origin and evolution of primates, from their very beginning some 55 mya to the dawn of human evolution. Primates are part of a great adaptive radiation of mammals, a radiation that continues to the present day. Understanding primate evolution provides the context for understanding who we are as biological organisms.

ANSWERING THE BIG QUESTIONS

What are fossils?

■ Fossils are the remains of once-living organisms, wholly or partially transformed into rock. The most common types of fossils are bones and teeth.

What do fossils tell us about the past?

■ Fossils provide an essential historical record for documenting and understanding the biological evolution of surviving and nonsurviving lineages.

■ Fossils provide information on chronology and geologic time.

■ Fossils and their geologic settings reveal past diets and environments, important contexts for understanding how past organisms evolved.

What methods do anthropologists and other scientists use to study fossils?

■ Geologic time provides the grand scale of the evolution of life. Both relative and absolute (numerical) dates place fossils and past events in chronological sequence on that scale.

■ Relative and absolute dates can be determined through various methods. Radioactive decay is central to some of the best methods of determining absolute dates.

■ Past climates and habitat in general can be reconstructed via two of the stable isotopes of oxygen.

■ Ancient animals' diets and their habitats can be reconstructed through two of the stable isotopes of carbon.

wwnorton.com/studyspace

KEY TERMS

amino acid dating
biostratigraphic dating
C_3 plants
C_4 plants
Cenozoic
chemical dating
cultural dating
dendrochronology
electron spin resonance dating
epochs
eras
fission track dating
fluorine
foraminifera
half-life
igneous
index fossils
isotopes

luminescence dating
Mesozoic
paleomagnetic dating
Paleozoic
Pangaea
pebble tools
phylogeny
polarized light
racemization
radiocarbon dating
radiopotassium dating
sedimentary
Steno's law of superposition
strata
stratigraphic correlation
taphonomy
tectonic

ADDITIONAL READINGS

Klein, R. G. 1999. *The Human Career: Human Biological and Cultural Origins*. 2nd ed. Chicago: University of Chicago Press.

Lanham, U. 1973. *The Bone Hunters*. New York: Columbia University Press.

Lee-Thorp, J. A., M. Sponheimer, and N. J. van der Merwe. 2003. What do stable isotopes tell us about hominid dietary and ecological niches in the Pliocene? *International Journal of Osteoarchaeology* 13: 104–113.

Marshak, S. 2005. *Earth: Portrait of a Planet*. 2nd ed. New York: Norton.

Mayor, A. 2001. *The First Fossil Hunters: Paleontology in Greek and Roman Times*. Princeton: Princeton University Press.

Taylor, R. E. 1995. Radiocarbon dating: the continuing revolution. *Evolutionary Anthropology* 4: 169–181.

Winchester, S. 2001. *The Map That Changed the World: William Smith and the Birth of Modern Geology*. New York: HarperCollins.

Wolpoff, M. H. 1999. *Paleoanthropology*. 2nd ed. New York: McGraw-Hill.

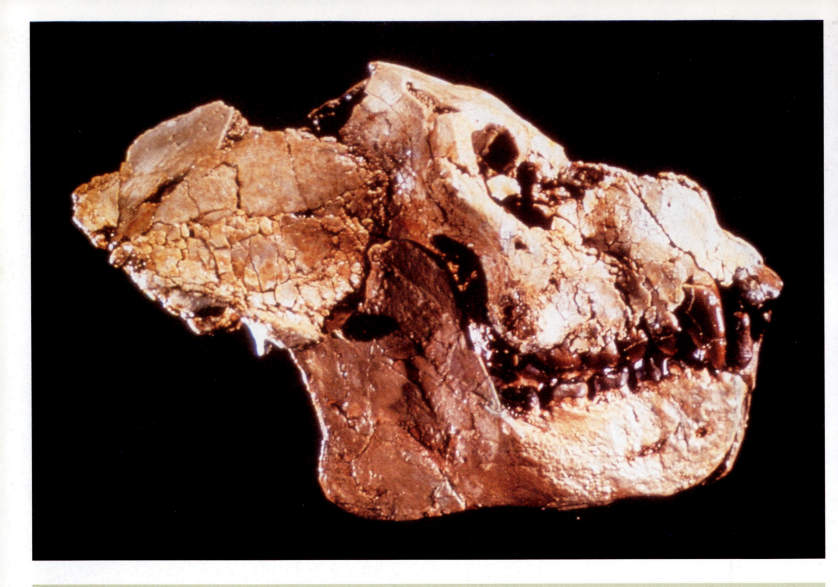

Also known as the "Dawn Ape," this fossil primate was an early ancestral catarrhine.
Aegyptopithecus lived approximately 29–32 mya, before the divergence of hominoids (apes) and
Old World monkeys. Like many catarrhines, this primate was likely an arboreal quadruped that
regularly consumed leaves and fruit.

CHAPTER 8

Primate Origins and Evolution: The First 50,000,000 Years

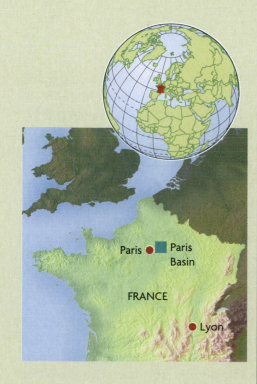

Paris ● ▪ Paris Basin

FRANCE

● Lyon

Remember Georges Cuvier, the Frenchman (introduced in chapter 2) who recognized that fossils are the remains of now-extinct animals and of plants? I bring him up again because of his central role in the study of primate evolution. The field would not have been the same had he not lived in the late eighteenth and early nineteenth centuries, when the scientific method, as we know it, began to take shape. As a child, Cuvier read the eighteenth-century biology luminaries Linnaeus and Buffon, and their works sparked in him a life-long interest in natural history. He went on to college at the University of Stuttgart, in Germany, and like many other bright college graduates at the time, he was recruited as a private tutor for a wealthy family, in his case in Normandy, France. While living with his host family, as luck would have it, he met France's leading naturalist and anatomist, Étienne Geoffroy Saint-Hilaire (1772–1844). Professor Geoffroy must have been impressed with young Cuvier, because he hired Cuvier as his assistant in comparative anatomy at the new National Museum of Natural History, in Paris. Cuvier became interested in the mammal fossils around Paris, and his encyclopedic knowledge of anatomy enabled him to recognize similarities between animals represented by fossils and living animals.

Among the hundreds of fossil bones and fossil teeth that he studied was a tiny skull, which he found in a gypsum quarry at nearby Montmartre. Dating to the Eocene, this specimen was unlike any skull Cuvier had ever seen. Was the animal it had come from living or extinct? When he published his description of the fossil in 1822, he did not recognize the creature he called *Adapis parisiensis* as a primate (**Figure 8.1**).

By the late nineteenth century, other French paleontologists had realized that Cuvier's fossil was that of an early primate, a finding that has been substantiated time and time again during the twentieth century, making *Adapis* the first primate fossil described by a scientist. Cuvier, the founder of paleontology, had good reasons for not recognizing this animal as a primate. For one thing, *no* fossil record of primates existed then—just about everything discussed in this chapter was found long after Cuvier's time. For another, taxonomists had very little understanding of living primate variation, and they had not yet defined the order much beyond Linnaeus's classification scheme (discussed in chapter 6).

BIG QUESTIONS

- Why become a primate?
- Who were the first primates?
- Who were the first higher primates?
- What evolutionary developments link past primate species and living ones?

Although Cuvier's assessment was wrong, his meticulous description of the *Adapis* fossil was very important. Stories like this happen often in science: the original discoverer may not recognize the finding for what it is, mostly because there is no context or prior discovery. Nevertheless, the discovery provides later scientists with important evidence. In this case, Cuvier's pioneering detailed description began the long process of documenting primate evolution, a process that continues today. Moreover, Cuvier set the bar high for future paleontologists by demonstrating the value of thorough description. Most importantly, Cuvier's careful work planted the seeds for asking key questions about primate origins.

In the two centuries since Cuvier, many thousands of fossils of ancient primates have been discovered in Europe, Asia, Africa, North America, and South America, providing a record—relatively complete for some time periods, frustratingly incomplete for others—of the origins and evolution of the earliest primates and their descendants. In this chapter, we address the big questions by examining the fossil record for evidence of three key developments: the first primates, the origins of higher primates (anthropoids), and the origins and evolution of the major anthropoid groups (monkeys, apes, and humans). The time frame for this chapter is expansive—50,000,000 years! We start in the early Paleocene, somewhere around 65 mya, and end in the late Miocene, around 6 mya, the dawn of human evolution. The record indicates that primates were highly successful and, like other mammals, underwent a cycle of adaptive radiations, followed by extinctions, and then new radiations of surviving lineages. These survivors are the primates occupying Earth today, including human beings (**Figure 8.2**).

WHY PRIMATES?

We know *what* primates are. For example, they are agile and adept at grasping, the claws have been replaced by nails, they have stereoscopic vision (the eyes are on the front of the head), they have a reduced sense of smell, and they have a big brain (**Figure 8.3**). *Why* they became what they are is far less clear. In the early 1900s, the British anatomists Sir Grafton Elliot Smith and Frederic Wood Jones proposed their **arboreal hypothesis** to explain primate origins. Smith and Jones hypothesized that primates' defining characteristics were adaptations to life in the trees: grasping hands and grasping feet were crucial for holding onto tree branches, binocular vision allowed much greater depth perception for judging distance in the movement from place to place in the trees, smell was no longer necessary for finding food, and greater intelligence was important for understanding three-dimensional space in the trees. The movement from life on the ground to life in the trees, Smith and Jones surmised, put into motion a series of selective pressures that resulted in the ancestral primate.

The arboreal hypothesis continues to influence profoundly the way anthropologists think about primate origins and evolution (e.g., the material in chapter 6). But in the early 1970s, the American anthropologist Matt Cartmill challenged the arboreal hypothesis. He pointed out that lots of mammals are arboreal (squirrels, for example), but except for primates none have evolved the entire set of characteristics that define the order *Primates*. (These characteristics include generalized structure, arboreal adaptation, and care of young; see chapter 6.) To account for primate origins, Cartmill proposed his **visual predation hypothesis.** He hypothesized that the first primate specialized in preying on insects and other small creatures, hunting

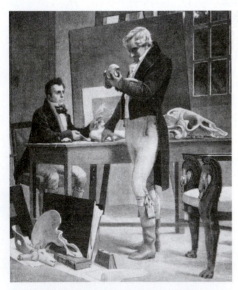

FIGURE 8.1 ■ Cuvier and *Adapis*
In describing the fossil remains of an animal he mistakenly thought was an ungulate or artiodactyl (hoofed mammal), Cuvier (here seated) named the specimen *Adapis,* Latin for "toward sacred bull." Later scholars realized that these remains were the first primate fossil ever recorded by a scientist.

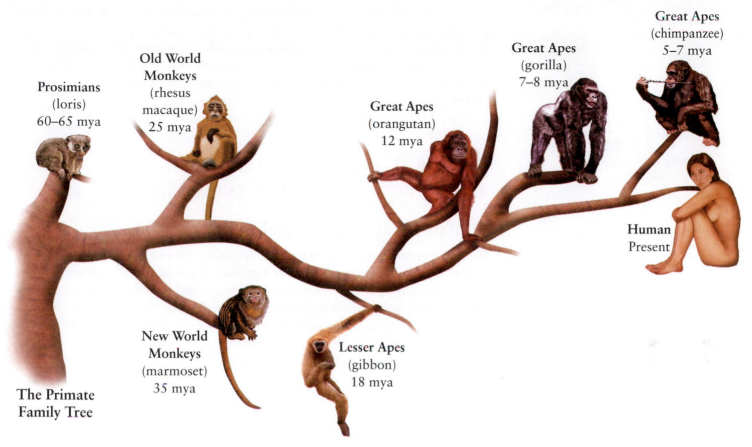

FIGURE 8.2 ■ Primate Family Tree
The variety of primates today is the result of millions of years of primate evolution. The different lineages represented by great apes, lesser apes, Old World monkeys, New World monkeys, and prosimians reflect divergences in primate evolution. For example, New World monkeys split off around 35 mya, and Old World monkeys diverged approximately 25 mya. The lineage leading to modern humans, however, diverged from the chimpanzee lineage much more recently, somewhere between 5 and 7 mya.

them in tree branches or in forest undergrowth. Cartmill argued that the shift to life in the trees was not the most important factor in explaining primate origins. Rather, the catching of small prey—using both a highly specialized visual apparatus and the fine motor skills of grasping digits—set primate evolution in motion.

Although the visual predation hypothesis elegantly explains the visual adaptations, intelligence, and grasping abilities of primates, it leaves an important question unanswered: *What role do the primate characteristics play in the acquisition and consumption of fruit, which many primates eat?* The American anthropologist Robert Sussman has hypothesized that the visual acuity, grasping hands, and grasping feet of primates were mostly adaptations for eating fruit and other foods made available with the radiation of modern groups of flowering plants called angiosperms. In other words, the original primate adaptation was about getting fruit and not about preying on insects. Sussman reasoned that because there was little light in the forest, early primates required visual adaptations for seeing small objects. Moreover, their grasping toes helped the animals cling to tree branches while they picked and ate fruit, rather than having to go back to more secure and larger branches, as squirrels do when they eat nuts. Sussman's **angiosperm radiation hypothesis** is grounded in the acquisition of a new food source available in the early Cenozoic: fruit.

arboreal hypothesis The proposition that primates' unique suite of traits is an adaptation to living in trees.

visual predation hypothesis The proposition that unique primate traits arose as adaptations to preying on insects and on small animals.

angiosperm radiation hypothesis The proposition that certain primate traits, such as visual acuity, occurred in response to the availability of fruit and flowers following the spread of angiosperms.

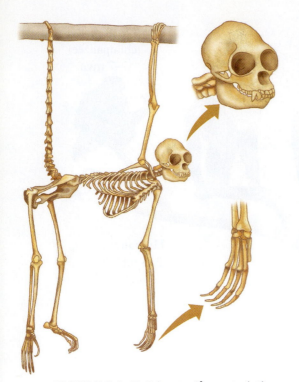

FIGURE 8.3 ■ **Primate Characteristics**
Primates differ from other mammals thanks to a unique combination of traits, such as forward-facing eyes, a postorbital bar or fully enclosed eye orbit, a large cranial vault, a reduced snout, and a versatile dentition. In the postcranial skeleton, primates usually have divergent big toes and divergent thumbs, grasping hands and grasping feet, and nails instead of claws on their fingers and their toes.

plesiadapiforms Paleocene organisms that may have been the first primates, originating from an adaptive radiation of mammals.

Proprimates A separate order of early primate ancestors from the Paleocene, such as the plesiadapiforms.

euprimates The first true primates from the Eocene—the tarsierlike omomyids and the lemurlike adapids.

adapids Euprimates of the Eocene that were likely ancestral to modern lemurs and possibly ancestral to anthropoids.

omomyids Eocene euprimates that may be ancestral to tarsiers.

In reality, elements of all three hypotheses may have provided the evolutionary opportunities that resulted in primate origins. Indeed, primates' most special feature is their adaptive versatility, especially in an arboreal setting. Primates have evolved strategies and anatomical features that enhance their ability to adapt to new and novel circumstances. That evolution constitutes primates' story of origin.

THE FIRST TRUE PRIMATE: VISUAL, TREE-DWELLING, AGILE, SMART

Primates in the Paleocene?

We know generally *when* primates first began—almost certainly in the early Cenozoic era. But just how early in the Cenozoic is debated by the paleontologists who study early primate evolution. They have reached no consensus as to whether the first primates appeared in the Paleocene epoch, which began 65 mya, or in the following epoch, the Eocene, which began 55 mya. The Paleocene candidate for the first primates is a highly diverse group called the **plesiadapiforms,** which lived in western North America, western Europe, Asia, and possibly Africa. These animals represent an adaptive radiation of primitive mammals that flourished over a 10,000,000-year period, beginning at the start of the Paleocene.

Despite their amazing diversity and geographic spread, by about 55 mya most of the plesiadapiforms had gone extinct. Were they primates? Probably not. The problem with attributing them to the primate order is that they lack the key characteristics that define primates today. That is, in contrast to primates, the plesiadapiforms lacked a postorbital bar and convergent eye orbits, their digits were not especially well-adapted for grasping tree branches (they lacked opposability), their digits lacked nails (they had claws), their teeth were highly specialized (some even have three cusps on their upper incisors, as opposed to the single cusp of most primates today), and their brain was tiny (**Figure 8.4**). Moreover, some plesiadapiforms lacked the auditory bulla, a part of the temporal bone that contains the middle-ear bones and is present in all primates. Because of their potential relationship with the first true primates, the American paleontologist Philip Gingerich has called them *Proprimates,* a separate order from *Primates.*

Eocene Euprimates: The First True Primates

Far better contenders for early primates are the **euprimates** (meaning "true primates"), which first appeared at the start of the Eocene, as early as 55 mya. Euprimates consisted of two closely related, highly successful groups, the **adapids** and the **omomyids.** Found in the western United States, western Europe, Africa, and Asia, they were the most common fossil prosimians, accounting for about 40% of the fossil primates, or about 200 species.

Were they primates? Almost certainly. Unlike the plesiadapiforms, adapids and omomyids had clear primate characteristics: the postorbital bar and convergent eye orbits, long digits with opposability for grasping, digits with nails (not claws), nonspecialized teeth, and a large brain relative to body size (**Figure 8.5**). These features indicate that vision was essential to their adaptation, they were agile and tree-dwelling, their diet was not as specialized as that of the plesiadapiforms, and

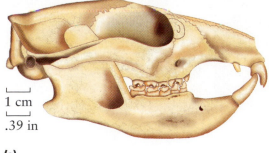

(a)

FIGURE 8.4 ■ *Plesiadapis*

These primatelike mammals were likely an ancestral lineage leading to true primate ancestors. **(a)** As this *Plesiadapis* skull illustrates, plesiadapiforms did not possess primates' postorbital bar. And while primates have a versatile dentition, plesiadapiforms had very specialized anterior (front) teeth, which were separated from the posterior (rear) teeth by a large gap. In addition, *Plesiadapis* and other plesiadapiforms had much smaller brains than did true primate ancestors. **(b)** This reconstruction of *Plesiadapis* reflects similarities to and differences from modern primates.

(b)

they were smarter than the earlier animals. Their body sizes were small but highly varied. Adapids were about the same size as some modern lemurs. One of the largest, *Notharctus,* weighed about 7 kg (15 lbs). *Adapis,* known from many skulls and other parts of the skeleton, weighed a little more than 1 kg (2 lbs). The adapids' incisors were flat and vertical, similar to those of many living anthropoids (**Figure 8.6**). In addition, like anthropoids, adapids had pronounced sexual dimorphism in body size and in canine size, some had lower jaws with two fused halves, and some had relatively short foot bones.

The omomyids differed from the adapids in having large and projecting central lower incisors, small canines, and wide variation in the other teeth. Unlike most adapids (and sometimes like living tarsiers), omomyids had a short skull, a short, narrow snout, and large eye orbits. Their large eye orbits held huge eyes adapted for night vision. Like the adapids, the omomyids consisted of widely diverse species and have left behind a great number of fossils, facts that speak to their high degree of success throughout the Eocene epoch.

From what primitive mammalian group did the adapids and omomyids evolve? Most of the plesiadapiforms are unlikely ancestors for the euprimates, because they either went extinct before the Eocene or were too specialized to have given rise to Eocene primates. However, one plesiadapiform, *Carpolestes,* whose skeleton was found in Wyoming's Bighorn Basin, had a number of characteristics that would be expected in a primate ancestor: it had a grasping foot, made possible by an opposable big toe; it had long, grasping fingers; and it had a nail on the end of the

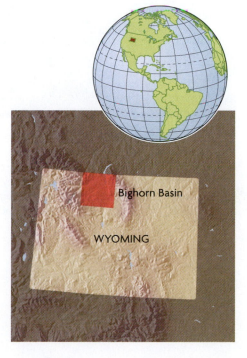

FIGURE 8.5 ■ **Adapids and Omomyids**

These two main groups of euprimates are likely related to lemurs and tarsiers, respectively. Unlike plesiadapiforms, adapids and omomyids are considered true primate ancestors because they possess many primate traits. **(a, b)** Omomyids, such as *Shoshonius* (shown here), had large eyes and large eye orbits on the front of the skull, grasping hands and grasping feet, and a reduced snout. Like tarsiers, these earliest primates were nocturnal. **(c, d)** Adapids, including Cuvier's *Adapis,* also had forward-facing eyes. However, adapids were diurnal and had longer snouts than omomyids.

first foot digit (**Figure 8.7**). This animal may be the link between proprimates of the Paleocene and euprimates of the Eocene.

The extinction of the plesiadapiforms, at the end of the Paleocene, and the appearance of the euprimates, at the beginning of the Eocene, coincided with a profound period of global warming. A rapid temperature increase around 55 mya

(a)

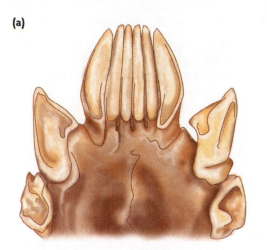

(b)

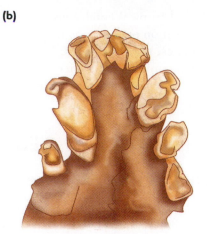

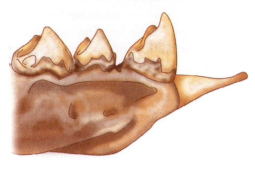

FIGURE 8.6 ■ **Incisor Variation**
(a) In modern lemur species, the lower incisors form a dental comb that projects horizontally from the mandible. **(b)** This feature was absent, however, in adapids, whose more vertical incisors resembled those of living monkeys and living apes.

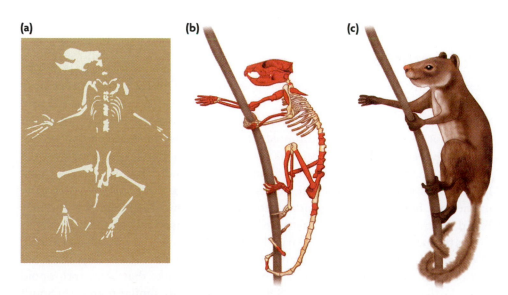

FIGURE 8.7 ■ *Carpolestes simpsoni*
(a) Fossilized remains such as these suggest that this species, a genus of plesiadapiforms, is the link between primatelike mammalian ancestors and the earliest true primate ancestors. **(b)** In this reconstruction of the full skeleton, the fossilized remains are highlighted. **(c)** This reconstruction depicts what *Carpolestes* might have looked like in life.

FIGURE 8.8 ■ *Eosimias*

This basal anthropoid, first discovered in 1999, represents one of the earliest genera of catarrhines (Old World monkeys and apes). *Eosimias* is the smallest primate ancestor discovered to date. Its smallest species is about the size of a human thumb and about one-third the size of the smallest living primate, the mouse lemur of Madagascar, which weighs approximately 28 gm (1 oz). The fossilized remains suggest they were arboreal insectivores and likely nocturnal.

Jiangsu Province

Shanghuang

CHINA

created tropical conditions virtually everywhere around the world. The resulting creation of new habitats triggered an adaptive radiation of modern-appearing primates, the euprimates. In particular, the high global temperatures and high global humidity led to an expansion of evergreen tropical forest, the environment that made possible many mammalian groups, including the primates.

THE FATE OF THE EUPRIMATES

The Anthropoid Ancestor: Euprimate Contenders

Like the Paleocene proprimates preceding them, many of the euprimates went extinct. Some of them may have provided the ancestral base for prosimians and anthropoids. Based on the kind of skull and tooth evidence described above, Philip Gingerich has made the case that adapids represent the ancestral group for living lemurs and anthropoids, with lemurs evolving a tooth comb (missing in adapids) and anthropoids not evolving the tooth comb. Their flat incisors, general similarity with anthropoids, and great diversity suggest that adapids had an evolutionary relationship with anthropoids. However, some (or even all) of adapids' anthropoid-like features could simply be unevolved (primitive) traits of all primates. If that is the case, then an ancestral-descendant link between adapids and later primates would be difficult to prove.

The American anthropologist Frederick Szalay sees a strong resemblance between omomyid fossils and living tarsiers and a greater similarity between tarsiers and anthropoids than between lemurs and anthropoids. Therefore, he regards the omomyids as more likely candidates for the ancestry of anthropoids than lemurs are. However, the anatomical similarities between omomyids and tarsiers are more suggestive than definitive. No single characteristic links these Eocene primates with anthropoids. While the adapids or omomyids may be ancestral to anthropoids, the lack of clear transitional fossils between these archaic primates and later primates makes it unclear who the anthropoid ancestor was more than 40 mya.

Basal Anthropoids

There is a third possibility for the anthropoid ancestor. During the Eocene, a group of primates called **basal anthropoids,** whose fossils have been found in Asia and Africa, had the kinds of characteristics that would be expected in an anthropoid ancestor or even the earliest anthropoid. One of the most interesting basal anthropoids is the remarkably tiny *Eosimias* (meaning "dawn monkey"), found near the village of Shanghuang, in Jiangsu Province, China, and dating to about 42 mya (**Figure 8.8**). Based on their observations of the teeth and the skeleton, especially of the foot bones, the American anthropologists Daniel Gebo and Christopher Beard regard *Eosimias* as the first true anthropoid. Especially convincing about their argument is the strong similarity between the shape and overall appearance of *Eosimias*'s tarsal (ankle) bones and those of fossil and living anthropoids. That is, *Eosimias*'s short calcaneus, or heel bone, was more like that of an anthropoid than like that of a prosimian (**Figure 8.9**). It was especially similar to those of South American monkeys, revealing that this primate moved in trees like a monkey. In addition, the upper canine and upper jaw would have given it a more monkeylike than prosimianlike face.

Another, later basal anthropoid is from the Fayum Depression, in Egypt. Called *Biretia* by the English paleontologist Erik Seiffert and the American anthropologist Elwyn Simons, it dates to the late Eocene, at about 37 mya. The presence of anthropoid characteristics in the teeth, such as the two-cusped (bicuspid) lower premolars, indicates that this animal, too, represents the beginnings of higher primates (**Figure 8.10**). If it is the first higher primate, then anthropoid ancestry began in Africa or the earlier primates from Asia immigrated to Africa and evolved into the African anthropoids. Based on the limited evidence, it is not possible to say whether Asia or Africa is the ancestral home of the higher primates, anthropoids. However, *Eosimias* and *Biretia* have the attributes that would be expected in an anthropoid ancestor. Given the earlier date for *Eosimias,* Asia could be the ancestral home for the higher primates.

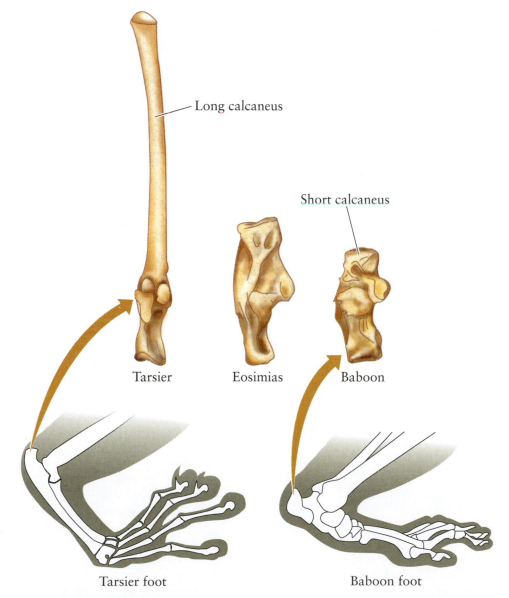

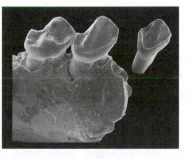

FIGURE 8.10 ■ *Biretia*
Its fossilized remains suggest that this animal was an anthropoid ancestor. For example, its lower premolars, with their two cusps, are structured like anthropoids'.

FIGURE 8.9 ■ **Calcaneus Variation**
Evidence for patterns of locomotion in *Eosimias* comes from some of the postcranial remains, especially bones of the ankle and foot. *Eosimias*'s calcaneus was more like that of an anthropoid (such as the baboon) than like that of a prosimian (such as the tarsier).

This discussion should make clear that anthropoids' origin is murky. Until recently, most authorities looked to either the lemurlike adapids or tarsierlike omomyids as the ancestor. But the incompleteness of the fossil record—and especially the lack of transitional fossils between these two early primate groups and true anthropoids of the Oligocene and later—makes it impossible to say whether either of these primitive primates is the higher primates' ancestor. Increasingly, anthropologists are looking to the basal anthropoids for answers and suggesting that the anthropoids may have evolved independently of the adapids and omomyids. If so, then adapids and omomyids were highly successful radiations of primates that had little to do with higher primates' origin.

EARLY ANTHROPOIDS EVOLVE AND THRIVE

Beginning in the Oligocene epoch, and coinciding with a period of widespread plant and animal extinctions, an episode of rapid global cooling occurred. With this shift in climate came new habitats and newly diverse primate taxa. The fossil record representing the evolution of these taxa is as remarkable in the Oligocene as the fossil

CONCEPT CHECK   When Were They Primates?: Anatomy through Time

Primates have a number of anatomical characteristics that reflect both an adaptation to life in the trees and related behaviors. Contenders for primate status in the Paleocene generally lack these characteristics; two groups of closely related Eocene mammals—adapids and omomyids—have these characteristics.

CHARACTERISTIC	PALEOCENE (65–55 MYA)	EOCENE (55–34 MYA)	PRESENT
Increased vision	no	yes	yes
Partially or fully enclosed eye orbits	no	yes	yes
Convergent eyes	no	yes	yes
Small incisors and large canines	no	yes	yes
Nails at ends of digits	no	yes	yes
Mobile, grasping digits	no	yes	yes
Short snout	no	yes	yes
Reduced smell	no	yes	yes
Large brain	no	yes	yes

FIGURE 8.11 ■ Fayum
Climatological and environmental reconstructions have provided a glimpse of what the Fayum was like when some of the earliest primates lived, at the end of the Eocene and the beginning of the Oligocene.

record is in the Eocene. However, whereas Eocene primate fossils have been found in a wide variety of settings around the world, most of the Oligocene primate fossils have come from one primary region, the Fayum, in the eastern margin of the Sahara Desert. Spanning about 8,000,000 years of evolution, roughly 37–29 mya, the fossil record consists of a wide and abundant variety of plants and of animals. From these remains, scientists have constructed a detailed picture of the environment in northeast Africa (**Figure 8.11**). In sharp contrast to the desert landscape of the Fayum today—it is among the harshest and driest places in the world—the late Eocene–early Oligocene landscape was much like contemporary Southeast Asia, namely wet, warm, and tropical. The Fayum's major feature, Birket Qarun Lake, was long the focus for all organisms in the region. In addition to diverse primates, all sorts of animals lived there, including the ancestors of rodents (the earliest porcupines are from the Fayum), bats, hippopotamuses, elephants, crocodiles, and various birds. Plants are also represented by a diverse array of tropical taxa, such as mangroves, water lilies, climbing vines, figs, palms, and cinnamon. It must have been an amazing place.

The Fayum primates included various prosimians and at least three groups of primitive (but unmistakable) higher primates: **oligopithecids, parapithecids,** and **propliopithecids.** The oligopithecids were the earliest, dating to about 35 mya. The later parapithecids, such as their namesake genus, *Parapithecus,* are among the most primitive early anthropoids. For example, parapithecids had three premolars, as did the primitive anthropoids. This condition may directly link parapithecids to platyrrhines (who also have three premolars), but having three premolars is more likely the ancestral condition that precedes the divergence of platyrrhines and catarrhines.

The propliopithecids consisted of several genera, but *Propliopithecus* and *Aegyptopithecus,* both dating to between 32 and 29 mya, are the most common of this group of primates. The propliopithecids had a more derived dental formula of 2/1/2/3, one fewer premolar than the parapithecids had. In this and other respects, they were more catarrhinelike than the parapithecids. *Aegyptopithecus,* the largest of the Fayum primates (it weighed 6–8 kg [13–18 lbs], or about the weight of a fox) is the best-known Fayum primate (**Figure 8.12**). *Aegyptopithecus* had a sagittal crest on the top of the skull where a large temporalis muscle was attached (see Figure 6.27). Its brain was larger than that of other Oligocene primates. The front and hind limbs were of relatively equal size, suggesting that the animal was a slow-moving, arboreal quadruped, similar to the modern howler monkey. Its overall appearance indicates that *Aegyptopithecus* was a primitive catarrhine—and a likely contender for the common ancestor of all later catarrhines.

oligopithecids The earliest anthropoid ancestors in the Oligocene, found in the Fayum, Egypt.

parapithecids Anthropoid ancestors from the Oligocene, found in Fayum, Egypt.

propliopithecids Anthropoid ancestors from the Oligocene, found in Africa.

Parapithecus A genus of later parapithecids from the Oligocene, found in Fayum, Egypt.

Propliopithecus Oligocene propliopithecid genus.

Aegyptopithecus A propliopithecid genus from the Oligocene, probably ancestral to catarrhines; the largest primate found in the Fayum, Egypt.

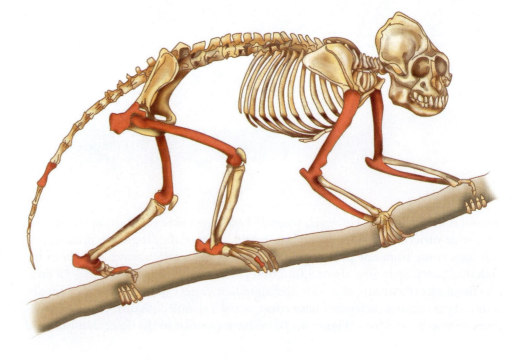

FIGURE 8.12 ■ *Aegyptopithecus*
Shaded in this reconstruction are the postcranial skeletal fossils of *Aegyptopithecus* that have been found in Fayum deposits. These recovered elements provide important information regarding the animal's mobility and form of locomotion: arboreal quadrupedalism.

COMING TO AMERICA: ORIGIN OF NEW WORLD HIGHER PRIMATES

Aegyptopithecus, the earliest definitive catarrhine, clearly evolved from some primitive anthropoid in the Old World. But where did the other anthropoids, the platyrrhines, come from? The first South American primate is a primitive monkey called ***Branisella,*** whose fossils were found near Salla, Bolivia, in geological deposits dating to the very late Oligocene, about 26 mya. It appears to have been a platyrrhine, given that it had three premolars and, especially, three upper molars with a four-cusp chewing surface strongly similar to that of the upper molars in living New World monkeys, such as the owl monkey (**Figure 8.13**). The fossil record for South America is generally sparse after the late Oligocene, but it shows the general patterns of platyrrhine evolution. The fossil platyrrhines bear a striking resemblance to living platyrrhines, represented by cebids and atelids.

Branisella A South American genus from the Oligocene, ancestral to platyrrhines.

How Anthropoids Got to South America

One important question about the origins of platyrrhines is just how they got to South America. Four alternative hypotheses have emerged to explain primates' presence in South America. First, platyrrhines evolved from a North American anthropoid, then migrated to South America in the late Oligocene. Second, platyrrhines evolved from an African anthropoid and migrated across the Atlantic to South America. Third, platyrrhines evolved from an anthropoid in Africa that migrated south (mainly) on land to Antarctica and then to Patagonia, at the southern tip of South America. Fourth, Old World and New World anthropoids evolved independently from different prosimian lineages in Africa and South America, respectively.

No evidence supports the first hypothesis—there were no anthropoids in North America during the Eocene or Oligocene. There were various euprimates, but none resembled the platyrrhines in South America during the late Oligocene.

Evidence supports the second hypothesis. There were early anthropoids in Africa (Fayum) beginning in the late Eocene, and they predated platyrrhines but looked remarkably similar to the earliest platyrrhines in South America (for example, they had three premolars). This resemblance indicates that platyrrhines originated in

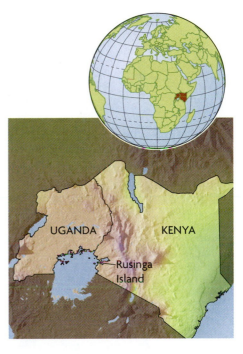

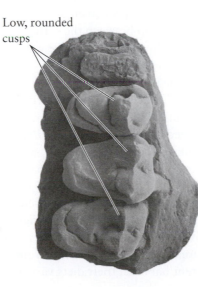

Low, rounded cusps

FIGURE 8.13 ■ *Branisella*
In the dental remains of this first definitive platyrrhine, the low, rounded cusps of its molars suggest that *Branisella* was frugivorous.

Africa *before* their appearance in South America. In addition, fossils indicate other similarities between animals in Africa and in South America.

The strong similarities between Old World and New World higher primates also support the third hypothesis. Migration across Antarctica would be impossible today, of course. However, for much of the Eocene, the continent's climate was much warmer and would have been conducive to migration.

Given the strong anatomical resemblance between African higher primates and South American higher primates, it is highly unlikely that anthropoids evolved independently in Africa and South America. DNA evidence that shows a strong relationship between Old World and New World higher primates is even stronger proof against the fourth hypothesis. In other words, these two groups did not evolve independently: they both originated in Africa.

On the face of it, it seems unlikely that primates migrated from Africa to South America via the Atlantic, especially in view of the wide and prohibitive expanse of open sea separating the west coast of Africa from the east coast of South America. At the time, however, areas of the ocean might have been shallow and dotted with series of islands. Moreover, primates might have crossed from Africa to South America via ocean currents, on natural rafts consisting of accumulated vegetation.

APES BEGIN IN AFRICA AND DOMINATE THE MIOCENE PRIMATE WORLD

proconsulids Early Miocene apes found in East Africa.

Micropithecus A genus of very small proconsulids from the Miocene, found in Africa.

Proconsul A genus of early Miocene proconsulids from Africa, ancestral to catarrhines.

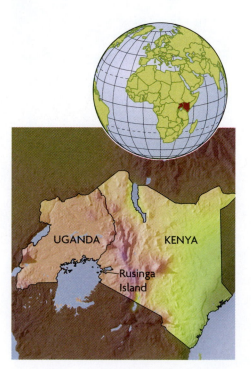

Following the Oligocene, the strength and completeness of the higher primate fossil record derives from rich Miocene geological deposits in East Africa, especially in the present-day countries of Kenya and Uganda. Just prior to this time, a warming trend in the late Oligocene provided the conditions for a shift in habitats and the appearance of a new and widespread radiation of a group of catarrhine primates called the **proconsulids,** mostly dating to roughly 22–17 mya. Recall that the last of the Oligocene primate fossils, in Egypt, date to about 29 mya. This means that about a 7,000,000-year gap exists between the last Oligocene propliopithecids (29 mya) and the first Miocene proconsulids (22 mya). As a consequence, the immediate ancestors of the proconsulids remain a mystery. However, the strong anatomical similarity in skulls and in teeth between the propliopithecids of the early Oligocene and the proconsulids of the Miocene indicates a likely ancestral-descendant relationship between the earlier and later groups. For example, both propliopithecids and proconsulids have a dental formula of 2/1/2/3, and their upper incisors are broad and flat.

The proconsulids are represented by a diversity of taxa—as many as 10 genera and 15 species—from the early and middle Miocene. In fact, the diversity of proconsulids is much greater than that of living apes today. For example, proconsulids ranged from the tiny *Micropithecus,* the size of a small New World monkey, to the namesake genus, *Proconsul,* a species of which, *Proconsul major,* was about the size of a modern male chimpanzee, weighing about 50 kg (110 lbs). *Proconsul* is the best-known of the early to middle Miocene apes from Africa, in part thanks to a nearly complete skeleton discovered on Rusinga Island, in western Kenya's Lake Victoria, in the late 1940s (**Figure 8.14**). Reflecting the proconsulids' biological diversity, their fossils have been found in a range of settings, representing different climates and environments, from open woodlands to tropics. Reflecting these different habitats, their diets varied considerably.

(c)

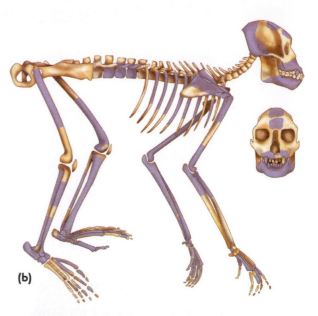

(b)

FIGURE 8.14 ■ *Proconsul*

This Miocene ape genus was first found in Kenya in 1909—it was the first fossil mammal ever discovered in that region of Africa. *Proconsul* literally means "before Consul"; Consul was the name given to chimpanzees that performed in European circuses. *Proconsul,* then, is considered an ancestor to apes, including chimpanzees. **(a)** The first skull of the genus was found in 1948 and was nearly complete. The cranial remains helped researchers determine that *Proconsul* was possibly an ancestor to apes. **(b)** Other fossil finds have helped researchers determine what *Proconsul*'s full skeleton was like. Note that it lacked a tail, like all modern apes. Here, areas shaded in blue represent the parts of the skeleton that have been discovered. **(c)** An artist's reconstruction illustrates *Proconsul*'s rainforest habitat and arboreal nature. (Figure 8.14c: "*Proconsul heseloni* Habitation," © 1992 by Jay H. Matternes.)

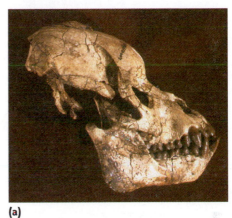

(a)

The skulls and teeth of the Miocene proconsulids were clearly like apes' in overall appearance (**Figure 8.15**). The molars have the Y-5 pattern, and the cusps are wide and rounded for eating fruit. There are well-developed honing surfaces on the backs of the upper canines and the fronts of the lower third premolars. Comparisons of tooth wear in living apes and in extinct Miocene apes suggest that some of the extinct apes ate leaves and some ate nuts and fruit, but that most of them routinely ate ripe fruit.

In contrast to the skulls and teeth, the rest of the skeleton of Miocene apes is generally like monkeys' (**Figure 8.16**). Unlike the living apes, these primitive apes had front and hind limbs that were equally long and that lacked specializations for knuckle-walking or arm-swinging. Moreover, like Old World monkeys, *Proconsul* had wrist bones (carpals) that articulated directly with the ulna, one of the two forearm bones. This direct articulation, a primitive characteristic, indicates relatively limited wrist mobility, whereas living apes have highly mobile wrists for arm-swinging and arm-hanging. Proconsulids' elbows could straighten only so far, whereas living apes' elbows can extend completely. Preconsulids' feet combined primitive and derived features—some of the ankle bones were slender, like monkeys', but the big toes were large, like apes'. The whole package suggests that *Proconsul,* unlike living apes, walked on the tops of tree branches on all fours.

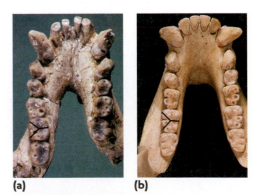

(a)   (b)

FIGURE 8.15 ■ *Dryopithecus*

(a) The mandible of *Dryopithecus,* a Miocene ape genus from East Africa, like that of **(b)** a modern gorilla, includes the Y-5 molar pattern and low, rounded cusps. Both also have large canines, plus the diastema between the canine and the first premolar.

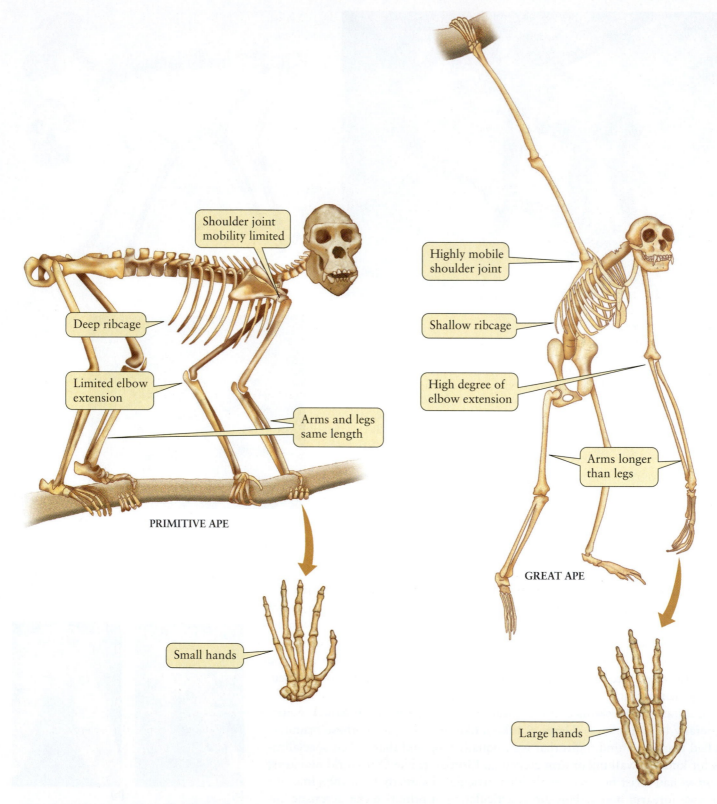

Shoulder joint
mobility limited

Deep ribcage

Limited elbow
extension

Arms and legs
same length

PRIMITIVE APE

Small hands

Highly mobile
shoulder joint

Shallow ribcage

High degree of
elbow extension

Arms longer
than legs

GREAT APE

Large hands

FIGURE 8.16 ■ Proconsulid Body Plan

The body plan of primitive, Miocene apes (left) differs from that of modern great apes (right). The Miocene apes had a more monkeylike body, with smaller hands, a more restricted hip joint, and a more flexible spine. The great apes have highly mobile shoulder joints and fully extendable elbow joints, enabling them to brachiate, or swing from branch to branch; the Miocene apes, by contrast, probably were arboreal quadrupeds, not needing the great mobility in their shoulders and their wrists. For the purposes of comparison, this Miocene ape, *Proconsul,* and this great ape, the modern gibbon, have been drawn the same size. In reality, *Proconsul* was about half the size of a gibbon.

Because these creatures lacked a number of anatomical features that living hominoids share, they can be used as a model of the animals that gave rise to the last common ancestor of all later hominoids.

APES LEAVE AFRICA: ON TO NEW HABITATS AND NEW ADAPTATIONS

The presence of ape fossils in Europe and Asia from about 17 mya (but not before) suggests that apes originated in Africa and then spread to Europe and Asia. The migration of primates (and other animals) from Africa to Europe and Asia was made possible by a land bridge created 23–18 mya by a drop in sea levels and the joining of the African-Arabian tectonic plate with Eurasia. Following their dispersal into Europe and Asia, apes became more diverse than ever before.

Apes in Europe: The Dryopithecids

By 13 mya, the early apes had successfully adapted to a wide range of new habitats. During this time, Europe was covered by a dense, subtropical forest that provided a rich variety of foods, especially fruit. *Dryopithecus,* the best-known genus within a group of apes called **dryopithecids,** lived in the area of Europe that is now France and Spain. Larger than earlier apes—about the size of a chimpanzee—it was first discovered and described by the eminent French paleontologist Edward Lartet (1801–1871), in 1856, in St. Gaudens, southern France. *Dryopithecus* and its contemporary taxa are known from other European regions, such as in Greece and Hungary.

Dryopithecus resembled living apes in many ways: its canines were sharp and tusklike; its cheek teeth were long and had very simple chewing surfaces, well-adapted for chewing fruit; and microscopic studies of the cross-sections of the teeth enamel indicate that these apes grew slowly. Their brains were larger than earlier primates', similar to the modern chimpanzee's. Their long forelimbs, grasping feet, and long, grasping hands were powerful and adapted for arm-hanging and arm-swinging, modern apes' main forms of locomotion.

Dryopithecus A genus of dryopithecid apes found in southern France.

dryopithecids Early Miocene apes found in various locations in Europe.

Apes in Asia: The Sivapithecids

In Asia, the **sivapithecids** were the counterpart of Europe's dryopithecids. The best-known sivapithecid is *Sivapithecus,* an ape ancestor that thrived about 12–8 mya. Whereas chimpanzees and gorillas have thin-enameled teeth, *Sivapithecus* had thick-enameled teeth, adapted for eating hard, tough-textured foods such as seeds and nuts. Its robust jaw bones were similarly adapted.

Because hominids also have thick-enameled teeth, primatologists once thought *Sivapithecus* was the ancestor of the Hominidae. This hypothesis was rejected in 1979, when the anthropologists David Pilbeam and Ibrahim Shah discovered a partial *Sivapithecus* skull (**Figure 8.18**). *Sivapithecus* skulls are strikingly similar to those of living orangutans, with concave faces, narrow nasal bones, oval eye orbits from top to bottom, projecting premaxillas (the *premaxilla* is the area of the face below the nose), large upper central incisors, and tiny lateral incisors. Even more similar to living orangutans, however, is the newly discovered *Khoratpithecus,*

sivapithecids Early Miocene apes found in Asia.

Sivapithecus A genus of Miocene sivapithecids, proposed as ancestral to orangutans.

Khoratpithecus A genus of Miocene apes from Asia, likely ancestral to orangutans.

FIGURE
8.17

Eocene-Oligocene-Miocene Habitats and Their Primate

Eocene 40–35 mya

Oligocene 33–29 mya

Convergent eyes and grasping hands

Quadrupedal, monkeylike primate with superb arboreal skills

Large eyes for nocturnal vision

Scenes from the late Eocene in the Paris Basin. *Top:* The diurnal *Adapsis* is feeding on leaves. *Bottom:* Several taxa of omomyids (*Pseudoloris, Necrolemur, Microchoerus*). Note the large eyes, a nocturnal adaptation, typical of both ancient and modern prosimians who are active at night.

Eocene-Oligocene-Miocene Habitats and Their Primates
Primate evolution began with primitive primates in the Eocene, setting the stage for the origin of all hominoids. Euprimates of the Eocene had the basic characteristics of living primates, such as convergent eye orbits and grasping digits. In the last 20,000,000 years, primates diversified in appearance and behavior. These changes included the shift, for some, from life in the trees to life on the ground, and eventually the beginning of bipedality in the late Miocene. (Based on Fleagle, J. G. 1999. *Primate Adaptation and Evolution*, 2nd ed. Academic Press.)

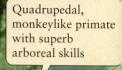

Miocene 18 mya

Quadrupedal, apelike primate. Note the lack of a tail, an ape characteristic.

Scene from the early Oligocene of the Fayum, Egypt. These anthropoid ancestors include *Aegyptopithecus*, *Propliopithecus*, and *Apidium*. These primates were adept arborealists, using their hands and feet for climbing and feeding.

Scene from the early Miocene of Rusinga Island, Kenya. Apes first appeared during this period, and these are the first apes (two species of *Proconsul*, *Dendropithecus*, *Limnopithecus*). These and other taxa form the ancestry of all later apes and hominids. Note the range of habitats occupied by these primates within the forest, including some in the middle and lower canopies and some on the forest floor. These primates show a combination of monkeylike and apelike features, in the skeleton and skull, respectively.

FIGURE 8.18 ◾ *Sivapithecus*
Originally found in the Siwalik Hills of modern-day India and Pakistan, this Miocene ape (center) has been proposed as ancestral to the orangutan (right). *Sivapithecus*'s facial features, for example, are far closer to the orangutan's than to those of other great apes, such as the chimpanzee (left). *Sivapithecus* has three species, any of which may be a direct ancestor to the orangutan; however, recent finds of another Miocene ape genus have called this ancestry into question.

a hominoid of the late Miocene (9–6 mya) in Thailand. Various features of this primate's teeth and lower jaw—for example, broad front teeth, canines with a flat surface on the tongue side—indicate that this Miocene primate is living orangutans' most likely ancestor.

Closely related to *Sivapithecus*, *Khoratpithecus*, and other Asian Miocene apes is a very interesting pongid, *Gigantopithecus*, also from Asia, dating to about 8–.5 mya (**Figure 8.19**). Appropriately named for its massive body, *Gigantopithecus* is the biggest primate that has ever lived, standing nearly 3 m (10 ft) tall and weighing as much as 300 kg (660 lbs)! Its massiveness would have limited this fossil primate to the ground for all its activities. Like some of the other Miocene apes, it had thick-enameled teeth and large, thick-boned jaws, adapted for eating very hard foods, likely nuts and seeds.

Gigantopithecus A genus of Miocene pongids from Asia; the largest primate that ever lived.

oreopithecids Miocene apes that were found in Europe.

FIGURE 8.19 ◾ *Gigantopithecus*
Bamboo was probably among the plant foods eaten by this enormous, herbivorous Miocene ape. Climate change and competition with other primate species likely brought about this ape's extinction.

Dead End in Ape Evolution: The Oreopithecids

Around the same time *Gigantopithecus* emerged, a group of apes called **oreopithecids** lived in Europe. They appear in the fossil record around 8 mya and disappear around 7 mya. *Oreopithecus,* the best-known of this group, has been found mostly in coal mines in Tuscany, Italy. (Oreopithecids were also present in Africa at the same time as the proconsulids on that continent.) Its Miocene habitat was dense, tropical forests, and its teeth were highly specialized for eating leaves (**Figure 8.20**). Also known as the "Swamp Ape," *Oreopithecus* was a medium-size primate, weighing an estimated 30–35 kg (66–77 lbs), but it had a tiny brain. Its relatively long arms indicate that it was adept at some form of suspensory locomotion, similar to that of a modern gibbon. Some of its hand adaptations foreshadow developments in hominid evolution.

Climate Shifts and Habitat Changes

During the period in which *Oreopithecus* and other later Miocene apes disappeared, Europe and Africa experienced dramatic changes in climate and ecology. Several factors coincided to cause these changes: a shift in tectonic plates created the Alps, the Himalayas, and the East African mountain chains; ocean currents shifted; and the polar ice caps began to reform. In Europe and then Africa, the once-lush tropical forests changed to cooler, dryer mixed woodlands and grasslands. As a result, tropical foods disappeared, including the apes' favored diet, fruit.

Miocene Ape Survivors Give Rise to Modern Apes

A handful of ape taxa survived these dramatic disruptions in habitat. *Khoratpithecus,* for example, thrived for a time and gave rise to the orangutan of Southeast Asia. The origins of the great apes of Africa and hominids are far less clear. In fact, only one small set of fossils—named *Chororapithecus* by their discoverer, the Japanese paleoanthropologist Gen Suwa—resembles similar parts of living great apes. These nine teeth from three individuals, found in Ethiopia and dating to about 10.5 mya, are remarkably similar to the modern gorilla's. Their existence suggests that late Miocene African pongids may have been the common ancestor of African apes and hominids. However, the fossil record in Africa between 13 mya and 5 mya is extremely sparse, leaving an 8,000,000-year gap until the first hominids' appearance, about 6 mya (discussed further in chapter 10). Therefore, the link between late Miocene African apes and later hominoids is unknown.

APES RETURN TO AFRICA?

Ape fossils from the late Miocene might be so scarce in East Africa because apes simply were not living there, at least not in great numbers, at that time. Unless the fossil record changes, somewhere other than Africa must be the source of living African apes' and humans' common ancestor. The Canadian primate paleontologist David Begun suggests that late Miocene Europe might yield that ancestor. He speculates that the similarities in dentition and skull between the Greek dryopithecid *Ouranopithecus* on the one hand and African apes and early hominids on the other indicates an ancestral-descendant relationship between European apes and African hominids. Begun argues that the climate changes in Europe prompted late Miocene

Oreopithecus A genus of oreopithecids found in Italy that was extinct within a million years of its appearance.

Ouranopithecus A genus of Miocene dryopithecids found in Greece

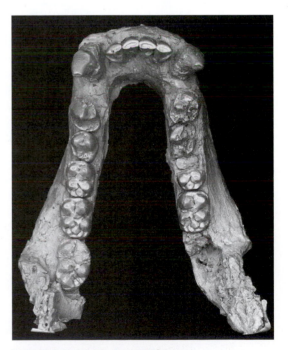

FIGURE 8.20 ■ *Oreopithecus*
The high, shearing crests on its molars suggest that this Miocene ape was folivorous. Like *Gigantopithecus,* this ancestral ape likely became extinct due to climate change.

The First Apes: A Remarkable Radiation

The apes' evolutionary glory days are in the Miocene epoch (23–5 mya), beginning in Africa and then spreading into Europe and Asia. Out of this remarkable adaptive radiation came the ancestors of living apes and of humans. All of these fossil primates had characteristics seen in living apes, especially in the teeth and the skull (Y-5 lower molars, 2/1/2/3 dental formula, broad incisors, large honing canines), but most were monkeylike in the postcranial skeleton (front and back limbs equally long).

GROUP	CHARACTERISTICS	AGE	LOCATION
Proconsulids	Large range in size Tropics to open woodlands Thin enamel (e.g., *Proconsul*)	22–17 mya	Africa (Kenya, Uganda)
Dryopithecids	Some size range Tropics Thin enamel (e.g., *Dryopithecus*)	14–9 mya	Europe (France, Spain, Germany, Greece, elsewhere)
Sivapithecids	Some size range Tropics Thick enamel Skull like orangutan's (e.g., *Sivapithecus*)	14–8 mya	Asia (Pakistan, India, China, Thailand, Africa)
Oreopithecids	Large body Tiny brain Specialized molars for eating leaves Suspensory locomotion (e.g., *Oreopithecus*)	9–7 mya	Europe (Italy) earlier form in Africa (Kenya)

apes to move from Europe back to Africa, essentially following the tropical forests, and the foods these forests provided, as forests and foods disappeared behind them. Some of the pongids adapted to forested settings, some lived in woodlands, and eventually one group, hominids, became committed to life on the ground. To date, the fossil record for the later Miocene is too incomplete to make clear whether early hominids descended from Miocene ancestry in Europe or in Africa.

MONKEYS ON THE MOVE

At the same time as the evolution and proliferation of ape taxa, an expansion and adaptive radiation of monkeys occurred, both in the New World (see "How Anthropoids Got to South America," above) and in the Old World. Primates recognizable as cercopithecoids—they have the distinctive bilophodont molars of Old World monkeys—first appeared during the early Miocene in North Africa and East Africa. These primitive primates are generally called **victoriapithecids.** *Victoriapithecus,* a prominent genus of the group, is just the kind of primate that would be expected for the ancestor of Old World monkeys.

Beginning in the late Miocene, especially in the Pliocene and Pleistocene, and continuing to the present day, monkey taxa have proliferated enormously. While ape species were far more prevalent and diverse during the early and middle Miocene, far outnumbering the living groups, monkey species are far more diverse since the end of the Miocene. Today's monkey taxa are for the most part the descendants of the fossil species from the Pliocene and Pleistocene. By contrast, most of the ape and apelike taxa from the Miocene went extinct and left no descendants.

The rise in monkey species and the decline in ape species were not due to competition between the two groups. Rather, the origin and diversification of monkeys reflect habitat changes. The climates and environments of the early Miocene seem to have favored the adaptive radiation of apes, with most taxa then going extinct as climates and environments changed. The climates and environments of the late Miocene, and into the Pliocene and Pleistocene, seem to have favored the adaptive radiation of monkeys.

The Pliocene and Pleistocene fossil monkeys are divided into the same two subfamilies as Old World monkeys, cercopithecines and colobines. The cercopithecines are represented by three major groups: macaques; mangabeys, baboons, and geladas; and guenons. The fossil monkeys were widespread, as living species of monkeys are. The fossil monkeys and their living descendants are similar in many respects, such

victoriapithecids Miocene primates from Africa, possibly ancestral to Old World Monkeys.

FIGURE 8.21 ■ Catarrhine Origins
This phylogeny represents catarrhine evolution. The circled numbers represent the estimated times of divergence. Old World monkeys and hominoids share a common ancestor; however, approximately 25 mya, Old World monkeys and hominoids split, each creating a separate evolutionary lineage. This last common ancestor, though, has not been discovered. Within the hominoid lineage, branching has occurred many times, including the branch leading to the lesser apes, around 18 mya, and most recently the branch leading to humans, approximately 6 mya. The Old World monkey lineage has also branched several times, most notably when colobines and cercopithecines split, approximately 14 mya.

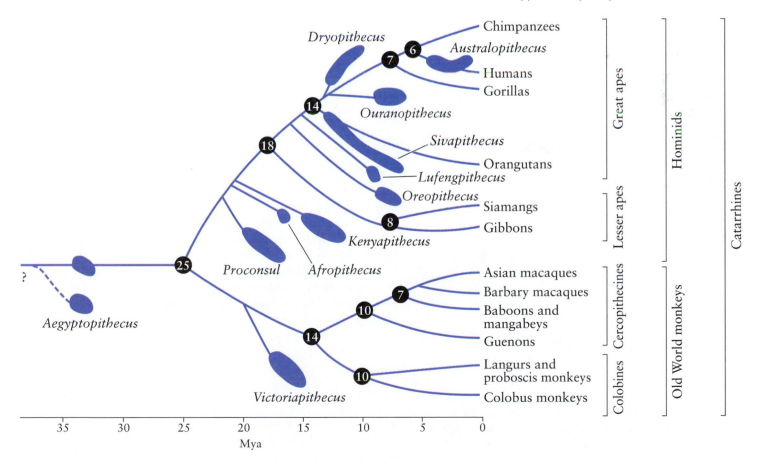

as skeletal and dental anatomy. For example, the fossil and living monkeys have virtually identical teeth (large, projecting canines) and cranial morphology.

The colobines included three geographic groups of species: European, Asian, and African. These species differed in many ways from their living descendants, in part reflecting their greater geographic distribution and the diverse environments they occupied. One clear evolutionary trend in many monkey species is a decrease in body size. In other words, around the world during the later Pleistocene there were widespread extinctions of large animals, including primates. These extinctions might have been caused by human hunting, climate change, competition with other mammals, or a combination of these factors (discussed further in chapter 13).

All of primate evolution is a dynamic story, peaking at different times and different places with key events, such as the origins of all the major groups of higher primates (**Figure 8.21**). The record becomes even more fascinating in the late Miocene, with the appearance of a new primate that is similar to but different from other primates. The first 50,000,000 years of primate evolution, from the beginning of the Eocene to the last several million years of the Miocene, set the stage for the appearance of this new taxa—a primitive, humanlike primate. This ancestor's origin begins the 6,000,000-year history of the appearance, rise, and dominance of humans. That story begins in the next chapter.

ANSWERING THE BIG QUESTIONS

Why become a primate?

- According to the predominant theory, primate origins represent the radiation of a primitive mammalian ancestor that adapted to life in the trees. Other theories suggest that the origins may be more closely linked to preying on insects or eating fruit.

Who were the first primates?

- The first radiation of primates included the appearance of two primitive primate groups: adapids and omomyids, both at about 55 mya. These animals may have given rise to modern prosimians and modern anthropoids, but the exact phylogenetic relationship between the Eocene groups and later ones is unknown.

Who were the first higher primates?

- In the Eocene, primate taxa possessing a combination of prosimian and anthropoid characteristics appeared in Asia and Africa. These basal anthropoids may have been the first anthropoids.
- Recognizable catarrhines (e.g., *Aegyptopithecus*) were present 30 mya in Africa, and platyrrhines (e.g., *Branisella*) were present 26 mya in South America. Platyrrhines likely descended from an early African anthropoid ancestor.

What evolutionary developments link past primate species and living ones?

- The evolution of apes began in Africa and continued in Europe and Asia. Recognizable African apes first appeared about 22 mya (e.g., *Proconsul*), and various Eurasian varieties (e.g., *Sivapithecus*) somewhat later with the opening of a land bridge connecting these continents. Most apes went extinct in the later Miocene, although a few survived, giving rise to modern apes and humans.
- Monkeys underwent a massive adaptive radiation in the Pliocene and Pleistocene, providing the foundation for the evolution of modern species.

KEY TERMS

adapids
Adapis
Aegyptopithecus
angiosperm radiation hypothesis
arboreal hypothesis
basal anthropoids
Biretia
Branisella
Carpolestes
dryopithecids
Dryopithecus
Eosimias
euprimates
Gigantopithecus
Khoratpithecus
Micropithecus
Notharctus

oligopithecids
omomyids
oreopithecids
Oreopithecus
Ouranopithecus
Parapithecus
parapithecids
plesiadapiforms
Proconsul
proconsulids
Propliopithecus
propliopithecids
Proprimates
sivapithecids
Sivapithecus
victoriapithecids
visual predation hypothesis

ADDITIONAL READINGS

Beard, C. 2004. *The Hunt for the Dawn Monkey: Unearthing the Origins of Monkeys, Apes, and Humans.* Berkeley: University of California Press.

Begun, D. R. 2003. Planet of the apes. *Scientific American* 289(2): 74–83.

Conroy, G. C. 1990. *Primate Evolution.* New York: Norton.

Fleagle, J. G. 1999. *Primate Adaptation and Evolution.* San Diego: Academic Press.

Miller, E. R., G. F. Gunnell, and R. D. Martin. 2005. Deep time and the search for anthropoid origins. *Yearbook of Physical Anthropology* 48: 60–95.

Rose, K. D. 1994. The earliest primates. *Evolutionary Anthropology* 3: 159–173.

Ross, C. F. 2000. Into the light: the origin of anthropoidea. *Annual Review of Anthropology* 29: 147–194.

Walker, A. and P. Shipman. 2005. *The Ape in the Tree: An Intellectual and Natural History of Proconsul.* Cambridge, MA: Belknap Press.

Often referred to as the "cradle of humankind," Olduvai Gorge is a ravine in East Africa's Great Rift Valley from which many hominid fossils have been recovered, providing insight into our evolutionary roots. Geologic activity and erosion have exposed some of the deepest and oldest layers of sediment, enabling paleoanthropologists to find fossils from strata that are nearly 2,000,000 years old.

CHAPTER 9

Early Hominid Origins and Evolution: The Roots of Humanity

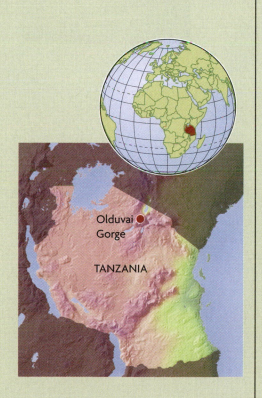

Olduvai Gorge

TANZANIA

Imagine yourself walking across the hot, desolate, and altogether inhospitable landscape of East Africa's Great Rift Valley. Imagine further that you have spent the better part of the last three decades—all your adult life—searching for early hominid fossils. Over those years, you have found evidence, such as stone tools, that early humans had lived in this place hundreds of thousands—even millions—of years. Still no fossils; not even a scrap. On this particular day, you see part of a bone sticking out of the ground, just like others you have seen over and over before. This one turns out to be different, though. Instead of being an animal of some sort, this fossil has *human* teeth—you have found a hominid, your first! In an instant, all your searching has been vindicated.

That scene describes exactly what happened to the English-born anthropologist Mary Leakey (1913–1996) one sunny morning in July 1959. She, along with her husband, the Kenyan anthropologist Louis Leakey (1903–1972), had searched high and low for early human bones in Olduvai Gorge, a side branch of the Rift Valley, 50 km (31 mi) long. Since beginning their searches in the early 1930s, they had found ancient stone tools and ancient animal remains scattered about the landscape—lots of them. They wanted more, however. They wanted the remains of the people who made the tools and ate the animals. Year after year, field season after field season, disappointment after disappointment, they searched for the bones and teeth that would represent our ancestors' roots.

What had motivated these two individuals to work so hard for so little payoff under such awful conditions? Simple. They were motivated by questions. In fact, the Leakeys were asking one of the fundamental questions of all time: *Who were the first humans?* The Leakeys demanded answers about human origins, and they were willing to do what had to be done to get those answers.

They started out with a pretty simple hunch about early hominids. Other scientists had found things in Olduvai Gorge—bones and tools, both in association with really old geologic strata—that strongly suggested the place would yield early hominid remains. Based on these findings, the Leakeys decided to investigate the gorge's geologic strata (**Figure 9.1**). Their work took a lot of time and resources, but it paid off well, laying the essential groundwork for our present understanding of the first humans and their place in evolution. In fact, the bits of bone and

BIG QUESTIONS

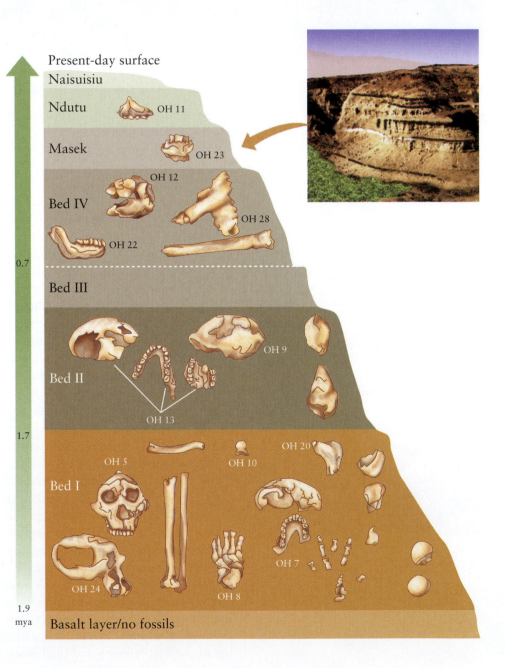

- What is a hominid?

- Why did hominids evolve from an apelike primate?

- Who were the first hominids?

- What was the evolutionary fate of the first hominids?

the teeth found in 1959 turned out to be a crucially important hominid skull. Not only did this discovery expand the territory in which early hominids were known to have lived—at that point, they were known just from South Africa—but it added a whole new dimension to their variability.

The Leakeys' pioneering work in East Africa was built around questions still central to paleoanthropology.

This chapter focuses on the fossil record of early human evolution. This record sheds light on the earliest humanlike ancestors. In order of origin and evolution, they are the pre-australopithecines (before the genus *Australopithecus*), which lived 7–4 mya, and the australopithecines, which lived 4–1 mya.

Present-day surface
Naisuisiu
Ndutu   OH 11
Masek   OH 23
OH 12
Bed IV   OH 28
OH 22
0.7
Bed III
OH 9
Bed II
OH 13
1.7
OH 20
OH 5   OH 10
Bed I
OH 7
OH 24   OH 8
1.9 mya
Basalt layer/no fossils

FIGURE 9.1 ■ **Geologic Strata at Olduvai** One key aspect of excavations at Olduvai is the exposed strata, dating back millions of years. The strata include volcanic rock, which can be radiometrically dated to provide accurate ages for each layer. Any fossils found in these layers can then be dated according to the stratum in which they were found. The ages of fossil hominids recovered from Olduvai Gorge help anthropologists reconstruct humans' family tree.

WHAT IS A HOMINID?

The morphological characteristics—and behaviors inferred from these characteristics—shared by living humans and their ancestors but not shared by apes reveal what is distinctive about hominids. For example, living humans speak, use language, depend fully on complex material culture, and have advanced cognition—living apes do not have these characteristics. Speech, advanced cognition, and complex material culture evolved in the human line long after the first hominids appeared in Africa, 7–6 mya, and so these characteristics do not define a hominid. Speech likely developed only in the last 2,000,000 years, and some authorities argue for late in that period. Evidence for material culture, in the form of primitive stone tools, dates to about 2.6 mya. As discussed in chapter 1, a hominid is much better understood as having two obligate behaviors—bipedal locomotion and nonhoning chewing—and the suite of associated physical characteristics that manifest these behaviors. The evidence is very clear: bipedal locomotion and nonhoning chewing preceded speech and material culture by several million years. Like large brains, speech and material culture help define humans today but were not attributes of the earliest hominids.

Bipedal Locomotion: Getting Around on Two Feet

In the 1800s, when the entire human fossil record was a very small fraction of what it is today, numerous authorities believed that the beginning of bipedalism was not the hallmark event distinguishing humans from the apes. Rather, these scientists believed that the most important initial evolutionary change was an increase in brain size, reflecting advanced (human) intelligence. They speculated that only with advanced intelligence would language, tool use, and the other behaviors that collectively define humanness have become possible. The focus on intelligence to the exclusion of other attributes helped bring about the rapid and uncritical acceptance of some purported early hominid ancestors that later turned out to be fake.

Since then, the large early hominid fossil record has proven that bipedalism—and not human intelligence—was the foundational behavior of the Hominidae, preceding most attributes associated with humans and with human behavior by *millions* of years. More than any other characteristic, the shift from walking with and running with four limbs (arms and legs) to walking with and running with two limbs (legs) distinguishes hominids from pongids (and other nonhuman primates).

Five distinguishing characteristics in the skeleton are associated with bipedalism (see also "What Is a Primate?" in chapter 6). The foramen magnum is positioned directly beneath the skull, the pelvis is short from front to back, the legs are long relative to the body trunk and arms, the foot has a double arch, and the big toe (the hallux) is not opposable. The position of the foramen magnum reflects the fact that the (bipedal) hominid carries its head atop its skull, in contrast to the (quadrupedal) ape, which carries its head on the front of the body. The shortened pelvis reflects anatomical changes that coincided with the shift from quadrupedalism to bipedalism. Especially important is the reconfiguring of the gluteal muscles for stabilizing the hip in walking on two legs (discussed in chapter 6). Bipeds have distinctively long legs, which provide the ability to stride, and to do so with minimal energy. The loss of opposability in the big toe reflects the use of this digit in helping propel the body forward during walking and running.

Nonhoning Chewing: No Slicing, Mainly Grinding

The second of the two major differences between living apes and humans (and human ancestors), a characteristic that defines the Hominidae, is the way the dentition processes food (again, see "What Is a Primate?" in chapter 6). Apes and humans have evolved different dental characteristics, reflecting how each uses the canine and postcanine teeth (**Figure 9.2**). When apes grab onto food with their front teeth, the upper canines and lower third premolars cut and shred the food. Through evolution, apes' upper canines have become large, pointed, and projecting, with a sharp edge on the back (**Figure 9.3**). When the jaws are fully closed, each canine fits snugly in the diastema, the gap located between the canine and the third premolar on the lower jaw and the canine and second incisor on the upper jaw. The sharp edge on the back of the upper canine hones, or rubs against, a sharp edge on the front of the lower third premolar, or sectorial premolar. This honing action helps maintain a sharp, shearing edge on both the canine and the premolar. The shearing edge is essential for slicing up leaves and fruit before they are chewed by the back teeth and swallowed. Apes' lower third premolar is also distinctive in having one large, dominant cusp on the cheek side of the tooth and a tiny cusp on the tongue side of the tooth.

In contrast, living and past hominids have small, blunt, and nonprojecting canines and no diastema. Hominid canines wear on the tips instead of the backs (see Figure 9.3). The cusps on both sides of the lower third premolars are similar in size, or at least more similar in size than are apes' cusps. Unlike apes, hominids do not hone their canines as they chew.

Apes' and humans' postcanine teeth have many similar anatomical characteristics. The third and fourth premolars, upper and lower, have two cusps each. Pongids' and hominids' upper molars have four cusps, and their lower molars have five cusps. Apes' and humans' back teeth crush and slice food, with a different emphasis: humans crush food more than apes do. Apes use their molars more for slicing than crushing, reflecting their plant-heavy diet.

In apes and humans, grinding and slicing are facilitated by powerful chewing, or masticatory, muscles, especially the temporalis, masseter, and pterygoid muscles (**Figure 9.4**). Hominids place more emphasis on the front portion of these muscles, to provide greater vertical force in crushing food. Apes place more emphasis on the

FIGURE 9.2 ■ **Nonhoning vs. Honing Chewing**

While humans have nonhoning chewing, primates such as gorillas (pictured here) have a honing complex, in which their very large canines cut food. The upper canines are sharpened against the lower third premolar.

FIGURE 9.3 ■ **Canine Wear**

(a) This gorilla's dentition reveals honing wear on the back of the upper canine, caused by the tooth's rubbing against the lower first premolar. **(b)** This human's dentition reveals wear on the upper canine's tip, which is the point of contact between the upper canine and the lower teeth when the jaws are closed.

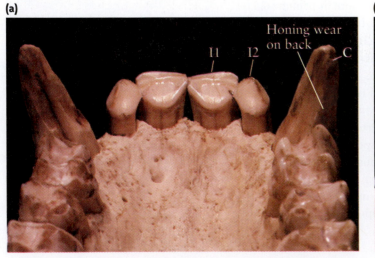

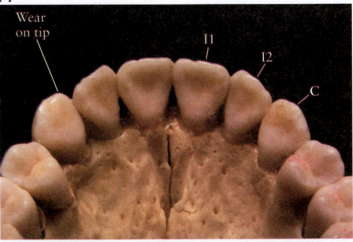

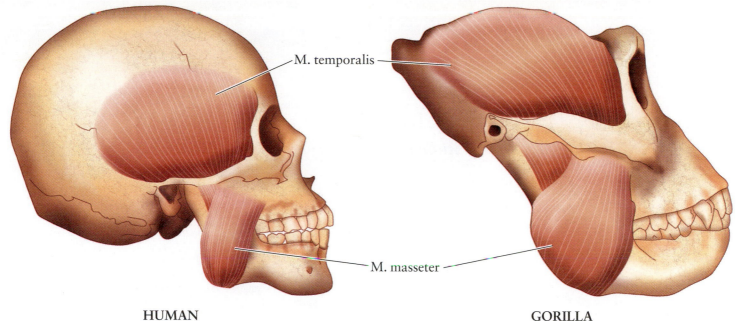

M. temporalis

M. masseter

HUMAN

GORILLA

back portion of the masticatory muscles because slicing requires more horizontally oriented forces. As an additional aid in powerful crushing, hominids have evolved thick enamel on their teeth (**Figure 9.5**). Pongids have evolved thin enamel, reflecting diets dominated by plants and soft fruit. Among the hominoids, the only exception is the orangutan, which has evolved thick enamel—its diet includes tough foods that require heavy crushing.

Like bipedalism, hominids' nonhoning masticatory complex evolved very early in the evolutionary record. Collectively, then, the distinguishing features of the Hominidae are located in the anatomical complexes associated with acquiring and transporting food (locomotion) and chewing food (mastication).

FIGURE 9.4 ■ Masticatory Muscles
Humans and other primates have powerful chewing muscles to process food. In humans, the temporalis muscle is vertically oriented, enabling a crushing ability. In nonhuman primates, this muscle is oriented horizontally, producing slicing motions.

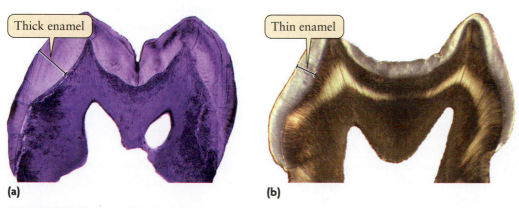

Thick enamel

Thin enamel

(a)

(b)

FIGURE 9.5 ■ Enamel Thickness
Enamel is the outermost layer of the exposed part of a tooth and is the hardest substance in the human body, enabling the tooth to grind and slice all types of food. Species with diets heavy in hard foods, such as seeds and nuts, have thicker enamel, allowing more of the enamel to be eroded or worn before the softer layers underneath are exposed. In these cross sections of **(a)** a human tooth and **(b)** a chimpanzee tooth, note how much thicker the human enamel is.

What Makes a Hominid a Hominid?

Hominids have a number of anatomical characteristics that reflect two fundamental behaviors: bipedal locomotion and nonhoning chewing.

BEHAVIOR	ANATOMICAL CHARACTERISTICS
Bipedalism	Foramen magnum positioned directly beneath the skull Short pelvis from front to back Long legs Double-arched foot Nonopposable big toe
Nonhoning chewing	Blunt, nonprojecting canine Small canine relative to size of other teeth No diastema Wear on tips of canines and of third premolars Cusps on lower third premolar equal size

WHY HOMINIDS?

The fossil record and genetic information gathered from it continue to fill in the story of hominids' first appearance on the scene, in the late Miocene epoch, some 5–10 mya. But *why* did hominids evolve? Central to most arguments is bipedalism, the focal point in the study of human origins.

Charles Darwin's Hunting Hypothesis

Charles Darwin offered the first serious hypothesis about the Hominidae's first appearance. It was a simple but elegant adaptive model for explaining human origins. Drawing on the great British naturalist Thomas Huxley's anatomical research on the living apes of Africa (both Darwin and Huxley are discussed in chapter 2), Darwin concluded that because of the remarkable anatomical similarity between humans and African apes, Africa was hominids' likely place of origin. The characteristics that distinguish living humans from living apes, Darwin reasoned, derive from one key evolutionary event in their common ancestor, namely the shift from life in the trees to life on the ground. He observed four characteristics that set living humans and living apes apart: (1) humans are bipedal, while apes are quadrupedal; (2) humans have tiny canines, while apes have large canines; (3) humans rely on tools in their adaptation, while apes do not; and (4) humans have big brains, while apes have small brains (**Figure 9.6**).

Building on these observations, Darwin asked what the advantages of bipedalism would be in a world where bipeds—early humans—ate mostly meat they acquired by killing animals with weapons. He concluded that bipedalism had freed the hands for carrying the weapons. To manufacture and use these tools, the early humans needed great intelligence. Once they had the tools, they did not need the big

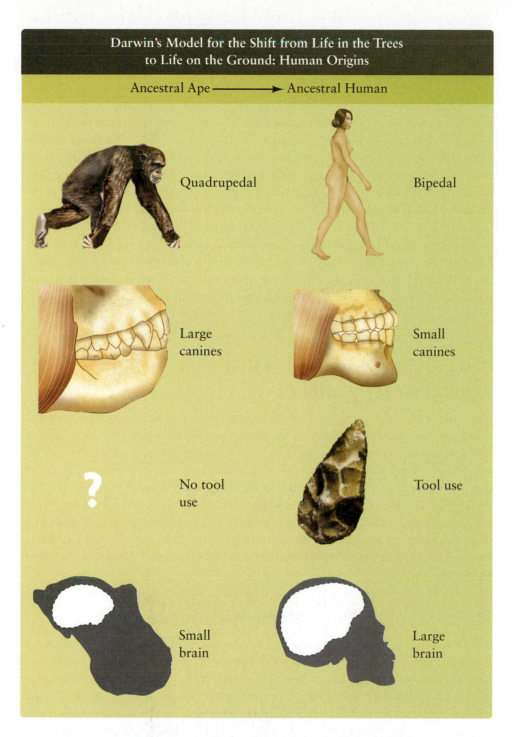

Darwin's Model for the Shift from Life in the Trees to Life on the Ground: Human Origins

Ancestral Ape ⟶ Ancestral Human

Quadrupedal — Bipedal

Large canines — Small canines

No tool use — Tool use

Small brain — Large brain

FIGURE 9.6 ■ **Four Key Differences** From Huxley's comparative studies of apes and humans, Darwin noted four differences between these two types of primates. In Darwin's time, there were no recorded instances of apes' making or using tools, so tools appeared a uniquely human phenomenon. Since then, however, apes have been seen making and using tools, such as when chimpanzees "fish" for termites with a rod and cracked hard nuts with a "hammer and anvil" (see "Acquiring Resources and Transmitting Knowledge: Got Culture?" in chapter 6).

canines for hunting or for defense. Although he saw tool production and tool use as essential factors in the development of human intelligence, Darwin believed that humans' large brain resulted mainly from the presence of language in humans.

Scientists now know that tool use and the increase in brain size began well after the appearance of bipedalism and the reduction in canine size. The earliest known tools date to about 2.6 mya, and evidence of brain expansion dates to sometime after 2 mya. Therefore, it now seems doubtful that canine reduction began with tool use. Although Darwin's hypothesis was refuted, it provided an essential first step toward an understanding of hominid origins.

Since Darwin, other hypotheses have emerged to answer the question of why there are hominids. After 17 mya, a massive adaptive diversification of apes occurred in Africa, resulting in many different taxa (see "Apes Begin in Africa and Dominate the Miocene Primate World" in chapter 8). At some point later, this diversity declined, perhaps due in part to competition between apes and to the rising number of monkey species that were also evolving in the late Miocene epoch. Changes in climate and in habitat also likely influenced the decline in the number of ape taxa. Most important about the evolution of Miocene apes is that somewhere out of this ancestral group of ape species arose the animal that was more human than ape.

Darwin proposed that hunting was at the basis of the divergence. However, the archaeological record suggests that hunting began much later in human evolution. Hunting, at least in the sense of cooperation among individuals to kill an animal, likely did not begin until after 2 mya, at about the same time the brain began expanding. It now seems likely that hunting played an important role in later human evolution but not in hominid origins.

Peter Rodman and Henry McHenry's Patchy Forest Hypothesis

The American anthropologists Peter Rodman and Henry McHenry have proposed that human origins and bipedality in particular may be related to the greater efficiency, in certain habitats, of walking on two feet rather than four feet. They suggest that bipedalism arose in areas where the forest was becoming fragmented, a process that began toward the end of the Miocene (**Figure 9.7**). Apes' quadrupedalism, they note, is not energy-efficient in Africa's patchy forests. As the forests became patchy and food became more dispersed, early hominids would have used their energy much more efficiently once bipedalism freed their hands to pick up food. The early hominids could then have fed in trees and on the ground, depending on the availability of resources.

Owen Lovejoy's Provisioning Hypothesis

The American anthropologist Owen Lovejoy has offered another alternative to Darwin's ideas about the arboreal-to-terrestrial shift and the origins of bipedalism. He has hypothesized that freeing the early hominids' hands was important in initiating bipedal locomotion, but not for the reasons Darwin cited. Lovejoy observes that in many species of monkeys and apes, males compete for sexual access to females. However, the young are cared for by the mother without any involvement of the father (see "What Is a Primate?" in chapter 6). Owing to the obligations of caregiving, such as the acquisition of food for her infant (and herself), the mother theoretically is not able to care for more than one infant at a time. Moreover, she is unreceptive to mating until the infant is able to find food on its own. In apes as in humans, the time from birth to the infant's independence can be rather long, upward of five years in chimpanzees, for example. The downside of this extended care period is that it gives apes a reproductive disadvantage, since so few offspring can be born to any female. Lovejoy hypothesizes that if infants and mothers were provided with more food, they would not have to move

FIGURE 9.7 ■ **East African Tree Cover** Around the time that humans and bipedality arose, East Africa had large amounts of discontinuous tree cover. Rodman and McHenry propose that the areas of open grassland, interspersed with some stands of trees, such as shown here, favored bipedalism over quadrupedalism.

around as much for resources. If males provisioned mothers and their offspring, each mother, again theoretically, would be able to care for two or more infants at a time. In other words, the mother could have more births—the time between births would be reduced.

Lovejoy makes the case that, for early hominids, a monogamous father enhanced the survival of the mother and her offspring by providing both food and protection from predators. This habitual provisioning required the male to have free hands for carrying food, and so bipedalism arose. This model focuses on the selective and simultaneous advantages of monogamy and of pair bonding, of food provisioning, of cooperation, and of bipedalism, all rolled into one distinctively human behavioral package.

Sexual Dimorphism and Human Behavior

Among all the hypotheses about hominid origins, Lovejoy's hypothesis had a unique focus, on differences in female and male body sizes and on the implications of behavior with a decidedly human bent. Through field and laboratory studies, anthropologists have observed that, in terms of body size, many living primate species are highly dimorphic sexually: males are considerably larger than females. This difference has come about because the larger the male, the more equipped it will be to outcompete other males for sexual access to females. Through natural selection, then, males in many primate species have maintained relatively large bodies. Some authorities argue that early hominids were highly dimorphic, in which case competing males were likely not involved in caring for their offspring. However, if early hominids were not especially dimorphic, then male competition for mates probably was not part of early hominid social behavior. The American anthropologist Philip Reno and his associates have studied early hominid bones to determine relative sizes of females and of males. Their analysis shows relatively little sexual dimorphism in body size. Such a low level of sexual dimorphism suggests that males were cooperative, not competitive. This cooperative behavior could have included pair bonding—one male paired with one female—a behavior pattern necessary for the kind of provisioning required in Lovejoy's hypothesis.

Bipedality Had Its Benefits and Costs:
An Evolutionary Trade-Off

All the hypotheses about human origins have suggested that an apelike primate evolved into an early hominid through completely positive adaptation. Bipedalism's advantages over quadrupedalism included an increased ability to see greater distances (thanks to an upright posture), greater ease of transporting both food and children, ability to run long distances, and the freeing of the hands for, eventually, such remarkable skills and activities as tool manufacture and tool use. However, the profound adaptive shift to bipedalism had its costs. Standing upright yields a better view across the landscape, but it also brings exposure to predators. Standing or walking on two feet while simultaneously lifting or carrying heavy objects over long periods of time causes back injury, such as that associated with arthritis and with slipped intervertebral disks. Bipedality also places an enormous burden on the circulatory system as it moves blood from the legs to the heart. The result of this

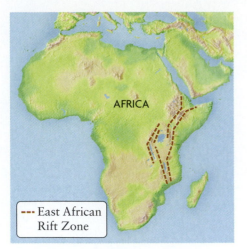

--- East African
Rift Zone

AFRICA

burden is the development of varicose veins, a condition in which overwork causes the veins to bulge. Lastly, if one of a biped's two feet is injured, then that biped's ability to walk can be severely reduced. Unable to move about the landscape, an early hominid would have had limited chances of surviving and of reproducing. In short, bipedality is a wonderful example of the trade-offs that occur in evolution. Only rarely do adaptive shifts, including one of the most fundamental human behaviors, come without some cost.

WHO WERE THE FIRST HOMINIDS?

Until a few years ago, the oldest hominid fossil dated to less than 4 mya. The earliest hominids were known from one genus, *Australopithecus,* found mostly in two key areas of Africa: a series of limestone caves in South Africa and in sedimentary basins and associated river drainages in the Eastern Rift Valley (part of the Great Rift Valley) in Ethiopia, Kenya, and Tanzania (**Figure 9.8**). As we saw in the previous chapter, the latest African Miocene apes—the group of hominoids out of which the first hominids evolved—date to about 8 mya. Thus, the crucial time period during which hominids and the last common ancestor with apes (chimpanzees) split into separate lineages has been an unknown because of the 4,000,000-year gap in the fossil record (8–4 mya). In the last few years, however, hominids predating *Australopithecus* have been discovered in north-central and eastern Africa. These hominids have closed the gap between late Miocene ape evolution and the first hominids, the pre-australopithecines.

Sahelanthropus tchadensis The earliest pre-australopithecine species found in central Africa with possible evidence of bipedalism.

The Pre-Australopithecines

Pre-australopithecine fossils are few in number and quite fragmentary, but they have provided critically important information about the origins and earliest evolution of the Hominidae. The pre-australopithecines had a number of primitive attributes, and in some respects they were more apelike than humanlike. They represent the first recognizable ancestors of the lineage leading to humans.

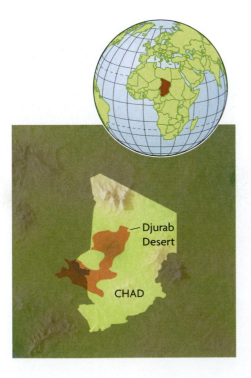

Djurab
Desert

CHAD

***SAHELANTHROPUS TCHADENSIS* (7–6 MYA)** The earliest pre-australopithecine is represented by most of a skull and other fossils found in central Africa, beginning in 2001, by the French paleontologist Michel Brunet and his colleagues (**Figure 9.9**). Named *Sahelanthropus tchadensis* (meaning "genus named for the region of the southern Sahara desert known as the Sahel") by its discoverers, this creature's fossils date to 7–6 mya. The finding's geographic location—the Toros-Menalla locality of the Djurab Desert, in Chad—surprised many, because it was 2,500 km (1,600 mi) from the Eastern Rift Valley, where all other early hominids in East Africa had been found for the last three-quarters of a century. The presence of early hominids in central Africa opens a third geographic "window" onto their evolution, the first two being later presences in East Africa and South Africa. In short, humans originated in Africa during the late Miocene and early Pliocene.

Cranial capacity, a rough measure of brain volume, is one important quantitative characteristic with which anthropologists determine the degree of humanness in individual fossil hominids. The fossil record of human evolution shows an increase in brain size, from the smallest in the oldest hominids (about 350 cubic

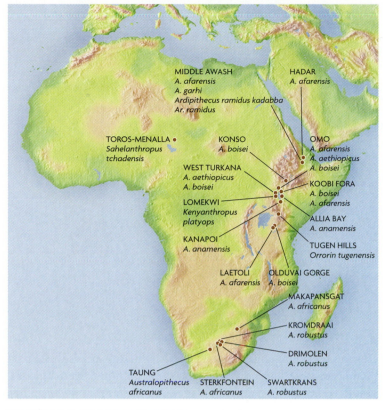

FIGURE 9.8 ■ African Hominids
Many hominid fossils have been found in East Africa and South Africa.

FIGURE 9.9 ■ *Sahelanthropus tchadensis*
Among the first and few hominid fossils uncovered in central Africa, this skull belonged to a primate with a small and primitive brain like that of apes. Note the large browridge.

centimeters, or cc) to the largest in *Homo sapiens* (about 1,450 cc). *Sahelanthropus* has a brain size of about 350 cc.

Its brain was primitive and like that of apes. Moreover, this hominid had a massive browridge, larger than that of modern gorillas. However, the two critical attributes that define the Hominidae are present in *Sahelanthropus*—the primate was likely bipedal (based on the position of the foramen magnum at the base of the skull) and the canine-premolar chewing complex was nonhoning. This combination of primitive (more apelike) and derived (more humanlike) features is to be expected in the oldest hominid, especially in apes' and humans' common ancestor. Its great age and primitive characteristics indicate that *Sahelanthropus* existed very close—the closest of any fossil known—to the divergence of their common ancestor into pongids and hominids.

Also found at the same site were the bones and teeth of nonprimate animals, fossils that create a picture of *Sahelanthropus*'s habitat. These remains—of hugely diverse animal species, including fish, crocodiles, and amphibious mammals associated with aquatic settings, and bovids (hoofed mammals), horses, elephants, primates, and rodents associated with forests and grasslands—indicate that *Sahelanthropus* lived in a forest near a lake.

ORRORIN TUGENENSIS (6 MYA) Dating to around 6 mya, the fossils of at least five pre-australopithecines were found in the Tugen Hills, on the western side of Kenya's Lake Turkana. The discoverers, paleoanthropologists Brigitte Senut and Martin Pickford, named these hominids *Orrorin tugenensis* (the genus means

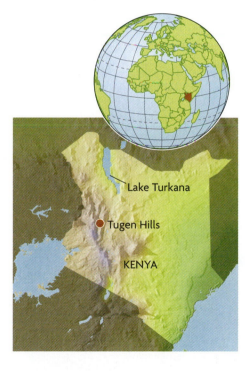

Orrorin tugenensis A pre-australopithecine species found in East Africa that displayed some of the earliest evidence of bipedalism.

FIGURE 9.10 ■ *Orrorin tugenensis*
The most important skeletal remain of this pre-australopithecine is a proximal, or upper, portion of the femur, which has a long femoral neck and a groove for the obturator externus muscle. These are the same as in humans and hominid ancestors, suggesting *Orrorin* was bipedal. By contrast, apes (such as the chimpanzee) have a short femoral neck and no groove.

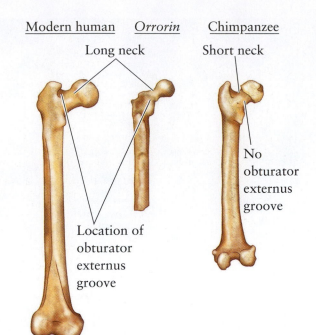

Modern human   *Orrorin*   Chimpanzee

Long neck   Short neck

No obturator externus groove

Location of obturator externus groove

"original man" in Tugen's local language). Among the 20 remains were several partial femurs, each missing the knee but indicating that these hominids were bipedal. For example, the femur's neck, the area that is at the top of the bone and articulates with the hip, was relatively long (**Figure 9.10**). A hand phalanx found at the site was curved like a living ape's, suggesting that *Orrorin* spent time in the trees. Like those of *Sahelanthropus,* the canines had wear on the tips and were nonhoning. The animal bones at the site indicated that *Orrorin* lived in a forest.

***ARDIPITHECUS KADABBA* AND *ARDIPITHECUS RAMIDUS* (5.8–4.4 MYA)** In Aramis, a site within the fossil-rich Awash River Valley of Ethiopia's expansive Afar Depression, the American anthropologists Tim White and Yohannes Haile-Selassie and their colleagues discovered the youngest pre-australopithecine species. The Middle Awash is an especially important place in the study of human evolution because it has yielded some of the most significant early hominid remains. Numerous pre-australopithecines, australopithecines, early members of *Homo*, and early modern *Homo sapiens* have been found in the area, providing a fabulous record of nearly continuous human evolution (**Figure 9.11**).

For a very long time, nearly 1,500,000 years, Aramis was occupied by at least two pre-australopithecines—an earlier and a later species of *Ardipithecus* known as, respectively, ***Ar. kadabba*** and ***Ar. ramidus*** (*Ardi* means "ground" or "floor" in the Afar's local language; *rama* means "root"). These pre-australopithecines date from the late Miocene (ca. 5.8 mya) to the early Pliocene (ca. 4.4 mya). The remains include a partial skeleton and other bones and teeth. The chewing in the earlier form of *Ardipithecus* (ca. 5.8–5.6 mya) was quite primitive. Although the dentition lacked functional honing, the presence of some polishing on the outside of the third lower premolar is a primitive trait consistent with its very early date (**Figure 9.12**).

The later form of *Ardipithecus* (4.4 mya) did not employ this primitive form of perihoning. Rather, its molars ground, and the tips of its canines chewed. *Ardipithecus* is unusual in being the fossil record's only hominid with thin enamel. Its curved foot phalanges reflect arboreal activity (**Figure 9.13**). Its femur and pelvic bones indicate bipedalism. *Ar. ramidus* was only about 1 m (somewhat over 4 ft) tall.

Ardipithecus kadabba An early pre-australopithecine species from the late Miocene to the early Pliocene; shows evidence of a perihoning complex, a primitive trait intermediate between apes and modern humans.

Ardipithecus ramidus A later pre-australopithecine species from the late Miocene to the early Pliocene; shows evidence of both bipedalism and arboreal activity but no indication of the primitive perihoning complex.

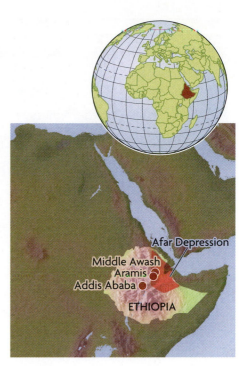

FIGURE 9.11 ■ **Middle Awash Valley, Ethiopia**
This hotbed of hominid fossil finds is located in the Afar Depression, an area of much geologic and tectonic activity. The Awash River flows through the depression, creating rich plant and animal life in the midst of an arid region. Because the Afar's floor consists of volcanic rock, radiometric dating methods can be used to provide age estimates for the fossils found in the geologic strata. The large amount of earthquake activity fissures the rock, allowing researchers to excavate layers that are millions of years old.

FIGURE 9.12 ■ *Ardipithecus kadabba*
The earlier form of this pre-australopithecine had an intermediate honing, or perihoning, complex in its dentition, while the later form lacked honing entirely. Shown here, the perihoning complex of an early form of *Ardipithecus* (right) as similar to chimpanzees' honing complex (left). Together, these forms suggest that *Ardipithecus* was an early hominid ancestor, as its dental morphology was intermediate between apes' and humans'. (Photo © 2003 Tim D. White/Brill Atlanta.)

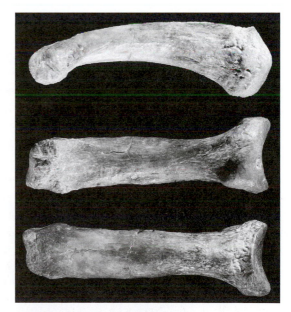

FIGURE 9.13 ■ **Foot Phalanges**
There is evidence that *Ardipithecus* was bipedal. However, its foot phalanges are curved like apes', suggesting that this pre-australopithecine was arboreal at least some of the time. Like its dentition, this anatomical evidence suggests *Ardipithecus* was an intermediate genus. (Photo © 2003 Tim D. White/Brill Atlanta.)

Who Were the First Hominids?   233

The Pre-Australopithecines

The first hominids spanned a 3,000,000-year period in Africa, about 7–4 mya. They had both apelike characteristics and the features that define hominids.

HOMINID	DATE(S)	LOCATION	HOMINID	DATE(S)	LOCATION
Sahelanthropus tchadensis	7–6 mya	Djurab Desert, Chad	*Ardipithecus kadabba*	5.8–5.6 mya	Awash River Valley, Ethiopia

Key features:
Skull and teeth found
Tiny brain (350 cc)
Skull like apes', with massive browridge
Lived in forest setting

Key features:
Skull, teeth, postcranial bones found
Small brain
Some tooth wear on outside of third premolar (perihoning)
Thin enamel
Curved foot phalanges
Femur and pelvis indicate full bipedalism
Less than 1 m (4 ft) tall
Lived in wooded setting

Orrorin tugenensis	6 mya	Tugen Hills, Kenya	*Ardipithecus ramidus*	4.4 mya	Awash River Valley, Ethiopia

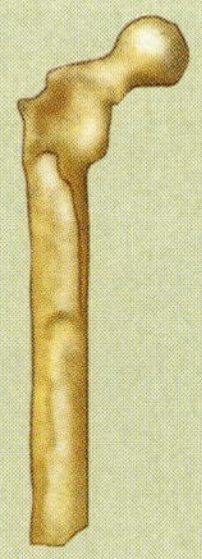

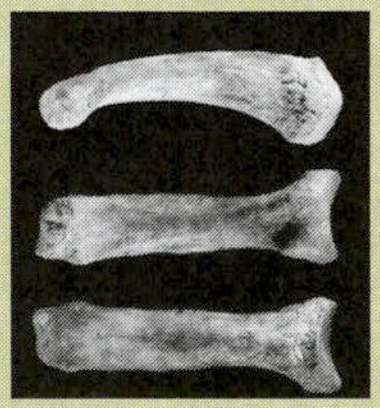

Key features:
Postcranial bones found
Femurs indicate likely bipedalism
Hand phalanx like apes' (curved)
Less than 1 m (4 ft) tall
Lived in forest setting

Key features:
Skull, teeth, postcranial bones found
Small brain
No perihoning
Thin enamel (only hominid with thin enamel)
Curved foot phalanges
Femur and pelvis indicate full bipedalism
Less than 1 m (4 ft) tall
Lived in wooded setting

Like those of *Sahelanthropus* and *Orrorin,* the Aramis fossils were found in a wooded setting, revealed by the presence of seeds, wood, and the bones and teeth of forest-dwelling monkeys and of forest-dwelling kudus. Thus, the pre-australopithecines share several key attributes: they were extraordinarily primitive, they were highly diverse, and they lived in wooded settings throughout Africa. They spent a lot of time on the ground, but also spent time in trees. The emerging picture of the first hominids as forest-dwellers calls into question the earlier notion that bipedality developed first in open grasslands. As far back as the 1800s, early hominids had been identified as having lived in a time period with a dryer climate. Bipedalism was thought to have been an adaptation to this new kind of climate and its associated open grasslands. It now seems unlikely, however, that early hominids first evolved in grasslands (**Figure 9.14**).

The Australopithecines (4–1 mya)

The australopithecines are represented by hundreds of fossils of at least seven species from one genus, *Australopithecus*. Some of the species represent members of ancestral-descendant lineages (**Figure 9.15**). For the other species, however, anthropologists are sorting out the lineage relationships. Compared with other mammals, australopithecines did not vary greatly. Their variation was mostly in size and robusticity—from relatively small and gracile to large and robust. As a group, the australopithecines had a small brain, small canines, large premolars, and large molars (**Table 9.1**). The later australopithecines' face, jaws, and teeth were very large.

FIGURE 9.14 ■ **Origins of Bipedalism**
The earliest hominid ancestors, the pre-australopithecines, lived in a forested setting, although it might have had a discontinuous tree cover. Contrary to earlier hypotheses, bipedalism appears to have originated not in open grasslands but in an environment with trees. ("*A. afarensis* Group Gathering Figs in an Ancient Hadar Forest," © 1985 by Jay H. Matternes.)

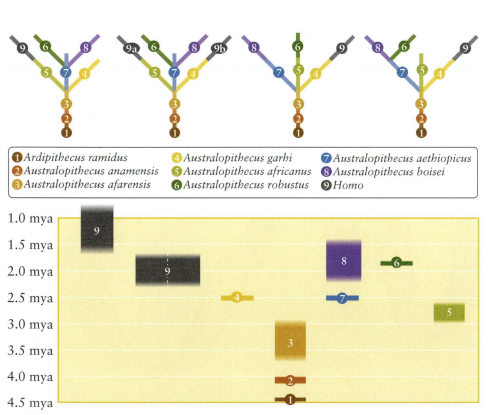

1 *Ardipithecus ramidus*   **4** *Australopithecus garhi*   **7** *Australopithecus aethiopicus*
2 *Australopithecus anamensis*   **5** *Australopithecus africanus*   **8** *Australopithecus boisei*
3 *Australopithecus afarensis*   **6** *Australopithecus robustus*   **9** *Homo*

FIGURE 9.15 ■ **Hominid Phylogenies**
These four alternative phylogenies depict the possible ancestor-descendant relationships among the many australopithecine species. In each tree, *Ardipithecus* is at the base, leading to its descendant *Australopithecus anamensis,* one of the earliest australopithecines. In the second tree, the 9a and 9b indicate that the *Homo* genus may have been the product of both ancestors.

TABLE 9.1	The Earliest Hominids Evolve		
	PRE-AUSTRALOPITHECINE	→	**AUSTRALOPITHECINE**
Teeth	Canine with modified honing	→	Nonhoning
Bones	Vestiges of apelike arboreal traits	→	Loss of traits
Brain	Small	→	Slight increase

Australopithecus anamensis The oldest species of australopithecine from East Africa and a likely ancestor to *A. afarensis*

Australopithecus afarensis An early australopithecine from East Africa that had a brain size equivalent to a modern chimpanzee's and was thought to be a direct human ancestor..

AUSTRALOPITHECUS ANAMENSIS (4 MYA) The oldest australopithecine species, *Australopithecus anamensis* (*anam* means "lake" in the Turkana language), was named and studied by the American paleoanthropological team of Meave Leakey, Carol Ward, and Alan Walker. *A. anamensis* dates to about 4 mya and was found within Allia Bay and Kanapoi, in, respectively, the eastern and southern ends of Lake Turkana, Kenya. Other remains, found at Asa Issie, Ethiopia, have been studied by the American anthropologist Tim White and his colleagues. This creature was broadly similar in physical appearance to *Ardipithecus,* enough to indicate a probable ancestral-descendant relationship between the two genera. Reflecting its relatively early place in australopithecine evolution, *A. anamensis* has a number of primitive, apelike characteristics, including very large canines, parallel tooth rows in the upper jaw, and a lower third premolar with both a very large outer cusp and a very small inner cusp (**Figure 9.16**). The fossils were created in woodland environments.

AUSTRALOPITHECUS AFARENSIS (3.6–3.0 MYA) Since the early 1970s, fossils representing *Australopithecus afarensis* have been found in two main sites: Laetoli, in Tanzania, Kenya; and Hadar, in Ethiopia (*Afar* is the name of the local tribe

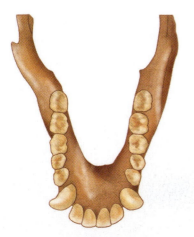

CHIMPANZEE

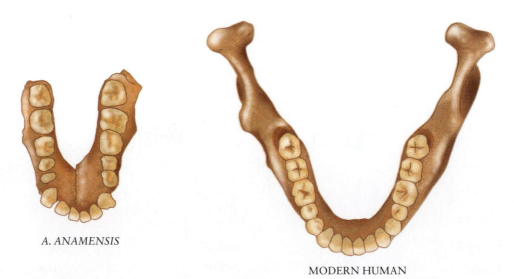

A. ANAMENSIS

MODERN HUMAN

FIGURE 9.16 ■ *Australopithecus anamensis*
Humans' mandible widens at the rear, causing the two rows of teeth to not be parallel to each other. By contrast, this australopithecine's mandible is like that of apes, U-shaped and with two parallel rows of teeth. Primitive features like this, combined with numerous hominid features, have led many researchers to conclude that *A. anamensis* is the earliest australopithecine.

where the fossils were found in Ethiopia). This hominid is the best-known australo-pithecine and is represented by hundreds of fossils from dozens of individuals, dating to 3.6–3.0 mya. The most spectacular of the *A. afarensis* fossils—discovered and described by the American paleoanthropologists Donald Johanson, Maurice Taieb, and Tim White—was a 40% complete adult skeleton, nicknamed **"Lucy"** after the Beatles' song "Lucy in the Sky with Diamonds." Recently, in Dikika, the partial skeleton of a three-year-old child was uncovered (**Figure 9.17**).

Especially important about *A. afarensis* is the remarkable representation of Lucy's postcranial skeleton, which includes both arms, much of the pelvis, a left femur and a right tibia, and hand and foot bones. The postcranial skeleton is primitive. Although she was an adept biped, her form of bipedalism differed from modern humans'. That is, her legs are short relative to the lengths of both the body trunk and the arms, and these shorter legs would have produced a somewhat shorter stride length than modern people's. The early hominids probably were striders, but perhaps with less skill than the longer-legged later hominids had. Lucy's arms are about the same as living humans' in the ratio of length to body size. Her fingers are the same length as modern humans', but the phalanges are curved, like pre-australopithecines'. The curvature suggests potential arboreal locomotion using the hands (**Figure 9.18**).

A. afarensis's skull is known from many fragments and teeth, as well as a child's skull and a nearly complete cranium, the latter found in the early 1990s at Hadar by Donald Johanson (**Figure 9.19**). The cranial capacity of this creature and others from the taxon is about 430 cc, that of a small brain, the size of an ape's. The hyoid

Lucy One of the most significant fossils: the 40% complete skeleton of an adult female *A. afarensis*, found in East Africa.

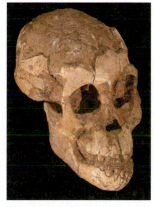

(b)

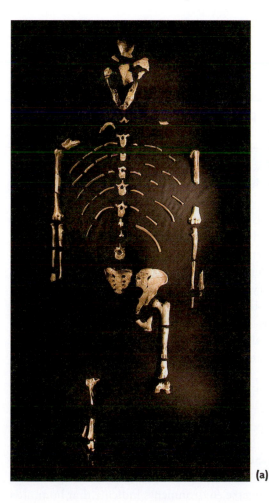

(a)

FIGURE 9.17 ■ *Australopithecus afarensis*

(a) As shown here, "Lucy" is a relatively complete skeleton, which helped researchers conclude that this species was bipedal. **(b)** Recently, the fossil remains of a three-year-old child were recovered and nicknamed "Lucy's baby." There are few children in the fossil record.

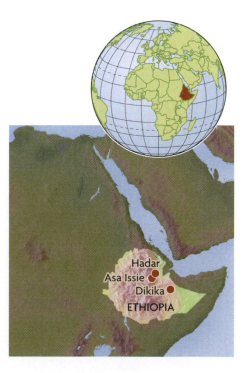

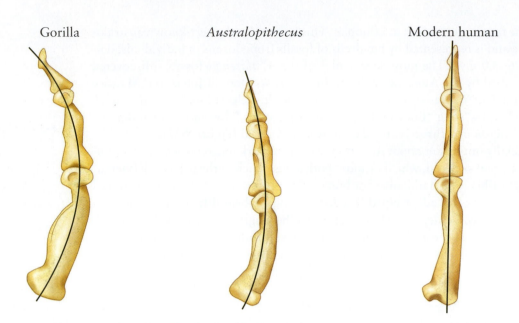

Gorilla   *Australopithecus*   Modern human

FIGURE 9.18 ■ **Finger and Toe Curvature**

Gorillas and other nonhuman primates have curved phalanges, which provide a better grip on tree branches and improve arboreal locomotion. In modern humans, this curvature has been lost in the hands and feet, as humans are adapted to life on the ground. The phalanges of early hominids, including Australopithecines, have an intermediate amount of curvature, which likely reflects an increasing adaptation to bipedalism but a retained ability to move through the trees.

bone of the child's neck is very much like an ape's. The apelike characteristics of the bone associated with speech indicates the strong likelihood that this hominid did not have speech. The canines are large in comparison with later hominids', the face below the nose projects like an ape's, and overall it looks primitive.

Its many similarities with *A. anamensis* indicate an ancestral-descendant link between the two. *A. afarensis* is not as primitive as the earlier hominid in that the two cusps of the lower third premolars are more equal in size. Moreover, *A. afarensis*'s canines are smaller than the earlier species', and the upper tooth rows are parabolic and not parallel—in other words, more like humans' than like apes'. *A. afarensis*'s mandibles are larger, perhaps reflecting an increased use of the jaws in chewing.

Of the two key *A. afarensis* sites, Laetoli is especially extraordinary because of its assemblage of fossil hominids and because of its spectacular preservation of thousands of footprints left by numerous species of animals, ranging from tiny insects to giant elephants. Geologic evidence indicates the eruption of a nearby volcano, which spewed a thin layer of very fine ash across the landscape. Soon after the eruption, a light rain fell, causing the ash to turn into a thin, gooey layer of mud. Animals then traversed the landscape, among them three hominids that left tracks indicating they had simultaneously walked across the muddy terrain around 3.6 mya (**Figure 9.20**). The footprints are remarkable for having been preserved for millions of years and with such clarity, a preservation made possible because the volcanic ash was wet carbonatite, which dries into a rock-hard substance. Physical anthropologists' study of these tracks reveals that the creatures were humanlike and had three key characteristics of bipedalism: round heels, double arches (front-to-back and side-to-side), and nondivergent big toes.

In contrast to earlier hominids, who were mostly associated with some type of forested environment, *A. afarensis* lived in various habitats, including forests, woodlands, and open country. These diverse environments indicate that hominids

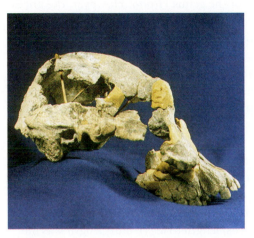

FIGURE 9.19 ■ *Australopithecus afarensis* **Cranium**
Although this species was bipedal, its brain size and canine size are more primitive and apelike. Other features of the dentition, however, are more hominidlike, illustrating the creature's intermediate position between the pre-australopithecines and other, later australopithecines.

FIGURE 9.20 ■ **Laetoli Footprints**
These footprints, found in Tanzania, resolved any doubt as to whether *A. afarensis* was bipedal. The tracks were made by three bipedal hominids, two adults and a child who walked in the footprints of one of the adults. In addition to the hominid footprints, many other prints were found at the site, including those of large animals, such as elephants and giraffes, and those of small animals, including rabbits and birds.

became more successful at this time, especially after 4 mya, in adapting to and exploiting new habitats. That *A. afarensis*'s tooth wear is more varied than that of earlier australopithecines indicates that *A. afarensis* probably had a more diverse diet than its predecessors did.

AUSTRALOPITHECUS (KENYANTHROPUS) PLATYOPS (3.5 MYA) *Australopithecus* (or *Kenyanthropus*) *platyops* is a lesser-known hominid from about the same time as *A. afarensis* (**Figure 9.21**). It was discovered by Meave Leakey and her colleagues, at Lomekwi, on the western side of Kenya's Lake Turkana, in deposits that date to about 3.5 mya. Its habitat was mainly woodlands. Its face was unusually flat (*platyops*, from the Greek, means "flat face"), a derived feature in hominids, but still retained some primitive characteristics.

Prior to that time, there had never been more than one hominid species. With the emergence of two contemporary australopithecine taxa, human evolution became more complex. This increasing complexity was related to the beginning of two adaptive patterns—evolutionary lineages—within human evolution.

Diversification of the Hominidae: Emergence of Two Evolutionary Lineages from One (3–1 mya)

Beginning more than 3 mya, two lineages of hominid evolution began to emerge from one. These two lineages likely reflect two different adaptations. One adaptive pattern is associated with the origin and evolution of the genus *Homo*. The other is represented by descendants of *A. afarensis*, leading to the evolution of two later australopithecine lineages, one in East Africa and the other in South Africa. The

FIGURE 9.21 ■ *Australopithecus (Kenyanthropus) platyops*
A contemporary of *A. afarensis*, this australopithecine was unique in having a flat face and small teeth. Its brain size, however, was similar to that of *A. afarensis*.

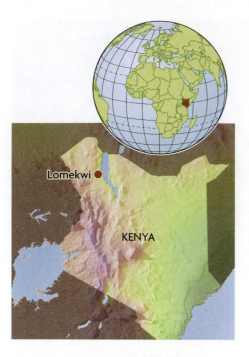

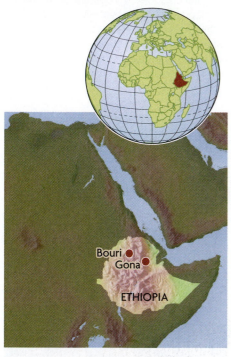

Australopithecus garhi A late australopithecine from East Africa that was contemporaneous with *A. africanus* and *A. aethiopicus* and was the likely ancestor to the *Homo* lineage.

Oldowan Complex The stone tool culture associated with *H. habilis* and, possibly, *A. garhi*, including primitive chopper tools.

Lower Paleolithic The oldest part of the period during which the first stone tools were created and used, beginning with the Oldowan Complex.

lineage leading to *Homo* survives to the present, whereas the australopithecine lineages became extinct by about 1 mya (**Figure 9.22**). Here, we look at the two emerging forms of early hominids.

AUSTRALOPITHECUS GARHI (2.5 MYA): THE FIRST MAKER, AND USER, OF TOOLS Soon after discovering *A. afarensis* at Hadar, Johanson and White began to suspect that *A. afarensis* was the most likely ancestor of the genus *Homo*. However, the ancestral-descendant linkage between the two taxa was difficult to identify, owing to the virtual lack of a hominid fossil record in East Africa dating to 3–2 mya, the time during which earliest *Homo* likely evolved (discussed further in chapter 10). In 1999, this picture changed dramatically, when the Ethiopian paleoanthropologist Berhane Asfaw and his associates discovered a new *Australopithecus* species, which they named *Australopithecus garhi* (*garhi* means "surprise" in the Afar language). Found in Bouri, in Ethiopia's Middle Awash region, it dated to about 2.5 mya.

A. garhi is represented by bones, teeth, a partial skeleton, and a skull (**Figure 9.23**). Its teeth were larger than the earlier australopithecines'. Its third premolar's two cusps were almost equal in size. As in *A. afarensis,* beneath the nose the face had a primitive projection, and the brain was small (450 cc). For the first time in hominid evolution, the ratio of arm (humerus) length to leg (femur) length was much more humanlike than apelike, resulting from the femur's lengthening. This more humanlike ratio indicates a decreased commitment to the arborealism of earlier australopithecines. These features combined—especially the chronological position at 2.5 mya and the cranial, dental, and postcranial features—suggest that *A. garhi* was ancestral to *Homo*. Environmental reconstructions based on animal remains and other evidence indicate that this hominid lived on a lakeshore, as was typical of later australopithecines and early *Homo*.

At least one or both early hominids made and used stone tools. Paleoanthropologists have found very primitive stone tools from a number of sites in East Africa dating to the early Pleistocene, 2.5–2.0 mya. These stone tools are part of the **Oldowan Complex,** the first hominid culture and the earliest culture of the **Lower Paleolithic,** named by Louis and Mary Leakey from their work at Olduvai Gorge. The Leakeys concluded that these crude stone tools must have been produced by the larger-brained early *Homo* found at the site, rather than by the contemporary smaller-brained australopithecines. Although no tools have been found at Bouri, the Belgian paleoanthropologist Jean de Heinzelin, the American anthropologist Desmond Clark, and their colleagues found mammal bones at the site having distinctive cutmarks and percussion marks that were produced by stone tools. This evidence indicates that *A. garhi* used stone tools to process animal remains for food (**Figure 9.24**). At the Gona River site, in the Middle Awash region, actual tools—the earliest known—have been found dating to around 2.6 mya. Though extraordinarily primitive, the tools would have been effective at cutting (**Figure 9.25**).

Archaeologists have long assumed that such primitive tools were used for cutting animal tissues to obtain the meat. Stone tools may indeed have been used this way. However, bone tools found in some South African caves show distinctively polished patterns of microscopic wear. Through experiments, the South African paleoanthropologist Lucinda Backwell and the French paleoanthropologist Francesco d'Errico have shown this kind of wear to be produced by digging in the ground, especially digging in termite mounds. Their finding supports the idea that early hominids ate insects (in addition to meat). While the idea of eating insects is

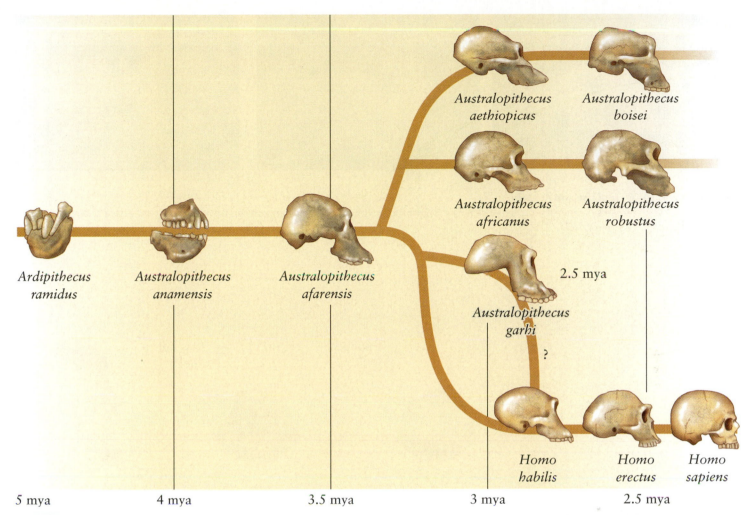

Ardipithecus
ramidus

Australopithecus
anamensis

Australopithecus
afarensis

Australopithecus
aethiopicus

Australopithecus
boisei

Australopithecus
africanus

Australopithecus
robustus

Australopithecus
garhi

2.5 mya

?

Homo
habilis

Homo
erectus

Homo
sapiens

5 mya   4 mya   3.5 mya   3 mya   2.5 mya

FIGURE 9.22 ■ Hominid Lineages
The evolutionary relationships among the various *Australopithecus* species suggest two
main lineages: one leading to modern *Homo sapiens* and the other leading to a number of
australopithecines. (This second lineage is shown here as two separate lines, one from East
Africa and the other from South Africa.) The ancestor to both lineages is hypothesized to
be *A. afarensis,* which may be a descendant of *Ardipithecus* and *A. anamensis.* (Fossil credit:
Ardipithecus ramidus and *Australopithecus garhi,* Middle Awash Research Project, redrawn from
photographs © David L. Brill.)

revolting to our Western tastes, insects would have provided important proteins
for our ancestors. Alternatively, the bone tools may have been used for digging up
edible roots.

Unlike Olduvai Gorge and other, younger sites where *Australopithecus* and early
Homo were found in the same general locality, Bouri has not yielded remains of
early *Homo.* In all likelihood, *Homo* had not yet evolved in East Africa, indicating
that *Australopithecus* was perhaps the first hominid to produce and use stone tools.
These tools were used both to butcher animals for food and for other functions.
Tool use might also have begun before 2.6 mya. Evidence of earlier tool use might
not have been found because tools had been made—and probably were made—out
of more ephemeral materials, such as wood and grass. In the kinds of environments

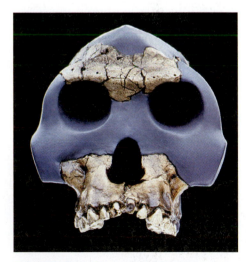

FIGURE 9.23 ■ *Australopithecus garhi*
This "surprise" hominid may be the link
between *A. afarensis* and the *Homo* genus.
That some of its traits are similar to those
of *A. afarensis* while others are similar to
features of *Homo* suggests its intermediate
status. (Photograph © 1999 David L. Brill.)

FIGURE 9.24 ■ **Tool Use and *A. garhi***

(a–c) Particular cutmarks on animal remains suggest that *A. garhi* used stone tools. The marks on this bovid mandible may have been made when the tongue was removed.

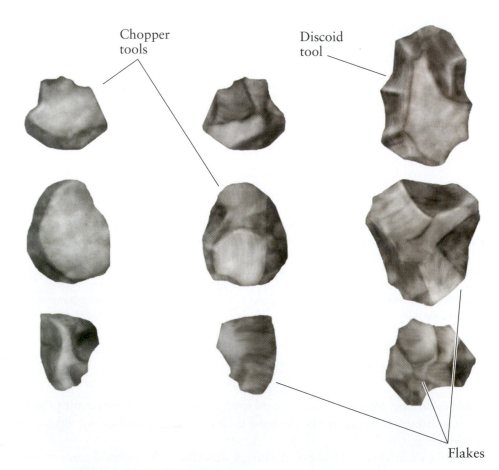

Chopper tools

Discoid tool

Flakes

FIGURE 9.25 ■ **Oldest Stone Tools**

A number of stone tools, known as Oldowan tools, were uncovered in the Middle Awash Valley. These primitive tools were not found in association with hominid remains, so it is unclear which genera or species produced them. Among the remains were flaked pieces and "chopper" tools; these may have had various functions.

in which the earliest hominids lived, these materials would not have survived. Other evidence suggests, though, that hominids living before 2.6 mya used tools. For example, australopithecines' hand bones have anatomical features associated with finer manipulation than that used by living apes. The paleoanthropologist Randall Susman has found evidence of a flexor muscle in australopithecines' thumb, very similar to a muscle in living humans that is absent in apes. The flexor muscle makes possible the finer precision use of the thumb and other fingers for tool production and tool use.

Evolution and Extinction of the Australopithecines

In addition to *A. garhi,* other australopithecine species lived in East Africa and South Africa. In East Africa, the species included earlier and later forms of robust australopithecines called *Australopithecus aethiopicus* (named for Ethiopia, the country where they were first found) and *Australopithecus boisei* (named for a benefactor who supported the discoverer's research), respectively. The earlier hominid, from the west side of Lake Turkana, dates to about 2.5 mya and had a brain size of about 410 cc. The later hominid, from Olduvai Gorge and around Lake Turkana, dates to 2.3–1.2 mya and had a brain size of about 510 cc. Compared with earlier australopithecines, these robust australopithecines had smaller front teeth, larger back teeth, and larger faces. Their most visually striking characteristic was a massive attachment area, on the skull, for the temporalis muscle, resulting in a well-developed sagittal crest. Both their premolars and their molars were enormous. These big teeth with large chewing surfaces, combined with large chewing muscles, made robust australopithecines the ultimate grinders (**Figure 9.26**).

Australopithecus aethiopicus An early robust australopithecine from East Africa, with the hallmark physical traits of large teeth, large face, and massive muscle attachments on the cranium.

Australopithecus boisei Formerly known as Zinjanthropus boisei; a later robust australopithecine from East Africa that was contemporaneous with *A. robustus* and *A. africanus* and had the robust cranial traits, including large teeth, large face, and heavy muscle attachments.

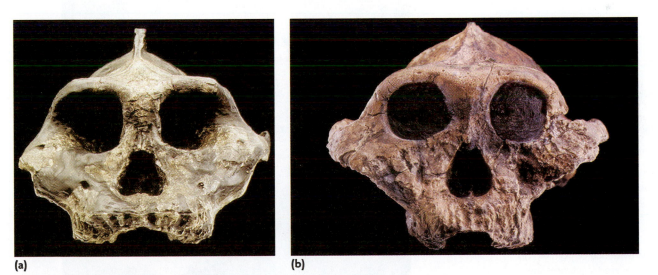

(a)   **(b)**

FIGURE 9.26 ■ **Robust Australopithecines**

(a) *Australopithecus aethiopicus* and **(b)** *Australopithecus boisei* had a large sagittal crest; large, flaring zygomatic, or cheek, bones; and large teeth. The description of these australopithecines as robust, however, applies only to their crania and is likely related to a diet rich in hard foods. Neither of these bipedal species had a robust postcranial skeleton. (Photographs [a] © 1995 David L. Brill and [b] © 1985 David L. Brill.)

Australopithecines' increasing cranial robusticity after about 2.5 mya indicates that they were increasingly focused on acquiring and eating foods that required more powerful chewing muscles than before. That is, they were eating harder foods. Robust australopithecines' presence in East Africa ended sometime before 1 mya, indicating that they became extinct at about that time.

In South Africa, a very similar trend of increasing cranial and dental robusticity began 3–2 mya. These changes coincided with a shift in habitat from forest to grasslands around 2.5 mya. At the Taung site in 1925, the Australian anthropologist Raymond Dart was the first to describe the earliest evidence of hominids in South Africa, a species he named *Australopithecus africanus* (**Figure 9.27**). Found also in Sterkfontein and Makapansgat, *A. africanus* dates to about 3–2 mya and had larger teeth than those of *A. afarensis* (**Figure 9.28**). After about 2 mya, a descendant species, ***Australopithecus robustus*** (sometimes called *Paranthropus robustus*) arose, and it is represented by fossils from Swartkrans, Kromdraai, and Drimolen.

South Africa's youngest-dating australopithecines had large premolars, large molars, big faces, and well-developed sagittal crests—these hominids were similar in many respects to their East African counterparts (**Figure 9.29**). Australopithecines' increasing robusticity in South Africa and East Africa indicates a widespread adaptation involving an increased focus on foods that required heavy chewing. Moreover, *A. robustus*'s teeth had more pits on the chewing surfaces and thicker enamel than *A. africanus*'s teeth, indicating that the later australopithecines specialized in eating harder food, such as hard fruits and seeds.

As in East Africa, the australopithecines in South Africa went extinct by 1 mya. The reasons for this extinction are unclear. However, the lineage leading to *Homo*

Australopithecus africanus A gracile australopithecine from South Africa that was contemporaneous with *A. aethiopicus*, *A. garhi*, and *A. boisei* and was likely ancestral to *A. robustus*.

Australopithecus robustus A robust australopithecine from South Africa that may have descended from *A. afarensis*, was contemporaneous with *A. boisei*, and had the robust cranial traits of large teeth, large face, and heavy muscle attachments.

FIGURE 9.27 ■ **Taung, South Africa**
Some of the earliest evidence of hominids in South Africa was discovered in a limestone quarry in Taung. For some time, the species found there, *A. africanus*, overlapped temporally with *A. afarensis*, of East Africa. In addition, the small, gracile species had a number of humanlike features.

FIGURE 9.28 ■ *Australopithecus africanus*
This *Australopithecus africanus* cranium was discovered in a series of limestone caves known as Sterkfontein. Located in South Africa, this site has been declared a UNESCO World Heritage Site. Unlike the robust australopithecines also discovered in South Africa, this *A. africanus* cranium is gracile.

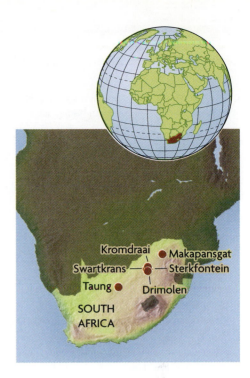

FIGURE 9.29 ■ *Australopithecus robustus*
Also discovered in South Africa, this robust australopithecine shares many traits with East Africa's robust species. One of these traits, dietary specialization, might have led to the eventual extinction of both *A. robustus* and the East African robust species, as they were not able to adapt to vegetation changes caused by climate change.

seems to have developed an increasingly flexible and generalized diet, whereas the later robust australopithecines' diets became less flexible and more specialized. This increasing focus on a narrower range of foods in the later robust australopithecines may have led to their extinction. Their brains show very little increase in size. The brains of South African *A. africanus* and *A. robustus* were only about 450 cc and 530 cc, respectively.

From the late Miocene through the Pliocene and into the Pleistocene—about 6–1 mya—the earliest hominids began to evolve. These diverse hominids had increasingly specialized diets, and their cranial morphology reflected this specialization. They experienced no appreciable change in brain size or body size, however. Thus, evolution focused on mastication. A new genus of and species of hominid, *Homo habilis*—having a larger brain and reduced chewing complex—made its appearance (**Table 9.2**). At that time, australopithecines were diverse, evolving, and a significant presence on the African landscape. This gracile hominid likely evolved from an australopithecine, and the ancestor may have been *A. garhi*. This point in human evolution is critically important because it is the earliest record of a remarkable adaptive radiation, leading to the most prolific and widespread species of primate: us.

Homo habilis The earliest *Homo* species, a possible descendant of *A. garhi* and an ancestor to *H. erectus*; showed the first substantial increase in brain size and was the first species definitively associated with the production and use of stone tools.

The Australopithecines

The australopithecines existed about 4–1 mya. Their fossils are from East Africa and South Africa. These creatures were still primitive in a number of ways, but they were more humanlike than apelike compared with the pre-australopithecines.

HOMINID	DATE(S)	LOCATION(S)
Australopithecus anamensis	4 mya	Lake Turkana, Kenya Awash River Valley, Ethiopia

Key features:
Skull fragments, teeth, postcrania found
Large outer cusp (like apes') on third premolar
Large canines
Parallel tooth rows in upper jaw (like apes')
Curved hand phalanx
Less than 1 m (4 ft) tall
Lived in wooded setting

HOMINID	DATE(S)	LOCATION(S)
Australopithecus platyops	3.5 mya	Lomekwi, Kenya

Key features:
Skull and teeth found
Flat face
Small brain (400–500 cc)
Contemporary with *A. afarensis,* signaling split of australopithecine lineage into two
Lived in woodlands

HOMINID	DATE(S)	LOCATION(S)
Australopithecus afarensis	3.6–3.0 mya	Hadar, Ethiopia

Key features:
Skulls, teeth, postcrania (hundreds of pieces) found
Partial adult skeleton (Lucy)
Partial juvenile (three-year-old) skeleton
Small brain (430 cc)
Hyoid like apes'
Mandible larger in earlier Laetoli than in later Hadar
Smaller canines than in earlier species
Equal-size cusps on third premolar (like humans')
Parabolic tooth rows in upper jaw
Curved hand phalanges
Short legs
Footprints indicate bipedal foot pattern
Lived in wooded setting, but a more open one than associated with *Ardipithecus* or *A. anamensis*

HOMINID	DATE(S)	LOCATION(S)
Australopithecus africanus	3.0–2.0 mya	Taung, South Africa Sterkfontein, South Africa Makapansgat, South Africa

Key features:
Skulls, teeth, endocast (impression of brain), postcrania, two partial adult skeletons found
Small brain (450 cc)
Moderate-size teeth
Equal-size cusps on third premolar
Phalanges not curved
Adult partial skeleton has apelike leg-to-arm ratio (short legs, long arms)
Lived in open grasslands

HOMINID	DATE(S)	LOCATION(S)	HOMINID	DATE(S)	LOCATION(S)
Australopithecus garhi	2.5 mya	Bouri, Ethiopia	*Australopithecus boisei*	2.3–1.2 mya	Olduvai, Tanzania Lake Turkana, Kenya

Key features:
Skull, teeth, postcrania found
Small brain (450 cc)
Equal-size cusps on third premolar
Teeth larger than in earlier *A. afarensis*
Ratio of upper arm length to upper leg length more humanlike
    than apelike
Curved foot phalanx (like *A. afarensis*'s)
Lived in grasslands, on lakeshore
Tool maker/user (animal butchering)

Key features:
Skull and teeth found
Small brain (510 cc)
Massive posterior teeth
Rubust skull with sagittal crest
Lived in open grasslands

| *Australopithecus aethiopicus* | 2.5 mya | Lake Turkana, Kenya | *Australopithecus robustus* | 2.0–1.5 mya | Swartkrans, South Africa Kromdraai, South Africa Drimolen, South Africa |

Key features:
Skull and teeth found
Small brain (410 cc)
Massive posterior teeth
Robust skull with sagittal crest
Lived in open grasslands

Key features:
Skull and teeth found
Small brain (530 cc)
Massive posterior teeth
Robust skull with sagittal crest
Lived in open grasslands

TABLE 9.2 Trends from Late Australopithecine to Early *Homo*

LATE AUSTRALOPITHECINE	→	EARLY *HOMO*

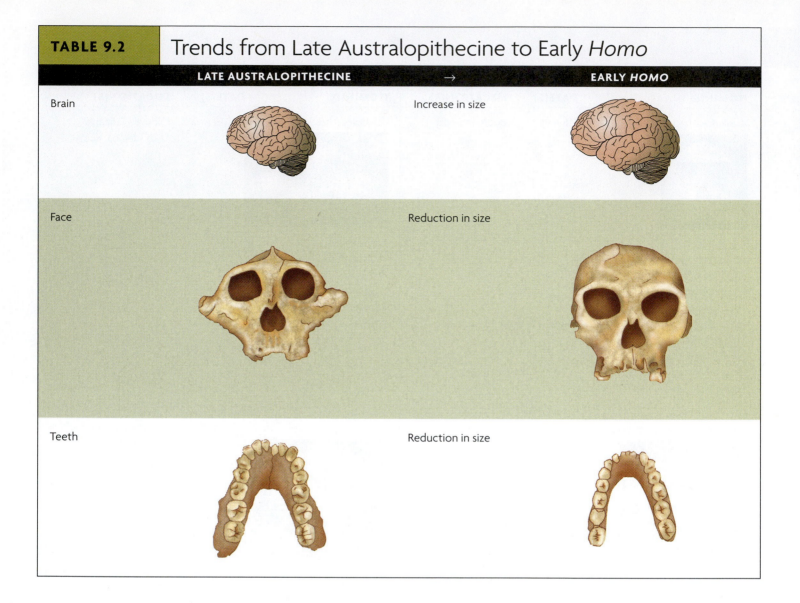

Brain — Increase in size

Face — Reduction in size

Teeth — Reduction in size

ANSWERING THE BIG QUESTIONS

What is a hominid?

■ Hominids are defined by two obligate behaviors: bipedal locomotion and nonhoning chewing.

Why did hominids evolve from an apelike primate?

■ The Hominidae's origin is closely tied to the origins of bipedal locomotion. This form of movement may have provided early hominids with a more efficient means of exploiting patchy forests, freeing the hands for feeding in trees and on the ground.

Who were the first hominids?

■ The earliest fossil hominids were the pre-australopithecines, dating to 7–4 mya. These hominids lived in forests.

■ The pre-australopithecines gave rise to the australopithecines, dating to 4–1 mya.

What was the evolutionary fate of the first hominids?

■ The evolution of the australopithecine lineages resulted in generally increased robusticity of the chewing complex, no change in brain size, and eventual extinction. The change in the chewing complex reflected an increasing emphasis on eating hard foods, especially plants.

■ By 2.5 mya, at least one australopithecine lineage gave rise to the genus *Homo*. Having evolved from earlier australopithecines, at least two other australopithecine lineages, one in East Africa and one in South Africa, went extinct around 1 mya.

ⓢ wwnorton.com/studyspace

KEY TERMS

Ardipithecus kadabba
Ardipithecus ramidus
Australopithecus aethiopicus
Australopithecus afarensis
Australopithecus africanus
Australopithecus anamensis
Australopithecus boisei
Australopithecus garhi
Australopithecus (or *Kenyanthropus*)
    platyops

Australopithecus robustus
Eoanthropus dawsoni
Homo habilis
Lower Paleolithic
Lucy
Oldowan Complex
Orrorin tugenensis
Sahelanthropus tchadensis

ADDITIONAL READINGS

Gibbons, A. 2006. *The First Human: The Race to Discover Our Earliest Ancestors*. New York: Doubleday.

Walker, A. and P. Shipman. 1996. *The Wisdom of the Bones: In Search of Human Origins*. New York: Knopf.

Ward, C., M. Leakey, and A. Walker. 1999. The new hominid species *Australopithecus anamensis*. *Evolutionary Anthropology* 7: 197–205.

White, T. D. 2002. Earliest hominids. Pp. 407–417 in W. C. Hartwig, ed. *The Primate Fossil Record*. Cambridge, UK: Cambridge University Press.

Wolpoff, M. H. 1996. *Human Evolution*. New York: McGraw-Hill.

Located at Zhoukoudian (Dragon Bone Hill), near Beijing, People's Republic of China, this cave was excavated in the 1920s–40s, revealing the remains of *Homo erectus*.

CHAPTER 10

The Origins and Evolution of Early *Homo*

FIGURE 10.1 ■ Eugène Dubois
A Dutch anatomist and anthropologist, Dubois discovered the first early hominid remains found outside Europe.

C harles Darwin was struck by the great anatomical similarity of living humans and African apes. In 1871, writing about human origins without having seen a human fossil, he settled on Africa as the birthplace of the earliest hominids. But he was not the only leading scientist in the nineteenth century to think about human origins and where humans first evolved. Ernst Haeckel (1834–1919), Germany's preeminent anatomist and evolutionary biologist of the late nineteenth century, came up with an entirely different origins scenario. He reasoned that the Asian great ape, the orangutan, is more anatomically similar to humans than are the African great apes. Asia, not Africa, he concluded, must have been the hominids' ancestral homeland. In his extensive scholarly work about human origins and evolution, Haeckel went to great lengths to describe what the first hominid would have looked like. He even went so far as to propose a genus name for the ancestor: *Pithecanthropus,* meaning "ape-man."

Haeckel's books on early human evolution and its Asian origins profoundly inspired a precocious Dutch teenager, Eugène Dubois (1858–1940; **Figure 10.1**). Fascinated by Haeckel's ideas about evolution, Dubois devoured Darwin's *On the Origin of Species.* He enrolled in medical school at the University of Amsterdam at age 19 and received his medical degree at 26. A superb scientist, he was hired as a lecturer in the university's anatomy department. At the same time, his interest in evolution deepened. He became convinced that to truly *study* human origins, he had to *find* human fossils. Within a year of being promoted to lecturer he quit his job, gathered his resources, got hired as a physician for the Dutch colonial government, and moved with his wife and their baby to the Dutch East Indies (the modern country of Indonesia, which includes the islands of Sumatra and Borneo; **Figure 10.2**). His friends, neighbors, and associates thought he was reckless at best to risk his family's well-being as he looked for something that might never be found. Soon after landing in Sumatra in December 1887, Dubois assumed his new responsibilities as a physician at a military hospital, spending his money and free time in the pursuit of fossils. After trying to juggle medicine and fossil hunting, he talked the Dutch colonial government into letting him leave his day job to work for the

BIG QUESTIONS

■ What characteristics define the genus *Homo*?

■ Who were the earliest members of the genus *Homo*?

■ What are the key evolutionary trends and other developments in early *Homo*?

Pithecanthropus erectus The name first proposed by Ernst Haeckel for the oldest hominid; Dubois later used this name for his first fossil discovery, which later became known as *Homo erectus*.

Dutch as a full-time paleontologist. With the help of two civil engineers and a group of 50 convicts, he searched the island, but found nothing. Meanwhile, he suffered from discomfort, fatigue, illness, and depression.

Desperate to avoid returning to Holland without having found fossils, Dubois pleaded with his superiors to let him shift his focus from Sumatra to nearby Java. The authorities accepted his assurances that Java would produce fossils. Soon after moving to Java, Dubois heard about bones appearing out of the eroding banks of the Solo River, near the village of Trinil. Soon after commencing excavations in the late summer of 1891, he and his field crew discovered a human molar. Within a couple of months, they had found a partial skull, and later in the following year they found a complete femur (**Figure 10.3**). The skull was extraordinary. It was clearly not from *Homo sapiens*—it had a low and long braincase, no forehead to speak of, and large browridges like apes'. Was it from an ape or a human or something between an ape and a human? By measuring the braincase's volume, he estimated that in life the brain had been about 1,000 cc, too big for a modern ape (a chimpanzee's brain is 400 cc) and too small for a modern human (the average human brain today is about 1,450 cc). He had found what he was looking for: the human ancestor. In fact, Dubois's anatomical study revealed that the femur was essentially identical to a modern human's—this primitive human ancestor was fully bipedal. Convinced that he had found what Haeckel had predicted, he called his fossil hominid *Pithecanthropus erectus,* meaning "upright-walking ape-man."

Dubois's ideas and the fossils he found met with mixed reactions, mostly negative. However, as the years went by, others found more hominid fossils in Java and

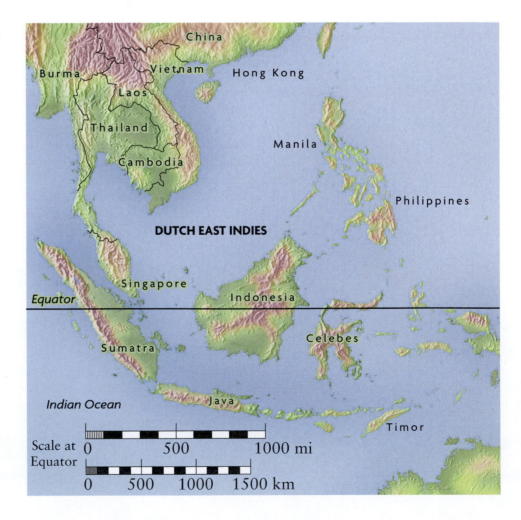

FIGURE 10.2 ■ **Dutch East Indies**
On the island of Java, one of the southernmost islands of what is now Indonesia, Dubois discovered the hominid fossil later identified as *Homo erectus*.

elsewhere in Asia. It became clear to most anthropologists that Dubois's fossils from Java were early members of our genus but a different species, and these hominids are now called *Homo erectus.* Dubois's fossil turned out to be not from the earliest hominid or even from the earliest species of *Homo* (see chapter 9 and below).

Dubois was wrong in thinking that evidence of the earliest human would be found in Southeast Asia, but he was working in a scientific vacuum. Without today's fossil record to guide him, he drew the best possible conclusion from the evidence available and made crucially important discoveries about the genus *Homo*'s evolution. The only scientist of the time who set out a research plan to test a hypothesis about early human ancestors, he sought fossil evidence to establish evolutionary relationships. In contrast to the great evolutionists of the nineteenth century—Darwin, Haeckel, Huxley, and others—he endeavored to use fossils, not living animals' comparative anatomy, to test his hypothesis. This revolutionary development in anthropology set the stage for paleoanthropology, the study of early human evolution.

FIGURE 10.3 ■ **Java Man**
Dubois originally named this hominid fossil *Pithecanthropus erectus,* though it was nicknamed "Java Man" after the island on which it was found. Dubois recovered **(a)** a cranium and **(b)** a nearly complete femur. **(b)**

This chapter focuses on the earliest members of our genus: *Homo habilis* and *Homo erectus.* These were the hominids that first began to develop the characteristic behaviors that we see in living humans, that increasingly employed intelligence and displayed adaptive flexibility, and that first depended on material culture. During early *Homo*'s evolution, hominids began to colonize areas of the world outside Africa. The earliest fossil evidence, from around 2.5–1.0 mya, indicates that *Homo habilis* and the earliest *Homo erectus* lived at the same time as the later australopithecines (discussed in chapter 9). Early *Homo,* however, adapted very differently than the other hominids, the australopithecines. These changes set the course for human evolution, the record of which is supported by abundant fossils.

Homo erectus An early *Homo* species and the likely descendant of *H. habilis;* the first hominid species to move out of Africa into Asia and Europe.

HOMO HABILIS: THE FIRST SPECIES OF THE GENUS HOMO

The Path to Humanness: Bigger Brains, Tool Use, and Adaptive Flexibility

Modern humans are distinctive in having large brains and in depending on material culture for survival. Rather than relying on their bodies for the collection, processing, and eating of food, modern humans rely on tools and technology as part of their adaptive strategy. These attributes are what scientists looked for in the fossil record when they sought the first species of our genus. Which of the multiple hominid species in the late Pliocene and early Pleistocene show brain size expansion? Which of the hominids with brain size expansion likely depended on tools and material culture for promoting adaptive success and behavioral flexibility?

Soon after the discovery of the massively robust australopithecine *Australopithecus boisei* (its cranium is known as "OH 5"), remains of a hominid having jaws,

teeth, and a face that were relatively smaller and a brain that was relatively larger were found, also in Olduvai Gorge. Its describers—Louis Leakey, Philip Tobias, and John Napier—recognized the significance of this combination of characteristics and named the new hominid *Homo habilis* (meaning "handy man"). *Homo habilis* is now known from Tanzania, Kenya, Ethiopia, Malawi, and South Africa—the same geographic distribution as that of the contemporary australopithecines (**Figure 10.4**). *Homo habilis* found on the eastern side of Kenya's Lake Turkana is sometimes called *Homo rudolfensis* (**Figure 10.5**). The major difference is that *Homo rudolfensis* is somewhat bigger than *Homo habilis*. Because they have the same general body plan and overall morphology (bigger brains, smaller faces), here the two species are discussed as *Homo habilis*.

As Leakey and his associates recognized, *H. habilis* differs in its anatomy from the robust australopithecines dating to about the same time in East Africa and South Africa. *Australopithecus boisei* had an enormous chewing complex—its back teeth, jaws, and face were very large—but it had a small brain. In sharp contrast, *H. habilis* had a smaller chewing complex and a larger brain. Combined, the reduced chewing complex and increased brain size gave *H. habilis*'s skull a more rounded, or globular, appearance. Most anthropologists agree that these attributes indicate that *H. habilis* began the lineage leading to modern humans.

Still unconfirmed is the identity of *H. habilis*'s immediate ancestor. The anthropologist Tim White's morphological comparisons between *H. habilis* and the earlier australopithecines suggests that the ancestor was *Australopithecus garhi*, because its face, jaws, and teeth are most similar to *H. habilis*'s. White suggests that the evolutionary transition took place sometime around 3.0–2.5 mya.

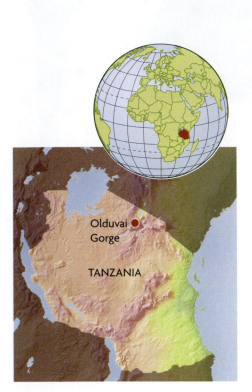

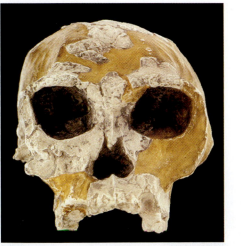
(a)

(b)

(c)

FIGURE 10.4 ■ *Homo habilis*
Many fossils of this hominid species have been recovered from East Africa and South Africa. **(a)** This specimen, known as "OH 24" or "Twiggy," was discovered in Tanzania in 1968. Dating to 1.8 million yBP, Twiggy had a larger brain and a less protruding face than australopithecines. **(b)** Slightly younger than Twiggy, this lower jaw, known as "OH 7," was found in Tanzania in 1960 and dates to 1.75 mya. Given its small dental size, researchers estimated that the brain size would have been smaller than in other *Homo habilis* fossils. **(c)** This cranium, "KNM-ER 1813," was discovered in Kenya in 1973 and dates to 1.9 mya. Its brain capacity is somewhat smaller than those of other, later *Homo habilis* specimens. (Photographs [a] © 1997 David L. Brill and [c] © 1985 David L. Brill.)

(a)   (b)

FIGURE 10.5 ■ *Homo habilis*
Owing to its larger size, this fossil hominid is believed by some researchers to be a separate species from *Homo habilis,* called *Homo rudolfensis.* (Photographs © 1985 David L. Brill.)

Homo habilis and *Australopithecus:* Similar in Body Plan

For many years, *Homo habilis* was known from just skulls and teeth. Anthropologists had no idea what the rest of the skeleton looked like. Excavations at Olduvai Gorge in the 1980s by Donald Johanson and his associates led to the discovery of a very fragmentary, but important, skeleton of *H. habilis*, known as "OH 62." The skeleton is from an individual who was short—about three and a half feet—like the australopithecines. Also like the australopithecines, this individual had short legs in comparison with the arms. Although *H. habilis* walked bipedally, these short legs would not have been involved in the kind of efficient striding performed by living people. The gait would have been shorter.

Homo habilis's Adaptation: Intelligence and Tool Use Become Important

Homo habilis's short legs indicate that the species retained a primitive form of bipedality, more australopithecine than human. Much more telling about *H. habilis*'s adaptation and evolution is skull and teeth morphology and evidence of the making and use of stone tools. Fossil skulls and fossil teeth reveal that this hominid ancestor had a larger brain, smaller chewing muscles, and smaller teeth than did earlier and contemporary hominids, the australopithecines. Both the brain enlargement and the masticatory changes may be linked to tools' growing importance. Anatomical

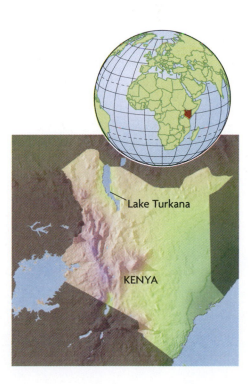

Lake Turkana

KENYA

CONCEPT CHECK

Homo habilis: The First Member of Our Lineage

Homo habilis was the first hominid to have anatomical and behavioral characteristics that foreshadowed the evolution of *Homo sapiens:* greater intelligence, reliance on tools, and dietary and behavioral flexibility.

LOCATION/SITES	Africa (Olduvai Gorge, Lake Turkana, Middle Awash, Omo, Uraha, Sterkfontein)	
CHRONOLOGY	2.5–1.8 mya	

BIOLOGY AND CULTURE (COMPARED WITH AUSTRALOPITHECINES)

FEATURE	EVIDENCE	OUTCOME
Tool use (Oldowan)	Skulls Teeth	Smaller face and smaller jaws Reduced size
Intelligence	Brain size	Increase (to 650 cc)
Diet (scavenging, plant collecting)	Plants available Body size	Perhaps more generalized No significant change
Locomotion	Leg length:arm length	No significant change

evidence from the study of hand bones, such as the presence of muscles that would have provided the necessary precision grip, suggests that *H. habilis* and at least some of the australopithecines made and used tools. For several reasons, toolmaking and tool use were likely more important in *H. habilis*'s adaptation. First, stone tools are more common in *H. habilis* fossil sites than in *Australopithecus* fossil sites. Second, *H. habilis*'s expanding brain size indicates that it was smarter than *Australopithecus,* with a kind of cognitive advancement almost certainly linked to toolmaking and tool use. That is, *H. habilis* and the lineage it founded became reliant on intelligence, toolmaking, and tool use as central means of adaptation. In contrast, the australopithecines became increasingly specialized, focusing on a narrower range of foods that required heavy chewing. They may have made and used tools, but tools were not as fundamental to their survival and adaptation. *H. habilis*'s behavioral advances laid the foundation for later hominids' success, including their rapid spread out of Africa and to other areas of the globe.

Habitat Changes and Increasing Adaptive Flexibility

Environmental reconstruction of the East African and South African landscapes at 2.5 mya provides some insight into early *Homo*'s adaptive shifts. This reconstruction indicates a spread of warm season (C_4) grasses, increasing habitat diversity, and increasing food resources for early hominids. Such information, along with skull and teeth morphology, suggests early *Homo*'s increasing dietary versatility. Tools may have played a central role in these early hominids' ability to exploit this increasingly diverse landscape. That is, stone tools were likely important for digging roots and tubers and for processing them for consumption. Such extremely primitive technology did not include the kinds of tools associated with later hominids that were clearly social, predatory hunters (discussed below). Still, tools increased these early hominids' *capability* of eating a greater range of food, most of it plants or small animals, the latter acquired by luck and opportunity and perhaps scavenging. This dietary shift may be what spelled adaptive success for early *Homo* and extinction for late *Australopithecus*.

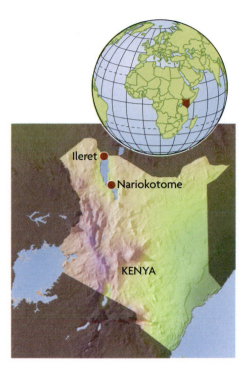

HOMO ERECTUS: EARLY *HOMO* GOES GLOBAL

Beginning around 1.8 mya, a new hominid appeared: *Homo erectus* had anatomical characteristics that distinguished it from *Homo habilis*. As discussed above, it was the only descendant taxon of *H. habilis* and was among the earliest fossil hominids described, having been found by Eugène Dubois at Trinil, in Java.

In the century since Dubois began his work in Java, many fossils with the same general attributes as the Trinil skull—large browridges, long and low skull, and bigger brain—have been found in Europe, Asia, and Africa (**Figure 10.6**). These hominids collectively date to about 1.8 mya–300,000 yBP. During this fascinating and dynamic period of human evolution, hominids first left Africa, colonized vast

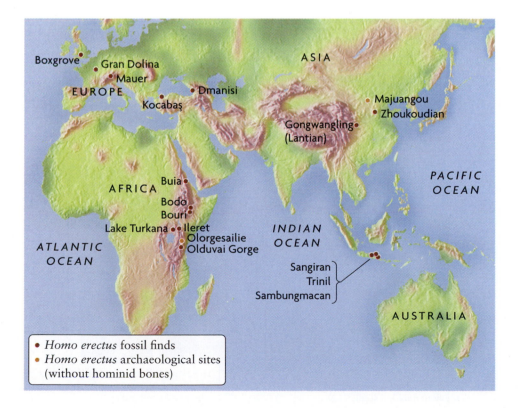

- *Homo erectus* fossil finds
- *Homo erectus* archaeological sites (without hominid bones)

FIGURE 10.6 ■ *Homo erectus* **Sites**
Fossils of *Homo erectus* have been discovered throughout Africa, Europe, and Asia.

areas of Asia and Europe, and underwent fundamental changes in culture and adaptation that shaped human biological evolution.

Homo erectus in Africa (1.8–.3 mya)

The earliest record of *Homo erectus* comes from Africa, less than 2 mya. At that time, the last australopithecines were still around in East Africa and South Africa, and their fossils reveal great differences in anatomy and adaptation from *H. erectus* (**Figure 10.7**). Among the earliest and the most spectacular of these fossils is an 80% complete juvenile skeleton from Nariokotome, on the west side of Lake Turkana (**Figure 10.8**). The skeleton dates to about 1.6 mya, placing it on the boundary between the Pliocene and Pleistocene epochs. In contrast to *Australopithecus* and *H. habilis,* the Nariokotome hominid has several quintessentially modern anatomical features. One of the most striking modern characteristics is the relatively short arms and long legs. That is, the *H. erectus* body plan is much more like that of a living human in its ratio of arm length to leg length. This change in limb proportions in *H. erectus* signals the beginning of a major alteration in the pattern of bipedal locomotion: *H. erectus* became completely committed to terrestrial life by adopting a fully modern stride. Life in the trees became a thing of the past.

Features of the pelvic bones and overall size indicate that the Nariokotome individual was likely a young adolescent male. He was quite tall, about 166 cm (66 in). Had he survived to adulthood, he would have grown to nearly 2 m (a little over 6 ft) in height. This change in height in comparison with *H. habilis* and the australopithecines indicates an enormous body size increase in this taxon (**Figure 10.9**). In addition, the Nariokotome boy's cranial capacity was about 900 cc. Even taking into account the body size increase (brain size and body size are roughly correlated), this expansion in brain size is large compared with similar changes in earlier hominids.

The presence of a sagittal crest to anchor large chewing muscles reflects this genus's hard diet of nuts and seeds.

The lack of a sagittal crest indicates this species had smaller chewing muscles, reflecting a much softer diet.

Australopithecus boisei

Homo erectus

The large premolars and molars enabled this genus to grind hard nuts and seeds.

This genus had much smaller molars and thinner enamel, reflecting its softer diet.

FIGURE 10.7 ■ *Australopithecus boisei* vs. *Homo erectus*
While both of these genera were contemporaneous for a period of time in Africa, there are important differences in their cranial and dental morphologies. (Upper left photograph © 1985 David L. Brill.)

The Nariokotome skeleton is just one of many *H. erectus* fossils from East Africa. At Ileret, on the eastern side of Lake Turkana, the partial skull of a very small *H. erectus*—possibly a female—was found in geologic strata dating to about 1.6 mya. The skull's diminutive size and small browridges indicate the very high degree of variation in *H. erectus*. Some *H. erectus*es had very large and robust bones, whereas others—such as the hominid from Ileret—were quite gracile.

Other key *H. erectus* fossils from Africa include a partial cranium found in Olduvai Gorge and dating to about 1.2 mya, partial crania found in Bouri and Buia and dating to about 1 mya, and a cranium found in Bodo and dating to about 600,000 yBP (**Figure 10.10**). The Bouri and Bodo crania are from the Middle Awash Valley, and the Buia cranium is from Eritrea. In contrast to the Nariokotome boy's skull and the skull from Ileret, the skulls from Olduvai Gorge, Bouri, Buia, and Bodo are very robust, having thick cranial bones and very large browridges. The Olduvai cranium's browridges are the largest of any known hominid,

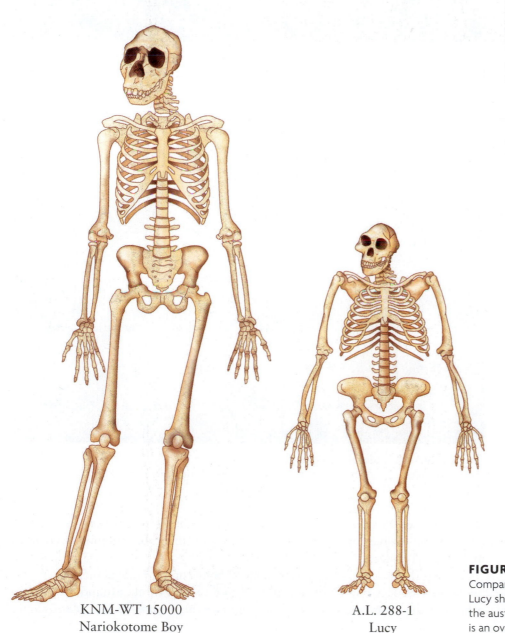

FIGURE 10.8 ■ Nariokotome
Researchers have debated the exact age of "Nariokotome Boy," also known as "Turkana Boy," but he was likely around 11 years old. Discovered in 1984, this *Homo erectus* fossil is one of the most complete early hominid skeletons ever found.

KNM-WT 15000
Nariokotome Boy

A.L. 288-1
Lucy

FIGURE 10.9 ■ Height Differences
Comparison of the heights of Nariokotome Boy and Lucy show how much taller *Homo erectus* was than the australopithecines. Together with brain size, there is an overall increase in body size with *Homo erectus*.

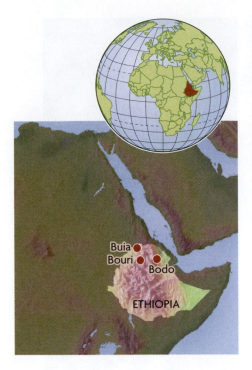

FIGURE 10.10 ■ **Bodo Cranium**
This *Homo erectus* fossil has different cranial features than other specimens of this species. Note the large browridges and thick cranial bones.

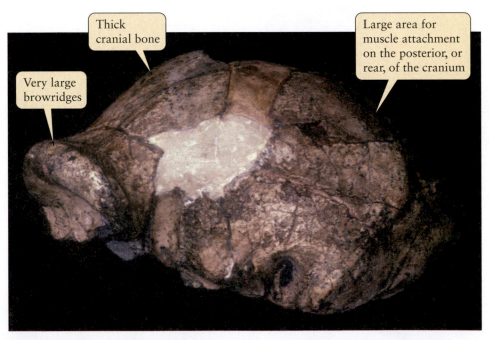

Thick cranial bone

Large area for muscle attachment on the posterior, or rear, of the cranium

Very large browridges

FIGURE 10.11 ■ **Olduvai Cranium**
This *Homo erectus* fossil, known as "OH 9," has the largest browridges of any hominid species.

before or after (**Figure 10.11**). Only some of this greater size can be accounted for by the Nariokotome boy's immaturity, because the other three hominids were fully mature adult males.

During the process of cleaning the facial bones of the Bodo skull, Tim White found a series of barely visible linear marks on the left cheek, around the left eye orbit and the nose, and elsewhere on the cranium (**Figure 10.12**). Microscopic

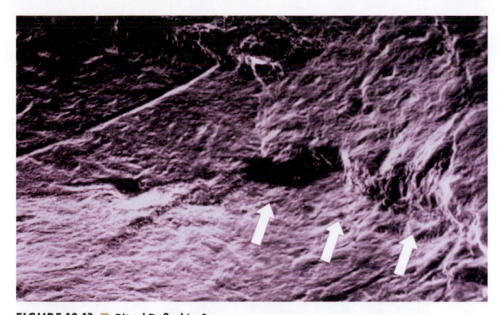

FIGURE 10.12 ■ Ritual Defleshing?
Viewed through a scanning electron microscope, cutmarks such as this one (arrows) indicate that stone tools were used to remove flesh from the Bodo skull.

analysis of the marks indicates that they were caused by a stone tool, perhaps as a contemporary hominid removed the soft tissue covering the facial bones. This activity may have been related to some ritual or to cannibalism. If so, it is the earliest evidence of body manipulation in human evolution.

Homo erectus in Asia (1.8–.3 mya)

The earliest evidence of *Homo erectus* in Asia consists of four skulls, other bones, and many stone tools found, by the Georgian paleontologist David Lordkipanidze and his colleagues, in Dmanisi, Republic of Georgia (**Figure 10.13**). The date for this important site, 1.7 mya, indicates that *H. erectus* colonized western Asia very soon after it first began to evolve in Africa (**Figure 10.14**). Compared with some members of the African *H. erectus*, these hominids' faces and jaws were smaller and their browridges were less developed—all *habilis*like facial characteristics. However, in overall shape the Dmanisi hominids' mandible and face strikingly resemble those of both the Nariokotome boy and the Ileret skull from East Africa. Also, like those of the Nariokotome skeleton, the leg bones are relatively long compared with the arm bones, at least as shown in the two partial skeletons—a child and an adult—found at the site. The oldest *H. erectus* from Dmanisi has a cranial capacity of only about 650 cc. The strong resemblance between the Dmanisi *H. erectus* and at least some of the East African *H. erectus*es indicates that the Asian *H. erectus* originated in Africa.

In a site dating to much later, workers discovered a partial *H. erectus* cranium—fragments of frontal and parietal bones—of an adult male dating to about 500,000 yBP, in a rock quarry near the village of Kocabaş, in the Büyük Menderes, a large valley system in western Turkey. Like many other *H. erectus* specimens from Africa and from Asia, the Kocabaş specimen has massive browridges and a **sagittal keel**. According to the American paleoanthropologist John Kappelman and his colleagues, the cranium's internal surface appears to have had a bone infection very

sagittal keel A slight ridge of bone found along the midline sagittal suture of the cranium, which is typically found on *H. erectus* skulls.

FIGURE 10.13 ■ Dmanisi

Extensive paleoanthropological investigations took place in Dmanisi after early stone tools were discovered there in 1984. Between 1991 and 2005, more than 20 hominid remains were found, including skulls and mandibles. One of the more complete crania (D-2282), shown here, was discovered in 1999 and enabled researchers to classify the hominid as *Homo erectus*.

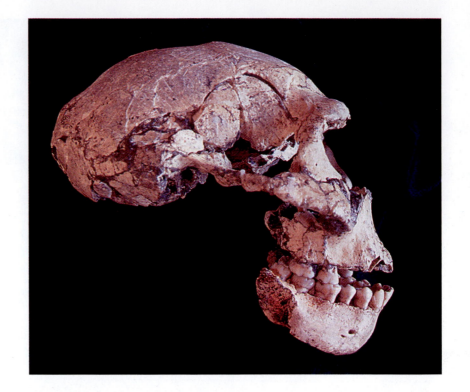

similar to that caused by tuberculosis. This hominid is doubly significant, first in being the only one found in this vast region of western Asia, second in being the first one showing signs of tuberculosis.

Since Dubois completed his fieldwork, in the 1890s, *H. erectus* fossils have been found in a number of sites in Indonesia, especially in Java. Some of these remains

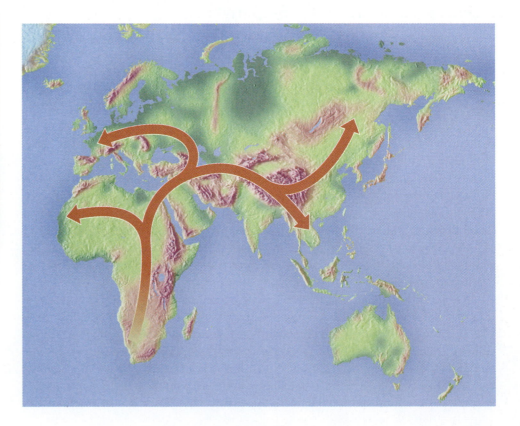

FIGURE 10.14 ■ First Migration

Homo erectus was the first hominid species to migrate out of Africa and expand into Europe and Asia, a movement this map illustrates.

are nearly as old as the Dmanisi remains. The earlier fossils, from the Sangiran site, date to as early as 1.8–1.6 mya. This early date shows that *H. erectus* rapidly spread eastward from western Asia. Thus, once the taxon had first evolved, it colonized areas outside Africa at a rapid pace, perhaps within less than a few hundred thousand years. The emerging picture is of *H. erectus*'s rapid, widespread movement throughout Asia. This rapid spread illustrates the Hominidae's high degree of adaptive success, a factor likely related to increasing intelligence, increasing reliance for survival on both material culture and tools, and overall greater ability at acquiring both food and other resources.

The most complete skull from Java is the Sangiran 17 cranium, from Sangiran, Indonesia. Like the African fossils, it has thick cranial bones and large browridges. Its cranial capacity is about 1,000 cc (**Figure 10.15**). A slight ridge, or "keel," runs along the sagittal suture atop the skull, and this sagittal keel appears on *H. erectus* skulls from Asia, Africa, and Europe.

Later *H. erectus* fossils from Java, dating to between 1 mya and 500,000 yBP, include remains from Sangiran and Sambungmacan, plus the original Trinil skull found by Dubois. These fossils show many of the same physical characteristics as the earlier ones but also some changes, such as larger brains and smaller teeth.

Some of the best information about the first hominids outside Africa comes from China. The earliest fossil is a partial skull from Gongwangling, near the village of Lantian, Shaanxi Province. The skull dates to about 1.2 mya. Like the fossils from Java, this specimen has large, well-developed browridges and thick cranial bones. Its cranial capacity is about 800 cc. The skull postdates the earliest evidence of hominids in north China, from Majuangou, by nearly 500,000 years. Both the animal bones with butchery marks and the stone artifacts found by the Chinese geologist R. X. Zhu and his collaborators date to nearly 1.7 mya, making them the earliest specimens from Asia.

The site yielding the most impressive *H. erectus* remains in East Asia is the cave in Zhoukoudian, on Dragon Bone Hill, near the modern city of Beijing (formerly Peking).

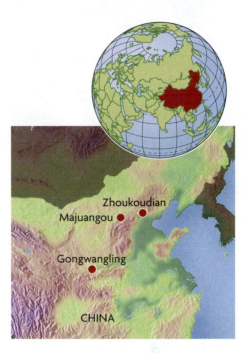

FIGURE 10.15 ■ **Sangiran *Homo erectus***
Excavations in Indonesia have uncovered many hominid fossils, including Dubois's Java Man and, shown here, the Sangiran 17 fossil. Note the long cranium, low forehead, and large browridges.

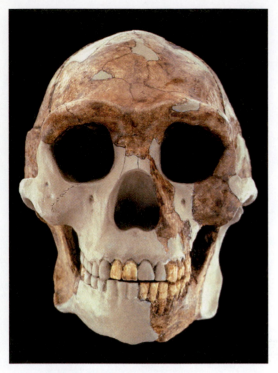

FIGURE 10.16 ■ **Peking Man**
Although the original remains of this *Homo erectus* fossil are lost, excellent casts, such as this reconstructed skull, enable modern anthropologists to study this important hominid. (Photograph © 1996 David L. Brill.)

FIGURE 10.17 ■ **Atapuerca 3**
These remains, from Gran Dolina, are the subject of debate as some researchers believe that the juvenile they came from belonged not to *Homo erectus* but to a new species of hominid, *Homo antecessor*. Others believe that despite its more modern appearance, this hominid belonged to *Homo erectus*.

After being discovered in the 1920s, the cave was excavated into the early 1940s. Deposits dating to 600,000–400,000 yBP contained, in fragments, the bones and teeth of 40–50 individuals, as well as many stone tools and food remains. Tragically, the entire collection of priceless bones was lost during World War II, late in 1941. Fortunately, shortly before the loss, the eminent German anatomist and anthropologist Franz Weidenreich (1873–1948) had thoroughly studied the bones and teeth, written detailed scientific reports, and made cast replicas, drawings, and photographs (**Figure 10.16**). This record has allowed scientists to continue studying the Zhoukoudian remains.

Fire: Expanding the Human World

Prior to the period represented by the Zhoukoudian fossils, humans had no or very minimal control of fire. They did not keep themselves warm with it, nor did they cook their food. Subsequently, however, fire has played a huge role in human adaptation. Without fire, heat-adapted animals, including humans, simply cannot survive in regions of the globe where the temperature is cold much or all of the year. The controlled use of fire was a remarkable development, because it allowed a major expansion in where people could live.

Excavations at Zhoukoudian revealed evidence for controlled fire use, including burned animal bones, burned stone tools, burned plants, charcoal, ash, ostrich egg shells, and hackberry seeds. The presence of burned plant and animal remains indicates that in addition to constructing fire to stay warm in a very cold climate, *Homo erectus* used fire to cook food. Prior to using fire, hominids ate both plants and animals raw. But cooking these foods made them easier to chew and, as a result, made their predecessors' very powerful jaws and large teeth less necessary. Indeed, the jaws and teeth of these Middle Pleistocene hominids were smaller than earlier hominids'. This size reduction was almost certainly related to the cultural innovations of the Middle Pleistocene, including both controlled use of fire and more advanced tool technology. Cooking also improved access to nutrients released by heating some foods to certain temperatures. These cultural developments were the harbingers of increasing environmental control and improved adaptive success, which form an ongoing theme of human evolution.

Homo erectus in Europe (800,000–400,000 yBP)

The earliest presence and subsequent evolution of *Homo erectus* were later in Europe than in Africa and Asia. The earliest fossil evidence of *H. erectus* in western Europe dates to about 800,000 yBP in Gran Dolina, Spain, and in Ceprano, Italy—a million years after the earliest hominids first left Africa. Of the half dozen sites in northern Spain's Sierra de Atapuerca, found by the Spanish paleontologist Juan Luis Arsuaga and his colleagues, the most important is Gran Dolina. In addition to many stone tools and animal remains, Arsuaga found the fragmentary bones and teeth of a half dozen hominids. Both animal bones and hominid bones had been cut with stone tools and purposely broken. This evidence indicates that hominids processed and consumed animals and other hominids (these practices are discussed further in chapter 11).

The most complete skull from Gran Dolina is Atapuerca 3, consisting of the left facial bones, upper jaw, and teeth of a child. This specimen provides a rare glimpse at what juveniles looked like at this point in human evolution (**Figure 10.17**). Juvenile or not, the cranium indicates that Atapuerca 3 appeared more modern than other members of *H. erectus*, but was clearly ancestral to later hominids in the Atapuerca region and elsewhere in Europe. Indeed, its bones and teeth are similar in a number of ways to those of hominids that lived in Europe later in the Pleistocene,

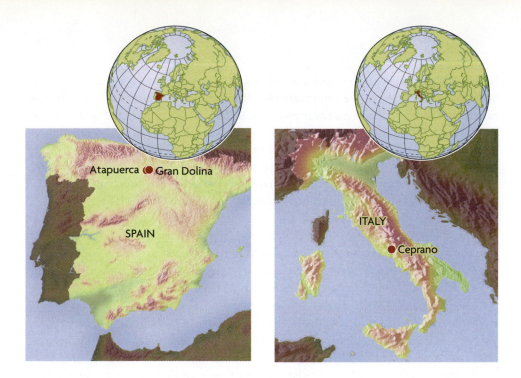

Homo sapiens. For example, like the later hominids, the Gran Dolina adults have a wide nasal aperture (opening for the nose).

The only other *H. erectus* remains in Europe date to about 500,000 yBP. They include the Mauer jaw—a mandible and most of its associated teeth, found near Heidelberg, Germany—and a tibia from Boxgrove, England.

Evolution of *Homo erectus*: Biological Change, Adaptation, and Nutrition

How did *Homo erectus* differ from earlier *Homo* species, such as *Homo habilis*? One of the most obvious differences is *H. erectus*'s remarkable body size and height.

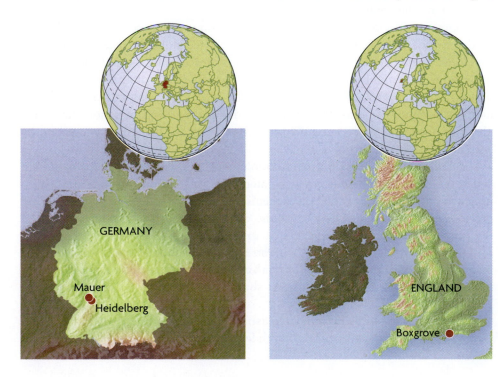

Moreover, the increase in body size occurred rapidly, perhaps in less than a few hundred thousand years. That is, at 1.8 mya *H. habilis* was about the size of an australopithecine, but by 1.6 mya another hominid, *H. erectus,* was considerably taller and heavier. The American physical anthropologists Henry McHenry and Katherine Coffing estimate that, from *H. habilis* to *H. erectus*, males' heights increased by 33% (to 1.8 m, or 5.9 ft) and females' heights by 37% (to 1.6 m, or 5.3 ft). In other words, *H. habilis*—like the australopithecines—was quite short (typically less than 1.2 m, or 4 ft), but *H. erectus* was considerably taller (more than 1.5 m, or 5 ft). Most of this increase took place 2.0–1.7 mya (**Table 10.1**).

What caused the rapid increase in body size from *H. habilis* to *H. erectus?* Various factors were likely involved, such as climate change and its impact on food supply. But the fundamental reason was likely increased access to animal food sources—protein—acquired from hunting. That some primitive stone tools date to 2.5 mya indicates that early hominids were able to cut meat and process it.

Cutmarks made with stone tools have been found on bones of animal prey in Kenya and Ethiopia, at the Olduvai Gorge and Bouri sites, respectively. Indeed, the pattern of cutmarks found at Bouri indicates that even some late australopithecines, ones that preceded *Homo,* were skilled in animal butchery.

As the American anthropologist Pat Shipman's work has shown, at Olduvai Gorge, stone tool cutmarks overlay animal tooth marks. This finding suggests that at least some of the behavior involving butchering was scavenging—eating animals killed by other animals—and not hunting. Other evidence of meat-eating has been documented in the bone chemistry of early hominids and in wear on their teeth.

Meat-eating likely started long before *H. erectus* appeared, but the technology available to earlier hominids and the minimal record of hunting prior to *H. erectus* suggest that meat was a minor part of this hominid's diet. Two things had to happen for early hominids to routinely acquire meat. First, to kill game hominids had to become able to manufacture the right tools, especially stone tools that could be thrown or thrust accurately, such as spears. Second, hominids had to develop the social structure whereby a group of individuals—older adolescent and adult males, primarily—could efficiently track and kill game. Both developments were part of the increase in hominid intelligence at this time, as recorded by brain size expansion and more complex technology. Once hominids had developed the technological and social means of accessing animal food sources daily, they likely had increased access to high-quality protein. This increased access to protein would in turn have produced *H. erectus*'s bump in height—these hominids were taller than their ancestors due to improved nutrition that came about by acquiring food (especially protein) through hunting and processing it by cooking.

Such increasingly sophisticated technology was an important factor in human evolution generally. The culture associated with this period of evolution, beginning around 1.5 mya, is called the **Acheulian Complex.** Acheulian stone tools are more sophisticated than Oldowan tools, were produced from a wider variety of raw materials, and were fashioned into a greater range of tool types, with a greater range of functions. This diversity suggests a greater familiarity with the necessary resources and with their availability. Within this diversity, the dominant tool is the **handaxe** (**Figure 10.18**). The handaxe's sharp edge was used in cutting, scraping, and other functions.

In addition, the tools became increasingly refined—better made than before, they clearly required a great deal of both learning and skill to produce. Acheulian

Acheulian Complex The culture associated with *H. erectus,* including handaxes and other types of stone tools; more refined than the earlier Oldowan tools.

handaxe The most dominant tool in the Acheulian complex, characterized by a sharp edge for both cutting and scraping.

TABLE 10.1	Trends from *Homo habilis* to *Homo erectus*	
H. HABILIS	→	**H. ERECTUS**

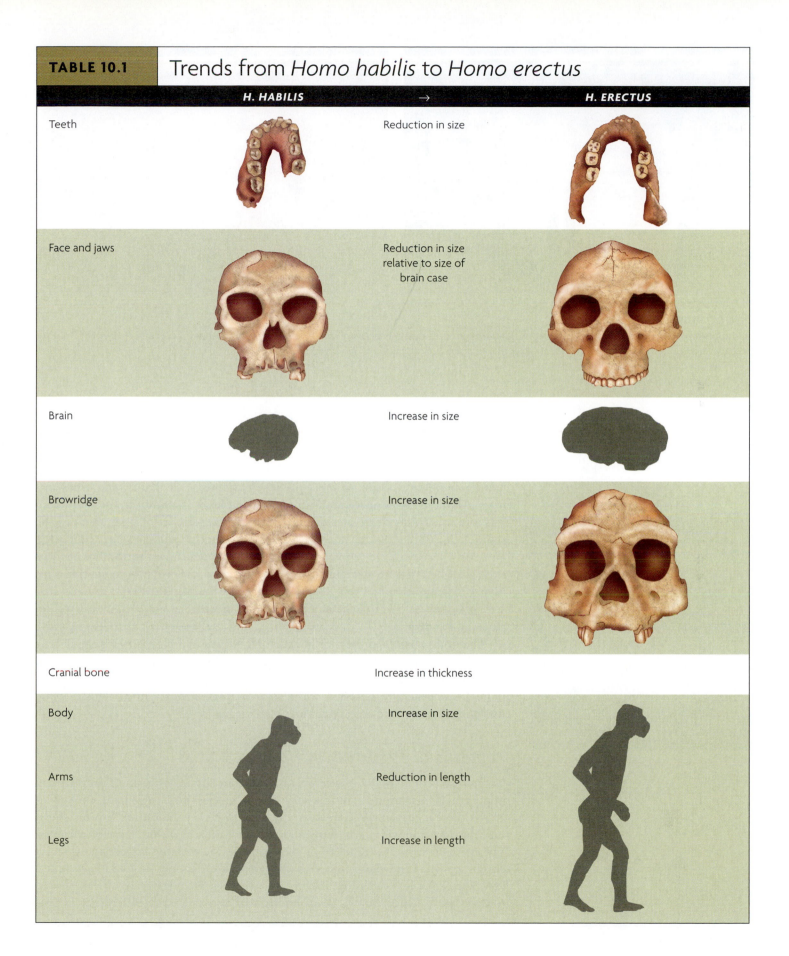

Teeth	Reduction in size	
Face and jaws	Reduction in size relative to size of brain case	
Brain	Increase in size	
Browridge	Increase in size	
Cranial bone	Increase in thickness	
Body	Increase in size	
Arms	Reduction in length	
Legs	Increase in length	

(a)

(b)

FIGURE 10.18 ■ **Olorgesailie**

(a) At this Acheulian site in Kenya, the remains of hundreds of butchered animals were found along with many handaxes and other tools. **(b)** This close-up shows the stone tools, with the handaxes in the middle. (Photographs © 1985 David L. Brill.)

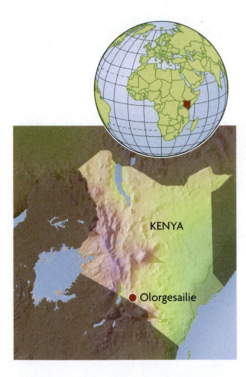

KENYA

● Olorgesailie

tools are found in association with large animals, suggesting that these tools were used to kill large animals and butcher them. In Ethiopia's Middle Awash region, for example, tools are commonly associated with hippopotamus bones. In Olorgesailie, Kenya, the South African archaeologist Glynn Isaac recovered many baboon bones in addition to those of hippopotamuses, elephants, and other animals. All these bones have cutmarks from stone tools. In addition, the tools from this and other Acheulian sites display microscopic patterns of wear that are the same as those seen in experimental studies where anthropologists have butchered animals. Clearly, *H. erectus* had killed, processed, and eaten the animals at these sites, well before 1 mya (**Figure 10.19**). This record, from Olorgesailie and sites like it, indicates that hunting was well in place by the Middle Pleistocene. If body size increase was tied to acquisition of animal protein via hunting, it was well in place by 1.5 mya.

The other obvious difference between *H. habilis* and *H. erectus* is the latter's much larger brain. From *H. habilis* to *H. erectus*, brain volume increased by 33% (from 650 cc to 950 cc). Some of the size increase was due simply to the increase in body size generally, but there was also an increase in brain mass. This increase was almost certainly due to increasing intelligence.

Patterns of Evolution in *Homo erectus*

Comparisons of all the *Homo erectus* fossils from Africa, Asia, and Europe reveal important information about this early *Homo* species, both in general similarities across these continents and in the individual forms' evolution. *H. erectus* skulls are long, low, and wide at the base, and they have thick bone and large browridges. The African *H. erectus* tends to be the most robust, with the largest and thickest cranial bones. The Dmanisi and African forms are strongly similar—the sagittal keel, for example, is missing in Dmanisi and present only rarely in the African representatives. Morphological variations are likely related to differences in time

FIGURE 10.19 ■ Butchering
This artist's reconstruction shows how early *Homo*, including *Homo habilis* and *Homo erectus*, likely processed animals in groups, using a variety of stone tools. ("*Homo habilis* Using Volcanic-Cobble Debitage to Rend a Carcass," © 1995 by Jay H. Matternes.)

and in geography, but the degree of variability is far smaller than that in other mammals.

Some authorities have interpreted the general similarity of *H. erectus* across Africa, Asia, and Europe and through time as representing evolutionary stasis. However, various morphological attributes show significant evolution in *H. erectus*, with earlier forms having considerably smaller brains than later forms. For example, the average Dmanisi skull is 650 cc, while the average Zhoukoudian skull is 1,200 cc. Overall, *H. erectus*'s brain size increased by some 30%. The American physical anthropologist Milford Wolpoff has also documented decreases in cranial bone thickness and browridge size. These characteristics indicate a decline in skull robusticity. Accompanying these changes is a reduction in tooth size, caused by the decreased demand on the face and jaws due to the increasing importance of technology and of cooking.

Homo erectus: Beginning Globalization

Homo erectus was the first hominid to inhabit territory all over the world. After first evolving in Africa, it spread rapidly to Asia and then to Europe. Increased intelligence, increased dependence on technology and on material culture, social hunting, and access to more protein and to better nutrition contributed to this early hominid's remarkable adaptive success.

LOCATION/SITES	Africa (Olduvai Gorge, Lake Turkana, Ileret, Bouri, Buia, Bodo, Olorgesailie); Asia (Dmanisi, Kocabaş, Trinil, Sangiran, Sambungmacan, Gongwangling, Majuangou, Zhoukoudian); Europe (Gran Dolina, Mauer, Boxgrove)
CHRONOLOGY	1.8 mya–300,000 yBP in Africa; 1.8 mya–300,000 yBP in Asia; .8–.4 mya in Europe

BIOLOGY AND CULTURE (COMPARED WITH *HOMO HABILIS*)

FEATURE	EVIDENCE	OUTCOME
Tool use (Acheulian)	Skulls Teeth	Smaller face and smaller jaws Reduced size
Fire and cooking	Ash in habitation sites	Smaller face and smaller jaws Smaller teeth
Intelligence	Brain size	Increase (to 950 cc)
Hunting and increased meat protein	Butchered large animal remains	Increased body size
Possible cannibalism	Cutmarks	New ritual or dietary innovation
Growth	Enamel perikymata	Slower growth but not modern
Locomotion	Leg length:arm length	Fully modern striding

Hominids' increasing reliance on tools profoundly affected human biology. As tools began to perform the face's and jaws' functions in preparing food for consumption—that is, in cutting up, cooking, and processing food—there was a commensurate decline in the robusticity of these body parts, the anatomical area associated with mastication. In terms of both culture and biology, *Homo erectus* evolved the contextual behavior—hunting, successful dispersal across large territory, adaptive success, and increasing dependence on and effective use of culture as a means of survival—that made possible the emergence and evolution of our species, *Homo sapiens*. The next chapter tracks and interprets the evolution of *H. sapiens*' primitive forms.

ANSWERING THE BIG QUESTIONS

What characteristics define the genus *Homo*?

◼ The genus *Homo* is defined on the basis of physical (biological) and behavioral attributes, including a relatively large brain, small face and jaws, and dependence on material culture for survival.

Who were the earliest members of the genus *Homo*?

◼ The earliest members of the genus *Homo* were *Homo habilis* and *Homo erectus*.

◼ Fossils of *Homo habilis* have been found in East Africa and South Africa and date to about 2.5–1.8 mya.

◼ *Homo erectus*, a geographically and morphologically diverse species, dates to about 1.8 mya–300,000 yBP. Its fossil record is represented in Africa, Asia, and Europe.

What are the key evolutionary trends and other developments in early *Homo*?

◼ Compared to the australopithecines, early *Homo habilis* experienced an enlargement of the brain and a general gracilization of the chewing complex. These developments were linked with an increased focus on tool production and tool use, increased dietary diversity, and increased intelligence.

◼ Compared with *Homo habilis*, *Homo erectus* experienced a continued reduction in size of the chewing complex (smaller face, jaws, and teeth), increased brain size, increased body size, and first evidence of modern limb proportions.

◼ *Homo erectus* developed an increasingly innovative and complex technology, including more elaborate tools, organized social hunting, and controlled use of fire. These developments facilitated greater access to protein and improved nutrition generally. Improved nutrition likely explains the rapid increase in body size around 2.0–1.7 mya. These developments are part of the larger picture of increasing adaptive flexibility, a central theme of human evolution.

◼ *Homo* increasingly became a predator genus in the early Pleistocene, and this change at least partly explains its remarkable and rapid geographic expansion. Successful predation was largely from hunting, but early *Homo* likely acquired food through hunting *and* scavenging.

◼ The evolution of *Homo erectus*—with its increased intelligence and full commitment to material culture as an adaptive strategy—set the stage for the emergence and evolution of *Homo sapiens*.

⊚ wwnorton.com/studyspace

KEY TERMS

Acheulian Complex
handaxe
Homo erectus

Pithecanthropus erectus
sagittal keel

ADDITIONAL READINGS

Antón, S. C. 2003. A natural history of *Homo erectus*. *Yearbook of Physical Anthropology* 46: 126–170.

Dunsworth, H. and A. Walker. 2002. Early genus *Homo*. Pp. 419–435 in W. C. Hartwig, ed. *The Primate Fossil Record*. Cambridge, UK: Cambridge University Press.

McHenry, H. M. and K. Coffing. 2000. *Australopithecus* to *Homo:* Transformations in body and mind. *Annual Review of Anthropology* 29: 125–146.

Rightmire, G. P. 1990. *The Evolution of* Homo erectus. Cambridge, UK: Cambridge University Press.

Shapiro, H. L. 1974. *Peking Man: The Discovery, Disappearance and Mystery of a Priceless Scientific Treasure*. New York: Simon & Schuster.

Shipman, P. 2001. *The Man Who Found the Missing Link*. New York: Simon & Schuster.

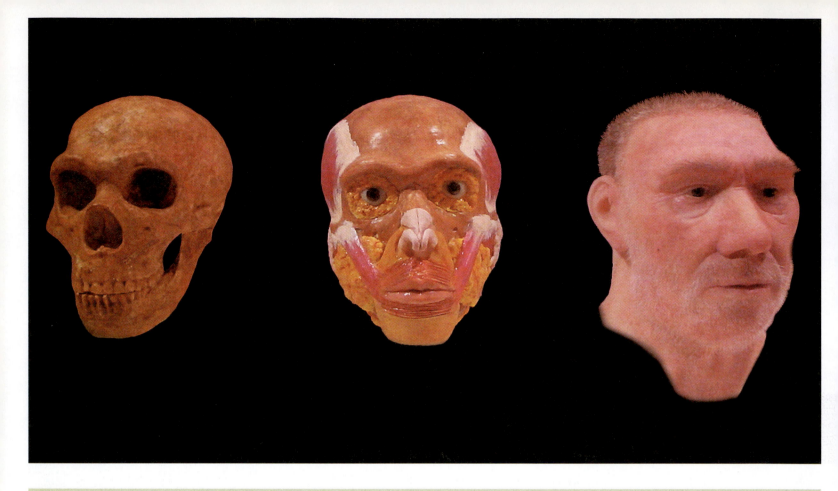

In this reconstruction, the Neandertal looks modern in some respects. Neandertals are central to our understanding of modern *Homo sapiens'* origins.

CHAPTER 11

The Origins, Evolution, and Dispersal of Modern People

GERMANY

● Feldhofer
Cave

The Feldhofer Cave Neandertal was the first fossil hominid to receive serious attention from scientists. Prior to its (accidental) discovery in 1856, answers to questions about the physical characteristics and behaviors of human ancestors were highly speculative owing in large part to a lack of a fossil record. The uncovering of this skeleton signaled a change for anthropology, beginning the scientific journey toward building our current understanding of the origins of modern people in particular and evolution in general. Feldhofer Cave is located in Neander Valley (in German, *Neander Tal*), near Düsseldorf, Germany. Workers happened upon the skeleton while removing clay deposits from the cave as part of a limestone quarrying operation. Sometimes accidental discoveries like this are reported; often they are not. The world of anthropology got very lucky because these workmen picked up the skull and bones and took them to a local schoolteacher. As luck further had it, the teacher recognized these remains as human and passed them on to the anthropologist Hermann Schaafhausen, at the University of Bonn. Schaafhausen studied the remains, quickly reported his findings to the German Natural History Society, and published a description in a leading German scientific journal. He described a skull having some archaic features, distinctive from modern humans'. In particular, the skull was long and low, different from modern people's but with some similarities, such as in brain size (**Figure 11.1**). Moreover, the skeletal remains of extinct Pleistocene animals also found in the cave indicated that this human had lived at the same time as these animals. At the time these breathtaking announcements were made, many authorities believed that humans had appeared very recently in the history of life, certainly postdating extinct animals associated with the great Pleistocene Ice Age.[1]

Schaafhausen and the Neandertal skeleton caught the attention of the leaders of science in Germany and around the world. One of these leaders was the top German anthropologist of the time, Rudolf Virchow (1821–1902). In addition to being a leading authority on evolutionary theory, archaeology, and cultural anthropology, Virchow started the discipline of cell pathology (diseases of cells). He helped

---

[1] Excavations at the Feldhofer Cave in 1997 and 2000 produced more than 62 new bone fragments that are part of the original skeleton, of at least one other adult, and of a young juvenile. Radiocarbon dates on these new bones indicate that this Neandertal is about 40,000 years old.

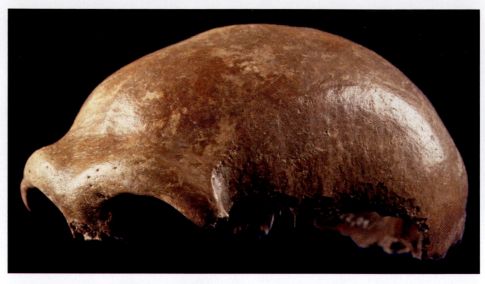

FIGURE 11.1 ■ **Feldhofer Neandertal**
This Neandertal's DNA has been used recently to test hypotheses concerning the genetic relationship between modern humans and Neandertals.

found several national scientific organizations and periodicals. He was a medical activist, a political leader known across Germany, and the teacher of others who would also become leaders in science and medicine. In short, his pronouncements about the Feldhofer Cave skeleton would be taken very seriously by the scientific community. After looking carefully at the cave remains, he summarily dismissed any notion that they belonged to an ancestor of living humans. He argued that their characteristics—a long, low skull and bowed, thick limb bones—were those of some modern human afflicted with rickets and arthritis. Others disagreed. Thomas Huxley (see Figure 2.18) argued that this was a primitive, potentially ancestral human. But Virchow was convincing to most, setting the course for years; later, scores of remains showing the same morphology as the Feldhofer Cave skeleton and dating to the same period of the late Pleistocene were found. Eventually, Virchow's pathology hypothesis was rejected, and debate centered around the role of the Feldhofer Cave skeleton and others like it—a group of hominids we call "Neandertals"—in later human evolution.

In this chapter, we look at *Homo sapiens'* evolution, from its origins in *Homo erectus* to its development into modern humans. Neandertals play a central role in this discussion, which is also based on rich records—of fossils, genetic variation, culture, and behavior—from around the world. First, though, we will explore which aspects of the fossil record define us as a modern species. Then we will examine those aspects, to understand just how anthropologists interpret the variation across the bones and teeth of *H. sapiens*.

WHAT IS SO MODERN ABOUT MODERN HUMANS?

What do physical anthropologists mean by *modern*? This question is very important, because the answer to it provides us with the baseline from which to assess the origins, evolution, and geographic distribution of modern *Homo sapiens*. Physical anthropologists define *modern* based on a series of distinctive anatomical characteristics

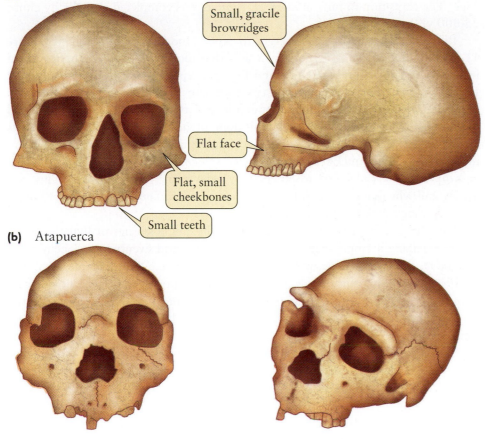

(a) Dolni Vestonice

Small, gracile browridges

Flat face

Flat, small cheekbones

Small teeth

(b) Atapuerca

FIGURE 11.2 ■ **Modern Human Features**
(a) Anatomically modern *Homo sapiens* possess a unique suite of traits that are absent in **(b)** archaic *Homo sapiens*.

that contrast with *archaic* characteristics found in earlier hominids (**Figure 11.2**). Modern people—people who essentially look like us—tend to have a high, vertical forehead, a round and tall skull, small browridges, a small face, small teeth, and a projecting chin (anthropologists call the latter a "mental eminence"). Below the neck, modern humans have relatively more gracile, narrower bones than their predecessors. Fossil humans having these cranial and postcranial characteristics are considered modern *H. sapiens*.

The immediate ancestors of modern people—archaic *H. sapiens*—are different from modern *H. sapiens* in a number of ways. Compared to modern *H. sapiens*, archaic *H. sapiens* have a longer, lower skull, a larger browridge, a bigger and more projecting face, a wider nasal aperture (opening for the nose), a more projecting occipital bone (sometimes called an **occipital bun** when referring to Neandertals), larger teeth (especially the front teeth), and no chin. The postcranial bones of archaic *H. sapiens* are thicker than modern people's.

occipital bun A cranial feature of Neandertals in which the occipital bone projects substantially from the skull's posterior.

MODERN *HOMO SAPIENS:* SINGLE ORIGIN AND GLOBAL DISPERSAL OR REGIONAL CONTINUITY?

Homo sapiens' evolution begins with the emergence of archaic forms, some 350,000 yBP. These early *H. sapiens* provide the context for modern *H. sapiens'* evolutionary development, which took place at different times in different places. The first modern *H. sapiens* appeared earliest in Africa, by 160,000 yBP, and latest in Europe. The transition to fully modern *H. sapiens* was completed globally by about 25,000 yBP.

Two main hypotheses have emerged to explain modern people's origins (**Figure 11.3**). The *Out-of-Africa* hypothesis states that modern *H. sapiens* first evolved in Africa and then spread to Asia and Europe, replacing the indigenous archaic *H. sapiens* populations living on these two continents. The *Multiregional Continuity* hypothesis regards the transition to modernity as having taken place regionally and without involving replacement. From this point of view, African archaic *H. sapiens* gave rise to African modern *H. sapiens*, Asian archaic *H. sapiens* gave rise to Asian modern *H. sapiens*, and European archaic *H. sapiens* gave rise to European modern *H. sapiens*. Both models seek to explain why today human beings consist of just one genus, and why that genus consists of just one species. The models differ, though, in accounting for that genus and species.

The Out-of-Africa model easily explains the single species of living humans by emphasizing a single origin of modern people and eventual replacement of archaic *H. sapiens* throughout Africa, Asia, and Europe. Quite a simple story. The Multiregional Continuity model emphasizes the importance of gene flow across population boundaries—separate species of humanity never arose owing to the constant interbreeding of human groups throughout human evolution. Not such a simple story.

Fossil and genetic records provide a wealth of information about modern human origins. We will now consider these records and draw some conclusions from

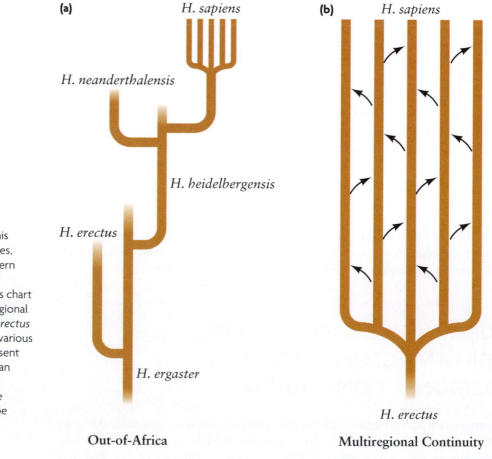

FIGURE 11.3 ■ **Out-of-Africa vs. Multiregional**
This important anthropological debate is about modern humans' origins. **(a)** This chart depicts one of the two hypotheses, Out-of-Africa, according to which modern humans originated in Africa and then migrated throughout the world. **(b)** This chart depicts the second hypothesis, Multiregional Continuity, according to which *Homo erectus* evolved into modern *Homo sapiens* in various geographic locations. The arrows represent continuous gene flow throughout human evolution. This hypothesis considers *H. ergaster* and *H. heidelbergensis* to be *H. erectus* and *H. neanderthalensis* to be *H. sapiens*.

(a) *H. sapiens*

H. neanderthalensis

H. heidelbergensis

H. erectus

H. ergaster

Out-of-Africa

(b) *H. sapiens*

H. erectus

Multiregional Continuity

them. We will then be ready to reassess the two hypotheses and to draw further conclusions about the origins of us—living people.

WHAT DO *HOMO SAPIENS* FOSSILS TELL US ABOUT MODERN HUMAN ORIGINS?

The fossil remains of archaic *Homo sapiens* have been found throughout Africa, Asia, and Europe. In Africa, archaic *H. sapiens* evolved into modern *H. sapiens* at least by 160,000 yBP, perhaps as early as 200,000 yBP. In Asia and Europe, the archaics consisted of an early group and a late group, divided very roughly at about 130,000 yBP. To understand the biological changes involved in hominid groups' evolution, we need to compare some details of a number of key fossils.

Early Archaic *Homo sapiens*

The earliest forms of *Homo sapiens* emerged around 350,000 yBP. They have been found in Africa, Asia, and Europe (**Figure 11.4**). Their evolution is clearly out of the earlier *Homo erectus* populations. Anthropologists have documented this evolutionary transition in the three continental settings, noting, for example, the similarly massive browridges in archaic *H. sapiens* and in earlier *H. erectus*. Although quite primitive in key respects, all fossils representing archaic *H. sapiens* and earlier *H. erectus* show continued reduction in skeletal robusticity, smaller tooth size, expansion in brain size, and increasing cultural complexity.

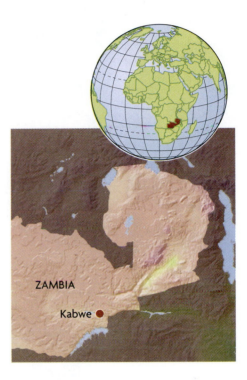

ZAMBIA

Kabwe ●

ARCHAIC *HOMO SAPIENS* IN AFRICA (350,000–200,000 YBP) One of several individuals found in the Kabwe (Broken Hill) lead mine in Zambia has enormous browridges, but the facial bones and the muscle attachment areas on the back of the skull for the neck muscles are quite small compared with those of *Homo erectus* in Africa (**Figure 11.5**). The cranial capacity is about 1,300 cc. The skull is similar in appearance to those of early archaic hominids from Europe. Both the Zambian and the European skulls have *erectus*like characteristics: a large face, large browridges, and thick cranial bones. However, *H. erectus* skulls, like their Asian counterparts, are higher, reflecting a brain expansion.

JAVA ●
Ngandong

EARLY ARCHAIC *HOMO SAPIENS* IN ASIA (350,000–130,000 YBP) Some of the best-known fossils representing early archaic *Homo sapiens* are from the Ngandong site, on the island of Java (**Figure 11.6**). The skulls are represented by the braincases only—the faces are missing. Ngandong 11 has a brain size of about 1,100 cc, well within the range for early archaic *H. sapiens*. The skull is long and low, but compared with its *Homo erectus* ancestor, the skull is somewhat higher, reflecting its larger brain. The browridge is massive, certainly on the order of many *H. erectus*.

The Ngandong skulls share a number of features with other Asian early archaic *H. sapiens,* especially with Narmada (Madhya Pradesh, India) and Dali (Shaanxi Province, People's Republic of China) skulls (**Figure 11.7**). The crania are large and robust. The browridges are quite large, although not as large as in *H. erectus*.

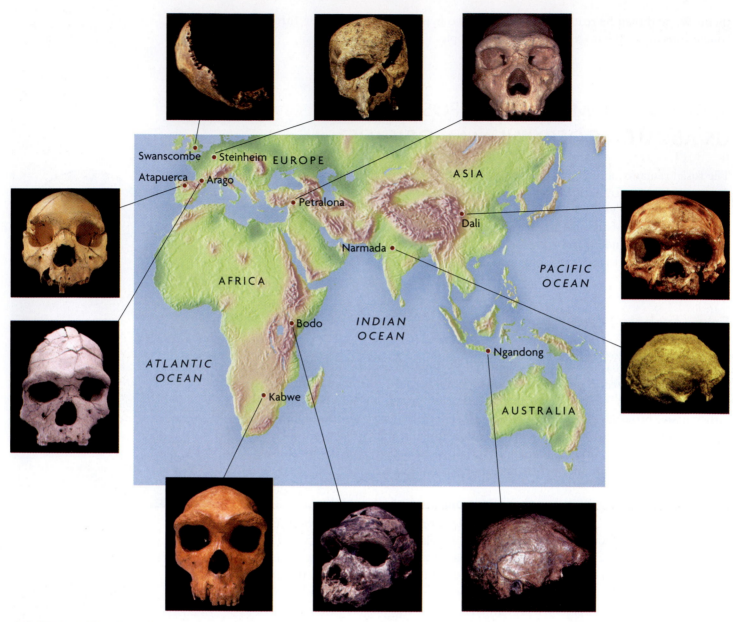

FIGURE 11.4 ■ **Early Archaic**
Homo sapiens

This map illustrates some of the sites in Africa, Asia, and Europe where the remains of archaic *H. sapiens* have been found. (Arago photograph © 1985 David L. Brill.)

EARLY ARCHAIC *HOMO SAPIENS* IN EUROPE (350,000–130,000 YBP) One of the most significant fossils for early archaic *Homo sapiens,* and for all of human evolution, is from the Sima de los Huesos cave site, in the Sierra de Atapuerca, near Burgos, Spain. Among the 32 individuals from the cave is a wonderfully preserved skeleton of an adult male, Atapuerca 5. This is one of the few instances ever in which a fossilized individual's skull (including the mandible) was found in direct association with the postcranial skeleton. The cranial capacity is about 1,125 cc. The skull has a large browridge and a pronounced facial projection. The nasal aperture is quite wide. These features foreshadow the facial characteristics of the late archaic *H. sapiens* in Europe and far western Asia, the Neandertals (discussed below). Other well-known early archaic *H. sapiens* fossils from Europe are the skull and other remains from Arago, France; the skull from Petralona, Greece; the skull from Steinheim, Germany; and the partial skull from Swanscombe, England (**Figure 11.8**). Their average cranial capacity

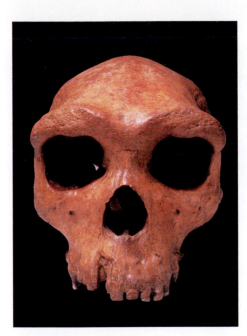

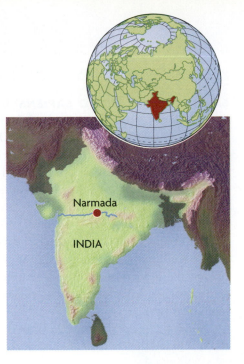

FIGURE 11.5 ■ Kabwe

This archaic *Homo sapiens,* also known as "Broken Hill Man" or "Rhodesian Man," was among the first early human fossils discovered in Africa. Found by miners searching for metal deposits in caves, it was originally thought to be less than 40,000 years old.

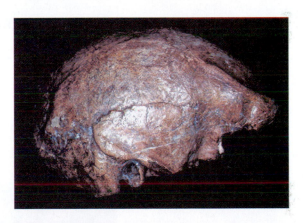

FIGURE 11.6 ■ Ngandong

Multiple skulls were found at this site in Java in the 1930s. The brain size of this early archaic *Homo sapiens* falls between those of *Homo erectus* and of modern humans.

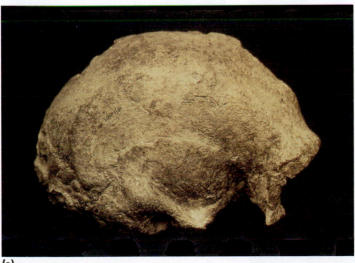

(a)

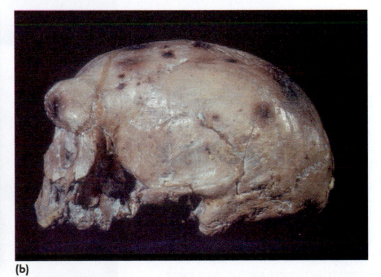

(b)

FIGURE 11.7 ■ Asian Early Archaic *Homo sapiens*

Like the Ngandong cranium, the crania of **(a)** Narmada and **(b)** Dali are robust with thick cranial bones. The cranial capacity, however, indicates the brain size was much larger than in *Homo erectus* but somewhat smaller than in modern humans.

is 1,200 cc. These early archaic *H. sapiens* illustrate the larger brain and rounder, more gracile skulls compared with *Homo erectus*.

EARLY ARCHAIC *HOMO SAPIENS'* DIETARY ADAPTATIONS The earliest archaic *Homo sapiens* had many of the same kinds of tools and material technology as the earlier *Homo erectus*, but *H. sapiens* used much more diverse tools to acquire and process food. Across the group, the face, jaws, and back teeth (premolars and molars) show a general reduction in size. The American physical anthropologist C. Loring Brace hypothesizes that selection for large back teeth lessened as tools became more important for processing food. Simply, with reduced selection, the teeth became smaller. Alternatively, as technological innovation changed the way teeth were used, the teeth may have been under *greater* selection for reduced size. Anthropologists have not reached a consensus on the mechanisms behind the reduction in tooth size except to say that cultural innovation and increased dependence on material culture likely played a role in this fundamental biological change.

About the same time that the importance of the back teeth diminished, the use of the front teeth increased. That is, during this period of human evolution, the front

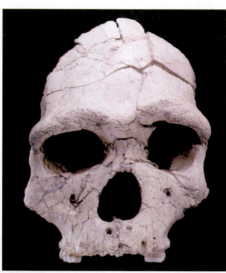
(a)

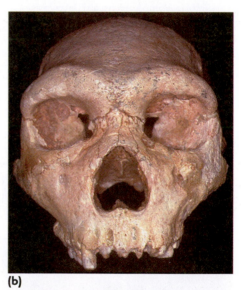
(b)

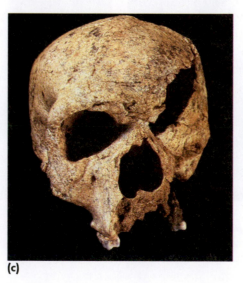
(c)

(d)

FIGURE 11.8 ■ **European Early Archaic** *Homo sapiens*
Cranial remains from four prominent European sites—**(a)** Arago, **(b)** Petralona, **(c)** Steinheim, and **(d)** Swanscombe—have somewhat larger cranial capacities than other early archaic *H. sapiens*. Although these crania reflect a more modern appearance, they retain primitive features such as larger browridges. (Arago photograph © 1985 David L. Brill.)

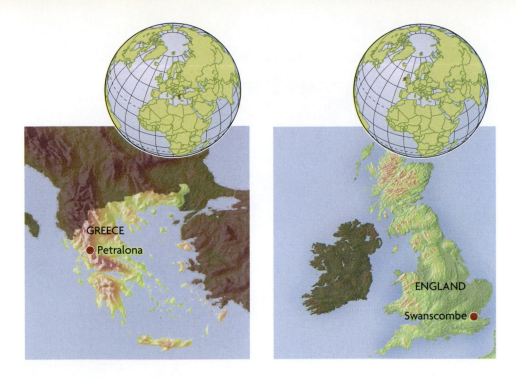

teeth—incisors and canines—underwent heavy wear. For example, in Atapuerca 5, from Spain, the front teeth are worn nearly to where the gums would have been in life (**Figure 11.9**). This evidence tells us that these hominids used their front teeth as a tool, perhaps as a kind of third hand for gripping materials. In European archaic *H. sapiens*, the front teeth show a size increase. The link between heavy use of the front teeth and increase in size of these teeth suggests the possibility of selection for large front teeth.

Late Archaic *Homo sapiens*

The hominids from this period show a continuation of trends begun with early *Homo*, especially increased brain size, reduced tooth size, and decreased skeletal robusticity. However, in far western Asia (the Middle East) and Europe a new pattern of morphology emerges, reflecting both regional variation and adaptation to cold. This new pattern defines the Neandertals. Neandertal features include wide nasal apertures; a projecting face; an occipital bun; a long, low skull; large front teeth (some with heavy wear); a wide, stocky body; and short limbs.

The fossil record of the late archaic *Homo sapiens* is fascinating. For the first time in human evolution, a number of fairly complete skeletons exist, allowing new insights into the biology and behavior of these ancient humans. Moreover, the material culture includes new kinds of tools, and reflects new behaviors, that are modern in several important ways.

LATE ARCHAIC *HOMO SAPIENS* IN ASIA (60,000–40,000 YBP) For Asian late archaic *Homo sapiens*, the record is fullest from sites at the far western end of the continent (**Figure 11.10**). Fossils from Israel form the core of discussions among anthropologists about modern people's emergence in western Asia. This record pertains to Neandertals from Amud, Kebara, and Tabun. The Amud Neandertals date to about 55,000–40,000 yBP and are best-known from the complete skeleton of an adult male. He had an enormous brain, measuring some 1,740 cc, larger than earlier humans' and the largest for any fossil hominid

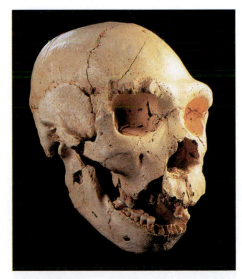

FIGURE 11.9 ■ **Atapuerca 5**
One of many human skeletal remains found in Sima de los Huesos, Atapuerca 5 represents a nearly complete adult male skeleton. Its cranial capacity falls within the range of other Pleistocene humans, but its cranium is unusual in its degree of tooth wear. Notice that the front tooth is worn—that it has very little enamel left.

FIGURE 11.10 ■ West Asian *Homo sapiens*

This map illustrates where late archaic *H. sapiens* remains have been found in western Asia, along the eastern Mediterranean Sea.

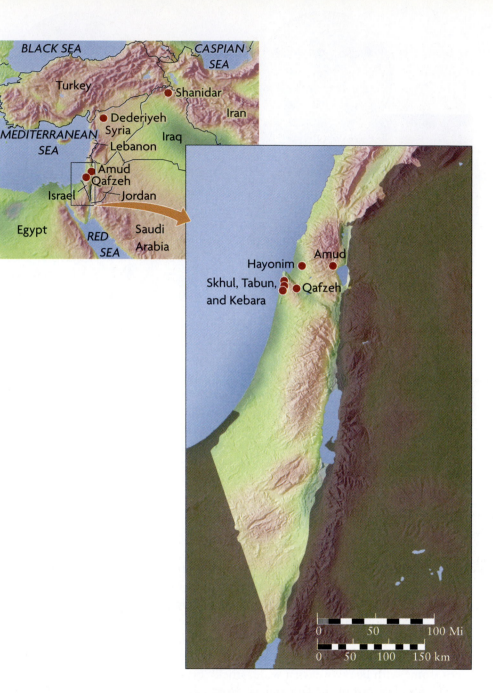

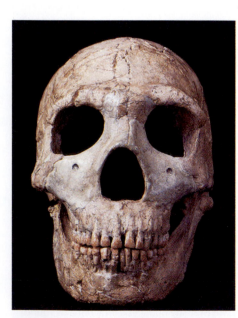

FIGURE 11.11 ■ Amud Neandertal

The exceptionally large cranial capacity of the Amud Neandertal indicates that this hominid's brain was at least as large as a modern human's. The large brain size suggests that Neandertals' intelligence was on par with modern *Homo sapiens'*.

(**Figure 11.11**). The Kebara Neandertals date to about 60,000 yBP and are represented by a complete mandible and body skeleton; the legs and cranium are missing (**Figure 11.12**). A nearly complete female Neandertal skeleton from Tabun was long thought to date to about the same time, but new thermoluminescence dating indicates that the skeleton may be as old as 170,000 yBP. Like the Amud male, she had a large brain.

The Amud and Tabun skulls have a number of anatomical characteristics that are strongly similar to those of contemporary populations of late archaic *H. sapiens* in Europe. For example, their eye orbits tend to be small and round, their nasal openings are large and wide, and their faces project forward. These two skulls share a number of modern characteristics, however, such as the lack of the occipital bun and the presence of relatively small teeth.

Some of the most interesting Neandertals are from the Shanidar site, in northern Iraq's Kurdistan region. These Neandertals—seven adults and three young children—have provided important insight into the lives, lifestyles, and cultural practices of late archaic *H. sapiens*. Shanidar 1, an older adult male dating to at least 45,000 yBP, is one of the most complete skeletons from the site (**Figure 11.13**). The face is that of a typical Neandertal, especially in its wide nasal aperture and projecting face. This individual's life history is written in his bones. A fracture on his upper face may have been severe enough to cause blindness. Severe arthritis in his feet might have resulted from the constant stresses of traversing difficult, mountainous terrain.

Shanidar 1's upper incisors are severely worn, probably from his use of the front teeth as a tool for grasping and holding objects in the same or a similar way as the much earlier hominid from Atapuerca. This extramasticatory wear on the front teeth is determined by culture—Neandertals used their front teeth as a part of their "tool kit." Use of the front teeth as a tool has remained a hallmark of human behavior into recent times in a wide variety of cultures, ranging from Eskimos, who chew hides for clothing and other material culture, to Native Americans, who chew plant material to prepare it for basketry.

Shanidar 1 may have had personal reasons for using his front teeth as a tool. When he was excavated by the American archaeologist Ralph Solecki in the late 1950s, his lower right arm was missing. The American physical anthropologist T. Dale Stewart suggested that the lower arm may have been either amputated or accidentally severed right above the elbow. The humerus was severely atrophied,

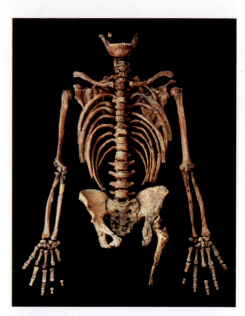

FIGURE 11.12 ■ **Kebara Neandertal**
The almost complete skeletal torso of this hominid was discovered in Kebara Cave, Israel. Even without a cranium and legs, this is one of the most complete Neandertal skeletons found to date. (Photograph © 1985 David L. Brill.)

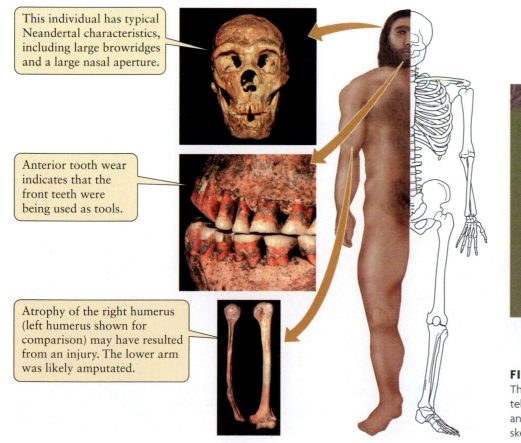

This individual has typical Neandertal characteristics, including large browridges and a large nasal aperture.

Anterior tooth wear indicates that the front teeth were being used as tools.

Atrophy of the right humerus (left humerus shown for comparison) may have resulted from an injury. The lower arm was likely amputated.

FIGURE 11.13 ■ **Shanidar 1 Neandertal**
The skeleton of this older adult Neandertal tells a life story of injury owing to accidents and violence. The majority of Neandertal skeletons have injuries.

FIGURE 11.14 ■ Neandertal Sites
This map illustrates the various locations of Neandertal discoveries throughout southern and middle Europe and the Middle East as well as the suggested boundaries of the Neandertal range.

probably owing to disuse of the arm during life. This meant that Shanidar 1 *had* to use his teeth to perform some simple functions, such as eating or making tools. His survival likely depended on the use of his front teeth.

LATE ARCHAIC *HOMO SAPIENS* IN EUROPE (130,000–30,000 YBP) The European late archaic *Homo sapiens*, Neandertals, are some of the best-known, most-studied fossil hominids in the world (**Figure 11.14**). Owing to the relative completeness of the fossil record, paleoanthropologists have been able to document and debate the meaning of their physical characteristics. The Neandertal record begins in eastern Europe, at the Krapina site in Croatia, dating to 130,000 yBP. The record ends with fossils from Vindija, Croatia, dating to 32,000 yBP or somewhat less.

Like many Neandertal remains, the Krapina fossils were excavated more than a century ago. Not all such early excavations were carefully done. Fortunately, the excavator of the Krapina site—the Croatian paleontologist Dragutin Gorjanvić-Kramberger (see Figure 7.10)—was extraordinarily meticulous in his recording of the excavation. During the period in which he excavated the site, 1899–1905, he kept detailed notes about where his workmen found fossils and stone tools. He was especially careful in recording the stratigraphic locations of the several hundred bones and teeth found at the site.

The Krapina remains were recovered from a series of strata inside a rock-shelter (not quite a cave—a rock overhang provides protection from the elements). The remains are highly fragmentary, making it difficult to identify key physical

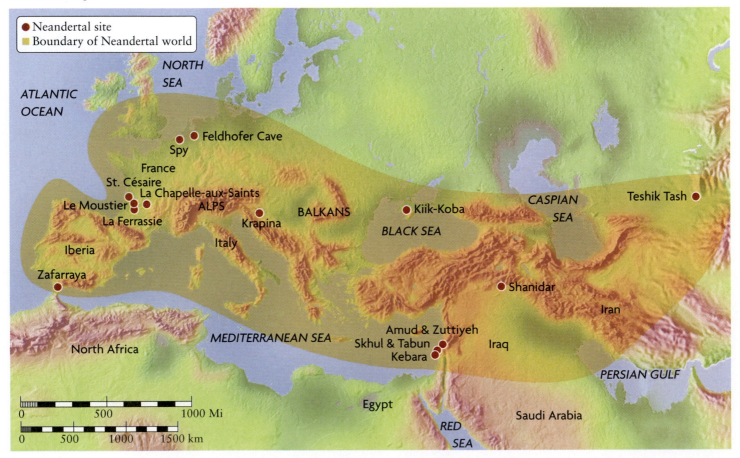

characteristics. The most complete cranium, Krapina has the typical Neandertal features: round eye orbits, wide space between the eye orbits, wide nasal aperture, and protruding midfacial region (**Figure 11.15**). The Krapina front teeth are the largest of any known fossil hominid. In fact, tooth size comparisons with earlier and later humans in Europe indicate that in these Neandertals the front teeth had increased and the back teeth had decreased.

The Krapina bones are mostly in fragments. The American anthropologist Tim White has found that some of these fragments display a series of distinctive cutmarks in places where ligaments (the tissue that connects muscle to bone) were severed with stone tools. The location and pattern of cutmarks on the Krapina Neandertal bones are identical to those on animal bones found at the site. That strategically placed cutmarks appear on human and animal bones strongly suggests that these people ate animal *and* human tissue.

The Krapina Neandertals were not the only ones to practice cannibalism. At the Moula-Guercy cave, in southeastern France, six individuals dating to about 100,000 yBP display cutmark patterns very similar to those on the animal remains at the site. Scientists cannot explain why cannibalism was practiced, but perhaps Neandertals ate human flesh to survive severe food shortages during their occupation of Ice Age Europe.

Many Neandertal skeletons, including some of the best-known from western Europe, are relatively late, postdating 60,000 yBP. The skeleton from La Chapelle-aux-Saints, France, is especially well-known because anthropologists used it as the prototype for all Neandertals in the early twentieth century. It has the characteristic Neandertal cranial morphology, including a very wide nasal aperture, a projecting midface, an occipital bun, and a low, long skull (**Figure 11.16**).

FIGURE 11.15 ■ **Krapina Neandertal**
This Krapina cranium has many features associated with Neandertals. Can you identify the key features that characterize it as Neandertal? (Photograph © 1985 David L. Brill.)

THE NEANDERTAL BODY PLAN: ABERRANT OR ADAPTED? The La Chapelle-aux-Saints skeleton is also one of the most complete Neandertals. The skeleton was first described in great detail by the eminent French paleoanthropologist Marcellin Boule (d. 1942) in the early 1900s. Professor Boule's scientific writings tremendously influenced contemporary and later scientists' interpretations of Neandertal phylogeny, behavior, and place in human evolution generally, basically continuing the earlier opinions expressed by Rudolf Virchow (discussed at the start of this chapter). Boule argued that the Neandertal cranial and postcranial traits were simply too primitive and too different from modern people's to have provided the ancestral basis for later human evolution (**Figure 11.17**). He concluded that the La Chapelle individual must have walked with a bent-kneed gait—as in chimpanzees that walk bipedally—and could not have been able to speak. Simply, in his mind, Neandertals represented some side branch of human evolution—they were too primitive, too stupid, and too aberrant to have evolved into modern humans.

Boule's interpretations led to the prevailing view at the time (still held by some authorities) that Neandertals were evolutionary dead ends, replaced by the emerging modern humans and representing distant cousins of humanity that were not able to survive. In rejecting this view, we should take a closer look at some topics Boule addressed in his study of the La Chapelle skeleton.

FRANCE

La Chapelle-aux-Saints

Moula-Guercy Cave

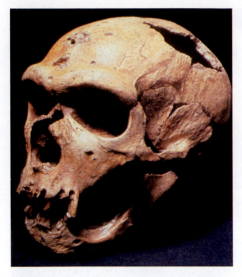

FIGURE 11.16 ■ La Chapelle-aux-Saints Neandertal
Like Shanidar 1, this skeleton shows evidence of healed injuries and arthritis.

One very distinctive feature is the *enormous* nasal aperture (**Figure 11.18**). The great size of the nasal aperture in many Neandertal fossils indicates that these people had huge noses, in both width and projection. Such massive noses were one of the cranial characteristics that led Boule to believe that Neandertals were not related to later humans in an evolutionary sense. However, nasal features are more likely part of an adaptive complex reflecting life in cold climates during the Upper Pleistocene. The shape and size of any nose is an excellent example of the human face's highly adaptable nature, especially in relation to climate. One of the nose's important functions is to transform ambient air—the air breathed in from the atmosphere—into warm, humid air. Large noses have more internal surface area, thus providing an improved means of warming and moistening the cold, dry air that Neandertals breathed regularly. Moreover, the projecting nose typical of Neandertals placed more distance between the cold external environment and the brain, which is temperature-sensitive. In any case, many people around the world today have wide, big noses, which are integral parts of their robust faces. These attributes are not uniquely Neandertal (**Figure 11.19**).

Other features of Neandertal skeletons are consistent with cold adaptation. For example, the infraorbital foramina—the small holes in the facial bones located beneath the eye orbits—are larger in European Neandertals than in modern people (**Figure 11.20**). The foramina's increased size is due to the blood vessels that tracked through them having been quite large. Some anthropologists speculate that the larger blood vessels allowed greater blood flow to the face, preventing exposed facial surfaces from freezing.

Most distinctive about the cold adaptation complex in Neandertals are the shape of the body trunk and the length of the arms and legs. Compared with modern humans, European Neandertals were stocky—the body was short, wide, and deep (**Figure 11.21**). Neandertals' limbs were shorter than earlier or later humans'. This combination—stocky trunk and short limbs—is predicted by Bergmann's and Allen's rules (see "Climate Adaptation: Living on the Margins" in chapter 5). That is, animals that live in cold climates are larger than animals that live in hot climates (Bergmann's Rule). The larger body trunk reduces the amount of surface area relative to the body size. This helps promote heat retention. Moreover, animals

FIGURE 11.17 ■ Neandertal Depictions
(a) The La Chapelle-aux-Saints skeleton, here fleshed out by an illustrator in 1909, reinforced the notion that Neandertals were too stupid and too brutish to have evolved into modern humans. **(b)** More-recent reconstructions show that Neandertals looked very similar to modern humans in many respects. In addition, estimates of brain size put them squarely within the modern human range.

(a)

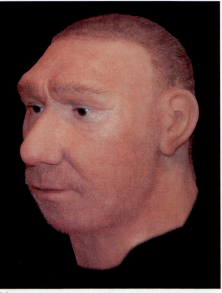

(b)

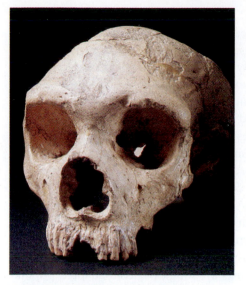

FIGURE 11.18 ■ Nasal Aperture
The large nasal aperture of Neandertal crania, such as this cranium from Gibraltar, may have been a cold adaptation.

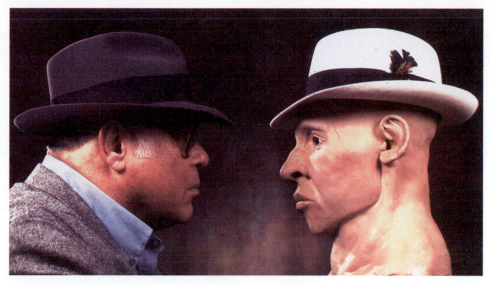

FIGURE 11.19 ■ Modern Human Relatives?
Some of the morphological traits associated with Neandertals can be found in modern humans, as illustrated by this photograph of the physical anthropologist Milford Wolpoff facing the reconstructed head of a European Neandertal. Might Neandertals have interbred with modern human ancestors, passing along some of these traits?

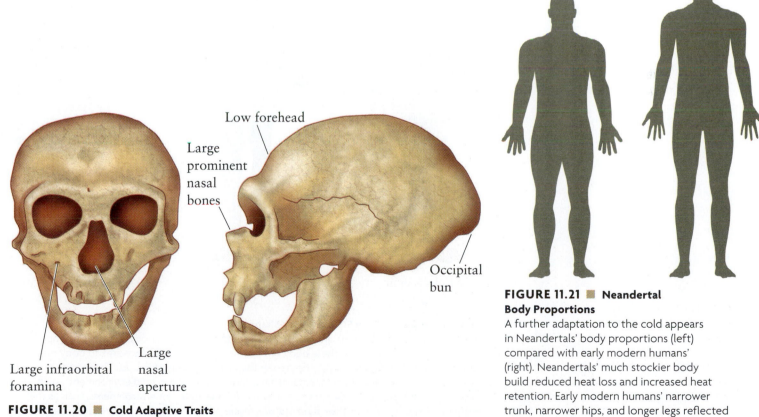

Low forehead

Large prominent nasal bones

Occipital bun

Large infraorbital foramina

Large nasal aperture

FIGURE 11.20 ■ Cold Adaptive Traits
Large infraorbital foramina are among the Neandertal traits that likely were responses to a cold environment during the later Pleistocene.

FIGURE 11.21 ■ Neandertal Body Proportions
A further adaptation to the cold appears in Neandertals' body proportions (left) compared with early modern humans' (right). Neandertals' much stockier body build reduced heat loss and increased heat retention. Early modern humans' narrower trunk, narrower hips, and longer legs reflected the warmer environment in which these people lived.

that live in cold climates have shorter limbs than animals that live in hot climates (Allen's Rule). This, too, promotes heat retention in cold settings.

The American physical anthropologist Christopher Ruff has further refined these concepts in interpreting human body shape morphology. He discovered that adaptation to heat or cold is not related to a person's height—some heat-adapted populations are quite tall, and some are quite short. Much more important is the width of the body trunk (usually measured at the hips), because the ratio of surface area to body mass is maintained regardless of height (**Figure 11.22**). This finding is borne out by a wide range of populations around the world today: Populations living in the same climate all have body trunks of the same width, no matter how their heights vary. Populations living in cold climates always have wide bodies; populations living in warm climates always have narrow bodies. These dimensions are always constant in adaptation to heat or cold. In addition, the ratio of tibia (lower leg) length to femur (upper leg) length differs between people that live in hot climates and people that live in cold climates. Heat-adapted populations have long tibias relative to their femurs (their legs are long), but cold-adapted populations have short tibias relative to their femurs (their legs are short). Neandertals

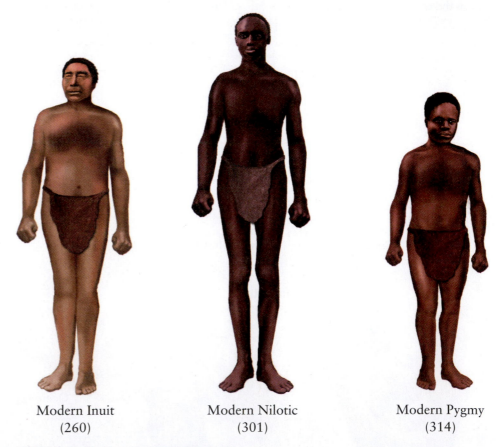

| Modern Inuit | Modern Nilotic | Modern Pygmy |
| (260) | (301) | (314) |

FIGURE 11.22 ■ **Body Size and Body Shape**
The refinement of Bergmann's and Allen's rules regarding body size, body shape, and temperature adaptations are illustrated by these body types. The ratio of body surface area to body mass (cm²/kg) is given below each type. The greater the ratio, the more that body shape and that body size are adaptations to high temperatures. Individuals living in cold environments, such as the modern Inuit, have a lower ratio than individuals living in hot environments, such as the modern Nilotic. Because of their short stature, modern Pygmies appear to contradict Bergmann's and Allen's rules. However, body surface ratio reveals that Pygmies are well adapted to hot environments.

fit the predictions for cold adaptation: their body trunks are wide, and their tibias are short. Simply, they were cold adapted.

NEANDERTAL HUNTING: INEFFICIENT OR SUCCESSFUL? The French paleo-anthropologists of the 1800s and early 1900s questioned Neandertals' humanness. They suggested that Neandertals were unintelligent, could not speak, and had a simplistic culture. Put in the vernacular expression, "Their lights were on, but nobody was home." Some paleoanthropologists continue to argue this point, viewing Neandertals as inefficient hunters and not especially well adapted to their environments. A growing body of archaeological and biological evidence demonstrates, however, that Neandertals were not clumsy mental deficients.

Neandertals were associated with the culture known as **Mousterian** or **Middle Paleolithic**. This culture's stone tool technology, lasting about 300,000–30,000 yBP, includes a complex and distinctive type of flaking called the **Levallois**. This technique involves preparing a stone core and then flaking the raw materials for tools from this core. Contrary to the opinions of early anthropologists, this Neandertal technology was complex and required considerable skill and hand–eye coordination. Moreover, anthropologists are learning that late Neandertals participated fully in the **Upper Paleolithic**, the earliest cultures associated mostly with early modern *Homo sapiens* in Europe, producing stone tools that were modern in many respects, and certainly as complex as those produced by early modern humans. Moreover, the size, shape, and articulations of the Neandertal hand reflect the kind of precise manual dexterity crucial for the fine-crafting of tools (**Figure 11.23**).

If Neandertals were not effective hunters, they might have been less successful adaptively than modern people. One way to measure hunting success is to determine how much meat Neandertals ate. Butchered animals' bones are abundant in Neandertal habitation sites, indicating that Neandertals hunted the animals and processed the carcasses for food. Suggestive though this evidence is, the mere presence of animal remains does not reveal how *important* animals were in the people's diet. To find out how important meat was in Neandertals' diets, anthropologists have

Mousterian The stone tool culture in which Neandertals produced tools using the Levallois technique.

Middle Paleolithic The middle part of the Old Stone Age, associated with Mousterian tools, which Neandertals produced using the Levallois technique.

Levallois A distinctive method of stone tool production used during the Middle Paleolithic, in which the core was prepared and flakes removed from the surface before the final tool was detached from the core.

Upper Paleolithic Refers to the most recent part of the Old Stone Age, associated with early modern *Homo sapiens* and characterized by finely crafted stone and other types of tools with various functions.

FIGURE 11.23 ■ Mousterian Tools
Neandertals made these tools out of flint. The use of such tools would have replaced the use of front teeth as tools, reducing the amount of anterior tooth wear in some later Neandertals. (Photograph © 1985 David L. Brill.)

applied the powerful tools of bone chemistry and stable isotope analysis. Measurement of stable isotopes of both nitrogen and carbon in the bones of Neandertals—from Scladina Cave (Belgium), Vindija Cave, and Marillac (France)—indicates that Neandertals ate lots of meat, at or nearly at the level of carnivores living at the same time and place (**Figure 11.24**). The chemical signature of diet, then, is a powerful indicator of Neandertals' effectiveness in acquiring and consuming animal protein. That is, it shows that Neandertals were successful hunters.

Another indicator of their effective adaptation is the measurement of stress levels. The American physical anthropologist Debbie Guatelli-Steinberg and her associates found that hypoplasias, the stress markers in teeth that reflect growth disruption due to poor diets or poor health, are present in Neandertals but at a frequency no different from that of modern humans. This finding, too, suggests that Neandertals dealt successfully with their environments.

NEANDERTALS BURIED THEIR DEAD In many Neandertal sites, the remains have been found scattered about, commingled and concurrent with living areas. For example, the Krapina Neandertal fossils are fragmentary and were scattered throughout the site. That is, the deceased were treated no differently than food remains or anything else being discarded. In contrast, a significant number of skeletons have been found in pits. That is, excavation of some Neandertal sites in Europe and western Asia has shown that pits had been dug, corpses had been placed in the pits, and the pits had been filled in. For example, the Neandertal skeletons from Spy, Belgium; ones from various sites in France, such as La Chapelle-aux-Saints; several Shanidar individuals; and the Neandertals from Amud and Tabun, both in Israel, were found in burial pits (**Figure 11.25**).

Was burial of the dead a religious or ceremonial activity having significant meaning for the living, those who buried the dead? Or was burial simply a means of removing bodies from living spaces? After all, the smell of a decaying body is quite

FIGURE 11.24 ■ **Neandertal Diet**
Measures of stable isotopes of both carbon and nitrogen, here labeled ^{13}C and ^{15}N respectively, can be used to determine the relative amounts of different kinds of foods consumed. This graph shows the isotope values for a variety of herbivores and carnivores. Herbivores generally have lower isotope values than carnivores. Neandertals' isotope levels are close to those of known carnivores, indicating that Neandertals ate plenty of meat.

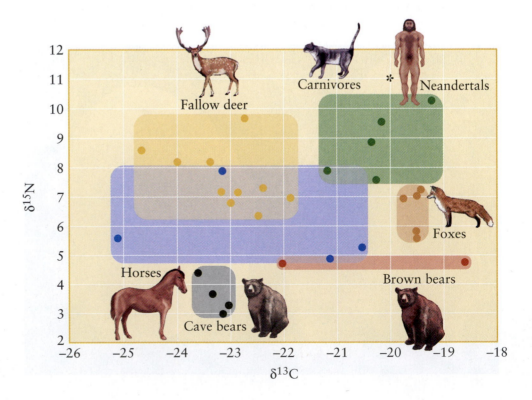

awful, and it would seem to make sense to bury it as soon as possible. Most of the intentionally buried skeletons were in flexed (fetal-oriented) postures. The hands and arms were carefully positioned, and the bodies were typically on their sides or backs. This vigilant treatment indicates that care was taken to place the bodies in the prepared pits. The skeletons' postures suggest, therefore, that these burials were not just disposals. They represented purposeful behavior linking those who died and those who were living.

NEANDERTALS TALKED Fundamental to human behavior is the ability to speak as part of the repertoire of communication. Conversation is a key way that we present information and exchange ideas. Because early anthropologists believed that Neandertals lacked the ability to speak, they argued that Neandertals were not related to modern people in an evolutionary sense. This idea continues to the present. The American linguist Philip Lieberman and the American anatomist Edmund Crelin, for example, have reconstructed the Neandertal vocal tract. Because their reconstruction resembles a modern newborn infant's vocal tract, Lieberman and Crelin conclude that, like human babies, Neandertals could not express the full range of sounds necessary for articulate speech. Although interesting, their reconstruction of the Neandertal vocal tract is conjectural. Based on skulls alone, it necessarily lacks the anatomical parts (soft tissues) important for speech production.

One compelling line of evidence strongly suggests that Neandertals were able to speak. The Kebara Neandertal skeleton includes the hyoid bone, a part of the neck that can survive from ancient settings. Various muscles and ligaments attach it to the skull, mandible, tongue, larynx, and pharynx, collectively producing speech (**Figure 11.26**). The morphology of the Kebara Neandertal's hyoid is identical to that of a living human's. The Kebara people talked.

The key point of this discussion of Neandertal characteristics—relating to climate adaptation, material culture, efficiency in hunting strategies, access to animal protein, treatment of deceased, and use of speech—is that Neandertals likely were not weird humanlike primates, less adaptable and less intelligent than modern humans.

Archaic *Homo sapiens*

Archaic *Homo sapiens* are the first of our species, beginning some 350,000 yBP globally and evolving locally from earlier *Homo erectus* populations. After 150,000 yBP, regional patterns of diversity emerge, followed later by simultaneous occupation of Europe by late archaic (Neandertals) and early modern *H. sapiens* by 40,000 yBP.

Locations (sites)[1]	Africa (Kabwe) Asia (Ngandong, Dali, Narmada, *Amud, Kebara, Tabun, Shanidar*) Europe (Sima de los Huesos, Swanscombe, Steinheim, Petralona, Arago, *Feldhofer Cave*, Atapuerca, *Spy, Krapina, Vindija, Moula-Guercy, La Chapelle-aux-Saints, Scladina Cave, Marillac, Les Rochers, Engis, El Sidron, Monte Lessini, Teshik Tash*)
Chronology	350,000–30,000 yBP
Biology	Mixture of *H. erectus* and *H. sapiens* characteristics 1,200 cc cranial capacity early 1,500 cc cranial capacity late Both skulls and skeletons less robust Reduced tooth size, but most of reduction in premolars and molars (front teeth increase in size) Appearance of Neandertal morphology after 130,000 yBP in Middle East and Europe (long, low skull; wide, large nose; large front teeth with common heavy wear; forward-projecting face; no chin; wide body trunk; short limbs) Distinctive mtDNA structure Distinctive nDNA structure, but overlapping with living humans'
Culture and behavior	Some evidence of housing structures Large-game hunting Fishing and use of aquatic resources after 100,000 yBP More advanced form of Acheulian early Mousterian late (Europe) Increased use of various raw materials besides stone after 100,000 yBP Skilled tool production Burial of deceased after 100,000 yBP Symbolic behavior Social care of sick and injured Articulate speech likely, perhaps much earlier

[1] Sites mentioned in text; italics denote sites where Neandertal (late archaic *H. sapiens*) remains have been found.

The record shows that their behaviors, both in form and in substance, were similar to modern humans'. The size and robusticity of their long bones show that Neandertals were highly physically active, more so than living humans. Such cultural and biological features reflect Neandertals' success in adapting to environmental circumstances of the Upper Pleistocene, not evolutionary failure. The empirical evidence disproves arguments that Neandertals were less than human.

FIGURE 11.26 ■ **Did Neandertals Speak?**
The Kebara skeleton's hyoid is identical to a modern human hyoid, indicating that Neandertals could speak.

Early Modern *Homo sapiens*

Modern *Homo sapiens* from the Upper Pleistocene are represented in the fossil record throughout Africa, Asia, and Europe. During this time, humans moved into other areas of the world. Later in this period, they spread into regions with extreme environments, such as the arctic tundra of Siberia in northern Asia. It was a time of significant increases in population size, increased ability through cultural means of adapting to new and difficult landscapes, and the development of new technologies and subsistence strategies. (**Table 11.1** lists the four major Upper Paleolithic cultures and important events associated with each.) The cultures of the later Pleistocene, grouped in the Upper Paleolithic, are also known from their stunning imagery, including hundreds of artistic works in caves throughout Europe but concentrated

TABLE 11.1	Timeline for Major Upper Paleolithic Cultures of Europe
The Aurignacian (45,000–30,000 yBP) • Associated with the first anatomically modern humans in Europe	
The Gravettian (30,000–20,000 yBP) • The Perigordian in France • Earliest art, in the form of carved figurines	
The Solutrean (21,000–17,000 yBP) • France and Spain during the last glacial peak • Made very fine stone points	
The Magdalenian (17,000–12,000 yBP) • Successful hunters of reindeer and horses • Spread out across Europe as conditions improved at the end of the Ice Age • Made many of the spectacular paintings and carvings	

FIGURE 11.27 ■ **Chauvet Cave Art**
(a) Chauvet Cave, in France's Ardèche River Valley, contains 400 painted images of late Pleistocene animals, especially lions, horses, cattle, and rhinoceroses. Dates of 32,000–30,000 yBP make this the oldest cave art.
(b) Upper Paleolithic tools, such as these, include some of the forms seen in earlier periods of human evolution. However, new tools reflect the procurement of additional types of food, such as the barbed harpoon for catching fish.

(a)

(b)

especially in France and Spain (**Figure 11.27**). This period of human evolution also includes the universal appearance of the modern anatomical characteristics discussed at the beginning of this chapter, namely a reduced face, small teeth, a vertical forehead, a more rounded skull, and gracile postcranial bones. Modern humans' evolution started much earlier in Africa than in Europe and Asia.

EARLY MODERN *HOMO SAPIENS* IN AFRICA (200,000–6,000 YBP) The African record for early *Homo sapiens* is especially important because it includes the earliest evidence of modern people's anatomical characteristics. Crucially important fossil hominids from this time come from the Herto, Aduma, and Bouri sites, in Ethiopia's Middle Awash River Valley, and from Omo, in southern Ethiopia. The remains from Herto—partial skulls of two adults and of a child, dating to 160,000–154,000 yBP—show a cranial capacity of about 1,450 cc, close to the average for modern humans (**Figure 11.28**). In addition, many of the characteristics are essentially

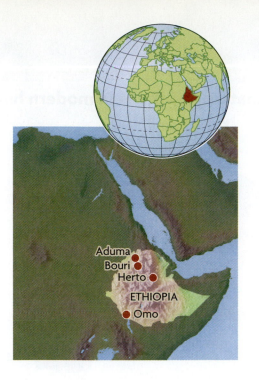

modern, including a relatively tall cranium, a vertical forehead, smaller browridges, and a nonprojecting face. Among the archaic features are significant browridges (though the trend is toward smaller) and a relatively long face. These remains may be from the earliest modern people in Africa or at least close to the earliest. The remains' overall appearance indicates that modern people emerged in Africa long before their arrival in Europe and western Asia. The remains from Omo may be as old as 195,000 yBP. If so, then they are the oldest evidence of anatomically modern humans. However, their dating is uncertain because the fossils were not positioned in the geological context as clearly as the Herto fossils were.

Belonging to later contexts are the partial skulls from Aduma and Bouri, dating to about 105,000–80,000 yBP. Like the Herto skulls, these skulls have both premodern and modern characteristics. However, the most complete Aduma skull is modern in nearly every characteristic.

Skulls from two key locations in southern Africa provide important information about early modern *H. sapiens* that date to after 100,000 yBP. Among the fragmentary remains from Klasies River Mouth Cave, anthropologists have documented the presence of a chin, a distinctively modern characteristic, that dates to at least 90,000 yBP (**Figure 11.29**). A nearly complete skull from Hofmeyr, dating to 36,000 yBP, bears a striking resemblance to Pleistocene modern Europeans.

Throughout the Pleistocene and well into the early Holocene, African hominids, although modern, retained some robusticity. For example, the skulls from Lothagam, Kenya, dating to the Holocene (ca. 9,000–6,000 yBP), are robust compared with living East Africans' (**Figure 11.30**). During this period, a number of characteristics seen in the region's living populations were present, such as wide noses. At Wadi Kubbaniya and Wadi Halfa, both in the Nile Valley, populations have some very robust characteristics, such as flaring cheekbones and well-developed browridges. These features contrast sharply with the gracile facial features seen later in the Holocene and in living people (these features are discussed further in chapter 12).

FIGURE
11.28

The First Modern Humans:
Biology and Behavior

Biology: Anatomy of the first modern humans

Kabwe skull

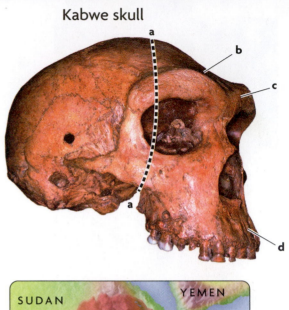

Behavior: Hunting and butchering

These early modern *Homo sapiens* were skilled hunters. They produced sophisticated stone tools (above) used for killing and butchering large game, such as hippopotamuses living along lake margins. At the Herto site, White's team found more than 600 stone tools. These tools had multiple functions, mostly relating to the killing and butchering of animals for food.

Herto Reconstruction

("*Homo idaltu* Portrait Bust Reconstruction," © 2005 by Jay H. Matternes.)

Herto skull

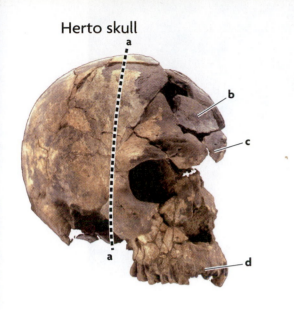

	Skull characteristics	Kabwe 300,000 yBP	Herto 160,000 yBP
a	Braincase	Shorter	Taller
b	Forehead	Less vertical	More vertical
c	Browridge	Larger	Smaller
d	Face	Projecting	Retracted
e	Brain size	Smaller	Larger

Homo sapiens' Big Brains Evolve

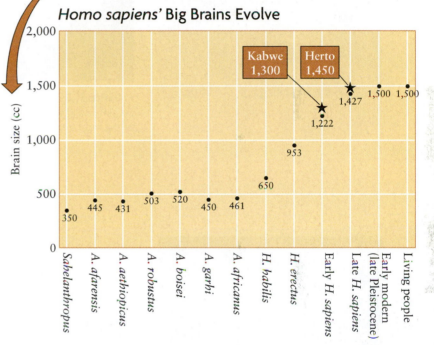

Kabwe 1,300
Herto 1,450

Brain size (cc)

2,000
1,500
1,000
500
0

350 — *Sahelanthropus*
445 — *A. afarensis*
431 — *A. aethiopicus*
503 — *A. robustus*
520 — *A. boisei*
450 — *A. garhi*
461 — *A. africanus*
650 — *H. habilis*
953 — *H. erectus*
1,222 — Early *H. sapiens*
1,427 — Late *H. sapiens*
1,500 — Early modern (late Pleistocene)
1,500 — Living people

Near the village of Herto, in the Middle Awash region of Ethiopia, a paleoanthropology team directed by Tim White discovered hundreds of hominid skull fragments dating to about 160,000 yBP. When pieced together, the skull proved to be remarkably modern (see reconstruction at left). In contrast to earlier hominids, such as Kabwe (found in Rhodesia and dating to 300,000 yBP), Herto has a tall braincase, a vertical forehead, small browridges, a retracted face, and a large brain. In combination, these are definitive characteristics of modern people. White and his team had found the first modern human.

Paleoanthropologists are learning that the stone tools used by the Herto people for butchering animals were also used for other purposes. The skull bones of the Herto man display cutmarks made by stone tools on the face, front, side, and back, all created when flesh was removed from the skull. This could have been done as part of some ancient ritual. The cutmarks are similar to ones found in skulls from New Guinea and from other places where the people were known to have practiced cannibalism.

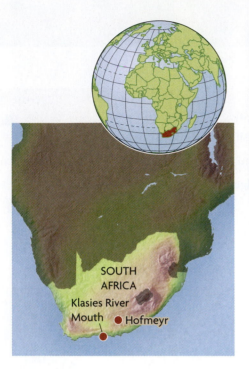

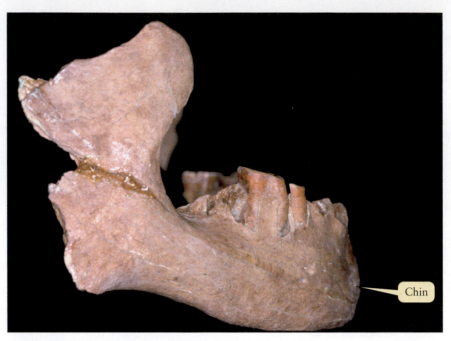

FIGURE 11.29 ■ **Klasies River Mouth Cave**
Excavations at this site in southern Africa revealed evidence of early modern *Homo sapiens*. One of the most important features found on these cranial remains is a chin on the mandible.

FIGURE 11.30 ■ **Lothagam Skull**
This Kenyan cranium illustrates early modern humans' rather robust nature. Note the projection both of the lower part of the front of the skull and of the mandible.

EARLY MODERN *HOMO SAPIENS* IN ASIA (90,000–18,000 YBP) The earliest modern *Homo sapiens* in Asia are best represented by fossils from the western part of the continent, in fact from the same region as the Amud and Kebara Neandertals in Israel. The 90,000-year-old remains from Skhul have distinctively modern characteristics, suggesting that the people living there were modern *H. sapiens*. Among the most prominent remains from the site are several male skulls, of which Skhul 5 is the most complete. That Skhul 5 dates to before the Amud fossils indicates that modern humans lived in the region before Neandertals (**Figure 11.31**).

Remains of the earliest modern people from eastern Asia are very scarce. Some of these remains are purported to be older than 60,000 yBP, but the dates are based on geologic deposits that are not clearly associated with the fossils. The earliest best-dated fossils are a mandible and partial skeleton, dating to about 41,000 yBP, from Tianyuan Cave, China. This individual's remains have archaic and modern features. Better-known are three skulls from the Upper Cave at Zhoukoudian, China, dating to 29,000–24,000 yBP (**Figure 11.32**; this site is discussed further in chapter 10). The Upper Cave skulls are robust compared with living Asians', but the facial flatness is characteristic of native eastern Asians today. Similarly, the early modern people from Minatogawa (Okinawa), dating to about 18,000 yBP, are gracile, but retain thick cranial bones and large browridges, especially compared with those of the later Holocene populations in East Asia.

EARLY MODERN *HOMO SAPIENS* IN EUROPE (35,000–15,000 YBP) Early modern people are known from various places throughout Europe. The earliest modern *Homo sapiens* in Europe is from Peştera cu Oase, Romania, and dates to 35,000 yBP. The Oase 2 skull from that site is distinctively modern, contrasting with Neandertals that lived during the same time. For example, Oase 2 has very reduced browridges and a generally gracile appearance. Almost as old are remains

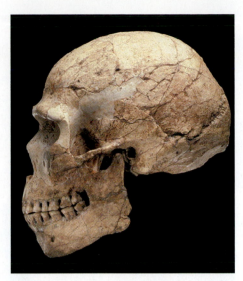

FIGURE 11.31 ■ **Skhul Cranium**
This skull possesses many characteristics associated with modern humans, including a chin, a less projecting face, small and gracile cheeks, and a high, vertical forehead. The browridges are still distinct, but are much reduced compared with archaic *Homo sapiens'*. (Photograph © 1985 David L. Brill.)

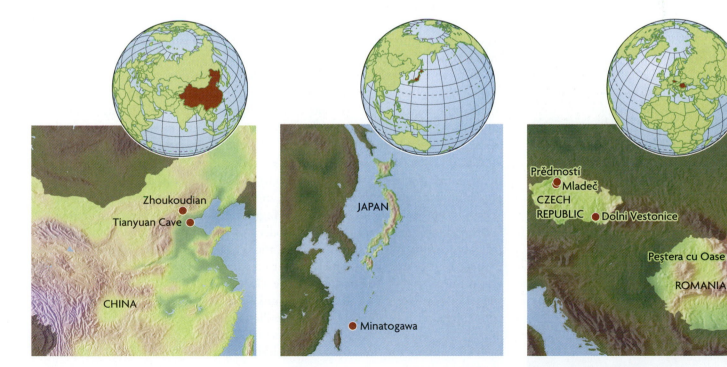

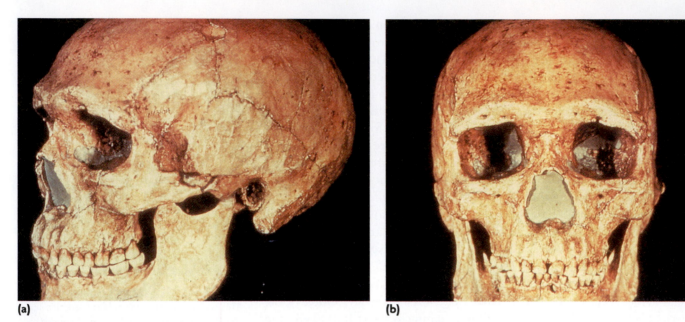

(a) **(b)**

FIGURE 11.32 ■ **Zhoukoudian Crania**
(a, b) One skull recovered from Zhoukoudian shows several modern human traits, but overall these crania are more robust than their modern Asian counterparts. In the older area of this site, the famous *Homo erectus* fossils were found, prior to World War II.

Lagar Velho

PORTUGAL

from Mladeč, Předmostí, and Dolni Vestonice, all in the Czech Republic, dating to 35,000–26,000 yBP. The half-dozen Mladeč skulls (35,000 yBP) show remarkable variability, including a mix of Neandertal characteristics in some (occipital bun, low skull, large browridges, large front teeth, and thick bone) and modern characteristics in others (nonprojecting face, narrow nasal opening). The Předmostí and Dolni Vestonice skulls retain a few Neandertal characteristics, but they are clearly more modern in appearance than the Mladeč people (**Figure 11.33**). Some Neandertal features persist well into recent times in eastern Europe, especially in the facial region (**Figure 11.34**).

Western Europe has virtually no fossil record for the earliest modern people, those contemporary with the populations represented by the Mladeč and Předmostí fossils. The skeleton of a five-year-old child from Lagar Velho, Portugal, dating to 24,000 yBP, has a number of archaic, Neandertal-like cranial and postcranial features, such as its limb proportions and robusticity (**Figure 11.35**).

The best-known western European representatives of early modern people are the remains of a half-dozen individuals from Cro-Magnon, in Dordogne, France, and remains from the Grimaldi Caves, in the Italian Riviera region, all dating to about 30,000–25,000 yBP. The Cro-Magnon remains are often presented as the archetypical example of the earliest modern people, but in fact people varied considerably during this time. Collectively, though, both ensembles of skeletons from western Europe have distinctively modern features: vertical forehead, narrow nasal aperture, and small browridges (**Figure 11.36**). In addition, unlike Neandertals', their tibias are long and their body trunks are narrow. Like Neandertals, these people lived in cold climates of the late Pleistocene, but their very different body morphology suggests adaptation to warmer climates. (The implications of these skeletal features for the origins of modern *H. sapiens* are discussed later in this chapter.)

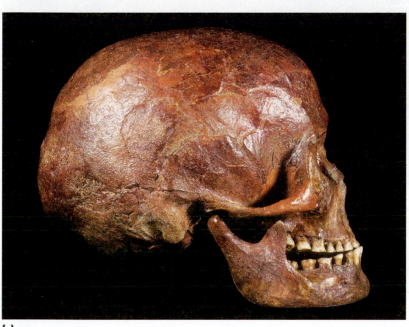

(a)

FIGURE 11.33 ◼ **Dolni Vestonice Skull**
(a, b) This cranium, from Dolni Vestonice, combines modern human and Neandertal characteristics.

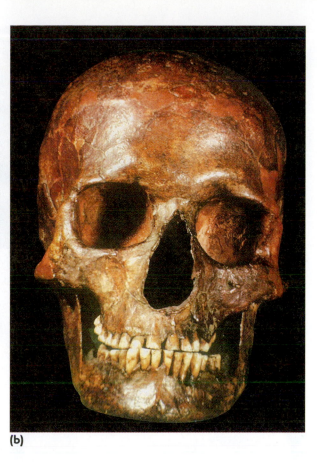

(b)

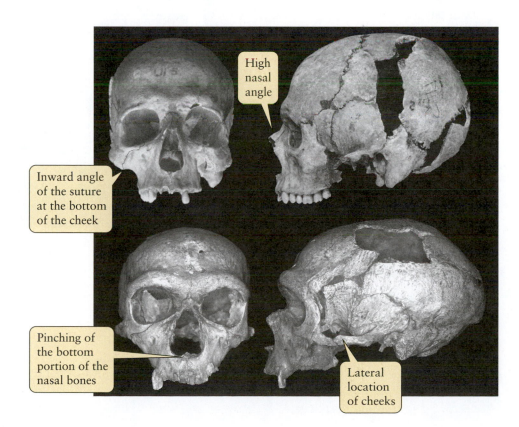

High nasal angle

Inward angle of the suture at the bottom of the cheek

Pinching of the bottom portion of the nasal bones

Lateral location of cheeks

FIGURE 11.34 ◼ **Neandertal Traits in Modern Humans**
The La Chapelle cranium (bottom, and see Figure 11.16) and a modern Croatian cranium (top) share four major facial similarities.

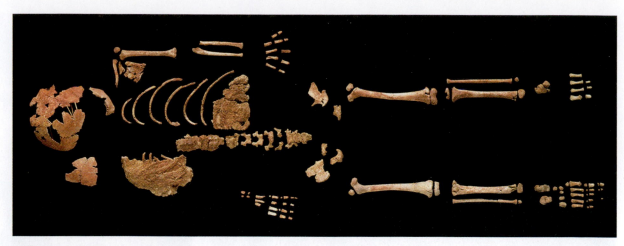

FIGURE 11.35 ■ **Lagar Velho**
This skeleton of a child was discovered at a rockshelter site in Portugal's Lapedo Valley.

(a)

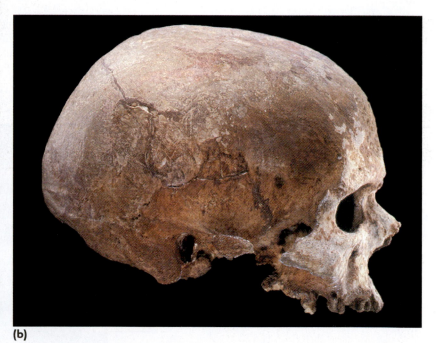
(b)

FIGURE 11.36 ■ **Cro-Magnon**
(a, b) In 1868, a geologist discovered skeletons in a rockshelter in Cro-Magnon, France. These remains are anatomically modern, with a number of features distinct from Neandertals', including a high, vertical forehead, flat browridges, a much narrower nasal aperture, and an overall gracile skull. (Photographs © 1985 David L. Brill.)

Overall, comparisons of earlier with later early modern *H. sapiens* in Europe indicate a trend toward gracilization—the faces, jaws, and teeth became smaller, and the faces became less projecting. In addition, comparison of early and late Upper Paleolithic heights reconstructed from the long bones shows that the later early modern people were shorter. The decrease in the height of early modern people may have been caused, at the very end of the Pleistocene, by both a decrease in quality of nutrition and resource stress. That is, during the last 20,000 years of the Pleistocene, food procurement intensified—more effort was put into acquiring and processing food for the same amount of caloric intake as before. This change may have occurred because human population size was increasing, placing increased pressure on food resources. An outcome of this change was a global increase in the range of foods eaten. Archaeological evidence shows that the later early modern humans hunted and collected smaller and less-desirable (because not as protein-rich) foods, such as small vertebrates, fish, shellfish, and plants. As the American anthropologist Trent Holiday has also shown, the late Upper Paleolithic people had wider body trunks and shorter legs than the early Upper Paleolithic people. The morphological shift indicates an adaptation to cold during the late Upper Paleolithic, a highly dynamic period of human adaptation and evolution.

Modern Behavioral and Cultural Transitions Happened First in Africa

Until recently, anthropologists identified a number of behavioral and cultural practices—such as painting and the use of symbolism (including the magnificent Upper Paleolithic cave art), the increased diversity of both hunting techniques and hunting technology, fishing and the use of aquatic resources, and the wider use of raw materials for tool production—as having developed in Europe during the late Pleistocene. Anthropologists are learning, however, that these practices developed tens of thousands of years earlier in Africa than in Europe. For example, fishing and the use of aquatic resources are first documented at Katanda, in Congo, where hominids were exploiting large catfish at 75,000 yBP. This early use of fishing in Africa is part of a larger package of behaviors associated with modern *H. sapiens*, including more specialized kinds of hunting, wider employment of raw materials (such as bone) for producing tools, use of advanced blade technology, trade, and art and decoration (**Figure 11.37**). By 80,000 yBP, personal ornamentation, such as with shell beads, was widespread in Africa, long before it appeared in Europe. Like the fossil record, then, the cultural record shows a much earlier appearance of modernity—the exploitation of both resources and material culture—in Africa than in Europe or Asia. In other words, modernity happened first in Africa, both biologically and culturally.

HOW HAS THE BIOLOGICAL VARIATION IN FOSSIL *HOMO SAPIENS* BEEN INTERPRETED?

At the beginning of this chapter, you read about the two key models that anthropologists use to explain modern *Homo sapiens'* origins, namely the Out-of-Africa model and the Multiregional Continuity model. After having learned what the fossil

FIGURE 11.37 ■ **Modern Human Tools**
Early modern humans used a variety of specialized tools, including harpoons and blades shaped for specific purposes. In addition to stone, bone and antler became common tool materials.

record reveals about the variation in late archaic *H. sapiens,* you should be starting to see what this record reveals about modern humans' origins. Now remember the question posed at the beginning of this chapter: Which of the two models best explains modern *H. sapiens'* origins?

The European fossil record from 40,000–30,000 yBP provides important clues about modern *H. sapiens'* origins in Europe. The earliest modern *H. sapiens* were present as early as 35,000 yBP at Mladeč (Czech Republic) and at Pestera cu Oase (Romania). The latest archaic *H. sapiens,* the Neandertals, survived until at least 32,000 yBP or so at Vindija (Croatia). The overlap in dates between Neandertals and early modern humans indicates that the two groups coexisted in eastern Europe for at least several thousand years. This finding argues against the Multiregional Continuity model, which sees archaic *H. sapiens* as having evolved locally into modern *H. sapiens.* That the earliest modern *H. sapiens* had clear Neandertal features (such as the occipital bun) strongly suggests interbreeding between Neandertals and early modern people. This finding argues against the Out-of-Africa model, which sees no gene flow between Neandertals and early modern humans. We will now see if the genetic record provides additional insight into modern *H. sapiens'* origins in Europe.

Ancient DNA: Interbreeding between Neandertals and Early Modern People?

Analysis of mitochondrial DNA, the DNA inherited only via the mother, offers potential clues about modern people's origins (mtDNA is among the topics of chapter 3). Comparisons of the mtDNA extracted from more than a dozen Neandertal skeletons—from Engis and Scladina in Belgium, Rochers de Villeneuve and La Chapelle-aux-Saints in France, Monte Lessini in Italy, El Sidron in Spain, Feldhofer Cave in Germany, Mezmaiskaya in Russia, Teshik Tash in Uzbekistan, and Vindija Cave in Croatia—with that of early modern humans and living humans shows *similarity* among the Neandertals and *dissimilarity* between the Neandertals and modern humans. The German molecular geneticist Matthias Krings and his associates found, for example, that 27 mtDNA base pairs of a sequence of 378 base pairs from the Feldhofer Cave Neandertal differ from living Europeans'. By contrast, living human populations have an average of just eight differences among them. Genetic differences between Neandertals and modern humans are consistent with the anatomical differences between Neandertals and early modern humans and lend support for the notion that Neandertals and modern humans are two different groups with different geographic ancestries. However, mtDNA is just a tiny part of the human genome and cannot reveal whether gene flow occurred between Neandertals and early modern humans.

Geneticists have begun to explore nuclear DNA's structure to address the possibility that gene flow occurred between the two groups in Europe during the late Pleistocene. So far, only the Neandertal from Vindija has yielded enough nuclear DNA to provide a picture of the Neandertal genome. Interestingly, the structures of Neandertal and modern DNA overlap somewhat. Because nuclear DNA better represents the total genome, these findings indicate the strong possibility of gene flow between Neandertals and early modern humans.

Based on the mtDNA evidence currently in hand, many authorities have concluded that Neandertals contributed nothing to the modern human gene pool. For several reasons, however, this conclusion may not be the best one. First, the Neandertal mtDNA is from only a dozen individuals—many more need to be studied to

Early Modern *Homo sapiens*

Early modern *Homo sapiens* occurred first in Africa, later in Asia and Europe. The peopling of Europe, Asia, and Africa by only modern *H. sapiens* was complete by 25,000 yBP.

Location/sites[1]	Africa (Herto, Aduma, Bouri, Omo, Klasies River Mouth, Lothagam, Wadi Kubbaniya, Wadi Halfa) Asia (Skhul 5, Tianyuandong, Minatogawa) Europe (Pestera cu Oase, Mladeč, Předmostí, Dolni Vestonice, Cro-Magnon, Grimaldi)
Chronology	160,000 yBP in Africa 90,000 yBP in western Asia 35,000 yBP in eastern Asia 32,000 yBP in Europe
Biology	Vertical forehead, high skull, rounder skull, reduced facial robusticity, smaller teeth, reduced midfacial prognathism, 1,500 cc cranial capacity Heat-adapted body morphology (small trunk, long limbs)
Culture and behavior	Upper Paleolithic Increased visible symbolic behavior (cave art) Burial of deceased with grave goods Decreased hunting, increased fishing, aquatic foods, likely more plants and reduced focus on big game animals Technology changes reflect increased focus on fishing (e.g., bone harpoons)

[1] Sites mentioned in text.

RUSSIA

Mezmaiskaya

fully understand the Neandertal genome and its differences with the modern human genome. Second, the mtDNA comparisons between Neandertals, early modern humans, and living humans are being made across many thousands of years. Genetic differences between these Neandertals and living people may simply reflect the fact that the Neandertals lived tens of thousands of years ago, plenty of time for these differences to emerge. Third, since mtDNA is only a small part of a person's genome, the failure of one part of the genome to survive to the present does not mean that the entire genome became extinct. The study of nuclear DNA in other Neandertals will presumably help fill out scientists' understanding of that genome.

Living People's Genetic Record: Settling the Debate on Modern Human Origins

Living people's genetic record helps settle the question about whether the Out-of-Africa model or the Multiregional Continuity model explains modern *Homo sapiens*' origins. The American geneticist and molecular biologist Rebecca Cann

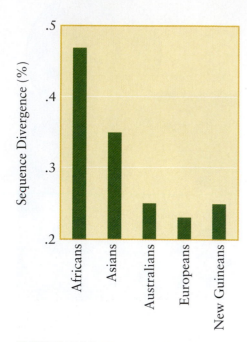

FIGURE 11.38 ■ **Genetic Diversity**
Patterns of genetic diversity have been used to assess the Out-of-Africa and Multiregional Continuity models of modern humans' origins. This graph shows genetic diversity within several major geographic groups, expressed as the average amount of genetic sequence divergence in percent. Note the much greater genetic diversity in Africans compared with other groups. (Source: Cann, R. L., M. Stoneking, and A. Wilson. 1987. Mitochondrial DNA and human evolution. *Nature* 325: 31–36.)

and her collaborators have found that sub-Saharan African populations are more genetically diverse than populations from any other region of the world. That is, genes of people living south of the Sahara desert today are more variable in frequency than are genes of people living in Europe, Asia, the Americas, and Australia (**Figure 11.38**). This pattern is also present in phenotypic variation of anatomical characteristics (e.g., cranial measurements).

Two explanations exist for Africa's greater genetic diversity. First, a population or group of populations that has been around a long time will have accumulated more mutations—hence, greater genetic variation—than a population or group of populations that has been around a short time. Therefore, Africa's greater genetic diversity may mean that modern people have existed longer there than in Asia or Europe.

Based on their assessment of mutation rates, Cann et al. came up with a figure of 200,000 yBP for the first early modern *H. sapiens'* appearance, and this date is consistent with the earliest record of modern *H. sapiens* in Africa. Calculations based on other sources of genetic material, such as from the Y chromosome, provide broadly similar results.

The alternative explanation for Africa's greater genetic diversity lies in Africa's population structure compared with other continents'. The American anthropological geneticist John Relethford observes that population size tremendously influences genetic diversity. As discussed in chapter 3, if the breeding population is small, genetic drift is a potentially powerful force for altering gene frequencies. Over time, genetic drift reduces genetic diversity in a small population (such as might have been the case in Europe and Asia). For example, if a group of 10 people splits off from a group of 1,000 people, the two resulting groups will show very different patterns of gene frequency change. The smaller population will be less variable, whereas its parent population will be more variable. Relethford argues that because in the remote past Africa had a significantly larger breeding population size than other continents did, Africa now has greater genetic diversity.

ASSIMILATION MODEL FOR MODERN HUMAN VARIATION: NEANDERTALS ARE STILL WITH US

The more modern characteristics of East African skeletons from the Upper Pleistocene (for example, Herto) suggest strongly that modern variation originated in Africa. The fossil record and (to a lesser extent) the genetic record indicate, however, that neither the Out-of-Africa model nor the Multiregional Continuity model adequately explains modern humans' origins. The Out-of-Africa model correctly accounts for the origin of modern human variation, but it incorrectly asserts that no gene flow occurred between Neandertals and modern *Homo sapiens*. The Multiregional Continuity model is not correct about modern *H. sapiens'* regional development. However, it is correct about gene flow and the notion that Neandertals have contributed to modern *H. sapiens'* gene pool.

In other words, elements of both models explain the emergence and evolution of fully modern people worldwide in the Upper Pleistocene. That is, sometime within 200,000–100,000 yBP, a population of modern heat-adapted *H. sapiens* migrated from Africa to Europe and Asia. Once arriving in Europe, this population encountered members of their species—the Neandertals—who were as behaviorally and technologically complex as they. Neandertals, cold-adapted people, had evolved from earlier *H. sapiens* populations in Europe—the early archaic *H. sapiens*—and they interbred with the newly arrived modern *H. sapiens*. Therefore, Neandertals' disappearance after 30,000 yBP or so likely resulted not from their extinction but from their *assimilation* by much larger, more genetically diverse populations of modern humans migrating into Europe from Africa during the late Pleistocene. Neandertals contributed to the gene pool of today's European and European-descended populations, leaving their genetic, behavioral, and adaptive legacy with modern humans in Europe and in Asia.

CONCEPT CHECK — Models for Explaining Modern *Homo sapiens*' Origins

Anthropologists have developed three models to explain modern humans' origins.

MODEL	FEATURES	PROPONENT
Out-of-Africa	Modern biology, behavior, and culture originated in Africa. Modern humans spread from Africa to Europe after 50,000 yBP. Modern humans replaced all populations once arriving in Europe, with no gene flow.	Christopher Stringer
Multiregional Continuity	Modern humans evolved from earlier archaic populations in their respective regions (Africa, Europe, Asia). Throughout evolution, there is always significant gene flow on the borders of populations. There is continuity of morphology in all regions of the globe.	Milford Wolpoff
Assimilation	Modern humans evolved first in Africa, then spread to Europe and Asia. Once they arrived in Europe and Asia, modern humans underwent gene flow with Neandertals.	Fred Smith, Erik Trinkaus

MODERN HUMANS' OTHER MIGRATIONS: COLONIZATION OF AUSTRALIA, THE PACIFIC, AND THE AMERICAS

The last 50,000 years of the Pleistocene saw fully modern people spread not only into Asia and Europe but also to continents that had previously not been occupied by people. Prior to 50,000 yBP, humans occupied only three of the six inhabitable continents: Africa, Asia, and Europe. After 50,000 yBP, populations migrated from the southeastern fringes of Asia to Australia, eventually fanning out from west to east across the hundreds of islands that dot the Pacific Ocean. In the last few millennia of the Pleistocene, humans spread to the Americas (**Figure 11.39**). These movements, and their accompanying adaptations to unfamiliar environments, are no less a part of human evolution than are bipedalism, language use, and all the other key developments discussed in chapters 10–11.

What motivated these early modern people to move? Among the multiple reasons, four are most important: population increase, disappearance of food resources, increased competition with neighbors for remaining resources, and climate deterioration. That is, a population's resources—food especially—are available in finite quantities. As Relethford has shown through genetic studies, African populations expanded rapidly during the late Pleistocene. These increases, as populations outgrew their carrying capacities, were the prime force stimulating anatomically modern people to move into Asia and Europe. Similarly, as population size expanded in Asia and Europe, humans continued to move and began to occupy vast regions of the globe.

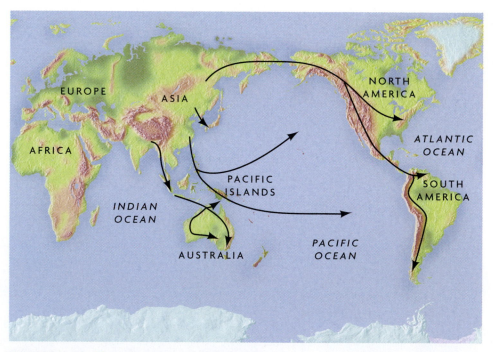

FIGURE 11.39 ■ **Modern Humans' Migrations**
Another major research question in physical anthropology focuses on modern humans' spread from Europe, Asia, and Africa into North America, South America, and Australia. This map shows modern humans' migration patterns from southern Asia to Australia and the Pacific Islands as well as from northern Asia to North America and, eventually, to South America.

Beginning in the very late Pleistocene, East Asia became the stepping-off point for migrations to previously unoccupied continents. Southeast Asia served as the stepping-off point for the movements to Australia and across the Pacific, as people eventually occupied most of the 20,000–30,000 islands between Australia and the Americas. Northeast Asia served as the stepping-off point for the spread to North America and South America.

Down Under and Beyond: The Australian and Pacific Migrations

In the late Pleistocene, sea levels were considerably lower than they are today, by as much as 90 m (300 ft), exposing land surfaces now submerged by water and making them available for human occupation and movement between landmasses (**Figure 11.40**). Even at the peak of the late Pleistocene's coldest period, when sea levels were at their lowest, a considerable distance of open water separated Australia from Asia. Late Pleistocene humans would have needed sophisticated boating technology.

The earliest archaeological evidence of humans in Australia is from Lake Mungo, in western New South Wales, dating to about 40,000 yBP. The two skulls from Lake Mungo, from an adult male and an adult female, have modern characteristics: the skulls are high and have rounded foreheads with small browridges. In overall

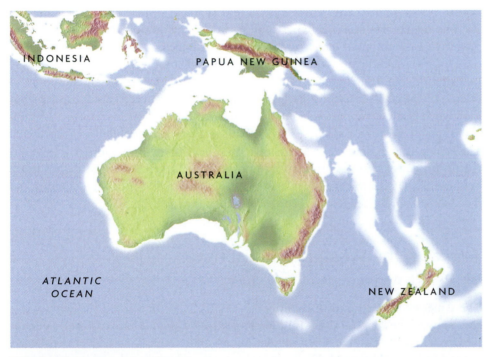

FIGURE 11.40 ■ Land Bridge
During the late Pleistocene, temperatures were much cooler and a great amount of seawater was locked in glaciers. As a result, sea levels were at their lowest, exposing shallow land, such as the Sunda shelf in Southeast Asia. On this map, the exposed land is white. Some of it connected the islands of Southeast Asia (Borneo, Java, and Sumatra) with the Asian mainland, and some of it connected Australia with New Guinea and Tasmania. Despite the increased land area, traveling to Australia would have required a sea voyage; however, there was much less distance between Southeast Asia and Australia. Modern researchers are unable to investigate evidence of the people who once inhabited the areas that are now underwater.

FIGURE 11.41 ■ **Kow Swamp**
This Australian site has yielded skeletons much more robust than those discovered at Lake Mungo. In fact, Alan Thorpe, who excavated the skull, originally believed the remains to be a *Homo erectus* skeleton rather than a modern human skeleton.

microcephaly A condition in which the cranium is abnormally small and the brain is underdeveloped.

Homo floresiensis Nicknamed "Hobbit" for its diminutive size, a possible new species of *Homo* found in Liang Bua Cave, on the Indonesian island of Flores.

appearance, the skulls resemble ones from Kow Swamp, in Victoria's Murray River Valley, which date to 13,000–9,000 yBP (**Figure 11.41**).

These early Australians also bear a strong similarity to native people who inhabit the continent today; the anatomical evidence indicates an ancestral-descendant relationship. However, mtDNA from the Lake Mungo and Kow Swamp skeletons differs substantially from living native Australians'. Based on the mtDNA evidence alone, one might conclude that the ancient populations represented by the Lake Mungo and Kow Swamp skeletons were not ancestral to living native Australians, but this conclusion runs counter to a range of cultural and archaeological evidence. As with the Neandertal mtDNA lineages discussed above, a more likely explanation for the disparity between ancient and modern genes in Australia is that the mtDNA sequence in ancient anatomically modern people has not survived to the present.

Southeast Asia is also the point of origin for populations that eventually dispersed throughout the Pacific Ocean. Unlike Australia, which was settled by 40,000 yBP, most of the Pacific Islands extending from east of New Guinea to Easter Island were not settled until well after 5,000 yBP.

Until recently, all human remains found in the East Asian region dating to around 40,000 yBP appeared to be fully modern *Homo sapiens*. The discovery of skeletal remains dating to about 18,000 yBP may challenge this long-held conclusion about human evolution in this region. In 2003, a very short and remarkably primitive skeleton was found in a cave on the Indonesian island of Flores (**Figure 11.42**). Dubbed "Hobbit" by the popular press, this hominid had an extremely tiny brain—about 400 cc. This size is close to that of an early australopithecine's brain, just one-quarter the size of a living human's brain! In addition, the wrist bones are primitive, resembling in many respects ape wrist bones.

This finding indicates that a group of primitive humans became isolated early in evolution, resulting in a pattern of biological variation previously unknown to scientists. Some scientists argue, however, that this creature was a modern human who suffered from **microcephaly** or some other genetic abnormality. Without evolutionary precursor species, it is difficult to say whether this fossil represents a dwarfed human species or a person with a developmental disorder. However, the primitive wrist bones and unusual morphology in general suggests that it is a new species—called ***Homo floresiensis*** by Peter Brown and colleagues. Additional discoveries will be needed to authenticate this new species name.

Arrival in the Western Hemisphere: The First Americans

The American physical anthropologist Aleš Hrdlička first noted the remarkable similarity in the shapes of the front teeth of East Asian and Native American peoples, past and present. He observed that Asians and Native Americans have **shovel-shaped incisors** (**Figure 11.43**). In these incisors and many other dental features, the American anthropologists Albert Dahlberg and Christy Turner have identified a common ancestry for East Asians and Native Americans.

Additional clues about the peopling of the Americas appear in modern and ancient Native Americans' mtDNA. For 95% of living Native Americans throughout North America and South America, mtDNA falls into any one of four haplogroups—A, B, C, or D. (As discussed in chapter 3, mtDNA is inherited just from the mother, so the haplogroup unit reflects the maternal line of inheritance.) Interestingly, the

FIGURE 11.42 ■ **Flores Man**
A recent discovery on Flores Island, Indonesia, has become the source of much debate in anthropology. Some researchers believe this "hobbit" represents a group of early humans, while others believe this individual suffered from a genetic or developmental abnormality.

The cranium is very small, especially compared with that of a modern human.

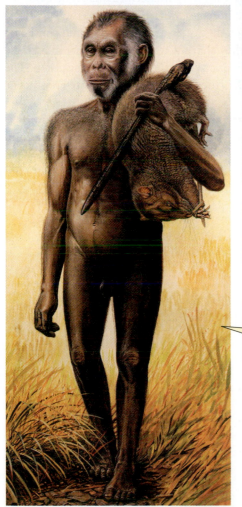

This artist's reconstruction shows what Flores Man may have looked like in life.

Based on measurements of the long bones, the Flores individual would have been approximately .9 m (3 ft) tall, considerably shorter than the average modern human.

FIGURE 11.43 ■ **Shovel-Shaped Incisors**
A dental characteristic often found in East Asians is the shoveled appearance of the back, or lingual side, of the incisors. That this trait has also been found in Native Americans likely reflects their descent from East Asians.

same pattern of four main haplogroups has been found in ancient Native American skeletons. This sharing of haplogroups by modern people and ancient skeletons indicates a common founding ancestry for present and past Native Americans. Moreover, Native Americans share haplogroups with northeastern Asians. The evidence indicates that the haplogroups were present in Asians who migrated to the Americas. The presence of all four groups throughout the Americas and the strong similarity of the nucleotide sequences suggest that they share a common ancestry in a single founding population that arrived in the Americas from Asia via one migration. The dental and the genetic evidence points to Northeast Asia during the late Pleistocene for native New World people's origin.

Migrations to the Americas occurred via a land route. This land route was across the Bering land bridge (which we call Beringea), connecting Siberia and Alaska. Like those in the western Pacific Ocean, this land route was created when sea levels reached a low point during the later Pleistocene, exposing areas of land that are now submerged.

INDONESIA

Flores

Folsom ●

NEW MEXICO

Clovis ●

WASHINGTON

Kennewick ●

Genetic dating based on mutation rates of mtDNA and Y chromosomes (see chapter 4) indicates that the migration from Asia to the Americas likely took place sometime around 15,000 yBP. The earliest people are called **Paleoindians** and are known from their distinctive stone artifacts, especially large spear points associated with the **Clovis** and later **Folsom** cultures. The Paleoindians hunted various animals, including **megafauna,** the large Pleistocene game such as the mammoth, steppe bison, and reindeer/caribou (**Figure 11.44**). Pleistocene megafauna became extinct in the early Holocene. Although humans may have contributed to the extinction of these large animals in Australia and the Americas, the more important factors leading to their decline and loss were climate change and the changes in habitats frequented by large mammals.

The Paleoindians differed anatomically from recent Native Americans. The Paleoindians' skulls were relatively long and narrow, and their faces were robust, with large attachment areas for the mastication muscles. In contrast, many late prehistoric and living Native Americans have short, round skulls with gracile faces. For example, the Paleoindian skull from Kennewick, Washington, dating to 9,300 yBP, is long and narrow and has large browridges; the face and jaws are robust (**Figure 11.45**). These differences between the Paleoindians and modern Native Americans have been interpreted to mean either that the Paleoindians are not the living Native Americans' ancestors or, alternatively, that the Paleoindians are the living Native Americans' ancestors but cranial morphology has changed due to evolutionary forces and other processes over the last 10,000 years in the Americas (discussed further in chapter 12). The more likely scenario is that the cranial morphology evolved and was shaped by later changes in use of the face and of the jaws. If so, then Paleoindians are the ancestors of living Native Americans.

FIGURE 11.44 ■ **Paleoindians**
The tools the Paleoindians used to hunt these animals included a specialized, fluted projectile point, called a Folsom point. An extraordinary amount of skill was required to make this tool.

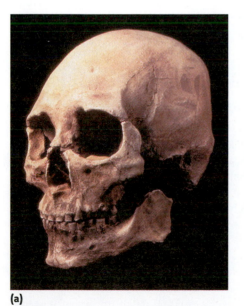

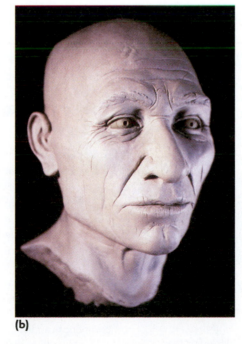

(a) **(b)**

FIGURE 11.45 ■ **Kennewick Man**
(a) Discovered on the banks of the Columbia River, Kennewick Man represents the Paleoindians.
(b) This artist's reconstruction shows the Paleoindians' likely facial appearance.

Paleoindians The earliest hominid inhabitants of the Americas; they likely migrated from Asia and are associated with the Clovis and Folsom stone tool cultures in North America and comparable tools in South America.

Clovis Earliest Native American ("Paleoindian") culture of North America; technology known for large, fluted, bifacial stone projectile points used as spear points for big game hunting.

Folsom Early Native American (immediately following Clovis) culture of North America; technology known for large, fluted, bifacial projectile points used as spear points for big game hunting.

megafauna General term for the large game animals hunted by pre-Holocene and early Holocene humans.

Modern humans' emergence and subsequent dispersal around the globe marks a remarkable period of population expansion and behavioral and biological diversification. The geographic biological diversity in the world today was likely well in place by the end of the Pleistocene. The rapid expansion of human population size resulted in increased types of foods eaten. The adoption and increased use of fish and aquatic life in general during the late Pleistocene likely reflects humans' need for alternative foods as population size expanded. Such dietary expansion set the stage for one of the most dramatic adaptive shifts in human evolution, the shift from eating plants that were gathered and animals that were hunted to eating plants and animals that were domesticated. In the next chapter, we will look at this important transition's biological implications for humans over the last 10,000 years of our evolution.

ANSWERING THE BIG QUESTIONS

What is so modern about modern humans?

- Modern humans have a number of anatomical characteristics that distinguish them from premodern humans. These include a small face, small jaws, small teeth, a vertical and high forehead, a narrow nasal aperture, a narrow body trunk, and long legs.

What do *Homo sapiens* fossils reveal about modern humans' origins?

- The *H. sapiens* fossil record shows early archaic *H. sapiens* evolving from a *Homo erectus* ancestor.
- There is evidence of regional diversification after 200,000 yBP. In Africa, early nearly modern people evolved 200,000–150,000 yBP. After 130,000 yBP, an archaic form of *H. sapiens* called Neandertals occupied much of Europe and of western Asia.
- From perhaps as long ago as 40,000–25,000 yBP, hominid groups occupied Europe—the Neandertals and modern *H. sapiens*. The former had various archaic features and a cold-adapted body morphology. The latter had modern characteristics and a heat-adapted body morphology.

How has the variation in fossil *Homo sapiens* been interpreted?

- The Out-of-Africa model argues that modern *H. sapiens* migrated from Africa to Asia and Europe. Once in Asia and Europe, they replaced indigenous late archaic *H. sapiens*, including the Neandertals in Europe and in western Asia.

- The Multiregional Continuity model argues that modern *H. sapiens* arose regionally in each of the three inhabited continents: Africa, Asia, and Europe.
- The combined presence of archaic (Neandertal) and modern anatomical characteristics in some late Pleistocene European skeletons and the overlap in DNA structure indicates that Neandertals were not replaced by modern *H. sapiens*. Rather, instead of disappearing through extinction, Neandertals were assimilated through substantial admixture with early modern *H. sapiens*. Thus the fundamental details of modern human anatomy probably have a single place of origin (Africa), but Neandertals later contributed to the European gene pool. Neandertals are part of modern humans' ancestry.

What other developments took place in *Homo sapiens'* evolution?

- Modern characteristics including more advanced tool technology, diversification of diet, and symbolism appeared first in Africa and later in Europe and Asia.
- Anthropologists do not know when spoken communication first began, but at least one Neandertal had the vocal anatomy consistent with speech.
- Neandertals and contemporary humans were the first species to intentionally bury their dead.
- An important theme in human evolution is migration and expansion into regions of the globe not previously occupied. Fully modern humans migrated to Australia about 40,000 yBP and to North American and South America by 15,000 yBP. By the beginning of the Holocene, humans lived on all inhabitable continents (Antarctica is the only uninhabitable continent).

KEY TERMS

Clovis
Folsom
Homo floresiensis
Levallois
megafauna
microcephaly

Middle Paleolithic
Mousterian
occipital bun
Paleoindians
shovel-shaped incisors
Upper Paleolithic

ADDITIONAL READINGS

O'Connell, J. F. and J. Allen. 1998. When did humans first arrive in greater Australia and why is it important to know? *Evolutionary Anthropology* 6: 132–146.

O'Rourke, D. H., M. G. Hayes, and S. W. Carlyle. 2000. Ancient DNA studies in physical anthropology. *Annual Review of Anthropology* 29: 217–242.

Relethford, J. H. 2001. *Genetics and the Search for Modern Human Origins.* New York: Wiley-Liss.

Ruff, C. B. 1993. Climatic adaptation and hominid evolution: the thermoregulatory imperative. *Evolutionary Anthropology* 2: 53–60.

Steele, D. G. and J. F. Powell. 1993. Paleobiology of the first Americans. *Evolutionary Anthropology* 2: 138–146.

Stringer, C. and R. McKie. 1998. *African Exodus: The Origins of Modern Humanity.* New York: Henry Holt.

Trinkaus, E. and P. Shipman. 1994. *The Neandertals: Of Skeletons, Scientists, and Scandal.* New York: Vintage.

Wolpoff, M. H. and R. Caspari. 1997. *Race and Human Evolution: A Fatal Attraction.* New York: Simon & Schuster.

Once humans began practicing agriculture, corn, wheat, and rice were three of the main crops they cultivated. The movement from procuring wild food to producing food has had many varied outcomes for modern *Homo sapiens,* including the decline of health.

CHAPTER 12

Our Last 10,000 Years: Agriculture, Population, Biology

One of my greatest disappointments as a kid was when my dentist told me my teeth were crooked and had to be fixed. My dentist was able to fix the problem by removing a lower third premolar on each side of my mandible, making room for other teeth to grow without crowding taking place. Most of my friends were not so lucky—the problems with their teeth required years of treatment, which involved painful throbbing after each orthodontic visit (in which the braces were tightened as in some kind of medieval torture); a tinny flavor no matter what was eaten; food stuck in the wiring; and perhaps worst of all, dietary restrictions: no gum, no caramel, nothing sweet and sticky—in short, none of the wonderful comforts of "civilization" (**Figure 12.1**).

Tooth crowding and malocclusion—improper fit of the upper and lower teeth, sometimes called underbite or overbite—are commonplace around much of the world today. Millions of people have crowded, misaligned teeth. This phenomenon has not always been the case, however. It has occurred mostly within the last 10,000 years—the Holocene. What happened?

This development, not present for most of human evolution, came about because of changes in *what* humans ate and *how* they prepared food for consumption. Namely, they switched from a diet of wild plants and wild animals to a diet partly based on domesticated plants and domesticated animals. In other words, in many areas of the world humans gave up hunting and gathering for agriculture (farming). Simply, they shifted from *foraging* for their food to *producing* their food. Moreover, they invented pottery, which was used for, among other functions, boiling food into soft mushes. As a result of this new technology, foods became much softer than ever before. These changes in what was eaten and how it was prepared reduced the stresses on humans' chewing muscles. This reduced stress, like that on any muscle, also reduced the underlying bone. Basically, we have smaller jaws because our ancestors began eating softer foods. (Remember Wolff's Law, discussed in chapter 5: bone develops where it is needed and recedes where it is unnecessary.)

Tooth size is under stronger genetic control than is bone size, and as a result tooth size is less affected by the environment. And as a consequence, humans' teeth had much less room to grow, resulting in the remarkable increase in crowded and poorly occluded teeth (**Figure 12.2**). The malocclusion epidemic, part of recent

BIG QUESTIONS

- When, where, and why did agriculture first develop?

- How did agriculture affect human living circumstances?

- How did agriculture affect human biological change?

- What are the most important forces shaping human biology today?

- Are we still evolving?

domestication The process of converting wild animals or wild plants into forms that humans can care for and cultivate.

Neolithic The late Pleistocene/early Holocene culture, during which humans domesticated plants and animals.

human evolution, is one of many consequences of our species' dietary change and but one example of our very dynamic biology.

THE AGRICULTURAL REVOLUTION: NEW FOODS, NEW ADAPTATIONS

Up until this point—to around 10,000 yBP or so—humans had acquired *all* their food through hunting and gathering. They hunted, trapped, fished, and otherwise collected animals big and small, terrestrial and aquatic, and they collected a huge variety of plants. During the later Pleistocene, they began to intensively exploit fish and shellfish, in oceans, lakes, streams, and so on. In the final centuries of that epoch, at the key environmental transition from the Pleistocene's cold and dry climate to the Holocene's warm and wet climate, people began to control animals' and plants' growth cycles, through a process anthropologists call **domestication**. Eventually, humans replaced nearly all the wild animals and wild plants in their diets with domesticated animals and domesticated plants. This dramatic change in lifeway—where people at the end of the Pleistocene and the early Holocene raised the animals and grew the plants they ate—is associated with the period called the **Neolithic.**

The shift from foraging to farming is among the most important adaptive shifts in hominid evolution. I rank it up there with bipedalism and speech as being fundamental to who humans are as an organism. As will be discussed in this chapter, this shift had important and long-lasting implications for *Homo* as an evolving organism. For example, many diseases we have today are linked in one way or another to this remarkable change in lifeway.

For 99.8% of the 7,000,000 years of human evolution, hominids had eaten plants of all kinds, but never before had they *grown* them. Domesticated plants

(a)

FIGURE 12.1 ■ **Braces**
(a) Straightening teeth has become so common that in the United States orthodontics is a multibillion-dollar industry. Among the braces used are **(b)** the standard wires and apparatus, both stainless-steel.

"Relax, Billy, they're just braces, even I had them when I was your age."

(b)

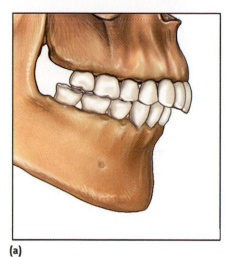
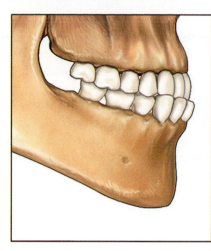

(a)

(b)

FIGURE 12.2 ◼ **Malocclusion**
Two major forms of malocclusion can be corrected with orthodontic treatments, including braces. **(a)** An overbite occurs when the maxillary teeth extend farther forward than the mandibular teeth. An underbite occurs when the mandibular teeth extend farther forward than the maxillary teeth. **(b)** This maxilla shows substantial crowding of the teeth from the prehistoric site in Windover, Florida. While dental crowding and malocclusion appear in some archaeological skeletal remains, both conditions became common only after humans adopted agriculture.

quickly became an integral part of food production across much of the globe, but that quickness is relative to the geologic timescale. Rather than happening overnight, in other words, the shift from foraging to farming took place over centuries and likely involved many successes and failures as the process unfolded for different human populations around the world (**Figure 12.3**). Compared with evolutionary changes that took place over thousands or hundreds of thousands of years, the

Evolution of Food Production from Plants			
Food Procurement from Wild Plants	Food Production from Wild Plants Dominant		Crop Production Dominant
Foraging, including use of fire	Incipient farming, with small-scale clearance of vegetation and minimal cultivation	Farming, with larger-scale land clearance and systematic cultivation	Full-blown agriculture, based largely or exclusively on domestic plants, with greater labor input into cultivation

Decreasing dependence on wild plants for food

Plant domestication: increasing dependence on domestic plants for food

15,000   11,000   9,000   6,000

Time (yBP)

FIGURE 12.3 ◼ **Adoption of Agriculture**
As this chart illustrates, humans did not simply abandon foraging and adopt agriculture. Initially, they foraged for wild plants to supplement their farming of cultivated plants. Over time, they depended less on wild plants and more on domesticated plants.

transitional process of domestication—the dietary changes, biological adaptations, and resulting health changes—was quite rapid.

Authorities agree on where and when domestication took place, based on the study of plant and animal remains found in archaeological sites. In addition, new breakthroughs in plant and animal genetics provide new windows on the origins of domesticated species. That is, the domesticated descendants of formerly wild plants and formerly wild animals have undergone genetic changes compared with the ancestral forms. These genetic changes have been documented via breeding experiments and by the extraction and study of DNA. The changes were brought about by humans' selecting food products that were beneficial to them. For example, they probably selected many plants with soft outer coatings and large seed yields. In a very real sense, the humans practiced artificial selection, as opposed to natural selection.

Authorities disagree on the *cause* for this dramatic, worldwide change in food acquisition. They are learning, however, that the change likely did not have only one cause. At least two factors probably brought about this agricultural revolution. First, the environment changed radically, going from cooler, drier, and highly variable during the later Pleistocene to warmer, wetter, and more stable during the Holocene (**Figure 12.4**). This abrupt environmental change brought about new conditions—local climates and local ecologies—suited to the domestication of plants and of animals. Second, almost everywhere agriculture developed, human population increased at the same time.

Population Pressure

Changes in climate and in ecology would not have resulted in plant and animal domestication, of course, without people. Almost everywhere agriculture developed, strong archaeological evidence indicates that the number and size of living sites increased. For example, on the Georgia coast (see the opening discussion in chapter 1) the beginning of agriculture coincided with an increase in number and especially size of villages. All over the world, wherever agriculture came into being, this pattern suggests that as human population size grew, people likely needed more food than hunting and gathering could provide. This population pressure model suggests that humans *had* to develop a new strategy for feeding the ever-growing world population. Domestication, especially of plants, produced more food per unit area of land than had hunting and gathering—more people could be fed from the same amount of land. In addition, agriculture provided food that could be stored for long periods. As an adaptive solution to population increase, domestication once again shows humans' remarkable flexibility in new and challenging circumstances.

Regional Variation

Plant and animal domestication was not just a one-time event, first occurring in one place and then spreading globally. Rather, domestication—in particular, plant domestication—started in at least 10 or 11 independent regions around the world (**Figure 12.5**). Out of these primary centers, the idea spread through a process of diffusion in some areas and through the movement of agricultural people in others. The process evolved slowly in some areas and fast in others. Eventually, every inhabitable continent except Australia saw the change. In some regions, newly domesticated plants replaced earlier ones. For example, in the American Midwest,

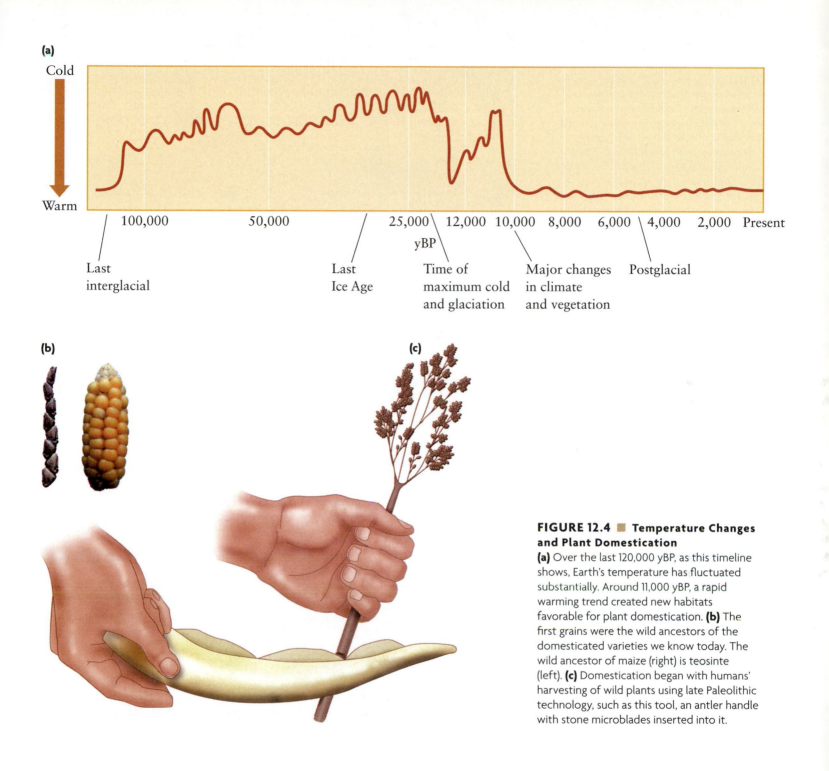

(a)

Cold

Warm

100,000   50,000   25,000   12,000 10,000 8,000   6,000   4,000   2,000   Present
                              yBP

Last   Last   Time of   Major changes   Postglacial
interglacial   Ice Age   maximum cold   in climate
                              and glaciation and vegetation

(b)

(c)

FIGURE 12.4 ■ **Temperature Changes and Plant Domestication**
(a) Over the last 120,000 yBP, as this timeline shows, Earth's temperature has fluctuated substantially. Around 11,000 yBP, a rapid warming trend created new habitats favorable for plant domestication. **(b)** The first grains were the wild ancestors of the domesticated varieties we know today. The wild ancestor of maize (right) is teosinte (left). **(c)** Domestication began with humans' harvesting of wild plants using late Paleolithic technology, such as this tool, an antler handle with stone microblades inserted into it.

native seed crops—goosefoot, sumpweed, and sunflowers—were farmed about 3,000–1,000 yBP. Later, corn replaced these crops, probably owing to its greater productivity and potential for feeding more people than before.

Archaeological evidence and genetic studies of domesticated plants indicate that prior to becoming agricultural at the end of the Pleistocene, people living in southwestern Asia, in a region called the Levant, began to intensively harvest the grains of wheat's and barley's wild ancestors. These grains provided food for the growing populations that were beginning to live in small, settled communities for at least part of the year. For the other part of the year, people were likely out and about, hunting

FIGURE 12.5 ■ **Worldwide Plant Domestication**

(a) This map shows the 11 separate centers of plant domestication. At each location, different types of domesticated plants were cultivated, including maize in Central America, sunflowers in eastern North America, cotton in South America, millet and sorghum in Africa, wheat in the Middle East, and banana trees in New Guinea.
(b) This chart illustrates the approximate times of plant and animal domestication in the major regions of the world.

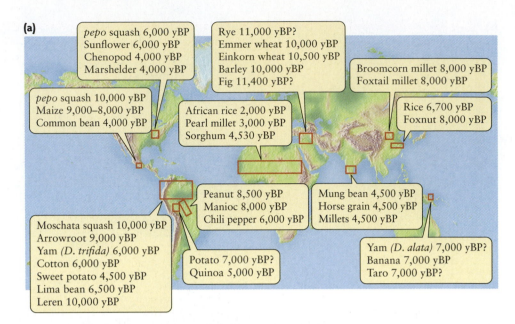

(a)

pepo squash 6,000 yBP
Sunflower 6,000 yBP
Chenopod 4,000 yBP
Marshelder 4,000 yBP

Rye 11,000 yBP?
Emmer wheat 10,000 yBP
Einkorn wheat 10,500 yBP
Barley 10,000 yBP
Fig 11,400 yBP?

Broomcorn millet 8,000 yBP
Foxtail millet 8,000 yBP

pepo squash 10,000 yBP
Maize 9,000–8,000 yBP
Common bean 4,000 yBP

African rice 2,000 yBP
Pearl millet 3,000 yBP
Sorghum 4,530 yBP

Rice 6,700 yBP
Foxnut 8,000 yBP

Peanut 8,500 yBP
Manioc 8,000 yBP
Chili pepper 6,000 yBP

Mung bean 4,500 yBP
Horse grain 4,500 yBP
Millets 4,500 yBP

Moschata squash 10,000 yBP
Arrowroot 9,000 yBP
Yam *(D. trifida)* 6,000 yBP
Cotton 6,000 yBP
Sweet potato 4,500 yBP
Lima bean 6,500 yBP
Leren 10,000 yBP

Potato 7,000 yBP?
Quinoa 5,000 yBP

Yam *(D. alata)* 7,000 yBP?
Banana 7,000 yBP
Taro 7,000 yBP?

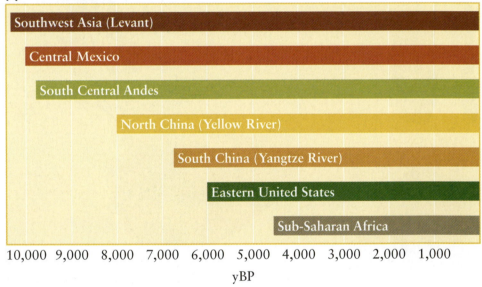

(b)

Southwest Asia (Levant)
Central Mexico
South Central Andes
North China (Yellow River)
South China (Yangtze River)
Eastern United States
Sub-Saharan Africa

10,000 9,000 8,000 7,000 6,000 5,000 4,000 3,000 2,000 1,000

yBP

and gathering. Within a thousand or so years following this combined practice of exploiting wild grains and foraging, sometime around 11,500 yBP, people began to manipulate plants' growth cycles. This manipulation was probably based on the simple observation that some seeds falling to the ground grew into new plants. People figured out what circumstances were conducive to the plants' growth, such as adequate water and protection from animals that might eat the plants. It would have been an important deduction for the people harvesting these plants to realize that if the seeds were placed in the ground, the seeds would sprout new plants that could grow to full maturity. These mature plants could then be harvested, just as the plants' wild ancestors were harvested generations before.

The archaeological record suggests that agriculture began first around lake margins in the Jordan Valley. By 8,000 yBP, early agricultural communities had sprung up across a vast swath extending from the eastern side of the Mediterranean across an arch-shaped zone of grasslands and open woodlands known as the

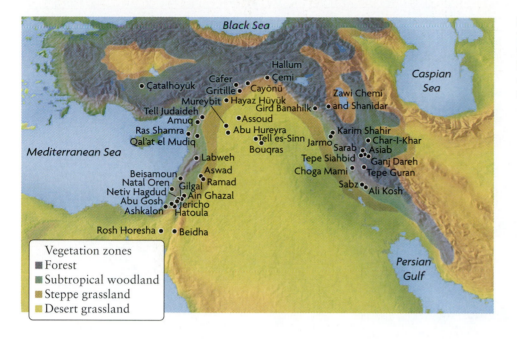

FIGURE 12.6 ◼ **Fertile Crescent**
This region of the Jordan valley has more than 50 major archaeological sites that date between 11,500 and 8,000 yBP and contain evidence of the earliest agriculture in southwestern Asia.

Fertile Crescent (**Figure 12.6**). Once domestication developed, within a short time villages sprang up; some of these villages developed into cities. For example, the early agriculture-based settlements of Jericho and Çatalhöyük, in Israel and Turkey, respectively, grew from tiny villages consisting of a few huts to the first cities, containing several or more thousands of people living in close, cramped settings (**Figure 12.7**).

Plant domestication may have been as early in China (millet and rice) as in the Levant (**Figure 12.8**). The earliest domestic rice from archaeological settings in China dates to about 6,700 yBP. By this time, the form of agriculture identified by archaeologists was well along in its development, so agriculture likely developed in

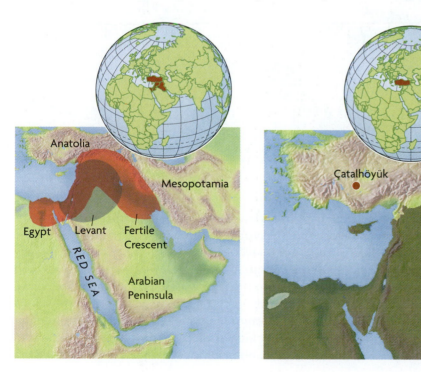

The Agricultural Revolution: New Foods, New Adaptations 323

(a)   (b)

FIGURE 12.7 ■ Çatalhöyük

(a) One of the earliest agricultural communities in southwest Asia, Çatalhöyük eventually grew into a city with a large sedentary population. (b) Skeletal remains have been discovered at the Çatalhöyük site, such as this Neolithic pregnant female. The fetus's remains can be seen in the abdominal area. Skeletons such as these provide an immense amount of information about life in this early city.

FIGURE 12.8 ■ Rice

There are more than 20 varieties of wild rice and two types of domesticated rice, the first of which was domesticated in southern Asia approximately 10,000 yBP. The second variety of domesticated rice was established in western Africa between 1500 BC and 800 BC.

China earlier than that, perhaps by several thousand years. Other early domesticated plants are from Mexico (bottle gourds, 10,000 yBP; corn, 6,300 yBP), New Guinea (taro and banana trees, 7,000 yBP), eastern North America (squash, sunflowers, and goosefoot, 6,000 yBP), South America (potatoes, sweet potatoes, and manioc, 5,250 yBP), and Africa south of the Sahara Desert (sorghum and yams, 4,500 yBP).

Like most other technological innovations, agriculture spread by diffusion out of the primary centers, usually for very long distances. Corn, for example, spread from its primary center in Mexico (probably in Oaxaca) to the American Southwest.

Eventually, corn agriculture reached North America's Atlantic coast about 1,000 yBP. The spread occurred not through people carrying corn, but through people describing their agricultural successes to neighbors, those neighbors telling their neighbors, and so forth, until the idea spread for thousands of miles over a series of generations. For some areas of North America, the adoption and intensive use of corn occurred very rapidly, perhaps within a few generations.

Another important area of the world where anthropologists have studied the origins and diffusion of agriculture consists of both far western Asia and Europe. From the primary center in the Levant, the domestication of wheat and of barley spread to central Turkey by 9,000 yBP, then to Greece by 8,000 yBP, and then throughout Europe. As in North America, agriculture spread mostly through cultural contact and the spread of knowledge—the spread of the idea of agriculture—rather than the spread of people. Some people moved, but the movement of early farmers was not widespread enough to account for the genetic diversity among humans in Europe today.

Animals were domesticated around the world, beginning with dogs at about 15,000 yBP. Some 7,000–8,000 years later, goats, sheep, cattle, and pigs were domesticated. These animals were important in Asia and later Europe, but domesticated plants were far more fundamental to the growing human populations' survival.

Survival and Growth

The importance of domestication for human evolutionary history cannot be overestimated. Domestication fueled humans' population growth in the Holocene, and it formed the foundation for the rise of complex societies, cities, and increasingly sophisticated technology. Archaeologists are learning that domesticated plants served as both a food staple and a source of drink, especially alcoholic drink. In China, for example, chemical analysis of residue inside ceramic vessels shows that as early as 9,000 yBP grapes and rice were fermented for wine.

The arrival of European explorers and colonists in the Americas had an enormous impact on the kinds of domesticated plants consumed by world populations. That is, beginning with Columbus's voyages, different plants were transported and grown throughout the world. Corn, for example, was taken back to Europe by early explorers. By the middle of the 1500s, its use as a food had spread widely, and it had become an important part of diets, especially in Africa.

Today, domesticated plants are crucial for sustaining human populations. Two-thirds of calorie and protein intake comes from the key cereal grains domesticated in the earlier Holocene, especially wheat, barley, corn, and rice. Rice has fed more people since its domestication than any other plant. It now accounts for *half* the food consumed by 1.7 billion people in the world whose diets include rice and more than 20% of all calories consumed by humans today. Rice and these other cereal grains are now aptly called **superfoods**.

superfoods Cereal grains, such as rice, corn, and wheat, that make up a substantial portion of the human population's diet today.

AGRICULTURE: AN ADAPTIVE TRADE-OFF

Most people assume that the adoption of agriculture was a highly positive development in human history. Indeed, agriculture's potential for supporting large numbers of people living in a concentrated setting, and its potential for creating surplus and thus wealth for some, laid the foundation for the great civilizations of the past—such as in China, South America, and Mexico—and those of today. Beginning with the earliest cities in the early Holocene, no complex society, anywhere in the world, would have been possible without an agricultural economic base. Writing, art, business, technology, and just about every other feature of modern life came about because of agriculture.

Population Growth

The rise of complex societies, of civilizations, and of technologically sophisticated ways to acquire both food and other resources also brought about a number of profoundly negative developments for humankind, however. Probably the single most visible characteristic associated with the shift from foraging to farming is the increase in population size and the demands that the increase places on the environment.

The growth of human population in the last 10,000 years is staggering. The world population around 10,000 yBP was probably no more than 2,000,000 or 3,000,000 people. By 2,000 yBP, population had likely increased to 250,000,000 or 300,000,000. By AD 1850, population had increased to one billion, and today it is well over six billion (**Figure 12.9**). Increasing population leads to competition for resources. As towns and cities began to compete for increasingly limited resources (e.g., arable land for crops), organized warfare developed. Interpersonal violence has a long history in human evolution, going back at least to Neandertals, in the late Pleistocene. But the level of violence in pre-Holocene hominids was nothing compared with the organized warfare of early civilizations in southwest Asia, Central America, or South America, or with the medieval wars in Europe, where up to thousands of people were killed. As the study of human remains shows, organized violence has likely been present in small societies as well.

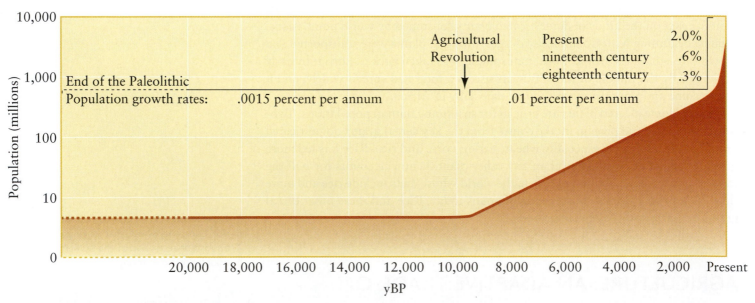

FIGURE 12.9 ■ **World Population Size**
This graph shows the trend in population size on a global scale. Until 10,000 yBP and the advent of agriculture, population remained constant, numbering less than 10,000,000 people. After the agricultural revolution, however, population skyrocketed.

Environmental Degradation

The consequences of environmental degradation, like those of extreme population growth, are well documented by historians and ecologists for recent human history. This degradation actually has a much more ancient origin, beginning with plant and animal domestication around 10,000 yBP. For much of the region surrounding the Mediterranean, including especially the Levant, landscapes have been substantially transformed and degraded. Dense settlement based on agrarian economies has contributed to soil erosion, making it increasingly difficult to produce food. Around 6000 BC, a number of large towns in the eastern Mediterranean were abandoned, probably due to a period of climate drying. Contributing to the abandonment was human activity, however, such as overgrazing with goats, which resulted in damaging erosion. Moreover, the amount of fuel, especially wood, needed to support the community resulted in the destruction of native vegetation and the desiccation of landscapes.

Likewise, the recent collapse of coastal ecosystems worldwide clearly had its start in overfishing—especially in that of large vertebrates (e.g., whales) and of shellfish—beginning thousands of years ago. Simply, the dramatically altered ecosystems worldwide have caused biodiversity to crash, a development that appears to be accelerating. The American anthropologist Jeffrey McKee argues that one primary force behind the reduction in biodiversity is expanding human population size. He predicts that if left unchecked, the population will outstrip the arable land available to produce the plants and animals consumed by humans. Thus, the increased food supply that resulted from the agricultural revolution in the Holocene could, in the not-too-distant future, lead to a food crisis.

CONCEPT CHECK | **The Good and Bad of Agriculture**

Agriculture had many advantages for human adaptation. But it also had drawbacks.

ADVANTAGES

Support for larger numbers of people
Creation of surplus food
Long-term food storage, especially of grains

DISADVANTAGES

Increased demands on the environment (land degradation)
Pollution
Conflict between populations competing for the same lands
Loss of wild species through overhunting
Decline of biodiversity
Health costs and quality-of-life implications

HOW DID AGRICULTURE AFFECT HUMAN BIOLOGICAL CHANGE?

A misperception shared by the public and anthropologists is that with the appearance of essentially modern *Homo sapiens* in the late Pleistocene, human biological evolution ground to a halt. That is, many think that humans stopped evolving biologically once they became modern, in the Upper Paleolithic. Unlike recent humans' cultural evolution (for example, increasing use of technology, development of the arts), humans' biological evolution since the closing days of the Pleistocene has gone largely unrecognized.

In the remainder of this chapter, we will examine the human biological changes that accompanied the agricultural revolution—changes linked directly or indirectly to the fundamental change, discussed above, in how humans have acquired resources, especially food. At the end of the chapter, we will revisit the question of why humans made this remarkable transition. Some very compelling reasons exist to believe that agriculture has contributed to *Homo sapiens'* evolutionary success, at least as measured by humankind's remarkable population increase since then.

Humanity's Changing Face

As discussed at the beginning of this chapter, the foods we eat and the manner in which they are prepared tremendously influence our physical appearance. The relationship between food and morphology is well illustrated by the major anatomical changes throughout human evolution. As discussed in chapter 9, the massiveness of the late australopithecines' face and jaws was clearly linked to the hard foods those hominids ate, such as seeds. Generating the power to chew hard foods required large masticatory muscles (and their boney support). Thus, the well-developed sagittal crests of some later australopithecines—such as *Australopithecus aethiopicus*—are adaptations related to chewing. Over the course of human evolution following the australopithecines, the face and jaws have continuously reduced in size and robusticity, reflecting a general decrease in the demand placed on the jaws and teeth as culture became increasingly complex and foodstuffs changed.

The reduction in size of the face and jaws is a general theme throughout human evolution, including during the Holocene and with the dietary adoption of domesticated plants. For example, in studying skulls from England that dated to the last couple of thousand years, Sir Arthur Keith documented a clear reduction in the size of the face and jaws. He believed that this reduction came about from eating soft foods, such as cooked cereal grains. Other physical anthropologists have noted similar changes in many other places of the world. In Sudan's Nile Valley—the region known as Nubia—hunter-gatherers living during the time immediately preceding agriculture had long and narrow skulls, whereas their descendants had short and wide skulls (**Figure 12.10**).

TWO HYPOTHESES To explain why the human skull changed shape in Nubia during the last 10,000 yBP, anthropologists in the 1800s and most of the 1900s offered a racial explanation. They believed that the change occurred because short-headed people invaded territory in Nubia occupied by long-headed people. These earlier anthropologists viewed head shape as unchanging and essentially a diagnostic racial marker. They were correct that humans living in specific areas of the

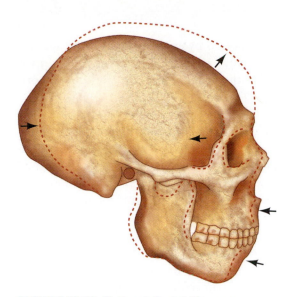

FIGURE 12.10 ■ **Craniofacial Changes**
The overall reduction in cranial size over the course of human evolution can be seen in Nubians' skeletal remains. Here, the dashed line indicates the craniofacial changes that have occurred between the Mesolithic foragers and the later agriculturalists. The skull has become shorter from front to back and, simultaneously, has gotten taller.

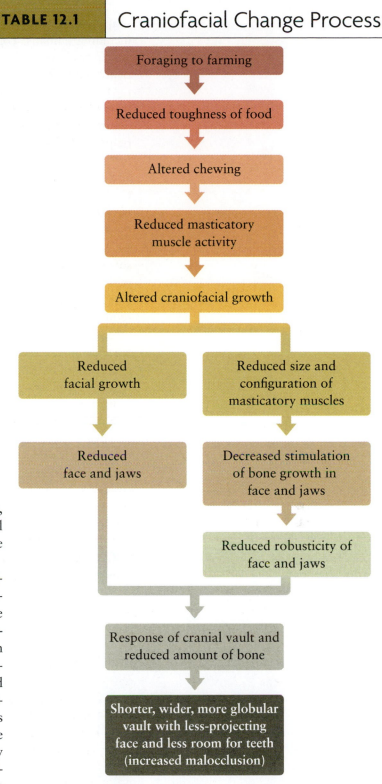

TABLE 12.1 Craniofacial Change Process

Foraging to farming

↓

Reduced toughness of food

↓

Altered chewing

↓

Reduced masticatory muscle activity

↓

Altered craniofacial growth

↓ ↓

Reduced facial growth | Reduced size and configuration of masticatory muscles

↓ ↓

Reduced face and jaws | Decreased stimulation of bone growth in face and jaws

↓

Reduced robusticity of face and jaws

↓

Response of cranial vault and reduced amount of bone

↓

Shorter, wider, more globular vault with less-projecting face and less room for teeth (increased malocclusion)

globe have physical characteristics in common. However, since then, anthropologists have learned that human facial and skull forms are highly plastic, as are other parts of the skeleton.

The American physical anthropologists David Carlson and Dennis Van Gerven have offered an alternative hypothesis, which explains differences in head shape in Nubia but can be applied globally. Their **masticatory-functional hypothesis** states that change in skull form represents a response to decreased demands on the chewing muscles—temporalis and masseter—as people shifted from eating hard-textured wild foods to eating soft-textured agricultural foods, such as millet. (**Table 12.1** lays out the hypothetical steps of this process.) To be sure, the millet grains eaten by ancient Nubians were not especially soft in their uncooked form. However, at that time, a critical change occurred in human technological evolution: the invention of pottery for storing food or cooking it. By cooking, I mean not a simple warm-up but cooking for hours until foods become soft mushes, rather easily chewed. The chewing of these mushes would have required far less-powerful muscles. Because light use of muscle produces limited bone growth, the later Nubians, eating soft foods, had reduced faces.

masticatory-functional hypothesis The hypothesis that cranial shape change during the Holocene was related to the consumption of softer foods.

Carlson and Van Gerven's explanation for much of the change in human head shape during the Holocene is strongly supported by evidence from living species, including humans. For example, experimental research shows that primates fed soft foods have a relatively shorter skull with a smaller face and jaws than do primates fed hard foods.

IMPLICATIONS FOR TEETH These changes in skull size and skull shape had enormous implications for our teeth. Today, the high numbers of people with orthodontic problems—malocclusions ranging from simple overbite to very poorly aligned teeth—contrast sharply with the few such problems found in ancient hominids and throughout much of prehistory. The American physical anthropologist James Calcagno has noted a number of exceptions, which may have influenced the size of our teeth, but malocclusions are rare prior to the modern era.

Why, then, do so many people around the globe have dental malocclusions? As with general skull shape, food plays an especially important role. Animals fed soft-textured foods develop far more occlusal abnormalities, such as crooked teeth, misaligned jaws, and chewing problems, than do animals fed hard-textured foods. The study of many thousands of skulls has shown that tooth size and jaw size have reduced in the last 10,000 yBP but at different paces. Bone is greatly subject to environmental factors, so a child fed softer foods than his or her parents ate will have appreciably reduced jaws. By contrast, teeth are controlled much more by genes, and so over the course of evolution teeth have reduced far less than jaws have. Simply, the greater reduction of the bones supporting the teeth has led to greater crowding of teeth. This disharmony underscores the complex nature of our biology, which involves an interplay between intrinsic (genetic) factors and extrinsic (environmental) factors.

Malocclusion is a clearly negative result of humans' eating soft foods. A positive result is that our teeth have very little wear, since eating soft foods places less stress on the chewing surfaces.

| CONCEPT CHECK | Soft Food and Biological Change |

The shift to agriculture and the eating of softer foods resulted in biological changes to the face, jaws, and teeth of modern people. Although not universal, some tendencies characterized the skulls and teeth of hunter-gatherers and of agriculturalists.

HUNTER-GATHERERS	AGRICULTURALISTS
Long cranial vault	Short skull
Large, robust mandible	Small, gracile mandible
Large teeth	Small teeth
Few malocclusions	Many malocclusions
Much tooth wear	Little tooth wear

Building a New Physique: Agriculture's Changes to Workload/Activity

One major debate in anthropology concerns the extent to which the agricultural revolution improved the quality of human life, including workload. Did people have to work more or work less to acquire food through agriculture rather than through hunting and gathering? The eminent American archaeologist Robert Braidwood characterized the lifestyle of a typical hunter-gatherer as "a savage's existence, and a very tough one . . . following animals just to kill them to eat, or moving from one berry patch to another." About the time Braidwood was writing this, in the 1960s, the Canadian cultural anthropologist Richard Lee and the American physical anthropologist Irven DeVore organized what turned out to be one of the most important conferences in the modern era of anthropology. They invited experts in different areas of anthropology from around the globe to determine the quality of life of hunter-gatherers, ancient and modern. A key component in assessing the quality of life was workload. If Braidwood was correct, hunter-gatherers had to work very hard, basically spending all waking hours in the food quest, getting food wherever and whenever possible. However, Lee and others reported that hunter-gatherers might not have had it all that bad when it came to workload. In fact, in his research on the Ju/'hoansi (!Kung) of southern Africa, Lee found that these hunter-gatherers had a great deal of leisure time (**Figure 12.11**).

Lee's work in the 1960s set in motion the work of a whole generation of anthropologists, who addressed both his observations and his hypotheses. Science works this way, of course—old hypotheses are often rejected as new observations are made, and new observations generate new hypotheses. Indeed, the subsequent work showed that hunter-gatherers have quite diverse workloads. Anthropologists realized that workload depended highly on the local ecology and the kinds of foods being eaten. For example, in how they acquire plants and animals, people living in the tropics differ greatly from people living in the arctic.

How do scientists know how hard or how easy a lifestyle was? Obviously, they cannot observe the behavior of dead people. Physical anthropology offers a way to reconstruct past behavior. Biomechanics, an area of great interest to physical anthropologists, provides enormous insight into the evolution of the body below the neck in relation to workload and to other activity. As with the bones of the face and of the jaws, the bones of the postcranial skeleton are highly plastic during the years of growth and of development, all the way through adulthood. The general shape and size of bones—the femur, in the leg, for example, or the humerus, in the arm—are determined by a person's genes. However, the finer details are subject to work/activity. Highly physically active people's bones tend to be larger and more developed than those of not so physically active people.

Borrowing from how engineers measure the strength of building materials—such as the "I" beam used in the construction of a bridge or of a house—physical anthropologists have developed a means for assessing the robusticity of bone cross-sections. Based on the simple premise that material placed farther away from an axis running down the center of the bone is stronger than material placed closest to the axis (**Figure 12.12**), it has become possible to look at the degree of bone development and

FIGURE 12.11 ■ Leisure Time
While foragers, such as this band of !Kung, must spend many hours searching for and hunting for food, their work does not preclude them from relaxing for periods of time. However, studies of numerous foraging groups have shown a great deal of variation in the workloads and amounts of leisure time of hunter-gatherers.

FIGURE 12.12 ■ Cross-Sectional Geometry

Using engineering principles, physical anthropologists can gain insight into activity patterns by examining the cross-sections of long bones, such as the femur and the humerus. The shapes of long bones, like those of I-beams (building materials used for structural support), maximize both strength and ability to resist bending, by distributing mass away from the center of the section.

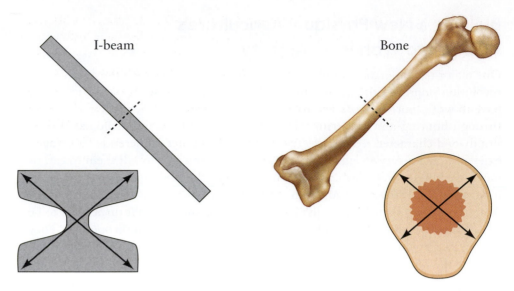

I-beam

Bone

determine by empirical means how bone strength has changed over the course of human evolution, to the present. Bone comparisons—from hunter-gatherers' to later agriculturalists' to modern peoples'—show a remarkable decline in bone size.

Physical anthropologists' studies have shown that populations respond differently to the adoption of an agricultural lifestyle. For example, in our research on

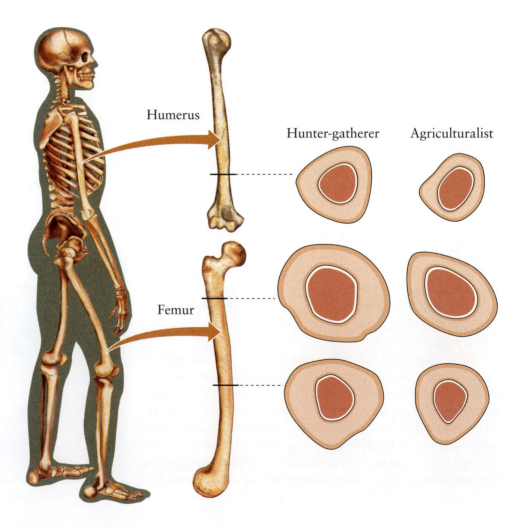

Humerus

Hunter-gatherer   Agriculturalist

Femur

FIGURE 12.13 ■ Activity Pattern Comparison

Physical anthropologists compared cross-sections of the femurs and humeri from prehistoric hunter-gatherers and agriculturalists living on the southeastern U.S. Atlantic coast (modern states of Georgia and Florida; see the opening paragraphs of chapter 1) to determine whether significant changes in the native populations' activity patterns had occurred with the shift to farming. The larger sections in the hunter-gatherers indicate greater bone strength than in their agricultural descendants. The reduced bone strength in the mission-era Indians reflects less mechanical stress in the prehistoric farmers in this setting.

skeletons from the Atlantic coast of Georgia and of Florida, Christopher Ruff and I have found that agricultural populations' bones became smaller, which we interpret to mean that those populations worked less hard than their hunter-gatherer ancestors (**Figure 12.13**). We have also found a decrease in **osteoarthritis,** a disorder of the skeletal joints that results from excessive stresses on places where the bones articulate (**Figure 12.14**). In contrast, the American physical anthropologist Patricia Bridges has discovered a clear increase in bone size in Alabama populations. Which is correct? Did workload increase or decrease? Actually, both are correct. Coastal settings involved very different means of food production than did noncoastal settings, reflecting the regions' differences in terrain and in other kinds of nonagricultural foods. On the Georgia coast, people collected seafood in addition to practicing agriculture. In noncoastal Alabama, people supplemented agriculture with terrestrial foods, such as deer.

osteoarthritis Degenerative changes of the joints caused by a variety of factors, especially physical activity and mechanical stress.

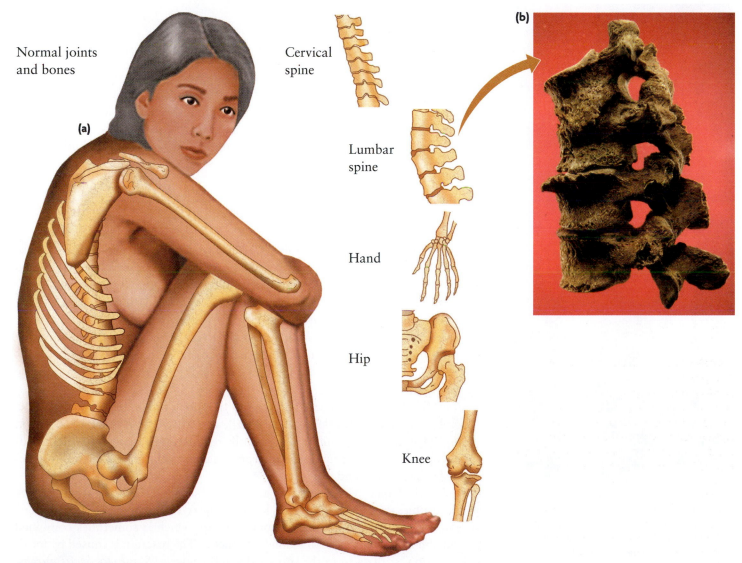

FIGURE 12.14 ■ Osteoarthritis
(a) Degenerative joint disease, or osteoarthritis, can occur in a variety of sites throughout the body, commonly in the vertebrae, hips, knees, and hands. **(b)** The lumbar vertebrae, toward the base of the spine, are often among the first bones affected by osteoarthritis. This condition results from stress on the back due to lifting and carrying, and its presence on a skeleton indicates the repetition of physically demanding activity.

Labor, Lifestyle, and Adaptation in the Skeleton

The human skeleton responds to activity, reflecting the person's lifestyle. Hunter-gatherers' skeletons and agriculturalists' skeletons vary in patterns that reveal different levels of activity, including that of workload, but hunter-gatherers' skeletons tend to show higher levels.

HUNTER-GATHERERS	AGRICULTURALISTS
Bones with higher second moments of area	Bones with lower second moments of area
Larger, more robust bones	Smaller, less robust bones
More osteoarthritis	Less osteoarthritis

FIGURE 12.15 ■ Periosteal Reaction The tibia is a common site of periosteal reactions. Here, the pathological tibia from St. Catherines Island, Georgia, on the left, has an irregular surface because new bone has been deposited unevenly. The normal tibia, on the right, has a smooth surface, free of any reactive bone.

In general, the reduction in human bone size represents an overall evolutionary trend in the last 20,000 yBP. Thanks to the increasing tool complexity and greater cultural sophistication, the biological changes came about as physical strength was replaced with technology. Ruff's studies of human remains from around the world indicate that the reduced bone mass reflects about a 10% decrease in body weight during this period.

Health and the Agricultural Revolution

POPULATION CROWDING AND INFECTIOUS DISEASE The population increase during the Holocene, discussed extensively above, was linked with agriculture and increased food production. As the population increased, communities grew more committed to raising crops and became more sedentary, living in one place the entire year. Before then, the smaller number of people had moved around at least on a seasonal basis. The increase in size and density of the population, especially when the population remained in place, had enormous, negative effects on people's health. In short, humans began to live in conditions crowded and unsanitary enough to support pathogens.

Consider the overcrowded cities around the globe today. In the urban slums of Bombay, India, or Rio de Janeiro, Brazil, or La Paz, Bolivia, or even within developed nations where sanitation is carefully regulated and monitored, the crowding sets up conditions for increased interpersonal contact and the spread of infectious microorganisms and of viruses.

During the Holocene, especially in agricultural settings, crowding seems to have produced illnesses and injuries. Any kind of injury to the outer surface of bone can cause a **periosteal reaction,** or bone buildup, which is sometimes combined with an abnormal expansion of a bone's diameter. The reaction is caused by localized infection, such as from the so-called staph bacteria, *Staphylococcus aureas.* The infection essentially stimulates new bone growth, hence the swollen appearance (**Figure 12.15**). Most periosteal reactions are nonspecific, so anthropologists cannot tell exactly what caused them. Anthropologists find, however, a general increase in periosteal reactions on the limb bones of skeletons from crowded settings in the Holocene. Such reactions are practically nonexistent in human groups predating that time.

Some infections identified on bones from Holocene populations have a specific pattern that suggests the diseases that caused them. In the American Midwest and Southeast, for example, tibias are swollen and bowed, while crania have distinctive cavitations (**Figure 12.16**). Both kinds of bone deformation are caused by a group of diseases called **treponematoses**, which include venereal syphilis, nonvenereal (also called endemic) syphilis, and yaws. Anthropologists, historians, and others debate the origin of venereal syphilis, some blaming native populations, some blaming Christopher Columbus and his ship crews, and some arguing for the appearance of a wholly new disease sometime following the initial European explorations of the New World. However, the pattern of bone changes in the New World prior to the late 1400s suggests a nonvenereal syphilis, one passed not by sexual contact but by casual contact, such as by a mother holding her child.

Many other infectious diseases likely affected Holocene populations worldwide. The skeletal indicators of tuberculosis, for example, are widespread in parts of the New World, of the Old World, and of Australia, well before the time of European exploration. For much of the mid-twentieth century, many medical practitioners thought this microbial infection had been conquered, but today, 2,000,000–3,000,000 people die annually from the disease. Other modern diseases made possible by overcrowding include but are not limited to measles, mumps, cholera, smallpox, and influenza. Some of these diseases have an Old World origin, but the New World was hardly a disease-free paradise before their introduction. Bioarchaeologists have documented many poor health conditions and evidence of physiological stress, before the Europeans' arrival, in North America and South America.

periosteal reaction Inflammatory response of a bone's outer covering due to bacterial infection or to trauma.

treponematoses A group of related diseases (venereal syphilis, yaws, endemic syphilis) caused by the bacteria *Treponema,* which causes pathological changes most often to the cranium and tibias.

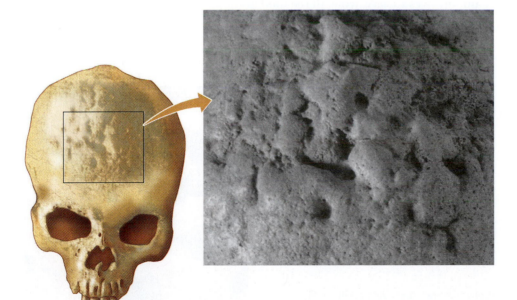

FIGURE 12.16 ■ Treponematosis
The lesions on this cranium indicate that this individual from the prehistoric southeastern United States suffered from treponematosis. The undulating surface of the skull shows active and healed lesions caused by the disease's long, slow progression.

dental caries A disease process that creates demineralized areas in dental tissues, leading to cavities; demineralization is caused by acids produced by bacteria that metabolize carbohydrates in dental plaque.

ameloblasts Cells that produce and secrete the material that becomes tooth enamel.

iron deficiency anemia A condition in which the blood has insufficient iron; may be caused by diet, poor iron absorption, parasitic infection, and severe blood loss.

heme iron Iron—found in red meat, fish, and poultry—that the body absorbs efficiently.

THE CONSEQUENCES OF DECLINING NUTRITION: TOOTH DECAY All domesticated plants have nutritional drawbacks. Because they are carbohydrates, they promote **dental caries**, commonly known as tooth decay or "cavities" (**Figure 12.17**). Caries is a process in which the natural bacteria in your mouth—common culprits are *Streptococcus mutans* and *Lactobacillus acidophilus*—digest the carbohydrates there. One end product of this digestive process is lactic acid, which literally dissolves teeth's enamel. In industrial societies today, dentists stabilize caries by removing diseased parts of teeth and filling the cavities with amalgam. In the ancient world, dentistry was mostly nonexistent, and cavities grew until the teeth fell out or, in some instances, people with cavities died from secondary infections.

Different domesticated plants promote tooth decay at varying rates. Rice does not seem to cause it to the same extent as other domesticated plants. Corn causes it considerably. Once post–AD 800 populations in eastern North America had adopted corn agriculture, the frequency of their dental caries rose dramatically (**Figure 12.18**).

NUTRITIONAL CONSEQUENCES DUE TO MISSING NUTRIENTS: REDUCED GROWTH AND ABNORMAL DEVELOPMENT The popular and the academic literatures suggest that agriculture has improved humans' nutrition. This conclusion makes sense given the huge worldwide investment in agriculture, even today. However, the assessment of superfoods' nutritional content argues otherwise.

All agricultural settings have the potential to impede normal growth and development, because of their nutritional limitation. Dietary reconstructions of past societies by archaeologists and studies of living agrarian populations in different settings indicate that agriculturalists' diets tend to overemphasize one plant or a couple of them, such as rice in Asia, wheat in Europe and temperate Asia, corn in the Americas, and millet or sorghum in Africa. Thus, many groups, especially in the later Holocene, received poor nutrition from an increasingly narrow range of foods. A well-balanced diet, as your parents and teachers have told you time and again, involves variety, from all the food groups.

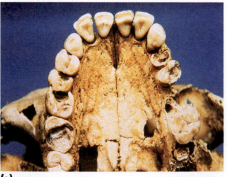
(a)

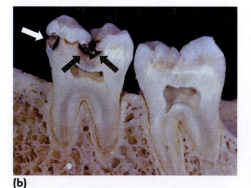
(b)

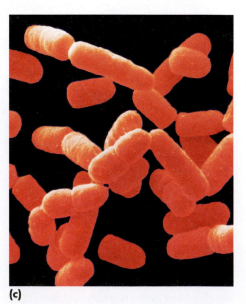
(c)

FIGURE 12.17 ■ **Dental Caries**
(a) Cavities are more common in individuals with carbohydrate-rich diets. As a result of the digestion of carbohydrates, carious lesions form as the teeth's enamel deteriorates. In extreme cases, the teeth's pulp can be affected. **(b)** This cross-section of a tooth affected by dental caries shows two common locations of cavities: the occlusal, or chewing, surface (black arrows); between successive teeth (white arrow). **(c)** *Lactobacillus* is one of the two main bacteria that cause dental caries.

Domesticated plants have nutritional value, of course, but they also present a range of negative nutritional consequences. For example, corn is deficient in the amino acids lysine, isoleucine, and tryptophan, and a person who does not receive the right amount of even one amino acid will neither grow normally nor develop properly. In addition, vitamin B_3 (niacin) in corn is bound chemically, and corn contains phytate, a chemical that binds with iron and hampers the body's iron absorption. Grains such as millet and wheat contain very little iron. Rice is deficient in protein and thus inhibits vitamin A activity.

Numerous societies worldwide have developed strategies for improving these foods' nutritional content. For example, corn-dependent populations commonly treat corn with alkali by cooking it with lime. This treatment increases the ratios of amino acids, improving the quality of the protein. Such treatments cannot, however, make up for the negative consequences of dietary overreliance on these plants.

One of the most obvious ways of assessing the impact of nutritional change in the Holocene is by looking at the growth of bones and of teeth. Like any other body tissues, bones and teeth grow to their full genetic potential only if they receive proper nutrition. Anthropologists are able to identify a few indicators of growth stress in skeletal and dental records from fossils, but these indicators are generally nonspecific—that is, they are not linked to a precise cause (for example, a particular vitamin that the person was deficient in). These stress indicators are also related to multiple factors that may or may not include nutrition. Nonnutritional factors often include infection or infectious disease. As studies of living populations have shown, nutrition and infection have a synergistic relationship: poor nutrition worsens the infection, and vice versa; essential nutrition is used to fight the infection and is taken away from the growth process. Despite such complications, anthropologists have found these indicators to be very informative about the history of stress both in individuals and in populations.

Deficiencies in dental enamel are one of the most important nonspecific stress indicators. Typically, the deficiencies appear as lines, pits, or grooves, any of which occur when the cells responsible for enamel production (called **ameloblasts**) are disrupted. As a result of the disruption, the cells do not deposit enough of the substance that turns into mature enamel. Consequently, when the disturbance ends (the illness or the infection is over) a defect, or hypoplasia, is left (**Figure 12.19**). Defects of this kind are commonplace in earlier humans' teeth—indeed, researchers have found them in australopithecines—but they are rare throughout most of human evolution. Some hunter-gatherer populations have high frequencies, but hypoplasias became relatively common in Holocene populations. The high frequency in agriculturalists around the world was caused by two factors: decline in nutritional quality and increase in infectious disease. (Other dental defects, visible in microscopic sections of teeth, reflect very short-term stress episodes, lasting several hours to several days. Virtually everyone has microscopic defects in the deciduous teeth, created as a result of birth stress.)

NUTRITIONAL CONSEQUENCES OF IRON DEFICIENCY Other markers of stress and of deprivation in agricultural populations can be linked to specific causes. **Iron deficiency anemia**, a problem that plagues many millions of people around the globe, results when the body receives limited iron. Iron is necessary for many body functions and is an essential element in hemoglobin, serving in the transport of oxygen to the body tissues. Iron—specifically, **heme iron**—enters the body easily through meat-eating, since meat does not require processing in the stomach, and since the amino acids from the digestion of meat promote iron absorption. Iron from

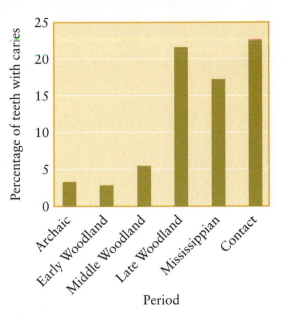

FIGURE 12.18 ■ **Changes in Oral Health**
This chart shows temporal changes in dental caries in eastern North America. During the Archaic, Early Woodland, and Middle Woodland periods, which predate AD 800, the region's native inhabitants were hunter-gatherers. During the Late Woodland, Mississippian, and Contact periods, which postdate AD 1000, the adoption of agriculture caused a large increase in dental caries.

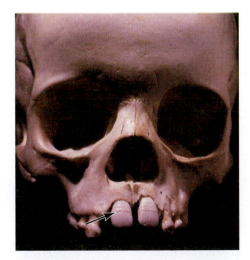

FIGURE 12.19 ■ **Enamel Hypoplasias**
These defects reflect stress episodes that occurred during tooth development. Individuals with multiple hypoplasias on each tooth underwent several stress episodes.

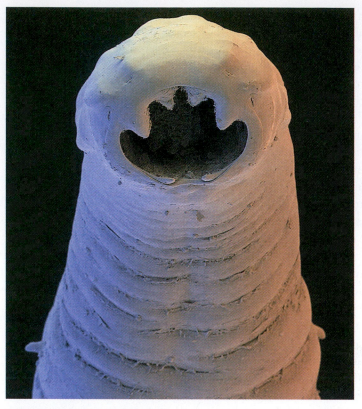

FIGURE 12.20 ■ **Hookworm**
Parasites, such as this hookworm, can cause iron deficiency. Today, hookworms are commonly found in subtropical regions such as North Africa and India.

nonheme iron Iron—found in lentils and beans—that is less efficiently absorbed by the body than is heme iron.

porotic hyperostosis Expansion and porosity of cranial bones due to anemia caused by an iron-deficient diet, parasitic infection, or genetic disease.

cribra orbitalia Porosity in the eye orbits due to anemia caused by an iron-deficient diet, parasitic infection, or genetic disease.

plants—**nonheme iron**—is not as readily available, because various substances in plants inhibit iron absorption (see the above discussion on corn). Citric acid found in various fruits, however, may promote iron absorption.

Some authorities believe that iron deficiency is rarely caused by dietary stress and is more often related to nondietary factors. Parasitic infections, for example, are a primary cause of iron deficiency anemia in many regions of the globe. One such infection, hookworm disease, is caused when someone inhales or ingests hookworm larvae. The worm (*Ancylostoma duodenale, Necator americanus*) extracts blood from its human host by using the sharp teethlike structures in its head to latch itself to the intestinal wall (**Figure 12.20**). When several hundred or more of these worms are present, severe blood loss—and therefore anemia—can result.

Abundant evidence of anemia exists among skeletons in numerous settings worldwide. In response to anemia, red blood cells increase in production, potentially leading to **porotic hyperostosis** in skulls and **cribra orbitalia** in eye orbits (**Figure 12.21**). These abnormalities were quite rare before the Holocene, but then suddenly appeared, especially in agricultural groups.

NUTRITIONAL CONSEQUENCES: HEIGHTS ON THE DECLINE In many regions where farming was adopted, adult heights declined appreciably. That people simply stopped growing as tall has been documented in western Europe, the eastern Mediterranean, Nubia, South Asia, the Ohio River valley, and central Illinois. The physical anthropologists Lourdes Márquez and Andrés del Ángel have found a general decline in height among the Maya of the first millennium AD, a time in which this

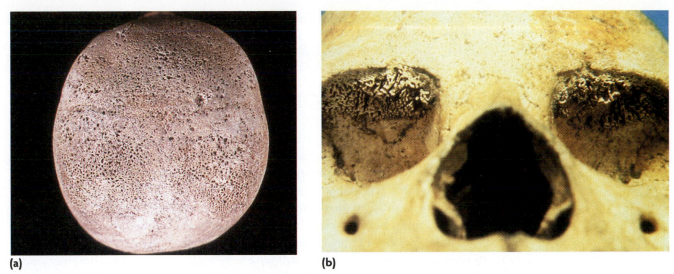

(a) **(b)**

FIGURE 12.21 ■ **Porotic Hyperostosis and Cribra Orbitalia**
(a) In porotic hyperostosis, which results from anemia, the cranial bones become porous as the marrow cavities expand from the increased production of red blood cells. **(b)** Anemia can also give the eye orbits a porous appearance, called cribra orbitalia.

ancient civilization experienced a deterioration in environment and in living circumstances. Thus, for some groups shorter height might have been the biological result of adopting agriculture, but for other groups it might have been an adaptation to reduced resources, since smaller bodies require less food. However, all the human populations whose height decreased due to stress also experienced elevated infectious disease loads, anemia, malnutrition and other factors indicating that a

CONCEPT CHECK	Health Costs of Agriculture	

Due to population increase, crowding, and poor nutrition, human populations' health declined in many settings globally.

HEALTH INDICATOR	HUNTER-GATHERERS	AGRICULTURALISTS
Infection (periosteal reactions)	Low	High
Dental caries	Low	High
Child growth and development	Normal	Reduced
Enamel defects (hypoplasias, microdefects)	Low	High
Iron deficiency (porotic hyperostosis, cribra orbitalia)	Low	High
Adult height	Normal	Reduced

smaller body does not confer an adaptive advantage. These people were smaller but not healthier.

IF IT IS SO BAD FOR YOU, WHY FARM?

This question brings us back to some points about evolution raised in earlier chapters. Namely, the key components of evolution are survival to the reproductive years and production of offspring. One documented fact about the Holocene is that during this time human fertility greatly increased. That women gave birth to more babies was likely made possible by the spacing out of births in agricultural groups. Simply, because women are settled and not spending time moving about the landscape, they can bear children more frequently. Therefore, a population with a reduced quality of life might still have very high fertility. This combination, of course, is present throughout much of the developing world, such as in Peru, Bangladesh, Mexico, and Thailand.

We have seen the evidence—a huge record—showing that the adoption of agriculture resulted in the development and spread of infectious disease and a reduction in health generally. Agriculture's positive side is that it provides both more calories per unit of land and the resources for population increase. And evolution dictates that organisms, including humans, engage in behaviors that increase the potential for and outcome of reproduction.

THE PAST IS OUR FUTURE

We can learn a lot about our future by paying attention to what has happened in the past. The global state of human health has been a driving force in our evolution and will continue to drive our future evolution.

This chapter has emphasized humans' foraging-to-farming transition and especially the domestication of plants, changes that laid the foundation for our continued population increase (today, there are more than 6.5 billion humans), the concentration of populations in large urban agglomerations (more than 50% of the 6.5 billion live in cities), and the shift in many regions of the globe from highly varied diets to diets focused on saturated fat and carbohydrates. This dietary shift is resulting in an epidemic of obesity. Obesity, in turn, along with humans' increasingly sedentary lifestyles, is an important factor in explaining the rising incidence of degenerative conditions including osteoporosis, cardiovascular disease, respiratory disease, diabetes, and depression.

We also face the threat of **global warming**. This alarming development is the result of "greenhouse gases" (carbon dioxide and methane, especially) brought about by the burning of fossil fuels, and it has been exacerbated by the increasing lack of vegetation and natural land cover. Concentrations of elevated heat, produced from roads and rooftops and other heat-storing materials, are producing abnormally high temperatures. These circumstances, in addition to putting an unprecedented strain on food resources, are yielding what the United Nations has recently called a global "silent tsunami" of deaths due to infectious disease. For example, higher temperatures and loss of land cover increase the breeding of mosquitoes, which in turn help spread pathogens such as those associated with malaria.

How might global warming, if left unchecked, affect future generations? Experts predict that the increasingly warmer planet will see major shifts in precipitation patterns, resulting in desertification in areas of the globe that are now productive. Those people most profoundly affected by the resulting decrease in the world food supply will be those already living in marginal circumstances, such as in vast areas of Africa, Asia, and Latin America.

OUR ONGOING EVOLUTION

Huge changes are affecting this planet and the human (and other) populations occupying it. These changes have real meaning for our future, including our evolution. But is there evidence of ongoing biological change in general and evolution in particular? In a word, plenty. Owing to technological innovations and their effects, humans are the most dominant evolutionary force on the other living organisms. Even before the Swiss chemist Paul Müller could receive the Nobel Prize in 1948 for his discovery that DDT killed insects, house flies' resistance to this chemical was being reported (**Figure 12.22**). By 1990, some 500 mosquito species had developed resistance to DDT, dashing the hopes that malaria could be eradicated. Bacteria associated with horrific infections have developed resistance to antibiotics, such as penicillin and tetracycline. Today, hospitals report that bacteria such as *Staphylococcus aureus* are almost always resistant to penicillin. The evolution of new, antibiotic-resistant strains of *Mycobacterium tuberculosis* is a big part of the dramatic rise in human deaths from this disease—more than 3,000,000 people die per year. Other human-influenced evolution is also reported in a range of other organisms. For example, fish are evolving slower growth and thinner bodies owing to overfishing. Salmon males are under strong selection for smaller size, and they are returning to the sea earlier to increase their survival. These are but a few of the many examples of the pervasive evolution resulting from human presence and activity. Thus the natural world is rapidly changing, in large part due to humans. The changes are **anthropogenic**.

Evolution began in the remote past, but it remains ongoing in humans and in other organisms. Few evolutionary biologists are comfortable with predicting future evolution, mainly because evolution is nonlinear and its course depends on

anthropogenic Refers to any effect caused by humans.

FIGURE 12.22 ■ DDT Resistance
Many countries have used DDT, the first modern pesticide, for decades. As a result, numerous insects, such as the fruit fly (shown here). have developed a resistance to it. In 1972, the United States banned DDT because its use caused a serious decline in birds, such as the bald eagle.

current—that is, ever-changing—circumstances. The pioneers of evolutionary biology, in the eighteenth century, could not have predicted the dramatic changes the peppered moth underwent in the nineteenth and twentieth centuries, for example. Today, the evolutionary record makes clear that evolution, whatever its forms, *will* continue.

Other inarguable predictions about the future world are that humans will continue to consume energy, human population size will continue to increase, and the global climate will continue to change. Left unchecked, these factors will present organisms with increasing challenges and perhaps new selective pressures. This chapter has painted a rather dark picture about our changing world—as we have more and more impact on the planet and its environment, we seem to be on a collision course with disaster. Just as humans have helped create these environmental changes, they will need to develop means of slowing global warming, most likely by modifying technologies and lifestyles to limit the production of greenhouse gases.

One key theme in this book is that humans adapt remarkably well to novel circumstances, and an enormous component of this resilience is culture, especially technology and material culture in general. Some technology has negatively influenced the world, including the technology associated with industrialization and the burning of fossil fuels. At the same time, human technology has produced a growing global economy and ways of producing more food, increasing the population, and living longer.

Scientists expect some regions of the world to be hit hard by temperature change and environmental disruption. Still, the record of human evolution over the last 5,000,000 yBP suggests that humans will develop means for dealing with such problems. Time will tell if humans are able to use culture, intelligence, and innovation to thrive in this changing world. That has been the story so far, and I believe it will continue.

ANSWERING THE BIG QUESTIONS

When, where, and why did agriculture first develop?

- The Holocene epoch—the most recent 10,000 years—was not a static period in human evolution or in biological change generally. During this time, *Homo sapiens* dramatically altered their diets to include for the first time domesticated plants and domesticated animals.
- The earliest agriculture occurred in the eastern Mediterranean (the Levant). It arose in at least 10–11 other centers independently around the world.
- Plant and animal domestication may have arisen to feed the ever-increasing human population.

How did agriculture affect human living circumstances?

- Agriculture (and associated population increase) resulted in population sedentism and crowding. Accumulation of waste and increased transmission of microbes owing to crowding provided the conditions conducive to the spread and maintenance of infectious disease.
- Agricultural foods shifted nutrition from a generalized diet to one focused on carbohydrates and poorer-quality protein.
- In most settings, agriculture caused a decline in workload/activity.

How did agriculture affect human biological change?

- Wherever the shift from foraging to farming occurred, quality of diet declined owing to a decrease in the breadth of diet and a reduction in the nutritional quality of foods eaten.
- Poorer-quality diets led to a decline in health as foragers became farmers.

- The shift from hard foods to soft ones resulted in a generally shorter and rounder cranial vault, along with a smaller face and smaller jaws. The bone supporting the teeth reduced in size faster than the teeth reduced. As a result, humans now have many more orthodontics issues requiring the artificial straightening of teeth.
- Decreased workload/activity resulted in a general tendency toward increased gracilization of the skeleton.
- The decline in health did not affect human populations' reproductive performance worldwide. For much of human evolution, population size was likely well under 1,000,000, but it perhaps grew to several million by the close of the Pleistocene. Today, the human population exceeds six *billion* people.

What are the most important forces shaping human biology today?

- Global warming is altering the environment. If left unchecked, it potentially will threaten food production and have continued negative impacts on health.
- Population increase is placing a burden on our resources and well-being.
- Population increase and associated crowding leads to poor sanitation and enhances the spread of existing and newly emerging infectious diseases.

Are we still evolving?

- There is abundant evidence of continued evolution in humans and other organisms.
- Little can be said about future evolution. If envirionmental circumstances (global warming, for example) continue in their predicted direction, almost certainly conditions eliciting evolutionary change will occur.

KEY TERMS

ameloblasts
anthropogenic
dental caries
domestication
global warming
heme iron
iron deficiency anemia
masticatory-functional hypothesis

Neolithic
nonheme iron
osteoarthritis
periosteal reaction
porotic hyperostosis
superfoods
treponematoses

ADDITIONAL READINGS

Bridges, P. S. 1996. Skeletal biology and behavior in ancient humans. *Evolutionary Anthropology* 4: 112–120.

Caballero, B. C. and Popkin, B. M. 2002. *The Nutrition Transition: Diet and Disease in the Developing World*. London: Academic Press.

Cohen, M. N. 1989. *Health and the Rise of Civilization*. New Haven: Yale University Press.

Garrett, L. 1994. *The Coming Plague: Newly Emerging Diseases in a World out of Balance*. New York: Farrar, Straus, & Giroux.

Larsen, C. S. 1995. Biological changes in human populations with agriculture. *Annual Review of Anthropology* 24: 185–213.

Palumbi, S. R. 2001. Humans as the world's greatest evolutionary force. *Science* 293: 1786–1790.

Ruff, C. B. 2000. Biomechanical analyses of archaeological human skeletons. Pp. 71–102 in M. A. Katzenberg and S. R. Saunders, eds. *Biological Anthropology of the Human Skeleton*. New York: Wiley-Liss.

Smith, B. D. 1995. *The Emergence of Agriculture*. New York: Scientific American Library.

Glossary

abnormal hemoglobin Hemoglobin altered so that it is less efficient in binding to and carrying oxygen.

Acheulian Complex The culture associated with *H. erectus,* including hand axes and other types of stone tools; more refined than the earlier Oldowan tools.

adapids Euprimates of the Eocene that were likely ancestral to modern lemurs and possibly ancestral to anthropoids.

Adapis A genus of adapids from the Eocene.

adaptations Changes in physical structure, function, or behavior that allow an organism or species to survive and reproduce in a given environment.

adaptive radiation The diversification of an ancestral group of organisms into new forms that are adapted to specific environmental niches.

adenine One of four nitrogen bases that make up DNA and RNA; it pairs with thymine in DNA molecules and uracil in RNA molecules.

adenosine triphosphate (ATP) An important cellular molecule, created by the mitochondria and carrying the energy necessary for cellular functions.

admixture The exchange of genetic material between two or more populations.

adult stage The third stage of life, involving the reproductive years and senescence.

Aegyptopithecus A propliopithecid genus from the Oligocene, probably ancestral to catarrhines; the largest primate found in the Fayum, Egypt.

aging The process of maturation.

allele One or more alternative forms of a gene.

Allen's Rule The principle that an animal's limb lengths are heat-related; limbs are longer in hot environments and shorter in cold environments.

altruistic Refers to a behavior that benefits others while being a disadvantage to the individual.

ameloblasts Cells that produce and secrete the material that becomes tooth enamel.

amino acid dating An absolute dating method for organic remains such as bone or shell, in which the amount of change in the amino acid structure is measured.

amino acids Organic molecules combined in a specific sequence to form a protein.

anatomical Pertaining to an organism's physical structure.

angiosperm radiation hypothesis The proposition that certain primate traits, such as visual acuity, occurred in response to the availability of fruit and flowers following the spread of angiosperms.

anthropogenic Refers to any effect caused by humans.

anthropology The study of humankind, viewed from the perspective of all people and all times.

anthropometry The study of the sizes and proportions of the human body.

antibodies Molecules that form as part of the primary immune response to the presence of foreign substances; they attach to the foreign antigens.

anticodons Sequences of three nitrogen bases carried by tRNA, they match up with the complementary mRNA codons and each designate a specific amino acid during protein synthesis.

antigens Substances, such as bacteria, foreign blood cells, and enzymes, that stimulate the immune system's antibody production.

Apidium A parapithecid genus from the Oligocene, possibly ancestral to anthropoids.

arboreal Tree-dwelling; adapted to living in the trees.

arboreal adaptation A suite of physical traits that enable an organism to live in trees.

arboreal hypothesis The proposition that primates' unique suite of traits is an adaptation to living in trees.

archaeology The study of historic or prehistoric human populations through the analysis of material remains.

Ardipithecus kadabba An early pre-australopithecine species from the late Miocene to the early Pliocene; shows evidence of a perihoning complex, a primitive trait intermediate between apes and modern humans.

Ardipithecus ramidus A later pre-australopithecine species from the late Miocene to the early Pliocene; shows evidence of both bipedalism and arboreal activity but no indication of the primitive perihoning complex.

artifacts Material objects from past cultures.

Australopithecus aethiopicus An early robust australopithecine from East Africa, with the hallmark physical traits of large teeth, large face, and massive muscle attachments on the cranium.

Australopithecus afarensis An early australopithecine from East Africa that had a brain size equivalent to a modern chimpanzee's and was thought to be a direct human ancestor.

Australopithecus africanus A gracile australopithecine from South Africa that was contemporaneous with *A. aethiopicus, A. garhi,* and *A. boisei* and was likely ancestral to *A. robustus.*

Australopithecus anamensis The oldest species of australopithecine from East Africa and a likely ancestor to *A. afarensis.*

Australopithecus boisei Formerly known as *Zinjanthropus boisei;* a later robust australopithecine from East Africa that was contemporaneous with *A. robustus* and *A. africanus* and had the robust cranial traits, including large teeth, large face, and heavy muscle attachments.

Australopithecus garhi A late australopithecine from East Africa that was contemporaneous with *A. africanus* and *A. aethiopicus* and was the likely ancestor to the *Homo* lineage.

Australopithecus (or *Kenyanthropus*) *platyops* An australopithecine from East Africa that had a unique flat face and was contemporaneous with *A. afarensis.*

Australopithecus robustus A robust australopithecine from South Africa that may have descended from *A. afarensis,* was contemporaneous with *A. boisei,* and had the robust cranial traits of large teeth, large face, and heavy muscle attachments.

autosomes All chromosomes, except the sex chromosomes, that occur in pairs in all somatic cells (not the gametes).

balanced polymorphism Situation in which selection maintains two or more phenotypes for a specific gene in a population.

basal anthropoids Eocene primates that are possibly ancestral to anthropoids.

basal metabolic rate (BMR) The rate at which an organism's body, while at rest, expends energy to maintain basic bodily functions; measured by the amount of heat given off per kilogram of body weight.

basal metabolic requirement The minimum amount of energy needed to keep an organism alive.

Bergmann's Rule The principle that an animal's size is heat-related; smaller bodies are adapted to hot environments, and larger bodies are adapted to cold environments.

bilophodont Refers to lower molars, in Old World monkeys, that have two ridges.

biocultural approach The scientific study of the interrelationship between what humans have inherited genetically and culture.

biological (physical) anthropology The study of the evolution, variation, and adaptation of humans and their past and present relatives.

biostratigraphic dating A relative dating method that uses the associations of fossils in strata to determine each layer's approximate age.

bipedalism Walking on two feet.

Biretia A later basal anthropoid genus found in the Fayum, Egypt, that may be ancestral to anthropoids.

blending inheritance An outdated, disreputed theory that the phenotype of an offspring was a uniform blend of the parents' phenotypes.

bone mass The density of bone per unit of measure.

brachiators Organisms that move by brachiation, or arm-swinging.

Branisella A South American genus from the Oligocene, ancestral to platyrrhines.

canine-premolar honing complex The dental form in which the upper canines are sharpened against the lower third premolars when the jaws are closed.

capillaries Small blood vessels between the terminal ends of arteries and the veins.

Carpolestes A plesiadapiform genus from the Paleocene, probably ancestral to the Eocene euprimates.

catastrophism The doctrine asserting that cataclysmic events (such as volcanoes, earthquakes, and floods), rather than evolutionary processes, are responsible for geologic changes throughout Earth's history.

Cenozoic The era lasting from 65 mya until the present, encompassing the radiation and proliferation of mammals such as humans and other primates.

C$_4$ plants Plants that take in carbon through C$_4$ photosynthesis, which changes carbon dioxide into a compound with four carbon atoms. These plants tend to be from warmer regions with low humidity and include corn, sugarcane, millet, and prickly pear.

chemical dating Dating methods that use predictable chemical changes that occur over time.

chromosomes The strand of DNA found in the nucleus of eukaryotes that contains hundreds or thousands of genes.

cline A gradual change in some phenotypic characteristic from one population to the next.

Clovis Earliest Native American ("Paleoindian") culture of North America; technology known for large, fluted, bifacial stone projectile points used as spear points for big game hunting.

coding DNA Sequences of a gene's DNA (also known as exons) that are coded to produce a specific protein and are transcribed and translated during protein synthesis.

codominance Refers to two different alleles that are equally dominant; both are fully expressed in a heterozygote's phenotype.

codons The sequences of three nitrogen bases carried by mRNA that are coded to produce specific amino acids in protein synthesis.

cognitive abilities Refers to the capacity of the brain to perceive, process, and judge information from the surrounding environment.

complementary bases The predictable pairing of nitrogen bases in the structure of DNA and RNA, such that adenine and thymine always pair together (adenine and uracil in RNA) and cytosine and guanine pair together.

cribra orbitalia Porosity in the eye orbits due to anemia caused by an iron-deficient diet, parasitic infection, or genetic disease.

cross-over The process by which homologous chromosomes partially wrap around each other and exchange genetic information during meiosis.

C$_3$ plants Plants that take in carbon through C$_3$ photosynthesis, which changes carbon dioxide into a compound having three carbon atoms. Tending to be from more temperate regions, these plants include wheat, sugar beets, peas, and a range of hardwood trees.

cultural anthropology The study of modern human societies through the analysis of the origins, evolution, and variation of culture.

cultural dating Relative dating methods that are based on material remains' time spans.

culture Learned behavior that is transmitted from person to person.

cytoplasm The jellylike substance inside the cell membrane that surrounds the nucleus and in which the organelles are suspended.

cytosine One of four nitrogen bases that make up DNA and RNA; it pairs with guanine.

data Evidence gathered to help answer questions, solve problems, and fill gaps in scientific knowledge.

deciduous dentition Also known as baby teeth or milk teeth, this is the first set of teeth, which form in utero and erupt shortly after birth.

deme A local population of organisms that have similar genes, interbreed, and produce offspring.

demic diffusion A population's movement into an area previously uninhabited by that group.

demography The study of a population's features and vital statistics, including birth rate, death rate, population size, and population density.

dendrochronology A chronometric dating method that uses a tree-ring count to determine numerical age.

dental caries A disease process that creates demineralized areas in dental tissues, leading to cavities; demineralization is caused by acids produced by bacteria that metabolize carbohydrates in dental plaque.

dental formula The numerical description of a species' teeth, listing the number, in one quadrant of the jaws, of incisors, canines, premolars, and molars.

deoxyribonucleic acid (DNA) A double-stranded molecule that provides the genetic code for an organism, consisting of phosphate, deoxyribose sugar, and four types of nitrogen bases.

diaphyses The main midsection, or shaft, portions of long bones; each contains a medullary cavity.

diastema A space between two teeth.

dietary plasticity A diet's flexibility in adapting to a given environment.

diploid A cell that has a full complement of paired chromosomes.

directional selection Selection for one allele over the other alleles, causing the allele frequencies to shift in one direction.

disruptive selection Selection for both extremes of the phenotypic distribution; may eventually lead to a speciation event.

diurnal Refers to those organisms that normally are awake and active during daylight hours.

domestication The process of converting wild animals or wild plants into forms that humans can care for and cultivate.

dominant Refers to an allele that is expressed in an organism's phenotype and that simultaneously masks the effects of another allele, if another one is present.

dryopithecids Early Miocene apes found in various locations in Europe.

Dryopithecus A genus of dryopithecid apes found in southern France.

electron spin resonance dating An absolute dating method that uses microwave spectroscopy to measure electrons' spins in various materials.

empirical Verified through observation and experiment.

endogamous Refers to a population in which individuals breed only with other members of the population.

Eoanthropus dawsoni The species name given to the cranium and mandible in the Piltdown hoax.

Eosimias A genus of very small basal anthropoids from the Eocene.

epiphyses The end portions of long bones; once they fuse to the diaphyses, the bones stop growing longer.

epochs Divisions of periods (which are the major divisions of eras) in geologic time.

equilibrium A condition in which the system is stable, balanced, and unchanging.

eras Major divisions of geologic time that are divided into periods and further subdivided into epochs.

essential amino acids Those amino acids that cannot be synthesized in the body; they must be supplied by the diet.

eukaryotes Multicelled organisms that have a membrane-bound nucleus containing both the genetic material and specialized organelles.

euprimates The first true primates from the Eocene: the tarsierlike omomyids and the lemurlike adapids.

evolutionary biology A specialty within the field of biology; the study of the process of change in organisms.

evolutionary synthesis A unified theory of evolution that combines genetics with natural selection.

exogamous Refers to a population in which individuals breed only with nonmembers of their population.

fission track dating An absolute dating method based on the measurement of the number of tracks left by the decay of uranium-238.

fitness Average number of offspring produced by parents with a particular genotype compared to the number of offspring produced by parents with another genotype.

fluorine dating A relative (chemical) dating method that compares the accumulation of fluorine in animal and human bones from the same site.

Folsom Early Native American (immediately following Clovis) culture of North America; technology known for large, fluted, bifacial projectile points used as spear points for big game hunting.

foraminifera Marine protozoans that have variably shaped shells with small holes.

forensic anthropology The scientific examination of skeletons in hope of identifying the people whose bodies they came from.

fossils Physical remains of part or all of once-living organisms, mostly bones and teeth, that have become mineralized by the replacement of organic materials with inorganic materials.

founder effect The accumulation of random genetic changes in a small population that has become isolated from the parent population due to the genetic input of only a few colonizers.

frameshift mutation The change in a gene due to the insertion or deletion of one or more nitrogen bases, which causes the subsequent triplets to be rearranged and the codons to be read incorrectly during translation.

free-floating nucleotides Nucleotides (the basic building block of DNA and RNA) that are present in the nucleus and are used during DNA replication and mRNA synthesis.

functional adaptations Biological changes that occur during an individual's lifetime, increasing the individual's fitness in the given environment.

gametes Sexual reproductive cells, ova and sperm, that have a haploid number of chromosomes and that can unite with a gamete of the opposite sex to form a new organism.

gemmules As proposed by Darwin, the units of inheritance, supposedly accumulated in the gametes so they could be passed on to offspring.

gene The basic unit of inheritance; a sequence of DNA on a chromosome, coded to produce a specific protein.

gene flow Admixture, or the exchange of alleles between two populations.

gene pool All the genetic information in the breeding population.

genetic drift The random change in allele frequency from one generation to the next, with greater effect in small populations.

genome The complete set of chromosomes for an organism or species that represents all the inheritable traits.

genomics The branch of genetics that studies species' genomes.

genotype The genetic makeup of an organism; the combination of alleles for a given gene.

genus A group of related species.

geology The study of Earth's physical history.

Gigantopithecus A genus of Miocene pongids from Asia; the largest primate that ever lived.

global warming The increase in the average temperature of Earth's atmosphere in response to the greenhouse effect; a cause of climate change.

glucose-6-phosphate dehydrogenase (G6PD) An enzyme that aids in the proper functioning of red blood cells; its deficiency, a genetic condition, leads to hemolytic anemia.

growth velocity The speed with which an organism grows in size, often measured as the amount of growth per year.

guanine One of four nitrogen bases that make up DNA and RNA; it pairs with cytosine.

habitat The specific area of the natural environment in which an organism lives.

habituate Refers to the process of animals becoming accustomed to human observers.

half-life The time it takes for half of the radioisotopes in a substance to decay; used in various radiometric dating methods.

handaxe The most dominant tool in the Acheulian complex, characterized by a sharp edge for both cutting and scraping.

haplogroups A large set of haplotypes, such as the Y-chromosome or mitochondrial DNA, that may be used to define a population.

haploid A cell that has a single set of unpaired chromosomes, half of the genetic material.

haplotypes A group of alleles that tend to be inherited as a unit due to their closely spaced loci on a single chromosome.

Hardy-Weinberg law of equilibrium A mathematical model in population genetics that reflects the relationship between frequencies of alleles and of genotypes; it can be used to determine whether a population is undergoing evolutionary changes.

heme iron Iron—found in red meat, fish, and poultry—that the body absorbs efficiently.

hemoglobinopathies A group of related genetic blood diseases characterized by abnormal hemoglobin.

hemolytic anemias Conditions of insufficient iron in the blood due to the destruction of red blood cells resulting from genetic blood diseases, toxins, or infectious pathogens.

heritability The proportion of phenotypic variation that is due to inheritance rather than to environmental influence.

heteroplasmic Refers to a mixture of more than one type of organellar DNA, such as mitochondrial DNA, within a cell or a single organism's body, usually due to the mutation of the DNA in some organelles but not in others.

heterozygous Refers to the condition in which a pair of alleles at a single locus on homologous chromosomes are different.

homeostasis The maintenance of the internal environment of an organism within an acceptable range.

homeothermic Refers to an organism's ability to maintain a constant body temperature despite great variations in environmental temperature.

homeotic (*Hox*) genes Also known as homeobox genes, they are responsible for differentiating the specific segments of the body, such as the head, tail, and limbs, during embryological development.

hominids A group of extinct and living bipedal primates in the family *Hominidae*.

hominin Humans and human ancestors in a more recent evolutionary taxonomy; based on genetics.

Homo erectus An early *Homo* species and the likely descendant of *H. habilis;* the first hominid species to move out of Africa into Asia and Europe.

Homo floriensis Nicknamed "Hobbit" for its diminutive size, a possible new species of *Homo* found in Liang Bua Cave, on the Indonesian island of Flores.

Homo habilis The earliest *Homo* species, a possible descendant of *A. garhi* and an ancestor to *H. erectus;* showed the first substantial increase in brain size and was the first species definitively associated with the production and use of stone tools.

homologous Refers to each set of paired chromosomes in the genome.

homoplasmic Refers to nuclear DNA, which is identical in the nucleus of each cell type (except red blood cells).

homozygous Refers to the condition in which a pair of alleles at a single locus on homologous chromosomes are the same.

Huntington's chorea A rare genetic disease in which the central nervous system degenerates and the individual loses control over voluntary movements, with the symptoms often appearing between ages 30 and 50.

hypercholesterolemia The presence of high levels of cholesterol in an organism's blood; this condition may result from the dietary consumption of foods that promote high cholesterol or through the inheritance of a genetic disorder.

hypothermia A condition in which an organism's body temperature falls below the normal range, which may lead to the loss of proper body functions and, eventually, death.

hypotheses Testable statements that potentially explain specific phenomena observed in the natural world.

hypoxia A condition in which an organism is not able to breathe in adequate amounts of oxygen, leading to low levels of oxygen in the blood, shortness of breath, and, in extreme situations, death.

igneous Rock formed from the crystallization of molten magma, which contains the radioisotope ^{40}K; used in potassium-argon dating.

index fossils Fossils that are from specified time ranges, are found in multiple locations, and can be used to determine the age of associated strata.

induced mutations Refers to those mutations in the DNA resulting from exposure to toxic chemicals or to radiation.

infanticide The killing of a juvenile.

intrauterine Refers to the area within the uterus.

iron deficiency anemia A condition in which the blood has insufficient iron; may be caused by diet, poor iron absorption, parasitic infection, and severe blood loss.

isotopes Two or more forms of a chemical element that vary in the number of neutrons in the nucleus and by the atomic weight.

karyotype The characteristics of the chromosomes for an individual organism or a species, such as number, size, and type.

Khoratpithecus A genus of Miocene apes from Asia, likely ancestral to orangutans.

kin selection Altruistic behaviors that increase the donor's inclusive fitness, that is, the fitness of the donor's relatives.

Klinefelter's syndrome A chromosomal trisomy in which males have an extra X chromosome, resulting in an XXY condition; affected individuals typically have reduced fertility.

lactation The production and secretion of milk from a female mammal's mammary glands, providing a food source to the female's young.

Lamarckism First proposed by Lamarck, the theory of evolution through the inheritance of acquired characteristics in which an organism can pass on features acquired during its lifetime.

language A set of written or spoken symbols that refer to things (people, places, concepts, etc.) other than themselves.

Law of Independent Assortment Mendel's Second Law, which asserts that the inheritance of one trait does not affect the inheritance of other traits.

Law of Segregation Mendel's First Law, which asserts that the two alleles for any given gene (or trait) are inherited, one from each parent; during gamete production, only one of the two alleles will be present in each ovum or sperm.

Levallois A distinctive method of stone tool production used during the Middle Paleolithic, in which the core was prepared and flakes removed from the surface before the final tool was detached from the core.

life history The details of an organism's existence from conception through senescence and death.

linguistic anthropology The study of the construction, use, and form of language in human populations.

linkage Refers to the inheritance, as a unit, of individual genes closely located on a chromosome; an exception to the Law of Independent Assortment.

locus The location of an allele, or gene, on a chromosome.

loph An enamel ridge connecting cusps on a tooth's surface.

Lower Paleolithic The oldest part of the period during which the first stone tools were created and used, beginning with the Oldowan Complex.

Lucy One of the most significant fossils: the 40% complete skeleton of an adult female *A. afarensis*, found in East Africa.

luminescence dating A relative dating method in which the energy trapped in a material is measured when the object is heated.

macroevolution Large-scale evolution, such as a speciation event, that occurs after hundreds or thousands of generations.

macronutrients Essential chemical nutrients, including fat, carbohydrates, and protein, that a body needs to live and to function normally.

masticatory-functional hypothesis The hypothesis that cranial shape change during the Holocene was related to the consumption of softer foods.

material culture The part of culture that is expressed as objects that humans use to manipulate environments.

matriline DNA, such as mitochondrial DNA, whose inheritance can be traced from mother to daughter or to son.

megafauna General term for the large game animals hunted by pre-Holocene and early Holocene humans.

meiosis The production of gametes through one DNA replication and two cell (and nuclear) divisions, creating four haploid gametic cells.

melanic Refers to an individual with high concentrations of melanin.

melanin A brown pigment that determines the darkness or lightness of a human's skin color due to its concentration in the skin.

melanocytes Melanin-producing cells located in the skin's epidermis.

menarche Refers to the onset of menstruation in an adolescent female.

Mendelian inheritance The basic principles associated with the transmission of genetic material, forming the basis of genetics, including the law of segregation and the law of independent assortment.

menopause The cessation of the menstrual cycle, signifying the end of a female's ability to bear children.

Mesozoic The second major era of geologic time, 230–65 mya, characterized by the emergence and extinction of dinosaurs.

messenger RNA (mRNA) The molecules that are responsible for making a chemical copy of a gene needed for a specific protein, that is, for the transcription phase of protein synthesis.

microcephaly A condition in which the cranium is abnormally small and the brain is underdeveloped.

microevolution Small-scale evolution, such as changes in allele frequency, that occurs from one generation to the next.

micronutrients Essential substances, such as minerals or vitamins, needed in very small amounts to maintain normal body functioning.

Micropithecus A genus of very small proconsulids from the Miocene, found in Africa.

microsatellites Specific loci in nuclear or organellar DNA that have repeated units of 1–4 base pairs in length; they can be used in various genetic studies.

Middle Paleolithic The middle part of the Old Stone Age, associated with Mousterian tools, which Neandertals produced using the Levallois technique.

mitochondria Energy-producing (ATP) organelles in eukaryotic cells; they possess their own independent DNA.

mitosis The process of cellular and nuclear division that creates two identical diploid daughter cells.

monogamous Refers to a social group that includes an adult male, an adult female, and their offspring.

monosomy Refers to the condition in which only one of a specific pair of chromosomes is present in a cell's nucleus.

morphology Physical shape and appearance.

motor skills Refers to the performance of complex movements and actions that require the control of nerves and muscles.

Mousterian The stone tool culture in which Neandertals produced tools using the Levallois technique.

mutagens Substances, such as toxins, chemicals, or radiation, that may induce genetic mutations.

mutation A random change in a gene or chromosome, creating a new trait that may be advantageous, deleterious, or neutral in its effects on the organism.

natural selection The process by which some organisms, with features that enable them to adapt to the environment, preferentially survive and reproduce, thereby increasing the frequency of those features in the population.

Neolithic The late Pleistocene/early Holocene culture, during which humans domesticated plants and animals.

noncoding DNA Sequences of a gene's DNA (also known as introns) that are not coded to produce specific proteins and are excised before protein synthesis.

nondisjunctions Refers to the failure of the chromosomes to properly segregate during meiosis, creating some gametes with abnormal numbers of chromosomes.

nonheme iron Iron—found in lentils and beans—that is less efficiently absorbed by the body than is heme iron.

nonhoning canine An upper canine that, as part of a nonhoning chewing mechanism, is not sharpened against the lower third premolar.

nonmelanic Refers to an individual with low concentrations of melanin.

nonmineralized Refers to bone reduced to its organic component.

nonsynonymous point mutation A point mutation that creates a triplet coded to produce a different amino acid than that of the original triplet.

Notharctus A genus of one of the largest adapids from the Eocene.

nucleotide The building block of DNA and RNA, comprised of a sugar, a phosphate group, and one of four nitrogen bases.

nucleus A membrane-bound structure in eukaryotic cells that contains the genetic material.

occipital bun A cranial feature of Neandertals in which the occipital bone projects substantially from the skull's posterior.

Oldowan Complex The stone tool culture associated with *H. habilis* and, possibly, *A. garhi*, including primitive chopper tools.

olfactory bulb The portion of the anterior brain that detects odors.

oligopithecids The earliest anthropoid ancestors in the Oligocene, found in the Fayum, Egypt.

omomyids Eocene euprimates that may be ancestral to tarsiers.

opposable Refers to primates' thumb, in that it can touch each of the four fingertips, enabling a grasping ability.

oreopithecids Miocene apes that were found in Europe.

Oreopithecus A genus of oreopithecids found in Italy that was extinct within a million years of its appearance.

Orrorin tugenensis A pre-australopithecine species found in East Africa that displayed some of the earliest evidence of bipedalism.

osteoarthritis Degenerative changes of the joints caused by a variety of factors, especially physical activity and mechanical stress.

osteoblasts Cells responsible for bone formation.

osteoclasts Cells responsible for bone resorption.

osteoporosis The loss of bone mass often due to age, causing the bones to become porous, brittle, and easily fractured.

Ouranopithecus A genus of Miocene dryopithecids found in Greece.

paleogenetics The application of genetics to the past, especially in anthropology and paleontology; the study of genetics in past organisms.

Paleoindians The earliest hominid inhabitants of the Americas; they likely migrated from Asia and are associated with the Clovis and Folsom stone tool cultures in North America and comparable tools in South America.

paleomagnetic dating An absolute dating method based on the random reversals of Earth's magnetic field.

paleontology The study of extinct life-forms through the analysis of fossils.

Paleozoic The first major era of geologic time, 570–230 mya, during which fish, reptiles, and insects first appeared.

Pangaea A hypothetical landmass in which all the continents were joined, approximately 300–200 mya.

parapithecids Anthropoid ancestors from the Oligocene, found in Fayum, Egypt.

Parapithecus A genus of later parapithecids from the Oligocene, found in Fayum, Egypt.

parental investment The time and energy parents expend for their offspring's benefit.

patriline DNA whose inheritance can be traced from father to daughter or son, such as the Y chromosome, which passes from father to son.

pebble tools The earliest stone tools, in which simple flakes were knocked off to produce an edge used for cutting and scraping.

peptide bond Chemical bond that joins amino acids into a protein chain.

periosteal reactions Inflammatory responses of the bones' outer covering due to bacterial infection or to trauma.

phenotype The physical expression of the genotype; it may be influenced by the environment.

phylogeny The evolutionary relationships of a group of organisms.

physical anthropology The original term for biological anthropology.

Pithecanthropus erectus The name first proposed by Ernst Haeckel for the oldest hominid; Dubois later used this name for his first fossil discovery, which later became known as *Homo erectus*.

pleiotropy Refers to one gene that affects more than one phenotypic trait.

plesiadapiforms Paleocene organisms that may have been the first primates, originating from an adaptive radiation of mammals.

point mutations Replacements of a single nitrogen base with another base, which may or may not affect the amino acid for which the triplet codes.

polarized light A kind of light used in amino acid dating because it allows amino acid changes to be observed and measured.

polyandrous Refers to a social group that includes one reproductively active female, several adult males, and their offspring.

polygenic Refers to one phenotypic trait that is affected by two or more genes.

polygynous Refers to a social group that includes one adult male, several adult females, and their offspring.

polymerase chain reaction (PCR) A technique that amplifies a small sample of DNA into a larger amount that can be used for various genetic tests.

polymorphism Refers to the presence of two or more separate phenotypes for a certain gene in the population.

polypeptide Also known as a protein, a chain of amino acids held together by multiple peptide bonds.

population genetics A specialty within the field of genetics; it focuses on the changes in gene frequencies and the effects of those changes on adaptation and evolution.

porotic hyperostosis Expansion and porosity of cranial bones due to anemia caused by an iron-deficient diet, parasitic infection, or genetic disease.

positive selection Process in which advantageous genetic variants quickly increase in frequency in a population.

postnatal stage The second stage of life, beginning with birth, terminating with the shift to the adult stage, and involving substantial increases in height, weight, and brain growth and development.

power grip A fistlike grip in which the fingers and thumbs wrap around an object in opposite directions.

preadaptation An organism's use of an anatomical feature in a way unrelated to the feature's original function.

precision grip A precise grip in which the tips of the fingers and thumbs come together, enabling fine manipulation.

prehensile tail A tail that acts as a kind of a hand for support in trees, common in New World monkeys.

prenatal stage The first stage of life, beginning with the zygote in utero, terminating with birth, and involving multiple mitotic events and the differentiation of the body into the appropriate segments and regions.

primates A group of mammals in the order *Primates* that have complex behavior, varied forms of locomotion, and a unique suite of traits, including larger brains, forward-facing eyes, fingernails, and reduced snouts.

primatologists Researchers that study nonhuman primates.

Proconsul A genus of early Miocene proconsulids from Africa, ancestral to catarrhines.

proconsulids Early Miocene apes found in East Africa.

prokaryotes Single-celled organisms with no nuclear membranes or organelles and with their genetic material as a single strand in the cytoplasm.

propliopithecids Anthropoid ancestors from the Oligocene, found in Africa.

Proprimates A separate order of early primate ancestors from the Paleocene, such as the plesiadapiforms.

racemization The chemical reaction resulting in the conversion of L amino acids to D amino acids for amino acid dating.

radiocarbon dating The radiometric dating method in which the ratio of ^{14}C to ^{12}C is measured to provide an absolute date for a material younger than 50,000 years.

radioisotopes Elements' unstable, radioactive isotopes.

radiopotassium dating The radiometric dating method in which the ratio of ^{40}K to ^{40}Ar is measured to provide an absolute date for a material older than 200,000 years.

recessive An allele that is expressed in an organism's phenotype if two copies are present, but is masked if the dominant allele is present.

recombination The exchange of genetic material between homologous chromosomes, resulting from a cross-over event.

regulatory genes Those genes that determine when structural genes and other regulatory genes are turned on and off for protein synthesis.

regulatory proteins Proteins involved in the expression of control genes.

replication The process of copying nuclear DNA prior to cell division, so that each new daughter cell receives a complete complement of DNA.

reproductive isolation Any mechanism that prevents two populations from interbreeding and exchanging genetic material.

rhinarium The naked surface around the nostrils, typically wet in mammals.

ribonucleic acid (RNA) A single-stranded molecule involved in protein synthesis, consisting of a phosphate, ribose sugar, and one of four nitrogen bases.

ribosomal RNA (rRNA) A fundamental structural component of a ribosome.

ribosomes The organelles attached to the surface of endoplasmic reticulum, located in the cytoplasm of a cell; they are the site of protein synthesis.

rigidity (bone) Refers to the strength of bone to resist bending and torsion.

sagittal keel A slight ridge of bone found along the midline sagittal suture of the cranium, which is typically found on *H. erectus* skulls.

Sahelanthropus tchadensis The earliest pre-australopithecine species found in central Africa with possible evidence of bipedalism.

scientific law A theory that becomes absolutely true.

scientific method An empirical research method in which data is gathered from observations of phenomena, hypotheses are formulated and tested, and conclusions are drawn that validate or modify the original hypotheses.

sectorial (premolar) Refers to a premolar adapted for cutting.

secular trend A phenotypic change, such as an increase in height, due to multiple factors.

sedimentary Rock formed when the deposition of sediments creates distinct layers, or strata.

senescence Refers to an organism's biological changes in later adulthood.

sex chromosomes The pair of chromosomes that determine an organism's biological sex.

sexual dimorphism A difference in a physical attribute between the males and females of a species.

sexual selection The frequency of traits that change due to those traits' attractiveness to members of the opposite sex.

shovel-shaped incisors A dental trait, commonly found among Native Americans and Asians, in which the incisors' posterior aspect has varying degrees of concavity.

sickle-cell anemia A genetic blood disease in which the red blood cells become deformed and sickle shaped, decreasing their ability to carry oxygen to tissues.

single nucleotide polymorphisms (SNPs) Variations in the DNA sequence due to the change of a single nitrogen base; also known as point mutations.

sivapithecids Early Miocene apes found in Asia.

Sivapithecus A genus of Miocene sivapithecids, proposed as ancestral to orangutans.

skin reflectance Refers to the amount of light reflected from the skin that can be measured and used to assess skin color.

sociolinguistics The science of investigating language's social contexts.

somatic cells Diploid cells that form the organs, tissues, and other parts of an organism's body.

species A group of related organisms that can interbreed and produce fertile, viable offspring.

spontaneous mutation Random changes in DNA that occur during cell division.

stabilizing selection Selection against the extremes of the phenotypic distribution, decreasing the genetic diversity for this trait in the population.

Steno's law of superposition The principle that the lower the stratum or layer, the older its age; the oldest layers are at the bottom, and the youngest are at the top.

strata Layers of rock, representing various periods of deposition.

stratigraphic correlation The process of matching up strata from several sites through the analysis of chemical, physical, and other properties.

stressors Any factor that can cause stress in an organism, potentially affecting the body's proper functioning and its homeostasis.

structural genes Genes coded to produce particular products, such as an enzyme or hormone, rather than for regulatory proteins.

structural proteins Proteins that form an organism's physical attributes.

sun protection factor (SPF) The rating calculated by comparing the length of time needed for protected skin to burn to the length of time needed for unprotected skin to burn.

superfoods Cereal grains, such as rice, corn, and wheat, that make up a substantial portion of the human population's diet today.

synonymous point mutation A neutral point mutation in which the substituted nitrogen base creates a triplet coded to produce the same amino acid as that of the original triplet.

systematics The study and classification of living organisms to determine their evolutionary relationships with one another.

taphonomy The study of the deposition of plant or animal remains and the environmental conditions affecting their preservation.

taxonomy The classification of organisms into a system that reflects degree of relatedness.

tectonic Refers to various structures on Earth's surface, such as the continental plates.

thalassemia A genetic blood disease in which the hemoglobin is improperly synthesized, causing the red blood cells to have a much shorter lifespan.

theory A set of hypotheses that have been rigorously tested and validated, leading to their establishment as a generally accepted explanation of specific phenomena.

Theropithecus A genus of primates ancestral to some Old World monkeys, found in Pliocene and Pleistocene Africa.

thymine One of four nitrogen bases that make up DNA; it pairs with adenine.

tooth comb Anterior teeth that have been tilted forward, creating a scraper.

total daily energy expenditure (TDEE) The number of calories used by an organism's body during a 24-hour period.

transcription The first step of protein synthesis, involving the creation of mRNA based on the DNA template.

transfer RNA (tRNA) The molecules that are responsible for transporting amino acids to the ribosomes during protein synthesis.

translation The second step of protein synthesis, involving the transfer of amino acids by tRNA to the ribosomes, which are then added to the protein chain.

translocations Rearrangements of chromosomes due to the insertion of genetic material from one chromosome to another.

transposable elements Mobile pieces of DNA that can copy themselves into entirely new areas of the chromosomes.

treponematoses A group of related diseases (venereal syphilis, yaws, endemic syphilis) caused by the bacteria *Treponema,* which causes pathological changes most often to the cranium and tibias.

triplets Sequences of three nitrogen bases each in DNA, known as codons in mRNA.

trisomy Refers to the condition in which an additional chromosome exists with the homologous pair.

type 2 diabetes A disease in which the body does not produce sufficient amounts of insulin or the cells do not use available insulin, causing a buildup of glucose in the cells.

uniformitarianism The theory that processes that occurred in the geologic past are still at work today.

Upper Paleolithic Refers to the most recent part of the Old Stone Age, associated with early modern *Homo sapiens* and characterized by finely crafted stone and other types of tools with various functions.

uracil One of four nitrogen bases that make up RNA; it pairs with adenine.

vasoconstriction The decrease in blood vessels' diameter due to the action of a nerve or of a drug; it can also occur in response to cold temperatures.

vasodilation The increase in blood vessels' diameter due to the action of a nerve or of a drug; it can also occur in response to hot temperatures.

victoriapithecids Miocene primates from Africa, possibly ancestral to Old World Monkeys.

visual predation hypothesis The proposition that unique primate traits arose as adaptations to preying on insects and on small animals.

weaning The process of substituting other foods for the milk produced by the mother.

Wolff's Law The principle that bone is placed in the direction of functional demand; that is, bone develops where needed and recedes where it is not needed.

Y-5 Hominoids' pattern of lower molar cusps.

zygote The cell that results from a sperm's fertilization of an ovum.

Glossary of Place Names

Primary research and/or findings are noted for each place.

Chapter 1
Baffin Island—Franz Boas research
St. Catherines Island, Georgia—Clark Larsen research

Chapter 2
Galápagos Islands—Charles Darwin trip and observations

Chapter 6
Gombe, Tanzania—Jane Goodall research
New World (primates)
Old World (primates)

Chapter 8
Bighorn Basin, Wyoming—*Carpolestes*
Fayum Depression, Egypt—*Aegyptopithecus, Parapithecus, Apidium, Biretia,* oligopithecids, parapithecids, propliopithecids
Paris Basin—*Adapis*
Salla, Bolivia—*Branisella*
Shanghuang, Jiangsu Province, China—*Eosimias*
St. Gaudens, France—*Dryopithecus*
Rusinga Island, Lake Victoria, Kenya—*Proconsul* (nearly complete skeleton)
Tuscany, Italy—*Oreopithecus*

Chapter 9
Afar Depression, Ethiopia—*Ardipithecus*
Allia Bay, Kenya—*Australopithecus anamensis*
Aramis, Ethiopia—*Ardipithecus kadabba* and *Ardipithecus ramidus*
Asa Issie, Ethiopia—*Australopithecus anamensis*
Awash River Valley, Ethiopia—*Ardipithecus* and *Australopithecus garhi*
Bouri, Middle Awash River Valley, Ethiopia—*Australopithecus garhi*
Dikika, Ethiopia—*Australopithecus afarensis*
Djurab Desert, Chad—*Sahelanthropus tchadensis*
Drimolen, South Africa—*Australopithecus robustus*
Eastern Rift Valley, Africa—*Australopithecus*
Gona River, Ethiopia—*Australopithecus garhi* tools
Hadar, Ethiopia—*Australopithecus afarensis*
Kanapoi, Kenya—*Australopithecus anamensis*
Kromdraai, South Africa—*Australopitheucs robustus*
Lake Turkana, Kenya—*Australopithecus anamensis, Orrorin tugenensis, Australopithecus (Kenyanthropus) platyops,* and *Australopithecus aethiopicus*

Laetoli, Tanzania—*Australopithecus afarensis*
Lomekwi, Kenya—*Australopithecus (Kenyanthropus) platyops*
Makapansgat, South Africa—*Australopithecus africanus*
Olduvai Gorge, Tanzania—various Australopithecines
Piltdown Common, East Sussex, England—Piltdown hoax
Sterkfontein, South Africa—*Australopithecus africanus*
Swartkrans, South Africa—*Australopithecus robustus*
Taung, South Africa—*Australopithecus africanus*
Tugen Hills, Kenya—*Orrorin tugenensis*

Chapter 10
Atapuerca, Spain—*Homo erectus*
Bodo, Middle Awash River Valley, Ethiopia—*Homo erectus* and evidence of cutmarks on bones
Bouri, Middle Awash River Valley, Ethiopia—*Homo erectus* and evidence of animal butchery
Boxgrove, England—*Homo erectus*
Buia, Eritrea—*Homo erectus*
Ceprano, Italy—*Homo erectus*
Dmanisi, Republic of Georgia—*Homo erectus*
Gongwangling, China—*Homo erectus*
Gran Dolina, Spain—*Homo erectus,* evidence of animal butchery, and cutmarks on *H. erectus* bones
Ileret, Kenya—*Homo erectus*
Lake Turkana, Kenya—*Homo habilis*
Majuangou, China—*Homo erectus*
Mauer, Germany—*Homo erectus*
Nariokotome, Kenya—*Homo erectus*
Olduvai Gorge, Tanzania—*Homo habilis, Homo erectus,* and *Homo rudolfensis*
Olorgesailie, Kenya—Acheulian tools
Omo, Ethiopia—*Homo habilis*
Sambungmacan, Java—*Homo erectus*
Sangiran, Java—*Homo erectus*
Sterkfontein, South Africa—*Homo habilis*
Trinil, Java—*Homo erectus*
Uraha, Malawi—*Homo habilis*
Zhoukoudian, China—*Homo erectus* and evidence of fire

Chapter 11
Aduma, Middle Awash River Valley, Ethiopia—early modern *Homo sapiens*

Amud, Israel—Neandertal and evidence of intentional burial
Arago, France—early archaic *Homo sapiens*
Bouri, Middle Awash River Valley, Ethiopia—early modern *Homo sapiens*
Clovis, New Mexico—Paleoindian sites
Cro-Magnon, France—early modern *Homo sapiens*
Dali, China—early archaic *Homo sapiens*
Dolni Vestonice, Czech Republic—early modern *Homo sapiens*
El Sidron, Spain—Neandertal
Engis, Belgium—Neandertal
Feldhofer Cave, Germany—Neandertal
Flores, Indonesia—early *Homo sapiens* ("Hobbit")
Folsom, New Mexico—Paleoindian sites
Grimaldi Caves, Italy—early modern *Homo sapiens*
Herto, Middle Awash River Valley, Ethiopia—early modern *Homo sapiens*
Hofmeyr, South Africa—early modern *Homo sapiens*
Kabwe (Broken Hill), Zambia—early archaic *Homo sapiens*
Katanda, Congo—early modern *Homo sapiens*
Kebara, Israel—Neandertal
Kennewick, Washington—controversial Paleoindian find
Klasies River Mouth Cave, South Africa—early modern *Homo sapiens*
Kow Swamp, Victoria, Australia—early modern *Homo sapiens*
Krapina, Croatia—Neandertal and possible evidence of cannibalism
La Chapelle-aux-Saints, France—Neandertal and evidence of intentional burial
Lagar Velho, Portugal—early modern *Homo sapiens*
Lake Mungo, New South Wales, Australia—early modern *Homo sapiens*
Lothagam, Kenya—early modern *Homo sapiens*
Marillac, France—Neandertal
Mezmaiskaya, Russia—Neandertal
Minatogawa, Japan—early modern *Homo sapiens*

Mladeč, Czech Republic—early modern *Homo sapiens*
Monte Lessini, Italy—Neandertal
Moula-Guercy, France—Neandertal and possible evidence of cannibalism
Narmada, India—early archaic *Homo sapiens*
Ngandong, Java—early archaic *Homo sapiens*
Omo, Ethiopia—early modern *Homo sapiens*
Peştera cu Oase, Romania—early modern *Homo sapiens*
Petralona, Greece—early archaic *Homo sapiens*
Predmostí, Czech Republic—early modern *Homo sapiens*
Rochers de Villeneuve, France—Neandertal
Scladina, Belgium—Neandertal
Shanidar, Kurdistan, Iraq—Neandertal, evidence of care of the sick, and evidence of intentional burial
Sima de los Huesos, Sierra de Atapuerca, Spain—early archaic *Homo sapiens*
Skhul, Israel—early modern *Homo sapiens*
Spy, Belgium—Neandertal
Steinheim, Germany—early archaic *Homo sapiens*
Swanscombe, England—early archaic *Homo sapiens*
Tabun, Israel—Neandertal and evidence of intentional burial
Tianyuan Cave, China—early modern *Homo sapiens*
Vindija Cave, Croatia—Neandertal
Wadi Halfa, Egypt—early modern *Homo sapiens*
Wadi Kubbaniya, Egypt—early modern *Homo sapiens*
Zhoukoudian, Upper Cave, China—early modern *Homo sapiens*

Chapter 12
Çatalhöyük, Turkey—evidence of early cities
Fertile Crescent, Jordan Valley—early agricultural communities
Jericho, Israel—evidence of early cities
Levant—early plant domestication

Bibliography

Abbate, E., A. Albianelli, A. Azzaroli, M. Benvenuti, B. Tesfamariam, P. Bruni, N. Cipriani, R. J. Clarke, G. Ficcarelli, R. Macchiarelli, G. Napoleone, M. Papini, L. Rook, M. Sagri, T. M. Tecle, D. Torre, and I. Villa. 1998. A one-million-year-old *Homo* cranium from the Danakil (Afar) depression of Eritrea. *Nature* 393: 458–460.

Abbate, E., B. WoldeHaimanot, Y. Libsekal, T. M. Tecle, and L. Rook. 2004. *A Step towards Human Origins: The Buia* Homo *One-Million-Years Ago in the Eritrean Danakil Depression (East Africa). Revista Italiana di Paleontologia e Stratigrafia* 110.

Adger, N. 2007. *Climate Change 2007: Climate Change Impacts, Adaptation and Vulnerability.* Washington, DC: Intergovernmental Panel on Climate Change.

Agarwal, S. C. and S. D. Stout, eds. 2003. *Bone Loss and Osteoporosis: An Anthropological Perspective.* New York: Kluwer Plenum Academic Press.

Ainsworth, C. and D. MacKenzie. 2001. Coming home. *New Scientist* 171(2298): 28–33.

Alemseged, Z., F. Spoor, W. H. Kimbel, R. Bobe, D. Geraads, D. Reed, and J. G. Wynn. 2006. A juvenile early hominin skeleton from Dikika, Ethiopia. *Nature* 443: 296–301.

Allison, A. C. 2004. Two lessons from the interface of genetics and medicine. *Genetics* 166: 1591–1599.

Alvarez, W. 1997. T. rex *and the Crater of Doom.* Princeton: Princeton University Press.

Alvesalo, K. and P. M. A. Tigerstedt. 1974. Heritabilities of human tooth dimensions. *Hereditas* 77: 311–318.

Ambrose, S. H., L. J. Hlusko, D. Kyule, A. Deino, and M. Williams. 2003. Lemudong'o: a new 6 Ma paleontological site near Narok, Kenya Rift Valley. *Journal of Human Evolution* 44: 737–742.

Ambrose, S. H. and J. Krigbaum. 2003. *Bone Chemistry and Bioarchaeology. Journal of Anthropological Archaeology,* special issue, 22(3).

Ankel-Simons, F. 2007. *Primate Anatomy: An Introduction.* Amsterdam, The Netherlands: Elsevier.

Antón, S. C. 2003. A natural history of *Homo erectus. Yearbook of Physical Anthropology* 46: 126–170.

Antón, S. C. and C. C. Swisher III. 2004. Early dispersals of *Homo* from Africa. *Annual Review of Anthropology* 33: 271–296.

Armelagos, G. J. and K. N. Harper. 2005. Genomics of the origins of agriculture, part one. *Evolutionary Anthropology* 14: 68–77.

Aron, J. L. and J. A. Patz. 2001. *Ecosystem Change and Public Health: A Global Perspective.* Baltimore: Johns Hopkins University Press.

Arsuaga, J.-L. 1997. Sima de los Huesos. *Journal of Human Evolution* 33: 105–421.

Arsuaga, J.-L., I. Martinez, C. Lorenzo, A. Gracia, A. Muñoz, O. Alonso, and J. Gallego. 1999. The human cranial remains from Gran Dolina lower Pleistocene site (Sierra de Atapuerca, Spain). *Journal of Human Evolution* 37: 431–457.

Ascenzi, A., I. Biddittu, P. F. Cassoli, A. G. Segre, and E. Segre-Naldini. 1996. A calvarium of late *Homo erectus* from Ceprano, Italy. *Journal of Human Evolution* 31: 409–423.

Asfaw, B., W. H. Gilbert, Y. Beyene, W. K. Hart, P. R. Renne, G. WoldeGabriel, E. S. Vrba, and T. D. White. 2002. Remains of *Homo erectus* from Bouri, Middle Awash, Ethiopia. *Nature* 416: 317–320.

Asfaw, B., T. White, O. Lovejoy, B. Latimer, S. Simpson, and G. Suwa. 1999. *Australopithecus garhi:* a new species of early hominid from Ethiopia. *Science* 284: 629–635.

Atsalis, S. and S. W. Margulis. 2006. Sexual and hormonal cycles in geriatric *Gorilla gorilla gorilla. International Journal of Primatology* 27: 1663–1687.

Backwell, L. R. and F. d'Errico. 2001. Evidence of termite foraging by Swartkrans early hominids. *Proceedings of the National Academy of Sciences* 98: 1358–1363.

Baker, C. 2006. *The Evolution Dialogues.* Washington, DC: American Association for the Advancement of Science.

Balter, M. 2005. Are humans still evolving? *Science* 309: 234–237.

Balter, M. 2006. Radiocarbon dating's final frontier. *Science* 313: 1560–1563.

Balter, M. 2007. Seeking agriculture's ancient roots. *Science* 316: 1830–1835.

Barker, D. J. P. 1996. The origins of coronary heart disease in early life. Pp. 155–162 in C. J. K. Henry and S. J. Ulijaszek, eds. *Long-Term Consequences of Early Environment: Growth, Development and the Lifespan Developmental Perspective.* Cambridge, UK: Cambridge University Press.

Barker, D. J. P. 1998. *In utero* programming of chronic disease. *Clinical Science* 95: 115–128.

Barker, D. J. P. 1998. *Mothers, Babies, and Health in Later Life.* Edinburgh and New York: Churchill Livingstone.

Barker, D. J. P. 2001. *Fetal Origins of Cardiovascular and Lung Disease.* Oxford, UK: Taylor & Francis.

Barker, D. J. P. and D. T. Lackland. 2003. Prenatal influences on stroke mortality in England and Wales. *Stroke* 34: 1598–1602.

Barnosky, A. D., P. L. Koch, R. S. Feranec, S. L. Wing, and A. B. Shabel. 2004. Assessing the causes of late Pleistocene extinctions on the continents. *Science* 306: 70–75.

Barsh, G. S. 2003. What controls variation in human skin color? *PLoS Biology* 1: 19–22.

Bar-Yosef, O. 2006. *Kebara Cave, Mt. Carmel, Israel.* Cambridge, MA: Harvard University Press.

Bar-Yosef, O. and A. Belfer-Cohen. 1989. The origins of sedentism and farming communities in the Levant. *Journal of World Prehistory* 3: 477–498.

Bar-Yosef, O. and B. Vandermeersch. 1993. Modern humans in the Levant. *Scientific American* 268(4): 94–100.

Barzun, J. 1965. *Race: A Study in Superstition.* New York: Harper & Row.

Beall, C., K. Song, R. C. Elston, and M. C. Goldstein. 2004. Higher offspring survival among Tibetan women with high oxygen saturation genotypes residing at 4,000 m. *Proceedings of the National Academy of Sciences* 101: 14300–14304.

Beall, C. and A. T. Steegmann Jr. 2000. Human adaptation to climate: Temperature, ultraviolet radiation, and altitude. Pp. 163–224 in S. Stinson, B. Bogin, R. Huss-Ashmore, and D. O'Rourke, eds. *Human Biology: An Evolutionary and Biocultural Perspective.* New York: Wiley-Liss.

Beall, C. M. 2001. Adaptations to altitude: a current assessment. *Annual Review of Anthropology* 30: 423–456.

Beall, C. M. 2006. Andean, Tibetan, and Ethiopian patterns of adaptation to high-altitude hypoxia. *Integrative and Comparative Biology* 46: 18–24.

Beard, C. 2004. *The Hunt for the Dawn Monkey: Unearthing the Origins of Monkeys, Apes, and Humans.* Berkeley: University of California Press.

Beard, K. C. 2002. Basal anthropoids. Pp. 133–149 in W. C. Hartwig, ed. *The Primate Fossil Record.* Cambridge, UK: Cambridge University Press.

Beard, K. C., T. Qi, M. R. Dawson, B. Wang, and C. Li. 1994. A diverse new primate fauna from middle Eocene fissure-fillings in southeastern China. *Nature* 368: 604–609.

Beck, T. J., C. B. Ruff, R. A. Shaffer, K. Betsinger, D. W. Trone, and S. K. Brodine. 2000. Stress fracture in military recruits: gender differences in muscle and bone susceptibility factors. *Bone* 27: 437–444.

Begun, D. R. 2002. European hominoids. Pp. 339–368 in W. C. Hartwig, ed. *The Primate Fossil Record.* Cambridge, UK: Cambridge University Press.

Begun, D. R. 2003. Planet of the apes. *Scientific American* 289(2): 74–83.

Behrensmeyer, A. K. and A. P. Hill. 1980. *Fossils in the Making: Vertebrate Taphonomy and Paleoecology.* Chicago: University of Chicago Press.

Bellwood, P. 2005. *First Farmers: The Origins of Agricultural Societies.* Malden, MA: Blackwell.

Benefit, B. R. and M. L. McCrossin. 1995. Miocene hominoids and hominid origins. *Annual Review of Anthropology* 24: 237–256.

Benton, M. J. 2003. *When Life Nearly Died: The Greatest Mass Extinction of All Time.* London: Thames & Hudson.

Benyshek, D. C., J. F. Martin, and C. S. Johnson. 2001. A reconsideration of the origins of the type 2 diabetes epidemic among Native Americans and the implications for intervention policy. *Medical Anthropology* 20: 25–64.

Berger, T. D. and E. Trinkaus. 1995. Patterns of trauma among the Neandertals. *Journal of Archaeological Science* 22: 841–852.

Bermúdez de Castro, J. M., M. Martinón-Torres, E. Carbonell, S. Sarmiento, A. Rosas, J. van der Made, and M. Lozano. 2004. The Atapuerca sites and their contribution to the knowledge of human evolution in Europe. *Evolutionary Anthropology* 13: 25–41.

Bhattacharjee, J. K., G. R. Janssen, and T. G. Gregg. 2006. Human genealogy: How wide and deep do our genetic connections go? *The American Biology Teacher* 68: 69–71.

Billman, B. R., P. M. Lambert, and B. L. Leonard. 2000. Cannibalism, warfare, and drought in the Mesa Verde region during the twelfth century A.D. *American Antiquity* 65: 145–178.

Bininda-Emonds, O. R. P., M. Cardillo, K. E., Jones, R. D. E. MacPhee, R. M. D. Beck, R. Greyner, S. A. Price, R. A. Vos, J. L. Gittleman, and A. Purvis. 2007. The delayed rise of present-day mammals. *Nature* 446: 507–512.

Bloch, J. I. and D. M. Boyer. 2002. Grasping primate origins. *Science* 298: 1606–1610.

Bloch, J. I., M. T. Silcox, D. M. Boyer, and E. J. Sargis. 2007. New Paleocene skeletons and the relationship of plesiadapiforms to crown-clade primates. *Proceedings of the National Academy of Sciences* 104: 1159–1164.

Blumenbach, J. F. 1775. *De Generis Humani Varietate Nativa.* Göttingen, Germany: Rosenbuschii.

Blumenbach, J. F. 1790–1828. *Decades suae craniorum diversarum Gentium, illustratae.* Göttingen, Germany: I. C. Dietrich.

Boas, F. 1912. Changes in bodily form of descendants of immigrants. *American Anthropologist* 14: 530–563.

Boesch, C. and M. Tomasello. 1998. Chimpanzee and human cultures. *Current Anthropology* 39: 591–614.

Bogin, B. 1999. *Patterns of Human Growth.* 2nd ed. Cambridge, UK: Cambridge University Press.

Bogin, B. and B. H. Smith. 2000. Evolution of the human life cycle. Pp. 377–424 in S. Stinson, B. Bogin, R. Huss-Ashmore, and D. O'Rourke, eds. *Human Biology: An Evolutionary and Biocultural Perspective.* New York: Wiley-Liss.

Bogin, B., P. Smith, A. B. Orden, M. I. Varela Silva, and J. Louky. 2002. Rapid change in height and body proportions of Maya American children. *American Journal of Human Biology* 14: 753–761.

Bouzouggar, A., N. Barton, M. Vanhaeren, F. d'Errico, S. Collcutt, T. Higham, E. Hodge, S. Parfitt, E. Rhodes, J.-L. Schwenninger, C. Stringer, E. Turner, S. Ward, A. Moutmir, and A. Stambouli. 2007. 82,000-year-old shell beads from North Africa and implications for the origins of modern human behavior. *Proceedings of the National Academy of Sciences* 104: 9964–9969.

Bowen, M. 2005. *Thin Ice: Unlocking the Secrets of Climate in the World's Highest Mountains*. New York: Henry Holt.

Bowler, P. J. 2003. *Evolution: The History of an Idea*. Berkeley: University of California Press.

Bowler, P. J. 2005. Variation from Darwin to the Modern Synthesis. Pp. 9–27 in B. Hallgrimson and B. K. Hall, eds. *Variation: A Central Concept in Biology*. Burlington, MA: Elsevier Academic Press.

Bown, T. M. and K. D. Rose. 1987. Patterns of dental evolution in early Eocene anaptomorphine primates (Omomyidae) from the Bighorn Basin, Wyoming. *Paleontological Society Memoirs* 23: 1–162.

Brace, C. L. 2002. The concept of race in physical anthropology. Pp. 239–253 in P. N. Peregrine, C. R. Ember, and M. Ember, eds. *Physical Anthropology: Original Readings in Method and Practice*. Upper Saddle River, NJ: Prentice Hall.

Brace, C. L. 2005. *"Race" Is a Four-Letter Word: The Genesis of a Concept*. New York: Oxford University Press.

Brace, C. L., S. L. Smith, and K. D. Hunt. 1991. What big teeth you had grandma! Human tooth size, past and present. Pp. 33–57 in M. A. Kelley and C. S. Larsen, eds. *Advances in Dental Anthropology*. New York: Wiley-Liss.

Bradley, R. S. 1999. *Paleoclimatology*. San Diego: Academic Press.

Brain, C. K. 1981. *The Hunters or the Hunted? An Introduction to African Cave Taphonomy*. Chicago: University of Chicago Press.

Brain, C. K. 1993. *Swartkrans: A Cave's Chronicle of Early Man*. *Transvaal Museum Monographs* 8.

Bribiescas, R. G. 2006. *Men: Evolutionary and Life History*. Cambridge, MA: Harvard University Press.

Bridges, P. S. 1996. Skeletal biology and behavior in ancient humans. *Evolutionary Anthropology* 4: 112–120.

Brown, K. 2002. Tangled roots? Genetics meets genealogy. *Science* 295: 1634–1635.

Brown, K. A. 2001. Identifying the sex of human remains by ancient DNA analysis. *Ancient Biomolecules* 3: 215–226.

Brown, P. 1992. Recent human evolution in East Asia and Australasia. *Proceedings of the Royal Society of London B* 337: 235–242.

Brown, P., T. Sutikna, M. J. Morwood, R. P. Soejono, Jatmiko, E. Wayhu Saptomo, and Rokus Awe Due. 2004. A new small-bodied hominin from the late Pleistocene of Flores, Indonesia. *Nature* 431: 1055–1061.

Brown, R. A. and G. J. Armelagos. 2001. Apportionment of racial diversity: a review. *Evolutionary Anthropology* 10: 34–40.

Bruner, E. and G. Manzi. 2007. Landmark-based shape analysis of the archaic *Homo* calvarium from Ceprano (Italy). *American Journal of Physical Anthropology* 132: 355–366.

Brunet, M., F. Guy, D. Pilbeam, H. T. Mackaye, A. Likius, D. Ahounta, A. Beauvilain, C. Blondel, H. Bocherens, J. R. Boisserie, L. De Bonis, Y. Coppens, J. Dejax, C. Denys, P. Duringer, V. Eisenmann, G. Fanone, P. Fronty, D. Geraads, T. Lehmann, F. Lihoreau, A. Louchart, A. Mahamat, G. Merceron, G. Mouchelin, O. Otero, P. P. Campomanes, M. P. De Leon, J. C. Rage, M. Sapanet, M. Schuster, J. Sudre, P. Tassy, X. Valentin, P. Vignaud, L. Viriot, A. Zazzo, and C. Zollikofer. 2002. A new hominid from the upper Miocene of Chad, Central Africa. *Nature* 418: 145–151.

Brutsaert, T. D., E. Parra, M. Shriver, A. Gamboa, J.-A. Palacios, M. Rivera, I. Rodriguez, and F. Leon-Velarde. 2004. Effects of birthplace and individual genetic admixture on lung volume and exercise phenotypes of Peruvian Quechua. *American Journal of Physical Anthropology* 123: 390–398.

Bufford, J. D. and J. E. Gern. 2005. The hygiene hypothesis revisited. *Immunology and Allergy Clinics of North America* 25: 247–262.

Buikstra, J. E. 1988. *The Mound-Builders of Eastern North America: A Regional Perspective*. Amsterdam, The Netherlands: Elfde Kroon-Voordracht.

Burger, J., M. Kirchner, B. Bramanti, W. Haak, and M. G. Thomas. 2007. Absence of the lactase-persistence-associated allele in early Neolithic Europeans. *Proceedings of the National Academy of Sciences* 104: 3736–3741.

Burke, A. 2004. *The Ecology of Neanderthals*. *International Journal of Osteoarchaeology*, special issue, 14(3–4): 155–342.

Caballero, B. and B. M. Popkin. 2002. *The Nutrition Transition: Diet and Disease in the Developing World*. London: Academic Press.

Calcagno, J. M. and K. R. Gibson. 1991. Selective compromise: evolutionary trends and mechanisms in hominid tooth size. Pp. 59–76 in M. A. Kelley and C. S. Larsen, eds. *Advances in Dental Anthropology*. New York: Wiley-Liss.

Cameron, D. W. 2004. *Hominid Adaptations and Extinctions*. Sydney: University of New South Wales Press.

Campbell, C. J., A. Fuentes, K. C. MacKinnon, M. Panger, and S. K. Bearder, eds. 2006. *Primates in Perspective*. New York: Oxford University Press.

Cann, R. L., M. Stoneking, and A. Wilson. 1987. Mitochondrial DNA and human evolution. *Nature* 325: 31–36.

Candela, P. B. 1942. The introduction of blood-group B into Europe. *Human Biology* 14: 413–443.

Caramelli, D., C. Lalueza-Fox, C. Vernesi, A. Casoli, F. Mallegni, B. Chiarelli, I. Dupanloup, J. Bertranpetit, G. Barbujani, and G. Bertorelle. 2003. Evidence for a genetic discontinuity between Neandertals and 24,000-year-old anatomically modern Europeans. *Proceedings of the National Academy of Sciences* 100: 6593–6597.

Carlson, D. S. and D. P. Van Gerven. 1977. Masticatory function and post-Pleistocene evolution in Nubia. *American Journal of Physical Anthropology* 46: 495–506.

Carlson, E. A. 2004. *Mendel's Legacy: The Origins of Classical Genetics*. Cold Spring Harbor, NY: Cold Spring Harbor Laboratory Press.

Carroll, S. B. 2005. *Endless Forms Most Beautiful: The New Science of Evo Devo*. New York: Norton.

Carroll, S. B. 2006. *The Making of the Fittest: DNA and the Ultimate Forensic Record of Evolution*. New York: Norton.

Cartmill, M. 1974. Rethinking primate origins. *Science* 184: 436–443.

Cartmill, M. 1975. *Primate Origins*. Minneapolis: Burgess.

Cartmill, M. 1992. New views on primate origins. *Evolutionary Anthropology* 1: 105–111.

Cartmill, M. 1996. *A View to a Death in the Morning: Hunting and Nature through History*. Cambridge, MA: Harvard Univerity Press.

Cartmill, M. 2002. Explaining primate origins. Pp. 42–52 in P. N. Peregrine, C. R. Ember, and M. Ember, eds. *Physical Anthropology: Original Readings in Method and Practice*. Upper Saddle River, NJ: Prentice Hall.

Caspari, R. 2003. From types to populations: A century of race, physical anthropology, and the American Anthropological Association. *American Anthropologist* 105: 65–76.

Caspi, A., K. Sugden, T. E. Moffitt, A. Taylor, I. W. Craig, H. Harrington, J. McClay, J. Mill, J. Martin, A. Braithwaite, and R. Poulton. 2003. Influence of life stress on depression: moderation by a polymorphism in the 5–HTT gene. *Science* 301: 386–389.

Cavalli-Sforza, L. L. and F. Cavalli-Sforza. 1995. *The Great Human Diasporas*. Cambridge, UK: Perseus.

Cerling, T. E., J. M. Harris, S. H. Ambrose, M. G. Leakey, and N. Solounis. 1997. Dietary and environmental reconstruction with stable isotope analyses of herbivore tooth enamel from the Miocene locality at Fort Ternan, Kenya. *Journal of Human Evolution* 33: 635–650.

Cerling, T. E., J. Quade, Y. Wang, and J. R. Bowman. 1989. Carbon isotopes in soils and paleosols as ecologic and paleoecologic indicators. *Nature* 341: 138–139.

Chaimanee, Y., D. Jolly, M. Benammi, P. Tafforeau, D. Duzer, I. Moussa, and J.-J. Jaeger. 2003. A middle Miocene hominoid from Thailand and orangutan origins. *Nature* 422: 61–65.

Chaimanee, Y., V. Suteethorn, P. Jintasakul, C. Vidthayanon, B. Marandat, and J.-J. Jaeger. 2004. A new orangutan relative from the late Miocene of Thailand. *Nature* 427: 439–441.

Chaimanee, Y., C. Yamee, P. Tian, K. Khaowiset, B. Marandat, P. Tafforeau, C. Nemoz, and J.-J. Jaeger. 2006. *Khoratpithecus piriyai*, a late Miocene hominoid of Thailand. *American Journal of Physical Anthropology* 131: 311–323.

Chalmers, J. and K. C. Ho. 1970. Geographical variations in senile osteoporosis: the association with physical activity. *Journal of Bone and Joint Surgery* 52B: 667–675.

Chaplin, G. 2004. Geographic distribution of environmental factors influencing human skin coloration. *American Journal of Physical Anthropology* 120: 292–302.

Chatters, J. C. 2001. *Ancient Encounters: Kennewick Man and the First Americans*. New York: Touchstone.

Check, E. 2006. How Africa learned to love the cow. *Nature* 444: 994–996.

Childe, V. G. 1925. *The Dawn of European Civilization*. London: Kegan Paul.

Churchill, S. E. 1998. Cold adaptation, heterochrony, and Neandertals. *Evolutionary Anthropology* 7: 46–61.

Churchill, S. E. 2001. Hand morphology, manipulation, and tool use in Neandertals and early modern humans of the Near East. *Proceedings of the National Academy of Sciences* 98: 2953–2955.

Churchill, S. E. and F. H. Smith. 2000. Makers of the early Aurignacian of Europe. *Yearbook of Physical Anthropology* 43: 61–115.

Ciochon, R. L. and G. F. Gunnell. 2002. Chronology of primate discoveries in Myanmar: influences on the anthropoid origins debate. *Yearbook of Physical Anthropology* 45: 2–35.

Ciochon, R. L. and G. F. Gunnell. 2002. Eocene primates from Myanmar: historical perspective on the origin of Anthropoidea. *Evolutionary Anthropology* 11: 156–168.

Clark, J. D., Y. Beyene, G. WoldeGabriel, W. K. Hart, P. R. Renne, H. Gilbert, A. Defleur, G. Suwa, S. Katoh, K. R. Ludwig, J.-R. Boisserie, B. Asfaw, and T. D. White. 2003. Stratigraphic, chronological and behavioural contexts of Pleistocene *Homo sapiens* from Middle Awash, Ethiopia. *Nature* 423: 747–752.

Clark, J. D. and S. A. Brandt. 1984. *From Hunters to Farmers: The Causes and Consequences of Food Production in Africa*. Berkeley: University of California Press.

Clark, J. D., J. de Heinzelin, K. D. Schick, W. K. Hart, T. D. White, G. WoldeGabriel, R. C. Walter, G. Suwa, B. Asfaw, E. Vrba, and Y. H.-Selassie. 1994. African *Homo erectus*: old radiometric ages and young Oldowan assemblages in the Middle Awash valley, Ethiopia. *Science* 264: 1907–1910.

Clarke, R. J. and P. V. Tobias. 1995. Sterkfontein Member 2 foot bones of the oldest South African hominid. *Science* 269: 521–524.

Clutton-Brock, J. 1999. *A Natural History of Domesticated Mammals*. Cambridge, UK: Cambridge University Press.

Cohen, J. M. 1992. *The Four Voyages of Christopher Columbus*. New York: Penguin.

Cohen, M. N. 1977. *The Food Crisis in Prehistory*. New Haven: Yale University Press.

Cohen, M. N. 1989. *Health and the Rise of Civilization*. New Haven: Yale University Press.

Cohen, M. N. 2002. Were early agriculturalists less healthy than food-collectors? Pp. 180–191 in P. N. Peregrine, C. R. Ember, and M. Ember, eds. *Archaeology: Original Readings in Method and Practice*. Saddle River, NJ: Prentice Hall.

Cohen, M. N. and G. J. Armelagos, eds. 1984. *Paleopathology at the Origins of Agriculture*. Orlando, FL: Academic Press.

Cohen, M. N. and G. Crane-Kramer, eds. 2007. *Ancient Health: Skeletal Indicators of Economic and Political Intensification*. Gainesville: University Press of Florida.

Colbert, E. 2007. *Field Notes from a Catastrophe: A Frontline Report on Climate Change*. London: Bloomsbury.

Collins, D. N. 2003. *Nature Encyclopedia of the Human Genome*. London: Nature.

Collins, F. S., M. Morgan, and A. Patrinos. 2003. The human genome project: lessons from large scale biology. *Science* 300: 286–290.

Conroy, G. C. 1990. *Primate Evolution.* New York: Norton.

Cook, D. C. 2006. The old physical anthropology and the New World: a look at the accomplishments of an antiquated paradigm. Pp. 27–71 in J. E. Buikstra and L. A. Beck, eds. *Bioarchaeology: The Contextual Analysis of Human Remains.* Burlington, MA: Academic Press.

Cook, L. M., R. L. H. Dennis, and G. S. Mani. 1999. Melanic morph frequency in the peppered moth in the Manchester area. *Proceedings of the Royal Society of London B* 266: 293–297.

Cook, L. M., G. S. Mani, and M. E. Varley. 1986. Postindustrial melanism in the peppered moth. *Science* 231: 611–613.

Coon, C. S., S. M. Garn, and J. B. Birdsell. 1950. *Races: A Study of the Problems of Race Formation in Man.* Springfield, IL: Charles C. Thomas.

Cooper, C., G. Campion, and L. J. Melton III. 1992. Hip fractures in the elderly: a world-wide projection. *Osteoporosis International* 2: 285–289.

Cordain, L., B. A. Watkins, G. L. Florant, M. Kelher, L. Rogers, and Y. Li. 2002. Fatty acid analysis of wild ruminant tissues: evolutionary implications for reducing diet-related chronic disease. *European Journal of Clinical Nutrition* 56: 1–11.

Costa, D. L. and R. H. Steckel. 1997. Long-term trends in health, welfare, and economic growth in the United States. Pp. 47–89 in R. H. Steckel and R. Floud, eds. *Health and Welfare during Industrialization.* Chicago: University of Chicago Press.

Covert, H. H. 2002. The earliest fossil primates and the evolution of prosimians: introduction. Pp. 13–20 in W. C. Hartwig, ed. *The Primate Fossil Record.* Cambridge, UK: Cambridge University Press.

Cowgill, L. W., E. Trinkaus, and M. A. Zeder. 2007. Shanidar 10: A middle Paleolithic immature distal lower limb from Shanidar Cave, Iraqi Kurdistan. *Journal of Human Evolution* 53: 213–223.

Crawford, M. H. 1998. *The Origins of Native Americans: Evidence from Anthropological Genetics.* Cambridge, UK: Cambridge University Press.

Crews, D. E. 2003. *Human Senescence: Evolutionary and Biocultural Perspectives.* Cambridge, UK: Cambridge University Press.

Critser, G. 2003. *Fat Land.* New York: Penguin.

Dagasto, M. 2002. The origin and diversification of anthropoid primates: introduction. Pp. 125–132 in W. C. Hartwig, ed. *The Primate Fossil Record.* Cambridge, UK: Cambridge University Press.

Darwin, C. 1859. *On the Origin of Species.* London, UK: John Murray.

Darwin, C. 1871. *The Descent of Man and Selection in Relation to Sex.* Akron, OH: Werner.

Davies, A. G. and J. F. Oates. 1994. *Colobine Monkeys: Their Ecology, Behaviour and Evolution.* Cambridge, UK: Cambridge University Press.

Deacon, T. W. 1997. What makes the human brain different? *Annual Review of Anthropology* 26: 337–357.

Dean, C., M. G. Leakey, D. Reid, F. Schrenk, G. T. Schwartz, C. Stringer, and A. Walker. 2001. Growth processes in teeth distinguish modern humans from *Homo erectus* and earlier hominins. *Nature* 414: 628–631.

Dear, P. 2006. *The Intelligibility of Nature: How Science Makes Sense of the World.* Chicago: University of Chicago Press.

De Bonis, L., G. D. Koufos, and P. Andrews. 2001. *Hominoid Evolution and Climatic Change in Europe: Volume 2, Phylogeny of the Neogene Hominoid Primates of Eurasia.* Cambridge, UK: Cambridge University Press.

De Heinzelin, J., J. D. Clark, K. D. Schick, and W. H. Gilbert. 2000. *The Acheulian and the Plio-Pleistocene Deposits of the Middle Awash Valley, Ethiopia. Musée Royal de L'Afrique Centrale, Annales Sciences Geologiques* 104.

De Heinzelin, J., J. D. Clark, T. White, W. Hart, P. Renne, G. WoldeGabriel, Y. Beyene, and E. Vrba. 1999. Environment and behavior of 2.5 million-year-old Bouri hominids. *Science* 284: 625–629.

Deino, A., P. R. Renne, and C. C. Swisher III. 1998. ^{40}Ar/^{39}Ar dating in paleoanthropology and archeology. *Evolutionary Anthropology* 6: 63–75.

Demment, M. W., M. M. Young, and R. L. Sensenig. 2003. Providing micronutrients through food-based solutions: a key to human and national development. *Journal of Nutrition* 133: 3879S–3885S.

Denham, T. P., S. G. Haberle, C. Lentfer, R. Fullagar, J. Field, M. Therin, N. Porch, and B. Winsborough. 2003. Origins of agriculture at Kuk Swamp in the highlands of New Guinea. *Science* 301: 189–193.

D'Errico, F. C. Henshilwood, G. Lawson, M. Vanhaeren, A.-M. Tillier, M. Soressi, F. Bresson, B. Maureille, A. Nowell, J. Lakarra, L. Backwell, and M. Julien. 2003. Archaeological evidence for the emergence of language, symbolism, and music—an alternative multidisciplinary perspective. *Journal of World Prehistory* 17: 1–70.

Derry, G. 2002. *What Science Is and How It Works.* Princeton: Princeton University Press.

Diamond, J. 2004. The astonishing micropygmies. *Science* 306: 2047–2048.

Diamond, J. 2005. Geography and skin color. *Nature* 435: 283–284.

Diamond, J. and P. Bellwood. 2003. Farmers and their languages: the first expansions. *Science* 300: 597–603.

Dixon, R. A. and C. A. Roberts. 2001. Modern and ancient scourges: the application of ancient DNA to the analysis of tuberculosis and leprosy from archaeologically derived human remains. *Ancient Biomolecules* 3: 181–194.

Dominguez-Rodrigo, M. and T. R. Pickering. 2003. Early hominid hunting and scavenging: a zooarchaeological review. *Evolutionary Anthropology* 12: 275–282.

Drapeau, M. S. M. and C. V. Ward. 2007. Forelimb segment length: proportions in extant hominoids and *Australopithecus afarensis. American Journal of Physical Anthropology* 132: 327–343.

Dressler, W. W., K. S. Oths, and C. C. Gravlee. 2005. Race and ethnicity in public health research: models to explain health disparities. *Annual Review of Anthropology* 34: 231–252.

Dronamraju, K. R. and P. Arese. 2006. *Malaria: Genetic and Evolutionary Aspects.* New York: Springer.

Ducrocq, S. 1998. Eocene primates from Thailand: are Asian anthropoideans related to African ones? *Evolutionary Anthropology* 7: 97–104.

Dunavan, C. P. 2005. Tackling malaria. *Scientific American* 293(6): 76–83.

Dunbar, R. 1977. Feeding ecology of gelada baboons: a preliminary report. Pp. 252–273 in T. H. Clutton-Brock, ed. *Primate Ecology: Studies of Feeding and Ranging Behaviour in Lemurs, Monkeys and Apes*. London: Academic Press.

Dunsworth, H. and A. Walker. 2002. Early genus *Homo*. Pp. 419–435 in W. C. Hartwig, ed. *The Primate Fossil Record*. Cambridge, UK: Cambridge University Press.

Duren, D. L., R. J. Sherwood, A. C. Choh, S. A. Czerwinski, W. C. Chumlea, M. Lee, S. S. Sun, E. W. Demerath, R. M. Siervogel, and B. Towne. 2007. Quantitative genetics of cortical bone mass in healthy 10–year-old children from the Fels Longitudinal Study. *Bone* 40: 464–470.

Eaton, S. B., S. B. Eaton III, and L. Cordain. 2002. Evolution, diet, and health. Pp. 7–17 in P. S. Ungar and M. F. Teaford, eds. *Human Diet: Its Origin and Evolution*. Westport, CT: Bergin & Garvey.

Eckhardt, R. B. 2003. Polymorphisms: past and present. *Human Biology* 75: 559–575.

Eimerl, S. and I. DeVore. 1965. *The Primates*. New York: Time-Life.

Ellison, P. 2001. *On Fertile Ground: A Natural History of Human Reproduction*. Cambridge, MA: Harvard University Press.

Ellison, P. T. 1994. Advances in human reproductive ecology. *Annual Review of Anthropology* 23: 255–275.

Ellison, P. T. and M. T. O'Rourke. 2000. Population growth and fertility regulation. Pp. 553–586 in S. Stinson, B. Bogin, R. Huss-Ashmore, and D. O'Rourke, eds. *Human Biology: An Evolutionary and Biocultural Perspective*. New York: Wiley-Liss.

Elton, S. 2006. Forty years on and still going strong: the use of hominin-cercopithecid comparisons in palaeoanthropology. *Journal of the Royal Anthropological Institute* 12: 19–38.

Ericson, P. A. 1997. Morton, Samuel George (1799–1851). Pp. 689–691 in F. Spencer, ed. *History of Physical Anthropology: An Encyclopedia*. New York: Garland.

Erikson, D. L., B. D. Smith, A. C. Clarke, D. H. Sandweiss, and N. Tuross. 2005. An Asian origin for a 10,000–year-old domesticated plant in the Americas. *Proceedings of the National Academy of Sciences* 102: 18315–18320.

Eriksson, J. G., T. Forsen, J. Tuomilehto, C. Osmond, and D. J. P. Barker. 2000. Early growth, adult income, and risk of stroke. *Stroke* 31: 869–874.

Eshleman, J. A., R. S. Malhi, and D. G. Smith. 2003. Mitochondrial DNA studies of Native Americans: conceptions and misconceptions of the population history of the Americas. *Evolutionary Anthropology* 12: 7–18.

Eveleth, P. B. and J. M. Tanner. 1990. *Worldwide Variation in Human Growth*. 2nd ed. Cambridge, UK: Cambridge University Press.

Fagan, B. M. 2004. *The Great Journey: The Peopling of Ancient North America*. Gainesville: University Press of Florida.

Falk, D. 2000. *Primate Diversity*. New York: Norton.

Falk, D., C. Hildebolt, K. Smith, M. J. Morwood, T. Sutikna, P. Brown, Jatmiko, E. W. Saptomo, B. Brunsden, and F. Prior. 2005. The brain of LB1, *Homo floresiensis*. *Science* 308: 242–245.

Feathers, J. K. 1996. Luminescence dating and modern human origins. *Evolutionary Anthropology* 5: 25–36.

Field, J. S., M. D. Petraglia, and M. M. Lahr. 2006. The southern dispersal hypothesis and the South Asian archaeological record: examination of dispersal routes through GIS analysis. *Journal of Anthropological Archaeology* 26: 88–108.

Feldman, M. W., R. C. Lewontin, and M.-C. King. 2003. Race: a genetic melting-pot. *Nature* 424: 374.

Finlayson, C. 2004. *Neanderthals and Modern Humans: An Ecological and Evolutionary Perspective*. New York: Cambridge University Press.

Fiorato, V., A. Boylston, and C. Knusel. 2000. *Blood Red Roses: The Archaeology of a Mass Grave from the Battle of Towton A. D. 1461*. Oxford, UK: Oxbow.

Fischman, J. 2005. Dmanisi find. *National Geographic Research* 207: 18–27.

Flannery, K. V. 1969. Origins and ecological effects of early domestication in Iran and the Near East. Pp. 73–100 in P. J. Ucko and G. W. Dimbleby, eds. *The Domestication of Plants and Animals*. Chicago: Aldine.

Fleagle, J. G. 1999. *Primate Adaptation and Evolution*. 2nd ed. San Diego: Academic Press.

Fleagle, J. G. 2000. A century of the past: one hundred years in the study of primate evolution. *Evolutionary Anthropology* 9: 87–100.

Fleagle, J. G. and R. F. Kay, eds. 1994. *Anthropoid Origins*. New York: Plenum Press.

Fleagle, J. G. and M. F. Tejedor. 2002. Early platyrrhines of southern South America. Pp. 161–173 in W. C. Hartwig, ed. *The Primate Fossil Record*. Cambridge, UK: Cambridge University Press.

Foster, E. A., M. A. Jobling, P. G. Taylor, P. Donnelly, P. de Knijff, R. Mieremet, T. Zerjal, and C. Tyler-Smith. 1998. Jefferson fathered slave's last child. *Nature* 396: 27–28.

Fragaszy, D., P. Izar, E. Visalberghi, E. B. Ottoni, and M. G. De Oliveira. 2004. Wild capuchin monkeys (*Cebus libidinosus*) use anvils and stone pounding tools. *American Journal of Primatology* 64: 359–366.

Freeman, A. S. and J. E. Byers. 2006. Divergent induced responses to an invasive predator in marine mussel populations. *Science* 313: 831–833.

Freeman, H. and R. D. Cox. 2006. Type-2 diabetes: a cocktail of genetic discovery. *Human Molecular Genetics* 15: R202–R209.

Frisancho, A. R. 1975. Functional adaptation to high-altitude hypoxia. *Science* 187: 313–319.

Frisancho, A. R. 1993. *Human Adaptation and Accommodation*. Ann Arbor: University of Michigan Press.

Fuller, D. Q., L. Qin, Y. Zheng, Z. Zhao, X. Chen, L.A. Hosoya, and G.P. Sun. 2009. The domestication process and domestication rates in rice: spikelet bases from the Lower Yangtze. *Science* 323: 1607–1610.

Futuyma, D. J. 2005. *Evolution*. Sunderland, MA: Sinauer Press.

Gage, T. B. 1998. The comparative demography of primates: with some comments on the evolution of life histories. *Annual Review of Anthropology* 27: 197–221.

Galik, K., B. Senut, M. Pickford, D. Gommery, J. Treil, A. J. Kuperavage, and R. B. Eckhardt. 2004. External and internal morphology of the BAR 1002'00 *Orrorin tugenensis* femur. *Science* 305: 1450–1453.

Garcia, R. S. 2003. The misuse of race in medical diagnosis. *The Chronical of Higher Education* May 9: B15.

Garrett, L. 1994. *The Coming Plague: Newly Emerging Diseases in a World out of Balance*. New York: Farrar, Straus, and Giroux.

Garruto, R. M., C.-T. Chin, C. A. Weitz, J.-C. Liu, R.-L. Liu, and X. He. 2003. Hematological differences during growth among Tibetans and Han Chinese born and raised at high altitude in Qinghai, China. *American Journal of Physical Anthropology* 122: 171–183.

Gebo, D. L., ed. 1993. *Postcranial Adaptation in Nonhuman Primates*. DeKalb: Northern Illinois University Press.

Gebo, D. L. 2002. Adapiformes: phylogeny and adaptation. Pp. 21–43 in W. C. Hartwig, ed. *The Primate Fossil Record*. Cambridge, UK: Cambridge University Press.

Gebo, D. L., M. Dagosto, K. C. Beard, and T. Qi. 2000. The smallest primates. *Journal of Human Evolution* 38: 585–594.

Gebo, D. L., M. Dagasto, K. C. Beard, T. Qi, and J. Wang. 2000. The oldest known anthropoid postcranial fossils and the early evolution of higher primates. *Nature* 404: 276–278.

Gebo, D. L., L. MacLatchy, R. Kityo, A. Deino, J. Kingston, and D. Pilbeam. 1997. A hominoid genus from the early Miocene of Uganda. *Science* 276: 401–404.

Gibbons, A. 2006. *The First Human: The Race to Discover Our Earliest Ancestors*. New York: Doubleday.

Gibbons, A. 2007. Food for thought: did the first cooked meals help fuel the dramatic evolutionary expansion of the human brain? *Science* 316: 1558–1560.

Gibbons, A. 2007. European skin turned pale only recently, gene suggests. *Science* 316: 364.

Gibson, R. 1990. *Principles of Human Nutrition*. Oxford, UK: Oxford University Press.

Gilby, I. C., L. E. Eberly, L. Pintea, and A. E. Pusey. 2006. Ecological and social influences on the hunting behaviour of wild chimpanzees, *Pan troglodytes schweinfurthii*. *Animal Behaviour* 72(1): 169–180.

Gillespie, J. H. 2004. *Population Genetics: A Concise Guide*. 2nd ed. Baltimore: Johns Hopkins University Press.

Gingerich, P. D. 1976. *Cranial Anatomy and Evolution of Early Tertiary Plesiadapidae (Mammalia, Primates)*. University of Michigan Museum of Paleontology, Papers on Paleontology 15.

Gingerich, P. D. 1976. Paleontology and phylogeny: patterns of evolution at the species level in early tertiary mammals. *American Journal of Science* 276: 1–28.

Gingerich, P. D. 1980. *Early Cenozoic Paleontology and Stratigraphy of the Bighorn Basin, Wyoming*. University of Michigan Museum of Paleontology, Papers on Paleontology 24.

Gingerich, P. D. 1990. Mammalian order Proprimates. *Journal of Human Evolution* 19: 821–822.

Gingerich, P. D. and G. F. Gunnell. 2005. Brain of *Plesiadapis cookei* (Mammalia, Proprimates): surface morphology and encephalization compared to those of Primates and Dermoptera. *Contributions of the Museum of Paleontology, University of Michigan* 31: 185–195.

Glass, B., M. S. Sacks, E. Jahn, and C. Hess. 1952. Genetic drift in a religious isolate: an analysis of the causes of variation in blood group and other gene frequencies in a small population. *American Naturalist* 86: 145–159.

Gluckman, P. D., M. A. Hanson, and A. S. Beedle. 2007. Early life events and their consequences for later disease: a life history and evolutionary perspective. *American Journal of Human Biology* 19: 1–19.

Godfrey, K. 2006. The developmental origins hypothesis: epidemiology. Pp. 6–32 in P. D. Gluckman and M. A. Hanson, eds. *Developmental Origins of Health and Disease*. Cambridge, UK: Cambridge University Press.

Godfrey, L. R. and W. L. Jungers. 2002. Quaternary fossil lemurs. Pp. 97–121 in W. C. Hartwig, ed. *The Primate Fossil Record*. Cambridge, UK: Cambridge University Press.

Goldberg, K. E. 1982. *The Skeleton: Fantastic Framework*. Washington, DC: U.S. News.

Goodall, J. 1986. *The Chimpanzees of Gombe: Patterns of Behavior*. Cambridge, MA: Harvard University Press.

Goodman, A. H. 1994. Cartesian reductionism and vulgar adaptationism: issues in the interpretation of nutritional status in prehistory. Pp. 163–177 in K. D. Sobolik, ed. *Paleonutrition: The Diet and Health of Prehistoric Americans*. Southern Illinois University at Carbondale, Center for Archaeological Investigations, Occasional Paper 22.

Goodman, A. H. 2005. Three questions about race, human biological variation and racism. *Anthropology News* 46(6): 18–19.

Goodman, A. H. and T. L. Leatherman. 1998. *Building a New Biocultural Synthesis: Political-Economic Perspectives on Human Biology*. Ann Arbor: University of Michigan Press.

Goodman, M., C. A. Porter, J. Czelusniak, S. L. Page, H. Schneider, J. Shoshani, G. Gunnell, and C. P. Groves. 1998. Toward a phylogenetic classification of primates based on DNA evidence complemented by fossil evidence. *Molecular Phylogenetics and Evolution* 9: 585–598.

Gore, A. 2006. *An Inconvenient Truth: The Planetary Emergency of Global Warming and What We Can Do about It*. New York: Rodale Press.

Goren-Inbar, N., N. Alperson, M. E. Kislev, O. Simchoni, Y. Melamed, A. Ben-Nun, and E. Werker. 2004. Evidence of hominin control of fire at Gesher Benot Ya'aqov, Israel. *Science* 304: 725–727.

Gould, S. J. 1982. Darwinism and the expansion of evolutionary theory. *Science* 216: 380–387.

Gould, S. J. 1989. *Wonderful Life: The Burgess Shale and the Nature of History*. New York: Norton.

Gould, S. J. 1992. *Ever since Darwin: Reflections on Natural History*. New York: Norton.

Gould, S. J. 1996. *The Mismeasure of Man*. New York: Norton.

Grant, P. R. and B. R. Grant. 2002. Adaptive radiation of Darwin's finches. *American Scientist* 90: 130–139.

Graves, J. L. Jr. 2004. *The Race Myth*. New York: Dutton.

Gravlee, C. C., H. R. Bernard, and W. R. Leonard. 2003. Heredity, environment, and cranial form: a reanalysis of Boas's immigrant data. *American Anthropologist* 105: 125–138.

Grayson, D. K. 2001. The archaeological record of human impacts on animal populations. *Journal of World Prehistory* 15: 1–68.

Grayson, D. K. and D. J. Meltzer. 2003. A requiem for North American overkill. *Journal of Archaeological Science* 30: 585–593.

Green, B. B., N. S. Weiss, and J. R. Daling. 1988. Risk of ovulatory infertility in relation to body weight. *Fertility and Sterility* 50: 721–726.

Green, R. E., J. Krause, S. E. Ptak, A. W. Briggs, M. T. Ronan, J. F. Simons, L. Du, M. Egholm, J. M. Rothberg, M. Paunovic, and S. Pääbo. 2006. Analysis of one million base pairs of Neanderthal DNA. *Nature* 444: 330–336.

Greene, M. 2005. *Jane Goodall: A Biography.* Westport, CT: Greenwood.

Gremillion, K. J. 2004. Seed processing and the origins of food production in eastern North America. *American Antiquity* 69: 215–233.

Grieco, E. M. and R. C. Cassidy. 2001. Overview of race and Hispanic origin. Pp. 1–11 in *U.S. Census Bureau, U.S. Department of Commerce* C2KBR/01-1.

Grine, F. E., R. M. Bailey, K. Harvati, R. P. Nathan, A. G. Morris, G. M. Henderson, I. Ribot, and A. W. G. Pike. 2007. Late Pleistocene human skull from Hofmeyr, South Africa, and modern human origins. *Science* 315: 226–229.

Grove, L. 1962. *Now It Can Be Told: The Story of the Manhattan Project.* New York: Harper.

Grün, R. 1993. Electron spin resonance dating in paleoanthropology. *Evolutionary Anthropology* 2: 172–181.

Grün, R. 2006. Direct dating of human fossils. *Yearbook of Physical Anthropology* 49: 2–48.

Guatelli-Steinberg, D., C. S. Larsen, and D. L. Hutchinson. 2004. Prevalence and the duration of linear enamel hypoplasia: a comparative study of Neandertals and Inuit foragers. *Journal of Human Evolution* 47: 65–84.

Guatelli-Steinberg, D., D. J. Reid, T. A. Bishop, and C. S. Larsen. 2005. Anterior tooth growth periods in Neandertals were comparable to those of modern humans. *Proceedings of the National Academy of Sciences* 102: 14197–14202.

Gunnell, G. F. and K. D. Rose. 2002. Tarsiiformes: evolutionary history and adaptation. Pp. 45–82 in W. C. Hartwig, ed. *The Primate Fossil Record.* Cambridge, UK: Cambridge University Press.

Haeckel, E. 1874. *The Evolution of Man.* 2 vols. Akron, OH: Werner.

Haeckel, E. 1889. *The History of Creation: Or the Development of the Earth and Its Inhabitants by the Action of Natural Causes.* New York: D. Appleton.

Haile-Selassie, Y. 2001. Late Miocene hominids from the late Awash, Ethiopia. *Nature* 412: 178–181.

Haile-Selassie, Y., B. Asfaw, and T. D. White. 2004. Hominid cranial remains from upper Pleistocene deposits at Aduma, Middle Awash, Ethiopia. *American Journal of Physical Anthropology* 123: 1–10.

Haile-Selassie, Y., G. Suwa, and T. D. White. 2004. Late Miocene teeth from Middle Awash, Ethiopia, and early hominid dental evolution. *Science* 303: 1503–1505.

Hallgrímsson, B. and B. K. Hall. 2005. *Variation: A Central Concept in Biology.* Burlington, MA: Elsevier Academic Press.

Hamada, Y. and T. Udono. 2002. Longitudinal analysis of length growth in the chimpanzee. *American Journal of Physical Anthropology* 118: 268–284.

Harper, G. J. and D. E. Crews. 2000. Aging, senescence, and human variation. Pp. 465–505 in S. Stinson, B. Bogin, R. Huss-Ashmore, and D. O'Rourke, eds. *Human Biology: An Evolutionary and Biocultural Perspective.* New York: Wiley-Liss.

Harris, E. E. and D. Meyer. 2006. The molecular signature of selection underlying human adaptations. *Yearbook of Physical Anthropology* 49: 89–130.

Harris, J. M. and T. D. White. 1979. *Evolution of the Plio-Pleistocene African Suidae. Transactions of the American Philosophical Society* 69(2).

Harrison, T. 2002. Late Oligocene to middle Miocene catarrhines from Afro-Arabia. Pp. 311–338 in W. C. Hartwig, ed. *The Primate Fossil Record.* Cambridge, UK: Cambridge University Press.

Harrold, F. B. 1980. A comparative analysis of Eurasian Paleolithic burials. *World Archaeology* 12: 195–211.

Hart, D. and R. W. Sussman. 2009. *Man the Hunted: Primates, Predators, and Human Evolution.* Expanded edition. Jackson, TN: Westview Press.

Hartwig, W. C., ed. 2002. *The Primate Fossil Record.* Cambridge, UK: Cambridge University Press.

Havill, L. M., M. C. Mahaney, L. A. Cox, P. A. Morin, G. Joslyn, and J. Rogers. 2005. A quantitative trait locus for normal variation in forearm bone mineral density in pedigreed baboons maps to the ortholog of human chromosome 11q. *Journal of Clinical Endocrinology and Metabolism* 90: 3638–3645.

Hawkes, K. 2003. Grandmothers and the evolution of human longevity. *American Journal of Human Biology* 15: 380–400.

Hawkes, K., J. F. O'Connell, N. G. Blurton Jones, H. Alvarez, and E. L. Charnov. 1998. Grandmothering, menopause, and the evolution of human life histories. *Proceedings of the National Academy of Sciences* 95: 1336–1339.

Hawks, J., E. T. Wang, G. M. Cochran, H. C. Harpending, and R. K. Moyzis. 2007. Recent acceleration of human adaptive evolution. *Proceedings of the National Academy of Sciences:* in press.

Hay, R. L. and M. D. Leakey. 1982. The fossil footprints of Laetoli. *Scientific American* 246(2): 50–57.

Heeney, J. L., A. G. Dalgleish, and R. A. Weiss. 2006. Origins of HIV and the evolution of resistance to AIDS. *Science* 313: 462–466.

Hernandez-Aguilar, R. A., J. Moore, and T. R. Pickering. 2007. Savanna chimpanzees use tools to harvest the underground storage organs of plants. *Proceedings of the National Academy of Sciences* 104: 19210–19213.

Higham, T., C. B. Ramsey, I. Karavanic, F. H. Smith, and E. Trinkaus. 2006. Revised direct radiocarbon dating of the Vindija G1 upper Paleolithic Neandertals. *Proceedings of the National Academy of Sciences* 103: 553–557.

Hill, W. C. O. 1972. *Evolutionary Biology of the Primates.* London: Academic Press.

Hlusko, L., N. Do, and M. C. Mahaney. 2007. Genetic correlations between mandibular molar cusp areas in baboons. *American Journal of Physical Anthropology* 132: 445–454.

Holden, C. 2004. The origin of speech. *Science* 303: 1316–1319.

Holliday, T. W. 1997. Body proportions in late Pleistocene Europe and modern human origins. *Journal of Human Evolution* 32: 423–447.

Holloway, R. L., D. C. Broadfield, and M. S. Yuan. 2004. *The Human Fossil Record, Volume 3: Brain Endocasts, The Paleoneurological Evidence*. Hoboken, NJ: Wiley-Liss.

Holman, D. J., M. A. Grimes, J. T. Achterberg, E. Brindle, and K. A. O'Conner. 2006. The distribution of postpartum amenorrhea in rural Bangladeshi women. *American Journal of Physical Anthropology* 129: 609–619.

Hudjashov, G., T. Kivisild, P. A. Underhill, P. Endicott, P. Sanchez, J. J. Sanchez, A. A. Lin, P. Shen, P. Oefner, C. Renfrew, R. Villems, and P. Forster. 2007. Revealing the prehistoric settlement of Australia by Y chromosome and mtDNA analysis. *Proceedings of the National Academy of Sciences* 104: 8726–8730.

Hunley, K. L., G. S. Cabana, D. A. Merriwether, and J. C. Long. 2007. A formal test of linguistic and genetic coevolution in native Central and South America. *American Journal of Physical Anthropology* 132: 622–631.

Hunley, K. L., J. E. Spence, and D. A. Merriwether. 2008. The impact of group fissions on genetic structure in native South America and implications for human evolution. *American Journal of Physical Anthropology*: in press.

Huss-Ashmore, R. 2000. Theory in human biology: evolution, ecology, adaptability, and variation. Pp. 1–25 in S. Stinson, B. Bogin, R. Huss-Ashmore, and D. O'Rourke, eds. *Human Biology: An Evolutionary and Biocultural Perspective*. New York: Wiley-Liss.

Huss-Ashmore, R., J. Schall, and M. Hediger. 1992. *Health and Lifestyle Change*. Philadelphia: Museum Applied Science Center for Archaeology, University of Pennsylvania.

Huxley, R. 2007. *The Great Naturalists*. New York: Thames & Hudson.

Institute of Vertebrate Paleontology and Paleoanthropology. 1980. *Atlas of Primitive Man in China*. Beijing, China, and New York: Science Press of the People's Republic of China and Van Nostrand Reinhold.

Irvine, W. 1955. *Apes, Angels, and Victorians*. New York: McGraw-Hill.

Isaac, G. L. 1977. *Olorgesailie: Archeological Studies of a Middle Pleistocene Lake Basin in Kenya*. Chicago: University of Chicago Press.

Jablonski, N. 2002. Fossil Old World monkeys: the late Neogene radiation. Pp. 255–299 in W. C. Hartwig, ed. *The Primate Fossil Record*. Cambridge, UK: Cambridge University Press.

Jablonski, N. G. 2004. The evolution of human skin and skin color. *Annual Review of Anthropology* 33: 585–623.

Jablonski, N. G. 2006. *Skin: A Natural History*. Berkeley: University of California Press.

Jablonski, N. G. and G. Chaplin. 2000. The evolution of skin coloration. *Journal of Human Evolution* 39: 57–106.

Jablonski, N. G. and G. Chaplin. 2002. Skin deep. *Scientific American* 287(4): 50–55.

Jablonski, N. G., M. G. Leakey, C. Kiarie, and M. Anton. 2002. A new skeleton of *Theropithecus brumpti* (Primates: Cercopithecidae) from Lomekwi, West Turkana, Kenya. *Journal of Human Evolution* 43: 887–923.

Jacob, T., E. Indriati, R. P. Soejono, K. Hsu, D. W. Frayer, R. B. Eckhardt, A. J. Kuperavage, A. Thorne, and M. Henneberg 2006. Pygmoid Australomelanesian *Homo sapiens* skeletal remains from Liang Bua, Flores: population affinities and pathological abnormalities. *Proceedings of the National Academy of Sciences* 103: 13421–13426.

Jaeger, J.-J. and L. Marivaux. 2005. Shaking the earliest branches of anthropoid primate evolution. *Science* 310: 244–245.

Jantz, L. M. and R. L. Jantz. 1999. Secular change in long bone length and proportion in the United States, 1800–1970. *American Journal of Physical Anthropology* 110: 57–67.

Jolly, A. 1985. *The Evolution of Primate Behavior*. New York: Macmillan.

Jones, M. 2003. Ancient DNA in pre-Columbian archaeology: a review. *Journal of Archaeological Science* 30: 629–635.

Kaestle, F. A. 1995. Mitochondrial DNA evidence for the identity of the descendants of the prehistoric Stillwater Marsh populations. Pp. 73–80 in C. S. Larsen and R. L. Kelly, eds. *Bioarchaeology of the Stillwater Marsh: Prehistoric Human Adaptation in the Western Great Basin. Anthropological Papers of the American Museum of Natural History* 77.

Kaestle, F. A. and K. A. Horsburgh. 2002. Ancient DNA in anthropology: methods, applications, and ethics. *Yearbook of Physical Anthropology* 45: 92–130.

Kaestle, F. A., R. A. Kittles, A. L. Roth, and E. J. Ungvarsky. 2006. Database limitations on the evidentiary value of forensic mitochondrial DNA evidence. *American Criminal Law Review* 43: 53–88.

Kaestle, F. A., J. G. Lorenz, and D. G. Smith. 1999. Molecular genetics and the Numic expansion: a molecular investigation of the prehistoric inhabitants of Stillwater Marsh. Pp. 167–183 in B. E. Hemphill and C. S. Larsen, eds. *Prehistoric Lifeways in the Great Basin Wetlands: Bioarchaeological Reconstruction and Interpretation*. Salt Lake City: University of Utah Press.

Kaifu, Y., H. Baba, F. Aziz, E. Indriati, F. Schrenk, and T. Jacob. 2004. Taxonomic affinities and evolutionary history of the early Pleistocene hominids of Java: dento-gnathic evidence. *American Journal of Physical Anthropology* 128: 709–726.

Kalaydjieva, L., B. Morar, R. Chaix, and H. Tang. 2005. A newly discovered founder population: the Roma/Gypsies. *BioEssays* 27: 1084–1094.

Kappeler, P. M. and C. P. van Schaik. 2006. *Cooperation in Primates and Humans: Mechanisms and Evolution*. New York: Springer.

Kappelman, J. 1993. The attraction of paleomagnetism. *Evolutionary Anthropology* 2: 89–99.

Kappelman, J., M. C. Alcicek, N. Kazanci, M. Schultz, M. Ozkul, and S. Sen. 2008. First *Homo erectus* from Turkey and implications for migrations into temperate Eurasia. *American Journal of Physical Anthropology*: in press.

Karavanic, I. and F. H. Smith. 1998. The middle/upper Paleolithic interface and the relationship of Neanderthals and early modern humans in the Hrvatsko Zagorje, Croatia. *Journal of Human Evolution* 34: 223–248.

Katzenberg, M. A. 2000. Stable isotope analysis: a tool for studying past diet, demography, and life history. Pp. 305–327 in M. A. Katzenberg and S. R. Saunders, eds. *Biological Anthropology of the Human Skeleton*. New York: Wiley-Liss.

Kay, R. F., C. Ross, and B. A. Williams. 1997. Anthropoid origins. *Science* 275: 797–804.

Kelley, E. A. and R. W. Sussman. 2007. An academic genealogy on the history of American field primatologists. *American Journal of Physical Anthropology* 132: 406–425.

Kelley, J. 2002. The hominoid radiation in Asia. Pp. 369–384 in W. C. Hartwig, ed. *The Primate Fossil Record*. Cambridge, UK: Cambridge University Press.

Kelly, R. L. 2003. Maybe we know when people first came to North America; and what does it mean if we do? *Quaternary International* 109–110: 133–145.

Kemp, B. M., R. S. Malhi, J. McDonough, D. A. Bolnick, J. A. Eshleman, O. Rickards, C. Martinez-Labarga, J. R. Johnson, J. G. Lorenz, E. J. Dixon, T. E. Fifield, T. H. Heaton, R. Worl, and D. G. Smith. 2007. Genetic analysis of early Holocene skeletal remains from Alaska and its implications for the settlement of the Americas. *American Journal of Physical Anthropology* 132: 605–621.

Kenneally, C. 2007. *The First Word: The Search for the Origins of Language*. New York: Viking.

Kennedy, K. A. R. 2000. *God-Apes and Fossil Men: Paleoanthropology in South Asia*. Ann Arbor: University of Michigan Press.

Kennedy, K. A. R., A. Sonakia, J. Chiment, and K. K. Verma. 1991. Is the Narmada hominid an Indian *Homo erectus*? *American Journal of Physical Anthropology* 86: 475–496.

Kettlewell, H. B. D. 1973. *The Evolution of Melanism*. Oxford, UK: Oxford University Press.

Kevles, B. H. 2006. *The Reluctant Mr. Darwin: An Intimate Portrait of Charles Darwin and the Making of His Theory of Evolution*. New York: Norton.

Keyser, A. W. 2000. The Drimolen skull: the most complete australopithecine cranium and mandible to date. *South African Journal of Science* 96: 189–197.

Khoury, M. J., R. Millikan, J. Little, and M. Gwinn. 2004. The emergence of epidemiology in the genomics age. *International Journal of Epidemiology* 33: 936–944.

Kim, U.-K., E. Jorgenson, H. Coon, M. Leppert, N. Risch, and D. Drayna. 2003. Positional cloning of the human quantitative trait locus underlying taste sensitivity to phenylthiocarbamide. *Science* 299: 1221–1225.

Kimbel, W. H., D. C. Johanson, and Y. Rak. 1994. The first skull and other new discoveries of *Australopithecus afarensis* at Hadar, Ethiopia. *Nature* 368: 449–451.

Kimbel, W. H., Y. Rak, and D. C. Johanson. 2004. *The Skull of Australopithecus afarensis*. New York: Oxford University Press.

King, T. E., G. R. Bowden, P. L. Balaresque, S. M. Adams, M. E. Shanks, and M. A. Jobling. 2007. Thomas Jefferson's Y chromosome belongs to rare European lineage. *American Journal of Physical Anthropology* 132: 584–589.

Kitchen, D. M. 2003. Alpha male black howler monkey responses to loud calls: effect of numeric odds, male companion behaviour and reproductive investment. *Animal Behaviour* 67: 125–139.

Klein, R. G. 1999. *The Human Career: Human Biological and Cultural Origins*. 2nd ed. Chicago: University of Chicago Press.

Klepinger, L. L. 2006. *Fundamentals of Forensic Anthropology*. Hoboken, NJ: Wiley-Liss.

Klitz, W., C. Brautbar, A. M. Schito, L. F. Barcellos, and J. R. Oksenberg. 2001. Evolution of the CCR5 delta 32 mutation based on haplotype variation in Jewish and northern European population samples. *Human Immunology* 62: 530–538.

Kolbert, E. 2007. *Field Notes from a Catastrophe: A Frontline Report on Climate Change*. London: Bloomsbury.

Kolman, C. J. 2006. Anthropological applications of ancient DNA: problems and prospects. *American Antiquity* 71: 365–380.

Komlos, J., ed. 1994. *Stature, Living Standards, and Economic Development: Essays in Anthropometric History*. Chicago: University of Chicago Press.

Kordos, L. and D. R. Begun. 2002. Rudabanya: a late Miocene subtropical swamp deposit with evidence of the origin of the African apes and humans. *Evolutionary Anthropology* 11: 45–57.

Kramer, A. 2002. The natural history and evolutionary fate of *Homo erectus*. Pp. 140–154 in P. N. Peregrine, C. R. Ember, and M. Ember, eds. *Physical Anthropology: Original Readings in Method and Practice*. Upper Saddle River, NJ: Prentice Hall.

Krause, J., L. Orlando, D. Serre, B. Viola, B. Prufer, M. P. Richards, J.-J. Hublin, C. Hanni, A. P. Derevianko, and S. Pääbo. 2007. Neanderthals in central Asia and Siberia. *Nature:* in press.

Krech, S. III. 1999. *The Ecological Indian: Myth and History*. New York: Norton.

Krogman, W. M. and M. Y. İşcan. 1986. *The Human Skeleton in Forensic Medicine*. 2nd ed. Springfield, IL: Charles C. Thomas.

Kunimatsu, Y., M. Nakatsukasa, Y. Sawada, T. Sakai, M. Hyodo, H. Hyodo, T. Itaya, H. Nakaya, H. Saegusa, A. Maxurier, M. Saneyoshi, H. Tsujikawa, A. Yamamoto, and E. Mbua. 2007. A new late Miocene great ape from Kenya and its implications for the origins of African great apes and humans. *Proceedings of the National Academy of Sciences* 104: 19220–19225.

Laitman, J. T. and I. Tattersall, eds. 2001. *Homo erectus newyorkensis. The Anatomical Record* 262(1).

Lamason, R. L., M.-A. P. K. Mohideen, J. R. Mest, A. C. Wong, H. L. Norton, M. C. Aros, M. J. Jurynec, X. Mao, V. R. Humphreville, J. E. Humbert, S. Sinha, J. L. Moore, P. Jagadeeswaran, W. Zhao, G. Ning, I. Makalowska, P. M. McKeigue, D. O'Donnell, R. Kittles, E. J. Parra, N. J. Mangini, D. J. Grunwald, M. D. Shriver, V. A. Canfield, and K. C. Cheng. 2005. SLC24A5, a putative cation exchanger, affects pigmentation in zebrafish and humans. *Science* 310: 1782–1786.

Lambert, D. M. and C. D. Millar. 2006. Ancient genomics is born. *Nature* 444: 275–276.

Lambert, J. E. 1999. Seed handling in chimpanzees (*Pan troglodytes*) and redtail monkeys (*Cercopithecus ascanius*): implications for understanding hominoid and cercopithecine fruit-processing strategies and seed dispersal. *American Journal of Physical Anthropology* 109: 365–386.

Lambert, J. E., C. A. Chapman, R. W. Wrangham, and N. L. Conklin-Brittain. 2004. Hardness of cercopithecine foods: implications for the critical function of enamel thickness in exploiting fallback foods. *American Journal of Physical Anthropology* 125: 363–368.

Lambert, P. M., ed. 2000. *Bioarchaeological Studies of Life in the Age of Agriculture: A View from the Southeast.* Tuscaloosa: University of Alabama Press.

Lambert, P. M. 2002. The archaeology of war: a North American perspective. *Journal of Archaeological Research* 10: 207–241.

Langdon, J. H. 2005. *The Human Strategy: An Evolutionary Perspective on Human Anatomy.* New York: Oxford University Press.

Lanham, U. 1973. *The Bone Hunters.* New York: Columbia University Press.

Larsen, C. S., ed. 1985. *The Antiquity and Origin of Native North Americans.* New York: Garland Publishing.

Larsen, C. S. 1994. In the wake of Columbus: native population biology in the postcontact Americas. *Yearbook of Physical Anthropology* 37: 109–154.

Larsen, C. S. 1995. Biological changes in human populations with agriculture. *Annual Review of Anthropology* 24: 185–213.

Larsen, C. S. 1997. *Bioarchaeology: Interpreting Behavior from the Human Skeleton.* Cambridge, UK: Cambridge University Press.

Larsen, C. S. 2000. *Skeletons in Our Closet: Revealing Our Past through Bioarchaeology.* Princeton: Princeton University Press.

Larsen, C. S. 2002. Bioarchaeology: the lives and lifestyles of past people. *Journal of Archaeological Research* 10: 119–166.

Larsen, C. S. 2003. Animal source foods and human health during evolution. *Journal of Nutrition* 133: 1S–5S.

Larsen, C. S. 2003. Equality for the sexes in human evolution?: Early hominid sexual dimorphism and implications for mating systems and social behavior. *Proceedings of the National Academy of Sciences* 100: 9103–9104.

Larsen, C. S., R. M. Matter, and D. L. Gebo. 1998. *Human Origins: The Fossil Record.* 3rd ed. Prospect Heights, IL: Waveland Press.

Larsen, C. S. and T. C. Patterson. 1997. Americas: paleoanthropology. Pp. 69–74 in F. Spencer, ed. *History of Physical Anthropology: An Encyclopedia.* New York: Garland.

Larsen, E. 2005. Developmental origins of variation. Pp. 113–129 in B. Hallgrímson and B. K. Hall, eds. *Variation: A Central Concept in Biology.* Burlington, MA: Elsevier Academic Press.

Larson, G., U. Albarella, K. Dobney, P. Rowley-Conway, J. Schibler, A. Tresset, J.-D. Vigne, C. J. Edwards, A. Schlumbaum, A. Dinu, A. Balacsecu, G. Dolman, A. Tagliacozzo, N. Manaseryan, P. Miracle, L. Van Wijngaarden-Bakker, M. Masseti, D. G. Bradley, and A. Cooper. 2007. Ancient DNA, pig domestication, and the spread of the Neolithic into Europe. *Proceedings of the National Academy of Sciences* 104: 15276–15281.

Lassek, W. D. and S. J. C. Gaulin. 2006. Changes in body fat distribution in relation to parity in American women: a covert form of maternal depletion. *American Journal of Physical Anthropology* 131: 295–302.

Latham, R. 1982. *The Travels of Marco Polo.* New York: Viking.

Lau, E. M., C. Cooper, C. Wickham, S. Donnan, and D. J. Barker. 1990. Hip fracture in Hong Kong and Britain. *International Journal of Epidemiology* 19: 1119–1121.

Leakey, M. 1984. *Disclosing the Past: An Autobiography.* Garden City, NY: Doubleday.

Leakey, M. G., C. S. Feibel, I. McDougall, and A. Walker. 1995. New four-million-year-old hominid species from Kanapoi and Allia Bay, Kenya. *Nature* 376: 565–571.

Leakey, M. G., F. Spoor, F. H. Brown, P. N. Gathogo, C. Kiarie, L. M. Leakey and I. McDougall. 2001. New hominin genus from eastern Africa shows diverse middle Pliocene lineages. *Nature* 410: 433–440.

Lee, S.-H. and M. H. Wolpoff. 2003. The pattern of evolution in Pleistocene human brain size. *Paleobiology* 29: 186–196.

Lee-Thorp, J. 2002. Hominid dietary niches from proxy chemical indicators in fossils: the Swartkrans example. Pp. 123–141 in P. S. Ungar and M. F. Teaford, eds. *Human Diet: Its Origin and Evolution.* Westport, CT: Bergin & Garvey.

Lee-Thorp, J. and M. Sponheimer. 2006. Distributions of biogeochemistry to understanding hominin dietary ecology. *Yearbook of Physical Anthropology* 49: 131–148.

Lee-Thorp, J. A., M. Sponheimer, and N. J. van der Merwe. 2003. What do stable isotopes tell us about hominid dietary and ecological niches in the Pliocene? *International Journal of Osteoarchaeology* 13: 104–113.

Leidy, L. E. 1994. Biological aspects of menopause: across the lifespan. *Annual Review of Anthropology* 23: 231–253.

Lemons, D. and W. McGinnis. 2006. Genomic evolution of Hox gene clusters. *Science* 313: 1918–1922.

Leonard, W. R. 2000. Human nutritional evolution. Pp. 295–343 in S. Stinson, B. Bogin, R. Huss-Ashmore, and D. O'Rourke, eds. *Human Biology: An Evolutionary and Biocultural Perspective.* New York: Wiley-Liss.

Leonard, W. R. 2002. Food for thought: dietary change was a driving force in human evolution. *Scientific American* December: 106–115.

Levy, S. 1994. *The Antiobiotic Paradox: How Miracle Drugs Are Destroying the Miracle.* New York: Plenum Press.

Lewin, R. 1988. *Bones of Contention: Controversies in the Search for Human Origins.* New York: Touchstone.

Lewontin, R. C. 1972. The apportionment of human diversity. *Evolutionary Biology* 6: 381–398.

Libby, W. F. 1952. *Radiocarbon Dating.* Chicago: University of Chicago Press.

Lieberman, D. E. 2007. Homing in on early *Homo. Nature* 449: 291–292.

Lieberman, L., R. C. Kirk, and A. Littlefield. 2003. Perishing paradigm: race—1931–1999. *American Anthropologist* 105: 110–113.

Little, B. B., P. H. Buschang, M. E. P. Reyes, S. K. Tan, and R. M. Malina. 2006. Craniofacial dimensions in children in rural Oaxaca, southern Mexico: secular change, 1968–2000. *American Journal of Physical Anthropology* 131: 127–136.

Little, M. A. and P. W. Leslie. 1999. *Turkana Herders of the Dry Savanna: Ecology and Biobehavioral Response of Nomads to an Uncertain Environment*. Oxford, UK: Oxford University Press.

Livingstone, F. B. 1958. Anthropological implications of sickle cell gene distribution in West Africa. *American Anthropologist* 60: 533–562.

Livingstone, F. B. 1962. On the non-existence of human races. *Current Anthropology* 3: 279.

Livingstone, F. B. 1967. *Abnormal Hemoglobins in Human Populations*. Chicago: Aldine.

Livingstone, F. B. 1971. Malaria and human polymorphisms. *Annual Review of Genetics* 5: 33–64.

Livingstone, F. B. 1973. *Data on the Abnormal Hemoglobins and Glucose-6-Phosphate Dehydrogenase Deficiency in Human Populations, 1969–1973. Museum of Anthropology, University of Michigan, Technical Reports 3, Contributions in Human Biology 1.*

Livingstone, F. B. 1985. *Frequencies of Hemoglobin Variants: Thalassemia, The Glucose-6-Phosphate Hydrogenase Deficiency, G6PD Variants, and Ovolocytosis in Human Populations*. Oxford, UK: Oxford University Press.

Lock, M. and P. Kaufert. 2001. Menopause, local biologies, and cultures of aging. *American Journal of Human Biology* 13: 494–504.

Lockwood, C. A., W. H. Kimbel, and D. C. Johanson. 2000. Temporal trends and metric variation in the mandibles and dentition of *Australopithecus afarensis*. *Journal of Human Evolution* 39: 23–55.

Londo, J. P., Y.-C. Chiang, K.-H. Hung, T.-Y. Chiang, and B. A. Schaal. 2006. Phylogeography of Asian wild rice, *Oryza rufipogon*, reveals multiple independent domestications of cultivated rice, *Oryza sativa*. *Proceedings of the National Academy of Sciences* 103: 9578–9583.

Long, J. C. and R. A. Kittles. 2003. Human genetic diversity and the nonexistence of biological races. *Human Biology* 75: 449–471.

Loomis, W. F. 1967. Skin-pigment regulation of vitamin-D biosynthesis in man. *Science* 157: 501–506.

Lordkipanidze, D., T. Jashashvili, A. Vekua, M. S. Ponce de Leon, C. P. E. Zollikofer, G. P. Rightmire, H. Pontzer, R. Ferring, O. Oms, M. Tappen, M. Bukhsianidze, J. Agusti, R. Kahlke, G. Kiladze, B. Martinez-Navarro, A. Mouskhelishvili, M. Nioradze, and L. Rook. 2007. Postcranial evidence from early *Homo* from Dmanisi, Georgia. *Nature* 449: 305–310.

Louwe Kooijmans, L. P., Y. Smirnov, R. S. Solecki, P. Villa, and T. Weber. 1989. On the evidence for Neandertal burial. *Current Anthropology* 30: 322–326.

Lyell, C. 1830–33. *Principles of Geology*. London: Murray.

Lynch, M. and B. Walsh. 1998. *Genetics and Analysis of Quantitative Traits*. Sunderland, MA: Sinauer.

Maddox, B. 2002. *Rosalind Franklin: The Dark Lady of DNA*. New York: HarperCollins.

Madrigal, L., B. Ware, R. Miller, G. Saenz, M. Chavez and D. Dykes. 2001. Ethnicity, gene flow and population subdivision in Limon, Costa Rica. *American Journal of Physical Anthropology* 114: 99–108.

Malthus, T. R. 1798. *An Essay on the Principle of Population*, ed. Philip Appleman, 2004. New York: Norton.

Maples, W. R. and M. Browning. 1994. *Dead Men Do Tell Tales*. New York: Doubleday.

Marks, J. 1994. Black, white, other. *Discover* December: 32–35.

Marks, J. 1995. *Human Biodiversity: Genes, Race, and History*. New York: Aldine de Gruyter.

Marks, J. 1996. Science and race. *American Behavioral Scientist* 40: 123–133.

Marlar, R. A., B. L. Leonard, B. M. Billman, P. M. Lambert, and J. E. Marlar. 2000. Biochemical evidence of cannibalism at a prehistoric Puebloan site in southwestern Colorado. *Nature* 407: 74–78.

Marquez, S., K. Mowbray, G. J. Sawyer, T. Jacob, and A. Silvers. 2001. New fossil hominid calvaria from Indonesia—Sambungmacan 3. *Anatomical Record* 262: 344–368.

Marshak, S. 2005. *Earth: Portrait of a Planet*. 2nd ed. New York: Norton.

Marshall, G. A. 1968. Racial classifications: popular and scientific. Pp. 149–166 in M. Mead, T. Dobzhansky, E. Tobach, and R. E. Light, eds. *Science and the Concept of Race*. New York: Columbia University Press.

Martin, D. L. and D. W. Frayer, eds. 1997. *Troubled Times: Violence and Warfare in the Past*. Amsterdam: Gordon and Breach.

Martin, L. 1985. Significance of enamel thickness in hominoid evolution. *Nature* 314: 260–263.

Martin, N., L. Eaves, and D. Loesch. 1982. A genetic analysis of covariation between finger ridge counts. *Annals of Human Biology* 9: 539–552.

Martin, R. A. 2004. *Missing Links: Evolutionary Concepts and Transitions through Time*. Sudbury, MA: Jones and Bartlett.

Martin, R. D. 1990. *Primate Origins and Evolution: A Phylogenetic Reconstruction*. London: Chapman & Hall.

Martin, R. D. 1993. Primate origins: plugging the gaps. *Nature* 363: 223–234.

Mayor, A. 2001. *The First Fossil Hunters: Paleontology in Greek and Roman Times*. Princeton: Princeton University Press.

Mayr, E. 1942. *Systematics and the Origin of Species*. New York: Columbia University Press.

Mayr, E. 1970. *Populations, Species, and Evolution*. Cambridge, MA: Harvard University Press.

Mayr, E. 2004. 80 years of watching the evolutionary scenery. *Science* 305: 46–47.

McBrearty, S. and A. S. Brooks. 2000. The revolution that wasn't: a new interpretation of the origin of modern human behavior. *Journal of Human Evolution* 39: 453–563.

McCorriston, J. 2000. Wheat domestication. Pp. 158–174 in K. Kiple and C. Ornelas, eds. *Cambridge World History of Food and Nutrition*. New York: Cambridge University Press.

McDougall, I., F. H. Brown, and J. G. Fleagle. 2005. Stratigraphic placement and age of modern humans from Kibish, Ethiopia. *Nature* 433: 733–736.

McGovern, P. E. 2003. *Ancient Wine: The Search for the Origins of Viniculture*. Princeton: Princeton University Press.

McGraw, W. S., C. Cooke, and S. Shultz. 2006. Primate remains from African crowned eagle (*Stephanoaetus coronatus*) nests in Ivory Coast's Taï Forest: implications for primate predation and early hominid taphonomy in South Africa. *American Journal of Physical Anthropology* 131: 151–165.

McGraw, W. S., K. Zuberbuhler, and R. Noe, eds. 2007. *Monkeys of the Tai Forest: An African Primate Community*. Cambridge, UK: Cambridge University Press.

McGrew, W. C. 1998. Culture in nonhuman primates. *Annual Review of Anthropology* 27: 301–328.

McGrew, W. C., L. F. Marchant, and T. Nishida. 1996. *Great Ape Societies*. Cambridge, UK: Cambridge University Press.

McHenry, H. M. 2002. Introduction to the fossil record of human ancestry. Pp. 401–405 in W. C. Hartwig, ed. *The Primate Fossil Record*. Cambridge, UK: Cambridge University Press.

McHenry, H. M. and K. Coffing. 2000. *Australopithecus* to *Homo*: Transformations in body and mind. *Annual Review of Anthropology* 29: 125–146.

McKee, J. K. 1996. Faunal evidence and Sterkfontein Member 2 foot bones of early hominid. *Science* 271: 1301.

McKee, J. K. 2003. *Sparing Nature: The Conflict between Human Population Growth and Earth's Biodiversity*. New Brunswick, NJ: Rutgers University Press.

McKee, J. K., F. E. Poirier, and W. S. McGraw. 2005. *Understanding Human Evolution*. 4th ed. Upper Saddle River, NJ: Pearson Prentice Hall.

McKee, J. K., P. W. Sciulli, C. D. Fooce, and T. A. Waite. 2003. Forecasting global biodiversity threats associated with human population growth. *Biological Conservation* 115: 161–164.

Meltzer, D. J. 1993. Pleistocene peopling of the Americas. *Evolutionary Anthropology* 1: 157–169.

Mercader, J., H. Barton, J. Gillespie, J. Harris, S. Kuhn, R. Tyler, and C. Boesch. 2007. 4,300-year-old chimpanzee sites and the origins of percussive stone technology. *Proceedings of the National Academy of Sciences* 104: 3043–3048.

Mercader, J., M. Panger, and C. Boesch. 2002. Excavation of a chimpanzee stone tool site in the African rainforest. *Science* 296: 1452–1455.

Merriwether, D. A. 2007. Mitochondrial DNA. Pp. 817–830 in D. H. Ubelaker, ed. *Handbook of North American Indians*. Washington, DC: Smithsonian Institution Press.

Mielke, J. H., L. W. Konigsberg, and J. H. Relethford. 2006. *Human Biological Variation*. New York: Oxford University Press.

Miller, E. R., G. F. Gunnell, and R. D. Martin. 2005. Deep time and the search for anthropoid origins. *Yearbook of Physical Anthropology* 48: 60–95.

Minugh-Purvis, N. 2002. Neandertal growth: examining developmental adaptations in earlier *Homo sapiens*. Pp. 154–173 in P. N. Peregrine, C. R. Ember, and M. Ember, eds. *Physical Anthropology: Original Readings in Method and Practice*. Upper Saddle River, NJ: Prentice Hall.

Mittermeier, R. A. 2000. Foreword. Pp. xv–xxiii in P. Tyson, ed. *The Eighth Continent: Life, Death, and Discovery in the Lost World of Madagascar*. New York: HarperCollins Publishers.

Moffat, A. S. 2002. New fossils and a glimpse of evolution. *Science* 295: 613–615.

Molleson, T. 1994. The eloquent bones of Abu Hureya. *Scientific American* 271(2): 70–75.

Molnar, S. 2002. *Human Variation: Races, Types, and Ethnic Groups*. Upper Saddle River, NJ: Prentice Hall.

Montagu, A. 1964. Natural selection and man's relative hairlessness. *Journal of the American Medical Association* 187: 356–357.

Monteiro, C. A., E. C. Moura, W. L. Conde, and B. M. Popkin. 2004. Socioeconomic status and obesity in adult populations of developing countries: a review. *Bulletin of the World Health Organization* 82: 940–946.

Moore, J. A. 1999. *Science as a Way of Knowing: The Foundations of Modern Biology*. Cambridge, MA: Harvard University Press.

Moorehead, A. 1969. *Darwin and the Beagle*. New York: Penguin Books.

Morris, L. N. 1971. *Human Populations, Genetic Variation, and Evolution*. San Francisco: Chandler.

Morwood, M., T. Sutikna, and R. Roberts. 2005. The people time forgot: Flores find. *National Geographic Research* 207(4): 4–12.

Mote, P. W. and G. Kaser. 2007. The shrinking glaciers of Kilimanjaro: can global warming be blamed? *American Scientist* 95: 318–325.

Motulsky, A. G. 1961. Glucose-6-phosphate dehydrogenase deficiency, haemolytic disease of the newborn, and malaria. *The Lancet* 1: 1168–1169.

Moura, A. C. A. and P. C. Lee. 2004. Capuchin stone tool use in Caatinga dry forest. *Science* 306: 1909.

Moya-Soya, S., M. Kohler, and L. Rook. 1999. Evidence of hominid-like precision grip capability in the hand of the Miocene ape *Oreopithecus*. *Proceedings of the National Academy of Sciences* 96: 313–317.

Muehlenbein, M. P., D. P. Watts, and P. Whitten. 2004. Dominance rank and fecal testosterone levels in adult male chimpanzees (*Pan troglodytes schweinfurthii*) at Ngogo, Kibale National Park, Uganda. *American Journal of Primatology* 64: 71–82.

Napier, J. 1993. *Hands,* rev. R. H. Tuttle. Princeton: Princeton University Press.

Napier, J. R. and P. H. Napier. 1967. *A Handbook of Living Primates: Morphology, Ecology and Behaviour of Nonhuman Primates*. London, UK: Academic Press.

National Academy of Sciences. 1998. *Teaching about Evolution and the Nature of Science*. Washington, DC: National Academy of Sciences.

Neufeld, A. H. and G. C. Conroy. 2004. Human head hair is not fur. *Journal of Human Evolution* 13: 89.

Newman, J. 2006. Allergies: a modern epidemic. *National Geographic* 209(5): 116–135.

Niewoehner, W. A., A. Bergstrom, D. Eichele, M. Zuroff, and J. T. Clark. 2003. Manual dexterity in Neanderthals. *Nature* 422: 395.

Nitecki, M. H. and D. V. Nitecki. 1994. *Origins of Anatomically Modern Humans*. New York: Plenum Press.

Noonan, J. P., G. Coop, S. Kudaravalli, D. Smith, J. Krause, J. Alessi, F. Chen, D. Platt, S. Paabo, J. K. Pritchard, and E. M.

Rubin. 2006. Sequencing and analysis of Neanderthal genomic DNA. *Science* 314: 1113–1118.

Nordin, M. and V. H. Frankel. 2001. *Basic Biomechanics of the Musculoskeletal System*. Philadelphia: Lippincott Williams & Wilkins.

Novembre, J., A. P. Galvani, and M. Slatkin. 2005. The geographic spread of the CCR5 Delta32 HIV–resistance allele. *PLoS Biology* 3: 1954–1962.

O'Connell, J. F. and J. Allen. 1998. When did humans first arrive in greater Australia and why is it important to know? *Evolutionary Anthropology* 6: 132–146.

Ogden, C. L., C. D. Fryar, M. D. Carroll, and K. M. Flegal. 2004. Mean body weight, height, and body mass index, United States 1960–2002. *Advance Data from Vital and Health Statistics* 337: 1–17.

Olsen, C. L., P. K. Cross, and L. J. Gensburg. 2003. Down syndrome: interaction between culture, demography, and biology in determining the prevalence of a genetic trait. *Human Biology* 75: 503–520.

Oota, H., W. Settheetham-Ishida, D. Tiwawech, T. Ishida, and M. Stoneking. 2001. Human mtDNA and Y-chromosome variation is correlated with matrilocal versus patrilocal residence. *Nature Genetics* 29: 20–21.

Oppenheim, A., C. L. Jury, D. Rund, T. J. Vulliamy, and L. Luzzatto. 1993. G6PD Mediterranean accounts for the high prevalence of G6PD deficiency in Kurdish Jews. *Human Genetics* 91: 293–294.

O'Rourke, D. H., M. G. Hayes, and S. W. Carlyle. 2000. Ancient DNA studies in physical anthropology. *Annual Review of Anthropology* 29: 217–242.

Overpeck, J. T. and J. E. Cole. 2006. Abrupt change in Earth's climate system. *Annual Review of Environmental Resources* 31: 1–31.

Oxenham, M. 2006. Biological responses to change in prehistoric Viet Nam. *Asian Perspectives* 45: 212–239.

Oxenham, M. and N. Tayles, eds. 2006. *Bioarchaeology of Southeast Asia*. Cambridge, UK: Cambridge University Press.

Pakendorf, B., I. N. Novgorodov, V. L. Osakovskij, A. P. Protod'jakonov, and M. Stoneking. 2007. Mating patterns amongst Siberian reindeer herders: inferences from mtDNA and Y-chromosomal analyses. *American Journal of Physical Anthropology* 133: 1013–1027.

Palumbi, S. R. 2001. Humans as the world's greatest evolutionary force. *Science* 293: 1786–1790.

Panger, M. A., A. S. Brooks, B. G. Richmond, and B. Wood. 2002. Older than the Oldowan?: rethinking the emergence of hominin tool use. *Evolutionary Anthropology* 11: 235–245.

Papathanasiou, A. 2001. *A Bioarchaeological Analysis of Neolithic Alepotrypa Cave, Greece. British Archaeological Reports Series* 961.

Parker, I. 2007. Swingers. *The New Yorker* 83(21): 49–61.

Parmesan, C. 2006. Ecological and evolutionary responses to recent climate change. *Annual Review of Ecology, Evolution and Systematics* 37: 637–669.

Partridge, T. C., D. E. Granger, M. W. Caffee, and R. L. Clarke. 2003. Lower Pliocene hominid remains from Sterkfontein. *Science* 300: 607–612.

Patterson, K. D. 2000. Lactose intolerance. Pp. 1057–1062 in K. F. Kiple and K. C. Ornelas, eds. *The Cambridge World History of Food*. New York: Cambridge University Press.

Patz, J. A., D. Campbell-Lendrum, T. Holloway, and J. A. Foley. 2005. Impact of regional climate change on human health. *Nature* 438: 310–317.

Patz, J. A., M. Hulme, C. Rosenzweig, T. D. Mitchell, R. A. Goldberg, A. K. Githeko, S. Lele, A. J. McMichael, and D. Le Seuer. 2002. Regional warming and malaria resurgence. *Nature* 99: 12506–12508.

Pennisi, E. 2006. The dawn of stone age genomics. *Science* 314: 1068–1071.

Perry, S. E. 2006. What cultural primatology can tell anthropologists about the evolution of culture. *Annual Review of Anthropology* 35: 171–190.

Peters, J. 1999. Urbanism and health in industrialised Asia. Pp. 158–172 in L. M. Schell and S. J. Ulijaszek, eds. *Urbanism, Health and Human Biology in Industrialised Countries*. Cambridge, UK: Cambridge University Press.

Peterson, D. 2006. *Jane Goodall: The Woman Who Redefined Man*. New York: Houghton Mifflin.

Peterson, J. 2002. *Sexual Revolutions: Gender and Labor at the Dawn of Agriculure*. Walnut Creek, CA: Altamira.

Pickford, M. and B. Senut. 2001. The geological and faunal context of late Miocene hominid remains from Lukeino, Kenya. *Comptes Rendus* 332: 145–152.

Pietrusewsky, M. 2006. The initial settlement of remote Oceania: the evidence from physical anthropology. Pp. 320–347 in T. Simanjuntak, I. H. E. Pojoh, and M. Hisyam, eds. *Austronesian Diaspora and the Ethnogenesis of People in Indonesian Archipelago*. Jakarta, Indonesia: Indonesian Institute of Sciences, LIPI Press.

Pietrusewsky, M. and M. T. Douglas. 2002. *Ban Chiang: A Prehistoric Village Site in Northeast Thailand I: The Human Skeletal Remains*. Philadelphia: University of Pennsylvania.

Pilbeam, D. R. 1982. New hominoid skull material from the Miocene of Pakistan. *Nature* 295: 232–234.

Pilbeam, D. R. 1996. Genetic and morphological records of the hominoidea and hominid origins: a synthesis. *Molecular Phylogenetics and Evolution* 5: 155–168.

Pilbeam, D. R. 2002. Perspectives on the Miocene Hominoidea. Pp. 303–310 in W. C. Hartwig, ed. *The Primate Fossil Record*. Cambridge, UK: Cambridge University Press.

Piperata, B. A. 2007. Nutritional status of Ribeirinhos in Brazil and the nutritional transition. *American Journal of Physical Anthropology* 133: 868–878.

Plummer, T. 2004. Flaked stones and old bones: biological and cultural evolution at the dawn of technology. *Yearbook of Physical Anthropology* 47: 118–164.

Pollan, M. 2003. The (agri)cultural contradictions of obesity. *New York Times Magazine* October 12: 41–48.

Pollitzer, W. S. 1999. *The Gullah People and Their African Heritage*. Athens: University of Georgia Press.

Popkin, B. M. 1998. The nutrition transition and its health implications in lower-income countries. *Public Health Nutrition* 1: 5–21.

Popkin, B. M. 2004. The nutrition transition: an overview of world patterns of change. *Nutrition Reviews* 62: S140–S143.

Portugal, F. H. and J. S. Cohen. 1977. *A Century of DNA: A History of the Discovery of the Structure and Function of the Genetic Substance.* Cambridge, MA: MIT Press.

Powell, J. F. 2005. *The First Americans: Race, Evolution, and the Origin of Native Americans.* Cambridge, UK: Cambridge University Press.

Prabhakar, S., J. P. Noonan, S. Paabo, and E. M. Rubin. 2006. Accelerated evolution of conserved noncoding sequences in humans. *Science* 314: 786.

Premack, D. 2007. Human and animal cognition: continuity and discontinuity. *Proceedings of the National Academy of Sciences* 104: 13861–13867.

Price, P. W. 1996. *Biological Evolution.* Fort Worth, TX: Saunders.

Pruetz, J. D. and P. Bertolani. 2007. Savannah chimpanzees, *Pan troglodytes verus,* hunt with tools. *Current Biology* 17: 412–417.

Quammen, D. 2006. *The Reluctant Mr. Darwin: An Intimate Portrait of Charles Darwin and the Making of His Theory of Evolution.* New York: Norton.

Quammen, D. 2007. Deadly contact: how animals and humans exchange disease. *National Geographic* 212(4): 79–105.

Rasmussen, D. T. 2002. Early catarrhines of the African Eocene and Oligocene. Pp. 203–220. in W. C. Hartwig, ed. *The Primate Fossil Record.* Cambridge, UK: Cambridge University Press.

Rasmussen, D. T. 2002. The origin of primates. Pp. 5–9 in W. C. Hartwig, ed. *The Primate Fossil Record.* Cambridge, UK: Cambridge University Press.

Reilly, P. R. 2006. *The Strongest Boy in the World: How Genetic Information Is Reshaping Our Lives.* Cold Spring Harbor, NY: Cold Spring Harbor Laboratory Press.

Relethford, J. H. 1995. Genetics and Modern Human Origins. *Evolutionary Anthropology* 4: 53–63.

Relethford, J. H. 1997. Hemispheric difference in human skin color. *American Journal of Physical Anthropology* 104: 449–457.

Relethford, J. H. 1998. Genetics of modern human origins and diversity. *Annual Review of Anthropology* 27: 1–23.

Relethford, J. H. 2001. *Genetics and the Search for Modern Human Origins.* New York: Wiley-Liss.

Relethford, J. H. 2002. Apportionment of global human genetic diversity based on craniometrics and skin color. *American Journal of Physical Anthropology* 118: 393–398.

Relethford, J. H. 2003. *Reflections of Our Past: How Human History Is Revealed in Our Genes.* Boulder: Westview Press.

Relethford, J. H. 2004. Global patterns of isolation by distance based on genetic and morphological data. *Human Biology* 76: 499–513.

Remis, M. J. 2000. Preliminary assessments of the impacts of human activities on gorillas (*Gorilla gorilla gorilla*) and other wildlife at Dzanga-Sangha Reserve, Central African Republic. *Oryx* 34: 56–64.

Remis, M. J. 2001. Nutritional aspects of western lowland gorilla diet during seasonal fruit scarcity at Bai Hokou, Central African Republic. *International Journal of Primatology* 22: 807–835.

Renfrew, C. and K. Boyle. 2000. *Archaeogenetics: DNA and the Population Prehistory of Europe.* Cambridge, UK: McDonald Institute Monographs.

Reno, P. L., R. S. Meindl, M. A. McCollum, and C. O. Lovejoy. 2003. Sexual dimorphism in *Australopithecus afarensis* was similar to that of modern humans. *Proceedings of the National Academy of Sciences* 100: 9404–9409.

Repcheck, J. 2003. *The Man Who Found Time: James Hutton and the Discovery of the Earth's Antiquity.* Cambridge, MA: Perseus Publishing.

Reynolds, V. 2005. *The Chimpanzees of the Budongo Forest: Ecology, Behavior, and Conservation.* New York: Oxford University Press.

Richard, A. F. 1985. *Primates in Nature.* New York: W. H. Freeman.

Richards, M. 2003. The Neolithic invasion of Europe. *Annual Review of Anthropology* 32: 135–162.

Richards, M., P. Pettitt, E. Trinkaus, F. Smith, M. Paunovic, and I. Karavanic. 2000. Neanderthal diet and Vindija and Neanderthal predation: the evidence from stable isotopes. *Proceedings of the National Academy of Sciences* 97: 7663–7666.

Richards, M. P., R. Jacobi, J. Cook, P. B. Pettitt, and C. B. Stringer. 2005. Isotope evidence for the intensive use of marine foods by late upper Paleolithic humans. *Journal of Human Evolution* 49: 390–394.

Richmond, B. G. 2007. Biomechanics of phalangeal curvature. *Journal of Human Evolution* 53: 678–690.

Richmond, B. G., D. R. Begun, and D. S. Strait. 2001. Origin of human bipedalism: the knuckle-walking hypothesis revisited. *Yearbook of Physical Anthropology* 44: 70–105.

Ridley, M. 2004. *Evolution.* Malden, MA: Blackwell Science.

Ridley, M. 2006. *Francis Crick: Discoverer of the Genetic Code.* New York: HarperCollins.

Rightmire, G. P. 1990. *The Evolution of* Homo erectus. Cambridge, UK: Cambridge University Press.

Rightmire, G. P. 1998. Human evolution in the middle Pleistocene: the role of *Homo heidelbergensis. Evolutionary Anthropology* 6: 218–227.

Robbins, A. M., M. M. Robbins, N. Gerald-Steklis, and H. D. Steklis. 2006. Age-related patterns of reproductive success among female mountain gorillas. *American Journal of Physical Anthropology* 131: 511–521.

Robbins, L. H. 1974. *The Lothagam Site. Michigan State University Anthropological Series* 1(2).

Roberts, M. B., C. B. Stringer, and S. A. Parfitt. 1994. A hominid tibia from middle Pleistocene sediments at Boxgrove, UK. *Nature* 369: 311–313.

Rodman, P. S. 1999. Whither primatology?: The place of primates in contemporary anthropology. *Annual Review of Anthropology* 28: 311–339.

Roff, D. A. 1992. *The Evolution of Life Histories: Theory and Analysis*. New York: Chapman and Hall.

Rolland, N. 2004. Was the emergence of home bases and domestic fire a punctuated event?: A review of the middle Pleistocene record in Eurasia. *Asian Perspectives* 43: 248–280.

Rose, K. D. 1994. The earliest primates. *Evolutionary Anthropology* 3: 159–173.

Rose, K. D. 2006. *The Beginning of the Age of Mammals*. Baltimore: Johns Hopkins University Press.

Roseman, C. C. 2004. Detecting inter-regionally diversifying natural selection on modern human cranial form using matched molecular and morphometric data. *Proceedings of the National Academy of Sciences* 101: 12824–12829.

Ross, C. F. 2000. Into the light: the origin of anthropoidea. *Annual Review of Anthropology* 29: 147–194.

Ross, C. F. and R. F. Kay, eds. 2004. *Anthropoid Origins: New Visions*. New York: Kluwer Academic/Plenum.

Rossie, J. B., X. Ni, and K. C. Beard. 2006. Cranial remains of an Eocene tarsier. *Proceedings of the National Academy of Sciences* 103: 4381–4385.

Rougier, H., S. Milota, R. Rodrigo, M. Gherase, L. Sarcina, O. Moldovan, J. Zilhao, S. Constantin, R. G. Franciscus, C. P. E. Zolliker, M. Ponce de Leon, and E. Trinkaus. 2007. Pestera cu Oase 2 and the cranial morphology of early modern Europeans. *Proceedings of the National Academy of Sciences* 104: 1165–1170.

Rowe, N. 1996. *The Pictorial Guide to the Living Primates*. Charlestown, RI: Pogonias.

Roy, S. R., A. M. Schiltz, A. Marotta, Y. Shen, and A. H. Liu. 2003. Bacterial DNA in house and farm barn dust. *Journal of Allergy Clinical Immunology* 112: 571–578.

Rubin, G. M. 2001. Comparing species. *Nature* 409: 820–821.

Rudwick, M. J. S. 1997. *Georges Cuvier, Fossil Bones, and Geological Catastrophes: New Translations and Interpretations of the Primary Texts*. Chicago: University of Chicago Press.

Rudwick, M. J. S. 2005. *Bursting the Limits of Time: The Reconstruction of Geohistory in the Age of Revolution*. Chicago: University of Chicago Press.

Ruff, C. B. 1991. Climate and body shape in hominid evolution. *Journal of Human Evolution* 21: 81–105.

Ruff, C. B. 1993. Climatic adaptation and hominid evolution: the thermoregulatory imperative. *Evolutionary Anthropology* 2: 53–60.

Ruff, C. B. 1994. Morphological adaptation to climate in modern and fossil hominids. *Yearbook of Physical Anthropology* 37: 65–107.

Ruff, C. B. 2000. Biomechanical analyses of archaeological human skeletons. Pp. 71–102 in M. A. Katzenberg and S. R. Saunders, eds. *Biological Anthropology of the Human Skeleton*. New York: Wiley-Liss.

Ruff, C. B. 2005. Mechanical determinants of bone form: insights from skeletal remains. *Journal of Musculoskeletal and Neuronal Interactions* 5: 202–212.

Ruff, C. B. 2006. Gracilization of the modern human skeleton. *American Scientist* 94: 508–514.

Ruiz-Pesini, E., D. Mishmar, M. Brandon, V. Procaccio, and D. C. Wallace, 2004. Effects of purifying and adaptive selection on regional variation in human mtDNA. *Science* 303: 223–226.

Sabeti, P. C., S. F. Schaffner, B. Fry, J. Lohmueller, P. Varilly, O. Shamovsky, A. Palma, T. S. Mikkelsen, D. Altshuler, and E. S. Lander. 2006. Positive natural selection in the human lineage. *Science* 312: 1614–1620.

Samson, M., F. Libert, B. J. Doranz, J. Rucker, C. Liesnand, et al. 1996. Resistance to HIV-1 infection in Caucasian individuals bearing mutant alleles of the CCR-5 chemokine receptor gene. *Nature* 382: 722–725.

Sapolsky, R. M. 2004. Of mice, men, and genes. *Natural History* May: 21–24, 31.

Sapolsky, R. M. 2004. Social status and health in humans and other animals. *Annual Review of Anthropology* 33: 393–418.

Sapolsky, R. M. 2005. The influence of social hierarchy on primate health. *Science* 308: 648–652.

Sapolsky, R. M. 2006. Social cultures among nonhuman primates. *Current Anthropology* 47: 641–656.

Sardi, M. L., P. S. Novellino, and H. M. Pucciarelli. 2006. Craniofacial morphology in the Argentine center-west: consequences of the transition to food production. *American Journal of Physical Anthropology* 130: 333–343.

Saunders, M. A., M. F. Hammer, and M. W. Nachman. 2002. Nucleotide variability in G6pd and the signature of malarial selection in humans. *Genetics* 162: 1849–1861.

Savolainen, P., Y. Zhang, J. Luo, J. Lundeberg, and T. Leitner. 2002. Genetic evidence for an East Asian origin of domestic dog. *Science* 298: 1610–1613.

Schmitz, R. W. 1997. Neandertal (Feldhofer Grotte). Pp. 710–711 in F. Spencer, ed. *History of Physical Anthropology: An Encyclopedia*. New York: Garland.

Schmitz, R. W., D. Serre, G. Bonani, S. Feine, F. Hillgruber, H. Krainitzki, S. Pääbo, and F. H. Smith. 2002. The Neandertal type site revisited: interdisciplinary investigations of skeletal remains from the Neander Valley, Germany. *Proceedings of the National Academy of Sciences* 99: 13342–13347.

Schoenemann, P. T. 2006. Evolution of the size and functional areas of the human brain. *Annual Review of Anthropology* 35: 379–406.

Schultz, A. H. 1969. *The Life of Primates*. New York: Universe.

Schurr, T. G. 2000. Mitochondrial DNA and the peopling of the New World. *American Scientist* 88: 246–253.

Schurr, T. G. 2004. The peopling of the New World. *Annual Review of Anthropology* 33: 551–583.

Schurr, T. G. and S. T. Sherry. 2004. Mitochondrial DNA and Y chromosome diversity and the peopling of the Americas: evolutionary and demographic evidence. *American Journal of Human Biology* 16: 420–439.

Schwartz, J. H. 1999. *Sudden Origins: Fossils, Genes, and the Emergence of Species*. New York: Wiley.

Schwartz, J. H. and I. Tattersall. 2000. The human chin revisited: what is it and who has it? *Journal of Human Evolution* 38: 367–409.

Schwartz, J. H. and I. Tattersall. 2002. *The Human Fossil Record, Volume One: Terminology and Craniodental Morphology of Genus* Homo *(Europe)*. New York: Wiley-Liss.

Schwartz, J. H. and I. Tattersall. 2003. *The Human Fossil Record: Volume Two, Craniodental Morphology of Genus* Homo *(Africa and Asia)*. New York: Wiley-Liss.

Schwartz, J. H. and I. Tattersall. 2005. *The Human Fossil Record, Volume Four: Craniodental Morphology of Early Hominids (Genera* Australopithecus, Paranthropus, Orrorin) *and Overview*. Hoboken, NJ: Wiley-Liss.

Scott, E. C. 2004. *Evolution vs. Creationism: An Introduction*. Westport, CT: Greenwood Press.

Scrimshaw, N. S. and E. B. Murray. 1988. The acceptability of milk and milk products in populations with a high prevalence of lactose intolerance. *American Journal of Clinical Nutrition* 48 (suppl): 1083–1159.

Seager, R., Y. Kushnir, C. Herweijer, and N. Naik. 2005. Modeling of tropical forcing of persistent droughts and pluvials over western North America. *Journal of Climate* 18: 4068–4091.

Segalen, L., J. A. Lee-Thorp, and T. Cerling. 2007. Timing of C_4 grass expansion across sub-Saharan Africa. *Journal of Human Evolution* 53: 549–559.

Seiffert, E. R. 2006. Revised age estimates for the later Paleogene mammal faunas of Egypt and Oman. *Proceedings of the National Academy of Sciences* 103: 5000–5005.

Seiffert, E. R., E. L. Simons, W. C. Clyde, J. B. Rossie, Y. Attia, T. M. Bown, P. Chatrath, and M. E. Mathison. 2005. Basal anthropoids from Egypt and the antiquity of Africa's higher primate radiation. *Science* 310: 300–304.

Selinus, O. 2005. *Essentials of Medical Geology: Impacts of the Natural Environment on Public Health*. Amsterdam, The Netherlands: Elsevier Academic Press.

Semaw, S. 2000. The world's oldest stone artefacts from Gona, Ethiopia: their implications for understanding stone technology and patterns of human evolution between 2.6–1.5 million years ago. *Journal of Archaeological Science* 27: 1197–1214.

Semaw, S., P. Renne, J. W. K. Harris, C. S. Feibel, R. L. Bernor, N. Fesseha, and K. Mowbray. 1997. 2.5–million-year-old stone tools from Gona, Ethiopia. *Nature* 385: 333–336.

Semino, O., G. Passarino, P. J. Oefner, A. A. Lin, S. Arbuzova, L. E. Beckman, G. De Benedictis, P. Francalacci, A. Kouvatsi, S. Limborska, M. Marcikiae, A. Mika, B. Mika, D. Primorac, A. S. Santachiara-Benerecetti, L. L. Cavalli-Sforza, and P. A. Underhill. 2000. The genetic legacy of Paleolithic *Homo sapiens sapiens* in extant Europeans: a Y chromosome perspective. *Science* 290: 1155–1159.

Senut, B., M. Pickford, D. Gommery, P. Mein, K. Cheboi, and Y. Coppens. 2001. First hominid from the Miocene (Lukeino Formation, Kenya). *Comptes Rendus* 332: 137–144.

Serre, D., A. Langaney, M. Chech, M. Teschler-Nicola, M. Paunovic, P. Mennecier, M. Hofreiter, G. Possnert, and S. Paabo. 2004. No evidence of Neandertal mtDNA contribution to early modern humans. *PLoS Biology* 2(3): 10.1371/journal.pbio.0020057.

Shackelford, L. L. 2007. Regional variation in the postcranial robusticity of late upper Paleolithic humans. *American Journal of Physical Anthropology* 133: 655–668.

Shang, H., H. Tong, S. Zhang, F. Chen, and E. Trinkaus. 2007. An early modern human from Tianyuan Cave, Zhoukoudian, China. *Proceedings of the National Academy of Sciences* 104: 6573–6578.

Shapiro, H. L. 1962. *The Pitcairn Islanders*. New York: Simon & Schuster.

Shapiro, H. L. 1974. *Peking Man: The Discovery, Disappearance and Mystery of a Priceless Scientific Treasure*. New York: Simon & Schuster.

Shea, J. J. 2003. Neandertals, competition, and the origin of modern human behavior in the Levant. *Evolutionary Anthropology* 12: 173–187.

Shea, J. J. 2006. Interdisciplinary approaches to the evolution of hominid diets. *Evolutionary Anthropology* 15: 204–206.

Shen, G., T.-L. Ku, H. Cheng, R. L. Edwards, Z. Yuan, and Q. Wang. 2001. High-precision u-series dating of locality 1 at Zhoukoudian, China. *Journal of Human Evolution* 41: 679–688.

Shen, G., W. Wang, Q. Wang, J. Zhao, K. Collerson, C. Zhou, and P. V. Tobias. 2002. U-series dating of Liujiang hominid site in Guangxi, Southern China. *Journal of Human Evolution* 43: 817–830.

Shipman, P. 2001. *The Man Who Found the Missing Link*. New York: Simon & Schuster.

Shipman, P. 2002. Hunting the first hominid. *American Scientist* 90: 25–27.

Shipman, P. 2002. *The Evolution of Racism: Human Differences and the Use and Abuse of Science*. Cambridge, MA: Harvard University Press.

Shipman, P. 2003. We are all Africans. *American Scientist* 91: 496–499.

Shipman, P. and P. Storm. 2002. Missing links: Eugene Dubois and the origins of paleoanthropology. *Evolutionary Anthropology* 11: 108–116.

Sholtis, S. and K. Weiss. 2005. Phenogentics: genotypes, phenotypes, and variation. Pp. 499–523 in B. Hallgrimson and B. K. Hall, eds. *Variation: A Central Concept in Biology*. Burlington, MA: Elsevier Academic Press.

Shoshani, J., C. P. Groves, E. L. Simons, and G. F. Gunnell. 1996. Primate phylogeny: morphological vs molecular results. *Molecular Phylogenetics and Evolution* 5: 102–154.

Shreeve, J. 1994. Terms of estrangement. *Discover* 15(11): 56–63.

Shriver, M. D., E. J. Parra, S. Dios, C. Bonilla, H. Norton, C. Jovel, C. Pfaff, C. Jones, A. Massac, N. Cameron, A. Baron, T. Jackson, G. Argyropoulos, L. Jin, C. J. Hoggart, P. M. McKeigue, and R. Kittles. 2003. Skin pigmentation, biogeographical ancestry and admixture mapping. *Human Genetics* 112: 387–399.

Shultz, S., R. Noe, W. S. McGraw, and R. I. M. Dunbar. 2004. A community-level evaluation of the impact of prey behavioural and ecological characteristics on predator diet composition. *Proceedings of the Royal Society of London B* 271: 725–732.

Sicherer, S. H., A. Muñoz-Furlong, and H. A. Sampson. 2003. Prevalence of peanut and tree nut allergy in the United States is determined by means of a random digit dial telephone survey: a 5-year follow-up study. *Journal of Allergy Clinical Immunology* 112: 1203–1207.

Sievert, L. L. 2006. *Menopause: A Biocultural Perspective*. Newark, NJ: Rutgers University Press.

Sigmon, B. A. and J. S. Cybulski, eds. 1981. Homo erectus: *Papers in Honor of Davidson Black*. Toronto: University of Toronto Press.

Simons, E. L. 1972. *Primate Evolution: An Introduction to Man's Place in Nature*. New York: Macmillan.

Simons, E. L. 1990. Discovery of the oldest known anthropoidean skull from the Paleogene of Egypt. *Science* 247: 1567–1569.

Simons, E. L. 1995. Skulls and anterior teeth of *Catopithecus* (Primates: Anthropoidea) from the Eocene. *Science* 268: 1885–1888.

Simons, E. L. and P. C. Ettel. 1970. *Gigantopithecus*. *Scientific American* 222(1): 77–85.

Simons, E. L. and T. Rasmussen. 1994. A whole new world of ancestors: Eocene anthropoideans from Africa. *Evolutionary Anthropology* 3: 128–139.

Simons, E. L., E. R. Seiffert, T. M. Ryan, and Y. Attia. 2007. A remarkable female cranium of the early Oligocene anthropoid *Aegyptopithecus zeuxis* (Catarrhini, Propliopithecidae). *Proceedings of the National Academy of Sciences* 104: 8731–8736.

Simpson, G. G. 1944. *Tempo and Mode of Evolution*. New York: Columbia University Press.

Simpson, G. G. 1967. *The Meaning of Evolution*. New Haven: Yale University Press.

Simpson, S. W. 1996. *Australopithecus afarensis* and human evolution. Pp. 3–28 in C. R. Ember, M. Ember, and P. Peregrine, eds. *Research Frontiers in Anthropology*. Needham, MA: Simon & Schuster.

Simpson, S. W. 2002. *Australopithecus afarensis* and human evolution. Pp. 103–123 in P. N. Peregrine, C. R. Ember, and M. Ember, eds. *Physical Anthropology: Original Readings in Method and Practice*. Upper Saddle River, NJ: Prentice Hall.

Smail, J. K. 2002. Remembering Malthus: a preliminary argument for a significant reduction in global human numbers. *American Journal of Physical Anthropology* 118: 292–297.

Smith, B. D. 1992. *Rivers of Change: Essays on Early Agriculture in North America*. Washington, DC: Smithsonian Institution Press.

Smith, B. D. 1995. *The Emergence of Agriculture*. New York: Scientific American Library.

Smith, B. D. 2001. Documenting plant domestication: the consilience of biological and archaeological approaches. *Proceedings of the National Academy of Sciences* 98: 1324–1326.

Smith, B. H. 1989. Dental development as a measure of life history in primates. *Evolution* 43: 683–688.

Smith, B. H. 1991. Dental development and the evolution of life history in the Hominidae. *American Journal of Physical Anthropology* 86: 157–174.

Smith, B. H. 1993. The physiological age of KNM-WT 15000. Pp. 195–220 in A. Walker and R. Leakey, eds. *The Nariokotome* Homo erectus *Skeleton*. Cambridge, MA: Harvard University Press.

Smith, B. H. 1994. Ages of eruption of primate teeth: a compendium for aging individuals and comparing life histories. *Yearbook of Physical Anthropology* 37: 177–231.

Smith, F. H. 2002. Migrations, radiations and continuity: patterns in the evolution of middle and late Pleistocene humans. Pp. 437–456 in W. C. Hartwig, ed. *The Primate Fossil Record*. Cambridge, UK: Cambridge University Press.

Smith, F. H., A. B. Falsetti, and S. M. Donnelly. 1989. Modern human origins. *Yearbook of Physical Anthropology* 32: 35–68.

Smith, F., I. Jankovic, and I. Karavanic. 2005. The assimilation model, modern human origins in Europe, and the extinction of Neandertals. *Quaternary International* 137: 7–19.

Smith, S. L. 2004. Skeletal age, dental age, and the maturation of KNM-WT 15000. *American Journal of Physical Anthropology* 125: 105–120.

Smith, T. M., A. J. Olejniczak, L. B. Martin, and D. J. Reid. 2005. Variation in hominoid molar enamel thickness. *Journal of Human Evolution* 48: 575–592.

Smith, T. M., A. J. Olejniczak, D. J. Reid, R. J. Ferrell, and J.-J. Hublin. 2006. Modern human molar enamel thickness and enamel-dentine junction shape. *Archives of Oral Biology* 51: 974–995.

Smuts, B. B., D. L. Cheney, R. M. Seyfarth, R. W. Wrangham, and T. T. Struhsaker, eds. 1987. *Primate Societies*. Chicago: University of Chicago Press.

Snodgrass, J. J., M. V. Sorensen, L. A. Tarskaia, and W. R. Leonard. 2007. Adaptive dimensions of health research among indigenous Siberians. *American Journal of Human Biology* 19: 165–180.

Soficaru, A., C. Petrea, A. Dobos, and E. Trinkaus. 2007. The human cranium from the Pestera Cioclovina Uscata, Romania. *Current Anthropology* 48: 611–619.

Spencer, F. 1990. *Piltdown: A Scientific Forgery*. London: Oxford University Press.

Spencer, F., ed. 1997. *History of Physical Anthropology: An Encyclopedia*. New York: Garland.

Spencer, F. 1997. Piltdown. Pp. 821–825 in F. Spencer, ed. *History of Physical Anthropology: An Encyclopedia*. New York: Garland Publishing.

Speth, J. D. 2005. News flash: negative evidence convicts Neanderthals of gross mental incompetence. *World Archaeology* 36: 519–526.

Sponheimer, M., B. H. Passey, D. J. de Ruiter, D. Guatelli-Steinberg, T. E. Cerling, and J. A. Lee-Thorp. 2006. Isotopic evidence for dietary variability in the early hominin *Paranthropus robustus*. *Science* 314: 980–981.

Spoor, F., M. G. Leakey, P. N. Gathogo, F. H. Brown, S. C. Anton, I. McDougall, C. Kiarie, F. K. Manthi, and L. N. Leakey. 2007. Implications of new early *Homo* fossils from Ileret, east of Lake Turkana, Kenya. *Nature* 448: 688–691.

Stafford, N. 2007. The other greenhouse effect. *Nature* 448: 526–528.

Stanford, C. B. 1995. Chimpanzee hunting behavior and human evolution. *American Scientist* 83(3): 256–263.

Stanford, C. B. 2001. *The Hunting Apes*. Princeton: Princeton University Press.

Stanton, W. 1960. *The Leopard's Spots: Scientific Attitudes toward Race in America, 1815–59*. Chicago: University of Chicago Press.

Steadman, D. W. 2003. *Hard Evidence: Case Studies in Forensic Anthropology*. Upper Saddle River, NJ: Prentice Hall.

Stearns, S. C. 1992. *The Evolution of Life Histories.* New York: Oxford University Press.

Steckel, R. H., J. C. Rose, C. S. Larsen, and P. L. Walker. 2002. Skeletal health in the Western Hemisphere from 4000 B.C. to the present. *Evolutionary Anthropology* 11: 142–155.

Steegmann, A. T. Jr. 2007. Human cold adaptation: an unfinished agenda. *American Journal of Human Biology* 19: 218–227.

Steele, D. G. and J. F. Powell. 1993. Paleobiology of the first Americans. *Evolutionary Anthropology* 2: 138–146.

Stewart, T. D. 1977. The Neanderthal skeletal remains from Shanidar Cave, Iraq: a summary of findings to date. *Proceedings of the American Philosophical Society* 121: 121–165.

Stewart, T. D. 1979. *Essentials of Forensic Anthropology.* Springfield, IL: Charles C. Thomas.

Stiner, M. C. 2001. Thirty years on the "Broad Spectrum Revolution" and paleolithic demography. *Proceedings of the National Academy of Sciences* 98: 6993–6996.

Stini, W. A. 1995. Osteoporosis in biocultural perspective. *Annual Review of Anthropology* 24: 397–421.

Stinson, S. 2000. Growth variation: Biological and cultural factors. Pp. 425–463 in S. Stinson, B. Bogin, R. Huss-Ashmore, and D. O'Rourke, eds. *Human Biology: An Evolutionary and Biocultural Perspective.* New York: Wiley-Liss.

Stinson, S., B. Bogin, R. Huss-Ashmore, and D. O'Rourke, eds. 2000. *Human Biology: An Evolutionary and Biocultural Perspective.* New York: Wiley-Liss.

Stocking, G., ed. 1974. *The Shaping of American Anthropology, 1883–1911: A Franz Boas Reader.* New York: Basic Books.

Stokstad, E. 2003. The Vitamin D deficit. *Science* 302: 1886–1888.

Stokstad, E. 2004. Forest loss makes monkeys sick. *Science* 305: 1230–1231.

Stone, A. C. 2000. Ancient DNA from skeletal remains. Pp. 351–371 in M. A. Katzenberg and S. R. Saunders, eds. *Biological Anthropology of the Human Skeleton.* New York: Wiley-Liss.

Stone, L., P. F. Lurquin, and L. L. Cavalli-Sforza. 2007. *Genes, Culture, and Human Evolution: A Synthesis.* Malden, MA: Blackwell.

Stoneking, M. 1993. DNA and recent human evolution. *Evolutionary Anthropology* 2: 60–73.

Stott, R. 2003. *Darwin and the Barnacle: The Story of One Tiny Creature and History's Most Spectacular Scientific Breakthrough.* New York: Norton.

Strachan, D. P. 1989. Hay fever, hygiene, and household size. *British Medical Journal* 299: 1259–1260.

Street, M., T. Terberger, and J. Orschiedt. 2006. A critical review of the German Paleolithic hominin record. *Journal of Human Evolution* 51: 551–579.

Strickland, S. S. and P. S. Shetty. 1998. *Human Biology and Social Inequality.* Cambridge, UK: Cambridge University Press.

Strier, K. B. 1994. Myth of the typical primate. *Yearbook of Physical Anthropology* 37: 233–271.

Strier, K. B. 2007. *Primate Behavioral Ecology.* 3rd ed. Boston: Allyn & Bacon.

Stringer, C. and R. McKie. 1998. *African Exodus: The Origins of Modern Humanity.* New York: Henry Holt.

Strum, S. C. and L. F. Fedigan. 2000. *Primate Encounters: Models of Science, Gender, and Society.* Chicago: University of Chicago Press.

Susman, R. L. 1994. Fossil evidence for early hominid tool use. *Science* 265: 1570–1573.

Susman, R. L. 1998. Hand function and tool behavior in early hominids. *Journal of Human Evolution* 35: 23–46.

Susman, R. L. 2004. *Oreopithecus bamboli:* an unlikely case of hominidlike grip capability in a Miocene ape. *Journal of Human Evolution* 46: 105–117.

Susman, R. L. 2005. *Oreopithecus:* still apelike after all these years. *Journal of Human Evolution* 49: 405–411.

Susman, R. L., J. T. Stern, and W. L. Jungers. 1984. Arboreality and bipedality in Hadar hominids. *Folia Primatologica* 43: 113–156.

Sussman, R. W., P. A. Garber, and J. M. Cheverud. 2005. Importance of cooperation and affiliation in the evolution of primate sociality. *American Journal of Physical Anthropology* 128: 84–97.

Suwa, G., R. T. Kono, S. Katoh, B. Asfaw, and Y. Beyene. 2007. A new species of great ape from the late Miocene epoch in Ethiopia. *Nature* 448: 921–924.

Swallow, D. 2003. Genetics of lactase persistence and lactose intolerance. *Annual Review of Genetics* 37: 197–219.

Swisher, C. C. III, W. J. Rink, S. C. Anton, H. P. Schwarcz, G. H. Curtis, A. Suprijo, and S. Widiasmoro. 1996. Latest *Homo erectus* of Java: potential contemporaneity with *Homo sapiens* in Southeast Asia. *Science* 274: 1870–1874.

Swisher, C. C. III, G. H. Curtis, and R. Lewin. 2000. *Java Man.* New York: Scribner.

Szalay, F. S. 1975. *Approaches to Primate Paleobiology.* Contributions to Primatology 5. Basel, Switzerland: S. Karger.

Szalay, F. S. and E. Delson. 1979. *Evolutionary History of the Primates.* New York: Academic Press.

Szalay, F. S., A. L. Rosenberger, and M. DaGosto. 1987. Diagnosis and differentiation of the order Primates. *Yearbook of Physical Anthropology* 30: 75–105.

Tabor, E., ed. 2007. *Emerging Viruses in Human Populations.* Amsterdam, The Netherlands: Elsevier.

Takai, M., F. Anaya, N. Shigehara, and T. Setoguchi. 2000. New fossil materials of the earliest New World monkey, *Branisella boliviana,* and the problem of platyrrhine origins. *American Journal of Physical Anthropology* 111: 263–281.

Tanner, J. M. 1978. *Fetus into Man: Physical Growth from Conception to Maturity.* Cambridge, MA: Harvard University Press.

Tattersall, I. 1995. *The Fossil Trail.* New York: Oxford University Press.

Tattersall, I. 2007. Madagascar's lemurs: cryptic diversity or taxonomic inflation. *Evolutionary Anthropology* 16: 12–23.

Taylor, R. E. 1995. Radiocarbon dating: the continuing revolution. *Evolutionary Anthropology* 4: 169–181.

Taylor, R. E. 2002. Dating archaeological materials. Pp. 15–35 in P. N. Peregrine, C. R. Ember, and M. Ember, eds. *Archaeology: Original Readings in Method and Practice.* Upper Saddle River, NJ: Prentice Hall.

Taylor, R. E. and M. J. Aitken. 1997. *Chronometric Dating in Archaeology*. New York: Plenum Press.

Teaford, M. F., P. S. Ungar, and F. E. Grine. 2002. Paleontological evidence for the diets of African Plio-Pleistocene hominins with special reference to early *Homo*. Pp. 143–166 in P. S. Ungar and M. F. Teaford, eds. *Human Diet: Its Origin and Evolution*. Westport, CT: Bergin & Garvey.

Teleki, G. 1973. *The Predatory Behavior of Wild Chimpanzees*. Bucknell, PA: Bucknell University Press.

Templeton, A. 2002. Out of Africa again and again. *Nature* 416: 45–51.

Templeton, A. 2005. Haplotype trees and modern human origins. *Yearbook of Physical Anthropology* 48: 33–59.

Teshler-Nicola, M., ed. 2006. *Early Modern Humans at the Moravian Gate: The Mladeč Caves and Their Remains*. New York: Springer.

Theunissen, B., L. T. Theunissen, and E. Perlin-West. 2006. *Eugène Dubois and the Ape-Man from Java: The History of the First Missing Link and Its Discoverer*. Berlin, Germany: Springer.

Thompson, J. L., G. E. Krovitz, and A. J. Nelson. 2003. *Patterns of Growth and Development in the Genus* Homo. Cambridge, UK: Cambridge University Press.

Thompson, L. G., E. Mosley-Thompson, M. E. Davis, K. A. Henderson, H. H. Brecher, V. S. Zagorodnov, T. A. Mashiotta, P.-N. Lin, V. N. Mikhalenko, D. R. Hardy, and J. Beer. 2002. Kilimanjaro ice core records: evidence of Holocene climate change in tropical Africa. *Science* 298: 589–593.

Thorne, A. G. and M. H. Wolpoff. 2003. The multiregional evolution of humans. *Scientific American* 2: 46–53.

Thuiller, W. 2007. Climate change and the ecologist. *Nature* 448: 550–552.

Tianyuan, L. and D. A. Etler. 1992. New middle Pleistocene hominid crania from Yunxian in China. *Nature* 357: 404–407.

Tidwell, J. 2004. Requiem for a primate. *Zoogoer* 33(5): 8–15.

Tishkoff, S. A., F. A. Reed, A. Ranciaro, B. F. Voight, C. C. Babbitt, J. S. Silverman, K. Powell, H. M. Mortensen, J. B. Hirbo, M. Osman, M. Ibrahim, S. A. Omar, G. Lema, T. B. Nyambo, J. Ghori, S. Bumpsted, J. K. Pritchard, T. B. Wray, and P. Deloukas. 2006. Convergent adaptation of human lactase persistence in Africa and Europe. *Nature Genetics* 39: 31–40.

Tishkoff, S. A., R. Varkonyi, N. Cahinhinan, S. Abbes, G. Argyropoulos, G. Destro-Bisol, A. Drousiotou, B. Dangerfield, G. Lefranc, J. Loiselet, A. Piro, M. Stoneking, A. Tagarelli, G. Tagarelli, E. H. Touma, S. Williams, and A. G. Clark. 2001. Haplotype diversity and linkage disequilibrium at human G6pd: recent origin of alleles that confer malarial resistance. *Science* 293: 455–462.

Tobias, P. V. 1967. *The Cranium and Maxillary Dentition of* Zinjanthropus (Australopithecus) boisei. Cambridge, UK: Cambridge University Press.

Tobias, P. V. 1997. Dart, Raymond A. (1893–1988). Pp. 314–315 in F. Spencer, ed. *History of Physical Anthropology: An Encyclopedia*. New York: Garland.

Tobias, P. V. 1997. Taung. Pp. 1022–1025 in F. Spencer, ed. *History of Physical Anthropology: An Encyclopedia*. New York: Garland.

Tocheri, M. W., C. M. Orr, S. G. Larson, T. Sutikna, Jatmiko, E. W. Saptomo, R. A. Due, T. Djubiantono, M. J. Morwood, and W. L. Jungers. 2007. The primitive wrist of *Homo floresiensis* and its implications for hominin evolution. *Science* 317: 1743–1745.

Tomasello, M. and J. Call. 1994. Social cognition in monkeys and apes. *Yearbook of Physical Anthropology* 37: 273–305.

Toth, N. and K. Schick, eds. 2007. *The Oldowan: Case Studies into the Earliest Stone Age*. Bloomington, IN: Stone Age Institute.

Trinkaus, E. 1983. *The Shanidar Neandertals*. New York: Academic Press.

Trinkaus, E. 2005. Early modern humans. *Annual Review of Anthropology* 34: 207–230.

Trinkaus, E. 2006. Modern human versus Neandertal evolutionary distinctiveness. *Current Anthropology* 47: 597–620.

Trinkaus, E., O. Moldovan, S. Milota, A. Bilgar, S. Sarcina, S. Athreya, S. Bailey, R. Rodrigo, G. Mircea, T. Higham, C. Ramsey, and J. van der Plicht. 2003. An early modern human from the Pestera cu Oase, Romania. *Proceedings of the National Academy of Sciences* 100: 11231–11236.

Trinkaus, E. and P. Shipman. 1993. Neandertals: images of ourselves. *Evolutionary Anthropology* 1: 194–201.

Trinkaus, E. and P. Shipman. 1994. *The Neandertals: Of Skeletons, Scientists, and Scandal*. New York: Vintage.

Trinkaus, E. and J. Svoboda. 2006. *Early Modern Human Evolution in Central Europe: The People of Dolni Vestonice and Pavlov*. New York: Oxford University Press.

Tubiello, F. N. and G. Fischer. 2007. Reducing climate change impacts on agriculture: global and regional effects of mitigation, 2000–2080. *Technological Forcasting and Social Change* 74: 1030–1056.

Ubelaker, D. H. and H. Scammell. 1992. *Bones: A Forensic Detective's Casebook*. New York: Edward Burlingame.

Ugan, A. 2005. Does size matter?: body size, mass collecting, and their implications for understanding prehistoric foraging behavior. *American Antiquity* 70: 75–89.

Ulijaszek, S. J., F. E. Johnston, and M. A. Preece. 1998. *The Cambridge Encyclopedia of Human Growth and Development*. Cambridge, UK: Cambridge University Press.

Ulijaszek, S. J. and H. Lofink. 2006. Obesity in biocultural perspective. *Annual Review of Anthropology* 35: 337–360.

Ulijaszek, S. J. and L. M. Schell. 1999. The future of urban environments. Pp. 311–322 in L. M. Schell and S. J. Ulijaszek, eds. *Urbanism, Health and Human Biology in Industrialised Countries*. Cambridge, UK: Cambridge University Press.

Ungar, P. S., F. E. Grine, and M. F. Teaford. 2006. Diet in early *Homo*: a review of the evidence and a new model of adaptive versatility. *Annual Review of Anthropology* 35: 209–228.

Ungar, P. S. and M. F. Teaford. 2002. *Human Diet: Its Origin and Evolution*. Westport, CT: Bergin & Garvey.

United Nations Human Settlements Programme. 2005. *2005 Annual Report*. Nairobi, Kenya: UN-HABITAT.

U.S.–Venezuela Collaborative Research Project and N. S. Wexler. 2004. Venezuelan kindreds reveal that genetic and environmental factors modulate Huntington's disease age of onset. *Proceedings of the National Academy of Sciences* 101: 3498–3503.

Vahakangas, K. 2004. Ethical aspects of molecular epidemiology of cancer. *Carcinogenesis* 25: 465–471.

Van Schaik, C. and C. D. Knott. 2001. Geographic variation in tool use on Neesia fruits in orangutans. *American Journal of Physical Anthropology* 114: 331–342.

Van Schaik, C. P., M. Ancrenaz, G. Borgen, B. Galdikas, C. D. Knott, I. Singleton, A. Suzuki, S. S. Utami, and M. Merrill. 2003. Orangutan cultures and the evolution of material culture. *Science* 299: 102–105.

Varea, C., C. Bernis, P. Montero, S. Arias, A. Barroso, and B. Gonzalez. 2000. Secular trend and intrapopulational variation in age at menopause in Spanish women. *Journal of Biosocial Science* 32: 383–393.

Vekua, A., D. Lordkipanidze, G. P. Rightmire, J. Agusti, R. Ferring, G. Maisuradze, A. Mouskhelishvili, M. Nioradze, M. P. de Leon, M. Tappen, M. Tvalchrelidze, and C. Zollikofer. 2002. A new skull of early *Homo* from Dmanisi, Georgia. *Science* 297: 85–89.

Vignaud, P., P. Duringer, H. T. Mackaye, A. Likius, C. Blondel, J.-R. Boisserie, L. de Bonis, V. Eisenmann, M.-E. Etienne, D. Geraads, F. Guy, T. Lehmann, F. Lihoreau, N. Lopez-Martinez, C. Mourer-Chauvire, O. Otero, J.-C. Rage, M. Schuster, L. Viriot, A. Zazzo, and M. Brunet. 2002. Geology and paleontology of the upper Miocene Toros-Menalla hominid locality, Chad. *Nature* 418: 152–155.

Villa, P. 1992. Cannibalism in prehistoric Europe. *Evolutionary Anthropology* 1: 93–104.

Visalberghi, E., D. Fragaszy, E. Ottoni, P. Izar, M. G. de Oliveira, and F. R. D. Andrade. 2007. Characteristics of hammer stones and anvils used by wild capuchin monkeys (*Cebus libidinosus*) to crack open palm nuts. *American Journal of Physical Anthropology* 134: in press.

Voland, E., A. Chasiotis, and W. Schiefenhovel, eds. 2005. *Grandmotherhood: The Evolutionary Significance of the Second Half of Female Life*. New Brunswick: Rutgers University Press.

Von Koenigswald, G. H. R. 1952. *Gigantopithecus blacki* von Koenigswald, a giant fossil hominoid from the Pleistocene of Southern China. *Anthropological Papers of the American Museum of Natural History* 43(4): 293–325.

Voris, H. K. 2000. Maps of Pleistocene sea levels in Southeast Asia: shorelines, river systems and time durations. *Journal of Biogeography* 27: 1153–1167.

Wagner, G. 1996. Fission-track dating in paleoanthropology. *Evolutionary Anthropology* 5: 165–171.

Wagner, G. A. 1999. *Age Determination of Young Rocks and Artifacts: Physical and Chemical Clocks in Quarternary Geology and Archaeology*. New York: Springer Verlag.

Walker, A. and R. Leakey. 1993. *The Nariokotome* Homo erectus *Skeleton*. Cambridge, MA: Harvard University Press.

Walker, A. and P. Shipman. 1996. *The Wisdom of the Bones: In Search of Human Origins*. New York: Knopf.

Walker, A. and P. Shipman. 2005. *The Ape in the Tree: An Intellectual and Natural History of Proconsul*. Cambridge, MA: Belknap Press.

Walker, A. and M. Teaford. 1989. The hunt for *Proconsul. Scientific American* 260(1): 75–82.

Walker, J., R. A. Cliff, and A. G. Latham. 2006. U-Pb isotopic age of the StW 573 hominid from Sterkfontein, South Africa. *Science* 314: 1592–1594.

Walker, P. L. 2001. A bioarchaeological perspective on the history of violence. *Annual Review of Anthropology* 30: 573–596.

Wang, E. T., G. Kodama, P. Baldi, and R. K. Moyzis. 2006. Global landscape of recent inferred Darwinian selection for *Homo sapiens. Proceedings of the National Academy of Sciences* 103: 135–140.

Ward, C., M. Leakey, and A. Walker. 1999. The new hominid species *Australopithecus anamensis. Evolutionary Anthropology* 7: 197–205.

Ward, C. V., M. G. Leakey, and A. Walker. 2001. Morphology of *Australopithecus anamensis* from Kanapoi and Allia Bay, Kenya. *Journal of Human Evolution* 41: 255–368.

Ward, S. C. and D. L. Duren. 2002. Middle and late Miocene African hominoids. Pp. 385–397 in W. C. Hartwig, ed. *The Primate Fossil Record*. Cambridge, UK: Cambridge University Press.

Waters, M. R. and T. W. Stafford Jr. 2007. Redefining the age of Clovis: implications for the peopling of the Americas. *Science* 315: 1122–1126.

Watson, J. D. 1980. *The Double Helix: A Personal Account of the Discovery of the Structure of DNA*. New York: Norton.

Watson, J. D. 2005. *Darwin: The Indelible Stamp*. Philadelphia: Running Press.

Watson, J. D. and F. H. C. Crick. 1953. Molecular structure of nucleic acids: a structure for deoxyribonucleic acid. *Nature* 171: 964–969.

Weaver, T. D. 2003. The shape of the Neandertal femur is primarily the consequence of a hyperpolar body form. *Proceedings of the National Academy of Sciences* 100: 6926–6929.

Webb, S. G. 2006. *The First Boat People*. Cambridge, UK: Cambridge University Press.

Weiner, J. 1994. *The Beak of the Finch: A Story of Evolution in Our Time*. New York: Knopf.

Weiner, J. S. and K. P. Oakley. 1954. The Piltdown fraud: available evidence reviewed. *American Journal of Physical Anthropology* 12: 1–7.

Weinstein, K. J. 2007. Thoracic skeletal morphology and high-altitude hypoxia in Andean prehistory. *American Journal of Physical Anthropology* 134: 36–49.

Weiss, K. M. 1995. *Genetic Variation and Human Disease: Principles and Evolutionary Approaches*. Cambridge, UK: Cambridge University Press.

Weiss, K. M. and A. V. Buchanan. 2003. Evolution by phenotype: a biomedical perspective. *Perspectives in Biology and Medicine* 46: 159–182.

Weiss, M. L. 2000. An introduction to genetics. Pp. 47–85 in S. Stinson, B. Bogin, R. Huss-Ashmore, and D. O'Rourke, eds. *Human Biology: An Evolutionary and Biocultural Perspective*. New York: Wiley-Liss

White, T. D. 1992. *Prehistoric Cannibalism at Mancos 5MT-UMR-2346*. Princeton: Princeton University Press.

White, T. D. 2001. Once were cannibals. *Scientific American* 265(2): 58–65.

White, T. D. 2002. Earliest hominids. Pp. 407–417 in W. C. Hartwig, ed. *The Primate Fossil Record*. Cambridge, UK: Cambridge University Press.

White, T. D. 2006. Early hominid femora: the inside story. *Comptes Rendus Palevolution* 5: 99–108.

White, T. D. 2006. Human evolution: the evidence. Pp. 65–81 in J. Brockman, ed. *Intelligent Thought: Science versus the Intelligent Design Movement.* New York: Vintage.

White, T. D., B. Asfaw, D. DeGusta, H. Gilbert, G. D. Richards, G. Suwa, and F. C. Howell. 2003. Pleistocene *Homo sapiens* from Middle Awash, Ethiopia. *Nature* 423: 742–747.

White, T. D., G. Suwa, and B. Asfaw. 1994. *Australopithecus ramidus,* a new species of early hominid from Aramis, Ethiopia. *Nature* 371: 306–312.

White, T. D., G. Suwa, W. K. Hart, R. C. Walter, G. Wolde-Gabriel, J. de Heinzelin, J. D. Clark, B. Asfaw, and E. Vrba. 1993. New discoveries of *Australopithecus* at Maka in Ethiopia. *Nature* 366: 261–267.

White, T. D., G. Suwa, S. Simpson, and B. Asfaw. 2000. Jaws and teeth of *Australopithecus afarensis* from Maka, Middle Awash, Ethiopia. *American Journal of Physical Anthropology* 111: 45–68.

White, T. D., G. WoldeGabriel, B. Asfaw, S. Ambrose, Y. Beyene, R. L. Bernor, J.-R. Boisserie, B. Currie, H. Gilbert, Y. Haile-Selassie, W. K. Hart, L.-J. Hlusko, F. C. Howell, R. T. Kono, T. Lehmann, A. Louchart, C. O. Lovejoy, P. R. Renne, H. Saegusa, E. S. Vrba, H. Wesselman, and G. Suwa. 2006. Asa Issie, Aramis and the Origin of *Australopithecus. Nature* 440: 883–889.

Whitten, A. 2005. The second inheritance system of chimpanzees and humans. *Nature* 435: 60–63.

Whiten, A., J. Goodall, W. C. McGrew, T. Nishidas, V. Reynolds, Y. Sugiyama, C. E. G. Tutin, R. W. Wrangham, and C. Boesch. 1999. Cultures in chimpanzees. *Nature* 399: 682–685.

Wild, E. M., M. Tescler-Nicola, W. Kutschera, P. Steier, E. Trinkaus, and W. Wanek. 2005. Direct dating of early upper Paleolithic human remains from Mladeč. *Nature* 435: 332–335.

Wilson, E. O. 2006. *From So Simple a Beginning: Darwin's Four Great Books* [*Voyage of the H.M.S. Beagle, The Origin of Species, The Descent of Man, The Expression of Emotions in Man and Animals*]. New York: Norton.

Winchester, S. 2001. *The Map That Changed the World: William Smith and the Birth of Modern Geology.* New York: HarperCollins.

WoldeGabriel, G., Y. Haile-Selassie, P. R. Renne, W. K. Hart, S. H. Ambrose, B. Asfaw, G. Heiken, and T. White. 2001. Geology and paleontology of the late Miocene Middle Awash valley, Afar rift, Ethiopia. *Nature* 412: 175–177.

WoldeGabriel, G., T. D. White, G. Suwa, P. Renne, J. de Heinzelin, W. K. Hart, and G. Heiken. 1994. Ecological and temporal placement of early Pliocene hominids at Aramis, Ethiopia. *Nature* 371: 330–333.

Wolfe, N. D., C. P. Dunavan, and J. Diamond. 2007. Origins of major human infectious diseases. *Nature* 447: 279–283.

Wolpoff, M. H. 1996. *Human Evolution.* New York: McGraw-Hill.

Wolpoff, M. H. 1999. *Paleoanthropology.* 2nd ed. New York: McGraw-Hill.

Wolpoff, M. H. 2006. *Neandertals on Our Family Tree.* Denver, CO: John Wesley Powell Memorial Lecture, Southwestern and Rocky Mountain Division of the American Association for the Advancement of Science.

Wolpoff, M. H. and R. Caspari. 1997. *Race and Human Evolution: A Fatal Attraction.* New York: Simon & Schuster.

Wolpoff, M. H., B. Senut, M. Pickford, and J. Hawks. 2002. *Sahelanthropus* or 'Sahelpithecus'. *Nature* 419: 581–582.

Wood, B. 1997. The oldest whodunnit in the world. *Nature* 385: 292–293.

Wood, B. 2002. *Palaeoanthropology:* hominid revelations from Chad. *Nature* 418: 133–135.

Wood, B. 2006. A precious little bundle. *Nature* 443: 278–280.

Wrangham, R. and D. Peterson. 1996. *Demonic Males: Apes and the Origins of Human Violence.* Boston: Mariner.

Wrangham, R. W. 1999. Evolution of coalitionary killing. *Yearbook of Physical Anthropology* 42: 1–30.

Yusupova, G., L. Jenner, B. Rees, D. Moras, and M. Yusupov. 2006. Structural basis for messenger RNA movement on the ribosome. *Nature* 444: 391–394.

Zeder, M. A. 1994. After the revolution: post-Neolithic subsistence strategies in northern Mesopotamia. *American Anthropologist* 96: 97–126.

Zeder, M. A. 1999. Animal domestication in the Zagros: a review of past and current research. *Paleorient* 25: 11–25.

Zeder, M. A. 2000. The goats of Ganj Dareh: identification of the earliest directly dated domestic animals. *Science* 287: 2254–2257.

Zeder, M. A. 2006. Central questions in the domestication of plants and animals. *Evolutionary Anthropology* 15: 105–117.

Zhivotovsky, L. A., P. A. Underhill, C. Cinnioglu, M. Kayser, B. Morar, T. Kivisild, R. Scozzari, F. Cruciani, G. Destro-Bisol, G. Spedini, G. K. Chambers, R. J. Herrera, K. K. Yong, D. Gresham, I. Tournev, M. W. Feldman, and L. Kalaydjieva. 2004. The effective mutation rate at Y chromosome short tandem repeats, with application to human population-divergence time. *American Journal of Human Genetics* 74: 50–61.

Zhu, R. X., K. A. Hoffman, R. Potts, C. L. Deng, Y. X. Pan, B. Guo, C. D. Shi, Z. T. Guo, B. Y. Yuan, Y. M. Hou, and W. W. Huang. 2001. Earliest presence of humans in northeast Asia. *Nature* 413: 413–417.

Zhu, R. X., R. Potts, F. Xie, K. A. Hoffman, C. L. Deng, C. D. Shi, Y. X. Pan, H. Q. Wang, G. H. Shi, and N. Q. Wu. 2004. New evidence on the earliest human presence at high northern latitudes in northeast Asia. *Nature* 431: 559–562.

Zilhao, J. and E. Trinkaus. 2002. *Portrait of the Artist as a Child: The Gravettian Human Skeleton from the Abrigo do Lagar Velho and Its Archeological Context. Trabalhos de Arqueologia* 22. Lisbon, Portugal: Instituto Portugues de Arqueologia.

Zimmer, C. 2006. *Smithsonian Intimate Guide to Human Origins.* Washington, DC: Smithsonian Books.

Zimmer, C. 2006. A fin is a limb is a wing: how evolution fashioned its masterworks. *National Geographic* 210(5): 111–135.

Zimmet, P., K. G. M. M. Alberti, and J. Shaw. 2001. Global and society implications of the diabetes epidemic. *Nature* 414: 782–787.

Permissions Acknowledgments

Front Matter

p. ii: David Sailors/Corbis; p. vii: © Will Owens; p. xi: © Dr. Alison S. Carson; p. xii (finch): © Ralph Lee Hopkins/National Geographic Image Collection; p. xii (chimp): © Oxford Scientific/Photolibrary; p. xiii: © Eye of Science/Photo Researchers, Inc.; p. xiv: © Massimo Borchi/Atlantide Phototravel/Corbis; p. xv: © Bettmann/Corbis; p. xvi: © Elwyn Simons; p. xvii ("Dawn Ape"): © Elwyn Simons, photo by Lee Boltin; p. xvii ("Olduvai Gorge"): © Buddy Mays/Corbis; p. xviii: © Russel Ciochon; p. xix: © Melanie Brigockas, Yale Peabody Museum; p. xx: © Royalty-Free/Corbis.

Chapter 1

Chapter opener: © Dr. Alison S. Carson; 1.1a: © Bettmann/Corbis; 1.1b: © AP Photo/The Field Museum; 1.1c: © Leslie Moore; 1.1d: © Horacio Villalobos/Corbis; 1.2a: © Associated Press/Argentine Forensic Anthropology Team, HO; 1.2b: © Phanie/Photo Researchers, Inc.; 1.2c: © Barbara Piperata; 1.2d: © Associated Press, AP; 1.2e: © Daniel Herard/Photo Researchers, Inc.; 1.2f: Getty Images; 1.4: © Associated Press; 1.5: © Bruce Coleman Collection; 1.6: © AKG/Photo Researchers, Inc.; 1.7: © Corbis.

Part I Opener

© W. Perry Conway/Corbis.

Chapter 2

Chapter 2 opener (a): © Galen Rowell/Corbis; (b): © Ralph Lee Hopkins/National Geographic Image Collection; (c–d): © Bettmann/Corbis; 2.1a: © Bettmann/Corbis; 2.1b: © Bettmann/Corbis; 2.2b, e, f: © Tim Graham/Getty Images; 2.2c: © Miguel Castro/Photo Researchers, Inc.; 2.2d: © Kevin Schafer/Corbis; 2.3: © Science Source; 2.4: © Stephen Marshak; 2.5: © Hulton Archive/Getty Images; 2.6a: © The Granger Collection, New York; 2.6b: Omikron/Photo Researchers, Inc.; 2.7a: © Bettmann/Corbis; 2.8a: © Time & Life Pictures/Getty Images; 2.8b: © Uppsala University Library, Sweden; 2.10: © Bettmann/Corbis; 2.11a: © SPL/Photo Researchers, Inc.; 2.12a: © David Ball/Corbis; 2.13: © Hulton Archive/Getty Images; 2.14: © Augustinian Abbey in Old Brno, Brno; 2.18a: © Royal Botanic Gardens, Kew;

2.15b: © Greg Mercer/Field Museum; 2.17: © Time & Life Pictures/Getty Images; 2.28a–b: © Eye of Science/Photo Researchers, Inc.

Chapter 3

Chapter 3 opener (left): © Will Owens; (right): © Oxford Scientific/Photolibrary; 3.2b: © Eye of Science/Photo Researchers, Inc.; 3.2c: © M. I. Walker/Photo Researchers, Inc.; 3.3a: © Roger Ressmeyer/Corbis; 3.3b: © Biophoto Associates/Photo Researchers, Inc.; 3.3c: © Michael Abbey/Photo Researchers, Inc.; 3.3c (insert): © SPL/Photo Researchers, Inc.; 3.3d: © Jim Zuckerman/Corbis; 3.4: © Eye of Science/Photo Researchers, Inc.; 3.5a: © Biophoto Associates/Photo Researchers, Inc.; 3.5b: *camel:* © Richard Nowitz/National Geographic Image Collection, *guinea pig:* © Royalty-Free/Corbis, *salamander:* © Wolfgang Thieme/dpa/Corbis, *house fly:* © Nigel Cattlin/Photo Researchers, Inc., *apple:* © Evans Caglage/Dallas Morning News/Corbis, *potato:* © DK Limited/Corbis, *petunia:* © Roy Morsch/Corbis, *algae:* © JP Nacivet/Getty Images, *ring-tailed lemur:* © Millard H. Sharp/Photo Researchers, Inc., *black-and-white colobus monkey:* © Mark Boulton/Photo Researchers, Inc., *orangutan:* © Robert Garvey/Corbis; 3.9: © Addenbrookes Hospital/Photo Researchers, Inc.; 3.10: © L. Willatt/Photo Researchers, Inc.; 3.12b: © Steve Gschmeissner/Photo Researchers, Inc.; 3.16a: © Clouds Hill Imaging Ltd./Corbis; 3.16b: © Visuals Unlimited/Corbis; 3.18a: © John Radcliffe Hospital/Photo Researchers, Inc.; 3.18b: © Bettmann/Corbis.

Chapter 4

Chapter 4 opener (a): © London School of Hygiene/Photo Researchers, Inc.; (b–d): © Eye of Science/Photo Researchers, Inc.; 4.1b: © Kevin Schafer/Corbis; 4.1c: © Mark Boulton/Photo Researchers, Inc.; 4.2a: © Scott T. Smith/Corbis; 4.2b, f: © Colin Keates/DK Limited/Corbis; 4.2c: © Tom Young/Corbis; 4.2d: © Jonathan Blair/Corbis; 4.2e: © Lynda Richardson/Corbis; 4.6a: © W. Perry Conway/Corbis; 4.6b: © Jane Burton/DK Limited/Corbis; 4.6c: © Anthony Bannister/Photo Researchers, Inc.; 4.6d: © Eye of Science/Photo Researchers, Inc.; 4.7: © 2004 by Blackwell Science Ltd., a Blackwell Publishing Company; 4.8: © Michael Willmer Forbes Tweedie/Photo Researchers, Inc.; 4.9 (top & bottom): © Roger Tidman/Corbis; 4.13: © Dr. Gopal Murti/Photo Researchers, Inc.; 4.16a: © Reuters/Corbis; 4.16b: © Paul Hilton/epa/Corbis; 4.22: © Conor Caffrey/Photo Researchers, Inc.; 4.21: © Time & Life Pictures/Getty Images.

Chapter 5

Chapter 5 opener: © Massimo Borchi/Atlantide Phototravel/Corbis; 5.1: Reprinted by permission of the New York Public Library; 5.3: © Pete Saloutos/Corbis; 5.5a: © SPL/Photo Researchers, Inc.; 5.6a: © Neil Borden/Photo Researchers, Inc.; 5.6b: © Gwen Robbins, Appalachian State University; 5.8a–b: © Barbara Piperata; 5.9b: © Biophoto Associates/Photo Researchers, Inc.; 5.12, 5.14: © Getty Images; 5.15: © David Turnley/Corbis; 5.19: © Associated Press.

Chapter 6

Chapter 6 opener: © Bettmann/Corbis; 6.4b: © Kennan Ward/Corbis; 6.4c: © Rich Reid; 6.6: © Frank Lukasseck/zefa/Corbis; 6.7a: © Theo Allofs; 6.8: © Michael Busselle/Corbis; 6.9: © Kornelius Kupczik, Max Planck Institute of Evolutionary Anthropology; 6.12a–b: © William K. Sacco; 6.13: © National Geographic/Getty Images; 6.14: © Martin Harvey; Gallo Images/Corbis; 6.16: *bushbaby:* © Clem Haagner; Gallo Images/Corbis, *loris:* © Martin Harvey/Corbis, *tarsier:* © Cheryl Ravelo/Reuters/Corbis, *lemur & colobus monkey:* © Kevin Schafer/Corbis, *indri:* © Wolfgang Kaehler/Corbis, *aye-aye:* © Nigel J. Dennis; Gallo Images/Corbis, *tamarin:* © Charles Krebs/zefa/Corbis, *spider monkey:* © Herbert Kehrer/Corbis, *mandrill & orangutan:* © DLILLC/Corbis, *gibbon:* © Anup Shah, *human:* © Steve Bowman/Corbis; 6.17: © Clark S. Larsen; 6.18a–b: © Elwyn L. Simons; 6.19: © Gallo Images/Corbis; 6.20a: © Frans Lanting/Corbis; 6.22: © Kevin Schafer/Corbis; 6.23a: © Art Wolfe/Photo Researchers, Inc.; 6.23b: © Theo Allofs/Corbis; 6.23c: © Gavriel Jecan/Corbis; 6.23d: © Associated Press; 6.23e: © National Geographic/Getty Images; 6.23f: © Art Wolfe/Photo Researchers, Inc.; 6.23g: © Tom Brakefield/Corbis; 6.23h: © Nevada Wier/Corbis; 6.24a–b: © National Geographic/Getty Images; 6.24c: © D. Robert Franz/Corbis; 6.24d: © Gallo Images/Corbis; 6.24e: © Adam Jones/Photo Researchers, Inc.; 6.26: © Kennan Ward/Corbis; 6.27a: © Pascal Goetgheluck/Photo Researchers, Inc.; 6.29: Bruce Latimer, figure: "Ape and Human Pelvis Mechanics." Reprinted by permission; 6.32: © David Tipling; 6.34a: © VEER John Giustina; 6.34b: © Tadashi Miwa; 6.35a: © Susanne Shultz; 6.35b: © W. Scott McGraw; 6.36: © William Wallauer/JGI (*www.janegoodall.org*); 6.37a: © Clark S. Larsen; 6.37b: © National Geographic Society; 6.38: © National Geographic Society.

Part II Opener

© John Reader/Photo Researchers, Inc.

Chapter 7

Chapter 7 opener: © Elwyn Simons; 7.1: © American Philosophical Society; 7.1 (inset): © Bettmann/Corbis; 7.2a: © Reuters/Corbis; 7.2b: © Henry Romero/Reuters/Corbis; 7.2c: © Chris Hellier/Corbis; 7.2d & h: © Tom Bean/Corbis; 7.2e: © Wolfgang Kaehler/Corbis; 7.2f: © Naturfoto Honal/Corbis; 7.2g: © James L. Amos/Corbis; 7.2i: © Philip Gould/Corbis; 7.4a: © John Reader/Photo Researchers, Inc.; 7.4b: "The Fossil Footprint Makers of Laetoli" © 1982 Jay H. Matternes; 7.8b: © SPL/Photo Researchers, Inc.; 7.10a: © Drazen Pomykalo; 7.11: "Pig Dating: Stratigraphic Correlations" © 1985 Jay H. Matternes; 7.12a–b: © Peter A. Bostrom; 7.12c: © John Reader/Photo Researchers, Inc.; 7.12d: © National Geographic/Getty Images; 7.12e: © Javier Trueba/Madrid Scientific Films/Photo Researchers, Inc.; 7.12f & k: © Martin Land/Photo Researchers, Inc.; 7.12g: © The Art Archive/Corbis; 7.12h: © World Museum of Man; 7.12i: © Peter A. Bostrom; 7.12j: © Sheila Terry/Photo Researchers, Inc.; 7.12l: © Archivo Iconografico, S.A./Corbis; 7.12m: © Steven Alvarez/National Geographic Image Collection; 7.12n: © Peter A. Bostrom;

7.12o: © Asian Art & Archaeology/Corbis; 7.12p–q: © Werner Forman/Corbis; 7.12r: © Bettmann/Corbis; 7.12s: © Remi Benali/Corbis; 7.13: © Ulmer Museum, photo by Thomas Stephan; 7.15a: R. H. Towner, figure: "Box 4. Constructing Chronologies" from "Archaeological Dendrochronology in the Southwestern U.S.," *Evolutionary Anthropology*, p. 73. Copyright © 2002, Wiley-Liss, Inc. Reprinted with permission of Wiley-Liss, Inc., a subsidiary of John Wiley & Sons, Inc.; 7.15b: © Doug Wilson/Corbis; 7.17a: BioArch, figure: "Amino Acid Dating" from "Amino Acid Racemization." Reprinted by permission; 7.17b: Fission-track geochronology, "Quaternary Geochronology: Methods and Applications," ed. J. S. Noller, J. M. Sowers, and W. R. Lettis, *American Geographical Union Reference Shelf,* Vol. 4, pp. 131–156. © American Geophysical Union. Reproduced by permission of American Geophysical Union; 7.17c (top): Davidson, Reed, and Davis, figure: "Earth's Magnetic Field Today" from *Exploring Earth: An Introduction to Physical Geology,* 2nd ed., Prentice Hall, 2001; (bottom): Philip L. Stein and Bruce M. Rowe, Figure 11-13: "The Geomagnetic Reversal Time Scale" from *Physical Anthropology,* 9th, ed. p. 280. Copyright © 2006, The McGraw-Hill Companies. Reprinted by permission; 7.17d: © James O. Hamblen; 7.20: © Ron Boardman; Frank Lane Picture Agency/Corbis; 7.27: © Getty Images.

Chapter 8

Chapter 8 opener: © Elwyn Simons, photo by Lee Boltin; 8.1: © Bettmann/Corbis; 8.5b & d: © Mark Klinger, Carnegie Museum of Natural History; 8.8: © Nancy Perkins, Carnegie Museum of Natural History; 8.10: © Erik Seiffert; 8.13: Courtesy of M. Takai; 8.14a: © Alan Walker; 8.14b: John G. Fleagle, Figure: "Proconsul Skeleton" from *Primate Adaptation and Evolution,* 2nd ed., p. 460, copyright Academic Press © 1998. Reprinted by permission of the publisher; 8.14c: "*Proconsul heseloni* Habitation: © 1992 Jay H. Matternes; 8.15a–b: © Eric Delson; 8.18: © David Pilbeam; 8.20: © Eric Delson; 8.21: Caro-Beth Stewart and Todd R. Disotell, figure reprinted from *Current Biology,* Vol. 8, No. 16, "Primate Evolution—In and Out of Africa," pp. 582–588, copyright © 1998, with permission from Elsevier.

Chapter 9

Chapter 9 opener: © Buddy Mays/Corbis; 9.1: Adrienne L. Zihlman, figure: "Olduvai Gorge," p. 61 from *The Human Evolution Coloring Book,* 2nd ed. Copyright © 1982, 2000 by Coloring Concepts, Inc. Reprinted by permission of HarperCollins Publishers; 9.2: © Martin Harvey/Gallo Images/Corbis; 9.3a–b: © William K. Sacco; 9.5a–b: © Tanya Smith, Donald Reid, Max Planck Institute for Evolutionary Anthropology; 9.7: © Fridmar Damm/zefa/Corbis; 9.11: © Institute of Human Origins/Nanci Kahn; 9.12–13: © 2003 Tim D. White/Brill Atlanta; 9.14: "*A. afarensis* Group Gathering Figs in an Ancient Hadar Forest" © 1985 Jay H. Matternes; p. 234 (clockwise from top left): © AFP Photos/Getty Images; © 2003 Tim D. White/Brill Atlanta; © Tim White; 9.15: Berhane Asfaw, et al., figure from "*Australopithecus garhi:* A New Species of Early Hominid from Ethiopia," *Science,* Vol. 284, pp. 629–635, April 23, 1999. Reprinted with permission from AAAS; 9.17a: Dave Einsel/Getty Images; 9.17b: © AFP/Getty Images; 9.19: © William Kimble/Institute of Human Origins; 9.20: © John Reader/Photo Researchers, Inc.; 9.21: © Fred Spoor; courtesy of National Museums of Kenya; 9.23: *Ardipithecus ramidus* and *Australopithecus garhi:* FOSSIL CREDIT: Middle Awash Research Project. Redrawn from photographs © David L. Brill; 9.29: ARTIFACT CREDIT: Original housed in National Museum of Ethiopia, Addis Ababa. © 1999 David L. Brill; 9.24a–c: © Tim White; 9.26a: ARTIFACT CREDIT: National Museums of Kenya, Nairobi. © 1995 David L. Brill; 9.26b: FOSSIL CREDIT: National Museums of Kenya, Nairobi. © 1985 David L. Brill; 9.27: © W. David Fooce; 9.28: © Jeffrey H.

Schwartz; 9.29: © Transvaal Museum, NFI; p. 246 (clockwise from top right): © Fred Spoor; courtesy of National Museums of Kenya; © Dave Einsel/Getty Images; Jeffrey H. Schwartz; p. 247 (clockwise from top left): ARTIFACT CREDIT: Original housed in National Museum of Ethiopia, Addis Ababa. © 1999 David L. Brill; FOSSIL CREDIT: National Museums of Kenya, Nairobi. © 1985 David L. Brill; Transvaal Museum, NFI; ARTIFACT CREDIT: National Museums of Kenya, Nairobi. © 1995 David L. Brill.

Chapter 10

Chapter 10 opener: (top) © Russel Ciochon; (bottom) © Bettmann/Corbis; 10.1: © Nationaal Naturhistorish Museum, Leiden, the Netherlands; 10.3a: © John Reader/Photo Researchers, Inc.; 10.3b: © Nationaal Naturhistorish Museum, Leiden, the Netherlands; 10.4a: ARTIFACT CREDIT: National Museum of Tanzania, Dar es Salaam. © 1997 David L. Brill; 10.4b: © John Reader/Photo Researchers, Inc.; 10.4c: FOSSIL CREDIT: National Museums of Kenya, Nairobi. © 1985 David L. Brill; 10.5a–b: FOSSIL CREDIT: National Museums of Kenya, Nairobi. © 1985 David L. Brill; p. 256: FOSSIL CREDIT: National Museums of Kenya, Nairobi. © 1985 David L. Brill; 10.7 (clockwise from top left): FOSSIL CREDIT: National Museum of Tanzania, Dar es Salaam. © 1985 David L. Brill; © Donald Johanson, Institute of Human Origins; © Human Origins Program at the National Museum of Natural History, Smithsonian Institution; 10.8: © Alan Walker; 10.10: © Tim White; 10.11: Courtesy of and © National Museum of Tanzania & Eric Delson (photo by C. Tarka); 10.12: © Tim White; 10.13 & 10.15: © Milford Wolpoff; 10.16: ARTIFACT CREDIT: American Museum of Natural History. © 1996 David L. Brill; 10.18a–b: © Tim White; 10.19: "Homo habilis Using Volcanic-Cobble Debitage to Rend a Carcass" © 1995 Jay H. Matternes; p. 270: ARTIFACT CREDIT: American Museum of Natural History. © 1996 David L. Brill.

Chapter 11

Chapter 11 opener: © Melanie Brigockas; 11.1: © Rheinisches Landesmuseum, Bonn; 11.4 (clockwise from top left): Swanscombe: © Jeffrey H. Schwartz, Steinheim: © Staatliches Museum für Naturkunde, Stuttgart, Petralona: © Milford Wolpoff, Dali: © Xinzhi Wu, Narmada: © Dr. K. A. R. Kennedy, Cornell University, and the University of Allahabad, India, Ngandong: © Milford Wolpoff, Bodo: © Tim White, Kabwe: © John Reader/Photo Researchers, Inc., Arago: FOSSIL CREDIT: Musée de l'Homme, Paris. © 1985 David L. Brill, Atapuerca 5: © Javier Trueba/Madrid Scientific Films/Photo Researchers, Inc.; 11.5: © John Reader/Photo Researchers, Inc.; 11.6: © Milford Wolpoff; 11.7a: © Dr. K.A.R. Kennedy, Cornell University, and the University of Allahabad, India; 11.7b: © Eric Delson; 11.8a: FOSSIL CREDIT: Musée de l'Homme, Paris. © 1985 David L. Brill; 11.8b: © Milford Wolpoff; 11.8c: © Staatliches Museum für Naturkunde, Stuttgart; 11.8d: © Jeffrey H. Schwartz; 11.9: © Javier Trueba/Madrid Scientific Films/Photo Researchers, Inc.; 11.11: © National Geographic/Getty Images; 11.12: FOSSIL CREDIT: Tel Aviv University, Sackler School of Medicine, Department of Anatomy and Anthropology. © 1995 David L. Brill; 11.15: FOSSIL CREDIT: Geolosko Paleontologi Musej. © 1985 David L. Brill; 11.16: © John Reader/Photo Researchers, Inc.; 11.17a: © The Granger Collection, New York; 11.17b: © Melanie Brigockas; 11.18: © John Reader/Photo Researchers, Inc.; 11.19: © Milford Wolpoff; 11.23: ARTIFACT CREDIT: Courtesy Denise de Sonneville Bordes, Centre Francois Bordes, Institut du Quaternaire, Batiment de Geologie, Université de Bordeaux I. © 1985 David L. Brill; 11.24: Hervé Bocherens, et al., figure from "Palaeoenvironmental and Palaeodietary Implications of Isotopic Biogeochemistry of Last Interglacial Neanderthal and Mammal Bones in Scladina Cave (Belgium)," Journal of Archaeological Science, Vol. 26, No. 6, June

1999. Copyright © 1999 Academic Press. All rights reserved. Reprinted by permission of the publisher; 11.25: Based on a photograph by Jacques Vainstain; 11.27a: © Associated Press; 11.28 (clockwise from upper left): "Homo idaltu Portrait Bust Reconstruction © 2005" Jay H. Matternes, Kabwe skull: © Milford Wolpoff, Herto skull: FOSSIL CREDIT: Housed in National Museum of Ethiopia, Addis Ababa. Photo © 2001 David L. Brill/Brill Atlanta, cutmarks: © Tim White; stone tool: © Tim White; 11.29a: © Ira Block/National Geographic Image Collection; 11.29b, 11.30: © Milford Wolpoff; 11.31: FOSSIL CREDIT: Peabody Museum, Harvard University. © 1985 David L. Brill; 11.32a–b: © Clark S. Larsen; 11.33a–b: © Eric Delson; 11.34: © Milford Wolpoff; 11.35a: © Instituto de Gestão do Património Arquitectónico e Arqueológico; 11.36a–b: FOSSIL CREDIT: Musée de l'Homme, Paris. © 1985 David L. Brill; 11.37: © Eric Delson; 11.41: © Milford Wolpoff; 11.42 (clockwise from left): reconstruction of Flores man: © Peter Schouten/National Geographic Society/Reuters/Corbis; map inset: © Handout/Reuters/Corbis; Flores man and human skulls: © Peter Brown; 11.43: © Ira Block/National Geographic Image Collection; 11.44: © Leland C. Bement; 11.45a: © James Chatters/Applied Paleoscience; 11.45b: © James Chatters/AFP/Getty Images.

Chapter 12

Chapter 12 opener (left to right): © David Frazier/Corbis; © Scott Haddow; © Jim Holmes/Getty Images; 12.1a: © Tom Grill/Corbis; 12.1b: © www.CartoonStock.com; 12.2a: Nucleus Medical Art, "Examples of Malocclusion." Medical illustration copyright © 2008 Nucleus Medical Art, all rights reserved. www.nucleusinc.com. Reprinted by permission; 12.2b: © A.D.A.M., Inc.; 12.2c: © John Lukacs; 12.4b: © John Doebley; 12.5b: Bruce D. Smith, figure: "The Approximate Time Periods When Plants and Animals Were First Domesticated," from The Emergence of Agriculture, p. 13, 1998. Reprinted by permission; 12.7a: John Swogger © Çatalhöyük Research Project; 12.7b: © Çatalhöyük Research Project; 12.8a: © Royalty-Free/Corbis; 12.9: Colin Renfrew and Paul Bahn, figure drawn by Annick Boothe. From Archaeology: Theories, Methods and Practice by Colin Renfrew and Paul Bahn, Thames & Hudson Inc., New York. Reprinted by permission of the publisher; 12.11: © Peter Johnson/Corbis; 12.13: Roberto Osti, figure: "Bones of the Postcontact Indians" from "Reading the Bones of La Florida" by Clark S. Larsen, Scientific American, Vol. 282, No. 6, p. 84. Reprinted by permission of Roberto Osti Illustrations; 12.14b: © Clark S. Larsen/Mark Griffin; 12.15: © Clark S. Larsen; 12.16: © Tracy K. Betsinger; 12.17a: © Clark S. Larsen; 12.17b: © Donald J. Ortner; 12.17c: © Scimat/Photo Researchers, Inc.; 12.18: Clark S. Larsen, figure 3.2: "Percentage of Teeth Affected by Dental Caries in Eastern North America" from Bioarchaeology: Interpreting Behavior from the Human Skeleton, p. 69, Cambridge University Press, 1997; 12.19: © Barry Stark; 12.20: © David Scharf/Photo Researchers, Inc.; 12.21a: © Clark S. Larsen; 12.21b: © Mark C. Griffin.

A34 Permissions Acknowledgments

Index

persistence, 58
lactation, **98**, 105
lactic acid, 336
Lactobacillus acidophilus, 336, *336*
lactose:
  intolerance, 58
  persistence, 58
Laetoli (Tanzania), 236, *237*
  fossil footprints at, *163,* 168, *170,* 238, *239*
Lagar Velho (Portugal), 300, *300,* 302
Lamarck, Jean-Baptiste de Monet, Chevalier de, 27, 30, *31*
lamarckism, **30**
land bridges, 211, 309, *309, 312*
language, **5**, 223
langurs, *145,* 152
Lantian (China), 263
La Paz, 334
Lartet, Edward, 211
Latin America, global warming in, 341
law, scientific, **15**
Law of Independent Assortment, *52,* **53**
Law of Segregation, **59,** *61*
leaf eaters, 144, *145,* 149, 209, 215, 224, *225*
Leakey, Louis, 123, 221–22, 240, 254
Leakey, Mary, 183, 221–22, 240
Leakey, Meave, 236, 239
Lee, P. C., 157
Lee, Richard, 331
leg-arm ratio, 223, 240, 258, 261
leisure time, 331, *331*
Lemudong'o (Kenya), 190
lemurs, 131, 137, 138, *140, 142, 143, 200, 201,* 202
  rhinarium in, 131
lesser apes, *see* hylobatids
lesser spot-nosed monkey, *126–27, 128*
leucism, 76
Levallois tools, **289**
Levant, 321–22, 323, *323, 325,* 327, 343
Lewontin, R. C., 97
Libby, Willard, 180
Lieberman, Philip, 291
life history, of humans, 98–105, *98*
  adaptation and, 105–20
  adult stage in, **98,** 103, 104
  food acquisition and, 104, 105
  postnatal stage in, **98,** 99–103, 104, 120
  prenatal stage in, 98–99, *98,* 104, 120
limb bones:
  of Neandertals, 281, 288–89
  periosteal reactions in, *334,* 335
  see also femur; humerus
limb proportion, in bipeds vs. quadrupeds, 149, *151*
Limnopithecus, 212–13
Lincoln, Abraham, *58*
linguistic anthropology, **5,** 6, 16
linkage, of genes, **53,** *53*
Linnaeus, Carolus (Carl von Linné), 27–28, *28, 96,* 124, 195
Lion Men sculptures, 179, *179*
living populations, *19,* 68, *70,* 89, 95–120, 163
Livingstone, Frank B., 82–83, 97–98
locomotion, suspensory (arboreal), 144, 147, *147, 151,* 188, *188, 209,* 237, *238*
locus, loci, on chromosomes, **58,** 63, 64, 75, 79, 84–85
Lomekwi (Kenya), 239, *240*
long bones:
  cross-sections of, *332*

growth of, 100–101, *101*
Loomis, William, 110
loph, **134**
Lordkipanidze, David, 261
lorises, 131, 138, *140,* 142, 143
Lothagam (Kenya), 295, *298*
Lovejoy, Owen, 228–29
Lower Paleolithic, **240**
Lucy (*A. afarensis*), **237,** *237, 259*
luminescence dating, *184, 185,* **186**
lung volume, 112, *112*
Lyell, Charles, 24, *25,* 27, 30
lysine, 337

macaques, 146, 154, 156, 217
  adaptive range of, 124
McGraw, Scott, 157
McHenry, Henry, 228, 266
McKee, Jeffrey, 327
macroevolution, **69,** *71*
macronutrients, **113**
Madagascar, 142
Madhya Pradesh, India, 277
Magdalenian culture, *293*
Magellan Strait, 22
Mahale (Tanzania), 159
maize, *see* corn
Majuangou (China), 263, *263*
malaria, 66, 70, 81–85, *83, 84,* 97, 340, 341
Malawi, 254
Malay race, 96
malnutrition, 114, *114, 115,* 117, 337, 341, 343
malocclusion, 317–18, *319, 329,* 330, 343
Malthus, Thomas, 27, 28–29, 30, *30*
mammals, 196, 218
mammoths, 177
Manchester, England, 78, 79
mandible, *242*
  of *A. afarensis,* 238
  of *A. anamensis, 236*
  of chimpanzees, *236*
  of early archaic *H. sapiens, 278*
  of early modern *H. sapiens,* 298, 299, 314
  of *H. erectus,* 261, 262, 264, 269–70, *271*
  of *H. habilis, 254*
  of *Homo,* 271
  of modern humans, 317, 328–30, 343
  see also skulls
mandrills, *145,* 146
mangabeys, 217
manioc, 324
Man's Place in Nature (Huxley), 149
Marco Polo, 96
Marfan syndrome, *58*
Marillac (France), 290
markers, genetic, 89
Márquez, Lourdes, 338–39
marriage, 104–5
masseter muscle, 224, *225,* 329
mastication, *see* chewing complex
masticatory-functional hypothesis, 329, **329,** 330
masticatory muscles, 224–25, *225,* 317, 328–29
material culture, **9,** *10–11,* 16
  of early modern *H. sapiens,* 304
  of *H. erectus,* 258, 264, 270, 271

monosomy, **53**, 75
Monte Lessini (Italy), 304
Moore, Leslie, 6
Morgan, Thomas Hunt, 35, *36*
morphology, **14**, 68, 138–39, *143*
   brain, 136–37, *137*, 138, 196, *198*, 204, 206
mosquitoes, *66*, 81–82, 83, *84*, 340, 341
motor skills, **99**
Moula-Guercy cave (France), 285
Mousterian culture, **289**, *289*
mRNA, **54**, 55, *56–57*
mtDNA, *see* mitochondrial DNA
Müller, Paul, 341
Multiregional Continuity evolutionary model, 275–77, *276*, 303–7,
   306, 314
Mungo, Lake, 309–10, *309*, *310*
Murray River Valley (Australia), 310
muscles:
   gluteal, 149, *150*
   masseter, 224, *225*, 329
   masticatory, 224–25, *225*, 328–29
   pterygoid, 224
   temporalis, 147, *148*, 206, 224, *225*, 329
mutagens, **75**
mutation(s), 36, **36**, 38, 72–75, *74*, 79, 82, 88, 90, 91, 306, 313
   frameshift, **75**
   induced, **75**
   point, **75**
   spontaneous, 75, *76*
Muybridge, Eadweard, *15*
Mycobacterium tuberculosis, 341

nails, 130, *130*, 196, *198*, 204
Napier, John, 254
Nariokotome (Kenya), 257, *258*
Nariokotome Boy (*H. erectus*), 258–60, *259*, 261
Narmada (India), 277, 279
nasal apertures, 265
   of early archaic *H. sapiens*, 278
   of early modern *H. sapiens*, 295, 300, *302*, 314
   of Neandertals, 278, 281, 282, *283*, 285, 286, *287*, 344
Native Americans, 283
   blood types of, 87–88, *88*
   bone strength (size) in, *332*, 333
   dental caries in, 336, *337*
   European contacts with, *2*, 3–4, *15*, 84–85, 89, 325, *332*, 335
   evolutionary change in, 3–4
   genetic variation in, 3–4, 306
   haplogroups of, 310, 312
   infectious disease in, 335, *335*
   malaria and, 84–85
   mtDNA of, 309, 313
   nonevolutionary change in, 4, 7
   Paleoindians vs., 313
   population growth in, 320
   as race, 96, *97*
   shovel-shaped incisors of, 310, *312*
   technology and tool use of, 313, *313*
   type 2 diabetes in, 116–17
   Y chromosomes of, 313
   see also Paleoindians
natural selection, 19, *20*, **22**, 28, 31–32, *32*, 35, 36, 38, 63, *66*,
   72, 95, 163
   adaptive advantage and, 76–77, 78–79, 83, 91, 104–5, 110,
     112, 264, 270, 280–81
   genetic variation and, 67–68, 72, 76–85, 90, 91

sickle-cell anemia and, 82–83
   types of, 77, *77*, 79
   workloads and, 119
nDNA, *see* nuclear DNA
Neandertals, 175–76, 281–92, *284*, 314
   in Asia, 281–84, *282*, *284*, 299
   body shape of, 281, 286–89, *287*
   brain size of, 273, 281, *282*, 283, *286*
   browridges of, 275, 278, *283*
   burials by, 290–91, *291*, 314
   cannibalism of, 285
   cold climate adaptation of, 286–89, *287*, 291–92, 307, 314
   early modern *H. sapiens*‘ coexistence with, 304, 307, 314
   in Europe, 284–85, *284*, 307
   as evolutionary dead ends, *276*, 285
   eye orbits of, 282, 285
   face morphology of, *272*, 275, 278, 281, 282, 283, 285
   height of, 281, 286–89
   hunting by, 289–90, 291
   incisors of, 283
   injuries to bones of, 283–84, *283*, 286
   intelligence of, 289–92
   limb bones of, 281, 288–89
   material culture of, 281, 283
   meat eating by, 289–90, *290*
   modern humans' genetic relationship with, *274*, 276
   Mousterian culture of, 289
   mtDNA of, 304–5, 314
   nasal aperture of, 278, 281, 282, *283*, 285, 286, *287*
   occipital bun of, 275, 281, 282, 285, 300, 304
   reconstructions of, *272*, *286*, *287*
   robustness of, 275
   skeletons of, 281–82
   skull morphology of, 273, 275, 278, 281, 282, 283, 285, *301*
   speech ability of, 291, 293, 314
   teeth of, 275, 281, 282, 283, *283*, 284, 285, *289*
   tool use and technology of, 281, 284, 285, 289, 314
   variation in, 281, 304
   violence of, *283*, 326
Neander Valley (Germany), 273
Necator americanus, 338
Necrolemur, 212–13
Neel, James V., 116
Negroid (African) race, 95, 96, *97*
Neolithic period, **318**, *324*
New Guinea, 310, *322*, 324
New South Wales, 309
New World monkeys, *see* ceboids; platyrrhines
Ngandong, Java, 277, *277*, 279
Ngandong 11 skull, 277
niacin (vitamin B₃), 337
Nile Valley, 295, 328
Nilotics, *288*
nocturnal adaptation, 142, 143, *143*, 148, 199, *200*
noncoding DNA, **55**, 73, 75
nondisjunctions, **51**
nonevolutionary change, in Native Americans, 4
nonheme iron, **338**
nonhoning canine teeth, **9**, *10–11*, 16, 224, 231, 232
nonhoning chewing, *see* chewing complex, nonhoning
non-insulin-dependent diabetes mellitus (NIDDM), 116
nonmelanic form, **78**, *78*, 79, *79*, 80
nonmineralized bone, **100**
non-radiometric dating, 183, *184*, 185–86
nonsynonymous point mutations, 75
North America:

Acheulian, 266, 268, *268,* 269–70
Clovis, **313**
Folsom, **313,** *313*
Levallois, **289**
Oldowan, **240,** *242,* 266
pebble, **179**
tool use:
by australopithecines, 240–43, *242,* 266
by chimpanzees, *12,* 123–24, 158–59, *158, 159*
in domestication of plants, *321*
by early archaic *H. sapiens,* 280–81, 314
by early modern *H. sapiens,* 294, 296–97, 303, *304,* 305, 314
by *H. erectus,* 261, *261,* 264, 266, 268, 269–70, 271
by *H. habilis,* 253, 254, 255–56, 257
by hominids, 226–27, *227,* 253, 263, 269–70
by *Homo, 9, 10–11, 12*–13, 16
by modern humans, 253, *321*
by Native Americans, 313, *313*
by Neandertals, 281, 284, 285, 289, 314
see also material culture; technology
tooth comb, **134,** *134,* 142, *201, 202*
Toros-Menalla, Chad, 230
total daily energy expenditure (TDEE), **113**
touch, in primates, *126,* 130, 132
towns, rise of, *see* villages, agriculture and rise of
traits, dominant/recessive, 61–62, *62*
transcription, in protein synthesis, **54,** *55, 56–57,* 74
transfer RNA (tRNA), *55,* **55**
translation, in protein synthesis, **54,** *55, 56–57*
translocations, **51**
transposable elements, **75**
treponematoses, **335,** *335*
Triassic period, *174*
trilobites, *167*
trimesters, 98–99
Trinil (Java), 252, 257, 263
triplets, **55**
trisomy, **53,** 75
tRNA, *55,* **55**
tryptophan, 337
tuberculosis, 261–62, 335, 341
Tugen Hills, 231, *231*
Tungusae, 97
Turkana, Lake, 231, *231,* 236, 239, 243, 254, *255,* 258, 259
Turkana boy, *see* Nariokotome boy
Turkey, 261, 323, *323,* 325
Turner, Christy, 310
turtles, *167*
Tuscany, 215, *215*
type 2 diabetes, **116,** 340
tyrannosaurus, *167*

Uganda, 208, *208*
ulna, 100, 209
ultraviolet (UV) radiation, 97, 109–10, 111, 120
undernutrition, 114, *114, 115,* 117, 120
UNESCO World Heritage Sites, *244*
uniformitarianism, **24,** 30
United Nations, 340
United States:
immigrants in, 97
obesity and overweight in, 114
Upper Paleolithic, *see* Paleolithic, Upper
Upper Pleistocene, *see* Pleistocene epoch, late
uracil, **54**
Ussher, James, 173

Utah, *24*
UV (ultraviolet) radiation, 97, 109–10, 111, 120

valine, 75
Van Gerven, Dennis, 329, 330
variation:
biocultural, *see* biocultural variation
mechanisms of, 41, 90
see also genetic variation
vasoconstriction, **108,** 111
vasodilation, **106,** 111
vertebrae, of primates, 130, *130*
vervet monkeys, *145*
Victoria, Lake, 208
victoriapithecids, **217**
Victoriapithecus, 217
Vikings, 89
villages, agriculture and rise of, 320, 321, 322–25
Vindija Cave (Croatia), 284, *284,* 290, 304
violence, in modern humans, 326
Virchow, Rudolf, 273–74, 285
Virginia, 165
viruses, 334–35
vision:
binocular (stereoscopic), *127,* 131, 132, 143, 196, 198, *198,* 204
color, 131, 132, 143
in primates, *127,* 130–31, *131,* 132, 143, *143,* 148, 160, 196, 197, 198, *198, 202,* 204
visual predation hypothesis, **196,** 197, 198
vitamin B₃ (niacin), 337
vitamin D synthesis, 109–10
vocalizations:
of chimpanzees, 159, 160
of prosimians, *143*
reproductive strategies and, 154, *154*
volcanic ash, 175, *177,* 238
volcanic rock, *233*
Vries, Hugo de, 35

Wadi Halfa (Sudan), *295, 298*
Wadi Kubbaniya (Egypt), *295, 298*
Walker, Alan, *235,* 236
Wallace, Alfred Russel, 32, *32*
Ward, Carol, 236
warfare, 326
water supply, 101–2
Watson, James, 37, 46
weaning, **99**
Weidenreich, Franz, 264
weight:
birth, 99
excess, 114–17, 340
Weinberg, Wilhelm, 70
West Africa, West Africans, 36, 70
wheat, *316,* 321, *322,* 325, 336
White, Tim, *177,* 232, 236, 237, 240, 254, 260, 285, 296–97
Wolff's Law, **118,** 317
Wolpoff, Milford, 269, *287*
wood, as fuel, 327
woolly monkeys, 144
woolly spider monkeys, 144
workload:
adaptation and, 117–19
agriculture and, 331–34, 343
effect on bones of, 117–19, *118,* 317, 329, 331–34, *332, 333*
of hunter-gatherers, 331–34